Othmar Schoeck: Life and Works

Eastman Studies in Music

Ralph P. Locke, Senior Editor
Eastman School of Music

Additional Titles on American Music and Musical Life

Analyzing Wagner's Operas
Stephen McClatchie

The Ballet Collaborations of Richard Strauss
Wayne Heisler, Jr.

"Claude Debussy As I Knew Him" and Other Writings of Arthur Hartmann
Edited by Samuel Hsu, Sidney Grolnic, and Mark Peters
Foreword by David Grayson

*Dane Rudhyar:
His Music, Thought, and Art*
Deniz Ertan

*Debussy's Letters to Inghelbrecht:
The Story of a Musical Friendship*
Annotated by Margaret G. Cobb

*Elliott Carter:
Collected Essays and Lectures, 1937–1995*
Edited by Jonathan W. Bernard

*French Music, Culture, and
National Identity, 1870–1939*
Edited by Barbara L. Kelly

Maurice Duruflé: The Man and His Music
James E. Frazier

The Music of Luigi Dallapiccola
Raymond Fearn

*Music's Modern Muse:
A Life of Winnaretta Singer,
Princesse de Polignac*
Sylvia Kahan

*Opera and Ideology in Prague:
Polemics and Practice at the
National Theater, 1900–1938*
Brian S. Locke

*Pentatonicism from the
Eighteenth Century to Debussy*
Jeremy Day-O'Connell

*The Pleasure of Modernist Music: Listening,
Meaning, Intention, Ideology*
Edited by Arved Ashby

*The Poetic Debussy:
A Collection of His Song Texts and Selected
Letters* (Revised Second Edition)
Edited by Margaret G. Cobb

*The Substance of Things Heard:
Writings about Music*
Paul Griffiths

A complete list of titles in the Eastman Studies in Music Series,
in order of publication, may be found at the end of this book.

Othmar Schoeck

Life and Works

CHRIS WALTON

R UNIVERSITY OF ROCHESTER PRESS

Publication of this book was supported in part by grants from the City of Zurich,
Switzerland, and the Ernst Göhner Stiftung.

First published 2009

University of Rochester Press
668 Mt. Hope Avenue, Rochester, NY 14620, USA
www.urpress.com
and Boydell & Brewer Limited
PO Box 9, Woodbridge, Suffolk IP12 3DF, UK
www.boydellandbrewer.com

ISBN-13: 978-1-58046-300-3
ISBN-10: 1-58046-300-2

ISSN: 1071-9989

Library of Congress Cataloging-in-Publication Data

Walton, Chris, 1963–.
Othmar Schoeck : life and works / Chris Walton.
    p. cm.—(Eastman studies in music, ISSN 1071-9989; v. 65)
"Concise work catalogue and discography": p.
Includes bibliographical references (p.) and index.
ISBN-13: 978-1-58046-300-3 (hardcover : alk. paper)
ISBN-10: 1-58046-300-2
    1. Schoeck, Othmar, 1886–1957 2. Composers—Switzerland—Biography.
I. Title.
ML410.S2827W35   2009
780.92—dc22
[B]

2009025847

A catalogue record for this title is available from the British Library.

This publication is printed on acid-free paper.
Printed in the United States of America

Cover photo colorization by Janus Anderson

Dedicated to Wolfgang, Salome, Luzia,
Konrad, Judith, Isabel, and Alvaro Schoeck,
and to the memory of Elisabeth
Schoeck-Grüebler and Georg Schoeck

Othmar Schoeck, ca. 1909. Courtesy of Zentralbibliothek Zürich.

Contents

Illustrations

Musical Examples

Acknowledgments

The origins of this book lie in the current copyright legislation. In 1988 I com-
pleted a biography of Othmar Schoeck as my doctoral dissertation at Oxford
University. The contract for its publication was signed with Atlantis Musikbuch-
Verlag shortly before that company was sold by its owner, Daniel Bodmer. The
next owner in turn sold Atlantis on within a matter of months. After a somewhat
meandering path through various hands, the company was bought by Schott of
Mainz, who was thereby under a contractual obligation to translate my book into
German and publish it. The translation was made by Ken Bartlett, and the book
appeared seven years after its completion. The publication process was as pleasant as any first-time author could have wished, and I retain happy memories of
my work with both Ken and the excellent personnel at Schott's. Several years
later, I decided to publish the original English version. However, my contract
with Atlantis/Schott meant that a large percentage of royalties from any other
edition of the book would by necessity go to the original publisher. There is
nothing in the least odd about this. But given that the market for a book on
Othmar Schoeck is not vast, the percentage in question was enough to deter any
English or American publisher from taking on the project.

As the fiftieth anniversary of Schoeck's death approached in 2007, and in
view of the fact that there was still no biography in English of the composer, I
decided to revisit the idea of publishing my original book. The matter of the
royalties remained, however. Furthermore, I had in the intervening two decades
published several articles and a further book on the composer (all in German).
Since my job as Head of the Music Division at the Zentralbibliothek Zürich had
made me responsible for the composer's archives for just over a decade, I had
in addition uncovered new source material that needed to be incorporated into
any biography. There were also several sources that I felt deserved an interpretation more nuanced than in my earlier book. In some cases the nuances were
such that can perhaps only arise from an author's getting older. Certain things
in the life of another that appear straightforward when one is twenty-four years
old and single can look quite different when one is forty-four, married, and a
father three times over, with two of the three on the cusp of puberty. In order
to circumvent the copyright problem and to do justice both to the new source
material and to my new interpretation of the old, I decided to write a new book.
There are naturally many parallels between the two "lives," for the main characters in the narrative are the same in each case, and I have not refrained from
quoting certain important source documents here just because I did so before.

But the first book had been restricted to the composer's life, with relatively little discussion of the music itself—that being the brief of my doctorate at the time. I wanted in the present case to allocate ample space to the music too. Both life and music are dealt with chronologically here, for the simple reason that it seems the most obvious decision. Chronology is a powerful thing. It reflects how we in general perceive our own lives, and it is perhaps the most useful anchor when considering the lives of others. So a straightforward "life and works," chronology and all, is what this is. The result is a book far longer than the first, though it took less than a third of the time to write. Getting older makes some things easier, too.

I append below a list of those individuals and institutions who have aided me in my Schoeck researches over the years. It is chastening for me to read through it, as many have died since the first book was written, though in my mind's eye and ear they and their voices remain as vividly real as when I met and spoke with them. Just as I completed the first draft I learnt of the death of Elisabeth Schoeck-Grüebler, the wife of the composer's nephew (and herself related to Schoeck through the Fassbind family); five weeks later her husband Georg also passed away. Elisabeth was—though to write about her and Georg in the past tense is both jarring and painful—one of the few historians to engage objectively with the life and music of Othmar Schoeck, and much in the present book is indebted to her work. She was also a witness at my wedding, and she became a much-loved godmother of our first daughter, who bears her name; Elisabeth's eldest daughter Salome in turn became godmother to our son, and he bears the names of her three brothers as his own. Georg Schoeck was a noted classical scholar and author with a range of intellectual interests as wide as those of his wife, and his reminiscences of his uncle are among the most vivid on record. The present book—as was intended from the start—is dedicated to Elisabeth, Georg, and their children, as a meager token of gratitude for their support and encouragement over many years.

Several friends and colleagues have in the course of my work given of their time, energy, and ideas to such an extent that merely to name them in a list would be unkind—which is not, of course, to imply that those listed below were in any wise of lesser importance to my project. If it were not for Robin Holloway's Cambridge lecture series of 1983 on twentieth-century music, I would not have become interested in Schoeck in the first place. And I particularly wish to express my gratitude to Martin Germann, Harry Joelson-Strohbach, Christoph Keller, Jürg Stenzl, and above all to my doctoral supervisors, John Warrack and the late Derrick Puffett, for my many conversations with them proved more stimulating to my work than they could possibly know. Assistance with typesetting the music examples was kindly provided by my student Fritz von Geyso. Permission to print those music examples was generously given by Universal Edition, Breitkopf & Härtel, Bärenreiter, and Hug Verlage.

I wish to record my thanks to the following for their assistance both direct and indirect with the research for this book: Janus Anderson, Richard Andrewes; Dorothea Baumann; Antony Beaumont; Charles Beer; Hansjörg Bendel; Ruth Berghaus; Günter Birkner; Daniel Bodmer; Angela Born; Alfred Bollinger; Ferdinand Bossart; Roman Brotbeck; Margrit and Georg Corrodi; Ulrich Cürten; John Deathridge; Stefan Dell'Olivo; Martin Derungs; Rainer Diederichs; Thomas Dünner; Sibylle Ehrismann; Kurt and Esther von Fischer; Beat Föllmi; Hanny Fries; Sylvia Gähwiller; Wolfgang Gartzke; Mireille Geering; Vreni Germann; Daniel Gloor; Sibyll Güntersperger; Hartmut Hell; Hans-Joachim Hinrichsen; Hans Peter Höhener; Hans Hubacher; Peter Hug; Hugo Hungerbühler; Ernst Isler; Corinna and Gerhard Jäger-Trees; Margrit Joelson-Strohbach; Max, Christa, and Katrin Käser; Wolfram Kinzig; Lotte Klemperer; Elisabeth Koch-Brun; Hermann Köstler; Georg Kreis; Thomas Krüger; Stefan Kunze; Hans Helmut, Irmgard, Christian, Peter, and Michael Kurz; Aygün Lausch; Fritz and Laurence Lendenmann; Glenys Linos; Hansrolf Loeffel; Hans Jürg Lüthi; Christoph Lüthy; Max Lütolf; Anna-Pia Maissen; Katharina Malecki; Yvonne Mörgeli; Peter Moerkerk; Renée Mouret; Charles, Eliane, and Sylvie Müller; Elsbeth Müller; Hans Müller; Verena Naegele; Magdalena Neff; Karl Neracher; Jörg Obrecht; Walter and Barbara Ochsenbein; Bernhard Päuler; Peter Palmer; Claudia Patsch; Guillermo Peretti; Gerhard Persché; Jim Reed; Vivian Rehman; Jeannell and Goetz Richter; Elsbeth Richter-Mutzenbecher; Rolf Urs Ringger; Paul Sacher; Frank and Ursula Schädelin; Elisabeth Schniderlin; Karin Schoeller; Meinrad Schütter; Willi Schuh; Franz Ludwig and Lesley von Senger; Sabrina Sonntag; Emil Staiger; Jonathan Steinberg; Ute Stoecklin; Hans Sturzenegger; Madeleine Sulzer; Peter Sulzer; Niklaus Tüller; Anna Katharina d'Uscio; Luzia van der Brüggen; Isobel van der Walt; Mario Venzago; Josef von Vintschger; Werner Vogel; Hans Vogt; Frédéric Wandeler; Margrit Weber; Viktor Weibel-Reichmuth; Marianne Zelger-Vogt; and Werner Gabriel Zimmerman.

Furthermore, I wish to express my thanks to the following institutions for their kind assistance: the Staatsbibliothek Preussischer Kulturbesitz; the Cambridge University Library and Pendlebury Library; the British Library; the Bodleian Library and Music Faculty Library in Oxford; Christ Church, Oxford; the Stadtarchiv Braunschweig; the University Library of Freiburg im Breisgau; the Institut de Musicologie in Fribourg; the Felix Mendelssohn-Bartholdy Conservatory in Leipzig; the Bayerisches Staatsarchiv and the Bayerische Staatsbibliothek in Munich; the Music Library of the University of Pretoria; the Musikkollegium, Stadtbibliothek, and Rychenberg-Stiftung in Winterthur; the Zentralbibliothek Zürich; the Othmar Schoeck-Gesellschaft; the Musikwissenschaftliches Seminar of the University of Zurich; the Eidgenössische Technische Hochschule Zürich; the Stadtarchiv and Staatsarchiv of Zurich; and the Tonhallegesellschaft Zürich.

The prime object of my gratitude, as always, is my family: my wife Riëtte and our children Elisabeth Irmgard Elena, Elza Lotte Glenys and Alvaro Wolfgang Konrad.

Abbreviations

CWZ   Chris Walton. *Othmar Schoeck und seine Zeitgenossen*. Winterthur: Amadeus, 2002.

DPS   Derrick Puffett. *The Song Cycles of Othmar Schoeck*. Bern: Peter Lang, 1982.

HCD   Hans Corrodi. Diary (manuscript; held by the Zentralbibliothek Zürich).

ISCM   International Society for Contemporary Music

KTV   Kantonsschulturnverein (cantonal school gymnastics association)

PSR   Peter Sulzer. *Zehn Komponisten um Werner Reinhart*. Vols. 1–3. Zurich: Atlantis Musikbuch-Verlag, 1979, 1980, and 1983.

SMZ   *Schweizerische Musikzeitung*. Zurich: Hug.

woo   without opus [no.] (German: WoO. Werk ohne Opuszahl)

WVG   Werner Vogel. *Othmar Schoeck im Gespräch*. Zurich: Atlantis, 1965.

WVZ   Werner Vogel. *Othmar Schoeck: Leben und Schaffen im Spiegel von Selbstzeugnissen und Zeitgenossenberichten*. Zurich: Atlantis Musikbuch-Verlag, 1976.

NB: almost all the extant correspondence to Schoeck, and most letters from Schoeck to others, are today held by the Zentralbibliothek Zürich. Where such correspondence is mentioned or quoted in the text without further reference, then the reader may assume that it is held by the Zentralbibliothek Zürich.

All letters to Hermann Burte mentioned here, and copies of correspondence from Burte to Werner Reinhart, are held by the Burte archives in Maulburg in Germany.

Note on orthography: The German "sz" ("ß") is printed throughout as "ss."

Introduction

Schoeck and the Swiss

Is there a topography of music? Some innate correlation between habitat and harmony, sound and space? Or is it mere conditioning that conjures up in our mind's eye the glories of Prague at the close of Smetana's *Vltava*, or swans circling above the endless Finlandian forests of Sibelius's Fifth Symphony? Is it wishful thinking that the music of Elgar seems to mirror the very contours of the Malvern Hills, while the ballets of Copland somehow summon up visions of the vast plains of the American West, even to those who have never seen them? And why do certain works by Grieg send us pining for the fjords? Of course, place is often depicted most vividly of all by those who do not belong there, but whose concern is to construct an exoticized Other. Spain seems to lie before us far more clearly in the Iberian fantasies of the French, China in the *chinoiserie* of Puccini, and Antarctica in the Seventh Symphony of Vaughan Williams than in anything any Spaniard, Chinese, or musicking penguin might contrive.

Of all the exotic locations popularized by travelers and travel writers of Europe since the heyday of the Grand Tour in the eighteenth century, one close to home proved to possess an appeal as powerful as it was lasting. Switzerland—to be precise, the sublime Switzerland of the Alps with its spectacular sunsets, lakes, and waterfalls—exerted an immense influence on the Western psyche. Byron, Shelley, Mark Twain, and Turner: the Anglo-Saxons in particular made of Switzerland an exotic, "imaginary" location, extolling both its natural virtues and the charmingly tenacious independence of its populace. But apart from those popularizing painters and printmakers who churned out engravings by the kitschy thousand of those Alpine sunsets, lakes, and waterfalls, Switzerland impinged upon the world of art in a manner at once more circumlocutory and yet far more immediate, namely as the point of origin for some of the most significant moments in Western culture. For without Switzerland, arguably, there would be no *Frankenstein*, no *Woyzeck*, no *Ring of the Nibelung*, no *Tristan und Isolde*, no *Rite of Spring*, no *Soldier's Tale*, no *Ulysses*, no *Zauberberg*, no Dada *entier*. Indeed, one could argue that modernism itself was born on the Gablerstrasse in the Zurich suburb of Enge in 1857, when Richard Wagner's stifled sexual urge found expression in the yearning prelude to *Tristan*. And what was perhaps the world's grandest modernist project of all—as grand in scope as in its failure—was also begun from there: the Soviet Union, brainchild of

Vladimir Ilyich Ulyanov, *aka* Lenin, who moved with ease from the Spiegelgasse to the Kremlin. His apartment in Zurich, as it happens, had been next door to the one in which a failed Hessian revolutionary of the previous century had lived and died: Georg Büchner, the dramatist of Danton and Woyzeck, buried today on the Zürichberg near the topmost stop of the nearby cog railway.

That Switzerland should have been home to the cutting edge of art might at first seem odd; but as much as it looks to us to be at the center of the map of Europe, it has, in a real sense, long been situated at its "borders." This is politically a fact today, on account of its self-imposed exclusion from the European Union, though this is merely the most obvious, contemporary signifier of a sense of "difference" that is much older. Switzerland has long remained a place of exile in the eyes of its neighbors, either as an exotic other for moneyed tourists, as a magic mountain for the tubercular, or as a temporary political elsewhere for foreign liberals and socialists unwanted or unsafe at home. All those prints, panoramas, postcards, and engravings were popular precisely because they signified a place, however geographically near, that was in fact far, far from one's own.

Musical depictions of Switzerland itself are more difficult to come by than the pictorial—perhaps not least because one cannot buy a symphony, sign it, stick a stamp on it, and send it home as proof of place—and they are usually unconvincing unless they include an alphorn, real or *faux* (such as the cor anglais in Rossini's *William Tell Overture*). There has been no Bartók or Kodály to take indigenous musical expression and merge it with the art and artistry of the West; there are no piano sonatas based on alphorn scales, no syncretic yodeling symphonies. Some have argued for the Swiss aura of those idyllic works of Brahms that were conceived by the Lake of Thun; but that too is a Swissness of the picture-postcard cliché, regardless of the actual, undeniable aesthetic worth of the music itself. The finest depictions of the Swiss landscape in music are perhaps to be found precisely where they have not generally been sought: in Wagner's *Ring*, where the composer's extensive Alpine wanderings through mountain passes, over glaciers, and alongside woodland torrents found a corollary in sound in the opening and close of the *Rheingold* with its swirling eddies and rainbow bridges in misty heights, and in the first act of the *Walküre* with its winter storms and balmy, moonlit nights.

In the reception history of the music of Arthur Honegger and Frank Martin, the two most widely known names in Swiss music, a hunt for traits specifically Swiss has never been of import, perhaps because they are seen both by their countrymen and by commentators abroad as essentially cosmopolitan in spirit. Indeed, Honegger is often, but mistakenly, regarded as having been French, though he was in fact a German Swiss who studied at the Conservatory of Zurich. But his home remained Paris for most of his life, and as a member of *Les Six* he was situated, if briefly, at the forefront of the musical avant-garde in the inter-War years. Frank Martin, who emigrated to Holland after World War II, was one of Switzerland's first composers to adopt the twelve-tone method (albeit in a highly personal, haphazard fashion), and this in itself served to stamp him as "international."

It is in the music of their slightly older contemporary, Othmar Schoeck (1886–1957), that the (German) Swiss themselves have most often, and most obviously, sought to find trace elements of a "national character" in music.[1] Regarded by many today as perhaps the finest talent of that twentieth-century Swiss triumvirate, Schoeck remained obstinately homebound, whereas Honegger and Martin gladly sojourned on foreign shores. Born in Brunnen by the banks of Lake Lucerne, Schoeck moved to Zurich in his early teens to attend school. With the exception of a year's study spent in Leipzig and extended holidays back in the family home, he never lived anywhere else. It was also in Zurich that he died, just a few months after his seventieth birthday. His music is almost all vocal, which has not aided its export: some four hundred songs and eight operas stand alongside half a dozen orchestral scores, a handful of chamber works, and a number of small, occasional pieces for piano, most of them weak. He was decidedly anti-modernist in his literary tastes, preferring by far to set the early German Romantic poets and later gravitating toward the Swiss Romantics Gottfried Keller and Conrad Ferdinand Meyer. But the hunt for his Swissness was, and is, if anything an attempt to deny the reality that he was in his music and biography as far removed as possible from the picture that the Swiss like to have of themselves, and which is largely shared by the rest of the world.

What, then, is "Swiss"? This is not so easy to answer, for while Switzerland as a unified, modern state is just a century and a half old, its much older political stability, neutral status, and freedom from outside oppression largely spared it from the war and strife that helped to cement those notions of nationalism current since the late eighteenth century in France, Germany, or the Slavic states. For the Swiss themselves, as for outsiders, "Swissness" is most commonly denoted by punctuality, cleanliness, a staunchly Protestant work ethic, a clockmaker's devotion to detail, fidelity to accepted, moderate moral and political beliefs, and carefulness with money. All these clichés are as unremarkably banal as they are, in fact, remarkably accurate. And Schoeck? Notoriously unpunctual and disorderly, with holes in his socks, his manuscripts strewn on the floor and trodden underfoot, he spent his money as it came in, borrowed it when it didn't, then didn't pay it back, took barely a thought of the morrow, never got up before midday unless he had to, never went to bed until the early hours unless he had to, frequently drank to excess, and was possessed of a voracious (hetero)sexual appetite, with one bed-partner at a time not always enough: in short, a Romantic Bohemian such as one might expect to find in the semi-mythical garrets of Montmartre, not on the serenely civilized Zeltweg in central Zurich. Self-consciously Bohemian, to be sure, with an obvious need to live against the grain and to be observed doing so, but a Bohemian nevertheless. This is not to say that the urge to subvert the Swiss "virtues" listed above has not been just as compulsive for others, if in different ways. It is surely, in part, the origin of those extremities in art already mentioned. As I can confirm from personal experience, a couple of years spent frequenting sedate coffee houses with spotless bathroom facilities can make anyone fantasize about booking a railway ticket to world revolution via the Finland Station. But in Schoeck, subversion and submission, resistance and acceptance play off each other in a myriad of ways that are responsible for much of the impact of his music. The extant recordings of his piano playing—as accompanist to his own songs and those of others—display in indubitable terms the extrovert Bohemian. The flexibility of tempo and immediacy of expression make the music sound as though it is being improvised before our very ears. And yet this merely demonstrates the immense control that the composer-as-performer was able to exercise over his material, a control so masterly that he was even able to conceal its existence. Regrettably, only one brief recording of Schoeck's conducting survives, though it supports the claims of those who insist that his art of interpretation was the same whether he sat at a piano or stood on the podium. His scores themselves, on the other hand—in their calligraphy probably as beautiful as those of any composer one could choose—display the archetypal Swiss clockmaker's ethos, being meticulously crafted for fullness of effect with economy of means. The late Derrick Puffett once remarked to me of his surprise upon at last procuring the score of a work by Schoeck that he had known for several years from a recording only. Certain passages with a particularly rich orchestral sound, he said, turned out to comprise just a few staves of music, exquisitely scored. The spacings, textures, and instrumental colors and combinations betray both the keenness of Schoeck's ear and the fact that, as the composer once admitted in an unguarded moment, this ostentatiously intuitive composer had in fact spent many hours studying in detail the orchestrations of Ravel, Stravinsky, and Strauss. Even in those of his late works where the inspiration is no longer at white heat, Schoeck's instrumentation still exudes a luminescence of which an Alban Berg would have been proud.

Schoeck has in Swiss writing also been celebrated as a typical example of so-called "helvetische Stilverspätung," or "Helvetic stylistic belatedness," namely that characteristic of much Swiss art by which trends from abroad do not properly impinge until at least a decade later than elsewhere.[2] There is assuredly an element of truth in this. Schoeck's best-known opera, *Penthesilea,* written 1923–25, is an example of bloodthirsty expressionism such as one found fifteen or twenty years earlier in the work of Strauss and Schoenberg. But if Schoeck came late to the modern, he caught up very quickly. There are passages in *Penthesilea* that one can explain as Schoeck's reaction to learning of Schoenberg's twelve-tone method, which had been formulated just a few months previously. But more than this: from 1923 to 1928 Schoeck underwent a stylistic evolution as astonishingly swift as it was extreme, covering in the space of some five years an aesthetic territory that took other composers decades to conquer. From a late-Romanticism rooted in Brahms and Wolf he moved through a vortex of expressionism and near-atonality to emerge in 1928, writing a ragtime-inflected sonata for bass clarinet as neoclassical as anything to be found in the worklists of his better-known contemporaries, and an equally neoclassical, ostentatiously tonal *Zeitoper* about a marital squabble that is in its topic akin to Strauss's *Intermezzo* and Schoenberg's *Von heute auf morgen*. In the mid- to late 1920s Schoeck's music was hardly "behind the times," and we can from today's perspective even interpret his retreat thereafter (though the noun is admittedly loaded) into a superficially more conservative position, as in the case of the post-*Elektra* Strauss, as merely one of the many strands of a nascent post-modern aesthetic.

If there is, however, a single trait that one can observe throughout the whole of Schoeck's oeuvre, then it is a sense of impermanence, even of loss. Be it the loss of a supposedly paradisiacal, innocent childhood, the tautological loss of love (real, imagined, or fearfully anticipated), or even, at the close, the loss brought about by waning creativity—the loss, as it were, of the ability to express loss itself—all this imbues Schoeck's music with a sense of fissure, of fracture, and with it a striking modernity, even when the musical building blocks themselves are superficially unassuming or just downright conservative. There is, again, nothing very Swiss about all of this, nothing local or parochial. The closer one looks at Schoeck's music, the less it surprises that in his day it occasioned admiration from a wide spectrum of leading musicians and literary figures, from Alban Berg, Ferruccio Busoni, Wilhelm Furtwängler, Arthur Honegger, and Ernst Krenek to James Joyce, Thomas Mann, and Hermann Hesse.

And yet, regardless of how we might wish to position Schoeck away from isolated Alpine heights and into the musical mainstream of the twentieth century, we must be frank: his music will probably never attain the broad appeal of a Honegger, if only because it is so resolutely situated in the world of (German) song, making no fewer demands on the audience than does, say, the vocal music of Hugo Wolf. But the past twenty years have nevertheless seen a marked increase in the frequency of recordings and performances: his opera *Penthesilea* has enjoyed a dozen different productions since the celebrations surrounding the centenary of his birth in 1986 (the most recent being the near-simultaneous productions in Basel and Dresden in early 2008), while almost all his music is now available on CD. These recordings feature many first-rate performances from singers and ensembles both home-grown-Swiss and international, including such names as Ian Bostridge, Lynne Dawson, and the English Chamber Orchestra. The only major works that have not been released on CD in their entirety are, regrettably, his two most stage-worthy operas, *Don Ranudo* and *Vom Fischer un syner Fru*.

The single most important man in the reception history of Schoeck's music was Hans Corrodi (1889–1972), who became friendly with the composer in 1912. They were for a while close enough for them to holiday together, and Schoeck also confided highly personal matters to him in these early years—until, that is, he realized that Corrodi was planning to write his biography. At this point Schoeck ceased their intimacy, and the distance between them became ever greater as time went on. Corrodi's biography of the composer appeared first in 1931, the second edition in time for Schoeck's fiftieth birthday in 1936, while the third, and last, edition came out in 1956, at the time of the composer's seventieth birthday. What Schoeck did not know was that Corrodi had been keeping a detailed diary from shortly after their first acquaintance, of which he alone formed the the subject matter. It was continued after Schoeck's death, to record the further reception history of the man and his music. Corrodi had it typed, copied, bound, and locked away in two Swiss libraries before he died, by which time it numbered some two thousand densely typed pages. He also used its contents as the basis for an expanded, unpublished biography, of which he made a second, condensed, version. He placed both in the Swiss National Library, under instructions that they were not to be published in full until after the death of Schoeck's wife and daughter. A copy of the shortened version has recently become available to scholars, though it contains nothing of substance that is not to be found in the (far more comprehensive) diaries. This confirms a statement by Corrodi's widow that these were in fact the principal source for the unpublished biography as a whole.[3]

Corrodi adored Schoeck's music and idolized the man. He was an equally devoted Wagnerian, and he despised the modernists, regarding Schoeck's music as the final peak of the Western tradition of which Wagner formed for him the highest summit; his devotion to Wagner also expressed itself in a pronounced anti-Semitism. Corrodi was by trade a German teacher, and he spent his working life at the Teachers' Training College in Küsnacht, just down the eastern shore of Lake Zurich, a few kilometers from the city itself. Corrodi published dozens of articles, almost all of them about Schoeck and his music; several dozen more remained unpublished. Schoeck's death did not stop Corrodi from writing about him, and he became one of the leading lights in the Schoeck Society that was formed just months after the composer's death.

The obsessive nature of Corrodi's passion cannot be denied, and it merits some attention here, not least because that obsession was also tolerated by Schoeck himself. Corrodi's widow even admitted to me that her husband—who was several years her elder—had made it clear before their marriage that she would always come second in his life, behind Schoeck. To what extent his partisanship for the composer had a homoerotic aspect is difficult to say. Corrodi's diary does record how on one occasion he found out that he was suspected of being homosexual. What is telling about his reaction is not that he found it absurd (which he did), but the fact that he felt no need to spend more than a few words denying it, which of itself suggests that there was little or no truth in it. It is likely in any case that he had been confused with his namesake Eduard Korrodi, the leading Zurich literary critic of the time, who was indeed gay.[4] No; much as we might today mock the romanticized male bondings of the late nineteenth and early twentieth centuries that we all know from the literature of the day, and much as we might write them off as a product of sublimated sexual desires (sublimated since "forbidden"), this is in some cases probably a matter of our imposing our own (pseudo-) psychoanalytical fads on a quite different era. For his day Schoeck was himself unusually liberal in sexual matters. When Corrodi once raised the topic of Oscar Wilde, Schoeck's reaction proves that he found nothing odd or "immoral" about homosexuality—it was "natural," he said, adding with characteristic bluntness that "every dog has it in him"[5]—though such remarks are also infrequent enough to suggest in turn that he had no particular interest in it. So the possibility of deconstructing him and his first biographer as homophobic, closet gays recedes rapidly from view. Wittgenstein once remarked caustically about Freud's fondness for spotting phallic symbols in dreams: sometimes, he said, a top hat is just a top hat, and nothing more.[6] Similarly, the few close male friendships that Schoeck enjoyed cannot really be construed as anything but just that: neither more nor less "sexual" in nature than the same-sex friendships in which the rest of humanity daily participates.

Corrodi stares at us from the available (German/Swiss) literature in a single stock photograph taken in his late middle age (see fig. I.1): balding, bespectacled, terribly stern, the archetypal Germanic schoolmaster, and possessed of a disturbing, obsessive stare that somehow correlates with the racist anti-Semite who emerges from the pages of many of his writings. But while Corrodi has offered many a commentator a suitable target for demonization, there was enough to the man to warrant a more subtle investigation of him. He had a play performed at the Zurich City Theater in the mid-1920s; not particularly successful, to be sure, but judged good enough to be performed on its own merits. He was a keen amateur photographer and a not ungifted amateur painter. And to judge from numerous reports of former students, he was a first-class teacher. His wife Margrit was intellectually at least his equal and under the pseudonym "Margo Markwalder" enjoyed a highly successful career as a novelist in the 1950s and 1960s. Their elder son had a phenomenal memory and was by all accounts a linguistic genius (the word is used with caution, though justified by the reports of those who knew him, such as Daniel Bodmer of Atlantis Verlag); he died early, not long after his father. Their other son won the coveted "Knabenschiessen" competition when a teenager—the traditional annual shooting match for the youth of all Zurich, the winning of which brings fame and glory of a kind any adolescent male would desire. The Corrodis were thus no average family, and whatever Hans's failings as a biographer, he is to be taken seriously. Unfortunately for the composer, Corrodi's long-time dominance of the field of Schoeck studies meant that the biographer's aesthetic became overlaid upon the composer's own. In his old age, Schoeck made many remarks that betray an anti-modernist stance almost identical to Corrodi's; but the latter in his writings conveniently omitted to mention that Schoeck had in his younger years espoused quite different views altogether, showing a keen interest in the latest music of Berg, Stravinsky, Schoenberg, Krenek, and their contemporaries. The obvious contradiction inherent in a composer's producing near-atonal works of music (as Schoeck did in the mid-1920s) while supposedly despising any hint

Figure I.1. Hans Corrodi in 1955.

of modernity went unquestioned for many years after Corrodi's death—indeed, until his diaries became available to researchers. As we shall see in due course, Corrodi's impact extended beyond Schoeck alone, for it seems likely that he also exerted a considerable influence on the figure of Zeitblom in Thomas Mann's novel *Doktor Faustus*.

Corrodi was not without his "competitors" (as he saw it). His younger contemporary Willi Schuh penned many articles on aspects of the composer's work, some of which were later gathered together in book form. Most of these, however, were originally reviews of first performances and eschewed anything biographical. Schuh was the most gifted of the early Schoeck commentators, but his proximity to the composer, both personal and geographical (they lived just a few streets apart), led him to avoid issues that could have muddied the waters of their friendship. It is a pity: Schuh would have been ideally placed to write the biography that could have put Schoeck studies on a firm foundation decades ago, but he chose not to. Corrodi's real successor was Werner Vogel, who in 1949 wrote the first-ever doctoral dissertation on Schoeck's music and in 1956 published a thematic catalogue of his works that remains valuable to this day. Now deceased, Vogel worked as a music teacher in Zurich, and he was by all accounts a fine pianist. He got to know Schoeck in the early 1940s when he began rehearsing with the composer's wife, Hilde, who was a soprano. Vogel's visits soon centered on the composer instead, and he began—in secret—to keep a diary of everything that Schoeck said and did. This was, *nota bene,* without knowing that Corrodi had already been doing the exact same thing for more than thirty years. Vogel published extensive excerpts from these diaries almost a decade after Schoeck's death.[7] They are fascinating, though since they record the views of the composer in his last few years, when he felt himself forgotten by the world, they record a man prone to bitterness and generally anti-modernist in his aesthetic ("I've never written a *single* measure of atonal music!" Schoeck insisted vehemently and erroneously a few months before his death).[8] This, however, when compared with earlier accounts, is but a small part of the story. It was only the "final chapter" of a life, though since it tallied with Corrodi's portrayal of the whole man, the unsuspecting reader had little choice but to read backwards, as it were, to construct a picture of a younger but equally anti-modernist Schoeck that was consistent with the man described by his diarists.

Vogel's documentary volume of 1976: *Othmar Schoeck: Leben und Schaffen im Spiegel von Selbstzeugnissen und Zeitgenossenberichten* ("Othmar Schoeck: Life and Work Reflected in His Own Words and Reports of His Contemporaries"), a kind of biography *manqué*, was, like Corrodi's book, a summation of its author's work and research of many years. In 1986, the year of the Schoeck centenary, Vogel published an edition of Schoeck's letters to his parents from his year of study in Leipzig (1907–8). That same year also saw the publication of a slim volume on Schoeck's childhood and youth by the composer's own nephew Georg (*Die Welt des jungen Othmar Schoeck*), which included not just fascinating family testimonies but a host of reproductions of artworks by Schoeck, his father, and his brothers. Also among the centenary celebrations was the first-ever Schoeck conference, held in Bern, of which the papers were published two years later. In 1991, Georg Schoeck's wife Elisabeth published *Post nach Brunnen,* an edition of letters from Schoeck to his parents subsequent to those already published by Vogel. Both Georg and Elisabeth published several other valuable articles on the composer in the ensuing years.

While the bibliography on him is not insubstantial, Schoeck's music has not yet prompted what one might term sustained musicological enquiry. Derrick Puffett's brilliant doctoral study of the song cycles from 1976 (long since remaindered) is to date the only book in English on the composer or his work, and it is by far the best book on the music in any tongue.[9] English contributions to Schoeck studies otherwise comprise a couple of fascinating articles from the pen of Robin Holloway and a number of articles and reviews by Peter Palmer. Since Vogel there have been a few other doctoral and undergraduate theses on Schoeck's music, though with the exception of Puffett none has had any lasting impact on Schoeck studies. There is one each on the song cycles by Charles Cattin (1973)[10] and Stefanie Tiltmann-Fuchs (1975);[11] Canisius Braun's fascinating thesis on Schoeck's conducting career with the St. Gallen Symphony Orchestra (1989) has sadly remained unpublished and, it seems, almost completely unnoticed.[12] Then there is a thesis by Michael Baumgartner on *Massimilla Doni,* written in tandem with his editing of that opera;[13] the same author's doctoral thesis on female statues in opera—"Exilierte Göttinnen: Die Darstellung der weiblichen Statue in Othmar Schoecks *Venus,* Kurt Weills *One Touch of Venus* und Thea Musgraves *The Voice of Ariadne*" (2005) was still unavailable at the time of writing. Despite these several theses, the most significant contributions of the past thirty years in the German-speaking world, besides those of Georg and Elisabeth Schoeck, are probably the few articles by Jürg Stenzl and, most recently, by Hans-Joachim Hinrichsen (for full details of all these titles, see the bibliography at the end of this book).

There does exist, however, one large-scale musicological project concerned with Schoeck, namely the *Sämtliche Werke* (Complete Works) set up at Zurich University under the auspices of the Othmar Schoeck Society in the late 1980s, first with the medievalist Max Lütolf as chief editor, and latterly with his former assistant Beat A. Föllmi in that position. But as Föllmi has himself remarked, the principal purpose of the edition is merely to "lay the necessary foundations for [Schoeck] research to come about."[14] The forewords to the volumes that have appeared thus far contain much useful documentary information on early performances and the like. The editors of the edition, again under the auspices of the Schoeck Society, initiated a book series in the 1990s (*Schriftenreihe der Othmar Schoeck-Gesellschaft*), of which four volumes have now appeared, though they contain in total more contributions about other composers than they do about Schoeck himself.

When one compares him with his contemporaries (even excluding the "big names" such as Strauss and Mahler), one sees just how poorly Schoeck has fared in the research stakes. Two simple means of comparison offer themselves: the RILM ("Répertoire International de Littérature Musicale") database of abstracts of music literature and the "Doctoral Dissertations in Musicology Online" (DDM), run by the School of Music of Indiana University, Bloomington. A search in RILM for "Schoeck" gives 127 hits for the past forty-one years. A sample of his contemporaries fares as follows: Hans Pfitzner, 558 hits; Arthur Honegger, 399; Alexander Zemlinsky, 285; and Ferruccio Busoni, 717. The DDM database confirms the trend: Schoeck, 5 hits; Pfitzner, 12; Honegger, 11;[15] Zemlinsky, 16; Busoni, 32.

As already outlined, Schoeck's name is no longer unknown outside his native country. But there have only been two biographies of Schoeck to date (not counting Vogel's collection of documents), namely Corrodi's and my own. Both were published only in German (the latter in 1994). At the time of writing, a further biography, in French, is being written by Beat A. Föllmi. However, there is as yet no biographical study of the composer in English, and it is this state of affairs that the present volume seeks to address.

Today, in our post-Barthesian era when the *auteur* is supposed to be *mort,* the biographer who determines nevertheless to resurrect him in words must inevitably be mistrustful of himself and his task. For what biographer does not in some way identify with his subject, for bad or for good, and how can one avoid (re)creating him in one's own image? The temptation is constantly to cut one's subject down to size, to doubt all that cannot be proven ineluctably true, and to explain the composer's personality as if by drawing up a list of specific attributes and calculating the sum of them one could unfailingly elucidate the workings of his psyche. To be sure, any serious biographer will wish to avoid hagiography and to "humanize" his subject. But a portrait of the artist today that hopes to do justice to his "humanness" must also allow for the possibility that certain aspects of his life will remain unexplained and inexplicable to both biographer and reader. Almost all first-hand reports of Schoeck, for example—whether written or verbal—tell of the composer's "magnetic personality." During my research on Schoeck in Switzerland in the late 1980s, the emotive power upon his contemporaries of the man and his music was still palpable. On one occasion I visited an old, bedridden woman up on the Zürichberg, after a student acquaintance who tended to her remarked that she had sung in a choir under the composer some seventy years earlier. Her whole being became animated as she spoke of Schoeck, and she sang his song "Das bescheidene Wünschlein" from memory, entire and unprompted. She also mentioned a "Martha Nabholz" with whom Schoeck had enjoyed a liaison—did I detect a note of envy in her voice? It is too long ago to remember precisely, and perhaps I am now reading things in that were not there. But throughout my research I observed similar reactions among those who had known the man. To write of the "personal magnetism" of one's subject goes decidedly against the grain for a biographer working in the early twenty-first century, attempting to scratch away the romanticized palimpsest to locate the "truth" lurking beneath the surface text. It smacks all too much of the cultic idolatry of the artist as perpetrated in the popular literature of the Romantics. And yet when intelligent, down-to-earth men and women, not otherwise given to hyperbole, idolization, or emotional indulgence, still speak of the composer's powerful personal aura, or of the mesmerizing effect of Schoeck's supposedly limpid blue eyes (even the cool, methodical, indubitably heterosexual Paul Sacher, billionaire conductor and patron, was one of those mesmerized thus, as he readily admitted), then one has little choice but to allow for certain aspects of the man that resist rational explanation (what on earth is an "aura"? And what, precisely, constitutes *mesmerizing eyes?* How does one describe or define them, except with the adjective thus?). These aspects were obviously vital to the manner in which the composer impinged upon his surroundings and engaged with his contemporaries. After all, it can hardly be a matter of mere chance that his every word and gesture was being recorded independently by two separate diarists at the same time, at opposite ends of Zurich. If I may generalize one last time: the Swiss on the whole are averse to wearing their hearts on their sleeves, to displaying excess of emotion, to erecting any cult of personality, and yet Schoeck prompted a good many of his contemporaries to do all of this for him. Perhaps his very "unSwissness" made his compatriots all the more keen to claim him as typically "Swiss," as if his example somehow freed them to postulate what they would really prefer "Swissness" to constitute, far away from all the clichéd norms.

In addition to the standard investigation of the facts of Schoeck's life and the notes of his music that are the topic of this volume, there must and will, therefore, also remain in the following biographical explorations a number of metaphorical rough edges, loose ends, and occasional subjective suppositions that will not be disguised as anything else. It is possible that some of these roughnesses are inevitable, as resulting in part from the friction between Schoeck's local specificity—that "Swissness" of his, at once dubious yet undeniable (for the geographical facts of his birth and life are fixed)—and his "generality," namely his position as a composer of significance within the musical traditions of Central Europe in the twentieth century. Perhaps locating those frictions themselves will make it possible to identify whatever correlations might actually exist between his music and his physical space. And perhaps—just perhaps—we might even find that Schoeck is indeed "Swiss" in some way after all.

Chapter One

Childhood and Youth

Birth may be an obvious place to begin the story of a life, but it is admirably finite; so we shall begin there. Othmar Schoeck was born in Brunnen in Canton Schwyz, in a villa overlooking Lake Lucerne, on 1 September 1886. The fact that the place of his birth is one of the most picturesque in Switzerland was no mere happenstance, for his father, an artist, had gone there in order to paint its landscapes. This Alfred Schoeck (1841–1931) was the only surviving child of a rich silk merchant from the city of Basel. His family, originally from the area around Heilbronn in southern Germany, had arrived there via France, where until the revolution a surgeon-Schoeck had been personal physician to the unlucky Princesse de Lamballe. Alfred had not inherited his family's business leanings, his ambitions being instead centered on the visual arts. This artistic streak was paired with a wanderlust such as one finds celebrated in the writings of the early German Romantics. So Alfred studied painting with Friedrich Horner and François Diday and thereafter spent a goodly portion of his considerable inheritance in traveling the northern hemisphere, hunting and painting. Photographs of him sitting at an easel, surrounded by trees and his own artwork, survive as testament to his exploits in Canada, the Lofoten islands, and the Dobruja.

When Alfred returned to Switzerland in the 1870s, it was not to his native city. Instead, he came to the region around Lucerne, which with its lakes, mountains, and forests is as good a spot for a painter as anything one might find in more extreme climes—after all, it had inspired Turner to some of his finest canvases thirty-odd years before. Alfred toyed with the idea of renting Wagner's former house in Tribschen but then went instead to Brunnen, on the other side of the Rigi mountain, booking himself a room in the fanciest hotel in the vicinity, the Waldstätterhof, which had hosted just about all the famous tourists that the nineteenth century could offer, including Queen Victoria. And it was here that Alfred finally fell in love and in 1876 married and quit his wanderings. His wife, Agathe Fassbind, was not just the daughter of the Waldstätterhof's wealthy owner but reputedly one of the prettiest girls in town. Her family history was also demonstrably Swiss, unlike Alfred's; one of her forefathers was Johann Rudolf Wettstein, who had been his country's representative at the negotiations for the Peace Treaty of Westphalia of 1648. Although the Fassbinds were Roman Catholic and Alfred Protestant, religious differences did not prove an unsurmountable hurdle. Agathe raised their children in her husband's faith, and she later converted, too.

In 1882, Alfred commissioned one Johann Meyer from Lucerne—the same architect responsible for the Waldstätterhof—to build him a villa on the "Gütsch," the cliff above Brunnen overlooking the lake.[1] He made sure that his "Villa Ruh-heim," as he called it, had enough room not just for a growing family but also for a large artist's studio on the top floor. Alfred and Agathe had six children alto-gether, of whom four boys survived into adulthood: Paul (1882–1952), who was an architect and a gifted watercolorist, but whose passion lay in writing; Ralph (1884–1969), who became an engineer but possessed a fine gift for portraiture; Walter (1885–1953), who took over the running of the family hotel, but whose real love was playing the cello; and Othmar, the youngest, and the only one who would live out his artistic inclinations to the full. They all inherited their father's artistic gifts to a greater or lesser extent—gifts passed on in turn to Walter's son, Georg, and to Georg's middle son, Wolfgang. But Alfred Schoeck was also a decent singer who had once sung the part of Max in a public performance of Weber's *Freischütz* in Basel.[2] So music was also actively cultivated in the Schoeck household. One of his earliest musical memories, so Schoeck recalled as an old man, was of his father singing the aria "to the evening star" from Wagner's *Tannhäuser*.[3]

Since painting was hardly going to support the Schoecks in the style to which they were accustomed, Alfred turned to the trade of his in-laws. In 1899 he had a hotel built that could cater for the growing tourist industry in Brunnen: the Hotel Eden, set into the side of the cliff beneath his villa (itself later to be renamed "Eden"). He left the running of it, however, to his wife and her right-hand woman, Mathilde Suter from nearby Ingenbohl, the daughter of the local composer and conductor Carl Suter.[4] So while the women ran his business, Alfred painted, and played with his children—by all accounts a model modern father, slow to chide and swift to bless. He now added portraiture to his activities, which proved to be perhaps his greatest talent. None of his many landscapes can match his charming portraits of his wife and children (see fig. 1.1). The family villa in Brunnen still houses the largest extant collection of Alfred's paintings, most of them in his for-mer studio on the top floor, the "atelier," where are also stored the fruits of his ear-lier, peripatetic existence—birds' eggs, a mineral collection, hunting rifles, stuffed deer heads, marble busts, lava from Vesuvius, mounted butterflies, and antique carpets. There is even a vulture that hangs in static flight at the top of the stairs as if guarding the entrance to this schoolboy's paradise: it is a fitting metaphor for the house, where time itself seems to have been captured, embalmed, and put on display for future generations. In a small side room to the atelier there still stands the modest upright piano on which Othmar many years later would compose when visiting for the summer holidays.

Even the casual visitor to Brunnen understands immediately why a painter would wish to settle there. One arrives at an unassuming railway station, the twin peaks of the Mythen looming vast above it, then one traverses a small underpass to reach the main road, from where it is a ten-minute walk to the center of town and the banks of the lake. The little town boasts nothing spectacular in its archi-tecture, with only a small, quaint chapel at its heart that gives any real sense of history to the place, the "Bundeskapelle," consecrated in 1636 and which features

Figure 1.1. Alfred Schoeck: Othmar Schoeck, aged ca. 8. Courtesy of the Schoeck family.

a superb altarpiece by Justus von Egmont, a student of Rubens.[5] But Brunnen's paucity of architectural splendor is inconsequential when one considers the stunning natural views offered from the lake's edge. The view is finer still from the terrace of the Schoecks' family villa, high up on the cliff—so fine that in the early twentieth century outside visitors were charged ten centimes per person to use the hotel lift that still runs from the ground floor up to the terrace.[6]

Brunnen lies at the place where Lake Lucerne merges into the Lake of Uri to form a single expanse of water. On the bank across from the town a steep incline rises to the Seelisberg, with a patch of green meadow at the halfway point. This is the Rütliwiese, the semi-mythical founding spot of Switzerland, where the representatives of the original three cantons gathered seven centuries ago to declare their independence from the Austrian yoke. But the weather is erratic, and mists often descend to obscure one's view. These can lift again, however, as quickly as they arrive. On some days, the air glows a marbled orange as the sun struggles to shine through the fog; at other times, the sun disappears in a blue haze that softens all contours of the opposite bank. And when all is clear, the forests below the Seelisberg shimmer a primeval green above the blue of the lake. It is no coincidence that the nearby Rigi was captured by William Turner in paintings known as the "Blue Rigi," the "Red Rigi" and the "Dark Rigi," for the ever-changing light in this region can at certain times of the year display a chameleon-like quality in which colors alternate with seeming incongruity.

When the weather is calm, the atmosphere of rest and quietness that the place exudes can easily make one forget its turbulent history. Brunnen's place near the head of the Gotthard Pass means that it has seen countless migrations through the ages. Here the armies of the Tsar and Napoleon lunged and parried, back and forth, more than a decade before Borodino—the Schoeck children still occasionally find the odd French coin in the soil of their garden today, presumably lost by some footsoldier slogging by with musket and pack. And when the Gotthard railway was built in the late nineteenth century, hundreds perished down in the hellish granite furrows that were groined beneath the green tranquility of the Alps. The luxurious Swiss transalpine trains carrying today's travelers from Zurich to Milan pass directly under the corner of Schoeck's villa, though they run too deep for even the slightest hum to be discernible on the surface.

Alfred's decision to enter the hotel business was an astute one, for during these years a flood of foreign visitors began that over the next century would be slowed only by two world wars. When one considers that this was also, in historical-geographical terms, a place of fracture—the site where little Switzerland had prised itself from the bosom of Austria—there is a certain logic in that this region drew to it many of the most significant aesthetic proponents of the modern in the decades before World War I. While Agathe Schoeck was pregnant with Othmar in the Villa Ruhheim in May 1886, Richard Strauss happened to be passing through the railway tunnel beneath her on his way back from Italy, about to stop off to view the Rigi and Lake Lucerne;[7] and in the days before Othmar's birth later that summer, August

Strindberg was in Weggis, just on the other side of the Rigi, finishing off the first version of his play *The Comrades*.[8] Over the coming years, the hotel guests who lodged at Eden and in the Fassbinds' Waldstätterhof would include aristocrats, musicians, writers, critics, publishers, translators, artists, and intellectuals from all over Europe. This cosmopolitan ambience would exert a considerable influence on Othmar and his siblings in their formative years.

It was Agathe Schoeck who took on the responsibility of starting her first three sons on the piano, but she had had her fill by the time Othmar's turn came. So he began piano lessons with a local teacher named Krieg instead, who soon stopped on account of claustrophobia. He was replaced by the excellent Marie Angele, a daughter of the music director in nearby Altdorf and herself a former student of the Royal Conservatory in Munich. This, however, was only one aspect of Schoeck's musical education. Together with various cousins and others, the Schoeck brothers put on Humperdinck's mini-singspiel *Seven Little Goats* for the seventieth birthday of their grandmother Fassbind in 1897. A charity concert they gave in the Waldstätterhof in August that same year even prompted a laudatory mention in the leading German music journal, *Die Signale der musikalischen Welt*, from its editor, Berthold Senff, a regular visitor to the hotel. It was at this time, too, that Alfred and Agathe first took their boys to the opera in Zurich, where Othmar saw Donizetti's *Fille du régiment*, Beethoven's *Fidelio*, and, a little later, Wagner's *Fliegender Holländer*. Alfred was no stranger to the Zurich Theater, for Othmar later recalled that he made a point of attending all the plays by Bjørnstjerne Bjørnson, an old acquaintance from his youthful hunting and painting trips to Norway.[9]

The childhood years of the four brothers in Brunnen are described in their various fragmentary reminiscences as having being utterly idyllic. Their tales of growing up amid the spectacular scenery of the region, of camping in a tent brought by Alfred from Canada, and of playing cowboys and Indians out in the woods behind the villa (with Othmar forced to play the squaw, as he was the youngest and the tubbiest) are irresistibly charming. The boys' fantasy was further stimulated by the books of Karl May, a German author immensely popular at the time, whose books were set in an invented Wild West that defined America for a whole generation of German-speaking children (even Adolf Hitler was a big fan, as Schoeck would discover over tea with the *Führer*'s sister many years later).

If their home in Brunnen was an "Eden" by name and nature, then Othmar by all accounts understood the onset of school as an expulsion from paradise. But his early school years hardly sound as disagreeable as commentators suggest he found it. He began his schooling with lessons from a Sister Marzelline from the nearby convent of Ingenbohl, progressed to the local primary school in Brunnen, and then completed his elementary education in Flüelen, just down the lake. We do not know much about Schoeck's forays into composition in these early school years. His first known piece was for piano, entitled "Mathilde [Suter] on Cleaning Day," written when he was about ten or eleven. Only a few such little

Figure 1.2. Anna Suter, Othmar, Mathilde Suter, Agathe, and Alfred Schoeck, mid 1890s. Courtesy of Georg and Elisabeth Schoeck.

piano pieces have survived from before the year 1990, none of them displaying any real sign of talent. His ambitions soon grew, however. His first attempt at anything larger-scale was an "opera" inspired by a book of Karl May's, *Der Schatz am Silbersee* ("The Treasure by Silver Lake"). He wrote it in about 1900 or 1901, to a libretto by brother Walter, with scenery organized by Ralph. It needed only a piano, a flute, two violins, and a cello and seems to have enjoyed a world premiere of sorts in the family home. It survives in only fragmentary form today but was at one time complete, for it is related that Grandmama Fassbind gave the boys a fee of twenty francs "for having finished it." Othmar attempted several other "dramatic" works at this time too (such as another May venture, *Der Ehri*, and the Grimm-inspired *Die Gänsehirtin am Brunnen*—"The Goose-Girl at the Well").

Alfred and Agathe had sent their three older boys to school at the *Evangelisches Pädagogium* in Bad Godesberg in Germany, but none of them liked it, so they were removed in 1900 and sent to finish their education in Zurich instead. Othmar was spared the experience of boarding abroad, and he followed them to Zurich at Easter 1901. There they lived under the watchful eye of Grandmother Fassbind, who had been despatched to act as their chaperone. Their apartment was at Moussonstrasse 12 in Fluntern, a suburb high up on the Zürichberg, though still within easy reach of the center—just a few streets from where, forty years earlier,

Brahms had holidayed and worked on his German Requiem. The city was still in the throes of the economic expansion enjoyed by so many central European cities in the late nineteenth century. Like most German towns, fin-de-siècle Zurich saw a huge building boom and the erection of neoclassical and art nouveau urban edifices that included its principal banks, the Conservatory, the Tonhalle (the city concert hall), the City Theater (renamed in the 1960s the "Opera House"), the marvellously mock-medieval National Museum, the new University premises and many private villas on the Zürichberg. But this was republican, Zwinglian Zurich, not royal Munich or imperial Berlin, so there are no grand spaces to complement the buildings or to allow one to stand too far back in admiration—public modesty has long been a civic virtue there. The Conservatory in particular, with its grand façade and beautifully ornamented great hall, is concealed from the main road by a cluster of eighteenth-century buildings, as if music were something to be practiced only in private among consenting adults.

Zurich further stood out from all the other cities on the periphery of German-speaking Europe, for it was situated in a democracy where freedom of speech was a long-held right, and where there was a tradition of accepting foreign nationals unwanted elsewhere. And although women would not have the vote for many decades to come, they nevertheless had far greater access to tertiary education in Zurich than was the case in the German empire to the north. Thus it was in Zurich that many of the finest minds of the day chose to study from the 1890s onwards, from Ricarda Huch to the future revolutionary Rosa Luxembourg.

Like his brothers, Othmar was sent to the so-called "Industrieschule," a cantonal high school where technical subjects were given preference. The vast majority of its school-leavers enrolled straightaway at the nearby Eidgenössische Technische Hochschule, the Swiss federal technical university. Othmar's artistic leanings were already dominant, and it seems his parents assumed that he might choose to study architecture as had his brother Paul before him. But the Industrieschule, not surprisingly, placed the greatest emphasis on math, and this had long been Othmar's worst subject. His parents received letters recommending private math lessons to help him catch up, and there were hours of detention with extra work, but all to no avail. He was finally expelled from school in March 1904.

Despite his problems at school, Othmar's compositional output had increased considerably after the move to Zurich. His surviving compositions from these years are mostly songs, one of which was deemed good enough to see its way into print several years later (the Uhland setting "Ruhetal," Op. 3, no. 1 of 1903), while others really should have been published but were not (such as "Kinderliedchen," woo 6, "Perlen," woo 67, and the Goethe setting "Gefunden" of summer 1904, woo 68). Schoeck later claimed that several of his songs dated "1903" were in fact composed much earlier, and that he had simply written them out neatly in this year.[10] While his models are both clearly audible and the same as for any young German-speaking composer of the day—Schubert, Schumann, and Brahms—his best songs of this time nevertheless demonstrate a burgeoning individuality and a high level of melodic inspiration. There is even a fragmentary piano trio entitled "Summer" (woo 61) from early 1903, whose Impressionistic harmony of regurgitated ninths, elevenths, and thirteenths proves that Schoeck was already familiar with Debussy's music.

Although they had ended in ignominy, Othmar's school years had not been in vain. His German teacher, one Hermann Bodmer, helped to confirm his love of literature, which had already been awakened by his parents and brothers back in Brunnen. There were also the joys of coeducation. Othmar arrived at school in Zurich at the age of fifteen, and the little available information that we possess suggests that he began to exert a considerable fascination upon the opposite sex. His blue eyes were counterpointed by a shock of blond hair, and his sense of humor—which by all accounts developed early—was paired with a boyish self-confidence. His physical needs, however, were for the moment being fulfilled in the sublimated fashion also beloved of English private schools, namely by the local school gymnastics association (the "Kantonsschulturnverein," hereafter "KTV"). Schoeck was a very good gymnast—for many years, his favorite after-dinner party trick, to the consternation of the more bourgeois of his colleagues, remained walking on his hands while smoking a cigar. But the KTV also provided access to alcohol by meeting once a week in the "Meierei" (the same bar where the Dada movement would be founded over a decade later). Furthermore, the association prompted a new foray into the world of musical theater when Schoeck assembled an "operetta" called *Josephine*, using popular melodies and home-grown tunes. It was performed in the "Ochsensaal," a hall on the Kreuzplatz, with the composer accompanying at the piano. Two of Schoeck's lifelong friends, Georges Treadwell and Armin Rüeger, first met him in the KTV. Treadwell remains peripheral in the story of Schoeck's life; Rüeger was anything but.

Schoeck and Rüeger had both the same year of birth and similar artistic leanings: where Schoeck painted and made music, Rüeger painted and wrote. Rüeger outlived his friend by only a few months and thus shared, too, his year of death. While Schoeck remained ever a highly social animal, surrounded by friends and admirers, his friendship with Rüeger went far deeper. Unlike his friend, Rüeger opted for a safe, bourgeois career, marrying early and running an apothecary's shop in the pretty little market town of Bischofszell, today an hour and a half by train to the north-east of Zurich. His artistic endeavors remained in the amateur sphere except for the three times when, at Schoeck's insistence, he wrote the libretti for his operas. These are all in different ways problematical, though their flaws are as much the fault of the composer as of the librettist. Both men knew that Schoeck's artistic gifts were the greater, and he dominated their artistic relationship from the start. But both also seem to have acknowledged that Rüeger's was the finer intellect, and he appears to have compensated for his artistic subservience by a readiness to pick an (intellectual) argument with Schoeck and pursue it mercilessly until his friend admitted complete defeat. The four Schoeck brothers were used to fierce debate within the family circle, but Rüeger seems to have been the only man from outside to have been willing and able to argue with Othmar, and to be respected for it.

Othmar's father took with ease the expulsion from school of his youngest son. Othmar later remembered him as saying, "Just wait until you've achieved something, then they'll all crawl back," though it was probably little more than an off-the-cuff remark intended to console his child.[11] Othmar's dual talents, in painting and in music, now left both him and his parents unsure as to which career path he should follow. We do not know whose idea it was that he should concentrate on the former, but he now enrolled in the oddly-named "Painting School for Ladies" run by two leading local artists, Ernst Würtenberger and Hermann Gattiker, in the Zurich studio where the pre-expressionist painter Arnold Böcklin had once worked. Schoeck retained happy memories of his studies there, and continued painting landscapes until well into middle age. But music was not forgotten, for he hedged his bets by studying harmony and counterpoint concurrently with Lothar Kempter Junior, the son of the chief conductor of the Zurich City Theater. Schoeck later claimed that he had never worked so hard.

As usual, Schoeck and his brothers returned to Brunnen for the summer holidays. We have a report of life in the family hotel at about this time from the pen of an Englishwoman, Ann Bridge, who many years later recalled her impressions as follows:

> It was very full and my Mother, Grace, and I had to be accommodated in Herr Schoeck's studio, a huge room on the top floor with a sky-light and stuffed birds and animals everywhere. . . . The Schoecks were a delightful family, cultivated and musical . . . their pleasant heavily furnished sitting-room was the scene of small private concerts, week after week. Othmar Schoeck—as I remember him the youngest and the stockiest of the three brothers—played the piano with something of the same cool, scholarly quality as did Donald Tovey; it was no great surprise to me to learn, thirty years later, that he had become a well-known composer.[12]

The pull of music soon grew too strong for Othmar to contemplate a career in painting any further. So his studies with Gattiker and Würtenberger were abandoned in time for him to enter the Zurich Conservatory in the autumn of 1904. It is possible that Schoeck's parents had foreseen such a step and had wanted their son to spend the six months between his expulsion from school and the start of the new academic year in trying out his different artistic inclinations. Many years later Georges Treadwell claimed that it was another member of the KTV who had convinced Othmar that his future lay in music, one Georg Lehmeier, though of him we know nothing except that Schoeck dedicated to him a violin sonata that he wrote in 1905.[13] Whatever the reasons, Othmar was the only one of the four Schoeck brothers who would dare to take the plunge and follow his real calling. There would be no more talk of anything but music.

Chapter Two

Wolf amidst the Sheep

When Schoeck returned to Zurich in the autumn of 1904, he and Ralph shared an apartment at Seegartenstrasse 14, not far from the lake, and a short bike ride from the conservatory. This institution had been founded in 1876 and was still run by its first principal, Friedrich Hegar, the long-standing conductor of the Zurich Tonhalle Orchestra, a violinist and composer, a friend of Brahms, and the dominant figure in the city's music life for over thirty years. He was also largely responsible for Zurich's reigning Brahmsian aesthetic. Only in the City Theater, under Lothar Kempter Senior, did the music of Wagner and the New Germans have the upper hand. It was with the elder Kempter that Othmar now took theory lessons at the conservatory. The teaching staff included many local lights: Hegar taught composition, Carl Attenhofer conducting, Johannes Luz organ, and Hans Häusermann singing. Schoeck also took violin lessons, though his teacher Alfons Grosser (the solo violist in the Tonhalle) found him so lazy that he seriously suggested he should return to painting instead.[1] Schoeck's favorite teacher was Robert Freund for piano. A Hungarian by birth, he had studied with both Carl Tausig and Franz Liszt, had enjoyed a career as a concert pianist, and had been among the first members of staff of the Zurich Conservatory back in 1876. Freund's wide circle of friends and acquaintances included many of the leading artists of the day, from Johannes Brahms, Gottfried Keller, and Arnold Böcklin to Richard Strauss and Friedrich Nietzsche. So it should not surprise us that he fascinated Schoeck, whose lessons were usually placed at the end of the day in order for the two men to retire to a café and talk into the evening. It was thanks to Freund, by all accounts, that Schoeck first became acquainted with the music of Hugo Wolf. This appears to have been in the autumn of 1905, for his influence appears suddenly, in the song "Himmelstrauer," Op. 5, no. 1, where Schoeck for the first time uses ostinato in the accompaniment, such as was typical of the mature songs of Wolf.

The Zurich Conservatory was hardly a hive of avant-garde activity—Kempter used the third act of Puccini's *Bohème* to warn his students of the horrors of parallel fifths, while Attenhofer referred to Reger's music as "dirt"—but it was probably no more conservative than any similar provincial institution in Germany or elsewhere. And in Friedrich Hegar the conservatory boasted a director who was highly regarded at home and abroad and was tolerant of aesthetic views different from his own. He encouraged his students to attend his rehearsals of the Tonhalle Orchestra, whose repertoire included modern German and French works, and where his interpretation of Debussy's *L'après-midi d'un faune* in particular made a huge impression on Schoeck.

Schoeck's studies included all the usual composition exercises and prompted him to venture for the first time into larger-scale chamber music and orchestral composition. There is the charming but impersonal Violin Sonata in D major (woo 22) of 1905 that Schoeck revised and published fifty years later, an equally charming but slightly more insipid Minuet and Trio for string quartet from 1906, and a cumbersome symphonic movement in E minor with the motto "I shall not let thee go unless thou bless me" (from the tale of Jacob and the angel in the Old Testament). There is little in any of these works that is more competent than one would expect from any above-average composition student. Schoeck's songs of these years are a different matter altogether, and they belie his later claim that he learned little at the conservatory. The years 1905 and 1906 saw the composition of some three dozen songs, most of which were later published, some showing real maturity (such as the setting of Goethe's "Diese Gondel vergleich ich," Op. 19b, no. 7.5, with its haunting, rocking accompaniment), despite the influence of Brahms, Schubert, Schumann, and Wolf being not yet properly digested. It is as if Schoeck felt that this or that poem would have attracted Brahms, and so deserved a more Brahmsian style, while another text reminded him of Schubert. But the youthful spontaneity of many of these songs is more than sufficient to sweep aside any aesthetic quibbles.

Wolf was not the only modern artist with whose work Schoeck came into contact during his conservatory years. Wilhelm Furtwängler arrived at the Zurich City Theater in 1906 to work for a few months as a lowly répétiteur, during which time he and Schoeck became friends—though we are not sure precisely when or how (and Schoeck was in any case away on his first annual stint of military service with Switzerland's militia army for two of those months, April and May). Schoeck and Furtwängler always remained on good terms, though it would be another half century before the latter would conduct anything by his friend. Of far more lasting significance to Schoeck was his discovery at this time of the poetry of Hermann Hesse. It seems that he and Hesse first met at a Tonhalle concert in about 1906, though they did not become properly acquainted for another five years. Of particular interest to us here is Schoeck's own (later) admission that his first-ever settings of Hesse songs, written over six months from late July 1906 onwards, were the result of an unhappy love for a fellow music student (the four songs Op. 8, plus Op. 24b, nos. 4 and 5, and woo 27). Her identity remains unknown, though the most likely candidate is one Marie Warpechovska, a student from Minsk whose mother worked as a midwife in Canton Vaud. Marie, a year younger than Schoeck, attended the Conservatory from 1903 to 1907, and Freund was among the lecturers whom they shared. Marie lived at the other end of town from Schoeck (on the Manessestrasse 69), though he often walked her home and once even organized a string quartet to serenade her from the pavement below her room. It is not clear why Schoeck should have singled out his Hesse settings as being a reflection of his lovelorn state, but perhaps the occasionally self-pitying tone of some of Hesse's poems had appealed to him. The last Hesse setting that he composed at the Conservatory, "Vorwurf" ("Reproach," woo 27) of 11 January 1907, remained unpublished until recently. It closes "in greatest passion" with a quotation from the quintet in Wagner's *Meistersinger,* and the music switches from ***ppp*** to ***fff*** within just a few measures as the singer cries "You spoke so much this evening / and broke the word that you never gave me." Another of this batch of Hesse songs, "Kennst du das auch" (Op. 24b, no. 4), also includes a quotation, this time of a popular dance tune of the day.[2]

Whoever the object of his affection might have been, and whatever the precise import of these musical quotations, these Hesse songs are of considerable significance for the composer's biography. The reminiscences of his fellow female students in Zurich make it clear that he was the center of much attention from the opposite sex. This failed affair with Miss X however (or, more probably, Miss W), seems to have been his first real crisis of the heart. It coincided, too, with the composition of some of his best songs to date, albeit with "Vorwurf" an exception. There is a more important "first" here, in that Schoeck himself acknowledged his inspiration to have come from an unhappy relationship. The notion of the Artist-Unlucky-in-Love who, purged by his sorrows, brings forth works of Great Art, might seem to us a hangover from the trivial literature of the nineteenth century, but it appealed to Schoeck himself. Throughout his life he would draw attention to the fact that his best music, as he saw it, was the product of a slump in his love life. Not only did the conjunction between emotional/ sexual frustration and the moment of inspiration become for Schoeck of great import, but it was in this specific case combined with the poems of Hesse. The memory of this experience was so powerful that during his greatest personal crisis, some forty years later, it seems to have been sufficient to lead Schoeck back from unfathomable depths of depression and the prospect of creative sterility.

Two days after he had composed his setting of Hesse's "Vorwurf" in Zurich, the world premiere of his first-ever commissioned work, two choruses for the carnival play *Das Glück in der Heimat* ("Happiness in the Home Country"), took place in Schoeck's native Canton Schwyz. This was the fiftieth anniversary of the so-called "Japanesen," a society in Schwyz—still in existence today—that organizes elaborate carnival theatricals every few years. Schoeck's choruses are not very adventurous (nor could they be, given the exigencies of an amateur, open-air performance), but they were well received in the press. Schoeck did not attend the premiere on 13 January 1907 but was represented by his elder brother Paul.

Schoeck's biggest professional opportunity to date also came thanks to connections at home. Mathilde Suter's elder sister Anna had studied singing at the Munich Conservatory in the late 1880s, and under the stage name of "Anna Sutter" she had become a favorite of the public at the Stuttgart Royal Opera House. Not even her colorful love life and the birth of two illegitimate children to different fathers proved a hindrance to her career (she was created "Kammersängerin" in February 1906). Othmar and Mathilde visited Anna in Stuttgart in late January 1907, where she introduced him to the high society of the Stuttgart music world, including Hugo Faisst—the wealthy lawyer who had been Hugo Wolf's patron—and the Klinckerfuss family of piano manufacturers. The latter in turn were friendly with Max Reger, who happened to be in Stuttgart as part of a nationwide concert tour.[3] Perhaps Anna had timed Schoeck's visit to coincide with Reger's. In any case, it was *chez* Klinckerfuss that Schoeck was now brought face to face with a man who was already one of the best-known composers in Germany. Schoeck had a bundle of songs with him that Reger went through one by one at the piano, putting the ones he liked in one pile, the others in another. When he had finished, he announced that a publisher must be found for the songs on his right and proposed that Schoeck join his composition class in Munich. Schoeck seems not to have treated this offer seriously. But six weeks later it was Reger who took the initiative, in a letter peppered with underlinings:

Dear Mr Schoeck!

. . . I have accepted the position of University Music Director in Leipzig, and I have also taken on the direction of a master class for composition at the Royal Conservatory. . . . I hereby insist most urgently that you immediately enter this masterclass for composition in Leipzig, i.e., on 8 April (the beginning of the summer term). Leipzig is for you a much, much, much better base than Munich! [. . .]
   That I shall always hold my hand over you, protecting and promoting you, I'm sure I don't need to tell you; but you must always work very, very hard! [. . .]
   I want to make something quite proper out of you. So you simply *must* [underlined four times] enter the class on 8 April in Leipzig!

Schoeck hesitated again, but Hegar declared: "If a man like Reger writes to you like that, you can't not follow him!" So follow he did. Schoeck's final act at the Zurich Conservatory was to make his debut as a conductor on 23 March 1907 in the first performance of his ten-minute-long "Spanish Serenade" for five wind instruments and strings. The geographical adjective was later jettisoned, no doubt to avoid the obvious comparison with Hugo Wolf's *Italian Serenade.* The critics were positive, though one "r.h." in the *Neue Zürcher Zeitung,* perhaps aware of Schoeck's imminent departure, declared that it was obviously influenced by Max Reger.[4] In fact, the piece is thoroughly Wolfian in style. Nevertheless, its youthful exuberance still makes it one of Schoeck's most successful orchestral works.
   Schoeck returned to Brunnen to rest for a few days then departed for Leipzig, stopping off on the way to visit Hugo Faisst and Anna Sutter in Stuttgart.

Chapter Three

Leipzig, Munich, and an
Awful Little Moustache

Schoeck arrived in Leipzig on 7 April 1907. As he had promised back in February, Reger soon put him in touch with his own publisher, Lauterbach and Kuhn, though after hearing Schoeck play to them for three hours they still showed no interest. By contrast, the Leipzig representative of the Zurich publishing house of Hug, Alexander Bartusch, was very keen indeed. Schoeck had met him on his second day in the city and was immediately impressed. Bartusch not only provided free coffee whenever they met at his apartment but also recommended a Zurich family from whom Schoeck could rent a room: a Mrs Eisele and her daughter Anny, a former student of the Zurich Conservatory who was now making a name for herself as a pianist. Schoeck moved in straightaway. He also promptly fell in love with Anny, though his letters to Armin Rüeger confirm his disappointment upon finding her possessed of firm moral fibre: "I'm not used to this!" he wrote.[1] A piano concerto for her was planned, though it was swiftly forgotten as it became clear that she had no intention of submitting to his charms. The link to Bartusch proved profitable, though: by 25 June 1907 Schoeck had signed a contract with Hug for his first eleven opus numbers. Opus 1 was his Serenade for small orchestra (for which he received one hundred marks), while the following ten numbers were of assorted lieder (at twenty marks per song).

Reger's tuition comprised reams of contrapuntal exercises that demanded precision of technique, posing limits in order to set the imagination free. Sadly, almost none of them have survived—Schoeck probably threw them away as of no artistic significance—but there is no doubt that his Leipzig studies provided an immense artistic stimulus. In his first weeks there Schoeck was producing more or less one new song a week alongside all his other work, and their quality was very fine indeed—they all soon found their way into print. Schoeck also became more adventurous in his choice of poet. Besides his staples such as Lenau and Uhland, he now set texts by Verlaine, Novalis, Michelangelo, and Li-Tai-Pe.

We know little of Schoeck's social life as a student in Leipzig, however, except that it resulted in a lifelong friendship with an older music student named Martin Kuntze-Fechner (1877–1950). But we do know that Hugo Faisst took the trouble to visit him, singing songs to Schoeck's accompaniment and wining and dining his young friend enough to be rewarded with the dedication of his six Uhland settings Op. 3—a rare honor, for Schoeck never allotted dedications

Figure 3.1. Stefi Geyer, ca. 1908.

easily. After his summer holiday back home in Brunnen, Schoeck returned to Leipzig in September via Stuttgart, in order to see Faisst and Anna Sutter again.

That same autumn of 1907, Schoeck came across the woman who would dominate the next five years of his life: the Hungarian violinist Stefi Geyer (1888–1956; see fig. 3.1). She had been something of a wunderkind, and her talent was exceeded only by her beauty ("she knew how to move so beautifully and to walk so beautifully," cooed Schoeck almost fifty years later).[2] In an undated letter of either late November or early December 1907, Schoeck wrote to his parents from Leipzig that "my crush, the young Stefi Geyer, was recently here; she played wonderfully and enchanted me more than ever. The rest is silence! I'd so like to get to know her; that would give me some more songs!"[3] Get to know her he would, though not for another half-year, and she would then inspire him to far more than songs.

Christmas 1907 saw Schoeck back in Brunnen, via Stuttgart again, though his return to Leipzig early in the New Year brought a detour via Munich instead. The reason was the novelist Friedrich Huch (a cousin of the more famous Ricarda), who had met Schoeck on holiday in Brunnen back in 1901. Huch had corresponded with Othmar intermittently over the next few years, requesting photos of the budding composer and sending him copies of his novels—all of them starkly homoerotic, full of beautiful young boys who spend their time in semi-closeted idolization of older male friends and tutors. Schoeck later claimed that he had not understood Huch's books and had given them to his father to read. But by early 1908 Huch was a well-known author, and Schoeck (or his parents) obviously felt that it was in his interest to renew the acquaintance. He played Huch his songs, they ate lunch together in the Torgelstube, and then they went for a walk, and Schoeck wrote proudly to his parents afterward to tell them of the grand impression that he had made. But Huch wrote in his diary:

> He has become somewhat ghastly, this beautiful 14-year-old boy with the big grey eyes, long blond hair, and pure face! His eyes are empty, his hair cut short and like a country coachman, his mouth has bad teeth and an awful little dandruff-laden moustache.[4]

This first impression was made worse by Schoeck's placing himself uninvited at the piano and playing through his songs and Serenade—he even managed to scare away the wife of the composer Paul von Klenau when she arrived to take Huch to lunch. It is noteworthy that Huch found Schoeck's moustache particularly "ghastly," referring to it only in the diminutive—"Schnurrbärtchen"—as if, by making this most visible mark of Schoeck's adulthood as small as possible, he might be able to make it disappear altogether. What probably disappointed him most of all was left unmentioned in the diary: the fact that Schoeck was heterosexual, which the sensitive Huch must surely have noticed, and which was perhaps why they never had any contact again. All the same, it is possible that Schoeck provided some inspiration for Huch's next book, *Enzio: A Musical Novel*, published in 1910. Enzio is blond and has lovely eyes, but spends much of the book having unhappy sex with passive women when it is implied he would be much better off with men instead. This is also the reason why he never realizes his early promise as a composer. While the similarities between Enzio and Huch's descriptions of the younger Schoeck are compelling, Enzio's death had a different source of inspiration: the near-drowning of Wilhelm Furtwängler, who once fell through the ice while skating on Zurich Lake. Furtwängler was now living in Munich and was in the middle of an affair with Huch's sister, and Schoeck would have bumped into him had he turned up at Huch's apartment a day earlier.

Schoeck's last term in Leipzig culminated in a visit to Dresden for the wedding of his friend Kuntze-Fechner in March 1908 (where to his delight he made the acquaintance of Marie Wieck, Clara Schumann's half-sister). Schoeck spent a week there in all and combined the festivities with a concert in nearby Greiz with the singer Frieda Hollstein. He wrote to his parents that the program had included a "new, long" song "that had to be encored." This can only have been his "Reiselied" ("Traveling song," Op. 12, no. 1), which he had written just a couple of weeks before. It is devoid of any harmonic complexity, being perhaps most akin to Schumann's "folksy" vein of songwriting. But its charm is irresistible, and it rapidly became one of Schoeck's most popular songs. It was also important to Schoeck—he would quote it twice in other works written over two decades later. He dedicated it to his best friend, Armin Rüeger (see ex. 3.1).

A Swiss musicologist once asked rhetorically what would have become of Schoeck if, say, he had gone to study with Arnold Schoenberg instead of Max Reger. Such "what ifs," while often banal, can also be thought-provoking. If one takes the case of Alban Berg, only a few months older than Schoeck, whose youthful oeuvre consisted almost wholly of songs, we see that his years of tuition with Schoenberg produced of him a composer in full command of large-scale forms. Schoeck had also written mostly songs, but his year of studies with Max Reger was followed by a return home to compose even more of them. For several years he would stumble whenever attempting anything bigger.

In fact, only three of Reger's students ever attained any real recognition as composers: Schoeck, Jaromir Weinberger (the composer of the opera *Schwanda the Bagpiper*), and Schoeck's direct contemporary Joseph Haas, who became well known for his church music. In Schoeck's letters home in late April 1907 his teacher was "My master Reger," who is inviting him to Sunday lunch, is willing to have his course fees waived if his parents can't afford it, and is pushing outside work his way in order for him to earn a little extra cash. But Reger is mentioned less and less, and by late autumn, if he is mentioned at all, he is but a surname, "master" no more: "Reger is away traveling this week. His students are glad of the break."[5] On Schoeck's final report of 8 April 1908 Reger wrote merely: "Is a very talented composer, for whom one can only wish that he gains more musical independence." With that their relationship ceased. Schoeck was soon maintaining that his studies at the Zurich Conservatory had proved more beneficial.[6]

Example 3.1. "Reiselied," Op. 12, no. 1. Copyright 1956 Hug & Co. "Through fields and beech forests, now singing, now happily quiet, he who chooses traveling will be happiest of all."

One might have imagined that Reger and Schoeck would understand each other well. For Reger was a fine song composer and fond of Eichendorff, to whose poetry Schoeck would soon become particularly attached. Schoeck even claimed in later years that it was Reger who had introduced him to the poet.[7] Reger was also a staunch champion of the music of Hugo Wolf, Schoeck's idol of the time. But according to the diary of a former fellow student at the Zurich Conservatory, Adele Zipkes-Bloch, Schoeck admitted in June 1908 that he and Reger had argued heavily and were no longer on good terms.[8] Five years after that, Schoeck told Hans Corrodi that Reger had made changes to certain of his songs and that this was why they had fallen out. In his reminiscences, Joseph Haas wrote that if, after Reger had explained his corrections to a student's work, "the student kept to his own standpoint out of vanity or because he was self-opinionated, then Reger could become furious. In such cases, scorn and derision took the place of humor and wit. And Reger's scorn was caustic;

it hurt."[9] Was Haas here thinking specifically of Schoeck? A letter to his parents of mid-March 1908 seems to confirm that Schoeck had withdrawn into silence: "Reger protests in nice terms about my simple manner of composition. I'm giving in diplomatically until I've got my final certificate. But he can't sway me from my inner conviction."[10] To what extent Reger's alcoholism might also have affected his teaching or his moods is not clear, though the smell of alcohol on his breath must have been obvious to all those in his class. The very fact that it remains unmentioned in the reminiscences of Schoeck and Haas suggests that they found it embarrassing.

Schoeck's attitude to Reger might also have changed if he had noticed that Reger's Novalis setting "Ich sehe dich in tausend Bildern," Op. 105, no. 1, written in early August 1907 and first performed in Leipzig later that month, is at the start virtually a paraphrase of his own song to the same text from the previous May (Op. 6, no. 5), which he had presumably shown to his teacher at the time. Or perhaps the obvious paternal concern demonstrated by the childless Reger meant that his student was from the start pushed unwillingly into a role of surrogate son. In any case, the Regers adopted their first child in July 1907, at which time Reger's fatherly attentions would, no doubt, have been directed away from his students. As he grew older, Schoeck's respect for Reger returned, he spoke less and less of their estrangement, and he even conducted his teacher's works with regularity. After a particularly fine piano performance (by whom is not recorded), Schoeck once remarked: "Only Reger could play like that."[11] Schoeck even took to placing a Reger volume under his manuscript paper when composing.

The year with Reger also saw Schoeck's first large-scale orchestral work since the "Symphonic Movement" of 1906: the *William Ratcliff Overture*, after Heinrich Heine. He did not think much of it later, claiming that he had been too distracted by an unhappy love experience (we know not with whom—perhaps Anny Eisele?) to have paid adequate attention to the writing of it.[12] But since it was his final task for Reger, perhaps it also brought back unhappy memories of their acrimony. Busoni once saw the score and somewhat unfairly declared the whole work a "printing mistake."[13] But although it was only performed twice within a year or so of its composition and then never again in Schoeck's lifetime, more recent performances have proved that it well deserves an airing. As it happens, orchestral writing was the one area where Reger had hardly more experience than his pupils, for it was only after moving to Leipzig that he began to busy himself seriously with composing for orchestra.

Some insight into the problematic relationship between master and pupil can perhaps be gained from Friedrich Huch's diary entry after his brief encounter with Schoeck in early 1908. For while Huch's response was presumably determined largely by sexual frustration, it nevertheless seems that Schoeck had in the meantime developed a strong sense of his own worth that others could take for sheer arrogance. As we have seen, this was not a trait that Reger liked in his students. Their paths crossed occasionally over the next few years—Reger's concert tours brought him now and then to Zurich—but there is no record of either man ever seeking out the company of the other. It seems that they never met again.

Chapter Four

Back in the Fold

In a letter of 31 March 1908 Schoeck wrote to his parents confidently of his future plans: he would seek out either a "little job" at an opera house, or, preferably, as a choral conductor, "which won't be so difficult at all in Switzerland."[1] Switzerland was certainly full of choirs. But while those in the metropolitan centers had the resources to put on occasional large-scale works with orchestra, their members were still amateurs and their repertoire largely dross. The principal alternative—a post at a small opera house in Germany—would have given Schoeck far more useful experience. Almost without exception, those composers before him who had excelled in orchestration had spent their galley years in small theaters: Wagner, Richard Strauss, and Gustav Mahler are the obvious examples. The leading composers of the nineteenth century whose orchestration has been most regularly criticized were those who had undergone little or no orchestral apprenticeship—Robert Schumann, Johannes Brahms, and Hugo Wolf. Schoeck must have known this, but still he chose the easier option of choral conducting back in his native land. With time, his powers of orchestration would be second to none—though only after he had abandoned choirs to conduct an orchestra instead. Schoeck's operas, however, would always lack the theatrical draughtsmanship that might have been learnt as a matter of course had he worked in an opera house.

Upon returning home from Leipzig in mid-April, Schoeck at least did not waste any time in presenting his talents to his countrymen. Within less than two months he was accompanying the baritone Rudolf Jung (cousin of the psychoanalyst C. G.) in several of his lieder at the annual festival of the Swiss Musicians' Association, the *Tonkünstlerfest,* held that year in Baden, just a few kilometers west of Zurich. And on 1 June he conducted the Zurich Tonhalle Orchestra in the world premiere of his *Ratcliff Overture.* It was during this festival that he first made the acquaintance of the Swiss composer Fritz Brun, with whom he became close friends. Back in Zurich he shared the podium with his old teacher Hegar in a concert of the Harmonie Chorus on 21 July. More importantly for Schoeck, the guest artist at that concert was none other than Stefi Geyer. Three weeks later he composed an "Albumblatt" for violin and piano (woo 70) for her, and they gave its world premiere that same month, when Schoeck acted as her piano accompanist in a concert in his native canton of Schwyz. He had now succeeded in making the personal acquaintance of the object of his desire, though she proved as elusive as he was persistent. What Schoeck could not have known was that Béla Bartók was also in the throes of a crisis of unfulfilment with Stefi.

As it happens, at that time Bartók was just a few kilometers away from them both, on his first-ever visit to Switzerland—though we have no proof that their paths might have crossed.

If Schoeck wished to live in Switzerland but was to have any real prospect of making a living from his art, Zurich was the obvious place to be. So he moved there for good at the end of the summer, renting an apartment at Freiestrasse 58. His success in the Harmonie's concert of the previous July had prompted them to offer him a job as their second conductor, and the contract was signed on 1 September 1908, with a salary fixed at fifteen hundred francs a year. An increasing self-confidence also became apparent in his dealings with Hug. Whereas just a year ago he had been over the moon that anyone was prepared to publish his works, now he was demanding royalties for each song, even though the publication of his first eleven opus numbers had been a financial disaster. Hug had invested four thousand marks in them, yet despite marketing them across Germany, they sold only fifty francs' worth.[2] They still recognized Schoeck's potential, however, for in late 1908 they agreed upon a contract for Opp. 12–15 that guaranteed Schoeck 5 percent on the second and all later editions.

One concrete sign of Schoeck's growing reputation was the first-ever concert devoted to his works (few as they still were in number), which took place on 28 October 1908 in Thun, the little lakeside town so beloved by Brahms. The instigator was Thun's music director, August Oetiker (1874–1963), a relative of Mathilde and Anna Suter's on their mother's side, and another sometime guest in the Eden Hotel. The concert featured Hans Kötscher, the leader of the Basel Symphony Orchestra, playing Schoeck's pre-Leipzig violin sonata, woo 22, with the composer accompanying; Schoeck and Rudolf Jung performed several of his songs, and Oetiker conducted his choir, the "Cäcilienverein," in several short choruses. Even after he became well known, Schoeck kept returning to perform for Oetiker in Thun, out of gratitude for his early recognition there.

Throughout the second half of 1908 Schoeck continued his pursuit of Stefi Geyer, later claiming that they had written "madly passionate" letters to each other. All his letters from former lovers were destroyed three decades later under the watchful eye of his wife. But the few of his letters that have survived in Stefi's papers are mild in character, and since we know that her correspondence with the equally lovelorn Bartók remained similarly measured, Schoeck was perhaps indulging here in an act of retrospective over-interpretation. He did admit that he only ever managed a single kiss with her (though Stefi probably regarded even that as platonic). It was, so Schoeck later related, as if her body were protected by a coat of armor.[3] All this merely seems to have further fueled his ardor, for he spent the Christmas holidays of 1908 composing a new violin sonata for her (Op. 16). He wrote of it to his brother Paul on 13 January 1909: "I had the second movement of the Violin Sonata finished, [but] tore it up yesterday in a fit of rage. It pains me a little, but for god's sake. It was too 'beautiful.'"[4]

If the dedication of the sonata had been intended to warm Stefi's heart, a sure sign that it didn't was Schoeck's decision to give the premiere to Willem de Boer instead, the leader of the Zurich Tonhalle Orchestra. It took place as part of a Schoeck concert held at the Zurich Conservatory on 29 April 1909. The same concert also saw the premieres of several of his newest songs with Rudolf Jung, Adele Zipkes-Bloch, and Alfred Flury, also to Schoeck's accompaniment. One of them must be numbered among the finest that he ever wrote: a setting of Mörike's *Peregrina II*, whose tale of lost love has an emotional impact all the greater for the composer's tight control over his musical means. He uses an obsessive Wolfian ostinato in the piano accompaniment and employs canon to great musical and dramatic effect. This ostinato bears more than a passing resemblance to a passage in the first movement of Brahms's Second Violin Sonata (Op. 100; see for example mm. 137–38), which Schoeck, given his acquaintance with Robert Freund, might well have known was regarded among Brahms's friends as inspired by the composer's (unconsummated) love for Hermine Spies.[5] "Peregrina"'s connection to Stefi is underscored by Schoeck's later admission that he quoted it in the slow movement of his new violin sonata as an intentional reference to her.[6] Canon is also employed in the sonata—the counterpoint exercises with Reger were apparently having a delayed but potent influence on his textures. This sonata so impressed one of the violin students in the Conservatory audience that he went out and bought it to play himself; it was Arthur Honegger.

The frustrations of Schoeck's love life were somewhat mitigated by good news on the career front. His success as deputy with the Harmonie had led to an offer from the Mens' Chorus of Aussersihl, a working-class quarter of Zurich to the southwest of the main station. After a trial rehearsal on 5 February 1909, Schoeck was unanimously elected principal conductor and successfully haggled up his annual fee to two thousand francs.[7] He conducted the chorus for the first time in public on 6 June 1909 at the Swiss Choral Festival in Glarus. His success was such that within six months of his taking on the job, the membership had already risen by more than a hundred.

June was the festival season, and Glarus was followed rapidly by the annual festival of the Allgemeiner deutscher Musikverein, held that year in Stuttgart, where Schoeck accompanied Hedwig Schmitz-Schweiker in eight of his songs (the Germans still regarded the nationals of other German-speaking nations as "German" enough to participate on an equal footing). It was also at this festival that Schoeck first met Richard Strauss, though it is unlikely that they did anything but exchange pleasantries.[8] The *Tonkünstlerfest*—the Swiss festival equivalent—followed two weeks later in Winterthur, to the northeast of Zurich. Schoeck's Violin Sonata was on the program, this time with de Boer accompanied by Fritz Brun.

Brun (1878–1959) was a native of Lucerne, had studied in Cologne, and had then moved to Bern in 1906. He rapidly established himself as the city's foremost conductor and was appointed director of its symphony concert series in 1909. He, too, was a composer, though his ambitions lay primarily in the field of absolute music. He composed ten symphonies, the earlier of which display the influence of Brahms, and the later ones that of Bruckner. Brun and Schoeck became particularly close in 1909, when the latter used the former as a soundboard for all his problems with Stefi Geyer. The age difference between the two men was only eight years, though when the one is twenty-three and the other thirty-one, the difference in life experience can be vast. What might also have bonded them together was the fact that Brun too had just been unlucky in love with a violinist: one Adele Bloesch-Stöcker. He had also recently written a violin sonata in which he had "encoded" his feelings (this time with the Schumannian trick of incorporating Adele's initials: "A–B[♭]"). Schoeck would later claim that Stefi was the girl he had always desired the most, though the intensity of that desire was perhaps directly proportional to its lack of fulfilment. Stefi later married—twice, in fact,—though many rumors still circulate in Zurich that her real desires were not of a nature that Schoeck or any other member of his gender could have satisfied.

Schoeck coped with his sexual frustration by living out one of the *topoi* of the German Romantics of whom he was so fond: he went to Italy, taking Brun along with him. He had visited the Italian-speaking parts of Switzerland before but had yet to discover Italy proper. Goethe, Wagner, and others had famously gone there to escape from unhappy love affairs, so perhaps Schoeck and Brun felt that they should do the same. The trip began in the Engadine, the plateau in eastern Switzerland beloved of numerous German artists, from Nietzsche to Ernst Ludwig Kirchner. Schoeck and Brun climbed the Piz Languard then continued, alternately on foot and by train, over the Bernina Pass to Tirano, Edolo, Pisogne, Verona, and finally to Venice. It was a revelation, as he wrote to Rüeger on 31 July 1909: "hundreds of gondolas, full moon, men with bells, sea, music, Italy, and above all *Venice*." If he was living out a Romantic Italian fantasy, it was to prove a potent one, for he returned to Italy every year that he could until World War I closed all the borders. It was at roughly this time that Schoeck wrote a four-minute waltz for piano (woo 32) that remained hidden in his papers for several decades and was only performed after his death. While there are figurations reminiscent of Chopin, and moments that bring Johann Strauss the Younger to mind, its atmosphere is highly Italianate and shows that Schoeck was well versed in the *fin-de-siècle* popular style of Paolo Tosti. His affinity for things Italian would rarely again express itself so clearly.

Schoeck's return to Switzerland a few days later brought a recurrence of his Stefi-inspired melancholy. He stayed for a few days with Brun in Thun, only to find, with the inevitability that haunts the lovelorn, that Stefi had decided to visit that same spot with her new fiancé: "a fashion-mad Viennese ponce," Schoeck called him.[9] Schoeck also visited Rüeger in Bischofszell during the summer, and he seems to have attempted to distract himself by the half-hearted, unsuccessful seduction of a local girl named Ida Kasper, whom he then forgot as swiftly as she had aroused his interest.

While his emotional life was in confusion, Schoeck's professional position seemed about to gain in clarity. In August 1909 Gustav Angerer—the principal conductor of the Harmonie—died, and Schoeck not unreasonably expected to inherit his job. He also moved into a new apartment, at Zürichbergstrasse 12, and busied himself with decorating it in between working on his first piece with orchestra since the *Ratcliff Overture*, namely *Der Postillon*, a choral setting of an elegiac poem by Niklaus Lenau. He soon found, however, that his position with the Harmonie was far from secure. He had dared to conduct in shirtsleeves during hot weather and had occasionally clowned around in rehearsal, and such conduct was deemed unseemly among the venerable ranks of Zurich's most history-laden choir. Relations became so fraught that Schoeck handed in his notice in December 1909, and he soon found out that another candidate for the directorship, Joseph Castelberg, had anyway been organized behind his back.

Despite this setback, Schoeck was establishing himself ever more firmly as a composer and accompanist on the local scene. On 20 October 1909 he accompanied the violinist Carl Flesch in a recital in the Zurich Tonhalle; six weeks later his former teacher Robert Freund accompanied de Boer in Schoeck's new Violin Sonata; 29 January 1910 then took Schoeck across the border to Frankfurt for a concert of his music with Rudolf Jung, while 28 February took him closer to home, to a music evening of the "Leserzirkel Hottingen," a cultural society to which the Zurich élite belonged, and where Schoeck accompanied several of his newest songs, to texts by Carl Spitteler. The writer was present, but he upset Schoeck by praising to his face the settings of his texts by the German composer Max von Schillings. In fact, two of Schoeck's settings—"Das bescheidene Wünschlein" and "Der Hufschmied"—are among the most tuneful songs that he ever wrote.

In January 1910 Schoeck moved apartments once again, this time to Zollikon, just outside the city boundary but a few minutes by bicycle from the city center. Here he shared a house with Engelbert Röntgen, a Dutchman his own age, who was the solo cellist in the Tonhalle Orchestra. Röntgen would a few years later be appointed solo cellist first at the Vienna Court Opera and then at the Metropolitan Opera in New York. Already widely traveled and well connected, he was one of Schoeck's prime contacts with the wider European music scene. But of more immediate significance for us is that he was also supposedly responsible for a "deterioration" in our composer's morals. While our principal source, the composer's later biographer Hans Corrodi, was admittedly quick in matters of moral censure, it does seem clear that Schoeck took to drinking heavily into the early hours while living with Röntgen and would soon enough abandon any qualms he might yet have harbored about venturing beyond the bounds of faithful monogamy.

In April 1910, however, Schoeck moved out, renting instead a chalet at Bergstrasse 36, high above the city, where he stayed for the next five years. Apart from the family villa in Brunnen, this was the one home he ever had that would haunt him in his dreams till he died. As an old man he reminisced about the years spent there as

Figure 4.1. The chalet on the Bergstrasse, with Schoeck's apartment on the top floor. Courtesy of Zentralbibliothek Zürich.

> a happy time . . . I had three small rooms on the top floor. From my bed, I could look out over a sea of houses. At the foot of the chalet lay an extended vineyard that stretched all the way down to the Pediatric Hospital. The Eichendorff songs that I wrote up there reflect my experience of the countryside, nature, and the world altogether.[10]

In June 1910 the musical world came to Zurich in the shape of that year's annual festival of the Allgemeiner deutscher Musikverein—the third time it had been held in Switzerland (after Zurich in 1882 and Basel in 1903). This year's festival was particularly cosmopolitan, for besides its regular quota of German, Austrian, and Swiss works—including the world premiere of Reger's Piano Quartet Op. 114 with the composer at the piano—the audiences heard Zoltán Kodály's First String Quartet, Béla Bartók's Rhapsody for Piano and Orchestra, Op. 1, played by the composer, and even *Brigg Fair* by Delius. There was nothing by Schoeck on the program, but we can be sure that he was there. For one thing, Stefi Geyer was there, and for another, his native Brunnen was in that month suffering under the worst flooding in living memory.[11] His family was safe up in their villa, but he will not have been overly keen to return home and wade through the knee-deep water in the streets to get to them. Stefi was still engaged to her "Viennese ponce," but when she invited Schoeck to visit her and her parents that summer in Budapest, he still said "yes." One cannot accuse him of lacking in persistence.

Schoeck set off for Budapest in late July, accompanied on the first leg of the journey by his cousin Léon Oswald. They spent a week in Salzburg before Schoeck ventured on alone to Vienna. He stayed there for about a week too, doing the same things that any musical tourist would do: he sauntered through the Prater, drank wine in the Rathauskeller, and went to the Central Cemetery to hunt out the graves of Beethoven, Brahms, Schubert, Hugo Wolf, and Johann Strauss—not an easy task, given that the cemetery covers an area larger than the old city of Zurich. Schoeck was apparently unsure if Stefi would actually be home when he got to Budapest, and he was determined to leave straightaway in a huff if she were not; but she was, so he didn't. He spent an enjoyable week with her and her family, though his postcard assurances to Rüeger that he had got over his infatuation merely suggest that he hadn't. He had hardly returned home when he confirmed it by embarking upon a violin concerto for her. Schoeck spent New Year in Grindelwald with Fritz Brun and Brun's friend Walter Schädelin (1873–1953), a forestry expert resident in Bern, whose diary over the following years provides us with many blunt insights into Schoeck's emotional life. Schädelin noted that the first movement of the new concerto was already finished in sketch; he also brought a Goethe poem to Schoeck's attention, which he then set just a fortnight later: "Dämmrung senkte sich von oben." This later became one of Schoeck's most popular songs, even eliciting praise from Richard Strauss.[12] Its popularity is far exceeded, however, by another song that Schoeck wrote at about the same time (its precise date is unknown), later published as the final song of his Opus 20 set: "Nachruf" ("Echo"), to a poem by Eichendorff (see ex. 4.1). Like "Dämmerung," it boasts an effortless melodic line with the simplest of accompaniments. It has been recorded at least ten times, by everyone from Karl Erb, Ilona Durigo, Heinrich Schlusnus, and Dietrich Fischer-Dieskau to Wolfgang Holzmair and Cornelia Kallisch.

It was at this time, too, that Schoeck began another orchestral work, variously entitled "Sinfonietta" or "Italian Sinfonietta" (woo 101), though only fragments of an opening movement survive. Hans Corrodi claimed many years later that Schoeck had played the entire work to him at the piano but had never written it all down. Whatever the reason for its incompleteness, committing anything to paper on more than a small scale was obviously still difficult for him. His Violin Concerto confirms this continuing uncertainty, for while it is intensely melodic, it more or less abandons any attempt at formal unity in favor of a meandering tunefulness. The opening, with its rapid violin figurations, makes more sense when one knows that Schoeck had in mind a high roof, bathed in sunshine, with swallows fluttering around it,[13] but its transition into the movement proper still jars. As a whole, the work is obviously modelled on the concerto by Brahms. The opening timpani strokes in the second movement recall Beethoven's Violin Concerto, while other passages remind one of Mendelssohn. There is in the first movement even an unmistakeable reminiscence (at original pitch) of the rising minor ninth from the second movement of Mahler's Fifth Symphony.

Example 4.1. "Nachruf," Op. 20, no. 14. Copyright Breitkopf & Härtel. Reprinted by permission. "You dear, faithful lute, how many a summer's night have I kept watch with you until the break of dawn."

The first movement of the Violin Concerto was premiered at the *Tonkünstler-fest* in Vevey on 21 May 1911—the other two were still not finished and would occupy Schoeck for more than a year still. It is an odd coincidence that Bartók's First Violin Concerto—the fruit of *his* passion for Stefi—had just had a partial world premiere too, when its first movement was performed alone, on 12 February 1911 in Budapest. Its second movement was not premiered until almost fifty years later, after Stefi's death. Bartók's planned third movement was never composed, but it was intended to have portrayed the "indifferent, cool and silent" Stefi.[14] Schoeck would have sympathized. This was the only time when either Schoeck or Bartók would allow a major work to be premiered piecemeal. That it was in each case a violin concerto inspired by a love for Stefi Geyer is a remarkable synchronicity. It is naturally fascinating to speculate how an incomplete, in a sense "unconsummated" concerto might have signified for each man the true nature of his respective relationship with her.

Schoeck must have felt uncomfortable with the form of his concerto, for he gave it the title: "Quasi una fantasia," no doubt as an attempt to defuse potential criticism of its formlessness. Even Wilhelm Furtwängler suggested to Schoeck at about this time that he should cut the last seventy measures of the second movement, as it was "far too long overall."[15] Schoeck's desire to work with large forms, and his discomfort with them, would soon come into conflict on a much bigger scale altogether.

Chapter Five

Hermann Hesse, via the Dentist

The first poet to offer Schoeck an opera libretto had been Hans Reinhart in 1908, whose "dramatic poem" *Der Garten des Paradieses* he had declined with all the tact necessary when dealing with a son of one of Switzerland's richest industrialists. It was not what he was looking for, claimed the composer—though in fact, it is full of undigested Wagnerisms, and words cannot describe its awfulness (a decade later, Arnold Schoenberg would turn it down with equal tact).[1] But like many a composer fresh from conservatory studies in Germany, Schoeck was on the lookout for a possible text. Friedrich Hegar urged him, unsuccessfully, to complete the operatic fragment *Francesca da Rimini* by Hermann Goetz (1840–76).[2] But in early 1911 Schoeck acquired a potential librettist of indisputably high calibre: Hermann Hesse. Their fleeting acquaintance of 1906 was renewed and deepened through the offices of a mutual friend, Alfred Schlenker, a music-loving dentist and amateur composer from Constance. Hesse invited Schoeck to his home in Gaienhofen in early March 1911 with the express intention of discussing an operatic collaboration. The topics he suggested included his novellas *Der verbannte Ehemann oder Frau Schievelbeyns Männer oder die Familie Schievelbeyn* and *Pater Matthias*. Hesse further suggested Eichendorff's novella *Das Schloss Dürande* as a possible basis for a stage work, and at this time he even wrote a libretto intended specifically for Schoeck: *Bianca*, a tale of jealousy, sex, and murder set in Florence in 1400. Schoeck rejected them all, though perhaps to sweeten the bitter pill he did set Hesse's poem "Frühling" to music a few days after his visit (Op. 24b, no. 6).

Hesse was no man of the theater. The only opera ever written to one of his texts was *Die Flüchtlinge*, on which Alfred Schlenker was already working. But since Schoeck made no attempt to engage with any of Hesse's proposals, it suggests that the problem really lay with the composer. Schoeck was struggling at the time with his Violin Concerto, the most "dramatic" of instrumental genres, so how could he have embarked upon a project on a far larger scale, in which the subtitle, "quasi una fantasia," would not suffice to mask a lack of dramatic trajectory? Hesse was placated with a free ticket to the first performance of Schoeck's *Postillon* a few days later (which, luckily, he adored). This ballad for tenor solo, chorus, and orchestra was perhaps in itself a quasi-operatic testing ground for its composer, for its lovely central tenor "aria" was the closest that Schoeck had yet come to writing anything even vaguely "theatrical." The choral writing in the outer sections is still very foursquare, but if the tempi are judged properly, there are also moments of real beauty.[3]

Schoeck's rejection of Hesse's offer of collaboration did not dim their mutual respect. Schoeck admired Hesse's stylistic brilliance, claiming that his prose was "perhaps the most beautiful that I know,"[4] while Hesse would write just before World War I that "of today's musicians, no one has composed Eichendorff settings as beautiful as those by the Swiss Othmar Schoeck."[5] Not even Schoeck's financial unreliability bothered him. When Schlenker once complained of Schoeck's laxity in debt repayment, Hesse wrote back: "That [Schoeck] is someone who makes debts is not something I knew, but I find it utterly comprehensible. He has that carelessness that both of us lack. . . . I wish good luck to every artist in our time who within himself can stand so very far from the business of the world."[6]

Within a month of the *Postillon*'s premiere, Schoeck embarked on a tour of the Tyrol with the Männerchor Aussersihl (see fig. 5.1). It had been planned meticulously by the chorus committee, even down to the type of hat to be worn by everyone ("in order to cater for different tastes, the hat is offered in two types, with either a narrow or a broad rim").[7] They left Zurich in a specially chartered train carriage at 7 A.M. on Sunday 16 April 1911, traveling to Innsbruck, Bolzano, Riva, Venice, Trieste, Verona, and then Milan, where Schoeck had arranged to meet up with Hesse and Fritz Brun in time to attend a performance of Bach's *St. Matthew Passion* by Volkmar Andreae and the Gemischter Chor of Zurich (also on an Italian tour). The Aussersihl Chorus now returned home without their conductor, who together with Brun and Hesse traveled on to Assisi, Spoleto, Orvieto, Siena, Pisa, Montepulciano, and Chiavari, indulging in adolescent pranks such as kicking a tin can around a town square at night or ringing doorbells and running away. On their way home Hesse and Schoeck stopped off in Brunnen to spend a few days with Schoeck's parents. Years afterward, the two men would still reminisce happily about their Italian exploits.

April 1911 also saw Schoeck's election as conductor of the Lehrergesangverein (Teachers' Singing Association), one of the most prominent choral societies in Zurich, which had previously been under the direction of his old teacher, Lothar Kempter Sr. His first rehearsal took place on 31 May and was by all accounts a success, despite Schoeck's late arrival after having forgotten about it altogether. The choir's president was one Jakob Corrodi, whose son Hans, also a schoolteacher, now joined the choir too. He and Schoeck soon became friends, and within just a few months of their first acquaintance Corrodi had begun the "Schoeck diary" mentioned in the introduction above.

Throughout all these months Schoeck had not ceased pining for Stefi—one of the (discarded) sketches from 1911 for the second movement of the Violin Concerto bears the words "Bloody Stefi" emblazoned on it ("Die chaibe Stefi"). But this did not stop him from seeking physical distractions elsewhere. In the second half of 1910 a Russian medical student named Bertha Liebert had moved into an apartment in Schoeck's house at Bergstrasse 36. The common use of a kitchen led with rapidity to the sharing of more intimate, anatomical spaces.

Figure 5.1. The Aussersihl Men's Chorus on the beach in Venice, April 1911.

Bertha was six years older than Schoeck, so perhaps she did not enter their relationship devoid of experience. With the emotional multi-tasking not uncommon in the post-adolescent male, Schoeck was for the moment content to covet Stefi while bedding Bertha. Rüeger later claimed that Bertha had been the dominant partner in their relationship, leading Schoeck on "with a firm hand." He added that she had "taught [Schoeck] everything that a man ought to know and be able to do."[8] While he was presumably referring to more than just the art of how to fry sausages, the evidence we have from Corrodi suggests that Schoeck had already learnt from his male housemates in Zollikon all about both girls and sausages. Those tales, however, were perhaps mere braggadocio intended for the easily shockable Corrodi. Since Rüeger was ever Schoeck's closest confidant, we should probably believe his testimony that it was Bertha who released Schoeck from the bounds of his virginity.

What we do know for sure is that Bertha became pregnant almost immediately. She kept the news from Schoeck throughout, which itself presupposes either uncommon stupidity on his part, or his acquiescence in the charade. Whatever his experience (or lack of it) hitherto, he cannot have been in complete ignorance of the biological goal of spermatozoa. So perhaps this was simply a matter of unquenchable desire aroused in the heat of the moment over Bertha's *pot-au-feu* in their common kitchenette, combined with the notorious age-old belief that a girl can't possibly get pregnant the first time (or the second or third). But we can surely assume that if Schoeck did not know of Bertha's pregnancy, then it was because he did not want to know and was quite happy to kick cans around Italian town squares with his buddies while back in Zurich Bertha coped with morning sickness and presentiments of social ignominy all on her own.

Bertha had moved out of her apartment sometime in the first half of 1911 when Schoeck was away, and upon his return she had merely claimed to be "sick." He thereupon alerted his apothecary friend Rüeger. Why Schoeck did not call a doctor we do not know. Perhaps Bertha was poor and could not afford one; or perhaps he suspected the truth and felt that his best friend would be the right man to deal discreetly with the situation. Rüeger indeed took charge of things, and had Bertha taken to hospital for the birth. On 11 June 1911, in the eighth month of pregnancy, she gave birth to a daughter. She was named after her mother, but died that same evening, having lived only fifteen hours. We do not know what Schoeck felt upon hearing the news of his daughter's birth and death, but we do know that Bertha moved back to her apartment on the Bergstrasse and shared Schoeck's bed for another two and a half years.

Just over a month after Bertha's birth trauma, Schoeck left her in order to spend the summer in Dachau, where his brother Paul was lodging while studying architecture in nearby Munich. Schoeck used Dachau as a base for trips to Salzburg and the Königssee, and spent the rest of his time working on his Violin Concerto. He returned to Zurich to rehearse for his first-ever concert with the Lehrergesangverein: an all-Schubert program on 1 October 1911. The concert tradition among the choirs of Switzerland had long been to present a medley of different pieces by different composers, interspersed with solos and duos, so Schoeck's choice of repertoire for his first concert was a somewhat daring statement of serious artistic intent.

Not long after this concert Schoeck had to undergo a minor operation for a perforated eardrum. The only negative long-term effect of this was to prevent him from diving while swimming, though there was a far more positive spin-off in that it had him consigned henceforth to the army reserves. Like every other Swiss adult male, he had hitherto reported each year to the army for his shooting practice, but hated every moment: "I curse a hundred times, oh, the whole patriotism business," he wrote to Fritz Brun in late September 1911.[9]

The year 1911 saw a drastic reduction in the number of songs that Schoeck wrote for voice and piano (only four in all). There is a single choral work from this year: *Dithyrambe,* to a brief text by Goethe, for double chorus, huge orchestra, and organ. At only ten minutes in duration, it is not easy to program today—it was, after all, composed in those heady prewar days when any self-respecting central European choral society could rustle up an orchestra with triple winds and brass. Schoeck's choral writing is far more idiomatic here than ever before, and while the *Dithyrambe* is unusually bombastic, its immense energy cannot fail to sweep one along. This work is also unique in Schoeck's oeuvre in that the influence of Gustav Mahler is clearly perceptible, his Eighth Symphony hovering constantly in the background (its score had been published just a few months earlier). Schoeck was only twenty-five, still searching for suitable models in large-scale composition, and *Dithyrambe* shows that his stylistic development could easily have taken him along more traditional late-Romantic, post-Mahlerian paths.

Schoeck's other concrete compositional achievement of 1911 was the completion of the Violin Concerto. Its orchestra is more modest that that of *Dithyrambe*—double winds, two horns, two trumpets, timpani, and strings—and despite its formal weaknesses, we do find in it presentiments of Schoeck's later brilliance as an orchestrator. It had taken him far longer to write than any other work hitherto. He now began work on a string quartet—almost as if he were ticking off a list of the major genres in which a young composer ought to test himself. It, too, would take over a year to complete. His next large-scale work, begun in late 1911, would take him even longer still. Hesse's operatic suggestions had been rejected, but when Léon Oswald brought Goethe's singspiel *Erwin und Elmire* to Schoeck's attention, he took the bait.

Goethe's little play with songs is typical of the pastoral topics beloved of the late Rococo—*Bastien und Bastienne,* set by Mozart, is very similar. Here, as there, the two lovers of the title succeed in overcoming the obstacles to their love through the intervention of a wiser, older man. Goethe has a fourth character in the shape of Elmire's mother, Olympia. There have been no convincing explanations as to why Schoeck chose such a flimsy text as his first libretto, but perhaps one major consideration was that his librettist was dead. Living librettists, especially well-known poets, have a tendency to make demands on their composers. Minor poets tend to be easier to work with, though their drawback is that they are minor. For a composer looking to write a first-time opera but as yet uncertain of his ability to fulfil his task, the best option by far would be to take a text by a well-known author who was by definition unable to tamper or cajole, or complain if the orchestration took too long. And although it would contain in total little more than an hour's worth of music, Schoeck would labor away at his mini-opera for a full five years. So dead was definitely best. *Erwin's* singspiel format had the further advantage of being a series of individual numbers linked by spoken dialogue. This meant that the song-composer Schoeck was not going to be challenged by the need to write a through-composed opera.

The premiere of the whole of Schoeck's Violin Concerto, albeit still only with piano accompaniment, took place in Berlin on 28 February 1912, with the composer accompanying de Boer. Just before the concert Schoeck discovered that he had left the black trousers of his evening dress at home. De Boer did not have a spare pair, nor did either of them have the money to buy a new one. Still wondering what to do, they wandered into the streets, only to bump into Engelbert Röntgen on his way back from a concert tour in Scandinavia, who promptly lent Schoeck his own trousers. The concerto's first performance with orchestra took place in Bern on 19 March, under Brun's baton, in a program that also included the first performance of the *Dithyrambe.* The first Zurich performance of the concerto took place exactly a week later under Volkmar Andreae, again with de Boer. Schoeck soon thereafter signed a contract with Hug for its publication, receiving seven hundred francs in return. Although de Boer had premiered it, the dedicatee—as with the Violin Sonata—was still Stefi. Schoeck gave her the manuscript of the second and third movements. She was by now also in possession of the manuscript of Bartók's (first) Violin Concerto. But whereas she never played the latter work—she sold the manuscript to Paul Sacher in her final months in order to pay for medical expenses, and Sacher conducted its premiere after her death—Stefi later took Schoeck's Concerto into her repertoire, and she even recorded it in Zurich in 1947, under Andreae's baton, with Walter

Legge as their recording engineer. The completion of his concerto did not stop Schoeck from pining for Stefi, and he began taking dual refuge in a bluntly misogynistic vocabulary on the one hand and drink and sex on the other. Nor did his drinking habits go unnoticed, for in mid-1912 he received a letter from an anonymous female admirer that ran: "Dear Mr Schoeck! You are a genius. You could achieve the highest things, but you should stop with your drinking. Then you could become a Swiss Beethoven."[10]

On 4 June 1912 we find Schoeck's name for the first time in the guest book of the "Fluh," a country house owned by the Reinhart family, situated by the shores of the Greifensee (literally "Lake Greifen") between Zurich and Winterthur. We can probably assume that Schoeck was this time the guest of Hans Reinhart, though in just a few years he would return with greater frequency as a guest of Hans's brother Werner. A trip to Neuchâtel to conduct the Männerchor Aussersihl at the Festival of the Swiss Singing Association (the *Eidgenössischer Sängerverein*) was a necessity in late July,[11] but apart from this Schoeck spent the summer in semi-monastic seclusion in Brunnen, working on *Erwin* in a little hut in the meadow behind the family villa. He had at his disposal an upright piano that had been wheeled out there for the duration of his stay. *Erwin* and his new string quartet seem to have absorbed most of his composing energies this year.

Before returning to Zurich for the usual autumn round of choir rehearsals and concerts, Schoeck headed back to northern Italy for a brief holiday, from where his postcards to Hermann Hesse wax lyrical about the architecture, wines, and women. But he was by no means sated with traveling, for at the close of 1912 he decided to visit Paul once more in Munich. His old Leipzig friends Martin and Jenny Kuntze-Fechner were also living there, so he paid them a visit too. He was back in Zurich long enough to attend the Swiss premieres of Mahler's *Das Lied von der Erde* in the Tonhalle and of Strauss's *Ariadne auf Naxos* at the City Theater before returning to Munich in early 1913 to experience *Fasching*, the local carnival. At one all-night party, the band went home at three in the morning; Schoeck—dressed as a Pierrot—sat at the piano and played Strauss waltzes so that everyone could carry on dancing. On Shrove Tuesday itself, dressed as Pierrot once again, he, Paul, and the Kuntze-Fechners spent the day wandering from pub to pub in the center of Munich.[12] His urge to return there was perhaps also prompted by an affair with a married woman that he had begun during the New Year festivities. We know neither her name nor how long the dalliance lasted, though its duration seems not to have extended beyond Carnival.

After his return from *Fasching*, Schoeck conducted his Lehrergesangverein in a concert of excerpts from Wagner's *Götterdämmerung, Lohengrin, Die Meistersinger,* and *Die Walküre,* all in commemoration of the thirtieth anniversary of the composer's death. This anniversary also freed the performance rights to *Parsifal*. Most countries had to wait until the end of the year for the copyright to lapse, but since Swiss laws were different, Zurich was able to schedule its first performance for April 1913. The conductor was Lothar Kempter Sr., and the scenery

Example 5.1. "Ravenna," Op. 24b, no. 9. Copyright Breitkopf & Härtel. Reprinted by permission. "I too have been in Ravenna. It is a small, dead town that has churches and many ruins. You can read of that in the books."

was designed by Gustav Gamper, a poet-cum-artist whom Schoeck had come to know through Friedrich Huch. Alfred Reucker, the enterprising director of the Zurich City Theater, even had a canvas "lid" constructed for the orchestra pit in order to reproduce as closely as possible the conditions in Wagner's *Festspielhaus* (though it did not last longer than the end of the season, for the heat in the pit was unbearable, the air stagnant, and the sound of the orchestra so loud down there that the conductor often could not hear the singers on stage).

While Zurich was sampling Wagner's last work, Schoeck was back in Italy with Hesse and the painter Fritz Widmann, watching *Cavalleria rusticana* at La Scala instead. His creative energies had recently been concentrated almost exclusively on his concerto, quartet, and opera, but this trip seems to have prompted him into song composition again. A few days after returning from Italy he set Hesse's poem "Ravenna" to music (Op. 24b, no. 9); it was an atmospheric portrait in sound of the old Italian city and deservedly became one of his most popular songs (see ex. 5.1). At this same time he also went to see *Parsifal* at last. The vocal score of *Parsifal* was observed on his piano for several months during this year (the transformation scene of act 1 might even have been one of the sources of the pseudo-modal harmony of "Ravenna"). Schoeck admitted to being particularly fond of the prelude to act 1, the prelude to act 3 (whose bass line he admired for years afterward[13]), and the Good Friday music. Schoeck protested that Wagner was a man of violence, "like Napoleon," but every time that he attended one of his operas, he would succumb to the music again. Perhaps for that reason, he made sure that he did so only rarely.[14]

The most significant event of spring 1913 for Schoeck was not, however, that first performance of *Parsifal*, but his first meeting with the Hungarian contralto Ilona Durigo (1881–1943). They had performed together once, just over a year before, but it was only now that she entered his circle of friends proper, apparently through the offices of her friend, the rich Zurich patroness Mathilde Schwarzenbach. Durigo had begun as a pianist, studying at the Budapest Conservatory before moving to Vienna to take singing lessons with Julius Stockhausen, Brahms's old friend. Not only did she become one of the most celebrated *lieder* and oratorio singers of her generation (Orfeo in Gluck's opera was her only stage role ever), but she was a formidable all-round musician, a faultless sight-singer, and a keen champion of contemporary music—among the works she premiered in the course of her career were Béla Bartók's songs Op. 16, with the composer at the piano. Ilona was also in love with Schoeck. Her feelings were not reciprocated, at least not yet, and the fact that she was already married (to the pianist Osman Kasics) was a further complication. Nevertheless, she soon became Schoeck's most prominent interpreter, and her love of Schoeck's music remained undimmed until her death. Their relationship would at times be turbulent, but in his old age, not long before he died, he finally admitted that he had never found a finer interpreter than her for his songs.[15]

Chapter Six

Look Back in Melancholy

Schoeck's String Quartet Op. 23 was premiered on 14 June 1913 at that year's *Tonkünstlerfest*, held in St. Gallen. It is cast in three movements and, like the Violin Concerto, is marvellously tuneful while somewhat aimless. The composer Hans Huber, Schoeck's elder by several years and one of the leading lights of the Swiss music scene, cried out after the quartet's premiere: "You're our Schubert!" referring to the work's effortlessly melodious qualities.[1] Its layout is at times reminiscent of the piano accompaniments to Wolf's Italian or Spanish songs, almost as if Schoeck had learnt to score for quartet, at least in part, from Wolf's piano writing. Perhaps tellingly, Schoeck remarked of his quartet almost two decades later that "someone should arrange it for the piano."[2]

The St. Gallen festival also saw two up-and-coming French-Swiss musicians conduct their own music: Ernest Ansermet with two orchestral songs, and Frank Martin with his Suite for Orchestra. More interesting in our context, however, was the debut of the composer/pianist Marcel Sulzberger. He was ten years older than Schoeck, though they had studied at the Zurich Conservatory at the same time. Sulzberger had then gone to study in Paris, where under the influence of Debussy he had become the first Swiss composer to cast tonality aside. Impecunity forced him back to Zurich, where his music was far too modern for local tastes (not for nothing did he later join the Dadaists). Sulzberger's output was highly uneven—a superb Violin Sonata jostles alongside near-incoherent dross—and he soon drifted into near-complete obscurity. But the piano pieces that he played in St. Gallen are significant because they were in part bitonal; and while we do not know for sure if Schoeck heard them, it would otherwise be an odd coincidence that he began to experiment with bitonality just a few weeks later in his overture to *Erwin und Elmire*, where a melody in E-flat major on the trumpet is accompanied in E major (see ex. 6.1).

Schoeck dashed off a brief piece for choir and orchestra in July—the jolly but rather vacuous *Wegelied*, to a patriotic text by Gottfried Keller (patriotism would always fail to inspire Schoeck)—before departing on a summer tour with the Lehrergesangverein to Austria, Hungary, and northern Italy. He took August Oetiker along to keep him company. In Salzburg Schoeck met up with Stefi Geyer (now Stefi Jung) and her husband. Schoeck was also supposed to conduct the Lehrergesangverein in front of Mozart's birthplace, but instead he went to a pub with Oetiker, where he demonstrated his powers of recall by playing and singing a whole act of the *Magic Flute* from memory, with Oetiker taking the cigar out of his mouth each time he came to an aria. Wild horses wouldn't drag him to

Example 6.1. *Erwin und Elmire*, Op. 25, opening of the overture.
Copyright Breitkopf & Härtel. Reprinted by permission.

conduct a men's chorus in front of his Master, he said. Once in Vienna, Schoeck went to see sights different from those of his first trip three years before. He took Oetiker along to the Schubert House, where they spent almost a whole day, and he ended with a "Schubertiade" from memory that the museum's curator remembered for years afterward.[3] Then Schoeck wandered round Beethoven's former dwellings and had lunch in the "Red Hedgehog," where Brahms had once been one of the regulars. He nearly missed the train to Budapest on account of a Russian girl he picked up in the Rathauskeller, and he also kept everyone waiting in their lunch break on the journey to Trieste, when he again picked up a girl and seriously considered staying to get better acquainted. After Trieste came Venice, where Schoeck visited the Palazzo Vendramin, where Wagner had died thirty years before. The tour had taken just two weeks in all, but Schoeck still felt he needed a holiday to recover, and so now he set off with Rüeger for southern Germany, visiting by rail, on foot, and by coach the towns where many of their favorite poets had lived—Mörike, Uhland, Hölderlin, and Hermann Hesse too. Not everyone on the choir tour this summer had been as happy-go-lucky as Schoeck, however; his erratic behavior throughout had placed such a strain on the choir's president, Jakob Corrodi, that he had suffered a nervous breakdown. He recovered this time, but it was not to be his last.

By the end of October 1913 Schoeck had finished *Erwin und Elmire* except for the orchestration (though this itself would take him over two more years to complete). The timing was fortuitous, for his new concert season was just beginning, and that always absorbed his creative energies. On 30 November he conducted Reger's recently composed *Römischer Triumphgesang* with the Männerchor Aussersihl and the Tonhalle Orchestra (proof that he was still keeping in touch with his teacher's newest music). But this was overshadowed by a much bigger local premiere, when Andreae conducted Mahler's Eighth Symphony for the first time on 13, 14, and 15 December, with some 750 participants in all. Schoeck was in the audience, but he told Corrodi afterward that he found it banal in comparison to *Das Lied von der Erde*.

Early 1914 saw Schoeck's private life in turmoil. His affair with Bertha had continued over the past months, despite the strain caused by his repeated infidelities. But she had failed her exams at the university, and a lack of funds now forced her to leave Switzerland. Although Schoeck was relieved that he was no longer threatened with permanent domestication, he told Corrodi that he had also grown used to having her around and now missed her. He compensated for his loss in what would over the years become a typical manner, namely by having as much sex as possible with as many women as took his fancy. Carnival time in February 1914 was ideal for this, and at the Saturday masked ball in the Tonhalle he managed to pick up two women: a Portuguese girl nicknamed "Fifi" and an Austrian divorcée. The latter's boyfriend almost scuppered Schoeck's chances when he followed her home one night, suspecting foul play—but Schoeck hid in a nearby doorway long enough for his rival to tire of waiting and leave, after which a key was dropped down to open his "gateway to paradise," as he called it.[4] Schoeck was now also determined to add Durigo to his list. On 30 January 1914 she sang several of his newest songs in a concert in Zurich that helped to cement her position as his principal interpreter. A few days later he told Corrodi that he had fallen in love with her, and for the next three months he penned a series of letters to her that were unusual in their frequency, their length, and their increasingly impassioned tone. By March he was complaining that he was busy with five different women, and a sixth was added on his annual Easter vacation in Brissago—her identity is not certain, but it seems to have been a Maria Giornelli, the wife of a tobacco factory owner. Schoeck's pursuit of Durigo also continued. She had complained of his easy virtue during Carnival, but a letter to her from Schoeck of April 26 leaves little doubt that she had finally resolved to sample it herself that same morning. This capitulation seems to have ended Schoeck's erotic interest in her, for the more distant tone of his earlier correspondence now returned.[5]

Schoeck's last trip to Germany before the outbreak of war was to the same year's festival of the Allgemeiner deutscher Musikverein, held in Essen, where his *Dithyrambe* received its German premiere under Hermann Abendroth on 24 May, just one day after the world premiere in Basel of his *Wegelied*. He traveled north in the company of the young Zurich composer Walter Schulthess (1894–1971), who a decade later would become one of his closest friends. Once he was back home a few days later, Schoeck returned to song composition with a setting of Gottfried Keller's "Jugendgedenken." Keller has rarely appealed to composers, for his otherwise often exquisite verse has always been regarded as somewhat unmusical. Schoeck himself had hitherto set only two of his texts to music, both from the more accessible *Alte Weisen* collection. But like any cultivated Swiss of his day, he had grown up with Keller's works—the poet's "presence" in the family being cemented by an anecdote of how Agathe Schoeck, the composer's mother, had in her youth caught the lascivious eye of the aging poet in a hotel corridor in Baden. Schoeck had renewed his interest in the poet in 1913 upon reading his famous bildungsroman, *Der grüne Heinrich* (*Green Henry*), and his love of the poet's works never left him. Years later, when his nephew remarked to him how little Keller had actually produced, Schoeck agreed, but quipped that "he only wrote his best works."[6]

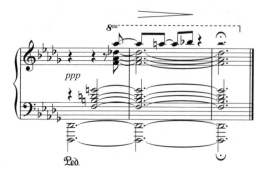

Example 6.2. The close of "Jugendgedenken," Op. 24b, no. 10. Copyright Breitkopf & Härtel. Reprinted by permission.

The Keller poem that Schoeck chose to set in June 1914, "Jugendgedenken," is a "look back in melancholy" at childhood days. It was his longest song to date, and unquestionably his finest. Nor did it did come easily, taking six months to finish. Schoeck found it so difficult to set that he even for a while considered having the fifth strophe recited. The close of the poem runs: "Nur noch einmal will ich rückwärts sehen"—"Just once more will I look back"; but Schoeck, typically, cannot relinquish his backward glances, and repeats "Nur noch einmal" six times in all. The haunting final cadence is the most "modern" that Schoeck had yet written (see ex. 6.2).

A song written in the second half of 1914 that bemoans things past seems to cry out to be placed in the historical context of the end of an era, and the lamps going out all over Europe. Yet there was little sense of an impending catastrophe at the time. The assassination of Archduke Franz Ferdinand on 28 June in Sarajevo had brought the Europe-wide system of alliances into play, setting France and Russia against Germany and Austria, while Germany's violation of Belgian neutrality ensured Great Britain's entry into the conflict. But there was no inkling of the slaughter to come, and the general opinion among all the belligerents was that (their own) victory would be confirmed by Christmas. So in the case of Schoeck's "Jugendgedenken," we might just as well read into it the composer's feelings of loss after Bertha Liebert's departure, or guilt about their dead child. Or perhaps he just found the poem beautiful and wanted to set it to music. Schoeck would in fact return to such expansive, poetic considerations of a lost youth several times again. Many years later, after setting Mörike's "Besuch in Urach"—another such example—Schoeck said to Corrodi that he could "remember exactly that he had looked back on his childhood with similar feelings when he was himself twenty years old, as if it already lay far, far behind him."[7]

Life in Zurich for Othmar and his fellow citizens was at first not unduly affected by the war. The army was mobilized on 31 July, and Schoeck with it, though since he was recuperating from a recent hernia operation he was soon

sent home. Before he could return to his division, the military situation stabi-
lized, his reserve unit was dissolved, and he remained a civilian for the moment.
But general mobilization did mean a temporary halt to rehearsals with the Männerchor Aussersihl, and thus also to Schoeck's payment as its conductor. Things
were more serious back in Brunnen, for the stream of tourists upon which the
family business depended had now halted. The hotel would only survive the war
by housing interned German prisoners of war. In the general confusion of the
times, it does not seem that Schoeck took notice of the death of an old friend,
Hugo Faisst from Stuttgart, who passed away there in early August 1914.

Chapter Seven

Chamber Music

Schoeck spent the weeks of his convalescence in Brunnen, where he completed the vocal score of *Erwin und Elmire* before embarking on its orchestration. A brief holiday in Brissago ensued before he had to return to Zurich for the autumn season. It was there, in October 1914, that he made the acquaintance of a young German violinist named Elsbeth Mutzenbecher (1891–1987). She had a teaching job in Italy, was on her way home to visit family in Hamburg, and had briefly stopped off in Zurich to visit a friend. The latter introduced her to Schoeck, only to find (to her apparent chagrin) that the two were immediately attracted. Elsbeth departed for Hamburg a few days later, leaving Schoeck moaning to Corrodi, while hugging her photo, that he'd been driven out of paradise before being allowed to indulge in original sin. He began to compose a violin sonata for her (though he never completed it), and also wrote a setting for her of Lenau's "Die Entfernte" ("The Distant Girl," Op. 24a, no. 3) in which the distance between two lovers is symbolized by bitonality.

Apart from the obvious disruptions to family, social, and economic life brought about by Switzerland's general mobilization, World War I soon began to cause grave divisions across Swiss society. The country's two main language groups, French and German, were split in their support for the opposing sides just across their borders. Matters were not helped by the fact that the head of the Swiss army, General Ulrich Wille, was German-born and had even married into the von Bismarck family. Although Switzerland remained neutral, the large numbers of German citizens resident in northern Switzerland who were called up to serve Kaiser and fatherland meant that almost everyone there will have known someone at the Front. The Aussersihl Chorus lost one of its German members to a grenade in the first months of the war (one Hermann Kaltenbach). Their Chorus bulletin subsequently published excerpts from his war diaries, with vivid descriptions of the dead, dying, and wounded, of mud and miserable provisions, and also of the famous Christmas truce.[1] Twenty years later the Swiss population would be almost unanimous in its detestation of German belligerence, but for now, the sympathies of most German-Swiss were decidedly with those neighbors with whom they shared a common language.

The Schoecks, however, were out of step. Paterfamilias Alfred led the way, for his youthful sojourn in North America had made him sympathetic to all things Anglo-Saxon.[2] And already in the summer of 1914, Othmar too was raging about Germany's violation of Belgian neutrality and had vented his anger at "Prussian militarism." His brothers—who were all on active duty in the Swiss

Army—felt the same. Othmar took to wearing a French beret in demonstration of his sympathies, while the main living and dining room in the Schoeck villa was soon referred to as the "Entente-Stübli" because of the family's sympathies for the Western Allies. But when the hotel's severe financial straits forced them to take in their first batch of some sixty German internees in 1916, the Schoecks had to be civil toward their guests' sensibilities. In a letter of 26 January 1917 to Hans Reinhart, Agathe Schoeck remarked mockingly that "the gong has just sounded to announce a theatrical performance of our son-in-grey [i.e., Paul] in honor of the birthday of the German Imperator."[3]

Schoeck's antagonistic attitude toward German militarism was in tune with Hermann Hesse's opinions, and the two men were closer in these years than ever before or after. In late 1914 Hesse sent him his latest book of poems: *Musik des Einsamen* ("Music of the Lonely Man"), and Schoeck promptly set three of them, at about the same time that he completed "Jugendgedenken": "Keine Rast," "Das Ziel" (Op. 24b, nos. 7 and 10) and "Die Kindheit," Op. 31, no. 2. Just a few weeks later, in early January 1915, his spirits were lifted by Elsbeth's return. He now made sure to penetrate those realms of original sin that had been previously prohibited to him. Unfortunately, his neighbors observed that the young lady with whom he had been playing chamber music did not surface again after the music had gone silent, nor did she emerge until the following morning. Cohabitation was illegal in Zurich, so Schoeck's contravention of cantonal law was immediately brought to the attention of his landlord, Herr Sprecher, who lived next door. He and his wife were fond of Schoeck and even kept his rent lower than the norm. But when faced with such flagrant disregard for Zurich's Zwinglian morals, Sprecher had no choice but to summon his delinquent tenant. The embarrassment was mutual, being compounded for Schoeck by the sight of his most recent unpaid bills lying on the table before them. Schoeck managed to extricate himself with assurances that his activities with the young lady had been restricted to musical intercourse; that she was from a good home, and so forth. The storm passed for the moment, and Schoeck was allowed to stay.

Elsbeth still had to return to her job in Turin, but the two of them managed to spend a few days together in Italian Switzerland before she left. Where Schoeck had found the money to go to the Ticino is unclear, as he was by all accounts in considerable financial trouble in early 1915. But the Aussersihl Chorus now began rehearsing again, bringing a resumption of his regular income, and he was asked to deputize for Andreae with the Gemischter Chor, which also brought in a little money (since Andreae was a high-ranking officer in the army, he was often called away during the war). Given the uncertainties of the time, it is astonishing that Schoeck's next choral concert, on 7 February 1915 (repeated on 9 February) featured Wagner's huge *Liebesmahl der Apostel,* which is one of the most taxing works of its kind in the repertoire. The Aussersihl Chorus was joined by both the Lehrergesangverein and the Harmonie Chorus, and the proceeds went to charity.[4] Schoeck then accompanied a choir concert in Bern in mid-February, and he was back there to give a *Liederabend* with Ilona Durigo on 23 March; it featured the premieres of several of his newest songs, including the Hesse settings "Keine Rast" and "Das Ziel." Hesse wrote a concert preview for the *Berner Tagblatt* of 19 March, in which he stated that Schoeck's songs were "the lasting creations of a great song composer . . . his songs are not promises of things to come, not of his talent, but are mature and perfect."

Chapter Eight

The Art of Counterpoint

In May 1915 Elsbeth returned to Zurich. Since she was a German citizen, Italy's declaration of war on Austria on the twenty-third of the month made it awkward for her to remain in Turin (though it took another three months before Italy took the next logical step by declaring war on Germany itself). The war just beyond Switzerland's borders was already intensifying. It was in spring 1915 that the Germans embarked upon chemical warfare on the western front and began their Zeppelin raids over London. The sinking of the Lusitania on 7 May, one of the major factors that turned American public opinion against Germany, even impinged upon Schoeck too, for the only manuscript of one of his songs—a Goethe setting—went down with the ship, lost for good in a watery oblivion.

Switzerland was a temptingly safe place to be at this time. And since Elsbeth and Schoeck were head over heels in love with each other and disinclined to part again so soon, she decided to stay, and rented an apartment at Steinwiesstrasse 1, a kilometer from Schoeck's own on the Bergstrasse. The renewed vigor of their "chamber music," however, resulted in his lease being terminated a few months later, and the loss of his chalet apartment for good. During the ensuing three years that Elsbeth spent in Zurich, she made some money by playing the violin part-time in the Tonhalle Orchestra and elsewhere but remained largely dependent upon Schoeck for her pecuniary survival. Schoeck's finances were already sorely stretched, though he still somehow found the extra funds to rent a little holiday apartment with Elsbeth in Strahlegg in the Zurich Oberland that summer. She did the cooking and read *Don Quixote,* while Schoeck read Goethe's *Wilhelm Meister,* painted small landscapes, studied Bach's *Well-Tempered Clavier* and practiced his fugue writing. He wrote to Rüeger on 30 July: "E. and I are quite alone up here and are having a truly beautiful time. We belong to each other in undisturbed joy, body and soul." They returned to Zurich in early August 1915, though Schoeck almost immediately abandoned Elsbeth to go home to Brunnen for a few days—he did not take a girlfriend home until long after Elsbeth had departed from his life.

In his few days spent back in Zurich, Schoeck set "Jünger des Weins I" by his friend the poet/painter Gustav Gamper (a "Jünger des Weins II" is undated but was probably composed at the same time). It was Gamper who had recently brought the poetry of Walt Whitman to Schoeck's attention, presumably the collection *Leaves of Grass* in the German translation by Johannes Schlaf (first published in 1907). When he arrived in Brunnen, Schoeck set a poem from that collection: "Drum Taps" (in German: "Trommelschläge"); the score is dated 16

August 1915. Eight days afterward, Schoeck wrote to Hesse: "I've vented all my anger about the present into a choral piece. It will perhaps break the neck of my position in Zurich." He was not far from the truth, as he found when he first played the piece to his Lehrergesangverein that autumn. One of the members even sat on the piano keyboard and claimed that *Trommelschläge* sounded just the same (see ex. 8.1). Schoeck's popularity was in any case becoming somewhat fragile with both his choirs, as he had grown bored and petulant in rehearsals, while his hatred of their bureaucracy meant he often did not bother to attend important meetings.[1] When he actually started rehearsals of *Trommelschläge* with the Lehrergesangverein, members accordingly began to drift away. Schoeck, too, became apathetic—though it probably did not help that he had a very busy concert schedule in the last three months of 1915, including assorted recitals with artists such as the violinist Joseph Szigeti and the Munich baritone Max Krauss. By January 1916 Jakob Corrodi, still the president of the LGV, was forced to beg his members to refrain from criticism of *Trommelschläge*, at least until after its first performance. This took place on 5 March 1916 in a concert devoted wholly to Schoeck's music; the program was repeated two days later. Besides *Trommelschläge*, the choral part of the program also included *Wegelied, Dithyrambe,* and *Postillon.* Schoeck furthermore accompanied Max Krauss in ten songs (eight of them world premieres), while Willem de Boer played the Violin Concerto. The Tonhalle Orchestra was augmented by many extra players, most of them needed for *Trommelschläge.* There were some negative comments in the press (Georg Herbst in the *Tages-Anzeiger,* for example, wrote of *Trommelschläge*'s "musical sadism"),[2] though the overwhelming impression was positive. Ernst Isler wrote a glowing review in the *Neue Zürcher Zeitung,* while Hans Reinhart wrote an even better one in the *Winterthurer Tagblatt.* But the man who, after Schoeck, should have been happiest at the work's critical reception, was unable to appreciate it. Jakob Corrodi had in the weeks before the concert become increasingly obsessed by the fear that it would be a financial disaster and that he would be held personally responsible. After it was over, he suffered another nervous breakdown, one from which he never recovered. He was eventually committed to a mental institution, where he died in 1930.

Schoeck used to say in later years that *Trommelschläge* was his "first piece of modern music." He was right, but it was arguably also his finest work thus far, and it has few peers in the choral repertoire of its time. It is hardly ever performed, for although it lasts only five minutes, it requires a massive choir and an orchestra that includes eleven percussionists, an organ, eight horns, and triple winds. The choral parts are in places highly dissonant, the men at one point have to shout (in rhythm), and the rapid, extreme changes of tessitura and dynamics would test even the best of vocal ensembles. Gone is the foursquareness characteristic of Schoeck's choral writing in the *Wegelied* or the *Postillon,* while instead the expressionist Strauss of *Elektra* now lurks in the background. But there is nothing derivative in *Trommelschläge.* The overall effect of the work is

Example 8.1. *Trommelschläge*, Op. 26. Copyright Breitkopf & Härtel. Reprinted by permission. "[. . . nor the] mother's entreaties; Make even the trestles to shake the dead, where they lie awaiting the hearses, So strong you thump, [O terrible drums . . .]."

breathtaking, as we can hear in the only recording of it, conducted by Mario Venzago and released in 2007.[3]

On Sunday 19 March 1916, two weeks after the premiere of *Trommelschläge*, Schoeck conducted his last concert with the Aussersihl Chorus. Their program comprised *Rinaldo* by Brahms, the "Gralserzählung" from Wagner's *Lohengrin*, and assorted works by Grieg. Schoeck had grown to detest conducting choirs, even fearing that their faulty tuning might ruin his perfect pitch, but they had provided a necessary source of income. It was Elsbeth above all who was now urging him to take the risk of devoting more of his time to composition. And as luck would have it, he soon gained access to other monies. He and Elsbeth had for a while been regulars at the Café Schneebeli on the Limmatquai, down by the river, where assorted artists used to meet. These included the sculptor Hermann Haller, who brought Schoeck's financial malaise to the attention of Werner Reinhart, the millionaire Winterthur industrialist and brother of the writer Hans (see fig. 8.1).[4] Schoeck had already met Werner on several occasions and had taken to dropping heavy-handed hints about his dire finances. Another man might have taken offense, but Reinhart decided instead to help. He informed Schoeck in writing on 12 April 1916 that he would for the next three years pay him an annual "scholarship" of three thousand francs. The money, he insisted, was not tied to any commission, and its purpose was to free Schoeck to compose as he saw fit. The first quarterly payment included an extra two hundred francs to help Schoeck pay outstanding debts. Extra money followed in July in order for him to go on holiday. Schoeck forgot to reply to this letter for three months, though Reinhart seems again not to have minded.

Schoeck's financial situation improved further when he was able to move into a cheaper apartment in April, at Dolderstrasse 93. Three months after that an apartment was found for Elsbeth in the house next door, with a connecting door leading to Schoeck. They were thus able to live together as man and wife without having to break the law by sharing the same address. Schoeck will have known his new house already, for Bertha Liebert had lived there four years earlier (something that he presumably kept quiet about). Elsbeth now played the good housewife, darning Schoeck's socks and trousers, cleaning, and cooking, though Schoeck's insistence on staying out late on his own with his drinking buddies would prove a frequent bone of contention.

In July Hans Corrodi went on holiday to Grimentz in the Val d'Anniviers in Canton Valais. Back in Zurich it had been raining more or less nonstop for two months, so when Schoeck heard that the Valais had the lowest rainfall in the country, he and Elsbeth decided to go too. They arrived at the Hotel Becs de Bossons on 21 July and stayed for three weeks (see fig. 8.2). Schoeck took along his score-in-progress of *Erwin und Elmire*, for a bare hotel room, he said, was conducive to the art of orchestration (it was proving intractable, and he later claimed to have spent up to two hours poring over a single measure). All three of them traversed the Moiry Glacier, but Elsbeth stayed in bed while Schoeck

Figure 8.1. Gustav Gamper (right) and Werner Reinhart (left). Courtesy of Winterthur Libraries (Switzerland), Special Collections.

Figure 8.2. Schoeck and Elsbeth in the Alps, July 1916. Courtesy of Zentralbibliothek Zürich.

and Corrodi got up early to ascend the 3000-meter-high Becs de Bossons. They moved to Zermatt for a few days in mid-August, by which time Schoeck had had his fill of mountain climbing.[5] But not long after their return home they were off on holiday again, this time for a week in Canton Ticino, with Rüeger along for company.

It is as well that Werner Reinhart had from the start guaranteed Schoeck a regular income with no strings attached, for if he had measured his money's success by the results of its first year he would have been disappointed. Schoeck had completed the instrumentation of *Erwin,* but his output for 1916 otherwise comprised a single movement for clarinet and piano—part of a projected sonata that was never completed.[6] His sudden interest in the clarinet is easy to explain: Reinhart was a competent clarinettist who played frequently as an extra in the Winterthur orchestra. Schoeck was by no means the only artist whom he funded. It was thanks to Reinhart's patronage that Stravinsky's *Soldier's Tale* was first performed, and it was for him that Stravinsky wrote his Three Pieces for Clarinet in 1918 (though Reinhart never played them in public). Reinhart later placed the tower of Muzot at Rainer Maria Rilke's disposal, and he was one of the founders of the International Society for Contemporary

Music. He gave generously to numerous other composers, and it was largely thanks to him that Hermann Scherchen was appointed conductor of the Winterthur Orchestra in 1923, in the face of opposition from several Swiss conductors.[7] Reinhart's private life, however, remains shrouded in mystery. Nor is it clear what he actually thought of Schoeck in human terms. "Not very much" was the answer suggested by one of Reinhart's acquaintances in conversation with the present writer, though that is perhaps belied by the scale of his financial support for Schoeck over the coming years.[8]

Toward the end of 1916, another potential source of income presented itself to Schoeck. Albert Meyer, the long-serving conductor of the City Orchestra of St. Gallen, in eastern Switzerland, had stepped down from his post in early 1915. His appointed successor, Karl Mannstädt, a German, had been forced to relinquish the position when called up into the army (he survived the war, becoming kapellmeister in Lübeck in 1920). The St. Gallen authorities decided to audition three possible replacements by assigning them each two or three regular concerts throughout the season. Schoeck was the first in the firing line in autumn 1916. For his opening concert he programmed Mozart's "Jupiter" Symphony and Beethoven's "Pastoral," with a sandwich filling of eight songs from Schubert's *Winterreise*, in which he accompanied Max Krauss. The chairman of the orchestra's board, Hans Bärlocher, could still remember twenty years later the enthusiasm that Schoeck generated straightaway. This first impression was cemented by the remaining two concerts assigned to him—even though he had taken the daring step of including two contemporary works in his third (Busoni's *Lustspielouverture* and Fritz Brun's Second Symphony). He was accordingly appointed permanent conductor at the close of the 1916–17 season. Schoeck insisted, however, on remaining resident in Zurich. Not only was it a more important musical and artistic center than St. Gallen, but keeping his distance meant that Schoeck could stay away from the administrative duties that had proved such a source of tension with his Zurich choirs. Yet while in the past he had on occasion delegated the choice of repertoire to his choir committees, St. Gallen saw him take great care in preparing each season's program in advance. Despite having only a small, semi-professional orchestra before him—the orchestra's permanent members had dwindled during the war to barely two dozen, and many of its string players for years to come were amateurs—right from the start Schoeck placed great emphasis on performing contemporary music. He even succeeded in bringing enough extra players from elsewhere to be able to perform a different symphony by Bruckner every year. St. Gallen would remain his orchestral home for the better part of the next thirty years.[9]

The climax of Schoeck's composing career thus far was the premiere of *Erwin und Elmire* on 11 November 1916. The conductor was Robert F. Denzler, a Swiss who is remembered today for conducting the premieres of Berg's *Lulu* and Hindemith's *Mathis der Maler* in Zurich in the late 1930s. Schoeck was at first little impressed: "Denzler is a cobbler, a pure amateur! . . . an immature little boy!" he raged in private the day after the premiere.[10] They never became close, though Schoeck's opinion later changed dramatically. He once even remarked that Denzler's ability to realize an orchestral score at the piano was exceptional, matched only by Walter Gieseking (he mentioned in the same breath that the least gifted in this regard was Furtwängler).[11] The cast for *Erwin* comprised Charlotte Sauermann as Elmire, Marie Smeikal as Olympia, August Richter as Erwin, and Alfred Jerger as Bernardo. Jerger had arrived at the theater as an operetta conductor, but director Reucker had soon discovered in him a fine baritone. Just a few months after his performance in *Erwin,* Jerger was "discovered" a second time, this time by Richard Strauss, who recommended him to the Munich Opera and would many years later make him the first Mandryka in *Arabella.*

Rehearsal time was in particularly short supply (perhaps a result of the wartime financial difficulties that all theaters were facing), and the singers did not get all their costumes until the first night. The director, Hans Rogorsch, had cobbled together the scenery from the leftovers of other operatic productions, with *Erwin*'s second scene taking place on what had hitherto been Brünnhilde's Rock in Wagner's *Ring des Nibelungen.* There were some—such as "Hsr" in the *Neue Zürcher Zeitung* (probably one Walter Haeser)—who found the discrepancy between the naiveté of the plot and the complexity of the musical means jarring, but the premiere was in general a success with public and critics alike. The *Schweizerische Musikzeitung* even brought two good reviews, the first by Georg Herbst, and the second by Ernst Isler, who stated openly that Herbst had not been nearly complimentary enough.

Schoeck made a few revisions to the score after the première, but in later years he finally admitted that his music for *Erwin* was just not "dramatic." The characters have no real problems, there is no drama, and the music itself, with hardly any attempt at motivic unity across individual numbers, is not intellectually demanding. But the orchestration is light and colorful—a considerable step forward from the Violin Concerto—and Schoeck's melodic gift, unencumbered by the need to express anything dramatic, comes marvellously to the fore. The final trio in particular is a gorgeous pseudo-Mozartian puff pastry. The individual numbers of *Erwin* must count among the most charming songs with orchestra to have been composed in the first two decades of the twentieth century. Yet aside from the sheer quality of its musical inspiration, this opera is of significance in Schoeck's biography because it is his first large-scale essay in a nascent musical neoclassicism. There was no theorizing on Schoeck's part about the "Mozartian" aspects of his music to *Erwin,* but his little opera deserves to be seen as an up-to-date example of trends that were beginning to emerge on the wider European music scene. Neoclassicism did in fact have a theorist at this time, and he was already living in Zurich. He went to see *Erwin* for himself, and would be responsible both for the topic of Schoeck's next opera and for the libretto of the one after it: Ferruccio Busoni.

Chapter Nine

Busoni

After Italy's declaration of war on Austria in 1915, Switzerland had found itself completely surrounded by warring powers. The trenches of the Western Front reached from Basel to the North Sea, while battles less famous—but hardly less bloody—raged on its southern borders (the chaos on that front being vividly depicted by Ernest Hemingway in his *A Farewell to Arms*). Switzerland's long-standing neutrality continued to be respected by the nations at war, so most of those in Central Europe who wished to avoid participation in the general slaughter inevitably endeavored to reach Swiss soil, with Zurich the city of choice for many of them. By the end of 1916, the city comprised just fewer than 150,000 Swiss citizens and almost 60,000 foreigners. The economy of the city suffered dreadfully during the four years of the conflict, so it is a considerable testament to the tolerance of the local populace that relations between Swiss and foreigners remained largely cordial throughout.

Such a wave of immigration also brings with it an immense stimulus to a city's intellectual and cultural life. Zurich had experienced a similar upswing after the European revolutions of 1848 and 1849 that had brought Richard Wagner, Gottfried Semper, and others to the city, but World War I brought a far greater number of artists and intellectuals than could have been imagined. They were joined in the cafés, restaurants, and theaters of the city by the leading Swiss artists of the day. A brief selective list of those artists resident in Zurich during World War I, both Swiss and foreign, will have to suffice here: there were the sculptors Hermann Haller, Hermann Hubacher, Ernesto de Fiori, Wilhelm Lehmbruck, and Bruno Heller; the painters Friedrich Hodler, Louis Moilliet, Wilfried Buchmann, Carl Hofer, Walter Helbig, Karl Walser, Ernst Morgenthaler, Oskar Lüthy, Augusto Giacometti, and Franz Wiegele; the actors Tilla Durieux and Alexander Moissi; the writers James Joyce, Franz Werfel, and René Schickele, and the composers Eugen d'Albert, Philipp Jarnach, Czesław Marek, and Ferruccio Busoni. Even Stefan Zweig moved to Zurich for the last months of the war, using the world premiere of his *Jeremias* at the City Theater on 27 February 1918 as a suitable pretext for leaving Austria. The most famous outlet for the passions and frustrations of the artistic community in Zurich was the "Dada" movement, founded with the opening of the Cabaret Voltaire in the Meierei pub on 5 February 1916, just a few houses down the Spiegelgasse from Lenin's apartment.

Ferruccio Busoni had been at home in Berlin when World War I had broken out, and he had left as planned for an American concert tour on 3 January 1915. But he missed Europe, so he moved to Italy instead. There, however,

his Austro-German parentage made his status no less awkward, and his support-
ers on either side of the current European divide expected him now to choose
between them. He refused to do so and decided that if he had to sit on the
fence, then Zurich was the most congenial place to do it. He accordingly arrived
there in October 1915, settling on the Scheuchzerstrasse, not far from the city
center, and—as it happened—just a couple of doors away from James Joyce.

Busoni was no stranger to Volkmar Andreae and the Tonhalle Orchestra, as
he had performed with them while on his various concert tours in the early years
of the century. He lost no time in making his presence felt anew, both as a pianist and on occasion as Volkmar Andreae's deputy when he was away on military
duty. The mammoth concerts that Busoni gave with the Tonhalle Orchestra to
illustrate the history of the piano concerto are now legend. He soon became
acquainted with the local musicians in Zurich, dispensing advice and encouragement wherever it was needed, and seeing talent where others didn't, thereby
exerting an even more lasting influence on the history of music in the city than
has perhaps hitherto been acknowledged. He was the only man ever really to
take Marcel Sulzberger as seriously as he deserved, while the exiled Polish composer Czesław Marek—whose music was only rediscovered by a wider public in
the 1990s—was another man who found in Busoni a firm supporter. Busoni's
impact on the musical life of Zurich was such that his spirit was still palpably
present as late as the 1990s. His last surviving piano pupil from Zurich, Anny
Roth-Dalbert (1900–2004), composed every day until well over a hundred,
remembering with perfect clarity how Giotto, Busoni's St. Bernhard dog, used
to sit in the corner of the room while his master taught her.

Most of the artists in Zurich, whether local or foreign, met at the Odeon or
the Café Schneebeli, but Busoni preferred to hold court in the "Bahnhofbuffet,"
the restaurant at the main station. Supping there also meant that Giotto could
sample the forbidden pleasures of splashing in the Alfred Escher Fountain on
the way out, drawing the furious attention of policemen whom Busoni could
then ignore ostentatiously, as he did.

Schoeck and Busoni first met in early 1916, probably through the offices of
Andreae. They did not have much in common. Schoeck adored the music of
Wolf, whereas Busoni openly disliked it. Schoeck also believed in the power of
the "Einfall," that mysterious, indefinable, quasi-mystical moment that in German signifies both the act of inspiration and the artifact that it generates, and
this Busoni found absurd yet intriguing. This stuck in Schoeck's mind, for over
thirty years later, he still recalled how "time and again, I argued with Busoni
about the nature of inspiration. In my opinion, inspiration must never quite
cross the threshold of consciousness."[1] But Schoeck was himself fascinated by
Busoni's technical mastery in all he did, whether playing, writing prose, or writing music, and Busoni treated him with the respect one accords to an equal. Nor
did Schoeck abandon his critical faculties in dealing with the older man. He
later remarked of Busoni's "Young Classicality" that "Busoni keeps coming along

with his Mozart scores, but when he writes something that works, it's out of *Meistersinger*." Another time, he referred to his friend's Violin Concerto as a "Concerto senza inspirazione."[2] Although cruel, his comments were not without a grain of truth. On at least one occasion in early 1916 Busoni joined Schoeck and Hermann Haller in an evening visit to a Dadaist show in the Waag guild house, though Busoni found little there to become enthusiastic about ("Dada-caca-popo" was his response—"popo" being German baby-language for one's hindquarters). Busoni's nature did not tend to the kind of frivolity in which the Zurich Dadaists excelled, so he will hardly have been thrilled by the performance of musical works with titles such as "Wet Dream Gavotte" (thus the name of one of the Dada cabaret pieces written and performed by the young Otto Luening). Busoni's son Benvenuto many years later recalled once hearing his father wander round his Berlin apartment in the dark, touching his *objets d'art* and muttering to himself in all seriousness: "Geschmack, Geschmack, verlass mich nicht"—"Oh, good taste, desert me not."[3]

Busoni was impressed enough with Schoeck to help him now find a new publisher. Not since Hug had brought out his last batch six years before had Schoeck published any more of his songs. Nor was he doing anything about it—on visiting Schoek's apartment Walter Schädelin had been horrified to find the manuscript of "Ravenna" lying on the floor with footprints on it. It was Schädelin who now took it upon himself to do something, even to the point of investing his own money in the project, despite being far from wealthy. Breitkopf & Härtel was one of the biggest music publishers in Germany, and Busoni one of their most prominent composers. At Schädelin's prompting, he now wrote to them to recommend Schoeck, and he was joined in his support over the coming months by Hegar, Eugen d'Albert, and others. Five volumes with some fifty of Schoeck's songs accordingly appeared in early 1917: Opp. 19a, 19b, 20, 24a, and 24b, some of which had been composed a full eleven years before. And Busoni's impact on Schoeck's oeuvre would now become more direct still.

A few days after the first performance of *Erwin*, Schoeck and Elsbeth bumped into Busoni walking along the Bahnhofstrasse. When asked the customary "How do you do?" Schoeck later recalled having said that he was fine, except that he was looking for a new opera topic. "How about Ludvig Holberg's *Don Ranudo de Colibrados*?" asked Busoni, and he whisked the couple into the Gotthard Restaurant to tell them the story. While this anecdote sounds almost too straightforward to be completely accurate—one can imagine it becoming increasingly fluent with each retelling—it was confirmed independently by Elsbeth Mutzenbecher almost seventy years later.[4] We might think it odd that Busoni should have been so familiar with a Danish playwright. Yet not only was Holberg generally popular in the early twentieth century, but Busoni also had a Swedish wife and had become familiar with Scandinavian culture through having lived there for several years himself.

Schoeck decided that *Don Ranudo* was just what he wanted. If he was going to make his mark in the music world, he had to find a topic for a "proper," through-composed music drama. More important still, a successful opera was the only way for a composer to achieve financial security, and Schoeck's finances were decidedly precarious. He was still waiting for confirmation of his appointment in St. Gallen, and the first year of his three-year scholarship from Werner Reinhart was already almost over. Although he had taken five years to write and score the sixty minutes of music that went into *Erwin und Elmire,* which even he admitted was not really an opera, Schoeck had perhaps calculated that the remaining two years of his Reinhart scholarship might be just enough to write an opera that could yet free him from financial dependence on others. So he began work on *Ranudo* straightaway in January 1917, even before he had a word of text. Zurich was at this time full of gifted writers whom Schoeck might have approached for a libretto. But he did not work well under pressure, so he needed a librettist gifted enough to provide whatever text he needed, but enough in awe of him to let him work at his own pace, free of any restrictions or deadlines. Armin Rüeger, he decided, fitted the bill. He had no experience of the theater, but he was widely read, possessed of a quick mind, and had long been writing for his desk drawer. And he would indeed defer to Schoeck in almost every respect.

Don Ranudo tells of an aging Spanish nobleman and his wife, Olympia. They live in abject poverty, and could save themselves by letting their daughter Maria marry the man she loves, the rich aristocrat Don Gonzalos. But his family tree is far too inferior for the Ranudos, so they refuse to allow it. Their servant Pedro decides to trick them by having a vegetable-selling Moor dress up and pretend to be the scion of an ancient noble Ethiopian family. Impressed by the black prince's suitably elaborate, immensely long family tree, Ranudo acquiesces in his marriage to Maria. At this, the ploy is revealed, and Ranudo is humiliated into allowing his daughter to follow the desires of her heart. He declares that, as her father, he can forgive her; but as a Colibrados, he has no choice but to disinherit her. The lovers are united, and the curtain closes on their happy ending.

Years later Rüeger told Werner Vogel that Schoeck had been fascinated by the peculiar idealism of the title role, and that the notion appealed to them of writing an opera in which the love story was of secondary importance. Corrodi's diaries confirm this—on 9 January 1917 Schoeck told him that he would not even write a proper love duet. He later claimed that he had "kept the love story in the background" in order to avoid the "sensual brutality" that he found in Franz Schreker's operas,[5] but the real reason probably lies with the man who had suggested the story in the first place, Ferruccio Busoni. Just three months before, he had completed his one-acter *Arlecchino* and was currently writing words and music to its companion piece, *Turandot* (after Gozzi). Not only did something of the irony from *Arlecchino* find its way into *Don Ranudo,* but the latter work follows closely Busoni's prescription for the opera of the future, in which love duets and the erotic in general were to be strictly avoided.[6]

Schoeck was unable to settle into his work on *Don Ranudo* until the following summer. For the first three months of 1917 he was busy with concerts—two *Liederabende* with Clara Wirz-Wyss in January, one each with Max Krauss and Durigo in February, two big concerts with the Lehrergesangverein in that same month, then off to Basel to conduct his Violin Concerto in early March. Concert life in Zurich was enlivened by a number of prominent guests at this time. The warring nations were making concerted efforts to enlist the sympathies of the neutral countries (and, by implication, to coax them out of their neutrality). Oddly enough, these efforts included major artistic events, and Switzerland was receiving special treatment. In January 1917 Richard Strauss arrived with the ensemble of the Mannheim Court Theater to put on the revised version of his *Ariadne auf Naxos,* and while there he also conducted the Tonhalle Orchestra in his *Also sprach Zarathustra, Don Quixote,* and his *Burleske.* On 17 February 1917 Schoeck wrote to his mother that *Erwin und Elmire* would "most probably" be given in Mannheim and that he had already spoken with the theater's artistic director—so we must assume that he had made direct contact with the Mannheimers when they came in January. He also had a direct contact in Mannheim, for the orchestra's first kapellmeister was his old acquaintance Wilhelm Furtwängler. But the planned production never came about.

While Germany was spending money on opera productions abroad, economic conditions among its populace were becoming ever worse—and since the Americans had just joined the conflict on the side of the Entente, the war was inexorably turning against the Kaiser and his allies. Switzerland, too, was struggling to maintain its economy. Prices were rising, fuel was scarce, and there had been socialist demonstrations the previous summer. The government became jittery and decided to remobilize some of the forces it had previously disbanded. Even Schoeck was called back into the Swiss Army, serving his country in the reserves in Canton Schwyz for four weeks from early April to early May 1917. Thanks to a sympathetic commanding officer, he had little to do except sit in an office and write a daily report of a few lines, but the experience still served to intensify his detestation of everything about the military. He was back in Zurich in time to see Busoni's *Arlecchino* and *Turandot,* which received their world premieres in a double bill at the Zurich City Theater on 11 May 1917. Despite his own recent conversion to a Busonian aesthetic (or perhaps because of it), Schoeck was not overly impressed by what he heard and saw. Nevertheless, he clapped "as if possessed," and according to one report bore much of the blame for the many curtain calls at the end.[7] Perhaps he might have noticed that Arlecchino's opening (spoken) words are a parody of an aria from *Erwin und Elmire:* "Ein Schauspiel ist's für Kinder nicht, noch Götter" ("This is theater neither for children nor for gods"), instead of Goethe's "Ein Schauspiel für Götter, zween Liebende zu sehen" ("It is theater for the gods to see two lovers"). Whether Busoni intended this as a reference to Schoeck's work—or a criticism of it—we cannot know, for we cannot be sure when his prologue assumed its final form.[8] But he would have had no obvious reason to engage in any way with Goethe's early singspiel except through Schoeck's recent setting of it.

May 1917 also saw the return of Richard Strauss, this time to conduct *Elektra* (with Anna Bahr-Mildenburg as Klytemnästra) and Mozart's *Don Giovanni*, both with the Zurich opera's own forces. Elsbeth many years later remembered Schoeck having attended the former, finding it a "tragic operetta" (Schoeck's gift for succinct put-downs often being directly proportional to the degree to which a work intrigued him). We know from Corrodi that Schoeck also attended one of the *Giovanni* performances. He spent the evening leaning out of their box, muttering "incredibly beautiful," occasionally singing along quietly, on other occasions complaining at what he found to be Strauss's "wrong" tempi. What really perturbed him was Strauss's omission of the final ensemble, which Schoeck found "a sin against Mozart"[9] (though it was in fact Strauss's custom otherwise to include it).[10]

It was also in May 1917 that Schoeck returned to song composition for the first time since October 1915, writing six Eichendorff settings. In June, however, he was determined both to get to work on his new opera and to go to Bischofszell himself to make sure that Rüeger was at last making proper progress on the libretto. He accordingly spent three months there in mid-1917. He first lodged with Rüeger, but his habit of working into the night, rising in the early afternoon, and demanding lunch at three did not endear him to Rüeger's wife Gret, so she threw him out. He rented a room two doors away from them instead and stayed there for the rest of the summer.

It is tempting to regard as hyperbole Schoeck's claim that he had composed his first act within the first two weeks of his stay, but we have no reason to doubt him. If he were in the mood and able to work undisturbed, he could compose astonishingly quickly. And that he now did, finishing three of his four acts by the time he left Bischofszell in September. The summer was not as easy for Rüeger. Apart from the altercation between his wife and his best friend, he had to work through the summer to earn his living but was continually interrupted whenever Schoeck wanted more text. The anecdotes that circulate still among Schoeck's family and friends tell of how he would nag Rüeger until the latter sat down to write the next instalment of verses, at which Schoeck would then run off to set them unquestioningly, even before the ink had dried. While this sounds farfetched, all the sources suggest that it is close to the truth. He was no Richard Strauss, with the patience to debate the finer points with his librettist before composing his opera steadily, "as a cow gives milk."[11] There were, however, certain advantages to composing a work as swiftly as this. While there are reminiscence motives of one sort or another here, as in all of Schoeck's post-*Erwin* operas (mostly of a kind akin to Puccini), there is little obvious large-scale formal planning in *Don Ranudo*. So the fact that the music still comes across as unified is probably due largely to the speed of its conception.

From the very moment since *Don Ranudo* first saw the light of day, however, Rüeger has suffered intense criticism, his libretto mocked as third-rate, a product merely of Schoeck's fidelity to his best friend. "Der dichtende Apotheker"—"the poetizing apothecary"—is the insult most frequently levelled at him, as if his main defect were his chosen profession. Rüeger was no Hofmannsthal, but to criticize him for that is as mean as it is pointless. Even without giving due consideration to the absurd circumstances of its genesis, the libretto to *Don Ranudo* in fact comes across as not merely coherent but also really rather amusing. When Rüeger was at last allowed more time to devote to a libretto for Schoeck—with *Massimilla Doni* twenty years later—the result was fine indeed.

Schoeck's first concert as the new conductor of the St. Gallen Symphony Orchestra took place on 25 October 1917, and he had made sure it would be one to remember by securing the services of Busoni as soloist in Mozart's Piano Concerto in D minor, K 466. Perhaps in order to tempt Busoni into participating, Schoeck had also programmed the Orchestral Suite from his friend's opera *Turandot*. He was obviously determined to make a splash. His second concert, just over a fortnight later, included Mahler's Fourth Symphony, with Charlotte Sauermann as his soprano soloist (his Elmire in Zurich a year before). Although he had to commute for his St. Gallen rehearsals and concerts, Schoeck was soon able to find a home from home in the family of the local judge and music lover Julius Gsell. They became acquainted through Gsell's son-in-law Hans Gonzenbach, whom Schoeck knew as the president of Andreae's Gemischter Chor in Zurich. Gsell seems to have come to regard Schoeck as a kind of substitute son, and he would play chess with him into the early hours. Gsell's unmarried daughter Clara (nicknamed "Lala" by all and sundry) fell at least half in love with their guest, though their relationship—despite frequent rumors to the contrary—remained to the end platonic. Schoeck would in future even confide in her when his love life went awry.

After his St. Gallen concert with Busoni, Schoeck went straight to Vienna to participate in a week-long festival of Swiss music. It was for him a train journey of over 34 hours, stopping at every godforsaken dot on the map along the way. It was all yet another futile propaganda effort to win the support of a neutral state at a time when the war and the nationalist passions it had inspired were tearing the Austro-Hungarian Empire apart. Schoeck's train arrived too late for the final rehearsal of his *Postillon,* which was conducted by another.[12] But he accompanied Stefi Jung-Geyer in his Violin Sonata (she and her first husband were now resident in Vienna), and Hans Duhan in fourteen of his songs (including several world premieres). His Violin Concerto was also on the week's program. Schoeck wrote to his parents that Vienna was terribly expensive but that everything was available, and that he and the other Swiss guests were being treated exceptionally well. Free tickets to the Court Opera and the Burgtheater were just some of their perks. Back in Zurich, however, things were in a dire state, with bread being rationed from 1 October and the heating turned off in all municipal buildings. Even the city crematorium, once an object of enthusiastic support from no less a figure than Gottfried Keller, was turned off. The events of the Bolshevik Revolution in early

November were followed with enthusiasm among the Zurich socialists, and violent demonstrations now left four men dead in clashes with the police.

The unrest in Zurich did not deter Schoeck from moving closer to the city center in October 1917. In the previous May, Elsbeth had moved from the Dolderstrasse to the Neumarkt, near the Conservatory. Schoeck now moved into a two-room apartment, just fifteen minutes' walk from Elsbeth. It was in the garden of Hermann Haller's studio at Zeltweg 53, a street that stretches from the Kreuzplatz to the Pfauen Restaurant and the City Art Gallery. Over the previous decades the street's inhabitants had included Richard Wagner, Gottfried Keller, and Johanna Spyri. Schoeck's home and Haller's studio were demolished in the second half of the twentieth century to make way for an apartment block. The park near it now features swings, slides, and round-abouts that fill with children whenever school is out. The only testament to the days when the Zeltweg was home to two of Switzerland's finest artists is a single bronze statue by Haller that stands there still, on a plinth that bears the artist's name, but with no plaque of explanation.

Chapter Ten

The Picture on the Wall

With St. Gallen under his belt—bringing Fr. 3000 per annum plus travel expenses—and increasing success at home and abroad, Schoeck now felt confident enough to give up his last choral conducting post, that with the LGV. Giving up the Aussersihl Chorus alone had not reduced the burden that choral conducting had become to him. He used to compare his choir's singing of a chord to the bullets peppered around the bull's-eye during target practice, and when he later heard of Alois Hába's experiments with quarter-tone music, he quipped: "We've had that in [Swiss] choirs for years." Against the wishes of many old members, the LGV had at Schoeck's insistence accepted the idea of bringing in women in order to venture into the broader repertoire for mixed choir. Now even this was not enough to tie him down any longer. He accordingly informed the LGV committee in mid-December 1917 of his decision to resign. His two final concerts, on 3 and 5 February 1918, were devoted to Mozart. The one comprised the Requiem followed by *Ave verum corpus,* while the other featured choruses from *König Thamos,* three solo arias, the clarinet concerto, and the oratorio *Davidde penitente.* As is often the case when a man has already tended his resignation, Schoeck's heart was not in the task, and his apathy began to drive members away. He even screamed and stamped his foot at the orchestra in one of the final rehearsals, and was amazed when they rose up in protest. Nevertheless, the concerts were a considerable success. Even his old teacher, Friedrich Hegar—the LGV's first-ever conductor, thirty years earlier—wrote to congratulate him ("Much [in the Requiem] I have never heard performed so beautifully").[1] Schoeck was now made an honorary member of the choir; his successor was Robert F. Denzler.

The effusive, rosy-fingered reports of Schoeck as a choral conductor (as collected, for example, in Vogel's volume of reminiscences) have obviously been filtered by the passing of time. "His success is thanks less to his outward appearance than to the strength of his inner qualities, which come to eloquent expression in his clear eyes . . . a swift hand, a firm fist, and hey, how the sparks jumped and flew!"[2] "His facial expressions constantly mirrored the smallest change of emotion, his hands moulded the sound as if it were molten wax, his baton drew the most delicate strands of the melody"[3] "In the famous 'Hallelujah' . . . such a daemonic fire appeared in his eyes that one felt as if overwhelmed by this explosion of temperament and passion, and as if swept off the ground."[4] We can smile at the latent sexual imagery of all this—Schoeck's swift hand, firm fist, and exploding baton sweeping his singers off their feet—not least because the singers quoted here were all male (the last of them being Corrodi). But we should also be grateful that the fulsome manner of expression of their age allowed these men to convey without embarrassment the fact that Schoeck's success on the podium was a result, not of technical mastery, but of intense (sexual) energy, the effect of which was apparently no less potent among his male charges than among the female.

The only surviving film of Schoeck in the process of music-making is of him playing the piano, and it is silent. While it would be unwise to draw too many conclusions from it, what immediately strikes one—all the more so for there being no sound to distract one's attention—is the fluidity of movement of hands, wrists, and arms. Much of the movement has no obvious necessity, for to play a note on the piano needs pressure from the fingers, supported only where necessary by the wrist and forearms. Schoeck's whole frame seems to be expressing something more sexual than musical, with his limbs performing a kind of pole-dance at the keyboard that nevertheless seems unconscious of itself and devoid of affectation. The extant recordings of Schoeck seem to offer a precise aural correlation of the film: all is ebb and flow, the center of the music seeming somehow to lie less in the notes than in the shifting tensions between them, in the constant fluctuations of tempo and dynamics that constitute his art of interpretation.

Further testimony of Schoeck's interpretative art is offered by Willy Tappolet, who in the spring of 1918 was on military duty, stationed in a country guesthouse in Mendrisio in Italian Switzerland. His captain was one Siegfried Fassbind, a cousin of Schoeck's on his mother's side. The guesthouse had an old piano among its furniture and so, on a whim, Fassbind—a passionate amateur cellist—rang Schoeck to invite him down to play chamber music. He turned up a day or two later, with Elsbeth and her violin in tow. The next few days were spent playing works by Schubert, Schumann, Brahms, and Mozart. Tappolet wrote that

> Schoeck was concerned with sharp contrasts. A powerful, energetic forte would alternate with a tender, gentle legato full of poetry. What he was able to conjure out of the old piano, with its worn-away keys, was astonishing. . . . Schoeck's daemonic, elementally healthy, powerful character was fired by an exuberant vitality. He seemed to us to be the purest incarnation of "Sturm und Drang."[5]

Nevertheless, all was not well between Elsbeth and Schoeck. She had a certain degree of independence—she was still playing as an extra here and there, occasionally in the Bern Orchestra under Brun, more often in the Zurich City Theater and the Tonhalle. On 12 February 1918, just a week after Schoeck's farewell concert with the LGV, she even played in Strauss's *Alpine Symphony* under the composer's direction on his latest trip to Zurich (seventy years later she still remembered "with terror" the opening of the work, with its long-held notes for the violins).[6] Schoeck would often arrive to pick her up after her orchestral stints, but after his move to the Zeltweg his passion for drinking into the early hours with his (male) friends only intensified. Legislation had been introduced during the war to fix early closing hours for pubs and restaurants—the so-called "Polizeistunde" or "policing hour" later immortalized by James Joyce in *Finnegan's Wake* ("Boumce! It is polisignstunter," 370.30). But Schoeck was now living close enough to his friends for them all to retire to someone's apartment late at night and continue carousing into the early hours, without his having the long walk back up the hill to the Dolderstrasse at the end of it. Elsbeth objected, but Schoeck was unwilling to compromise. Corrodi mentions in his diary how they would bicker like an old married couple. Marriage, however, was the last thing on Schoeck's mind. Whether it was on Elsbeth's we cannot know. But most of her female friends will have been married already, and she must have wondered what her future might hold once the war was over. She found comfort at about this time in the arms of Rüeger, whose wife even contemplated separation and divorce as a result.[7] This did not happen; but Corrodi wrote years later that Elsbeth had found solace, too, in the bed of the Austrian exile painter Franz Wiegele, one of Schoeck's drinking friends.[8] Whatever the precise dynamics of these relationships, what we know for sure is that Elsbeth traveled back to Hamburg in April 1918 and never returned. This seems an odd time for her to have left for Germany. To be sure, the economic situation in Zurich was far from rosy, with inflation far outstripping wage increases and many in the population suffering real financial hardship. There were even "hunger demonstrations" by local women in June, by means of which they managed to bring about a reduction in the price of milk.[9] But conditions back in Germany were already far, far worse. It is unclear whether Elsbeth or Schoeck understood her departure as a complete break. Perhaps she thought that booking a ticket home and the prospect of separation would jolt Schoeck into begging her to stay. This was a tactic that another of Schoeck's girlfriends would use with success seven years later. But if this was what Elsbeth had calculated, then it was fuzzy math.

At about the same time as Elsbeth's departure, Schoeck completed his sketches for *Don Ranudo*. He now set about orchestrating it, and it was painfully slow. He turned to Busoni for advice, and even to Busoni's pupil Philipp Jarnach, another wartime immigrant, who was six years Schoeck's junior. Schoeck needed peace and quiet to work, so in June 1918 he withdrew once more to Bischofszell to finish the job. He was interrupted in the task by a package from Busoni. It contained a brief libretto: *Das Wandbild* ("The Mural") and the following lines:

Whether Othmar Schoeck
might be attracted
by what I took from
ancient times,
the present writer
asks himself, in doubt;

Whether you take it
or leave it undone,
accept this bundle
of words
and gestures
as a sign of my esteem.

Jarnach had discovered the story in a volume of Chinese fairy tales and brought it to Busoni's attention, as he thought it might be suitable for a libretto. Without consulting his pupil any further, Busoni wrote the text and sent it to him in June 1917. But Jarnach became uncomfortable with its mixture of pantomime, song, and spoken dialogue, so he gave up after finishing just the prelude and the first scene. Busoni sent it to Schoeck instead, who accepted the challenge and set the libretto to music within three days.[10]

The plot is as follows: It is Paris, 1830. Two young men, Novalis and Dufait, are being shown round an antique shop in the Rue St. Honoré. There is a mummy that dances to a mechanical clock, an ancient Chinese suit of armor, and a mural that depicts a strange, beautiful girl who fascinates Novalis. Dufait and the antique dealer move on, but Novalis remains transfixed by the picture. The girl in it comes to life and runs away; he follows her into the picture. Suddenly we are standing in a Chinese landscape, in front of a temple. Young girls are dancing round the image of a deity. An old priest sings; the girls join him in chorus, and then they leave. One of the girls remains: the one from the picture. She beckons to Novalis; a love scene ensues, and the other girls return to rearrange the hair of their companion. A giant then appears dressed in the Chinese suit of armor from the shop; Novalis flees; the giant discovers that the girl's hair has changed, claps her in irons, and disappears with her. We are suddenly back in the shop. Dufait and the antique dealer return, and Dufait notices a change in the picture on the wall: the girl's hair is now arranged differently from before. Novalis, horrified, runs out into the street, the antique dealer closes his shop, and the curtain descends.

Schoeck seems to have forgotten *Das Wandbild* almost as quickly as he wrote it. Its form certainly does not recommend it to theaters. Apart from a strange, almost minimalistic, dance for the mummy played on the celeste, the music only begins with Novalis's entrance into the picture. The ending—being devoid of music, like the opening—is something of an anticlimax. But the work is of interest for several reasons. It is Schoeck's first foray into the "supernatural," a field that Busoni maintained was ideal for opera. In his article "On the Future of Opera" of 1913, he had written:

Opera should grasp the supernatural and the unnatural as being regions of appearances and feelings that are ideal for it. Opera can thus create a fictitious world that reflects life in either a magic or a comic mirror, a world that should consciously offer what one cannot find in real life . . . and let dance and masks and grotesque charades ["Spuk"] be woven into it.[11]

Elements of this, and even of the *Wandbild* plot itself, would find their way into Schoeck's next opera project, too. But for the moment he returned both to the orchestration of *Don Ranudo* and to Zurich at the end of June.

This was hardly an ideal time for Schoeck to return to the city, for the so-called "Spanish flu" was raging across Europe and had just reached Switzerland. The flu of 1918 was no mere sniffle to be cured by hot whiskey and a warm bed. It brought death: deaths by the millions, as if during the war Nature had taken offense that man should pride himself on being so skilful at slaughter and had decided to humble him by an enterprise far more vast in scale. After four years of economic privation, the populations of the warring world were so weakened that some fifty million of them would die in the epidemic—far more than were killed in the war itself. Schoeck too was struck down, though only with hypochondria. Despite being perfectly healthy and devoid of symptoms, he retired to bed for three days in July 1918. Corrodi paid him a visit shortly afterward, finding him with pockets brimful of all manner of pills and scouring his apartment with a wetted finger in order to identify any hole or crack through which infected air might penetrate from the outside. Schoeck had also suddenly become a vociferous adherent of socialism. The reason he gave, in all earnestness, was that the capitalist Swiss government was so intent on exporting cheese to fund its armaments factories that the cheese ration for the average Swiss had had to be reduced. And Schoeck did so like his cheese. The flu epidemic did not spare all of Schoeck's friends: in Vienna, Stefi Jung-Geyer's husband was one of its victims. Their marriage had not been happy, with Jung resorting to alcohol to console himself. He had also begun to confide in Schoeck's acquaintance Walter Schulthess, who had recently taken up a job as a répétiteur at the Vienna Court Opera. Schulthess was now assigned the task of escorting Jung to his office in the morning to ensure that he did not make any detours via the watering holes along the way.[12] Two years after Jung's death, Schulthess would marry Stefi and bring her back to Zurich for good.

When we consider that the flu epidemic had closed all the schools in Zurich, that some were soon being converted into makeshift hospitals (as was the Tonhalle, too), and that the daily death rate in the city reached forty by the autumn of 1918 (necessitating the reopening of the crematorium), we can better understand Schoeck's apparent paranoia. His thoughts now, according to Corrodi, were back with Elsbeth (perhaps intensified by his hypochondriacal fear of imminent demise). He now even entertained, however distantly and reluctantly, the remote notion that marriage with her might not be a complete impossibility—if only he had enough money to marry, then he might, he said.[13] But these waverings were all swept aside on 12 August 1918, when a Genevan pianist visited him for an audition with a view to a concerto engagement in St. Gall.

Chapter Eleven

Touch of Venus

Her name was Mary de Senger. She played him Bach's *Italian Concerto* as her audition piece. He said just two words: "Quite perfect." They then played piano duets together and presumably exchanged pleasantries of some kind. Then they had sex. And then she took the evening train home to Geneva, with Schoeck following, also by train, the next morning.

Mary was the daughter of the Bavarian composer, conductor, and pedagogue Hugo von Senger (1835–92), who had settled in Geneva in 1869. He had assimilated swiftly, his "von" becoming a "de." For the next twenty-three years of his life he was the dominant figure in the music life of his adopted city. Hugo numbered some of the most notable men of the time among his acquaintances, including Wagner, Tchaikovsky, and Nietzsche. It was while visiting him in 1876 that Nietzsche met and proposed to one of de Senger's pupils, one Mathilde Trampedach. She refused and later married her teacher instead, becoming his third, and last, wife (the incident was later immortalized by Thomas Mann when he used it as the basis for the love triangle of Adrian Leverkühn/Marie Godeau/Rudi Schwerdtfeger in his novel *Doktor Faustus*).

"Louise Maria von Senger"—she too later swapped the "von" for a "de," but then also adopted as her first name the English version of her second one—was nine months younger than Schoeck. She had studied at the Paris Conservatoire, had married a Frenchman and borne a daughter, Renée, but had separated not long after. Her messy divorce proceedings were still in progress when she met Schoeck in 1918 (she would in fact lose custody of her daughter at the end of it all). Her family had come down in the world since the days of her father's fame, and she was at this time living in a tiny house on the edge of Geneva along with a great-aunt, her mother Marie, and her brother Ernst (a bank clerk who supported the family on his small salary).

Schoeck already knew Mary's other brother, the architect Alexander, who had studied at the ETH in Zurich at about the same time as Paul Schoeck, and it was he who had organized the audition for his sister. Schoeck and Mary spent three days together in the Hotel Bristol in Lausanne in early September. Schoeck boasted to Corrodi afterward that they hadn't had a wink of sleep and never got around to eating anything until four in the afternoon. He could not praise Mary enough: she combined German aristocratic charm with the arts of love of the French, he said. He felt bad about being unfaithful to Elsbeth, but relieved all the same, as the events had now given him a sense of release, and expunged for good the notion that he might be better off marrying her.[1]

After arriving back in Zurich, Schoeck had to leave almost immediately for Leipzig to take part in a "Swiss music week" that lasted from 15 to 21 September 1918. Germany was on the verge of both economic collapse at home and defeat in the war. Just six weeks later, Leipzig too would be caught up in the wave of revolution that swept across the land. It seems in retrospect absurd that the city should now indulge in a musical celebration of Switzerland, but the authorities still somehow managed to maintain a semblance of normality for their festival. Schoeck conducted his Violin Concerto with Alphonse Brun as soloist (no relation to Fritz) and accompanied Durigo in a *Liederabend*. She had managed to organize Elsbeth's presence at the festival, though it is not clear if it was done with Schoeck's foreknowledge. Schoeck conducted miserably, Fritz Brun later told Walter Schädelin, "half an hour behind" the soloist. His *Liederabend* was also peppered with wrong notes, and he played "like a hysterical woman [Frauenzimmer]." Schoeck himself complained of being utterly exhausted—mentally, emotionally, and sexually. He said to Walter Schädelin, with reference to his exploits with first Mary, then Elsbeth: "the days in Lausanne, then in Leipzig—I'm a proper Popacatapetl, or is there one that's worse? Etna or another one?"[2]

Schoeck called in to see Martin and Jenny Kuntze-Fechner in Munich on his return from the festival, and he was back in Zurich before the end of the month. The flu epidemic was still raging, with all public gatherings cancelled in the city—including rehearsals and concerts. So Othmar left instead for the family nest in Brunnen. It was a wise step, for the political situation was becoming increasingly polarized. The Swiss Social Democrats felt sidelined, and together with other leftist groups they planned a general strike to commemorate the first anniversary of the Bolshevik Revolution in Russia. The strike took place on 11 November 1918 (also the day of the Armistice on the Western Front). But within three days it had crumbled, and its organizers recommended a return to work. The government had mobilized its troops in response to the strike threat, but the effect of this was merely to spread the influenza virus among the soldiers. Back in Brunnen Othmar would notice nothing of these events, however, except for the ringing of the bells to announce the beginning of the general strike. He had sprained his foot and so spent a good part of October confined to the Villa Eden. He finished the vocal score of *Don Ranudo,* which he then sent to Rüeger for him to make any necessary corrections to the text ("Much of it is not difficult to play and might give you pleasure," he wrote).[3] There had been interest from Vienna in the world premiere of their work, though since the Austro-Hungarian Empire was now disintegrating, it was clear even to a man as unpractical as Schoeck that there was little hope of its happening.

Schoeck interrupted his work on *Ranudo* at Brunnen from 4 to 9 October in order to write six new Eichendorff songs. He placed these together with the six he had written back in May 1917 to form a set of twelve. For the first time in any set of Schoeck's songs, these Eichendorff Songs Op. 30 convey a real sense of a quasi-dramatic trajectory, moving from the other-worldliness of the beginning to the strangely bittersweet jollity of the closing song (though ironically, Schoeck would still premiere them piecemeal). The six songs from October 1918 furthermore strike a more personal tone that is new to Schoeck's oeuvre.[4] In these and in the works that follow, it is particularly notable how the bass line plays an increasingly independent role in the musical argument. This is at once a result of Schoeck's growing interest in harmonic experimentation and also a prerequisite for it. It would be tempting to read some biographical import into this musical trait, given that Schoeck was in the process of setting himself free of his primary "emotional bass line" of the past four years—namely his relationship with Elsbeth. But it is probably too neat and tidy a notion for it to be wholly accurate.

The general tenor of the 1918 set is the transience of all things: "the tree stands deserted in the field, its leaves long scattered" ("Winternacht"); "we all must leave behind all we love" ("Ergebung"); "Ah, who knows how soon, how soon everything must fade" ("Nachklang"). Yet the mood is neither depressive nor sentimental, but rather one of gentle acceptance. One might want to read immediate relevance into a song such as "Sterbeglocken" ("Passing bells"), though it is probably no more a reference to the influenza epidemic than to those dying as cattle in the mud of Flanders. For Schoeck seems as much concerned with his own plight as he is with anyone else's. There again, artistic expression is often at its most potent when dealing with the all-too-human in the here-and-now, and at its weakest when shouting out to future generations the injustices of the world. Schoeck was depressed, exhausted, temporarily celibate, the world around him falling apart—except in the womb of Brunnen—and it seems he felt he had to choose between two women who represented on the one hand quotitudinal, domestic commitment (Elsbeth) and on the other, consequence-free, wild weekend sex (Mary). He would choose the latter, but for the moment he could not make up his mind and so decided to withdraw completely in order not to have to choose at all. Years later, after his death, Schoeck's widow discovered reams of letters that Elsbeth had sent him, begging him to write to her. But he did not. Toward the end of the year Mary wrote too, asking that a beautiful memory not be turned into an ugly one. He wanted to reply, but again he couldn't. And besides, he offered to Corrodi in paltry excuse, he was too busy with the orchestration of *Don Ranudo*. By the end of the year the flu epidemic had subsided, the ban on public meetings was lifted, and concert life was able to resume. Schoeck had his first St. Gallen concert of the season on 16 January 1919. In this same month he acquired yet another girlfriend, a pretty young painter from Winterthur by the name of Lise Stiefel, whose parents used to run the Gotthard Restaurant there, just opposite the train station. She was eight years younger than he was and had studied both in Florence and with Lovis Corinth in Berlin. Since Winterthur lay conveniently on the railway line between Schoeck's home in Zurich and his job in St. Gallen, Lise had the advantage of being closer than either Elsbeth or Mary. "Are you always this quick?" Schoeck claimed she had asked of his seduction routine. "Only recently," he had replied. But she disappeared from his life almost as swiftly as she had entered it.[5]

Schoeck was now juggling his concert commitments with frantic efforts to finish the orchestration of *Don Ranudo*, whose world premiere was planned for April at the Zurich City Theater. He did not complete the task until 30 March, just two weeks before the premiere, which was then moved from 10 April to the sixteenth. There were further problems. Max Hirzel, the tenor due to sing Don Gonzalo, became ill and withdrew, whereupon Rudolf Jung—originally a baritone—learnt the part in three days and sang it without a hitch (though he concealed his text in his hat, just in case). The part of Olympia, too, was reassigned at the dress rehearsal. According to Schädelin, a total of five roles had to be recast in the weeks before the premiere because of different singers being indisposed, and he was not a little astonished that, of everyone involved, Schoeck was the one who never abandoned his optimism. The conductor, as with *Erwin* over two years before, was Robert F. Denzler. The house was sold out (even Schädelin almost didn't get a seat), and everyone who was anyone on the Zurich artistic scene seems to have been there: the Hermanns: Haller, Hesse, and Hubacher, the Reinharts: Werner, Hans, and Georg, Gustav Gamper, Ermanno Wolf-Ferrari, and many others. Schädelin wrote in his diary how the audience warmed up from act to act, with stormy applause at the close. The press reaction was excellent, with Alois Jerger's portrayal of Ranudo receiving especial praise. There were comments about the lack of prominence of the love interest, as in the *Neue Zürcher Zeitung* of 19 April, but even this criticism was muted, and Schoeck had every reason to be happy.

Only Busoni was annoyed, for Schoeck had forgotten to provide him with a free ticket. His anger was not of the lasting kind, however, and he wrote to Andreae shortly afterward: "I'm so sorry about the little disgruntlement between Schoeck and me! I hope he still had a thoroughly unspoilt evening."[6] The day after the premiere he wrote to his wife: "Schoeck's Ranudo was very gratifying yesterday, in some moments very good, and the production was scenically and musically satisfactory."[7]

Schoeck's allowance from Werner Reinhart should now have come to an end: the three years promised had elapsed. But the money continued. There is no correspondence to explain why, though it is hardly a mystery: Reinhart, it seems, simply liked Schoeck's music. Since the beginning of the "scholarship," Schoeck had written numerous songs and a full-length opera and was making a name for himself abroad. Reinhart was a businessman, and it must have been obvious to him that his investment had produced considerable returns. The sums in question were negligible to him but had helped to transform Schoeck's working life. The money would continue to flow until Schoeck's dying day.

Chapter Twelve

Silent Bronze

"Oh, if only I had you here! I've already composed half the opera . . ."

To compose the final scene of an opera before a word of the libretto has been written—indeed, before there is even really a plot—is one of the oddest things a composer could do. But this is precisely what Schoeck did in May 1919. He had set off for the Ticino once more, this time with Rüeger and their mutual friend Paul Loewensberg, his intention being presumably to relax after the turmoil of the *Ranudo* premiere. But just as had been the case with *Erwin,* the experience of seeing a new opera take to the stage had fired Schoeck anew with enthusiasm for the theater.

According to a postcard home, Schoeck and his friends first spent a few days in Lugano with Hesse and Andreae before moving on to Brissago, where he felt so at ease that he did not even return for the next performances of *Ranudo* in Zurich.[1] He was not alone in his delight in the region. The nearby Monte Verità had in the previous twenty years become a place where vegetarians, socialists, Communists, anarchists, pacifists, theosophists, spiritualists, nudists, and adherents of the freest kinds of love could and did give equally free expression to their assorted inclinations. This was a world away from Zurich, and it was to find freedom from that city's everyday Germanic grind that Schoeck, too, had kept coming here. It had also been for him a place of sexual adventure, so in his current unattached state he might have hoped that his escapades of yore might now repeat themselves. It should therefore not surprise us that it provided the stimulus for an opera in which the hero throws off all shackles of conventional morality.

It was apparently Loewensberg who drew to Schoeck's attention the operatic possibilities of Mérimée's novella *La Vénus d'Ille.* Rüeger was immediately assigned the task of writing the text, but he had to return to job and family in early May (hence the lines quoted above, taken from Schoeck's letter to him of 12 May). But Schoeck was not to be deterred—when the muse arrived, her way could not be barred—and so he sat down at a piano in an old garage and composed the opera's final scene. Rüeger would just have to write the words for it later.

Mérimée's novella tells of a young bridegroom named Alphonse, who thoughtlessly places his wedding ring on the finger of a bronze statue of Venus, only to find that he can't prise it off again. That night, Venus comes to him and claims her "husband" by strangling him. As Elisabeth Schoeck-Grüebler has pointed out, the motive of the ring and the promise of marriage stretches back into the Middle Ages (it has recently resurfaced, in slightly altered form, in Tim Burton's movie *The Corpse Bride*). The idea of the female statue that comes to life is even older (Pygmalion is an obvious example). Nor was Mérimée's novella the only telling of this tale in the first half of the nineteenth century; it was but one strand in a whole nexus of sources. Joseph von Eichendorff's *Das Marmorbild* ("The Marble Statue") of 1819 is the best known of them, and it too figured as a source for Schoeck's opera, as the latter freely admitted. Here the statue is also of Venus, but it is marble, not bronze. She is discovered by Florio, a young aristocrat, and exerts a strange fascination upon him. Matters are complicated by a girl he meets at a masked ball, whose face seems to have the features of the statue. Venus then comes to life in order to lure Florio for ever into her castle. But in the nick of time he hears his friend Fortunato singing in the distance, comes to his senses, utters a prayer, and Venus and her castle disappear. It then turns out that the girl from the ball has nothing supernatural about her, and she and Florio end the tale in happy harmony. The novellas by Mérimée and Eichendorff are related not just through the matter of Venus and the ring; they are similar even in several small details—there is a tennis game in Mérimée, for example, and badminton in Eichendorff.

Heinrich Heine—who knew Eichendorff's *Marmorbild* and moved in the same Parisian circles as Mérimée—also offered a retelling in his "Florentinische Nächte" ("Florentine Nights"), published in 1837, the same year as Mérimée's novella (Heine's statue is marble, like Eichendorff's). In fact, both Mérimee and Heine were probably influenced more directly by the opera *Zampa, or the Betrothed of Marble,* composed by Ferdinand Hérold (1791–1833) to a libretto by Mélesville (aka Anne-Honoré-Joseph Duveyrier). It was first performed in Paris in 1831 and soon became a staple of even the smallest theaters across Germany and Switzerland. In Hérold, the evil pirate Zampa plans to marry Camille, the fiancée of his younger brother Alphonse (the same name as Mérimée's hero). But Zampa foolishly places his ring on the finger of a statue of Alice, a long-dead girl he had seduced years before. At the close of the opera (shades of Mozart's *Don Giovanni,* too), the statue comes to life and strangles him, and the two are then swallowed up by the molten lava of an ejaculatory Mount Etna. Hérold and Mérimée were also well known to each other—indeed, Hérold's next opera was based on one of the latter's stories.

In his reminiscences of the Brissago trip, Rüeger many years later wrote that the works of Mérimée "were well known to us," though given his wide literary tastes, he more likely meant "to me." Schoeck's knowledge of French was that of the average German Swiss of his day, able to grasp the gist of a newspaper and order a meal in a restaurant, but little more. The novella had been published in German translation a decade before, so it is not completely impossible that Schoeck had known of it. But what does seem clear is that none of the friends had a copy of it with them in Brissago. So we can safely assume that Schoeck was dependent upon his friends to describe the details of the story to him.

Schoeck's final plot, as developed over the ensuing months with Rüeger, runs as follows: On the morning before the marriage of Horace and Simone, the old Baron de Zarandelle gives them a wedding present of an old statue of Venus, recently unearthed on his estate. Horace is fascinated by the statue's beauty, but everyone else feels only unease. The act ends as the couple goes off to the wedding ceremony, accompanied by a jubilant crowd. The second act takes place at the post-nuptial masked ball that evening. Here Horace meets and falls madly in love with a beautiful woman whom he does not know, but who seems familiar. He places his wedding ring on her finger. To his horror, he now notices that the plinth outside, upon which the Venus had stood, is empty. The woman disappears, and Horace rushes out to find her. In the third act, Horace finds the statue back on its plinth once more; but she now wears his ring on her finger. He realizes the truth, but his only desire is still to give himself to her. He sinks at her feet; she embraces him; he dies. Simone rushes on, determined to give up her husband if that is what he wants, but finds only his corpse at the foot of the statue.

The fact that Schoeck took almost nothing from Mérimée except the ring and its placing on the finger of a statue would seem to reinforce our supposition that his knowledge of Mérimée's story was dependent upon the second-hand explanations of Rüeger and Loewensberg. There is undoubtedly a Busonian aspect to the story, at least in its earliest projected form, for it is in perfect accord with Busoni's exhortation, already mentioned above, to include "the supernatural and the unnatural . . . and dance and masks and grotesque charades."[2] But it has most in common with Eichendorff's *Das Marmorbild*. Schoeck knew his Eichendorff exceptionally well—here we have no need of supposition or second-guessing—and had even mentioned the story on a postcard to Hesse when he visited Lucca in 1914, signing himself "Florio Schoeck." It is clear that it was this story that provided the idea for the masked ball in the second act and the overall German-Romantic ambience of the opera.

Venus's castle in Eichendorff is "built almost like a heathen temple," but it is in fact a phantom, for on the spot there really stand only the ruins of an old temple to the goddess. And here we have an odd correlation to the area around Brissago where Schoeck's opera was conceived. For it was well known at the time that on one of the Brissago Islands, just a few hundred meters away from the town of Brissago itself, there stood the ruins of a Roman temple to Venus (the belief was in fact erroneous, but our hindsight is of no consequence here). It is quite plausible that the three friends, sitting in Brissago and looking out onto the islands, might have come to talk first about the local "Venus," and then, only by association, about Mérimée. Schoeck will have been reminded immediately of Eichendorff's story, and we can assume that the different sources were fused together in his mind from the very start. Schoeck admitted years later that he had wanted to write on the title page of his opera "after Mérimée and Eichendorff," but Rüeger had insisted on naming only the former.[3]

This maze of related sources is not complete, however, without considering the lady who actually lived on the Brissago Islands. Just a few months after Schoeck's stay, the area was visited by Rainer Maria Rilke, who on 22 October 1919 wrote: "The villa [on the island] is inhabited, and there are legends upon legends about the woman who owns it . . . at present, she is said to have a Japanese man staying, with whom she creates dolls."[4] A few days later he pondered the rumors that circulated about the "baroness" on the island, who was said "to be an evil, female Bluebeard and buries a new husband every three years, putting a laconic inscription on their graves."[5] Six months after Rilke, the German diplomat Harry Graf Kessler actually visited the islands and met the baroness, who, he said, was rumored to be a "Circe." She showed him her dolls:

> lifelike little girls and boys in fantastic costumes with bright, doll's eyes . . . she took each little being into her arms, introduced it, and had it move and bow to us; this seemed to be her world . . . that there had once been a temple of Venus here, then a monastery . . . she confirmed to us, and showed us reproductions of inscriptions.[6]

This "Baroness of Saint-Léger" had been born as Antonietta Beyer in St. Petersburg in 1856, and it was rumored that she was an illegitimate daughter of Tsar Alexander II (which by all accounts might just be true). She studied at the "Smolny Institute for Noble Maidens," the prestigious girls' school in St. Petersburg, but for reasons unknown had to flee Russia after having been given only forty-eight hours to do so.[7] She married at least four times, her third husband being the rich Irishman Richard Flemyng de St. Leger. It was with him that she bought the Brissago Islands and there built a villa and a park. She had supposedly studied with Liszt in Rome in her youth; she certainly cultivated friendly relations with artists of different kinds thereafter. The composer Ruggiero Leoncavallo and the artists Giovanni Segantini and Daniele Ranzoni were on occasion her guests on the island, and in later years she apparently corresponded with James Joyce. Her interests were wider still, however: in 1913 she published an article about her park in the *Journal of the Royal Horticultural Society* (in English),[8] and she was busy learning her fourteenth language when she died in Intragna several years later, bankrupt.

Given the notoriety of the baroness, it is hardly likely that Schoeck and his friends will have spent their holiday a few hundred meters away from her villa without her ever being mentioned in their conversation. The Brissago Islands thus offered all the ingredients for Schoeck's new opera: Venus herself (or, rather, a supposed temple to her honor), a beautiful park, a "Circe" who supposedly murders her husbands, and even "lifelike" representations of the female form, albeit in the shape of dolls instead of a statue. And, like the Venus in Schoeck's opera, the baroness was "silent" in that she lived a hermit-like existence. We can even postulate that Schoeck's friends first spoke of the baroness

Figure 12.1. Schoeck's entry in the guestbook of the Fluh. Courtesy of Winterthur Libraries (Switzerland), Special Collections.

and then thought of the Mérimée story by a banal matter of word association. For the step from "The Venus of the [Brissago] Islands"—*La Vénus des Îles*—to "La Vénus d'Ille" is but a small one.

After a brief appearance at that year's Swiss *Tonkünstlerfest* in Burgdorf at the end of May, accompanying the contralto Hanna Brenner in five of his songs, Schoeck left for another holiday, this time for a week as Werner Reinhart's guest at the "Fluh." It was his first visit since the renewal of his "scholarship," and when he left, he drew a caricature of himself in the house's guestbook with a broad smile extending over almost half his head. He is staring through a telescope and has his right hand raised, as if in greeting to a now secure golden future (see fig. 12.1).

In June, too, Elsbeth made contact once more, offering by telegram to help organize a production of *Don Ranudo* in Hamburg. But Schoeck again took the path of least resistance and left her without an answer. Ironically, it might well have been Elsbeth's move that prompted him to make some kind of decision in his love life. He now, somehow, summoned up the energy to contact Mary in Geneva. She answered immediately by telegram that she had found him a room and that he could come and visit. He had been thinking of spending the summer in the Ticino again—he had received fifteen hundred francs in royalties for the *Ranudo* production in Zurich and so could easily afford another holiday—but instead he now rang Mary to confirm that he would be coming to Geneva. He arrived there on 3 July 1919, taking with him all he needed to spend the summer working on his new opera.

Chapter Thirteen

Sucking Sweet Folly

Geneva, 14 August 1919

Dear Mama,

... just think! Von Senger's Mama *insists* that I eat at her home for the whole duration of my stay in Geneva.... It was she, too, who found me my room, with the help of her daughter.

Liar, liar—and through his teeth, no less. Ever deceitful toward his parents in matters of love, he outdoes himself this time. "Von Senger" refers implicitly to Alexander, the only member of that family known to the rest of the Schoecks. Mama von Senger "insisted" on feeding Schoeck because the room "she" had found him was in fact in her own house, and it would have been impolite to have denied food to the man who for two months was happily rogering her daughter on the other side of a thin wall. Although sixty years later her nephew remembered her as being very religious, Mama von Senger—Mrs von Senger no. 3, *née* Trampedach, and the could-have-been Mrs Nietzsche—had lived her life in artistic and intellectual circles and so can hardly have been that much of a prude. Anyway, given that Schoeck was devoid of all inhibitions in bed (according to a deathbed confession from a later lover);[1] given that (by his own account) Mary was highly inventive between the sheets; and given that the house was tiny—so tiny that the meals Schoeck mentions had to be eaten in the cellar—then the nights will have been noisy enough for Mama von Senger not to have been able to live in denial about her daughter's nice new friend.

Nocturnal distractions aside, Schoeck now made good progress with his *Venus,* for which Rüeger had somehow managed to deliver a large chunk of text by early July. Since the opera begins in a park, Schoeck had at first thought of incorporating a song he had begun in 1915, namely Eichendorff's "Berg und Täler fingen ringsumher zu blühen an" ("Mountain and valleys began to blossom around [us]")—another sign that Eichendorff exerted an early influence on the opera—but then decided that it was too melancholy for that context[2] (its music seems nevertheless to have left its traces on the opera's opening bars). Schoeck seems to have more or less completed the sketch of the first act during the summer, with the exception of the closing bridal chorus, which he put to one side until he was in the right mood for it.

It was now that Schoeck did something that for him was completely normal, yet whose repercussions would in large part determine the next four years of his life and haunt him for many years thereafter. He interrupted his stay in Geneva to go on a walking holiday in Canton Valais with his brother Ralph and cousin Léon. He had always liked holidaying with his brothers and close male friends, and in the past he had never bothered to ask his girlfriends how they felt about being left alone when it suited him. Elsbeth had merely been the latest in a series of women from whom puppy-dog devotion had been unquestioningly expected. So when Schoeck returned to Geneva from the Valais, he was shellshocked to find that Mary had in turn decided to go off on her own. If he could, then so could she. He now acted on impulse in a manner that might be considered as part of the everyday give-and-take in any average relationship but was for Schoeck such an unheard-of step that it seems to have altered for good the balance of power between him and Mary. He found out where she was, went to the station, and took the train to go and beg her back. It is ironic that the opera on which Schoeck was working was a fantasy of complete (male) sexual freedom, for as it progressed it would become more and more divergent from his own experience (and would profit greatly in emotional impact as a result).

After having made up, Schoeck and Mary spent another week together before his autumn commitments made his return home to Zurich a necessity. He stopped off on the way to visit Alexander von Senger in Zurzach. After he arrived home, Schoeck tried phoning Mary. Eight times; no answer. No letter, no telegram, nothing from Geneva. Doubt and jealousy consumed him. "Now I've found my master" ("Meisterin"), he said to Corrodi. "Now I have to do penance for my sins . . . this woman is stronger than I, highly intelligent, a marvellous artist, with an incomparable temperament and an exceptional will—a fantastic woman."[3] Two weeks later he called Corrodi to him, asking him to bring a bottle of wine. He had caught a cold and could not go out, he said. When Corrodi arrived, Schoeck poured out his heart. He wasn't himself any more, he couldn't work on his new opera, he couldn't do anything except think of Mary. He rummaged around in his bric-a-brac until he found a photograph of himself that he deemed handsome enough to send to her. All he had managed to compose was a little piano piece entitled "Consolation" based on a theme from the final scene of *Venus* (see ex. 13.1)—the same scene that he had sketched out in Brissago six months before (see ex. 13.2). This theme circles obsessively around a fixed central point, reaching out to ever greater intervals on either side; the opening bass line of the piano piece offers, with one or two interruptions, a descending scale over two octaves before it returns in the eleventh measure to its point of origin. The effect can be either mesmerizing or claustrophobic, depending upon one's mood, but hardly "consolatory." If Schoeck had meant this little piece to depict his own passion, then it seems to be a passion obsessed with itself rather than with anything or anyone "other" or "outside." This opening theme of "Consolation" now came to be associated in Schoeck's mind directly with Mary, and its

Example 13.1. Opening of the piano piece "Consolation," Op. 29, no. 1. Copyright Breitkopf & Härtel. Reprinted by permission.

Example 13.2. Horace's final monologue from the last act of *Venus*, Op. 32. Copyright Breitkopf & Härtel. Reprinted by permission. Schoeck conceived the music in Brissago in 1919, before he had any text. The theme that he extracted for "Consolation" is marked by a bracket.

contours would repeatedly insinuate themselves into the fabric of his music over the next two decades.

Schoeck's opinion of women had undergone a sea change. He had once delighted in proclaiming that woman is the blank page upon which man has to write. Now what was most important to him, he claimed, was that a woman should be intelligent. He had decided that he had to marry Mary and had written to tell her so. She sent a telegram back that she would think about it. In any case, her divorce proceedings were not over and were still as acrimonious as they can come. But Schoeck was serious enough about it to tell his parents. While his mother had her doubts, the other members of the family took the news in their stride.

Don Ranudo was given its German premiere under Fritz Busch in Stuttgart on 26 November 1919, though Schoeck did not attend. Not only was he hesitant to cross the border when Germany was still beset by food shortages, but he had near-concurrent performances of Mozart's *Figaro* in St. Gallen (on 24 and 25 November). Schoeck's brother Walter went instead, and he was joined for the journey by Corrodi, who had to write a review for the *Neue Zürcher Zeitung*. They both judged the musical aspect of the production excellent (one would expect nothing else from Busch), but as Walter wrote home on 28 November,

> The success was not as great as one expected . . . the text received no praise. The director [Ludwig Hörth] said it was stupid, but I in turn think that he's an idiot. . . . No one could understand why the composer wasn't there. Even Dr Hase, Othmar's publisher [from Breitkopf & Härtel] was there.[4]

Ranudo's lack of luck in Stuttgart was compounded when the tenor became ill and the rest of the performances were cancelled. Schoeck was depressed about the news when Corrodi reported back to him, but a letter from Mary one day later served to dispel all thoughts of anything but her.

Schoeck's composing was already profiting from his experience with the St. Gallen Symphony Orchestra, for the years after his appointment coincide with a clearly audible increase in the felicity of his orchestration. His *Figaro* in St. Gallen was his first-ever experience of conducting from the pit. He would never take on any permanent post in the theater and would only conduct some two dozen performances in the St. Gallen City Theater over the next five years. Nevertheless, the experience will have taught him much: not just in how to balance one's scoring for voices and orchestra, but also in matters of basic stagecraft. Only when one has worked on a stage production throughout the rehearsal process can one appreciate even simple issues such as how much time one must calculate for a scene change, how long it takes for a character to walk on, across, or off the stage, or—as John Barbirolli once put it, the musical consequences when "a character has to rush in and sing something and the door sticks."[5]

Schoeck spent Christmas at the family home in Brunnen, and while there he composed another piano piece for Mary: a toccata possessed of intricate cross-rhythms and far from easy to play, but which really ought to be in the standard repertoire (its admirers later included Georg Solti in the days before he abandoned his pianism for the podium).[6] Schoeck began sketching another piece for her, a rondo, though it remained unfinished and was later incorporated into the masked ball in the second act of *Venus*. In late December 1919 Schoeck traveled to Bern to discuss a planned production of *Ranudo* at the City Theater, though his real reason was to enjoy a few days there with Mary. They spent three evenings in the company of Schädelin, who wrote in his diary: "I received a significant impression of this rare woman, who is a striking, harmonious mixture of unusual qualities of intellect and spirit. And possessed of a culture and grace that are captivating."[7]

Schoeck's newfound love of French Switzerland was further confirmed when Ernest Ansermet invited him to conduct four concerts with the Orchestre de la Suisse Romande while he was away conducting the Ballets Russes in Paris. The first three took place on 7, 8, and 9 February 1920, while the fourth and final concert in early March featured Durigo as the soloist in several of Schoeck's songs as orchestrated by Fritz Brun. It was apparently in late March that Schoeck completed his next song set, begun in late 1919, namely the *Twelve Hafez Songs* Op. 33 (whose texts are in fact not by Hafez but are free reworkings of his poetry by Georg Friedrich Daumer). Although Schoeck gave the manuscript of only one of them to Mary (no. 8), they are obviously written with her in mind and might even have been meant as a birthday present—for what would be more appropriate for her thirty-third birthday on 12 May 1920 than to give her his own Opus 33? They are all in praise of wine, the night, music, and love, with metaphors of taste and scent that are at times overtly sexual, even without allowing for the interchangibility of bodily orifices that is common in erotic lyrics. "My love said: Come and gently suck sweet folly, sin, and youth from my rosy mouth" (no. 6); "I smelt the heavenly aroma of love, and in its breeze I would like to dissolve and die gently in soul, mind, and body" (no. 7; see ex. 13.3). The song that Schoeck gave to Mary is no less explicit: "I abjured salvation, and in so doing was born into it . . . I only found myself when I lost myself wholly in you." But aside from any private messages, desires, or instructions that Schoeck might have wished to convey to his lover in his music, what is of prime consideration for us is that the irrationality of passion and the lack of inhibition that characterized Schoeck's relationship with Mary here seem reflected in the very fabric of his music. In the context of Schoeck's oeuvre to date, these songs are at times surprisingly experimental. Never before had he written such consistently advanced harmony, nor passages of such complex rhythmic content. Something fundamental seems to have changed in him since he had finished the first act of *Venus* a few months earlier. The "heavenly aroma" song even casts itself adrift from any notion of barlines or firm tonality, its only point of reference being an obsessive F$\sharp$ that lasts throughout the piece.

Example 13.3. "Ich roch der Liebe," no. 7 of the *Hafez Songs,* Op. 33. Copyright Breitkopf & Härtel. Reprinted by permission. "I smelt the heavenly aroma of love, and in its wafting [scent] I would like to [. . . disappear and die]."

Schoeck also experiments freely with the rhythms of the text. Sometimes the voice expands certain syllables unexpectedly, while at other times it comes in "too soon" (which might itself have unfortunate connotations in the context of erotic song). The piano accompaniments explore the full range of the keyboard and employ all manner of ostinati (such as the eighteen-note passacaglia that opens no. 9). The final song quotes the opening melody of Brahms's love song "Wie Melodien zieht es" ("Like melodies it wanders through my senses," Op. 105, no. 1), though what it might have signified for either Schoeck or Mary remains unknown to us.

Don Ranudo enjoyed a repeat run in Zurich in spring 1920, with its final performance timed to feature on the program of the Swiss *Tonkünstlerfest,* which took place there that year. Mary came too, having joined the association the previous October. That year's festival boasted an impressive list of performers, including Joseph Szigeti and Stefi Geyer, while the composers represented included Philip Jarnach, Paul Müller-Zürich (fresh from studies in Paris), Emil Frey (formerly of the Moscow Conservatory), Walter Schulthess, and Bruckner's sometime pupil Friedrich Klose. Schoeck's *Trommelschläge* was on the program of the final concert. At the dress rehearsal the leading lights of the Musicians' Association—Hermann Suter, Fritz Brun, and Gustave Doret—had seated themselves in the front row, joined by Busoni. But when the work's twelve military drummers struck up, they all fled to the back of the hall. Schoeck claimed—with a dash of hyperbole, perhaps—that Busoni was afterward to be found in the artists' dressing room, lying on a sofa, quite exhausted. *Trommelschläge* certainly made an impression, inspiring the enmity of one of French Switzerland's otherwise most perceptive music critics, Aloys Mooser. Unable to perceive the irony of the text in its musical setting, he found instead that it reeked of Teutonic glory in slaughter and declared that it would have been more appropriate on the "Siegesallee" in imperial Berlin.[8] Schoeck never quite forgave him for that.

On 2 June 1920 Schoeck left to spend the summer in Geneva. He sent Werner Reinhart the manuscript score of *Don Ranudo* as a gift on 4 June, and his accompanying letter suggests that he had again moved in with Mary and her family. Five days later, however, he wrote to his mother: "I couldn't move into the room I'd planned to take. Now I'm right outside Geneva, in a wonderful area with the best air. Address O.S. chez Madame Freyre, chemin de bel-air, Villa Marcel Chène Bourg près Genève." We do not know the reasons. The most plausible would be that Mary's mother did not want him there any more, but since we know from other sources that Schoeck and Mary met at her home throughout the summer, it would not seem that there had been any irreparable breakdown of relationships. Schoeck and Mary spent a few nights in Bern in mid-June, their purpose being an audition for Mary that Schoeck had arranged with Brun, presumably for a potential solo engagement. Walter Schädelin was also there, and he noted in his diary that Brun was "not particularly gallant" toward her. Schädelin also left us a description of the couple's morning routine.

> Today I picked up Schoeck at the Bernerhof, for lunch together with Daettwyler. That is: I wanted to pick him up. At 12.15 he was still in his crumpled nightshirt. We had arranged lunch for 1 o' clock. . . . Schoeck's room, no. 132, was in a gypsylike order: The breakfast tray, half a cup of coffee, here an egg, there half a roll, meat spread in greaseproof paper, cigarette butts, ash everywhere, Schoeck in his shirt with a cigarette, washing himself and shaving with his Gillette, bit by bit getting into the swing of things so that he is close to being ready by 1 o'clock, while Mary still needs time.[9]

After they had left for Geneva the next day, 15 June, Schädelin noted: "I can't believe that a marriage between the two of them would have the right foundation. She is too clever for it, and he is too much of an artist and a Bohemian, unfit for marriage."[10]

Chapter Fourteen

Self Portrait, with Sandwich

"Damned Rüeger has left me in the lurch!" Schoeck wrote to his mother on 12 August 1920. Rüeger had delivered the second act of *Venus* before Schoeck's departure for Geneva in June, but within only six weeks Schoeck was bombarding him with requests for the third. He managed to oblige, but in a letter of 19 August, Schoeck insisted on various changes and cuts. His description of what he needs—a duel between the hero Horace and his brother-in law Raimond, plus the latter's curse on Horace—makes one wish that Rüeger had not given in so easily, for every production of the opera at this point exudes a whiff of melodrama.

It seems that Rüeger's original idea of *Venus* had been of something slightly ironic, even comical, not too far removed in spirit from their *Don Ranudo* (and thus much closer to both Mérimée and a Busonian "Young Classicality"). His conception seems to have been shared by Schoeck, for the first act bristles with stock operatic characters and situations: the absurd old Baron Zarandelle, the moralizing mother-in-law, the wedding chorus at the close, and so on. There are some lovely passages, such as Simone's opening aria to spring, but the overall idiom is closest to the more conservative of the Eichendorff songs Op. 30, and there is little to suggest that either composer or librettist was really inspired by the topic. Rüeger later recounted that Schoeck had even considered dropping the opera after completing the first act, in order to take on another topic altogether. But then *Venus* tightened her grip, as it were, and when the two men discussed the opera on a post-concert nocturnal march from St. Gallen to Rüeger's home in Bischofszell, Rüeger realized how the story had in the meantime seized hold of Schoeck with "hundredfold intensity."[1] The ironic tone disappears altogether in the second and third acts, as the focus moves ever more onto Horace alone. Given this trajectory, it seems perfectly logical that the drama should climax in a long monologue for the hero (the one for which Rüeger still had to write the text). The music shifts gear immediately at the beginning of the second act, which with its brilliant cross-rhythms is far more arresting than anything to be found in the first.

This change from Rüeger's original interpretation into an exploration of an all-consuming passion is also essentially a shift away from Mérimée and toward Eichendorff—or, rather, to the latently Wagnerian resonances that abound in Eichendorff's story. While it might seem chronologically suspect to postulate such "resonances" in a novella written when Wagner was himself a toddler, it would be impossible for a composer of Schoeck's generation to read a story about the goddess "Venus" without it being colored, retrospectively, by a knowledge of *Tannhäuser*. There are also specific correlations between *Tannhäuser* and *Das Marmorbild,* for in each a young knight is torn between the opposing forces of spiritual and erotic love, the virginal and the demonic. Furthermore, as Dieter Borchmeyer has observed, the beautiful women that in Eichendorff rise up from out of the fields of flowers in Venus's castle inevitably bring to mind the Flower Maidens in Wagner's *Parsifal,* just as her castle is more reminiscent of Klingsor's magic garden than of the Venusberg.[2]

Schoeck's treatment of the topic differs in one crucial aspect from Wagner's *Tannhäuser,* however. For, unlike Venus in the latter, Schoeck's goddess represents a spiritualized, aesthetized attraction, a paragon of perfection with whom physical congress is by implication an impossibility. For Schoeck, it is Simone, the bride, who embodies fleshly physicality. There is no "redemption" for Schoeck's hero, no flowering of papal staffs, but submission to an ideal of perfection and its only possible consummation, in death. One cannot blame Rüeger if he suddenly felt out of his depth. His easy-flowing verse had worked well in *Ranudo,* which was a straightforward tale to tell. But to write an essentially tragic opera in which the "heroine" is silent throughout, one that diverges more and more from the source material, leaving the poet with no crutch except his own imagination: that is a different task altogether. And he will have guessed that Schoeck would again bombard him with demands for text at the most awkward of times, that he would again capitulate, and that criticism of the "poetizing apothecary" would again circulate. On the other hand, Schoeck remained confident of Rüeger's abilities and on some level really needed his collaboration. And as Rüeger will have noticed—for his ears were not untrained—Schoeck's music was growing rapidly in maturity. Who could resist when a fine composer insists on a libretto? The only surprising fact is that Schoeck seems never to have contemplated writing an opera together with his brother Paul, who was becoming an experienced dramatist and was at this time preparing for the world premiere of his *Täll,* a drama based on the William Tell legend. Othmar returned to Zurich for the opening night at the *Schauspielhaus* on 6 September 1920. Walter Schoeck, too, was master enough of the written word to have been capable of providing Othmar with a decent libretto. The brothers were also all very close; but perhaps that was reason enough for Othmar not to work with them on any creative project.

Schoeck returned to Geneva after *Täll,* but he had to visit Bern again on account of the preparations for its production of *Ranudo.* Basel also staged *Ranudo* at the beginning of this season, with one "G. R." remarking upon its "extraordinary success" in the *Neue Zürcher Zeitung* of 4 October. The first concert of the St. Gallen concert season was on 7 October, and just a week later (on 13 and 15 October), Schoeck conducted two performances of *Fidelio* as the St. Gallen Theater's contribution to the festivities surrounding Beethoven's 150th birthday. He had a world-class cast, including Alfred Jerger (now based in Munich) and Karl Erb—all thanks to the Swiss franc's being the only hard currency left in Central Europe amid the economic chaos of the postwar years. These performances are also noteworthy because they occasioned a flurry of critical activity in the local press. "F. K." (Fritz Kreis) of the *St. Galler Tagblatt* criticized putting together a production with soloists "shipped in from afar, in two to three rehearsals," and found the chorus to have been particularly awful.[3] This prompted an adverse reaction from Schoeck's St. Gallen fans, which in turn led Kreis to defend himself against those "in whom every criticism of O. Schoeck seems to bring about a nervous shock."[4] The chairman of the board of the St. Gallen Symphony Orchestra, Hans Bärlocher, wrote a stern letter to Kreis, admonishing him that "public discussions are unfruitful and damage the matter itself,"[5] and then even the theater committee jumped into the fray with a long, harshly worded letter to the press that lambasted Kreis as a "Beckmesser." In his response, Kreis—who obviously had his own reliable sources of information—stated that the committee had published their letter "at the express request of Mr Othmar Schoeck."[6] Just three years into his career in St. Gallen, Schoeck had already built up a coterie of admirers for whom he was virtually untouchable, and he was apparently willing to use them to defend himself. Their tactic worked, for it would be over two decades before a local critic would dare to utter any such complaint again.

Despite his hectic concert and opera schedule, Schoeck still commuted to visit Mary as often as possible. In a letter to Hermann Hesse of 16 December 1920, he quipped that he was now on first-name terms with all the ticket collectors on the Swiss railways. As a footnote to Schoeck's Genevan experiences in the latter half of 1920, we should note that he recalled over thirty years later that he had met Rilke there, for the first and last time, and had spent a whole afternoon in his company. Rilke was a finely organized man, he remembered; perhaps "too finely organized." But Schoeck took no liking to his poetry, openly admitting that he found it difficult to understand.[7] Rilke's poetry, he said, was an artistic achievement without being great art.[8]

Schoeck had now completed the second and third acts of his new opera. The cross-fertilization between *Venus* and his "Consolation" had also taken a new turn, for while the latter begins with a quotation from the final scene of the opera, Schoeck in his second act quoted the same melody in the form found in "Consolation." It sets the hero's words: "Now Cupid should be gracious to me, the ungrateful one—he disappears and leaves me to the pain of love that your beauty here inflamed" (see ex. 14.1). To a later passage taken from the piano piece, Horace sings: "How shall I hold you eternally in my heart? I wish to surrender myself to you!" It seems that Schoeck was already beginning to see in Horace's all-consuming obsession a mirror image of his love for Mary. There is no denying the passion embodied in the love music of the second act, which verges at times on a Korngoldian lusciousness, though since the "heroine" is silent, the passion in question is solely that of Horace. It is thus wholly male in origin and expression and cannot be contradicted by its object.

Scene 9

Example 14.1. Horace's aria in the second act of *Venus,* Op. 32. Copyright Breitkopf & Härtel. Reprinted by permission. The theme from "Consolation" is marked with a bracket. "Now Cupid should be gracious to me . . ."

"If only the monster were already orchestrated!" Schoeck had written to Rüeger on 30 August, just as he was about to begin work on the full score. Over the ensuing weeks he seems to have made concerted efforts to improve his knowledge of scoring for the stage. He went to hear his own *Ranudo* in Bern—Mary joined him for the first performance on 7 November—and returned to the pit of the St. Gallen Theater later that month for productions of Mozart's *Figaro* and *Die Entführung aus dem Serail.* "My opera activities in St. Gall will be useful to me," he had remarked to Rüeger in that letter of late August. Schoeck did not, however, travel to Halle in Germany for the world premiere of his *Das Wandbild* at the City Theater on 2 January 1921, conducted by Oskar Braun. Nor did Busoni, who was in Berlin preparing to conduct two concerts of his own works on 7 and 13 January in the Philharmonie. The *Neue Zürcher Zeitung* featured a measured review of *Das Wandbild* on 21 January by one "M. U.," who praised Schoeck's "exotic touch" but remarked oddly that, when one actually heard the music, it "wasn't half as bad" as could be expected from merely studying the vocal score.

Later that month, Schoeck went to Bern to conduct the first performance of the "storm" interlude that leads from the second to the third acts of *Venus.* He made no mention to anyone of his reasons for finishing this piece ahead of the rest of the opera. But it was his first-ever piece of orchestral tone painting, so perhaps the opportunity to try it out in concert was a means of allaying his fears about his scoring (it is in fact very fine and makes one wish that Schoeck had not been so averse to writing for orchestra alone). Schoeck was back in the opera pit in St. Gallen in February, March, and April, conducting Rossini's *Barber of Seville* and then sharing a double bill of his own *Erwin* and Ermanno Wolf-Ferrari's *Susanna's Secret,* in which the composers themselves conducted their respective works (Wolf-Ferrari had praised *Don Ranudo* after its world premiere in Zurich, so perhaps Schoeck wanted to repay the favor).

By May 1921 Schoeck had orchestrated a large chunk of the first act of *Venus,* and now also at long last completed his setting of Eichendorff's "Angedenken," which he had begun in 1915 and briefly considered for the opening of his opera. This same month affords us Hans Corrodi's first description of Mary—for only now, over two years into her relationship with Schoeck, were they introduced. Corrodi wrote as follows in his diary for 19 May 1921:

> She had bright, clear, pretty, intelligent brown eyes, but her cheeks [were] rather thin and sunken, though rouged in compensation for it. Her teeth were heavily filled with gold and were long and somewhat irregular; she tried to hide them as best she could with her lips, not showing them when she laughed, and this made her whole mouth seem somewhat stiff. What bound Schoeck so passionately to her was incomprehensible to me. I couldn't find her beautiful—it seemed as though she had been rather consumed by life.[9]

We cannot comment on his description, for the only known photos of Mary show her at an advanced age and are also of miserable quality (see fig. 14.1).

A few days later Schoeck left for Weimar, where his *Erwin* was being performed at a Goethe festival. He also took the opportunity of visiting his publisher Breitkopf & Härtel in Leipzig, where he was allowed to see their music manuscripts, with Beethoven's Fifth Symphony making the biggest impression. Schoeck moved south to Heilbronn to visit Mathilde Suter (she had married and left the Hotel Eden several years earlier), and then went on a walking tour to Cleversulzbach, making sure to visit the local graveyard where the mothers of both Mörike and Schiller were buried.[10] Stuttgart was next. Fritz Busch had a guilty conscience about the truncated first run of *Ranudo* in 1919 and was planning more performances (though none came about). Schoeck was not his only visitor: the young Paul Hindemith was there, too, for Busch was about to conduct the world premiere of his one-acters *Das Nusch-Nuschi* and *Mörder, Hoffnung der Frauen* on 14 June 1921. Busch played through one of these works at the piano (presumably *Mörder,* since the piano score of the other is on four staves and difficult to realize as a solo). Schoeck was horrified by Oskar Kokoschka's expressionist libretto and whispered to Busch: "But—this text!," which Hindemith overheard and with the confidence of youth took for a compliment, replying "Yes, isn't it marvellous!"[11]

Schoeck had intended to spend the summer of 1921, or at least part of it, with Mary at the Wörthersee in Carinthia. But they disagreed about something—we know not what—so she left to visit relatives at the Chiemsee instead, while Schoeck went home to Brunnen. We do know that tension had arisen when Mary had cancelled plans for performing a concerto with the St. Gallen Symphony Orchestra in the previous concert season. We also know that Mary's

Figure 14.1. Mary de Senger with dog, date unknown.

mother was becoming increasingly antagonistic toward her daughter's lover, finding him far too Bohemian. Perhaps she feared that Mary, fresh from an acrimonious divorce, would be badly hurt all over again. Whatever her reasons, Schoeck was soon claiming that his prospective mother-in-law was intriguing against him, sending meddling letters to his parents and even to Léon Oswald. According to Mary's nephew Franz Ludwig von Senger, who lodged with them in Geneva in the early 1920s, the whole family was devoted to his grandmother, with none of them willing to offend or contradict her. Her wishes were at least realized for the summer of 1921. After a few weeks in Brunnen, Schoeck moved to Engelberg to stay in the Terrasse Hotel, which was owned by relatives. On 9 August, he wrote to Rüeger:

> I'm sitting here in Engelberg, alone with my Venus (if only the other one were here too!) and working like a clock on my score. It's good that I have the work, otherwise I'd feel pretty lonely. Wherever I look, everyone has a partner, but I have to *mourn* this summer away. I have more and more the feeling that I am working on a self-portrait.

Schoeck was adamant that he wanted to marry Mary, and he insisted that it was impossible only because he did not earn enough to support them both (the same excuse he had given two years earlier for not marrying Elsbeth). Yet he did: he received five thousand francs a year from St. Gallen, about another four thousand from his other concerts, and three thousand from Werner Reinhart, which together put him squarely in Switzerland's upper-middle income bracket and was sufficient for a married man to live comfortably.[12] He nevertheless considered applying for a better-paid kapellmeister job at the Zurich Theater that had just become free. But his bad-temperedness in rehearsal with his Zurich choirs had not been forgotten, and when Hans Corrodi quietly used his contacts to sound out Schoeck's chances at the theater, he was told that they were nil. Schoeck then decided not to try at all.

Mary's mother knew of Schoeck's supposed lack of money, though it must have been obvious to her, as to everyone else, that if a musician as active as Schoeck had little of it, then he must be spending it unwisely. She had already observed with disdain his delight in spending what she regarded as large sums on alcohol. Nor was she far from the truth. Schoeck had never grown accustomed to budgeting for anything and usually spent his money as soon as it came in. When it ran out, he depended on his natural charm to help him borrow money from friends and colleagues, and in many cases never paid it back. And he drank a lot. Never beer; it was always wine, preferably an expensive one. Yet despite the many reports of Schoeck's heavy drinking, it does not seem that he ever became dependent on alcohol. There are no witnesses to his ever having been drunk, which would suggest that his intake was regularly high. But when asked specifically about Schoeck's drinking, a former concertmaster of the St.

Gallen Orchestra stated that he had never smelled alcohol on Schoeck's breath during rehearsals or concerts.[13] There are no reports of his keeping a bottle by his bed or in his briefcase for private antemeridian imbibing or for the breaks between rehearsals. His drinking seems to have remained for him a purely social activity, if a regular one.

In early September 1921 Mary returned from the Chiemsee, stopping off in Zurich on the way. Schoeck had planned to travel on to Geneva with her but he said something to offend her, so she decided to leave immediately on her own. He accompanied her to the station, they exchanged a few bitter words, and she got on the train to leave. But then she changed her mind, got off, and told Schoeck that they could not end it all that way. So they returned to Schoeck's apartment for several days. Things seem to have improved rapidly thereafter, for by mid-September Schoeck was in a good enough mood to compose the wedding chorus for the end of the first act of *Venus*—a task he had been postponing for two years.

On 7 October, Schoeck and Durigo gave the world premiere in Zurich of his latest work, a setting for voice and piano of Goethe's ballad *Der Gott und die Bajadere,* composed that summer. It was only one item in a program of world premieres, including the String Quartet in E Flat, Op. 44, by Karl Heinrich David and a Serenade for Flute, Viola, and Harp by Hermann von Glenck.[14] Goethe's *Bajadere* is a poem that today seems almost unbearably sexist. It is set in India. A god descends to traverse the earth in the guise of a man and comes upon a "Bajadere," a dancing-girl-cum-prostitute, who invites him into her hut for sex. He accepts, but first makes her serve him in all kinds of ways (verging on physical abuse, it is implied), and in so doing somehow breaks through her outer, "professional," shell to reveal a loving girl beneath. Then they have sex and fall asleep. But in the morning she wakes to find him dead at her side. The priests come to take him to the funeral pyre, at which she begs to be allowed to join him in an act of "sati." The priests refuse, for she was not his wife. In defiance of them, she throws herself on the pyre to be with the man she loved—and at this the god ascends from the fire, taking her with him into heaven (see ex. 14.2).

It is convenient to interpret this as Schoeck's fantasy of womanly self-abasement and uncomplaining acquiescence to the whims of man, a kind of corrective to the dominance of woman enshrined in *Venus*. But convenience does not preclude truth. There might well be a further underlying biographical significance, however, for while Schoeck always had high praise for Mary's bedroom technique, many years later he confessed to Corrodi his fears that "French women" (meaning in this case Mary) always remained "alien" to one ("fremd"), even in the "most intimate" of moments.[15] It is precisely this alienation that the god strips away in the song. The music to this ballad is some of the most compelling that Schoeck ever wrote, consolidating the advances in rhythm and harmony made in the *Hafez Songs,* but within a large-scale narrative structure

Example 14.2. The climax of the ballad *Der Gott und die Bajadere*, Op. 34, for voice and piano. Copyright Breitkopf & Härtel. Reprinted by permission. ". . . [fiery] death. But the godly youth rises [up . . .]."

(the song lasts for over a quarter of an hour). In its use of canon it also displays a tendency to constructivism that will intensify in Schoeck's music over the next decade.

Work on *Venus* was now nearing completion, and Schoeck was keen to have the work performed the following year. In late October 1921 the director of the Zurich City Theater, Paul Trede, came to Schoeck's apartment to hear him play through the opera. Also present were Robert Denzler, still the main conductor at the theater, and the baritone Karl Schmid-Bloss. Schoeck told Corrodi afterward that they had listened in silence, except for Trede's occasional complaints about how difficult the main tenor role was. Schoeck finally got up, enraged, left the room, slammed the door behind him, and lit a cigarette. After he had pulled himself together, his visitors informed him that they would accept the opera, though they would not perform it until the following autumn (1922). In fact, the premiere was to be brought forward to May 1922.

Relations with Mary now took a turn for the worse. She was to have played Schumann's Piano Concerto in St. Gallen but called it off. She then wrote to Max Thomann of the St. Gallen Concert Association to ask him to inform Schoeck that she was undergoing medical treatment and would have to avoid any contact with him for several months. Schoeck fell into a deep depression, believing that any chance of talking through their problems was rapidly disappearing. His spirits lifted shortly thereafter when he set Eichendorff's "Nachklang" to music, but he was soon once more as depressed as ever. On 5 November Corrodi found Schoeck sitting in the Pfauen Restaurant with his brother Ralph, morbidly depressed. He had received a letter from Mary in which she declared her determination to break off all contact with him. He read the letter, put it in his pocket, then took it out again, read it again, put it back in his pocket, then took it out once more—and so on throughout the evening. Now he was suspicious, and his jealous mind wandered over all the worst possible explanations. Perhaps she wasn't really sick at all; perhaps she'd taken another lover; perhaps the doctor treating her was a psychiatrist she had admitted to having loved before him; perhaps it was *he* who had forbidden her to see him; and one jealous thought led to another until he could bear it no longer and resolved to take the train straight to Geneva, that same evening. He asked Corrodi to come with him, and he agreed—not least out of fear that Schoeck might do something stupid. Ralph agreed to come along too. Schoeck continued reading and rereading the letter in the train, and what had begun as a series of jealous, free-association fears turned in his mind to logical certainties: it *was* the psychiatrist to blame, he *was* her lover, he *had* forbidden them from seeing each other. Once in Geneva they went straight to Mary's house, with Ralph and Corrodi barely able to stop him from hammering on the door at half past one in the morning. "There's someone up there in her room!" cried Schoeck when he saw that Mary's light was still on, though neither Corrodi nor Ralph had noticed anything of the sort. They dragged him away to spend the night with them in a hotel.[16]

The next morning Ralph was allotted the task of going to Mary to ask if she were prepared to meet Othmar, while the latter and Corrodi killed time by moping along the banks of Lake Geneva. Mary agreed, Ralph brought her to the others, and they all retired to a café—Ralph and Corrodi in one corner, Mary and Othmar in another. Mary told Othmar that she could not bear to marry anyone without her mother's blessing, but this would only be forthcoming if he agreed to a "trial year" in which he would have to refrain from seeing her so often. Schoeck protested that the last few years had been trial enough for him, and so they agreed to continue writing to each other, but in secret, via a mutual friend, a "Miss Fehrmann" (probably one Emma Martha Fehrmann from St. Gallen[17]). The four now left the café. Schoeck told Ralph and Corrodi that he would take Mary "for a walk," though it soon became clear to them that the walk took them straight to Schoeck's hotel room for sex. Later that afternoon, Ralph took Mary home and convinced her that it would not be wise for her to see Othmar again that evening. She agreed, but Othmar was furious with Ralph when he found out. He accused his brother of stabbing him in the back, even intimating that he was trying to steal Mary for himself. Ralph then told Othmar to his face that he was a "brutal egoist," ready to exploit others ruthlessly just to satisfy his own urges. Mary, he claimed, had said the same of him. Othmar now swore that he had never even asked the two men to join him in Geneva anyway. The three of them parted in anger, taking different trains home the next day.[18] Schoeck had to be back in St. Gallen to rehearse his orchestra for an all-French program scheduled for the following Thursday, 10 November, comprising Ravel's *Ma mère l'oye* and *Introduction and Allegro,* Debussy's First Clarinet Rhapsody with Edmond Allegra as soloist, and Edouard Lalo's Overture to *Le roi d'Ys.*

On Friday 11 November 1921 Schoeck was back in Zurich and went straight to pour his heart out to Corrodi. He said he had cried through all his afternoons in St. Gallen, was hopelessly depressed, and would now do anything that was asked of him by Mary's mother or anyone else. He just could not exist any more without her. Only in composition had he found some consolation. It was another Eichendorff setting, "Vesper," but he refused to show it to Corrodi, claiming that it was "too terrible" to play, though it was probably because Corrodi would have straightaway noticed that it quotes the piano piece "Consolation" when the words speak of "the old, beautiful time." Schoeck now admitted to having written his Hesse song "Was lachst du so" in a similar depression back in 1906. But this was different, he said, for he had now, for the first ever time, been able to console himself through the act of composition.

Mary also relented, and they began seeing each other again in Geneva. Schoeck now had to stay in hotels, however, and they presumably had to find excuses for Mary's absences from the family home. After conducting Bruckner's Ninth Symphony and Te Deum in St. Gallen, then the usual family Christmas at Brunnen, Schoeck went back to Geneva for a week over New Year. Things were at least improving for him on the professional front. At the end of 1921 Hug brought out a new, two-volume edition of his most popular songs from the many that they had published individually over a decade before. Then the Zurich City Theater announced that *Venus* would be produced in May as part of the Zurich International Festival. Just as important for his later career, though Schoeck did not know it yet, was his meeting with the Bern bass Felix Loeffel in January 1922. It was thanks to August Oetiker, who had organized a concert in which Loeffel sang some songs from *Erwin* under Schoeck's direction. Loeffel would soon become Schoeck's preferred male interpreter, just as Durigo had established herself as the leading female singer of his lieder. Several recordings survive of Loeffel in his prime. His voice had a grainy, occasionally nasal quality, and listening to it can at times be almost unpleasant. But he was a highly intelligent singer—a rare animal—and was able to offer such a compelling interpretation that one almost forgets about the sound of the voice itself.

Early 1922 brought Schoeck into contact with yet more contemporary music. In St. Gallen he conducted Mahler's *Das Lied von der Erde* on 19 January for the first time, with Durigo and Karl Erb as soloists. The audience included the young Elsa Cavelti, who although just into her teens was a regular attendee of Schoeck's concerts, and upon whom this work made a tremendous impact (in the 1950s, she herself became one of the work's leading interpreters, even recording it under Otto Klemperer).[19] It was also in early 1922 that Schoeck became properly acquainted with Arthur Honegger, who in the early 1920s was dividing his time between his home in Paris and his family back in their native Zurich. Honegger had achieved great success with his oratorio *Le roi David* at its world premiere in Mézières the previous July, and he had recently joined the list of Werner Reinhart's protégés. Schoeck presented him to his friends in the Pfauen in early March 1922 and told Corrodi, to the latter's surprise, that he had "complete trust in this man, trust that he's capable and really *is* someone."[20] For his part, Honegger recounted vivid tales of the music life of Paris, a city that Schoeck did not yet know.

In spring 1922 Schoeck was once again in the throes of despair and jealousy over Mary, who had yet again left him without any word for weeks on end, except for a single telegram to say that she was going away from Geneva for some time. Just after Palm Sunday he raged against marriage as "idiotic, the despotism of the mediocre and the stupid, an institution against nature," but his mood swung back again within days. On Maundy Thursday (13 April), he received a letter from Mary instructing him not to contact her, but in the same envelope he found a card on which she had written: "It's all for show, I'm still your Mary, stay calm." The implication was that her mother had either dictated the letter, or at least instructed her what to write, and that Mary had subverted her mother's intentions by smuggling an extra note into the envelope. This cheered Schoeck immensely, and he celebrated by going out to get his hair cut and generally sprucing himself up.[21] But apart from the absurd logistics of who wrote the letter, who sealed and posted the envelope, and of how a contradictory note got inside it, what thirty-five-year-old divorcée allows her mother to dictate the words she is to write to her lover? Schoeck considered none of this, proving how unreceptive passion is to logic. The more illogical his passion became, the more it was obvious to everyone else that his relationship was careening toward catastrophe. And the more he insisted that he could not live without Mary, the less he did to keep her.

Maundy Thursday passed; Good Friday came and went. No word from Mary. Schoeck began to rage about his mother, who he was sure was conspiring with Mary's mother to keep them apart. Easter Saturday came and went. No word. On Easter Sunday he took the train to Geneva and went straight to Mary's house. He arrived just as she was leaving home with a suitcase under her arm, on her way to stay with a friend in order to avoid him should he decide to turn up. Too late; when she saw him, she tried to run away but then stopped as he called to her. So she stayed, and Schoeck took a hotel room until the next Tuesday. When he left, he was utterly certain once more that all was now in order. The notion that Mary might want more from their relationship than occasional weekend bouts of all-day sex does not seem to have occurred to him.

Schoeck was at this time very much occupied with his "other" Venus. The world premiere was set for 10 May 1922, Schoeck was to conduct, and Horace was to be sung by Curt Taucher, the star tenor of the Dresden Opera. He had demanded a fee of five thousand francs, and when the theater in Zurich could offer only three, the Schwarzenbach family had stepped in to provide the missing two thousand.[22] Neither Schoeck nor anyone else seems to have remembered until almost the last moment that the opera demands that there be a statue on stage (though the opera has in more recent times been performed without one). With just days to go before the premiere, he approached his friend Hermann Hubacher, who after forty-eight hours and several dozen cups of coffee managed to produce a plaster statue that would be adequate for the task (Hubacher ensured, however, that his rushed job would not survive to embarrass him, and personally supervised its dumping into the Zurich Lake after the second and last performance). The "live" Venus was portrayed by a dancer. The cast list, largely unremarkable apart from Taucher, deserves a footnote in that one of the smaller roles was sung by the same Heinrich Gretler who just over a decade later became one of Switzerland's most famous screen actors, renowned for his performance as the grandfather in the first film version of *Heidi*.

Despite high ticket prices the evening was sold out. The audience included not just Schoeck's usual friends and colleagues—Hesse, Brun, Gamper, Haller, Durigo, Hermann Suter, Wilfried Buchmann, Franz Wiegele, Stefi Geyer, Walter Schulthess, among others, but also representatives of the press from Switzerland, Germany, England, and elsewhere. To judge from the reviews and the several surviving accounts of Schoeck's friends, the premiere was a complete success, with ovations for Schoeck and Taucher.

Schoeck had waited for Mary since the early afternoon, but there was no sign of her, and he had conducted the performance in the belief that she was not there. But after the final curtain, he turned round to find her standing on the empty stage. She had been there the whole time but had not wanted to be seen. Schoeck spent just a few minutes with her before going to the post-premiere get-together in the Corso Restaurant behind the theater. He and his friends then celebrated into the early hours at the nearby Kronenhalle Restaurant before he walked home to Mary up the hill, therewith to disappear for several days of quasi-conjugal bliss. He surfaced once, to accompany seven of his *Hafez Songs* at that year's *Tonkünstlerfest* in nearby Zug, only to return and submerge himself in Mary once again.

Among the journalists present at *Venus* was the eminent critic Ernest Newman, whose review for the *Sunday Times* summed up succinctly the work's strengths and weaknesses:

After hearing two performances of [Schoeck's] *Venus* I am sure that here is a composer whose reputation will soon extend beyond the frontier of his native land. . . . The opera begins excellently, and then, for the remainder of the first scene [i.e., act], falls off somewhat. Perhaps in another production it would go better,—I cannot say; but it seems to me that the composer's touch is not so sure here as in the rest of the work.

The second and third scenes [acts] I found very interesting, and, I was glad to observe, still more interesting at the second performance than at the first.

S[c]hoeck strikes me as a conservative radical. It is evident that he knows a good deal of modern music, but he is never as extravagant as some of his contemporaries. On the other hand, while he develops out of the great German tradition, he is not a slave to it; he handles the transmitted tools with independence, and expresses through them what is evidently a decided personality. I . . . shall follow S[c]hoeck's further career with interest.

The opera, from the practical point of view, will be rather handicapped, I imagine, by the fact that Horace has to carry the bulk of it on his own shoulders. The part is surely as trying as any in opera, for the tenor has not only to sing almost continuously through the second and third acts but has to have an enormous reserve for the finish.[23]

Newman was right about the part of Horace, which verges on the inhuman, as even Taucher discovered. He swore afterward that he would never sing it again, not even for ten thousand francs, and would urge any fellow tenors to avoid it, should they care to ask him.[24] The problem with the role of Horace lies perhaps in the fact that his last scene was composed first. The vocal part circles around the tenor's top G and A♭, rising repeatedly to a top B♭ and above. Such a tessitura is not uncommon in the earlier Italian repertoire, though in Rossini or Donizetti a tenor might sing his highest notes in a semi-falsetto. The late-Romantic orchestra of Schoeck's *Venus,* however, playing its accompaniment *forte* or *fortissimo,* would drown out any tenor who did not sing with a full chest voice, and the number of tenors alive at any one time who could manage the role can be counted on the fingers of one hand. In the context of the plot, an element of striving at the end of the opera is not out of place. But since Horace is singing a hymn to "Vollendung"—"perfection"—the raucous squawking that most singers would produce after an hour and a half on stage is hardly appropriate.

What is this "perfection" to which Horace aspires? Ostensibly, the physical and aesthetic perfection incarnate in the Venus figure. Unlike her, Horace's wife Simone is decidedly earthbound, allowing herself to be dominated by the male sex. When she realizes at the wedding ball that her husband loves another woman, she faints; at the end of the opera—the next time we see her—she is suddenly ready to give up her husband if it makes him happy. She is too late, as he has already "left" her by dying in the arms of Venus; so she again collapses. But is Venus herself that much different, at least at the start? As a statue, she is implicitly a direct product of man's fantasy and artifice, and by remaining silent and immobile she remains subject to him. Horace's desire for the statue—kindled long before she comes to life—is thus little more than a male masturbatory fantasy in which the superiority of his gender is confirmed. Venus might just as well be a blow-up doll (how long, one wonders, before an opera director thinks of that?). By coming to life, however, Venus calls that supposed superiority into question. When Horace pulls off his wedding ring and puts it on her finger, this signifies not just the abandonment of his wife but also an attempt to declare proprietary rights over this new woman. In the end, however, it is she who takes possession of him, and the price he pays is death.

Only on a superficial level is *Venus* a hymn to beauty; it is really far more the composing-out of the male fear of woman's emancipation. One could even argue that the real "dream woman" in *Venus* is not the title heroine at all but the subservient Simone. If Venus did not come to life, and if Horace did not die, one could imagine a happy-ever-after in which Simone would play the archetypal Swiss housewife, cleaning and polishing, making cups of tea for her husband, bringing him his slippers and carrying in his TV-supper on a tray while he ogles bronzed goddesses in *Baywatch* instead of bronze goddesses in the park.

Schoeck found notions of domestic bliss both fascinating and repellent, and it is tempting to draw parallels between Simone and the real-life Elsbeth (who had been lover to both composer and librettist). As we have seen, Elsbeth had been content to play the obedient (quasi) wife: cleaning, polishing, darning, and opening her legs, depending upon whichever service Schoeck required. His near-acquiescence in matrimony with her, as he admitted at the time, had been thwarted only by his having sex with Mary. But Mary was a different kettle of fish (let us not forget that her mother had once turned down Nietzsche as a husband). Schoeck was now prepared to marry her—for it seemed the only way not to lose her—but he still feared that by institutionalising their relationship he would enter into the same kind of monotone bourgeois monogamy that is intimated by the wedding chorus at the close of the first act of *Venus,* whose jubilation always sounds hollow.

There is, however, more to *Venus* than this. On a superficial level the opera tells us that if a man gives himself to an independent woman, then he must give up everything to her—in this case, his life included—and there is here also a parallel with Schoeck's next opera, *Penthesilea,* in which the hero is not just killed by his beloved but torn to pieces and half-eaten, too. *Venus* and *Penthesilea* are a realization on stage of the metaphorical "man-eating woman." But while Schoeck's "self portrait" Horace, like Achilles in the later opera, finds death by giving himself in his entirety to the woman he loves, Schoeck himself seems to have feared that by submitting to Mary in marriage he would be killing off his creative energies. His horror of bourgeois morality had somehow become fused in his mind with his recurrent fears of compositional sterility. One can even detect Schoeck's hesitation to "abandon" himself in the very music to the final scene of his opera. This is probably the most overtly Straussian music that he ever wrote, with whooping horns and all their concomitant sexual connotations as the music surges from one climax to the next. But while Horace sings in full awareness of his fate—"[For he] who has known perfection wholly, yearning will drive him to your divine heart, and beauty must kill him out of love"—the conviction conveyed by the text is subverted by the insertion of several pauses. These prevent the music from achieving the sense of continuity and eventual climax to which we are accustomed from those examples in Wagner and Strauss in which the death of a character coincides with a musical depiction of the biological imperative. In fact, the music here breaks off just *before* Horace throws himself into the arms of Venus, which he does to a general pause. Only when Simone arrives on stage to find him dead and cries "Tot!" does the music erupt—but it subsides just as quickly, ending six measures later on a triple *piano* and in the "wrong" key—a mixed chord of B-flat major and minor, which is the dominant of Horace's closing monologue (E flat). What could better signify a hesitation to achieve consummation than a refusal to cadence properly? Robin Holloway has written of this ending that "the inner frenzy within the decorum and the refinement of silky orchestral finish achieves maximal strangeness . . . Webern himself could not have done more with less."[25]

Oddly, Schoeck himself helped to ensure that after these first performances *Venus* remained unperformed for over a decade. Breitkopf & Härtel—so Schoeck's wife would discover eight years later—had offered a double premiere of the opera at two renowned houses (we do not know which). But instead, be it out of impatience or out of a desire to control his *Venus* to the last in compensation for his growing loss of control over (in his words) "the other Venus," he had performed the work in Zurich from the manuscript, without the involvement of his publisher. To make matters worse, Schoeck had sold the Zurich Theater the parts and his only copy of the score—all of which had to be bought up by Breitkopf afterward.[26] One can hardly blame his publisher for showing little interest in promoting the work, once the publicity value of the world premiere had been lost. And by the time Breitkopf came to publish the vocal score, because of burgeoning German inflation it cost them 80 million marks.[27]

After *Venus* Schoeck had the perfect opportunity to provide a perfect cadence, as it were, to his relationship with Mary. His friends were aware of the financial hurdles that were supposedly preventing him from popping the question, and so—led by Stefi Geyer—they made a collection of almost five thousand francs and presented it to him at the festivities after his opera premiere. Now there was no reason why he should not marry, and Mary agreed. But he couldn't. A few weeks later, Corrodi met Schoeck and Mary on the street. They went off to the Pfauen Restaurant together, where Mary said: "I declare herewith, and you [Corrodi] are my witness: I am ready to marry Othmar." Schoeck replied: "No, Mary, you know we can't get married." When Schoeck left them alone for a few minutes, Mary told Corrodi everything. Schoeck had promised to marry her, her mother had at last agreed, and he had taken her to Brunnen to present her to his parents as his fiancée. But when they arrived, the words "fiancée," "engagement" and "marriage" never crossed his lips. He became nervous and depressed, and when they went out on an afternoon walk, he burst into tears. She did not know how to react, or how to face her mother when she returned to Geneva. Furthermore, she had seen written reports from "information bureaux" on his infidelity to her, with precise descriptions of illicit behavior in St. Gallen (though whether private detectives had been engaged by her, her mother, or their go-between, we do not know). They recorded that he was nicknamed "Sandwich" there, on account of his having supposedly slept with more than one woman at a time. The accusation was true, as Schoeck would boast to Corrodi just three weeks later (he had suggested it to a couple of girls, he said; they had agreed, and it had been a very curious feeling. Not a trace of love, just "raging sensuality").[28] But still Mary could not bring herself to end their relationship. Nor could Schoeck; and after she left for home, his regular visits to Geneva began once more. Nothing, it must have seemed, had changed at all.

Chapter Fifteen

Elegy

The summer of 1922 brought another bout of depression for Schoeck—not helped by Mary's mother writing full of reproaches after his broken promise of marriage to her daughter. But again emotional turmoil brought songs in its wake. In July and August 1922 Schoeck wrote a total of seventeen—three to texts by Eichendorff, the rest by Lenau. In the midst of writing them he decided to add the two songs he had written the previous November and turn them all into a song cycle with orchestral accompaniment. It was at the beginning of this bout of prolonged activity that Schoeck allowed Corrodi one of his rare insights into the compositional process, which he interpreted, not surprisingly, in sexual terms. Corrodi wrote:

> Schoeck maintained that you can in fact compel inspiration. Often he will sit down without any stimulus, sometimes with no result, but then sometimes the moments of inspiration ["Einfälle"] would come suddenly after three or four hours of strenuous work. . . . He compared this process, of compelling and winning, to one's path to a lover. However far and difficult that path might be, the happiness at the end is no less on that account.[1]

Schoeck's mood throughout these two months was highly changeable. His work would lift his spirits, but then he would plunge back into depression and bitterness. In one moment he could rage against marriage as an unnatural institution, and in the next against Mary's mother for not wanting him to marry her daughter. Mary should just leave her mother, come and live with him for a few weeks, then everything would be fine, he insisted. He wrote to her every day and rang her as often as he could. He had recently given her number through to the operator, only to be asked: "Will it be another long call?"[2] All the while that he was fantasizing about marriage with Mary, he was frittering away the money gathered by Stefi and co. that was supposed to make it possible. It was now being spent on expensive meals and champagne in the Hotel Elite, and once it was gone, Schoeck began complaining again that he did not have enough money to get married. His anger at the institution of marriage culminated in his insistence that it should be banned altogether, as should the education system and all other "bourgeois" institutions. One of Schoeck's friends, the medical doctor Toni Schucany, who was present during these rages, bluntly told him that he was suffering from a neurosis, wished him a speedy recovery, and left in disgust. Schoeck was certainly possessed of a combative spirit, and even into old age he would occasionally adopt extreme positions in discussions in order to stimulate debate. But his arguments in this summer seem to have gone beyond the pale of playful conversational sparring. It is almost as though he were so excited by his new-found ability to convert depressive depths into creative energy that he had decided—whether consciously or no—to intensify his inner conflict in order to prolong his creative surge. In the meantime anyway, Mary had changed her mind about marriage. Walter Schädelin and Fritz Brun met Alexander von Senger in September 1922, and afterward Schädelin wrote in his diary: "Brun told me that [von Senger] had said of Mary that she was unusually intelligent, highly cultivated, but calculating and heartless and it would be a great calamity if she were to marry Schoeck; but *she* [his emphasis] does not want to."[3] And so Schoeck's commuting to and from Geneva continued, as did his work on the new cycle. In late September, he approached Felix Loeffel to ask if he would sing the premiere of the work, which now comprised twenty-three songs, including the setting of "Angedenken" that he had completed in May 1921 and had inserted into the cycle. The twenty-fourth and last song to join the others, "Warnung und Wunsch," was composed later (it was placed fifth in the overall scheme). He considered various titles for the song cycle—his first ever—but finally decided on one suggested by his brother Paul: *Elegie*. He sent the songs to Mary as he composed them, with love messages scribbled around the margins. Much later he had to ask for them back in order to send them to the publisher, and in one of his least tactful gestures he roped in Lala Gsell—still in the grip of an unrequited love for him—to help tape over all the messages before posting the songs to Breitkopf & Härtel.[4]

The new concert season brought a number of first performances of contemporary music in Zurich, ranging from Korngold's opera *Die tote Stadt* and excerpts from Stravinsky's *Petrushka* in October to Schoenberg's *Pierrot lunaire*, conducted by the composer in both Winterthur and Zurich, in late November and early December 1922. Since Schoenberg was Reinhart's houseguest, it is not impossible that Schoeck was invited along, though we have no proof either way. But his own schedule was so heavy this autumn and early winter that he could have had little time to listen to other men's concerts. Beethoven's Ninth Symphony in St. Gallen on 9 and 10 December was followed by a run of Puccini's *La Bohème* at the city's theater on 14, 15, and 17 December.

Schoeck's programs this season demonstrated his increasing interest in the music of his contemporaries, for they included Richard Strauss's *Bürger als Edelmann* suite and Honegger's *Pastorale d'été*. March 1923 was particularly strenuous. Schoeck conducted Mozart's *Così fan tutte* and *Don Giovanni* in the St. Gallen City Theater (with Elisabeth Schumann as a guest in both), then came back to Zurich to conduct the Tonhalle Orchestra on 12 and 13 March in a concert that paired Mozart arias (also sung by Schumann) with Schubert's "Great" C-major Symphony; then he went back to St. Gallen for two orchestral concerts on 15 and 18 (the latter including his own Violin Concerto), returning to Zurich again to conduct the world premiere of his *Elegie* in the smaller hall in the Tonhalle on 19 March (also the date of Werner Reinhart's thirty-ninth birthday). Although the concert was not sold out, it was a great success, and the reviews were highly complimentary. Isler even claimed in the *Schweizerische Musikzeitung* on 31 March: "No composer has ever received such unanimous, spontaneous, and prolonged homage in Zurich as after the close of this work by Othmar Schoeck; not even Strauss or Reger." Schoeck was also lucky in having excellent players on the night. Besides de Boer and the other members of the Zurich String Quartet, the chamber orchestra included the pianist Walter Lang and Busoni's favorite wind players from his time in Zurich, namely the flautist Jean Nada and the clarinettist Edmond Allegra (the latter has also entered the annals, for having given the world premiere of Stravinsky's Three Pieces for Clarinet five years earlier). Only Schoeck's father was unhappy, for to him the autobiographical aspect of the work was clear. He said that he found it distressing to experience how his child was losing himself in a nirvana of grief.[5] Mary did not come, though we should not read too much into this, as they met up in Bern just three weeks later.

The *Elegie* became one of Schoeck's most frequently performed works in the ensuing years, primarily thanks to Felix Loeffel, its first interpreter, who sang it some fifty times across the German-speaking world. It is both Schoeck's first song cycle and his most mature work to date. The twenty-four poems are arranged so as to evoke a loose narrative of the loss of love. As Isler pointed out in his review, its principal model was Schubert's *Winterreise,* which Schoeck had accompanied many times. Schoeck's cycle progresses from spring to autumn; from day to night; from "here" to an unstated "elsewhere"; from the presence of the beloved to the vaguest memory of her; and (implicitly) from life to death. The narrative, however, is more inferred than clearly stated, and the opening numbers, depicting "love's spring" (the actual title of the second song) have a bittersweet quality that seems to speak of times past, even when describing a purportedly happy present. There is here no moment of unalloyed joy, for loss is somehow omnipresent. Schoeck even incorporates overtly Schubertian major-minor alternations, though in a manner that makes Schubert, too, seem just a distant memory. And in many of the songs, the voice obstinately repeats fragments of scalic passages or arpeggios, circling round just a few notes. It is at times as if the very building blocks of melody and harmony were themselves receding into distant memory, with the singer/narrator holding on obsessively to the only fragments over which he has any control. Some of the songs can work with a mere piano accompaniment, but most then sound lifeless, for the orchestral timbres are an essential element of the affect. Schoeck had decided to orchestrate the cycle because the piano alone does not have the sustaining power that he desired— a piano's notes, he told Corrodi, would die away too quickly for the sound he had in mind.[6] This is telling, for in a work that embodies "loss" to such a high degree, the orchestration creates "echoes" in timbre that become themselves the very signifiers of transience. Corrodi noted that the orchestration seemed to recreate the textures that Schoeck was able to draw from the piano when he accompanied his songs.[7]

Only in the final song, "Der Einsame," does Schoeck allow his melodic gift to take flight (see ex. 15.1). Here at last we find resolution, "solace," both in word and music. The text itself—by Eichendorff—begins "Komm, Trost der Welt, du stille Nacht" ("Come, solace of the world, you silent night"). Stylistically, this is perhaps the most "backward-looking" song in the cycle. Gone are the obsessive Wolfian ostinati that dominate the orchestral accompaniments for much of the cycle; gone are the repetitive melodic fragments that dominate much of the vocal part; gone is the syllabic devotion to the prosody. Instead, we have a seamless melodic flow that is straightforwardly periodic in its structure and compelling in its simplicity. Here, at last, the voice leads the orchestra, whose function is now solely to accompany. And the most complex chords are those with a seventh that is added for purely coloristic reasons. The orchestration sounds fuller than in most of the other songs in the cycle, though it is as subtle as ever. The "model" for this song (though not for its actual music) is the final song of Schubert's *Winterreise*, which demonstrates how resolution and closure can be attained through a drastic reduction in musical complexity. In each song, the "closure" is also implicitly that of death.

Example 15.1. The opening of "Der Einsame," the final song of the *Elegie*, Op. 36. Copyright Breitkopf & Härtel. Reprinted by permission. "Come, solace of the world, you silent night! How you rise up gently from the mountains, the breezes all [fall silent]"

The *Elegie* needs a sensitive interpretation, as otherwise the mood of despondency that so troubled Schoeck's father can teeter on the brink of self-pity. But Schoeck achieves in this work a dramatic trajectory that is all the more powerful for remaining oblique in its actual narrative. It is arguably his most "dramatic" work to date, and proof that he was perfectly capable of realizing large-scale forms. It was undoubtedly writing *Venus* that made it possible, for there he had for the first time endeavored to write a real drama in music, and one in which the drama is slowly but surely stripped away to leave the hero alone at the end with his embrace of oblivion. But Horace's death at the close is intended to be heroic in the Romantic, Wagnerian tradition, and for all its whooping horns, it is not nearly as convincing as the narrator's anti-heroic acceptance of his extinction at the close of the *Elegie*. The heroic was simply not a natural mode of expression for Schoeck. *Venus* and the *Elegie* also provide the first intimation that Schoeck's gift for drama in music, with few exceptions, found its finest expression when it tended to monodrama.

At the time that Schoeck wrote his *Elegie,* its modest instrumentation meant that it was not difficult to program, whereas today, an hour-long cycle with chamber orchestra is seen as too short for an evening's concert and too long for one half of a program. But if the *Elegie* is now something of a white elephant because of its impracticability, it is to be regretted. For it has few peers in the genre of the orchestral song cycle in the first half of the twentieth century.

Chapter Sixteen

Goodbye to Geneva

In spring 1923 Schoeck was again contemplating an opera: this time his challenge was how to combine the Grimm fairy tales *Meister Pfriem* and *Bruder Lustig* into a single plot. Franz Wiegele wrote on his behalf to Hugo von Hofmannsthal, in the hope of procuring for him the man everyone acknowledged as the leading librettist of the age.[1] It was not to be, for Hofmannsthal was committed to Strauss alone, and he had in any case just begun working on his libretto for their *Ägyptische Helena*. So for now Schoeck put all his opera plans to one side. In the meantime he had begun work on a suite for string quartet that was partly programmatic in intent. Its scherzo is a "burlesque serenade" in which bitonality is used for humorous effect, depicting how one of the players of a serenade gets stuck in the wrong key and provokes laughter from the other instruments.[2] The second movement, apparently a "rain song" ("Regenlied"), is visually reminiscent of the opening of the fourth movement of Schoenberg's Second Quartet, with its wide ascending arc in which one instrument takes over from the next. But when one hears it, Schoeck's quartet instead confirms the increasing influence on him of contemporary French music. In its first movement there are distinct similarities—not least in its sarabande rhythms—both to the final movement of Ravel's *Ma mère l'oye* (which Schoeck had conducted just seventeen months before) and to Honegger's First String Quartet.

Three weeks after the premiere of the *Elegie*, Schoeck also had the opportunity of hearing one of his recent stage works for the first time. This year's *Tonkünstlerfest* was being held—serendipitously for him—in Geneva, and it was there that Ernest Ansermet conducted a concert performance of *Das Wandbild* on 7 April. Schoeck's reaction is not known, and he seems to have been more interested in meeting up with Mary in Bern in advance of the festival. Their relationship had regained stability since late 1922. However, since Schoeck's notion of stability was still defined primarily by whether or not they were having regular sex, things were perhaps not as calm as he thought they were. We know that he was back in Geneva in early June 1923, for he wrote a card to Reinhart, saying "As you see, the 'sun' has brought me to Geneva for a few days."[3] He left for Paris shortly afterward—his first visit to the city. He had wanted to take Mary with him, but her mother had forbidden it. His host in the city was Arthur Honegger, of whom he had been seeing much in Zurich in recent months. Honegger had not only attended the rehearsals and premiere of the *Elegie* but by his own admission was also consulting Schoeck on the orchestration of his new symphonic poem, *Pacific 231*.[4]

We do not have many concrete details of Schoeck's visit to Paris. This is regrettable, because our lack of information seems to stand in inverse relation to the impact that the city's music life had upon him. Upon his return to Zurich Schoeck told Corrodi that he had viewed Paris's immense art treasures with much enjoyment and had moved among the circles of *Les Six*—Honegger will have been keen to impress his older companion with the company that he kept. Honegger himself reminisced about Schoeck's visit, briefly, many years later. They dined exquisitely, he recalled, and on one evening went to the Moulin Rouge, where the local girls heard them speak in Swiss German dialect and mistook it for Russian. Honegger then compounded the mistake by passing off Schoeck as the Russian émigré "Grand Duke Schoeckinskoff," after which they did not want for female attention all night. On another occasion during this trip, Schoeck ordered a "marc" after dinner (a *digestif* known as "grappa" in Italy; the final "c" in the name is silent). It was a particularly fine one, and when Schoeck praised it to Honegger, the latter exclaimed, with reference to their mutual colleague Andreae: "Then it's an Oth-mar[c], not a "Volk-mar!"[5]

Honegger further recalled that they attended the premiere of Stravinsky's *Les noces*, conducted by Ansermet, at the Gaîté-Lyrique Theater on 13 June. Perhaps they had even timed Schoeck's visit to coincide with it—once again, Reinhart might have played an intermediary role, for he was in direct contact with Stravinsky about the *Noces* and had even received the manuscript of the work as a gift; however, he was unable to attend the premiere himself. On a postcard sent to Reinhart on 22 June and signed by Schoeck, Honegger, Paul Hoehn, and Honegger's lover (and later wife) Andrée Vaurabourg, Schoeck's contribution is the sentence: "The *Noces* were wonderful, besides others things too!"[6] But that was not all that they saw, for the premiere of *Les noces* was coupled with a performance of *Petrushka*. Schoeck might have heard it when Ansermet had performed excerpts from it in Zurich in late October 1922, but we can be sure that he now took the trouble to study the score, for certain passages would heavily influence the opening scene of his next opera. Schoeck was also impressed enough to include the suite from *Petrushka* in his St. Gallen concerts several years later.

Back in Zurich in late July 1923, Schoeck told Corrodi that in general there had been much to admire in Paris, but that the avant-garde there was creating a "house of cards" that would tumble down with the first gust of wind.[7] Such negative comments, of which several more of similar import would follow, were usually a sign that Schoeck had been far more impressed than his urge for artistic self-preservation would allow him to confess. A few days later, Schoeck left Zurich to spend a few days in the Engadine with Walter Schulthess, Stefi Geyer's husband, with whom he had now become close friends. Schulthess later recalled him praising *Les noces* to the skies, in particular its ensemble of pianos and percussion. The Engadine was followed by a trip to Geneva to see Mary. We have no testimony from either Schoeck or Mary as to the state of their relationship, though the simple fact that it would soon alter for good suggests that it was again precarious. Some sixty years later, Mary's nephew Franz could still remember the final stages of the affair, for Mary's mother would refuse to allow Schoeck to cross her threshold, and he would then pace the opposite side of the route de Chêne until Mary came out to speak to him. The money that Stefi had collected was all long spent, and Schoeck was again claiming that he did not have enough money to marry. His financial woes were not all self-made, however, for his German publishers were able to pay him next to nothing in royalties. That year saw the worst of the postwar German hyperinflation, peaking at an exchange rate of several billion marks to the dollar, so even though Breitkopf had just increased what they owed him by 500 percent, the resultant 140,000 marks were worthless.[8]

Schoeck only had a couple of days to spend with Mary in Geneva before he had to join Werner Reinhart, Alma Moodie, Honegger, and Andrée Vaurabourg on a trip to Salzburg. The occasion was a chamber music festival of the International Society for Contemporary Music. They set off on Monday, 30 July, traveling in Reinhart's "big white car," as Honegger recalled several years later, spending a night in the Hotel Tyrol in Innsbruck along the way, and arriving in Salzburg on the Wednesday. The society had been founded just months earlier. Reinhart had attended the first "Delegate's Conference" in London in January 1923 and a few weeks later had hosted the first jury meeting, with Ansermet, André Caplet, Hermann Scherchen, and Egon Wellesz. He was deeply involved in details of the organization of this Salzburg festival, even down to procuring an E-flat clarinet from Geneva for a performance of the Clarinet Quintet by Paul Hindemith— another composer whose acquaintance Reinhart had recently made, and who would benefit from his occasional patronage.[9] Salzburg was also an opportunity for Schoeck to renew his own acquaintance with Hindemith from May 1921, and the two became firm friends.

The Salzburg festival program was absurdly full: thirty-six works by thirty-five composers were performed in six days, including Bartók's Second Violin Sonata, Berg's String Quartet Op. 3, William Walton's String Quartet, Stravinsky's Concertino and Three Pieces for String Quartet, Alois Hába's String Quartet no. 2, Ravel's Sonata for Violin and Cello, Poulenc's *Promenades* for piano, Darius Milhaud's Fourth String Quartet, Sergei Prokofiev's *Overture on Jewish Themes* for clarinet, string quartet, and piano, Kodály's Solo Cello Sonata, Schoenberg's *Buch der hängenden Gärten,* and Ernst Krenek's Third String Quartet. And much more, too. Schoeck accompanied the baritone Heinrich Rehkemper in five of his *Hafez Songs,* Op. 33—oddly, Karol Szymanowski's contribution to the festival comprised two of his own *Hafez Songs.* Honegger reminisced thus about the festival over twenty years later:

There we found again the whole of the international music world, but also Ansermet, R[udolph] Ganz, and even Aloys Mooser, Schoeck's bitter, unjust adversary. However, a truce seemed to be established between them. One saw them lift their glasses to their mutual health, though at that moment, Schoeck's had only water in it. "That Mooser," he confided to me afterward, "has a head like a snake" [*Schlangegrind*].

Every morning and afternoon we listened resignedly to the interminable concerts in which atonal quartets followed on unremittingly from polytonal *Klaviermusiks*, followed in turn by cycles of monodicotonal [*sic*] songs. In order to console ourselves, we went to meet *Schlangegrind* for aperitifs, either at the Österreichischer Hof or at the Schloss Mirabell. There Ansermet met Stefan Zweig, Casella conversed with Alban Berg, and the Hindemith and Pro Arte quartets fraternized by playing Mozart serenades in order to purge their instruments of the quarter-tones that risked still being stuck there from the afternoon before.[10]

The only really prominent Central Europeans who could not be present were Webern and Schoenberg. The press was there in great number, and almost all judged Krenek and Berg to be the stars of the festival. In the *Schweizerische Musikzeitung,* however, Ernst Isler wrote his usual patriotic hymn of praise: "Our Othmar Schoeck . . . represented another musical sphere from the one that dominated the festival. The musicians who were there reacted perhaps too little to the pure, clear air of this wonderfully imagined, masterfully formed, pure music."[11] But for all Isler's joy in Schoeck's supposed purity, the composer himself was not as happy. His songs had been third on the program of the evening concert of 3 August in which Krenek's Third Quartet was featured last, and the latter work had drawn almost everyone's attention. Edwin Evans wrote in the *Musical Times* that "Schoeck's songs proved pleasant enough in their way, which, however, is so small a way that one wonders a little at their inclusion, save for contrast."[12] Alban Berg went further, writing to his wife that "the first four numbers [of that concert] were indescribable muck."[13] Although Berg will no doubt have refrained from thus expressing himself in public, similar sentiments were obviously being openly expressed in Salzburg about the more "conservative" composers. Schoeck himself told Corrodi afterward how Paul Bekker, the leading German critic, had told him to his face that "well, in fifty or a hundred years, Switzerland might also have a little say in things."[14]

Schoeck had been thoroughly upstaged at Salzburg, and by Krenek in particular. This is in itself not surprising, given that the ISCM's thrust was decidedly toward a Schoenbergian understanding of aesthetic progress, and that the five *Hafez Songs* that Schoeck had accompanied were the more conservative of the set. But Schoeck's reaction was quite different from Isler's, and in conversation he did not for a moment wish to detract from Krenek's success. He judged Krenek and Hindemith to have been the best of the bunch, though he also had nothing but praise for Stravinsky's "fabulous ear" and his "razor-sharp sense of rhythm." He felt that his contemporaries were opening up new paths for music thanks to their emancipation of the dissonance, and he regretted not having chosen the more progressive of his songs for performance. He now even took to showing his friends certain carefully chosen passages from his *Venus* in order to prove that he, too, was capable of writing extreme dissonance.

Schoeck's lack of street credibility among the avant-garde was not his only worry. Straight after returning from Salzburg he had gone to Geneva to see Mary. On Sunday 12 August he had waited "for hours" for her, but in vain. He waited again on Monday, but again in vain, and then decided to go and look for her in Lausanne and Ouchy, further up the lake—though precisely why he thought she could be there we do not know. Still he could not find her, and he became so desperate that he began asking passing postmen and anyone else on the street who looked vaguely helpful. He even went to a police station to report her missing. Eventually, a mutual friend rang him to say that Mary was still in Geneva but did not wish to see him. Schoeck would not relent and insisted upon seeing her. She finally agreed, but she brought her brother Ernst along "so I don't weaken again." Their meeting was brief: she simply told him that their relationship was over. Over a decade later Mary met Lala Gsell in Geneva and told her: "One can't marry a man like that. He has to stay free."[15]

Schoeck now returned home to Zurich, but he still seems to have assumed that Mary would once more capitulate and invite him down for a weekend of make-up sex. But a week later, their go-between, "Miss Fehrmann," informed him that Mary had said, "cold-bloodedly, it's all over."[16] And indeed it was. They would not meet again for a decade.

Chapter Seventeen

The Bee in the Rose

How does one cope with losing the love of one's life, the woman whose very existence seems to define one, and without whom the mere fact of being seems to lose its purpose? The answer, felt Schoeck, was to have lots of sex with lots of other women as soon as possible. That is precisely what he did within a fortnight of losing Mary. In compensation for his loss, he also began to display a heightened sexual bravado among his (male) friends, once more claiming that fidelity was different for men and women: women remained faithful by remaining faithful, while men could sleep around without being unfaithful *per se*. Furthermore, he claimed, not one of his friends' wives had ever failed to make a pass at him, with the sole exception, he remarked pointedly, of Stefi Geyer. He now boasted for weeks on end of how many women he was sleeping with, and of how many came to beg him for sex. All this *macho* posturing was presumably to compensate for the fact that the one woman he really wanted was the one he had lost—through no one's fault but his own—and would never win back. And while he might have somewhat exaggerated the number of his conquests, he nevertheless was indeed consoling himself in the arms and orifices of several women. The least fleeting of them was Annie Gottlieb-Sallenbach, whom Schoeck called "Angelie." She was Swiss, was married to a Dane, and had two children. Although resident in Dresden, she frequently visited her mother back in Zurich, into whose care she had placed her children during the inflation years in order to spare them the economic privations inevitable in Germany. Angelie's family knew the local music scene well. Her mother's home on the Bellerivestrasse was used as a rehearsal venue by de Boer's Zurich String Quartet, and Angelie had probably got to know Schoeck through one or both of their mutual friends Ilona Durigo and Stefi Geyer.[1] She had been in love with Schoeck for some time—she would later claim that he had been the love of her life—and when she appeared at his apartment two weeks after the break with Mary and found him in need of consolation, she bestowed it amply.

At about the same time that Angelie appeared, Schoeck composed the song "Die Entschwundene" ("The Girl Who Disappeared"), a setting of the first poem in Gottfried Keller's cycle *Erstes Lieben* ("First Love"). If it was meant as a farewell to Mary, its obsessive two-measure ostinato accompaniment and its vocal line hovering around the notes of a broken chord make it just as much a farewell to the soundworld of the *Elegie*. But it also points the way forward, inasmuch as Schoeck's songs for the next five years would be to poems by Gottfried Keller alone—a poet whom he had long avoided. While we must be suspicious of spotting all-too-convenient parallels between biography and work, Schoeck's life "post-Mary" undeniably coincides almost exactly with a phase in his compositional life that was breathtakingly new. It is not really "the girl" who disappears, for it is the Schoeck of the *Elegie* who is "der Entschwundene." The first signs of the new direction in his music are to be found in a "Lento" movement that he added in early September to his suite for string quartet (soon to be renamed simply "Second String Quartet"), in which sustained dissonant chords in parallel motion suspend tonality for much of the time; he called it an "Abendbild" ("Picture of Evening").[2]

This summer also brought Schoeck in closer contact with one of the leading proponents of modern music, Hermann Scherchen, whose appointment as conductor of the Winterthur City Orchestra Reinhart had ensured just a few months before. To judge from a letter that he sent his wife at this time, Scherchen seems to have been somewhat swept off his feet by the strength of Schoeck's personality:

> I love Schoeck. . . . The fellow has all the marks of the exceptional in his overflowing personality, in the fire of his eye. A highly robust chap, but without being crude. Talented down to the tips of his fingers. Full of eroticism, wit, and with it all, above all, likeable . . . not intelligent in the sense of "clever," but at times almost enlightened in his physical/emotional intelligence. That's the source of his marvellous judgments and insights.[3]

A performance of the *Elegie* that Scherchen had scheduled in Frankfurt in September 1923 had to be cancelled because of a lack of rehearsal time, but his passion for Schoeck and his music would remained undimmed over the coming decades.

Besides finishing his new string quartet in autumn 1923, Schoeck now also planned a setting of Keller's narrative cycle of fourteen poems entitled *Lebendig begraben* ("Buried Alive"). It proved intractable, however, and after considering having certain sections spoken, not sung, he put it to one side (he would return to it three years later). He turned instead to Keller's *Gaselen* ("Ghazels"), a brief cycle of ten poems that mix erotic love lyrics with satire, and whose only real unifying factor is the verse form (aa–ba–ca–da, etc.). These poems are even more abstruse and awkward than those of the *Lebendig begraben* cycle, and Schoeck at first found them just as intractable. He considered setting them to an accompaniment of cello and piano, with the most difficult verses once more spoken, not sung; but he soon decided instead to have all the verses sung to the accompaniment of an ensemble of trumpet, flute doubling piccolo, oboe, bass clarinet, piano, and percussion. Derrick Puffett has suggested that this "top and bottom" instrumentation was influenced by Stravinsky's *Soldier's Tale*,[4] though the opening of the work, with its brash solo trumpet followed by the nasal, almost "vulgar" sound of the woodwind scoring, actually takes us into a soundworld that is perhaps most reminiscent of Kurt Weill. Once Schoeck had begun, the floodgates opened by themselves, for five of the ten poems were apparently sketched in the space of two hours, and the cycle was finished by early November 1923, with the exception of the very ending. Schoeck claimed to have been disturbed by a visitor just as his moment of inspiration came (his "Einfall"), and it took him till December to find an ending that truly satisfied him.

The opening poem of *Gaselen* runs: "Ours is the fate of the Epigones who live in the vast halfway-world; look how you squeeze one more drop from old lemon rinds!" the final poem tells of the poet's old hat whose rim is crumpled and attracts the mockery of passers-by; so he turns it round, but then people only laugh behind his back; and he then turns it round again, as he would rather face down his critics than have them mock him out of sight. Schoeck's friends assumed that it was such satirical verses that had attracted him to the cycle, but if the strength of the music is a reliable guide, then it was the love songs that appealed to him the most. They contain some of the most blatantly erotic imagery that he would ever set to music. The central poem runs thus:

> I hold you in my arms, tenderly you hold the rose,
> And the rose holds deep within it a young bee;
> Thus we arrange ourselves like pearls on life's single thread,
> Thus we rejoice as petal upon petal gathers round the rose,
> And when my kiss glows on your mouth, a flame darts
> Into the heart of the bee as it mates with the chalice of the rose.

—and its music is suitably erotic, the flute and bass clarinet weaving a canon around the voice to a background of luscious triplet figurations in the piano. The song climaxes on a top F for the voice as the flame darts into the heart of the mating bee before subsiding into "an expansive Straussian postlude" (thus Puffett[5]), whose aesthetic effect is, obviously and intentionally, the musical equivalent of the post-coital cigarette.

Gaselen was also Schoeck's first continuous song cycle. The model he chose, as Puffett has demonstrated cogently, was *An die ferne Geliebte*, "Beethoven's continuous cycle with interludes, a recapitulation, and a well-balanced tonal scheme. All these devices [Schoeck] incorporated into *Gaselen,* almost as if he were afraid that the work would not stand up without them."[6] What Puffett did not know was that *An die ferne Geliebte* was the song cycle that Schoeck admired above all others and already knew well as an accompanist—he had played it just over a year before, on 30 March 1922 in St. Gallen, with Alfred Jerger as soloist. "Weisch," Schoeck once said to his nephew Georg, "d'bescht Zyklus isch d'*ferni Geliebti*" ("You know, the best cycle is the *Distant Beloved*").[7] The significance of the model might even go beyond the merely musical, given that Schoeck's longings were still very much for his own beloved in distant Geneva. He had interrupted his composition of the cycle to go on a brief concert tour to Holland with Ilona Durigo and had summoned up the courage to write to Mary from The Hague. He received no answer.

Example 17.1. *Gaselen* Op. 38, opening song. Copyright Breitkopf & Härtel. Reprinted by permission. "Ours is the fate of the Epigones who live in the vast halfway-world; look, how you squeeze one more drop from old lemon rinds." The "note row" is bracketed.

Puffett has also remarked at length on the latently serial implications of Schoeck's compositional technique in *Gaselen*, in particular the manner in which the opening melody takes a "series" of notes that is repeated, the rhythm being altered at each repetition (see ex. 17.1).

Puffett writes that "the comparison with serial music is not gratuitous. In both methods the notes are conceived as sound objects, independent of durations and stresses," and further points out that in the *Hafez Songs* and elsewhere Schoeck "had already started to organize series of chords, as well as series of notes, in this way. But so far as the 'serial' organisation of melody is concerned, this is his most rigorous experiment so far."[8]

Puffett's analysis of Schoeck's compositional technique here circles around a possibility that remains unspoken, probably because the historical sources that would have allowed its consideration (Corrodi's diaries) were unknown to researchers at the time of writing. For Schoeck's "serial" technique here is at once so close to Schoenberg's theory and yet so far removed from it (in its refusal to acknowledge all its harmonic implications), that it is almost as if he had overheard those theories, misunderstood them, and then put those misunderstandings into practice. But if we investigate the chronology of Schoeck's sudden surge of interest in a quasi-serial organization of his musical material, then this is precisely one possibility that we must consider. Schoenberg wrote his first twelve-tone piece in 1921, the prelude for the Suite Op. 25. He informed his students

Joseph Rufer and Erwin Stein of his "discovery," but it was not until early 1923, when he had completed the Suite Op. 25 and the Piano Pieces Op. 23, that he told his other students about the "method."[9] In his old-age reminiscences of the Salzburg festival of 1923, Schoeck recalled that "the atmosphere back then was already Schoenbergian."[10] His word is "verschönbergt," which has a pejorative implication; but what is noteworthy is not his apparent resentment but the fact that the Schoenbergian aspect of the festival is what remained uppermost in his memory. Besides Alban Berg, several other figures from Schoenberg's immediate circle were certainly prominent at the festival, such as Paul Pisk, Fritz Kaltenborn, Alexander Zemlinsky, Joseph Rufer, Egon Wellesz, and Heinrich Jalowetz. So although the first published explanation of Schoenberg's "method of composition with twelve tones" did not appear until 1924,[11] the "method" itself will surely have been a matter of eager discussion in the coffee houses and concert hall foyers of Salzburg in August 1923. However, since the prime players had not yet begun to realize the consequences of Schoenberg's theory and would in any case have been hesitant to share their knowledge in detail with a foreigner (Schoeck's Swiss accent would have stuck out like a sore thumb among the Viennese), we can safely assume that Schoeck will have learnt of it primarily through overhearing festival gossip. How else are we to explain the sudden leap from the techniques of the *Hafez Songs* to those of the first song of *Gaselen,* which was written just after Schoeck's first contact with Schoenberg's students, and which has what even Puffett terms a "manifesto-like quality"?[12] There is no doubt that Schoeck intended *Gaselen* to be his answer to the modernists of Salzburg, for he put it on the program for the next festival of the Allgemeiner deutscher Musikverein in June 1924 and—more tellingly—on the program for the next festival of the ISCM, one year after his first. But *Gaselen* was not a one-off experiment, for similarly quasi-"serial" passages are to be found in his next works too, as we shall see.

The ironic, satirical element in *Gaselen* is what has received most comment over the years. Corrodi maintained that Schoeck's target was the modernists of Salzburg and Paris—but this was another example of his own wish-fulfilment, for Schoeck's satire in *Gaselen* is as much directed at himself as anyone else. He seems to have felt himself situated in that "vast halfway-world" of which the first poem speaks, between the Romantics and the moderns, with the music of *Gaselen* an attempt to bridge the two. Puffett, with no reason to doubt Corrodi's assurances, complained of the work's thematic material that it was in places of a "triviality . . . that debases the composer more than it does the enemies he wishes to satirise."[13] But Schoeck was unaware of having any enemies; on the contrary, he was keen to ally himself with the modernists. If the thematic material is in places uncomplicated, it is surely because the composer was not yet wholly comfortable with the processes of thematic transformation that he had begun to employ. A comparison with Schoenberg's earliest twelve-note works is perhaps not inappropriate, for in each case the composer was engaging with new compositional techniques. Those twelve-tone works too have something of a "manifesto" about them, and their thematic content is times arguably no less "trivial."

Puffett felt that the love songs of *Gaselen* blunt the edge of the satire; but if one accepts that the latter was never the *raison d'être* of the cycle, then one can find, on the contrary, that it only serves to heighten the impact of the erotic lyrics. The stylistic plurality of the work thus becomes, not a weakness, but one of its major strengths.

Chapter Eighteen

Raging Queen

Since Mary had left him, Schoeck had on the one hand been stilling his physical needs with numerous willing women, but on the other hand he had begun to make loud pronouncements to his male friends about the wickedness of the weaker sex. It was in early November 1923, in the midst of one of these misogynistic tirades, that Corrodi suggested the drama *Penthesilea* by Heinrich von Kleist (1777–1811) as an opera topic. Schoeck was immediately attracted by the idea, so Corrodi set to work on a libretto. Kleist's play is a variant of the story of Achilles and Penthesilea, the Queen of the Amazons. According to Greek myth, they met on opposite sides on the battlefield of Troy, where Achilles killed Penthesilea but fell in love with her upon seeing her dead body. In Kleist, however, Achilles wounds Penthesilea, who flees, then faints. He captures her and falls in love. But in order to awaken her feelings for him, he pretends that he is in fact *her* prisoner when she regains consciousness. Their love scene is interrupted as the battle nears again. Penthesilea is rescued by her troops and is compelled to face the reality of her situation. Achilles now sends a message that they should meet in single combat, for he intends to give himself up to her. Convinced that he has betrayed her love, she rides out in the full panoply of battle. Her mind now quite unhinged, she joins her dogs, who tear apart her unarmed lover with their teeth. When she finally comes to her senses, she explains her actions with a Freudian slip: "Küsse, Bisse, das reimt sich, und wer recht von Herzen liebt, kann schon das eine für das Andre greifen"—"Kisses, bites: that rhymes, and whoever really loves from the heart can easily mistake the one for the other"—though Penthesilea's idea of giving a hickey has left her with flesh dripping from her molars. The play ends with her *Liebestod* over the mangled body of her lover. The play is all the more harrowing for being written in a language of rare emotive power and complex, tightly controlled syntax.

The fact that Schoeck's misogyny should have prompted Corrodi to suggest an opera on *Penthesilea,* and that Schoeck should have found it so apposite, is noteworthy, because it is not *per se* a misogynistic work. Rather does it present all of man's fears of inadequacy toward the opposite sex. Here man is at the mercy of woman and is subject to her complete control—sexually, emotionally, and physically. For could there be a sexual consummation more complete, or more perverse, than one in which "death" is no metaphor for (male) orgasm, but in which the woman takes full possession of the man by devouring him? As is usual with misogynists, Schoeck's anger at womankind was a result, it seems, of fear:

specifically his fear that in having lost Mary he had also lost the long-standing sense of control upon which he had earlier prided himself in his sexual relationships. But apart from reflecting his own current mental and emotional state, the play may well have attracted him because of its superficial similarity to the topic of Hindemith's *Mörder, Hoffnung der Frauen,* whose modernity had so appealed to Fritz Busch back in Stuttgart in 1922. Schoeck, let us not forget, was still very keen to be "modern" himself.

A few days after Corrodi had suggested the topic, Schoeck composed Penthesilea's principal motive and decided upon the chords that were to characterize both Achilles and Penthesilea's confidante, Prothoe. Within a week of deciding to write the opera, Schoeck was already able to recite large chunks of the original Kleist from memory. He would horrify waitresses by loudly declaiming at them: "Staub lieber, als ein Weib sein, das nicht reizt!" ("Better to be dust than a woman without charms!"). By the end of the month he had decided to jettison Kleist's whole exposition and compress everything into a single act, so that the opera would, in his words, "rush past like a tempest."[1] Corrodi could not agree with this drastic change to his conception of the work, so their collaboration was abandoned before it even started. Schoeck mentioned no more of the project for several weeks.

In the meantime Schoeck had been busy in the St. Gallen City Theater once again, conducting the ensemble of the Munich State Opera (including Maria Ivogün and Karl Erb) in two performances of Donizetti's *Don Pasquale* on 15 and 16 November 1923—one could hardly imagine a topic further removed from his projected *Penthesilea.*[2] His *Elegie* received its first Winterthur performance two weeks later, on 28 November, sung by the Dutchman Thomas Denijs (and with no less a figure than Arthur Honegger in the audience), and then one day after that, on 29 November, his Second String Quartet was given its world premiere in the Zurich Tonhalle. The ensemble, as for his First Quartet a decade earlier, was the Zurich String Quartet, led by Willem de Boer. At the party in the Kronenhalle afterward, the composer's friends included the "Miss Fehrmann" who had served as a go-between for him and Mary. She was also interested in him, though he ignored her the whole evening. Also present was Angelie. Although she receives little mention in the literature, she was important enough for Schoeck to give her the manuscripts of both "Die Entschwundene" and *Gaselen.* The former was given its first performance by Ilona Durigo in Zurich, in a *Liederabend* with Schoeck on 9 January 1924. Relations between them were no longer good. Perhaps Durigo was for some reason offended that Schoeck had begun an affair with her friend Angelie (though she should by now have been accustomed to his serial conquests), or perhaps Schoeck had allowed his current misogyny to come to the fore in conversation with her. In any case, he seems now to have found her manner of interpretation "too Romantic" (proof once more that he was now determined to be "modern"). He made his dissatisfaction clear to her, and she felt deeply wounded—after all, she had done more than anyone to promote his songs. At that concert in January 1924, he even refused to go back on stage to accompany her encores, so she went on and accompanied herself instead. Durigo would sing in Gluck's *Orfeo* under Schoeck at the St. Gallen City Theater one year later, but their relationship would never be the same again. She later claimed that Schoeck had said to her face that she "had been more of a hindrance than a help" to him.[3]

February 1924 was a busy month for Schoeck in St. Gallen. On the eighth he conducted Strauss's *Bürger als Edelmann* Suite and Honegger's *Pastorale d'été*, and on the 22nd he conducted Emanuel Feuermann in a Haydn cello concerto. In between the two he was able to realize a long-held desire by putting Hugo Wolf's opera *Der Corregidor* on stage. He had come across the opera several years earlier, and something of its Mediterranean ambience is to be found in his own *Don Ranudo*. It is not unlikely that Schoeck saw in Wolf's fate a mirror of his own—that of a song composer whose greatest wish was to become a successful opera composer. He later admitted that the *Corregidor*'s orchestration was faulty, and that its dramatic proportions were badly balanced. But for the moment he remained convinced that the work's neglect on the part of the operatic establishment was a travesty of justice. Among those present at the work's St. Gallen premiere on 20 February 1924 was Ernst Krenek, the darling of the previous Salzburg festival. Werner Reinhart had provided him with a scholarship to enable him and his wife Anna (Mahler's daughter) to spend two years in Switzerland—and he was rewarded within weeks of Krenek's arrival by the dedication of the Little Suite for Clarinet and Piano, Op. 28, in time for his fortieth birthday. Krenek was fourteen years younger than Schoeck and, despite his own recent immense success, he seems to have been in awe of the older man. Corrodi later recalled how Krenek's obvious deference to Schoeck in the company of others seemed excessive to his Swiss colleagues. Krenek moved to Zurich soon after the *Corregidor* in St. Gallen, and during the next months he was a frequent visitor to Schoeck's coffee circle at the Pfauen restaurant on the Zeltweg. He followed Schoeck's progress on *Penthesilea* with particular interest, and Schoeck was gracious in return, openly defending the younger generation's desire to create something new.

Given their common patron, we can assume that Krenek was also present at the world premiere of *Gaselen* on 23 Feburary in Winterthur, just three days after *Corregidor*. It came at the end of a concert that also included a suite by Karl Heinrich David for flute, oboe, clarinet, horn, and bassoon and seven songs by Schoeck for voice and piano. The baritone soloist was Felix Loeffel; the bass clarinet part in the ensemble was played by Reinhart himself. It is noteworthy that the first of the solo songs on the program was "Nicht düstre, Theosoph, so tief" from the *Hafez Songs*, Op. 33, for it is one of the most extreme of the set, and one that Schoeck had not performed in Salzburg. It is as if he wanted to smooth his audience's passage into *Gaselen* by demonstrating its stylistic proximity to his existing music. The evening, however, was not a success. Loeffel sang flat, Schoeck accompanied badly, and to cap it all, a power failure meant that the concert had to be interrupted. It was only concluded once enough candles had been found and lit. The invited audience was more polite than enthusiastic, and showed it by its restrained applause.[4] It was not an auspicious start to Schoeck's career as a would-be modernist. Karl Heinrich David's own impressions of the evening were conveyed by letter to his friend Hermann von Glenck four days later; they are noteworthy because the critical tone he adopts is a far remove from the praise he would bestow in his printed reviews of Schoeck's music for the next twenty years.

> Schoeck's *Gaselen* . . . disappointed somewhat. The good fellow dabbles in modernism there, which neither suits him nor is something that he can actually do. It's a pity that his vanity seduces him into making such concessions; he wants to be first in line everywhere. His successes of last year have rather spoilt him, and he now plays the Lord God all too much, and in the process offends many a good friend. He exaggerates his importance, for to be the Lord God in Zurich isn't anything at all, and I fear that if he carries on like this, then he will run quite wild, and will also alienate his supporters here.[5]

A few weeks later Schoeck returned to work on his operatic project, *Penthesilea*. After the disagreement with Corrodi over the libretto, Schoeck decided to set Kleist's original text itself, and assigned his cousin Léon Oswald the task of cutting it down into a manageable shape. Although it had been drastically shortened—the opera begins with Penthesilea's first appearance after her defeat in battle (Kleist's scene 8)—Schoeck was proud that the text still "did not contain even a comma that was not by Kleist." He now also decided to have certain passages recited, not sung—just as he had planned before with "Jugendgedenken" and *Gaselen* but had not carried out. This time, however, he did not change his mind. Although he had barely started on the music, he already knew the timbres that he was aiming for, and he was going to include two pianos in the orchestra "in order to achieve a metallic sound." He also said that "there'll not be much left of traditional tonality."[6] Walter Schulthess told Corrodi that he was sure their friend was strongly influenced by the pianos and percussion of Stravinsky's *Les noces*, about which he hadn't been able to stop talking the year before. In fact, the most obvious influence of *Les noces* might well have been the first note that the listener is aware of: an E, which is the top note of the first chord of each work. The opening of *Les noces* is undeniably striking, and since Schoeck had perfect pitch, the impact of its first page probably remained associated in his mind with that particular note, as well as with the acciaccaturas that follow it (in *Penthesilea*, it is the first two chords in the orchestra that feature an acciaccatura; see ex. 18.1). The play *Penthesilea* was itself a point of contact between Schoeck and Schulthess, for the latter had begun (but never completed) a symphonic poem based on it back in 1915.

Example 18.1. The opening of *Penthesilea,* Op. 39, with "not . . . much left of traditional tonality." Copyright Bärenreiter.

Easter fell late in 1924, on 20 April, and Schoeck now went to Brissago for a spring break. Perhaps he hoped to summon up the muses that had inspired him to begin his *Venus* there, for it was in Brissago that he now composed the opening scene of his new opera. He told Corrodi upon his return: "The opera will be very homophonic; the real melody is formed by Kleist's words. The music gives them no more than harmony and rhythm." He had also decided to include eight clarinets in his orchestra (the number employed by Strauss in *Elektra;* Schoeck in the end trumped him by using ten). By early June Schoeck had finished the opening scenes up to Achilles' entrance, plus Penthesilea's final monologue, and parts of the scene between Achilles and Diomedes. One passage was giving him particular trouble, namely Penthesilea's lines "Der Mensch kann gross, ein Held im Leiden sein, doch göttlich ist er, wenn er selig ist" ("Man can be great in suffering, even a hero; but when he is happy, he is like a god"). The music for it came to him at seven o'clock in the morning, after an all-night drinking session with Hermann Hubacher, and is one of the lyrical highpoints of the opera. Hubacher reminisced several years later about how Schoeck had often visited him at this time:

> We sat through many a night, discussed everything over wine, and you played [*Penthesilea*] scene by scene at the piano. My old grand piano couldn't cope with it any more and perished under the Penthesilea motive. I see you still, when after such a night you rode on my bicycle along the Zollikerstrasse toward the city on a bright spring morning: a traveling musician, the score on the handlebars, and you waved back one last time with your straw hat.[7]

A few days later Schoeck traveled to Frankfurt am Main to conduct his *Gaselen* with Loeffel at the annual festival of the Allgemeiner deutscher Musikverein—his first appearance as a "modernist" among modernists. There was some surprise at the stylistic turn that he had taken, and in *Die Musik* the critic Walter Schenk even went so far as to describe the work as "purely cerebral."[8] Schoeck was delighted at the reception accorded to him, probably because he felt he was now being taken seriously by the people who mattered on the contemporary scene. But the star of Frankfurt—and in this, Schoeck agreed with everyone else—was Alban Berg, with his *Three Fragments from "Wozzeck,"* conducted by Scherchen on 15 June. Werner Reinhart had ordered two copies of the vocal score of the opera when Berg had published it privately in late 1922, so it is not wholly impossible that Schoeck might have perused it in the meantime. He was bowled over upon hearing it, not least by Berg's use of the orchestra. Several years later he could still remember precise details of the work's instrumentation. He was just as enthusiastic about Berg himself, with whom he had now become a little better acquainted. He was, he told Corrodi: "A decadent fellow à la [Oscar] Wilde, oversensitive, in Schoenberg's entourage, but more sincere and genuine then he, a man who has suffered much and really empathized with what he has written."[9] Berg's use of instrumental forms in his opera was a matter of intense discussion (fueled by Berg himself with his own program notes), and it is probably no coincidence that Schoeck's *Penthesilea* was soon including scenes based on ostinati, on a repeated rhythm and on a kind of "tone row."

When Schoeck returned to Zurich, the city's music lovers were being enthralled by Arturo Toscanini, who was on tour with the orchestra of La Scala Milan. The second and last of their concerts in the Tonhalle took place on 17 June. Schoeck declined to attend, but he did not want to be alone and so spent the early evening with his brother Ralph before wandering down to the Kronenhalle Restaurant, where he knew his friends would appear after the concert. And so they did. One of them was Carl Friedrich Wiegand, a schoolteacher and dramatist whose speciality was improvising in verse for anything up to half an hour at a time. He had brought along with him a young German soprano by the name of Hilde Bartscher. She had spent the previous few months singing at the Zurich Theater, her roles including that of the Christelflein in Pfitzner's opera of the same name, and she was soon due to leave for an engagement at a theater in Germany. Hilde recalled the evening in detail fifty years later, as follows:

> [Wiegand spots Schoeck amidst the clouds of smoke in the Kronenhalle, and cries:] "The whole winter I've been wanting to introduce you to this tender blue butterfly who can sing too!" Schoeck looked at me intensely, then pushed a few chairs, waved to the left and the right, and suddenly I was sitting at his side. I really only saw the unusually big, beaming blue eyes when he asked me what I did, what my plans were, and made me promise to visit him without fail before I left Zurich, also stipulating the day and the hour.
>
> There was not much time before last orders at midnight. . . . There was a unison chorus of: "Schoeck, we'll go to your place!" and my attempts at taking my leave were to no avail! My arms linked to the left and right, I arrived

at Schoeck's home on the Zeltweg. Where could everyone find space in that cramped room?—it was almost filled up by a large grand piano, which had already begun to sound under Schoeck's hands before the last guests had climbed the stairs. One felt that he could hardly wait to play what he had most recently composed in the opera *Penthesilea,* on which he was currently working. He often repeated the same passage, singing the text softly, a cigar in the corner of his mouth, his gleaming eyes turned to his listeners, putting them under the spell of his completely new sounds and the compelling aura of his personality. After *Penthesilea,* suffused with passion, Schoeck suddenly entered his world of song—and how different it was! . . . this Schoeck-Schubert sat before me at the piano and played half the night with an intensity of expression that no one could evade. Unnoticed, I slipped onto the small balcony in order to get some air and to be alone a little with all the unusual impressions of this overlong night. Dawn was breaking and the birds began to twitter. Schoeck suddenly stood next to me and said gently: "I have difficult years behind me and am grateful to have met you. Perhaps I could even become a happy man once more . . ." Schoeck insisted on taking me home, taking care to place his coat over my light summer dress, and thus we walked without speaking along the Zeltweg to the nearby [Hotel] Florhof, where I was living. "You will definitely come, as agreed" were his last words as we took our leave. Did we perhaps suspect that fate had already made its decision?[10]

Hilde's recollection of the evening is in many aspects identical to that of Corrodi, who was also present. It would nevertheless seem—how could it be otherwise?—that time's rosy spectacles had somewhat transfigured her night. In Corrodi's more nuanced recollections, Schoeck placed Hilde on the chaise longue, directly opposite the piano—"where others of similarly sympathetic type had sat before her." Schoeck obviously had no intention of letting Hilde demonstrate her singing prowess, wrote Corrodi, and he began playing from the manuscript of *Penthesilea* that was lying on the piano. It was the passage shortly after the entrance of the wounded Amazon queen: "Oh, my soul is weary unto death"—and he soon put it to one side as inappropriate for his intentions. He then reached for his *Venus,* singing Horace's final aria, staring longingly at Hilde all the while. Then he moved on to the twelfth song of the *Elegie,* "Herbstklage." "Watch out," said Léon Oswald to Hilde, "now he's casting out his most effective bait." Schoeck overheard him, broke off, and stood up angrily, refusing to continue. But his guests smoothed his ruffled feathers, and so he resumed the *Elegie,* singing from "Welke Rose" until the end of the cycle. He accompanied Hilde home afterward, as she herself recalled.[11]

Two weeks after this first meeting Schoeck took Hilde for a three-day holiday on St. Peter's Island in the Bienne Lake, to the north of Bern. Corrodi later heard that Hilde had demonstrated a fondness for nude bathing, which was no doubt intended to fire Schoeck's passion, as it did. But Hilde was no easy fish to catch. Her adamant refusal to "go all the way" outside the bounds of matrimony both repelled and fascinated him. Not since Stefi Geyer over a decade earlier, it seems, had his arts of seduction failed him. A few days later Hilde was at the center of another all-night "Schoeckiade" for the composer and his friends, when he (unusually) played from Wagner's operas, though all the while denouncing him as a "magician . . . but dangerous; woe to the musician who succumbs to him! He's a vampire who sucks our blood! . . . a Lucifer, a fallen angel."[12] He proceeded to sing several songs by Brahms and concluded by playing the whole finale of Bruckner's Fifth Symphony—from memory, as was everything else that evening. The "magician" in this context was Schoeck himself, and his demonstration was obviously intended to prompt Hilde into succumbing. She clearly fell under his spell; but still she did not let him bed her. "If only she weren't German," he moaned to Corrodi.[13]

Hilde's sister had also been in Zurich at this time, and she now returned to Frankfurt to give their parents risqué reports of her sister's attendance at all-night parties. Their faith in Hilde's virtue was considerably weaker than her own resolve, and they wrote her a letter full of reproaches. Hilde showed it to Schoeck in the presence of his friends, at which he cried out "Just look what I'd be marrying into"—which is our only proof that the nuptial question had been raised this early in their relationship. It suggests that Hilde was considering quite specific goals. Corrodi wrote in his diary at this time that she appeared to everyone "an innocent, harmless child," though her subsequent behavior suggests instead a steely determination on her part to get what she wanted.[14]

Hilde returned home to Frankfurt for the summer, but she was intent on returning in the autumn. Schoeck's more immediate concern was his appearance at that year's Salzburg Festival of the ISCM. The program was perhaps not as exciting as it had been the year before, though it did include Stravinsky's Octet and Hindemith's String Trio Op. 34 (the latter work a world premiere). Composers of a more moderate modernism were well represented this time. The works performed included Arnold Bax's Viola Sonata, Erik Satie's *Socrate* (in the version with chamber orchestra), John Ireland's Cello Sonata, and works by Georges Auric, Darius Milhaud, Francis Poulenc, and Karol Szymanowski. *Socrate* very nearly proved the undoing of the ISCM itself, when the French section refused to pay for its performance and threatened to leave the organization altogether. Reinhart paid the costs from his own pocket and saved the day.[15] Of interest to us here is the fact that the program also featured two extended works for voice, in which a string quartet was the core accompaniment: Peter Warlock's *The Curlew,* in which the quartet is joined by a flute and a cor anglais, and Ralph Vaughan Williams's *On Wenlock Edge,* where it is supported by a piano.[16] Eight years later Schoeck would himself embark on a song cycle with string quartet accompaniment, the *Notturno,* and it is not impossible that his experiences in Salzburg in 1924 exerted a certain influence in his choice of accompanying medium—the *Notturno's* fourth movement in particular shares certain autumnal resonances with Warlock's work.

Schoeck again traveled with Reinhart, though this time they took the sleeper train. His contribution to the festival was his *Gaselen*, which Heinrich Rehkemper sang under his direction. Reinhart himself played the bass clarinet in it; the piano part was assigned to Walter Frey, the younger brother of the brilliant composer-pianist Emil Frey. Walter Frey would remain one of Schoeck's most dedicated interpreters over the years and in fact owed his reputation as one of the leading pianists for contemporary music largely to his ISCM appearances (his most famous world premiere would be that of Berg's Chamber Concerto two years after Salzburg, together with Stefi Geyer). This Salzburg festival occasioned one of the briefest, and oddest, reviews of Schoeck's career, when the unnamed critic of the *Musical Times* wrote of *Gaselen:* "This seems to me a mass of humbug. More I cannot say." But since he also judged Satie's *Socrate* a "sacrilege" and was sure that "the Hindemith-Jarnach type of music is wrong . . . the condemnation of itself," Schoeck was at least in good company.[17]

After their return from Salzburg Schoeck paid Reinhart a visit at the Fluh; he seems otherwise to have spent the summer working on his *Penthesilea*. It was the first time since *Erwin und Elmire* that he had worked on a large-scale opera whose text lay complete before him at the moment of his beginning its composition (though in this case, "complete" needs to be qualified somewhat, as Schoeck had still not made his final decision on which sections would be excised in the later part of the play). Work was not progressing as swiftly as he would have liked. To be sure, Kleist's syntax is at times tortuous, and few composers have ever ventured to set him to music. But perhaps Schoeck also missed the very cajoling and nagging that had characterized his working relationship with Rüeger on *Ranudo* and *Venus*. Working "with" a dead librettist, it seems, just did not fulfil him in the same way. By the end of October 1924 the new opera was sketched up to the end of the love scene. Another year would pass before work on it was completed.

Chapter Nineteen

Storms in the Pigeon Loft

Hilde Bartscher returned to Zurich in autumn 1924 with the consent of her parents, whom she had apparently convinced of her continued innocence. But the object of her attraction seemed to have lost interest in her. Schoeck's thoughts were again with Mary, though his bodily needs were still being satisfied by Angelie and numerous other women—"wie in einem Taubenschlag," as he boasted to Corrodi.[1] The literal translation thereof is "as in a pigeon loft," though its meaning in English is conveyed more idiomatically by saying that his bedroom was "like Grand Central station." Whether or not his lack of interest and his boasting were together intended to prompt Hilde into joining the other pigeons in his loft, she nevertheless remained adamantly unfluttered and untouchable. It was Angelie who was in tow when Schoeck attended a performance of Stravinsky's Concerto for Piano and Winds in Winterthur on 26 November 1924. Angelie years later could still recall fragments of their conversation after the concert. Schoeck remarked to Stravinsky that he found his music "rather cool," to which Stravinsky replied, with sovereign disregard for the accusative case: "Ich liebe der Frost"—"I love the frost."[2] Toward the end of the year Schoeck attended a lieder recital that Angelie herself gave in Bishofszell. It was part of a Mörike evening organized by Rüeger, who gave a brief lecture on the same occasion. Schoeck was afterward full of praise for both singer and speaker.

At Christmas, 1924 Schoeck went home to Brunnen—without female accompaniment—and it was there that his brother Paul drafted for him the text for the final scene of *Penthesilea*. Why this had not been done by his original collaborator, their cousin Léon, is not clear. But in any case, the words were all Kleist, and neither of Schoeck's literary helpers was later featured on the title page of the opera. Schoeck now felt advanced enough in the composition of his opera to begin contemplating where it should be performed. The conductor of *Ranudo*'s German premiere, Fritz Busch, visited Zurich in this winter, and expressed a wish to be assigned the premiere. He was now music director of the Dresden State Opera and was continuing that house's long tradition of presenting world premieres of contemporary works. By the beginning of January 1925 Schoeck had reached Achilles' departure for battle, and he was assuring Corrodi that the whole opera would soon be finished. But shortly thereafter he fell into a depression and was unable to compose anything for some four months. He was not inactive, however, for he still had his regular conducting commitments at St. Gallen, where his programs reflected his increasing interest in contemporary music. On 3 February 1925, for example, he conducted a program that included

Strauss's *Macbeth*, Stravinsky's *Pulcinella* Suite, Honegger's *Pacific 231*, and the Swiss premiere of Krenek's Violin Concerto Op. 29, played by Willem de Boer. It was less than a month since Krenek's concerto had received its world premiere in Dessau, and the composer himself was in attendance in St. Gallen. So was Reinhart, who was playing clarinet as an extra in the orchestra. Nor was this concert a one-off occurrence, but merely one of several all-contemporary programs that Schoeck put on in St. Gallen in these years, in which works by Krenek, Hindemith, and Honegger were regular features. In several cases—as with Krenek's Concerto Grosso No. 2, Op. 25, performed later in 1925—Schoeck conducted these works many years before they were heard in either Winterthur or Zurich.[3] His policy of programming so much contemporary music was daring by any standards, let alone for a provincial town like St. Gallen. Even Reinhart was impressed and wrote to Hans Bärlocher to say so, adding that in Winterthur they had resorted to bringing modern works in "homeopathic doses" in order for them not to be rejected out of hand by the public.[4]

On 4 February 1925 the Zurich City Theater mounted a production of Schoeck's *Das Wandbild*—the first scenic production, in fact, since its world premiere four years earlier. Among those in the audience were Hilde and Corrodi, who both, independently of each other, decided not to attend the post-performance convivialities and ended up walking home together. Hilde poured out her heart to him—it must be wonderful, she said, for a young woman to leave her father's house and be taken up straightaway in the "protecting hands of an older man."[5] But Schoeck still seemed to have no intention of cementing their relationship with a wedding ring, and she was unable to cope with his moods. She was persistent, however, and had no intention of diverting from her dual tactic of temptation and denial. Schoeck still did not want for female attention. After he conducted Loeffel in a performance of the *Elegie* in Zurich on 4 May, Karl Heinrich David wrote of it to Hermann von Glenck on the fifteenth of the month as follows:

> Recently Schoeck's *Elegie* was performed here. It was terrible. The whole hall full of hysterical amateurs, women in particular, milking their tear ducts . . . I'm afraid I can't go along with this overestimation and doting. Even as a person, Schoeck is going to seed more and more. For weeks, he spends afternoons and evenings and nights in the pub, and his mornings in bed.[6]

Reinhart invited Schoeck to join him at the ISCM festival in Prague but had his offer turned down, for Schoeck was working hard on *Penthesilea*. With the exception of Janáček's *Cunning Little Vixen*, Bartók's *Dance Suite*, and Vaughan Williams's Third Symphony, Schoeck did not miss much. The work that might have really interested him, Stravinsky's *Symphonies of Wind Instruments*, with its montage-like construction, was dropped from the program at short notice[7]— though Schoeck might already have got to know the score via Reinhart.

According to Corrodi's diary, Schoeck finished the composition sketch of *Penthesilea* on 13 May 1925. He had in the meantime received word from the theater in Dessau that its director, Franz von Hoesslin, was interested in being given the premiere of the work.[8] But Schoeck was still hoping for the more prestigious venue of Dresden. Luckily for him, the Dresden Opera visited Zurich in June to give a number of guest performances, and Schoeck was able to play his new opera to both Fritz Busch and the theater's director, Alfred Reucker—the same man who had for over a decade been in charge of the Zurich Theater, and thus had been responsible for the world premieres of *Erwin* and *Don Ranudo*. Schoeck's impression was that they did not like it, but he nevertheless received written confirmation within a month that they would accept the work for performance, with the premiere planned for 1926 (it would in fact be postponed until early 1927). Schoeck attended the third performance that the Dresden Opera gave of Strauss's *Intermezzo* but claimed afterward to have liked the music only for the toboggan ride. Perhaps he was smarting over what he perceived as a lack of interest in his own work. He must have paid attention to *Intermezzo* all the same, for just three years later he would embark on an opera that would also depict a marital squabble, and whose origins were just as autobiographical as the opera by Strauss.

In anticipation of an impending first performance of *Penthesilea*, Schoeck worked hard to finish the full score by the end of the year. Schädelin wrote the following in his diary on 14 October 1925:

> Yesterday I visited Schoeck with Brun and Loeffel. We find him working on a page of the score of his *Penthesilea*. And what a page! Schoeck had a desk of pinewood made especially in Brunnen, arranged quite steeply, at some 30°, broad and spacious like an architect's drawing board. At the top there's a frame attached to a hinge, on which he can place his sketches, which he thus has nicely in front of him. The manuscript paper lies on this desk: very large in format, much bigger than double folio, and what is remarkable is: it has been printed especially, with all the instruments listed on the left. Breitkopf & Härtel printed them for him. . . .
>
> Brun plays the first movement of his Fourth Symphony, which he has just finished orchestrating, while Schoeck reads the score, following it on his desk . . . [at one point Schoeck says:] "The bassoon, swathed in violas and cellos, won't be heard, because it's not playing in its beautiful register." . . . As we walk home, Brun says that he thinks extraordinarily highly of Schoeck's judgment, also in matters of orchestration, for there he possesses an unerring genius for accuracy.
>
> Schoeck is now working as a rule from 4 in the afternoon until 9 or 10 at night, then goes to bed between 2 and 5, and sleeps until the afternoon. It struck me how seriously submerged Schoeck is in his work.[9]

The full score of *Penthesilea* was completed on 28 December 1925. Busch and Reucker had requested that the parts be ready early in the New Year, so Schoeck went ahead with commissioning a copyist to write out the parts, without first negotiating with his publisher Breitkopf to secure their rights to the work and their concomitant duties with regard to producing and hiring out the performance materials. This broke at the least the spirit of a contract that he agreed with Breitkopf in January 1926, which stated clearly that he was not to offer them any work that had already been "exploited" in artistic or business terms without their consent. Breitkopf subsequently refused to have anything to do with the opera. Instead, Schoeck's friend Alfred Hüni, a local piano dealer, stepped in to help. He was fully aware of Schoeck's incompetence in financial and organizational matters and was soon acting as coordinator for the preparation of the vocal score and parts—the cost of the latter alone was already running to several thousand marks. Busch's second-in-command, Hermann Kutzschbach, offered to help with preparing the vocal score so that it would be straightforward enough to use in rehearsal; its final layout would owe much to his input.[10]

It is not without irony that the last quarter of 1925 saw both the completion of Schoeck's "battle of the sexes" and the beginning of just such a battle on his own territory—though at the time it seemed to him as though such battles were to be a thing of the past. Hilde Bartscher had remained in Zurich throughout 1925, still pursuing Schoeck, still determined to domesticate him, and still a virgin. He in turn had become increasingly fascinated by her, by her beauty, and—above all—by her chastity. She cajoled him, claimed she would leave him for another man, and finally threatened to leave Switzerland unless they married. Only when she was able to show him her train ticket home—booked, bought, and tucked safely away in her handbag—did he capitulate.[11] Their engagement was made public in the *Tagblatt der Stadt Zürich,* the official organ of the city authorities from which all municipal announcements are made to this day, including impending changes in the marital status of its citizens. The *Tagblatt* is read by many, so anyone hoping to marry in secret in Zurich will be sorely disappointed. We do not know how many people Schoeck confided in before the *Tagblatt* conveyed the knowledge of his planned nuptials to the wider world along the Limmat, but we know for certain that he told three: Corrodi; Karl Heinrich David, who was to be best man; and—of course—Hilde herself. He presumably told his brothers too. Years later, David recalled Schoeck's decision:

> It seems as if it were today that Schoeck said to me, alone in the Pfauen, that it had to be. I felt a sudden surge of joy, but don't know why, for everything spoke against it. Unconscious emotion was in this case stronger than reason.[12]

Schoeck had no intention of telling his parents in advance, "because otherwise things will just be messed up again"—it seems that he still blamed his mother, in part, for his having lost Mary.[13] As chance would have it, he had spent the night before the *Tagblatt*'s announcement in the company of Wiegand, the very man who had introduced him to Hilde sixteen months earlier. But he had said nothing;

Wiegand recalled later only that Schoeck had been in a strange mood all night, playing the piano alternately with his hands and his posterior.

A few days after the publication of the banns, Schoeck's parents were informed by a third party. Although he was now thirty-nine, one cannot really blame his parents for being somewhat peturbed that their youngest was about to marry a woman of whom they knew absolutely nothing. We do not know the wording of their reaction, but we do have Schoeck's reply, written on 16 November, just a day before he left to conduct Loeffel in a performance of his *Elegie* in Karlsruhe:

> Nothing could have been further from my intention than to hurt you in any way with this; if this is nevertheless the case, then I am truly sorry, for I really did not think that embarrassing misunderstandings would be caused by a third party (who has nothing to do with the matter at all). That was a mistake that I readily admit . . . to write about [Hilde] goes against everything inside me, for I love her too much for it. I have every inner confidence that you will all appreciate and love her, as I do.[14]

Schoeck's insistence that the source "has nothing to do with the matter at all" suggests some involvement from a jealous party. One possibility would be Angelie. Although she was still married, she had not contemplated having to give up Schoeck. We cannot be sure that she was one of the many who had remained oblivious to his marriage plans, though it is likely. What we do know for certain is that she attempted suicide when she found out.[15] She survived, and she and Schoeck even managed to establish a platonic relationship in the 1930s.

The wedding took place on 14 December 1925. Schoeck thanked the city official in charge of the ceremony for doing his duty without any sermonizing or unnecessary bureaucracy. "If I'd known it were so easy," he quipped, "I'd have tried it many a time before." David wrote of the occasion: "I was best man, and in my memory this scene is enveloped in a blood-red sheen, for the registry office is lit by the brilliant colors of [Augusto] Giacometti's windows."[16]

Hilde had been warned in advance of Schoeck's ingrained bachelor habits—his convivial evenings with his male friends, his drinking, his going to bed late and sleeping into the afternoon, and so on. "Oh," she had smiled, "that will all change once we're married."[17] Poor Hilde. It didn't. There was no stag night, no hen night, no wedding reception, and no honeymoon. And while Hilde presumably kept her part of the bargain and on her wedding night at last allowed Schoeck to excise her ingrowing virginity, her husband had not taken the trouble to find a bigger apartment. It would be cruel to suggest that he might not even have waited twenty-four hours before packing her off to her apartment down the road in order to continue scoring his *Penthesilea* in peace, but it is probably not far from the truth. Not for another three months would they move in together. Hilde went to see him at three in the afternoon, though on evenings he would often leave her alone to go out drinking with his friends in the Kronenhalle. Schoeck took her to Brunnen to see his parents (see fig. 19.1), but his mother's reaction to her new daughter-in-law, Hilde recalled after her husband's death thirty years later, "was ghastly. I can even now think of it only in horror."[18] Schoeck stood up for her this time, and she found support, too, in her father-in-law, whom she remembered always with affection. Whether or not this first visit bore the brunt of the blame, Hilde's relationship with the Schoeck family home was to remain problematical. Brunnen was central to Schoeck's understanding of himself and his place in the world, and he refused to give it up. In the years to come, when he went to Brunnen to relax or to compose during the summer, Hilde would usually holiday somewhere else. Matters were complicated by Hilde's increasing dislike of Walter, the brother who ran the family hotel, whom she regarded as having all of her husband's bad qualities and none of his good ones[19]—though other reports of the man paint a quite different, sympathetic portrait. The extant photographs make it evident that he bore a greater facial resemblance to Othmar than did the other brothers, so perhaps he simply formed a convenient object upon whom Hilde could project her many marital frustrations.

Just a few days after Schoeck completed *Penthesilea,* he embarked on another large-scale work, this time the setting of Keller's narrative cycle *Lebendig begraben* that he had contemplated over two years earlier. By the end of January he was able to play Corrodi six of the fourteen songs, with only his volume of Keller's poems open at the piano, not a note committed to paper. Just a few days later he played Walter Schädelin eleven of the songs.[20] He soon finished the sketches, though the orchestration of the work would take him till the end of the year. Early February saw the arrival in the post of the privately printed vocal score of *Penthesilea,* and it was followed shortly afterward by the vocal score of *Venus,* which had just been published by Breitkopf at a cost of some eighty million marks.[21] Both were the work of one Karl Krebs, whose skill Schoeck greatly admired, though in fact both scores were closely based on the format of Schoeck's own composition sketches. It was Krebs, too, who would be assigned the vocal score of *Lebendig begraben.*

Schoeck and Hilde now began to look at possible apartments to rent. Since he got up at about three in the afternoon and was working constantly on his new cycle when he was not out drinking with friends, we can only surmise that he was still devoting very little attention to his new wife. He still had his regular concert duties in St. Gallen, and we have no record of Hilde accompanying him to them. He was soon also busy with rehearsals in the Zurich Tonhalle, for he conducted his *Erwin und Elmire* in concert there on 15 and 16 February 1926. Schoeck's friends found him surprisingly happy with his new marital state, though matters changed within a few months of their moving at last into a common apartment in May—a very small one. It was also on the Zeltweg, further along toward the Kreuzplatz, at no. 83, and thus lay roughly between the apartments that he and

Figure 19.1. Meeting the in-laws. Hilde, Othmar, and Walter Schoeck in Brunnen, 1926. Courtesy of Georg and Elisabeth Schoeck.

Figure 19.2. Othmar and Hilde during their "war of attrition." Courtesy of Zentralbibliothek Zürich.

Hilde had hitherto occupied separately. Karl Heinrich David later recalled the early months at no. 83 thus:

> In these primitive rooms a bitter war of attrition is fought out, an incredible, tenacious, heroic battle, of which no one knows a thing. It is made more difficult for the woman, because in her heightened passion she is so similar to Schoeck—but that is precisely the reason why she could keep up the fight.
>
> At the beginning, she does not have much terrain to defend—in any sense. His friends come in whenever they want, on afternoons and evenings, stay to eat, or they all go out. It could drive one to despair.[22]

From late May to early June Schoeck and Hilde spent two weeks at the Fluh—perhaps Reinhart realized that the couple needed time together, in an atmosphere where they were free of everyday domestic cares. But it did little good as far as Hilde was concerned. After their return, in mid-June 1926, she confessed to Corrodi that everything was going wrong. She was astonished that Schoeck had not changed his life's habits upon marrying her. Now she realized that what she had seen as the solution to everything—marriage—had in reality altered nothing. Othmar was ruining her health, she said, and she felt unable to continue their present life together. Night after night he sat drinking with his friends until two in the morning, and she was unable to live like that for more than a few days at a time. He had left her at home one night recently, at which she had gone to bed alone. When he had arrived back in the early hours, she had woken with a start, had failed to recognize him, and screamed out in fear of the supposed intruder. It took Schoeck several minutes to calm her down. Since then he had refrained from disturbing her whenever he returned late, sleeping next to his piano instead. Sometimes he would then work for a while before going to bed, which meant that he would get up even later the next day, and Hilde's days thus became as lonely as her nights. Over the course of the coming months she would resort to bouts of crying and semi-fainting fits when he wanted to leave at night, but it never stopped him from going out of the door.[23] In July, she became ill and was hospitalized briefly in the nearby Neumünster Clinic, where Schoeck went to visit her every day.

Fritz Busch was back in Zurich in mid-1926 for that year's ISCM Festival, which took place from 18 to 23 June. He informed Schoeck that he would be on tour in the United States later that year and thus would be unable to conduct the premiere of *Penthesilea* that was planned for October. It was assigned to Kutzschbach instead, which pleased Schoeck not a whit. The most advanced works on the ISCM program were Schoenberg's Wind Quintet, Op. 26 and Webern's Five Pieces for Orchestra, Op. 10, but we have no record of whether Schoeck attended.[24] The ISCM also seems to have brought Furtwängler once more to Zurich (he was the president of its German section), for he paid Schoeck a visit in the early summer. He was at the height of his fame in Germany, being chief conductor of both the Berlin Philharmonic and the Leipzig Gewandhaus Orchestras. Despite their acquaintance of some twenty years, Furtwängler had hitherto shown no interest in conducting Schoeck's music. But he had no doubt heard of Schoeck's impending operatic premiere at the prestigious Dresden State Opera, and perhaps he thought it was time to pay greater attention to his old colleague. He expressed an interest in *Lebendig begraben,* so Schoeck played it for him at the piano. But Furtwängler was taken aback by its modernity, exclaiming: "What about my good German public?" which Schoeck naturally assumed to signify a refusal.[25]

On 1 September 1926 Schoeck celebrated his fortieth birthday with just a few close friends. He and Hilde holidayed afterward at Rigi-Klösterli, where Carla Fassbind, one of Schoeck's relations on his mother's side, ran the "Krone" and "Sonne" hotels. As we have already noted, the Rigi had been popular with tourists since the nineteenth century—it was Richard Wagner's favorite mountain—and Klösterli, situated over halfway up on the route of the cog railway *Rigibahn,* is today still a popular tourist destination. At that altitude the vegetation becomes sparse, the air rarefied but invigorating, and the view spectacular. The Fassbinds in Rigi-Klösterli were in-laws with whom Hilde felt comfortable (the fact that Carla too married a creative artist—the painter Adolph Milich—might have helped), and it became one of the few places where she and Othmar would holiday together over the years to come. Since it lies not too far from Brunnen, it was perhaps yet another geographical compromise for the couple. Compromises, however, were proving difficult to find in all other aspects of their married life. Hilde was not working, and Schoeck's largely freelance career provided little more than their basic financial foundation. Schoeck will hardly have calculated that marrying a woman also means investing in more than the bare necessities of food, drink, shaving cream, a piano, and a bed. One day in November 1926 Corrodi called on the Schoecks, only to walk in on a huge argument. Schoeck had accompanied a second-rate (female) singer in a concert, simply for the three hundred francs that it brought, which he had placed at Hilde's disposal for her to invest in new curtains and furniture. But Hilde was furious, accusing him of having made a fool of himself by working with an untalented woman. She then left the two men alone, at which Schoeck grumbled to Corrodi: "Beware of women, don't marry . . . they're all bad in some way, all despicable."[26] What is obvious to us, though Schoeck had somehow remained oblivious to it, is that the sex of the singer in question was surely the point of conflict. For Hilde, too, was a singer. She would probably have had little problem with Schoeck accompanying tenors, baritones, or basses, regardless of their talent or lack thereof, and will also have accepted his working with established female partners-in-song such as Ilona Durigo. But for Schoeck to be "acquired" by a new female singer, and to work with her for extra-musical reasons, was bound to suggest to Hilde that he might have been attracted by more than mammon. Just one week later, the tables were turned, and Schoeck was jealous because Hilde had begun to enjoy singing to Karl Heinrich David's accompaniment.[27]

We have no proof that Hilde had expected her marriage to Schoeck to boost her singing career, though Schoeck came to believe it himself, and Willi Schuh later had the same impression.[28] They had met because of their musical connections, and there have been enough examples in history of composers marrying performers for her to have expected, not unreasonably, that their union might result in some form of musical partnership. It is also possible that Schoeck was attracted by the idea of having a soprano constantly at hand to try out his latest songs before he presented them to the general public. Whatever their respective hopes or expectations of musical collaboration, however, none was to be fulfilled for the next twenty years. By November 1926 Hilde was already refusing to sing at home with Schoeck because he was too critical of her.[29] It would soon seem as if each of them was determined to thwart the other's expectations out of mere spite.

Chapter Twenty

Into the Vortex

In October 1926, out of the blue, Furtwängler wrote to ask for the score and parts of *Lebendig begraben*. Unfortunately Schoeck was still struggling with the scoring of the work and had to turn him down. Furtwängler never did conduct it. But then an opportunity for advancement of a different kind presented itself to Schoeck with the death of Hermann Suter, the conductor of the orchestra in Basel. This was a far more prestigious post than the one Schoeck currently held in St. Gallen, and several people now recommended him for the job, including Furtwängler. But Schoeck refused to kowtow to the authorities and waited instead for them to approach him. He was invited to conduct a concert there in February of the following year, which he had assumed would be to test his competency. But he had made a complete miscalculation. Long before his concert, the city of Basel achieved a small coup by procuring Felix Weingartner for the post, one of the most respected conductors in the world. The job was officially coupled with the directorship of the city theater and of the city conservatory. Not only had Schoeck never run any institution, but he had as far as possible avoided managerial duties with his choirs in Zurich and with his orchestra in St. Gallen. If he had seriously thought himself a viable candidate in Basel, then he was not a little deluded.

In late November 1926 Schoeck completed the orchestration of *Lebendig begraben,* which had proved his most difficult work yet to score. He had hoped to have the experience of hearing his new opera before finalizing the scoring of his cycle, but *Penthesilea* had been postponed until January 1927. Schoeck was still consistently exploring the modern repertoire in St. Gallen. December 1926 saw him conduct a work by Bartók for the first (and only) time, though since it was only the early Second Suite, he will have learnt little from its orchestration that could be of help to him now. Schoeck's last work for solo voice and orchestra had been the *Elegie,* and although it is superbly scored, its music is largely tonal. Every student of instrumentation learns how to score tonal, functional harmony so that the textures have the necessary density. But for long stretches, the harmony of *Penthesilea* and *Lebendig begraben* is devoid of any real tonal connotation, and perhaps Schoeck was wary that this might in turn demand a different kind of balance in the scoring. There are in fact occasional miscalculations in *Penthesilea*—though nothing that a sensitive conductor cannot overcome. If Schoeck suspected this, then it would explain his nervousness at embarking upon the score of *Lebendig begraben* before having heard the opera. He need not have worried, for the orchestration of the cycle is of a subtlety hitherto unparalleled in his oeuvre, and arguably the equal of anything scored by his contemporaries at the time.

Schoeck's self-doubts were never far from the surface in late 1926. He had pinned many of his hopes on his *Penthesilea*, and he was nervous both as to how it would sound and how it would be received. He was right to be apprehensive, for once again he was going into an opera premiere with no backing from a publisher, with no one representing his interests to ensure that the world's press was there, no one to lobby other theaters to take up the work afterward, and no one to look after his royalties. If the work were not a success big enough to attract attention on its merits alone, then it risked suffering the same fate as *Venus* five years earlier. Schoeck was further afraid that, in allotting the premiere to Kutzschbach, Busch had fobbed him off with something second-best. And when Kutzschbach wrote to him in December to reassure him that all was progressing well, he became even more nervous, because Kutzschbach had not expressly stated that the *orchestral* rehearsals were going well. The Dresden authorities had asked him for an introductory text to his opera and a brief autobiography, but he refused. His "official" reason was that all his work needed was a good performance, though in fact he was terrified that anything he might write would be taken and used against him by the critics. It was with no little trepidation that he left for Dresden just after Christmas. Hilde went too. When they arrived, Schoeck was relieved to find that all was well. Friedrich Plaschke was perhaps a little old for the part of Achilles but was in excellent voice, while Irma Tervani as Penthesilea was just as good, if also a little on the gray side, and somewhat better at depicting the raging queen than the tender lover. The director was Waldemar Staegemann.

The world premiere of *Penthesilea* took place on 8 January 1927. It was the biggest premiere that Schoeck had ever experienced, and the forces at the disposal of the opera house were greatly superior to those he had ever enjoyed in Zurich. Not surprisingly, many of his friends and colleagues came to support him. Reinhart came, bringing with him as his guests the painter Wilfried Buchmann and the German writer Hermann Burte. Walter Schoeck was there on behalf of the rest of their family; Ernst Isler was there to report for the *Neue Zürcher Zeitung*, while the others included Hans Corrodi and the Zurich kapellmeister Max Conrad. Many German critics were there, as were (apparently) even a few French journalists. There were eighteen curtain calls afterward, and the applause lasted some ten minutes. When he heard the first reports of the evening, Rüeger wrote in his diary:

> [I] repeated to myself: "the composer enjoyed 18 curtain calls," and alongside my joy for him I also had the bitter realization that the time would inevitably come when our lives would part ways completely. . . . I pondered the possible conversations about me. The first big operatic success—of course, because the librettist didn't make a mess of it this time.[1]

He wrote too soon. For it seems to have been obvious to everyone present that the premiere was not the overwhelming success that Schoeck had hoped for. On 11

January Reinhart wrote to Hermann Wilhelm Draber, the secretary of the Zurich branch of the ISCM, saying that *Penthesilea* had been given an excellent production, and adding that: "since I am so close to both the work and its creator, my judgment is perhaps all too subjective. But *my* impression was a strong one. With the general public, however, the work seems not to have achieved more than a *succès d'estime.*"[2] After the premiere, Schoeck was apparently at first in good spirits, but then quickly came down to earth. Walter sent a telegram home, saying "Very nice success." When Schoeck asked him what he would have written if it had flopped, he answered—truthfully, but tactlessly—"Probably the same."

The reviews did not serve to raise Schoeck's spirits. Ludwig Misch, writing in the *Berliner Lokalanzeiger* of 10 January, remarked that Schoeck's drastic editing down of Kleist should not be of concern *per se*, for a libretto has to be judged on its own terms; his use of the word "Verstümmelung" ("mutilation") for the editing process leaves the reader in little doubt, however, of Misch's real opinion. He continued that "the question arises whether the musician has provided with his [musical] means a replacement for what he took from the drama to achieve his ends. The answer, sadly, has to be in the negative . . . this composer, possessed of a fine sensibility, and whom we have learnt to appreciate in many fields, is no dramatist." He further complained that the music served to illustrate and comment on the action, but that there was "no sense of large-scale line." Achilles was "pale and anemic," while Penthesilea herself was "from start to finish a perverse, hysterical woman." He did praise Schoeck's treatment of the orchestra, however, and judged the standard of performance overall to have been excellent. "J.F.W." in the *Dresdner Neueste Nachrichten* of 11 January also wrote of a "mutilation" of Kleist, finding Schoeck's use of the spoken word a sign of his "capitulation before Kleist's poem," and he bemoaned the fact that the song composer Schoeck had allowed his melodic muse to soar only in the love scene and in the final monologue. Adolf Aber, in the *Leipziger Neueste Nachrichten* of 10 January, also had a problem coming to terms with the mixture of singing and speaking in the work, and wrote of Schoeck as "more than ever an adherent of that radical direction that sees the well-being of art as lying in the dissolution of every larger form, in the juxtaposition of the smallest motives, filled with the most intense expression." A more positive response came from Hans Schnoor in the *Dresdner Anzeiger* on 18 January. He found some of the battles both empty and loud, but he praised several scenes, including that between Achilles and Penthesilea, and the latter's final monologue. He noted the heavy applause for all concerned but doubted whether the work would really hold its place in the repertoire. The reviews that Ernst Isler published in the *Neue Zürcher Zeitung* were predictably laudatory: the first was a short one, sent by telegram, that appeared on 10 January, while the second was much longer and appeared a day later. He wrote of a "glorious premiere" and continued with a long list of positive adjectives.

The reviews were, then, a not uncommon mixture of contradictory statements—some finding that the work lacked any real trajectory, others finding the opposite, and so on. But the general tenor of the major papers was reserved. The critics were surprised that this Swiss song composer, possessed of an obvious melodic gift, should write an opera that largely seeks to eschew traditional melody. Whether or not the style of the opera would have bothered them had they not known Schoeck's songs, we cannot say. But all this was of little import to Schoeck, who fell into a rage that lasted two days, as Hilde recalled many years later.[3] She claimed that she had feared for his sanity—though we also cannot know if the passing of time had altered her recollection of events. If the reviews were not as Schoeck had hoped, then worse was still to come, for Tervani soon fell ill and was able to give just four performances in all.

Schoeck's *Penthesilea* was in every sense his most ambitious work to date. It was not his longest opera, for *Don Ranudo* in its original, four-act version lasts a good forty minutes more. But *Penthesilea* is in a single act and so demanded a quite different sense of dramatic timing and musical climax. Like Alban Berg in his *Wozzeck* (and, before him, Strauss and Debussy with *Salome* and *Pelléas et Mélisande* respectively), Schoeck was also faced with the problem of how to shorten and structure a spoken play so that it made sense as a libretto. Although some critics complained that the whole exposition of the play had been cut, with the result that the audience really had to have some advance knowledge of Kleist's plot, the alterations to the play were on the whole made with considerable skill. The cuts concentrate one's attention on the love story itself, with the result that the opera resembles a "Romeo and Juliet" with Greeks and Amazons instead of Montagues and Capulets. The Trojan war recedes decidedly into the background, and the warring parties running on and off stage can seem somewhat aimless. But the music and Kleist's text together are more than enough to carry the drama.

The orchestration, however, looks on paper more inventive than it actually sounds. Despite Walter Schulthess's belief that *Les noces* was a major influence, Stravinsky's Concerto for Piano and Winds (plus double bass) might have had an even greater impact on Schoeck's orchestration (the work that he had heard in Winterthur in November 1924). For the orchestra of *Penthesilea* has plenty of lower strings—double basses, cellos, and violas—but only four solo violins; then there are two pianos, three flutes doubling piccolos, a single oboe (doubling cor anglais), two E-flat clarinets, six "normal" clarinets, two bass clarinets, contrabassoon, four horns, four trumpets, three more trumpets behind the scenes, four trombones, tuba, *Stierhorn*, timpani, and numerous percussionists. The instrumentation is thus ostentatiously "lop-sided." But the actual choice of instruments seems somewhat arbitrary—Schoeck might almost as easily have chosen ten horns, four oboes, and one clarinet. It is the oddness itself that is the defining characteristic of the score's modernity. And in those passages where the harmony is thoroughly tonal, the music is at times notated to appear fragmentary (for which read "modern"), such as the excerpt given below from figure 19 (ex. 20.1a), with its huge, quasi-expressionistic leaps on the flute that one does not hear in performance (one of several such passages in the score):

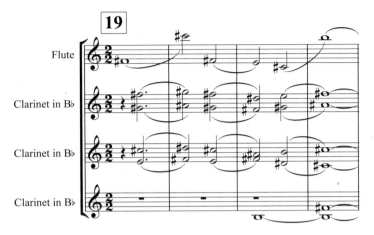

Example 20.1a. *Penthesilea*, Op. 39, figure 19. Copyright Bärenreiter.

sounding as:

Example 20.1b. Copyright Bärenreiter.

This somewhat superficial striving to be up-to-date is also noticeable in other areas. Even the work's vocal score, which is printed on several staves, not just the usual two, has a distinctly complex, contemporary appearance. No single pianist could play it as written; but the added staves in any case really only eluci-date what is happening in the orchestra and are thus, in a sense, "for show." In purely visual terms, *Penthesilea*'s vocal score is most reminiscent of that of Berg's *Wozzeck*, to which Schoeck had long had easy access through Reinhart. Given that Schoeck was closely involved in the drafting of *Penthesilea*'s vocal score, we can probably assume that this was intended to show to the world that he too was now very much a "modern" composer.[4]

In order to maintain coherence in the opera, Schoeck also resorts to techniques not unlike those employed in *Wozzeck*. There is thus a scene based solely on a rhythm (though in Schoeck it is simply repeated as an ostinato, not varied and combined with itself as in Berg); there are scenes based on other ostinati; and the primitive "note row" technique developed in *Gaselen* is also employed extensively, so that a melody can be repeated throughout a scene, with its rhythm varied as necessary. Aspects of *Penthesilea*'s scoring and structure prove that Schoeck had also been studying Stravinsky's scores assiduously. In its first scene (just before figure 3), the texture is underpinned by a six-note ostinato given simultaneously in canon and in diminution— a technique all but copied from the opening scene of the 1911 version of *Petrushka*.[5] The opening scenes of *Penthesilea* as a whole are reminiscent of the "montage" technique of Stravinsky, already mentioned above as being at its most obvious in his *Symphonies of Wind Instruments,* though also to be found *in ovo* in those same opening tableaux of *Petrushka*. Thus Penthesilea and Prothoe (Penthesilea's confidante) are both assigned reminiscence motives that can be, and often are, reduced to a single, characteristic chord to be inserted into the fabric of the music whenever necessary in order to signify its bearer (Penthesilea's motive is also a linear version of her chord). Achilles himself is assigned no motive, but just a single chord that is, however, immediately recognizable, as much on account of its distinctive orchestration as for its harmony. This all helps to impart to Schoeck's opera a directness that is veritably cinematic in effect.

For long stretches the music of *Penthesilea* is devoid of any real tonality— Hans-Joachim Hinrichsen has pointed out that no major or minor triad is heard in the opera until measure 124.[6] The harmonic extremes of the work have from the very start been much remarked upon—dominant seventh chords a tritone apart are repeatedly superimposed on each other, symbolizing the "battle of the sexes," just as the keys associated with the two lovers—F sharp and C—are also a tritone apart. But for all its apparent constructivism, the music of *Penthesilea* is probably also a direct result of its having being conceived "manually"—in other words, its textures and spacings reflect the lie of the hands, fingers, and thumbs on the keyboard. Many of the work's most complicated harmonies can be generated by sitting at the piano, playing a straightforward chord in both hands (say, a dominant seventh), and then sliding one of the hands up or down a semitone. Schoeck would not have been the first to create his dissonances like this; the famous, often-quoted dissonant chord at the climax of the final scene of Strauss's *Salome* was probably conceived in just this manner. If this is indeed how Schoeck created his harmonies, it merely confirms his intent to create a "modernist" sound, for it entails actively choosing to distort consonance into dissonance.

As we have already noted, the very topic of *Penthesilea* was probably chosen by Schoeck with a view to being "up-to-date," on account of its vague similarity to Hindemith's *Mörder, Hoffnung der Frauen*. Kleist's play was certainly en vogue with composers at this time. The Czech composer Vincenc Maixner and the German Rudo Ritter each wrote a *Penthesilea* opera almost exactly concurrently with Schoeck, while Richard Rosenberg and Klaus Pringsheim independently wrote incidental music for Kleist's play in the early 1920s, for Mainz and Berlin respectively. Unfortunately, however, some two decades had elapsed since Strauss had put his murderous women on stage in *Salome* and *Elektra,* and the world had in the meantime seen more than enough real blood shed—except, of course, in Switzerland. By the time that Schoeck's *Penthesilea* was staged, a quite different aesthetic from his own had dawned, and the man whose work had probably served as his model was again leading the way. On 9 November 1926 the premiere of *Cardillac* at the Dresden State Opera gave Hindemith his first major operatic success. Although based on a story by E. T. A. Hoffmann—himself roughly contemporary with Schoeck's "librettist" Kleist—*Cardillac* nevertheless exemplified Hindemith's personal brand of neoclassicism, with more than a dash of Handel, Bach, Verdi, and *neue Sachlichkeit.* This was what the *Zeitgeist* wanted, not late-Romantic gore. Within just a few months *Cardillac* had been taken up by opera houses all over Germany.

Penthesilea was overshadowed even more by Krenek's *Jonny spielt auf,* which was given its world premiere in Leipzig under Gustav Brecher on 10 February 1927. Although more or less ignored today, *Jonny*'s success trumped that of *Cardillac.* With its jazz ambience, its special stage effects—including glaciers and railway trains—and its black jazz-band-violinist-as-hero, it offered a heady brew of modernity that had never been experienced before on the operatic stage. Indeed, it appears in retrospect to be one of the most representative works of the whole Weimar era (not for nothing was it reviled by the Nazis). In its first season alone *Jonny* was given over four hundred performances at dozens of opera houses, was soon being performed in Paris and New York, and brought its composer the kind of fame of which others could only dream. Schoeck's premiere was thus sandwiched between two of the biggest operatic events of the decade. Perhaps it was made even worse for him by the fact that he knew both composers personally—and liked them—and that they all shared the same patron, Werner Reinhart.

When Schoeck returned home from Dresden in the second half of January, the wild success of *Jonny* was still to come. But if he was not upset enough by the middling reception of his opera, he had to face yet another blow, for his mother died on 21 January, some twenty-four hours before he arrived back in Brunnen. She had already been seriously ill in December, but he had nevertheless refrained from visiting her. They had been on poor terms for some time—we have already seen how Schoeck had blamed her for the break with Mary—though it must also be mentioned that she suffered from Grave's (Basedow's) disease, which affects the thyroid and can, in turn, be responsible for mood swings in the person affected. Her death, as is the wont of such events, seems at least briefly to have swept aside all residual bitterness in her youngest son. A day later, on 22 January, he was already writing to his old friend Martin Kuntze of the "irreplaceable loss" of his "unforgettable Mama."[7]

It had all seemed so rosy, just a year before. His married life had started off well (or so he had felt), he was composing fluently, his opera had been accepted by one of the world's top houses, and leading conductors were taking him seriously as a modern composer. He had finished an opera that represented everything modern that he wanted to be. But it now must have seemed as if all his worst fears were being realized. His opera had no prospect of finding an international publisher, he was heavily in debt over the cost of producing the orchestral parts, and there was no immediate possibility of another theater's taking up the work. It seemed as if the tag of "Swiss song composer" was going to stick for good, with all the incapacities that it implied. To cap it all, his mother had just died, and his marriage was becoming the disaster that his closest friends had prophesied. His finances suffered another, indirect, blow in early 1927 when it became public that Lala Gsell was pregnant. She was unmarried, and since her house was Schoeck's domicile whenever he visited St. Gallen, his reputation as a womanizer was sufficient to convince everyone that he must be the father. As it happens, he was innocent—Lala had become aware of the ever-louder ticking of her biological clock, had happened upon a suitable (German) man, and had accordingly done the deed, sown the seed, and in due course borne a daughter. Her family was upper-class enough to bear the social stigma with impunity, but the gossip made it impossible for Schoeck to continue as a regular guest under their roof. He now had to stay in hotels instead, which was a huge drain on his already modest income. Lala missed his company too; she would content herself in future with placing a single rose in his hotel room whenever he was about to arrive.

Given that here was a man prone to recurrent periods of deep depression, one might expect that these extraordinarily depressing circumstances would have paralysed his creative spirit for many months to come. It is therefore surprising that precisely the opposite now seems to have been the case.

Chapter Twenty-One

Wrong-Note Rag

Schoeck did not have time to mope, for he had to conduct a concert performance of *Erwin und Elmire* in Lausanne on 10 February 1927. His spirits might have already been buoyed by a concert of his works in Zurich on 6 February (repeated on the eighth), in which his old choir, the Lehrergesangverein, sang his *Wegelied, Postillon,* and *Dithyrambe* under his successor, Robert F. Denzler; the concert also included excerpts from *Erwin* and the whole first act of *Venus.* His *Don Ranudo* was then performed again at the Zurich opera on 13 February, receiving praise in the press both at home and abroad. In any case, his depression seems to have lifted enough for him soon to embark on revisions to *Penthesilea.* We know that he had been offended by the critics after the premiere, so we also know that he had read them. He had also taken to heart those who complained that he had not allowed his lyrical imagination to take flight, for on 17 February he wrote a duet for Achilles and Penthesilea to be inserted into the middle of the love scene. He told Corrodi that he had felt he would like "to hear more" at that point. He had, however, come into conflict with his desire to set "no comma that is not in Kleist," so he had himself chosen a few phrases from Kleist's fifteenth scene—sketched onto the back of a letter from one Louis Neher in Bern, which was probably the nearest piece of paper to hand—and juggled them around a little in order to produce a text whose words were "by" Kleist, if not all in their original order. Since the characters are both singing at the same time, the words are in any case neither particularly audible nor of real importance to the listener. And the music, which seems to change gear at the onset of the duet, has an immense *Schwung* that sweeps one along regardless—though it is not without the same odd, deflatory moments such as characterized Horace's final monologue in *Venus.* The duet is also closer in idiom to that work than to the rest of *Penthesilea,* and its harmonic rhythm is more stable and conventional than in the rest of the score. Commentators remain divided as to whether or not the duet was a positive addition, though audiences are usually more than happy to bathe in its forty-nine measures of late-Romantic harmonic repose.

Two weeks later, on 2 March, Schoeck conducted the world premiere of his latest work, *Lebendig begraben,* in the Winterthur City Church. The venue was chosen because the orchestra requires an organ, but since the Zwinglian morals of the local ecclesiastics forbade clapping in church, the work ended without anyone the wiser as to its success or failure. The solo part was sung by Thomas Denijs, whose interpretation of the *Elegie* had so impressed Schoeck. But *Lebendig begraben* is a different score entirely. Where the former is Romantic and lyrical, the latter is modernist and declamatory, demanding both an intense dramatic presence and immense stamina (there is only one brief orchestral passage halfway through to give the singer a rest). The ensemble for the *Elegie* is a chamber orchestra, but *Lebendig begraben* needs double wind (plus an extra bass clarinet and contrabassoon), four horns, two trumpets, three trombones, tuba, percussion, harp, piano, and organ, plus strings. Toward the close, the soloist even has to contend with a wordless semi-chorus. Denijs's voice was strained in its upper register (the solo part has a range of two octaves), but he was nevertheless already engaged to sing the work twice more under Schoeck that same month, with the Tonhalle Orchestra in Zurich on 14 and 15 March. Schoeck's conducting schedule was particularly hectic. Before the Zurich performances of *Lebendig begraben,* he had to conduct Reger's *Mozart Variations,* his own Serenade, Op. 1, and Stravinsky's *Firebird* Suite in St. Gallen on 10 March, and on the last day of the month he would return there for an all-Beethoven program that included the "Eroica" Symphony and the Third Piano Concerto (with Edwin Fischer as soloist). It was also, it seems, in this season that Schoeck gave a helping hand to a teenager who would later become one of Switzerland's finest dodecaphonic composers, Edward Staempfli (1908–2002), a schoolboy in nearby Trogen who regularly attended Schoeck's orchestral concerts. Staempfli's first large-scale orchestral work was a symphonic poem entitled *Pan,* written in June 1926, and Schoeck allotted some of his normal rehearsal time to a run-through of the work—a gesture that Staempfli still remembered with gratitude over sixty years later.[1]

While the Winterthur performance of *Lebendig begraben* had been something of a damp squib, its Zurich premiere was greeted with a quarter-hour of applause. Nevertheless, Schoeck was again smarting over the reaction to *Penthesilea* in Dresden. He had convinced himself—and repeated many times over the ensuing months—that Ernst Isler's hymn of praise to *Penthesilea* in the *Neue Zürcher Zeitung* had been a negative review, and he now became equally convinced that *Lebendig begraben* too, was a failure. He admitted that he should rather have offered the solo part to Loeffel, and it was he who became Schoeck's soloist of choice over the next decade and a half. Loeffel gave the German premiere in Frankfurt in the summer of 1927 under Walter Herbert. Schoeck was this time delighted with both the performance and its reception—and nor was he alone, for it even received a positive review from Theodor Adorno.[2]

Lebendig begraben was for Derrick Puffett "the central work of [Schoeck's] career." It is difficult to disagree. It sets Keller's complete narrative cycle of fourteen poems, depicting the thoughts of a man mistakenly buried alive after he falls into a coma and is pronounced dead. The opening poems depict the narrator's random, panic-stricken thoughts, but then his memories of childhood, youth, and first love gain the upper hand, his imagination takes flight, and at the close, he metaphorically casts his soul into eternity in a strangely pantheistic acceptance of his fate. The music reflects perfectly the trajectory of the narrative,

Example 21.1. *Lebendig begraben,* Op. 40, fifth song. Copyright Breitkopf & Härtel. Reprinted by permission. "[. . . sits in front of his] house, crows a psalm, but she's barely heard it when his wife storms out to berate him, tells him to go inside . . ."

utilizing techniques taken from instrumental music in order to impart greater musical coherence as the cycle progresses. Ostinati abound, and Schoeck uses passacaglia and chaconne to even better effect than in *Penthesilea.* In fact, *Lebendig begraben* is in almost every way an advance on the opera. It is also even more direct in the manner in which it comments upon the "action." In the fifth song, for example, the narrator—singing for four verses on a repeated C♯ only—tells us how he hears the drunken, psalmodizing sexton wander past above, how he hears his wife chide and nag him, then the door of the house slammed shut after them (see ex. 21.1). We hear all this in the orchestra just as it happens (and sometimes just before it happens). The use of the high bassoon for the sexton is wonderfully absurd—an ironic reference, perhaps, to the opening of Stravinsky's *Le sacre?*—as are the two clarinets in thirds that depict his wife. The fragmentary textures do not dissolve into incoherence because everything is underpinned by a six-note passacaglia in the bass.

Schoeck was fully aware that he was attempting something quite new in this work. At the time that he had begun its composition, Corrodi noted:

> Before beginning work every time, [Schoeck] seems to himself to be a beginner once again. The form has to be conquered anew every time because it is a new form each time. . . . he said that Max Reger, who really endeavored to fill old forms with new content, is a dangerous example.[3]

Keller's text provides more opportunities for coloristic effect than did that of Kleist. The narrator's memories of wandering through forests and of his first adolescent infatuation are set to a music whose scoring is of exquisite subtlely. Birdsong fragments come and go, more reminiscent of Ravel's *Daphnis* than of Wagner's "Forest Murmurs." There are occasional references to other music—the opening motive of Wagner's *Parsifal* surfaces just after the narrator eats the rose that had been placed in his coffin; and fragments of Schoeck's own *Elegie*—though only just recognizable—can also be heard. The only moment in the cycle that disappoints is the very close, primarily because the long, superb build-up to it raises expectations that Schoeck, oddly, cannot satisfy. As in *Venus*, Schoeck is unable to sustain the momentum to the very end: he continually interrupts the orchestral texture with little pauses that make it difficult to regain momentum. It is a pity; but *Lebendig begraben* is nevertheless a *tour de force* in every respect: formally, in its orchestration, in its narrative power and expressive subtlety. Puffett refers to its "almost Ivesian abundance of ideas" and writes that "Schoeck's invention was rarely so rich."[4] Schoeck himself referred to the work as his "first symphony," though it is more "operatic" than symphonic. It would not be unfair to call *Lebendig begraben* Schoeck's "best opera" by far.

We cannot investigate *Lebendig begraben* without considering Schoeck's reasons for setting the cycle to music in the first place. It was long interpreted as being of autobiographical significance, reflecting Schoeck's frustration at seeing his treasured Romantic values trodden underfoot by the wicked avant-garde. But since we now know that Schoeck was himself keen to be as wickedly *avant* as any of the *garde,* with *Lebendig begraben* partial proof of his contemporary credentials, that explanation rings hollow. Not long before his death Schoeck discussed the work in conversation with Werner Vogel, summing it up thus: "*Lebendig begraben* in my opinion has as its theme: What is man? What is our life? Where do we come from, where are we going?"[5] This is all very well, though it sounds more like something from the *Hitchhiker's Guide to the Galaxy* and was probably no more than a smokescreen. In fact, Vogel remarks that Schoeck "did not give away what really prompted its composition," which suggests, naturally, that there was something particular behind it.

That "something" was quite possibly Mary. She suffered from an inordinate fear of being buried alive and even stipulated that her veins should be opened after her death in order to ensure that she would not wake up in her coffin.[6] We cannot know for certain if she discussed this with Schoeck, but it would offer a cogent argument as to why Schoeck would have considered setting Keller's cycle just after the end of their relationship, and why the cycle should have held such sway over him (it might also explain the musical references to the *Elegie*). It has often been remarked how odd it was that Schoeck began work on *Lebendig begraben* just three or four weeks after getting married. But his marriage gave obvious closure to his relationship with Mary, who was now to all intents and purposes "buried" for him, and by him. She was far from "dead" to him, however, and we shall see later how her presence haunts Schoeck's music for many years to come.

After the premiere of *Lebendig begraben* in Winterthur Schoeck's mind turned once more to opera. He pondered *Meister Pfriem* and *Bruder Lustig* again before deciding instead to continue with the revisions to *Penthesilea* that he had begun in February. So when he and Hilde spent a few weeks in April and early May in San Mamette by the shores of Lake Lugano (as guests of Hans Bärlocher from St. Gallen), he took with him, not just paintbrush and palette, but also the sketches for the love duet, and some spare manuscript paper. He now composed a further interpolation: twenty-five measures for Penthesilea herself at the end of the love scene (unlike the love duet, there has been no debate about this brief lyrical addition—from figure 111 to 114 in the Breitkopf vocal score). He and Hilde spent a few days in Lugano, Verona, and Venice before returning home via Lake Garda. In June Hilde went to Rigi-Klösterli, and Schoeck to Brunnen to visit his aged widowed father. It was there that his tinkering with *Penthesilea* turned into a wholescale revision of the work. Perhaps writing the duet and Penthesilea's little interlude had made him aware of how far he had come from his original intention that the work should "rush past like a tempest." If still a tempest, then it was now one with prolonged languid spells. Schoeck wanted, so he said, to bring the work back in line with his original "ideal." But he also wanted to revise it so that "even a bad conductor could not ruin it."[7] The notion that one can build failsafe mechanisms into an orchestral score is one that shows how insecure Schoeck had become. Perhaps, however, he was worried in concrete terms about the work's first Swiss performance, which was due to take place the next season.

Schoeck now took his copy of the vocal score and spent a month revising it. This score is held today by the Zentralbibliothek Zürich and bears all his annotations and corrections in red ink. He not only shortened several scenes in order to improve the dramatic flow but also went about shortening actual note values throughout, in order to bring the tempo of the singing closer to that of the spoken word. The original version of the opera has never been performed since its premiere and has never been recorded, but a glance at the score shows how much tighter the revised version is and how much more impetus the work now possesses. Schoeck also altered the ending. *Penthesilea* had originally ended softly, in a manner reminiscent of *Venus,* but Schoeck now added a sudden closing *fortissimo* chord of F sharp minor. The reason was probably quite simple: he was desperate for success, and with a big-bang ending, the audience would at least know when to clap. The chord is, in a sense, the anticipated tumultuous response of the audience, composed back into the music itself.

It is as well that Schoeck was not a practically minded man, for had he given any thought to the cost of revising the score and parts, he might never have undertaken the work. Alfred Hüni now offered to publish *Penthesilea,* despite having no experience in the field. So it was he who had to organize the complete rewriting of the performance materials. Schoeck did not want to do it himself and asked that the job be given to Karl Krebs, whom he felt he could trust enough to follow his revisions accurately. But just six days after Hüni wrote to Krebs to ask him if he could do the work "in perhaps two to three weeks" (which would probably have meant at least an eighty-hour week for the poor chap), Hüni wrote back to Schoeck to say: "Mrs Penthesilea isn't making things easy for me. . . . Krebs has died."[8] Schoeck wrote back to Hüni on 27 August: "the early death of Krebs is very sad; he was a decent fellow."

Hüni had written to Werner Reinhart as early as February 1927 with the idea of finding enough donors to create a fund of some Fr. 50,000, to be invested so that Schoeck could be paid a monthly income supplement, and which could also be used to pay the cost of the parts for *Penthesilea* and other works. Not surprisingly, Hüni failed to generate enough support. So Reinhart himself stepped in and paid not only the ten thousand francs outstanding for *Penthesilea* in Dresden but also a further fourteen thousand francs by the end of the year toward his further costs in matters Schoeckian.[9] Reinhart had already paid for the vocal score and the writing out of the orchestral parts for *Lebendig begraben,* which was about to be published by Breitkopf & Härtel.[10] Nevertheless, Schoeck had been complaining to his friends that Reinhart was placing whole castles ("Schlösser") at the disposal of foreigners while he had to make do with mere alms (he was referring to the tower of Muzot—hardly a "Schloss"—where Reinhart allowed Rainer Maria Rilke to spend his final years rent-free). It was thus to Schoeck's utter horror that Reinhart halted his quarterly payments in October 1927 on account of the monies he was already giving to Hüni. But it was only a brief hiatus, and he soon began paying again. We can better comprehend just how privileged Schoeck's position with Reinhart was when we consider that Alban Berg's cry for help on behalf of a poverty-stricken Anton von Webern in mid-1925 was at first turned down. Only after a further appeal, several months later, was it met with a gift of some nine hundred francs.[11]

Schoeck's current moodiness did not merely express itself in ingratitude toward Reinhart: the problems surrounding *Penthesilea* were having an adverse effect on his relations with many others. Even Schulthess, to whom he had been especially close, complained "bitterly" to Corrodi in June 1927 of Schoeck's unreliability, his lack of fidelity to his friends, and the constant ebb and flow of his opinions. "Even his best friends are distancing themselves from him," noted Corrodi.[12] Some proof that Schoeck was not always ungrateful is to be found in the dedications that he made to Reinhart. Mary had received the dedication of just two piano pieces; Hilde would wait for over twenty years before being accorded such an honor; nothing was ever dedicated to Elsbeth (except unofficially), nor were Ilona Durigo and Felix Loeffel, his two champions in song, rewarded thus. Even Armin Rüeger, his closest friend, and his brothers Walter, Ralph, and Paul received in total the dedication of just a few songs, almost all of them early works. But it was Reinhart who now received the dedication of *Penthesilea*. And in the last quarter of 1927 Schoeck embarked on another work that he would dedicate to his patron, and which was also intended for him to play: a sonata for bass clarinet and piano.

As was often the case whenever Schoeck was about to compose a piece of absolute music, this new sonata was preceded by numerous pronouncements against instrumental music *per se:* "the time of absolute music is over," he had declared the previous July, "and perhaps it was altogether only a mistake. . . . all music, from first to last, is song."[13] But he spent his August holiday at Rigi-Klösterli practising his fugal writing and studying Bach's *48* as a prelude to embarking on his new work. It is more tonal than not, though for much of the time the music meanders in and out of various tonalities. The textures are highly contrapuntal, often quite spare—the second movement even begins with a fugato of sorts (hence, no doubt, the study of the *48*)—and there is much three-part writing in it, often imitative.

In the light of the works that followed it, we can now see that this sonata was a kind of testing ground for a Schoeckian neoclassicism, the very oddness of the instrumental combination perhaps according its composer the freedom that he needed for his experiments. The sonata also provides us with clear evidence that Schoeck was intrigued by the musical trends coming from across the Atlantic. Its third and final movement is a strangely Hindemithian, slightly comical "wrong-note" ragtime that highlights what most musicians—apart, perhaps, from bass clarinettists—would regard as the instrument's innate silliness. It juggles with all kinds of banal, trashy fragments, ranging from jazz-like syncopations to a hilarious "hunting horn" passage in $\frac{6}{8}$ time (beginning in m. 73) that veers off into a different key in almost every measure. Schoeck had surely had enough opportunity to hear ragtime recordings—his family, after all, ran a hotel that was particularly popular with Anglo-Saxon tourists. But he will also have been familiar by now with the jazz-influenced works of Stravinsky and Krenek, and perhaps he had taken the trouble to look at Hindemith's *Suite 1922* for piano, whose last movement is a ragtime with even more "wrong" notes than Schoeck's. But it was maybe Krenek's success with *Jonny spielt auf* that had spurred him on to dabble in a spot of Americanized music of his own. While Schoeck's Bass Clarinet Sonata (see ex. 21.2) will always remain a peripheral work, it is nevertheless both amusing and very clever.

In February 1928 Hilde went to visit the soprano Felicie Hüni-Mihacsek in Munich; she was the wife of Alfred Hüni, though the couple led relatively independent lives. Schoeck stayed in Switzerland, for he had three concerts in St. Gallen in the space of as many weeks. On 9 February he conducted a concert that included no less than three works written since 1914: Ravel's *La valse*, Busoni's

Example 21.2. The Bass Clarinet Sonata, Op. 41, opening of the last movement with its "wrong-note" ragtime (here notated in C). Copyright Breitkopf & Härtel. Reprinted by permission.

Indian Fantasy, and Stravinsky's Suite for Small Orchestra. This was followed by a *Winterreise* with Loeffel on the twenty-third and Bruckner's First Symphony on 1 March. It was after this that Schoeck and Alfred Hüni set off to join their wives in Munich, taking their time on a motor tour across southern Germany, via Ulm, Dinkelsbühl, Augsburg, and Rothenburg ob der Tauber (which the Anglo-Saxon cinema-goer knows best as the village backdrop for the film *Chitty Chitty Bang Bang*). Armin Rüeger accompanied them as far as Ulm before returning home.

The Bass Clarinet Sonata received its first performance on 22 April 1928 at the Swiss *Tonkünstlerfest* in Lucerne. It was to have been played by the Zurich clarinettist Carl Pathe, but his place was taken at relatively short notice by one Wilhelm Arnold from Munich. The accompanist was Fritz Müller, to whom Schoeck had said in advance of the performance: "The piece isn't painted, it's drawn. . . . You have to take, as it were, a harder pencil! . . . Play hard!"[14] Unfortunately, Müller did just that, to such an extent that one could barely hear the bass clarinet. In his otherwise positive review of the work in the *Neue Zürcher Zeitung* of 25 April, Ernst Isler suggested that the instrument perhaps was just not capable of keeping a line above the sound of the piano. Arnold himself blamed the bad acoustic in Lucerne for the work's mediocre success,[15] and more recent performances (and recordings) have proved that Schoeck's original conception was in no wise a miscalculation. Schoeck did, however, consider performing the work with harpsichord accompaniment instead of the piano—and it is a shame that neither he nor anyone since has followed this idea through, for such a combination would serve to underline the neoclassical aspects of the work.

The Swiss premiere of *Penthesilea*—also the world premiere of the revised version—took place on 15 May 1928 at the Zurich City Theater. Max Conrad conducted; the director was Paul Trede, Penthesilea was sung by Marie Mülkens, and Karl Schmid-Bloss played Achilles. The house was sold out and the performance was, according to the reviews, highly successful. Alfred Hüni did his best to stimulate interest in the opera by publishing a brief "guide" to it by Ernst Isler, and this, too, received suitable praise in the local press (as in the *Neue Zürcher Zeitung* of 9 May). But not everyone was thrilled by the opera, nor by the continuing special treatment that Schoeck seemed to be receiving from the local critics. Among them was Hermann von Glenck, who wrote as follows to Karl Heinrich David on 3 July:

I confess that I was annoyed by the sloppy writing, not just of the music itself, but of the way it is notated. I'd allow myself something like that in a sketch, but not in a finished, published work. . . . such a sloppy manner repels me on account of its lack of discipline, which is far from being proof of invention or genius. It can be that the reason lies in the astonishing, regrettable unkemptness of Schoeck. . . . But just think of these constant syncopated entries and rhythms—something that when used in certain places and in moderation (*Gott und die Bajadere*) has an excellent, convincing effect. But here it is raised to being a general precept, all the way through. It becomes a "recipe" and degenerates into a mania, it becomes all too subjective, because it can be traced back to the first sketches in the work's genesis, as Schoeck hummed it to himself at the piano. . . . As I say, that can all be explained by Schoeck's undisciplined, unruly manner—one that he himself emphasizes with vain obstinacy.[16]

David replied on 5 July:

The man is on the one hand far more elemental than you think—you see him through a veil—and on the other hand, he is far too mature and experienced in practical matters of composition not to know exactly what he wants, and he is also capable of achieving it. His heavy bouts of emotional depression, his inability to shape many external aspects of life in a practical manner, have led to him "running wild" in all kinds of ways—at times, anyway—but have not hindered him from writing his scores pretty well. . . . Schoeck is much more naïve than you think.[17]

While Glenck's opinion is colored by his own conservativism, he was a fine composer and conductor, who knew the contemporary repertoire well. And he also astutely put his finger on an important point, for the "rough edges" of Schoeck's *Penthesilea* form part of its intentional modernity. It is as if Schoeck allows traces of the compositional process to remain as a "grain" on its surface, as tangible proof of its modernist aesthetic. *Penthesilea,* as it were, wears its modernist construction on its sleeve. The demonstrative nature of its craftsmanship, particularly obvious, as already postulated above, in its intentionally unplayable vocal score, arguably extends beyond the music into the very carpentry of the wooden desk that Schoeck had commissioned and into the typesetting of his specially printed manuscript paper, both of which he had deemed necessary in order to embark on the scoring of the opera (and which were prominently displayed for his friends to observe and remark upon).

If one wanted real "street credibilty" as a modernist, the ISCM still offered the best place to mingle and mix. Volkmar Andreae was on the jury for the next ISCM chamber music festival, which was to take place in Siena from 10 to 15 September 1928. The others on the jury were Alban Berg, Alfredo Casella, Karel B. Jirák, and Schoeck's old friend Philipp Jarnach. Andreae suggested to Schoeck that he submit his Bass Clarinet Sonata for the festival, which he then did. However, it was turned down. Instead, Switzerland was represented by Ernest Bloch's Quintet for Piano and Strings and an octet by the young Robert Blum, a former Busoni pupil. Schoeck was horrified, as much at being "replaced" by Blum (as he saw it) as by the fact that he was turned down at all (though Blum's subsequent compositional career would thoroughly justify the faith put in him by the ISCM jury).

We know that Berg's main concern for the Siena Festival was to push through Webern's String Trio and Alexander Zemlinsky's Third String Quartet, and in this he was successful.[18] But since the jury meeting took place in Zurich, and since Reinhart took it upon himself to entertain Berg and others during their visit, one might have expected Reinhart's most privileged composer to have enjoyed a smidgeon of "special treatment." Yet there is nothing odd about a work being rejected for an ISCM festival, and the final selection will always be more or less of a compromise.[19] The only odd thing is that we do not know when Andreae suggested to Schoeck that he submit his new sonata. The extant sources would seem to suggest that it was after the work's first performance, though the jury had already met in late March, at just about the time that Schoeck was completing the work. Perhaps Andreae had thought he might push the work through as a late entry, and had miscalculated. Whatever the reason, Schoeck's reaction was one of fury. To be "rejected" by the ISCM seems to have called into question for him not just the validity of the organization but all it stood for, namely: musical modernism. This might seem petulant in the extreme, but it is likely that Schoeck had already entertained some doubts about his rapid forays into the world of the avant-garde. He had abandoned traditional tonality for long stretches in his recent works; he had toyed with jazz and ragtime; but he had never been a likely candidate to pursue the modernist road toward, say, complete atonality or the twelve-note system. Schoeck had friends among the modernists—Krenek, Hindemith, and Scherchen—but he was neither suited to joining the frivolous Parisian neoclassicism of *Les Six,* nor Austrian enough to fit in with the Viennese twelve-note crowd. The Swiss, having rent themselves from the bosom of Austria in the late Middle Ages, have never been particularly fond of their eastern neighbors, who are as much the butt of jokes to the German Swiss as are the Irish to the English. Schoeck does seem to have got on particularly well with Hindemith, who played under his baton in St. Gallen several times over the next ten years (Schoeck's friend Josef von Vintschger related in the 1980s how their post-concert drinking sessions would be enlivened by everyone present testing Hindemith's infallible encyclopaedic knowledge of the Central European railway timetables).[20] It was Hindemith who proved the most influential of the modernists among Schoeck's Swiss colleagues in the 1930s, several of whom took to writing neo-Bachian, wrong-note concerti grossi and the like. But Hindemith himself was no member of a specific clique or "school," and he had as a young man enjoyed early contact with Switzerland and the Swiss. So perhaps it was easier for Schoeck to relate to him than to their avant-garde contemporaries. One gets the impression that Schoeck saw the modernists otherwise as a kind of schoolyard clique: a self-appointed club of the fashionable to which he, as a Swiss, would never be allowed full access. When Schoeck learnt through Reinhart that there were moves afoot in the ISCM to put his *Penthesilea* on the program of their 1929 festival in Geneva, he exercised his right of veto (so he later claimed), out of sheer spite. If true, then it was a decision one can only describe as idiotic, for poor Hüni was still vainly trying to get theaters interested in the work (he was claiming that his correspondence in the matter now ran to some five hundred pages).

We can never know his precise reasons, but what is clear is that Schoeck's music now suddenly makes an about-turn, back to tonality. The latent neoclassicism of the Bass Clarinet Sonata, with its spare, contrapuntal textures, soon dominates his music altogether, in a context in which dissonance plays a far less significant role. Schoeck had never abandoned tonality altogether, but now it takes on the ambience of something "after the fall." Schoeck's use of tonality from here on bears within it, as it were, the knowledge of a world without it.

Chapter Twenty-Two

Hildebill

In late June 1928 Schoeck and Hilde retired to the Fluh for a few days. They were not alone. As usual, other guests of Reinhart were present, this time Hermann Burte and Wilfried Buchmann. On the evening of 29 June there was a heated discussion in which Schoeck vented his anger on the vogue for honors and titles, honorary doctorates in particular—"You just have to look at the people who've got them!" he cried. The next morning he was woken early and emerged at half past ten to go down to bathe in the lake. A line of fancy cars was pulling up out-side—"Bloody hell [*Herrgott-Sterne-Cheib*], not even here can you get any peace away from it all," he grumbled, only to find that the men who emerged in dress suits were from the University of Zurich and had come to surprise him with an honorary doctorate. The rector began his speech, though at the point where he was supposed to give the specific reason why they were honoring Schoeck he for-got his lines and had to be prompted by one of his colleagues. Schoeck accepted meekly, embarrassed but with good grace.[1]

The trip to the Fluh also brought creative results, for Schoeck was now working on a new opera. Twenty-five years later he recalled how he had vis-ited Rüeger in Bischofszell in early summer 1928—presumably just before his outing to the Fluh—and was once more looking for a new plot. Together they flicked through the pages of Grimm's *Fairy Tales*. Schoeck was yet again thinking of "Bruder Lustig," but then late one night he came across the tale "The Fisherman and His Wife" and asked Rüeger to write out its dialogue for him "if he had nothing to do in his shop the next morning." Rüeger obliged, and Schoeck claimed to have begun work that same afternoon.[2] One matter is missing from the telling, however, for the version of the tale in Grimm is, to be precise, the one committed to paper by the early Romantic writer and painter Philipp Otto Runge. It is written in Low German (*Plattdeutsch*), the dialect spoken in the very north of Germany that in a westward-flowing linguis-tic continuum merges into Dutch. *Vom Fischer un syner Fru* is a tale that many Anglo-Saxon children still have read to them today. A poor fisherman catches a flounder that turns out to be an enchanted prince. He tosses it back in the sea, but his nagging wife Ilsebill is desperate to leave their hovel and has him go back to ask the fish to grant them a little house instead. The fisherman does so, but Ilsebill is not satisfied, so she asks for more. Her wishes become increas-ingly preposterous—to be king, emperor, then pope—but when she wishes to be like God himself, her world collapses and she and her husband find them-selves back in their old hovel.

Figure 22.1. Othmar and Hilde lounging by a lake, late 1920s. Courtesy of Zentralbibliothek Zürich.

For his libretto Schoeck set the dialogue as recorded by Runge, with just three characters: the fisherman, his wife, and the fish. Richard Wagner had once considered an opera on just this topic when he was living in Tribschen, as Cosima's diary makes clear,[3] while Schoeck's countryman Friedrich Klose had actually gone ahead and written one, entitled *Ilsebill* (it had been performed at the same Zurich Festival in 1922 that had seen the world premiere of *Venus*). Schoeck conceived of his new opera as a possible partner to *Penthesilea*, presumably in the hope that opera houses would find a double bill a more attractive proposition than the former work alone. The two works in fact have a similar premise, namely a "battle of the sexes," except that the one is tragic and ends in death, while the other is (more or less) comic and ends with the implicit acceptance of their lot on the part of the two main characters (a happy end that is not in the original tale). It was hardly a coincidence that Schoeck began work on the opera at precisely a time when Hilde was nagging him about the small size of their apartment on the Zeltweg (she was soon being dubbed "Hildebill" behind her back by several of Schoeck's friends).

As so often before, it was Reinhart who provided at least a temporary solution to the Schoecks' continuing marital problems, by giving them extra money for a holiday. Schoeck and Hilde decided to spend the summer by Lake Morat in northwestern Switzerland, one of the most picturesque spots that the country has to offer. They went first to Vallamand but soon moved to the little town of

Figure 22.2. "Fahrewohl," Op. 35, no. 2. Copyright Breitkopf & Härtel. Reprinted by permission.

Morat itself, where Schoeck found a room with a piano so that he could work. Three short songs for voice and piano date from 1928—his first for five years—two of which were composed this summer (they later became his opus 35). For all their brevity, they are strangely diverse. While the first of them to be composed ("April," from February 1928, Schoeck's only-ever setting of Theodor Storm) is in its declamatory style the closest to *Lebendig begraben* or *Penthesilea*, the other two ("Fahrewohl," Keller, and "Gottes Segen," Eichendorff), although more overtly tonal, also bear the traces of his recent works in their harmony and text-setting (see fig. 22.2). With hindsight, they were perhaps a small-scale, first inkling of a desire on Schoeck's part for a change in aesthetic direction.

It was at Morat this summer that Schoeck wrote a new ten-minute song cycle, *Wandersprüche* ("Aphorisms of Wandering"), to eight poems by Eichendorff, which is even more a testament to his current urge to experiment, both in its instrumentation and in its structural organization. It is written for high voice with an accompanying ensemble of piano, clarinet, horn, and percussion. The poems do not form any kind of narrative, being linked solely by the theme of travel. Musically this is reflected in an extensive use of thematic transformation, in which a "motto theme" given at the beginning is constantly modified—it is, as it were, constantly "in motion." The cycle is constructed upon a scheme of linked keys and related tempi, the latter carefully calculated in ratios of 2:3 and 3:2. The technique of "metric modulation" utilized here (the term is Elliott Carter's) is something that Schoeck might have culled from Berg's *Wozzeck,* or even from Berg's String Quartet Op. 3, which had been performed at the Salzburg ISCM festival, back in 1923. Schoeck's interest in variation and his desire to combine vocal and instrumental forms would find further expression in his opera *Vom Fischer,* which is cast as a set of symphonic variations.

In mid-August 1928 the excessive heat in Morat became too much to bear, so Schoeck and Hilde withdrew together to Rigi-Klösterli, up in the mountains. Schoeck then returned home in order to conduct Bruckner's Fourth Symphony in Winterthur on 31 August. His autumn schedule included lieder recitals in Zurich and St. Gallen with Karl Erb and Durigo in commemoration of the hundredth anniversary of Schubert's death, plus the St. Gallen premiere of *Lebendig begraben* with Loeffel as soloist; the two men also performed the *Elegie* in Zurich again that autumn. Schoeck had been one of many composers to receive an invitation from the Columbia Gramophone Company to participate in a competition to provide a completion of Schubert's "Unfinished" Symphony in honor of the composer's centenary. Unusually for the letter-shy Schoeck, he had written straight back, stating bluntly: "the "Unfinished" is finished enough."[4]

At Christmas Schoeck left for Brunnen, while Hilde went ice-skating in Arosa. He had reached the point in his new opera where the anti-heroine asks to become king (although the work was only forty minutes in length when finished, it would take Schoeck more than another year to complete). He was then back home in January 1929 for yet more concerts, including one on the twenty-fourth in St. Gallen, with Paul Hindemith as soloist in his own Viola Concerto (the *Kammermusik* No. 5) and a concerto by Vivaldi. The season reached a climax for Schoeck with the world premiere of *Wandersprüche* in the Zurich Tonhalle on 16 March. He had originally intended the work for tenor voice, but instead he gave the premiere to Felicie Hüni-Mihacsek. We can probably assume that Hilde felt slighted at being passed over, and it was perhaps the reason that she left for Berlin in April, where she spent two months looking in vain for an engagement at one of the city's opera houses before returning home again, still jobless. In the meantime Schoeck had decided that he needed to get away, too, and so in early April he went on a brief motoring trip to the Rhone Valley in southern France with his friends Toni Schucany and Josi Magg. Only after seeing these landscapes, he told Magg afterward, did he understand the art of Jean-Baptiste Camille Corot (whose use of color remained a topic of his conversation for many years to come[5]). Schoeck returned soon after in order to finish his season at St. Gallen, and he spent the next weeks moping on account of Hilde's absence. Thus was established a pattern that would not change for years: they would squabble, find each other impossible to live with, take time off on their own, and then Schoeck would soon be wishing Hilde back again.

Schoeck now resumed work on *Vom Fischer* and also began to set some new poems of Hesse's to music. By July 1929 the ten Hesse songs that make up his Opus 44 were complete. They do not form a cycle—the songs of the set are highly heterogeneous—but nevertheless benefit from being performed together. Some (such as "Nachtgefühl," "Emotions of the Night") display a greater sense of dissonance than was now usual in Schoeck's music, while others (for example, "Magie der Farben," "The Magic of Colors") have a contrapuntal accompaniment that approaches the neo-Bachian counterpoint of Schoeck's more overtly neoclassical contemporaries. The finest are arguably "Mittag im September" ("Midday in September"), with which Schoeck was particularly pleased, and "Sommernacht" ("Summer Night"), which boasts one of the most beautiful cadential passages to be found in any of his songs (see ex. 22.1). Schoeck mentioned to Corrodi that he had quoted his "Reiselied," Op. 12, no. 1, in this same passage, on the word "Sterne"—though no one else has ever noticed it, and the "quotation" is barely one at all. What its significance might have been to the composer remains a mystery. But the "Reiselied" was for some reason particularly important to Schoeck (he would quote it again, a decade and a half later, in "Der Reisebecher" in the cycle *Das stille Leuchten,* only this time openly, with an appropriate footnote upon its publication).

Schoeck wrote to Hesse on an unusually cold 6 June, in the middle of his work on Opus 44, referring ironically to the previous winter's unusual *Seegfrörni* (the local name for the freezing over of the Zurich Lake):

> The lake will soon be freezing over again; in front of our window on the meadow there stands an intrusive tent of the Salvation Army that's freezing over too, and down by the lake, the Circus Knie and its lions are freezing. Everything at the wrong place at the wrong time, as usual. But I've brought your marvellous "Mittag im September" under cover, and that gives a little warmth.[6]

Example 22.1. "Sommernacht," no. 8 of the *Hesse Songs,* Op. 44, mm. 10–12. Copyright Breitkopf & Härtel. Reprinted by permission. (See also the opening of the "Reiselied," Example 3.1.) "O summer night, and half-overcast stars . . ."

Schoeck and Hilde spent the summer of 1929 on Sylt, the northernmost of Germany's East Frisian Islands, traveling via Colmar, Strasbourg, Kassel, and Hamburg. Then, as now, Sylt was popular with holiday-makers, though since Schoeck had aways preferred southern climes, the choice of destination lay perhaps in a desire to experience directly the north German "platt" dialect that he was setting to music in his new opera. Schoeck had never before seen the North Sea, and he found it both fascinating and terrifying. His general frame of reference remained an Alpine one, for he wrote to Hesse, oddly, that "Sylt and the sea smell of high mountains."[7] Schoeck did some painting while there, and in what one might interpret as an odd gesture of solidarity with his current operatic hero he also delighted in the acquisition of a fisherman's outfit, sou'wester and all. They returned in late August via Lübeck (whose "wonderfully sharpened pencil-point towers" delighted him[8]) and the island of Rügen, famous for its chalk cliffs. They spent a few days in Würzburg, where Hilde went to sing some more auditions—also unsuccessful—and then they returned together to Zurich.

Autumn 1929 brought what was arguably the biggest change to Schoeck's life since moving to Zurich over a quarter of a century before. Hilde had long been insisting that they move house, away from the center of town. But Schoeck had lived on or near the Zeltweg for a decade. It offered his inner circle easy access to him, and to Hilde's chagrin they had not ceased their bachelor-era habits of coming and going as they pleased. Schoeck still liked most of all to go out drinking late in the Kronenhalle, from where it was then only a short walk home, with no worries about catching the last tram. But now, somehow, Hilde got her way. Perhaps Schoeck had finally realized that more and more of his friends had acquired wives whose approach to marriage differed not a great deal from Hilde's. All the same, it was a bitter fight, and one that Schoeck lost without grace. He simply left for Brunnen, leaving Hilde to organize the move all on her own (probably in the vain hope that it would prove beyond her ability). Werner Reinhart helped out again, this time in the form of a cash gift into their bank account. Hilde wrote to him on 2 October to express her thanks, adding that "Othmar was in Brunnen the whole time; he would have suffered so much at such a cheerless move. . . . I hope that he gets well used to the changed situation; as far as he is concerned, I still have some unspoken fears."[9]

Nordstrasse 377, their new house—not an apartment—was further away from the city center than Schoeck had ever lived before. It lay about a hundred meters within the city boundary, though Schoeck referred to it disparagingly as "out in the Black Forest."[10] There was not (and still is not) a tramline nearby, so if Othmar took the tram home, he would still have quite a way to walk. But if he were to stay out carousing in the Kronenhalle and miss the last tram, it would take him about an hour to walk back. This was perfectly clear to Hilde, who wanted him to make a statement that she, not his drinking circle, was now at the center of his life. It had taken Schoeck four years to realize that the freedom of bachelorhood and the commitment of marriage are not compatible states of being. Marrying at a relatively late age, when his ways were set, was no doubt the greater part of the problem. Furthermore, he had probably imagined that having a much younger woman as a wife would allow him to impose his will on their relationship and that it would bring the benefit of ready sex with a willing, nubile partner without the inconvenience of having to trawl bars, buy dinner, drinks and flowers, or take a train to Geneva. He was dreadfully wrong on all fronts, as now seems to have dawned upon him. As Schoeck's various remarks to Corrodi over the years confirm, Hilde did not take long to learn that sexual abstinence was her most potent weapon of all.

The move to "the Black Forest" meant that "Hildebill" had won the most significant battle thus far in their marriage. But Othmar was going to make her suffer for it. It would take another fifteen years before a truce would be declared, and that would only happen under conditions of extreme duress. For the moment, however, it must have looked as though Hilde had gained the upper hand. Schoeck would never live near his friends again.

Chapter Twenty-Three

Variations and Fugue on an Age-Old Theme

A rocky marriage in an unwanted house was not Schoeck's only problem in late 1929. He had offered his latest works to Breitkopf & Härtel, his most regular publisher of the past decade: the three songs Opus 35, the Bass Clarinet Sonata, Op. 41, *Wandersprüche*, Op. 42, and the *Hesse-Lieder*, Op. 44. But Breitkopf only agreed to take on the songs with piano, offered a one-off fee of 750 marks, and asked for more time to consider the sonata and the song cycle, which it deemed "difficult works in publishing terms."[1] Schoeck was furious, withdrew all four works, and thus essentially broke off his relationship with Breitkopf.

He had picked just about the worst possible time for a business argument. Gustav Stresemann, the chancellor largely responsible for creating Germany's current economic stability, died of a heart attack on 3 October 1929, and the twenty-ninth of the same month saw the New York stock market collapse on "Black Tuesday." While the worst repercussions of these events only became apparent over the ensuing months, the economic downturn did nothing to improve the lot of music publishers or their composers. Karl Heinrich David tried to help Schoeck by asking Hindemith for advice. The latter replied on 29 October 1929 that he knew of "a whole number of composers" who were having similar difficulties with their publishers, and that the blame lay simply with the current state of the music industry. He added: "I do not know if it is advisable to leave a publisher unless he is absolutely incompetent."[2] He helped to broker a discussion with his own publisher, Schott's, but they turned Schoeck down in early 1930, stating that there was now hardly any interest in songs in Germany.[3]

Schoeck spent the New Year at the family home in Brunnen, working on *Vom Fischer*—a set of "Variations and Fugue on an Age-Old Theme" as he joked in a letter to Reinhart—while Hilde remained at home, looking after a visiting brother of hers.[4] Absence, however, did little to make the heart less hostile, and when Corrodi ventured out to the Schoecks for tea in January 1930, he walked into the latest minefield. Schoeck had procured a copy of Krenek's *Reisebuch aus den österreichischen Alpen*, Op. 62 ("Travel Journal from the Austrian Alps"), a song cycle written to texts by the composer himself the previous summer. Schoeck did not like it, though this was probably at least in part a natural, equal, and opposite reaction to the fact that Hilde did. After tea Schoeck wanted her to try out his new Hesse songs. But she refused, complaining that they were written against the voice, not for it. Schoeck managed to convince her to try out "Mittag im September," but afterward she pointed out how much more effective Krenek's songs were by comparison. "That's where all discussion stops," cried Schoeck, who refused to continue. Hilde presumably knew that Felicie Hüni-Mihacsek was going to sing the world premiere of the Hesse songs that coming March and was piqued at being good enough to try out her husband's songs at home but overlooked—for the second time in a year—when a soprano had to be found to sing them in public. *Wandersprüche* was performed again on 19 January in Zurich, just a week after the *Reisebuch* squabble, and again Hilde was not involved. This time, the soloist was Julius Patzak. Schoeck had not heard him before but was highly impressed, so Patzak was engaged to sing Schubert's *Schöne Müllerin* in St. Gallen in the autumn of that same year, to Schoeck's accompaniment. They would perform together often in the coming years, with Patzak as delighted with Schoeck's playing as was Schoeck with his singing. One anecdote relates how, when rehearsing for a Schubert concert not long after they had become acquainted, Patzak simply said: "Just play, and I'll sing how you play."[5]

Schoeck's conducting career also continued to keep him busy. His St. Gallen season for 1929/30 included his usual judicious mixture of the old and the new: there were the Concertino for Piano and Orchestra by the young Paris-trained Swiss composer Conrad Beck, Bruckner's Sixth Symphony, Honegger's *Rugby*, Brahms's Fourth Symphony, Schumann's First Symphony, and Hindemith's Organ Concerto. The outside soloists engaged included the cellist Emanuel Feuermann (for the Dvořák Concerto) and the pianist Robert Casadesus (for Beethoven's Fourth Concerto). Schoeck was also called upon to conduct two performances of the Zurich Tonhalle Orchestra in late February 1930 (including Beethoven's *Eroica*) when Andreae was indisposed due to illness.

In May *Penthesilea* received its first production for two years, this time in the Basel City Theater. At about the same time, Schoeck completed the scoring of *Vom Fischer* and decided to offer it to Fritz Busch in Dresden. It was immediately accepted, and the world premiere was planned for the coming 3 October as part of a conference of the "Reichsverband deutscher Tonkünstler und Musiklehrer" ("Imperial Union of German Musicians and Music Teachers"). Busch decided to present the opera as a double bill with a shortened version of *Don Ranudo,* omitting the second act of the latter, and with the hero, Don Gonzalo, impersonating the fictitious Ethiopian prince instead of the job being done by the vegetable-selling Moor. The only person who was unhappy about this turn of events was Hilde. She had good reason, for Schoeck had once again arranged an operatic premiere without consulting any of his publishers. Even worse, this was just as he was opening negotiations once more with Breitkopf & Härtel. It was cheaper for Dresden to deal with Schoeck directly, but this also made the opera far less attractive to any potential publisher, who would normally expect to earn money from a world premiere.

It was at this point that the musicologist and journalist Willi Schuh stepped in to save the day. Schuh was born in Basel in 1900, had studied in Munich (under

Walter Courvoisier and others) and at Bern University (under Ernst Kurth), and had in 1928 begun to write reviews for the *Neue Zürcher Zeitung*. Schoeck had first met him in 1926 in a restaurant on the Kreuzplatz in Zurich, and Schuh soon became one of his most tireless advocates—though without descending into the hagiography that so characterized the writing of Corrodi and Isler. In his diary of Schoeck's later years, Werner Vogel recorded an instance when Schuh criticized the enharmonic notation of a particular chord in one of Schoeck's works. This prompted a long explanation from the composer, but only after Schuh had left. When questioned about that particular occasion in the mid-1980s, Schuh was asked if he was the only person who had ever dared to criticize Schoeck in musical matters. He smiled for the first time during the conversation, and said, "Almost."[6]

Schuh was possessed of considerable diplomatic skills (as his later dealings with Richard Strauss would prove), and he now helped Schoeck to negotiate with Hellmuth von Hase of Breitkopf. By September they had agreed to take on all four works that Schoeck had withdrawn twelve months before, plus *Vom Fischer,* for a total sum of one thousand marks—though this would be the last time that Breitkopf would take any of his music under contract.[7] Schuh even offered to make the vocal score of the opera, though it remains unclear whether he ever got any money for the task. Schuh's brother Gotthard would also be drawn into the Schoeckian periphery. As one of Switzerland's finest photographers, he would over the next three decades be responsible for some of the most evocative photographic portraits that we have of the composer.

Willi Schuh was not the only important new friend to enter Schoeck's inner circle at this time. In June 1930 Schoeck paid an extended visit to a mother-and-daughter pair by the name of Hedwig and Esther Weydmann, who lived in a house called the "Weidhof" in the little town of Landschlacht on the banks of Lake Constance. They had become acquainted through their relatives the Gsells in St. Gallen, which was the nearest city of any consequence, and their house now became a refuge where Schoeck could compose undisturbed. The Weydmanns were wealthy and happy to "mother" Schoeck (after Hedwig's death in 1933 Esther continued the tradition alone). Hilde seems to have realized that neither of them offered her cause for jealousy—she would even on occasion spend time there with her husband. Despite their generosity, Schoeck never rewarded them with a work dedication. In July Schoeck left for a brief visit to Dresden in order to discuss details for his forthcoming premiere, then returned to spend the rest of the summer in Brunnen and in Engelberg. He took the opportunity to go on a walking tour with his brother Ralph, from Engelberg over the Jochpass (which lies at well over two thousand meters), and the experience prompted him in September to write a short song cycle, dedicated to Ralph, called *Wanderung im Gebirge,* Op. 45 ("Walking Tour in the Mountains"), to texts by Nikolaus Lenau. It was his answer to Hilde's advocacy of Krenek early in the year. "I wanted to show Krenek how to do that kind of thing," Schoeck later said to Felix Loeffel.[8] It is cast for baritone and piano—quite possibly to make sure that Hilde would be unlikely to sing it (or criticize it). Schoeck's finest a cappella choral piece also dates from this summer: "Die drei" ("The Three," woo 39) for three-part male-voice chorus. It is a searingly chromatic setting of a morbid Lenau poem depicting the conversation of three mortally injured horsemen after defeat in battle. They are watched by three vultures who are already dividing up their own spoils: "You can eat that one; you the other, and I'll eat this one" they cry as the piece ends. Schoeck did not assign an opus number to "Die drei," which suggests that it was of little lasting significance to him. But its atmosphere of constriction is of an intensity that he never bettered, and it deserves to be in the standard chamber choir repertoire today (though its extreme difficulty will probably always count against it).

Schoeck and Hilde traveled to Dresden in late September 1930, where Schoeck (but not Hilde, it seems) stayed as a guest of Annie Gottlieb-Sallenbach and her husband, with whom he was once more on good terms. Schoeck was delighted with Busch's preparations thus far and wrote to Rüeger five days before the premiere to say so. He even found nothing to object to in the shortened version of *Ranudo,* and when Busch mentioned that it would be nice to have some music linking the first and third acts where once the second act had stood, Schoeck sat down and in the space of an afternoon had written and scored a new "serenade" for oboe, cor anglais, and strings that was given its premiere on the opera's first night. It has since become one of Schoeck's most popular orchestral pieces; it is short and tuneful, and it has a wonderfully atmospheric strumming accompaniment (something that Schoeck had perhaps remembered from Busoni's *Arlecchino* over a decade before).

The double bill of *Vom Fischer* and the revised *Don Ranudo* on 3 October was a great success. Max Hirzel sang the role of the fisherman, Claire Born Ilsebill, and Ivar Andresen the flounder; in *Ranudo,* Jessika Koettrik sang Olympia, while Friedrich Plaschke (Schoeck's erstwhile Achilles) sang the title role. Busch conducted, and the director was Waldemar Staegemann. The reviews in the press were on the whole better than had been the case for *Penthesilea* three years earlier. Some critics (such as Karl Schönewolf in the *Dresdner Neueste Nachrichten*) expressed reservations regarding Schoeck's dramatic gifts, but others wrote of his "grandiose polyphony" (*Neues Wiener Journal*) and his "unerring assurance and warm-blooded strength" (*Leipziger Volkszeitung*). Schoeck left for home in a good mood, though he was piqued by Hilde's decision to stay longer in order to visit a friend (it is tempting to suppose that it was her way of punishing him for staying with an ex-girlfriend, though we have no proof of it).

Stylistically *Vom Fischer* continues the trend toward neoclassicism that we have already noted with regard to the Bass Clarinet Sonata. It is decidedly tonal and abounds in counterpoint (even aside from the obvious example of the fugue toward the end). A particularly neoclassical touch is provided by the use of solo piano to accompany the recitatives and ariosos that form the dialogue between the fisherman and his wife. In many other ways, the work is as "modern" as could

Example 23.1. The opening of *Vom Fischer un syner Fru,* Op. 43. Copyright Breitkopf & Härtel. Reprinted by permission.

be. Despite its fairy-tale subject matter, it is highly constructivist, while the storyline itself has less in common with the Romanticism of Klose than with the *Zeitoper* of the day (its similarity to the marital squabbles depicted in Strauss's *Intermezzo* and in Schoenberg's exactly contemporaneous *Von heute auf morgen* has already been noted in the introduction above). One can also interpret *Vom Fischer* as a late homage to Schoeck's old teacher Max Reger, for, as mentioned, it really belongs to the genre of symphonic variations with closing fugue—with Schoeck bringing a new variation at Ilsebill's every wish. Although "created" by Brahms, this was a genre that Reger had made his own. If one listens attentively, then the A-major opening of *Vom Fischer,* which toys with the interval of E–C♯ and in its harmony tends to gravitate toward the submediant with an added seventh, sounds almost like a paraphrase of the (A-major) opening of Reger's *Mozart Variations* (see ex. 23.1). It is worth remembering that Schoeck had conducted that work in St. Gallen in March 1927, just over a year before he began his opera.

Schoeck's music follows the structure of the text very closely. The storm before the final catastrophe is set as a fugue, and when the couple are banished back to their hovel, the music recapitulates the previous wishes in reverse order, presenting in some four seconds a précis of the music of the previous half hour (only the music from the "wife-as-king" scene is given obliquely, with little remaining except its principal rhythm in diminution, and its descending octave leap; otherwise, each wish is represented by its main motive, albeit truncated, at original pitch) (see ex. 23.2).

Schoeck later claimed to have written seventeen different endings to *Vom Fischer.* As we have already noted, he would often struggle with the close of a large-scale work, as with *Lebendig begraben* and *Gaselen.* In the case of *Vom Fischer,* Schoeck simply recapitulates the opening material and brings the whole to a close with a simple plagal cadence, and one could not imagine a more satisfying rounding-off. This return to the work's beginnings also means that the characters are in effect trapped, "imprisoned" in the work, with the variations acting as metaphorical bars of their highly constructivist prison. It reflects Schoeck's current view of his own marriage with uncanny accuracy.

Example 23.2. The "cataclysm" in *Vom Fischer un syner Fru*, Op. 43 (notated in C). Copyright Breitkopf & Härtel. Reprinted by permission. This is where Ilsebill's wishes appear, condensed, in reverse order, before the flounder sends her and her husband back to their original hovel: 1: to be pope 2: to be emperor 3: to be king 4: for a castle 5: for a cottage.

There are also musical gestures in this opera that point back toward the recent, "expressionist," Schoeck. This is particularly audible, interestingly enough, in the composer's own recording of the work—which is unfortunately only a fragment.[9] The entry of stopped horns at the very beginning of the first scene (measure 84), playing parallel major thirds that have the effect of a false relation (E/C–C♯/A–E/C, etc.), even seems to conjure up a distant memory of similar false relations in muted horns in Stravinsky's *Rite of Spring* (at figure 89 in the Boosey score). In fact, as Derrick Puffett observed, Schoeck's thirds are most likely a reminiscence of the false-related parallel sixths to be found in Hindemith's Viola Concerto (*Kammermusik* No. 5).[10] Since Schoeck conducted that work in January 1929, he will have started learning the score in the previous summer when he decided to program it in St. Gallen. This was precisely the time when he began work on *Vom Fischer*.

Whereas the fisherman and his wife find reconciliation at the end of their forty minutes' worth of marital strife, Schoeck and Hilde were having no such luck. Their squabbling and bickering continued, regardless of whether they were on their own or in company. Hilde maintained repeatedly that in a modern marriage the man and the woman should be equal partners. Schoeck was far more conservative and felt this to be merely an excuse for the wife to intrude on the husband's rights. In January 1931, Corrodi once again walked in on a fight. Hilde claimed to have sacrificed her youth to Schoeck. He countered: "So am I to blame as well that you're getting older? Haven't I given you anything in return? Did I marry you, or you me?"[11]

Chapter Twenty-Four

Put to the Wheel

Schoeck conducted the first-ever concert performance of *Vom Fischer* on 16 January 1931, in St. Gallen. The Swiss staged premiere followed eight days later at the Zurich City Theater, coupled with the revised *Ranudo*, as in Dresden, and on 7 February Schoeck conducted a concert performance of his new opera in Winterthur, as part of a "Schoeck evening" that also included the world premiere of his new song cycle, *Wanderung im Gebirge*. Stravinsky was also around this month, in order to conduct his *Apollon musagète* and *The Fairy's Kiss* in Winterthur, and he stayed with Reinhart from 17 to 22 January. We do not know if Reinhart brought the two men together, though since Schoeck was due to conduct Stravinsky's *Capriccio* for Piano and Orchestra in St. Gallen on 5 February (with Fritz Müller as soloist), perhaps he had scheduled it in the hope that the composer might attend (though he did not). Stravinsky's was not the only modern work on the bill, for the same concert also included Kodály's *Háry János* Suite, Manuel de Falla's *Nights in the Garden of Spain*, and Roussel's Concerto Op. 34 for Small Orchestra. Schoeck's programs had lost none of their inventiveness.

In the midst of the January jubilation around *Vom Fischer,* however, Schoeck was called back urgently to Brunnen. Hilde wrote to Reinhart the next day, 27 January:

> Just a few minutes after he arrived, his dear father died there, of a mild flu and of old age. He passed away very gently. Othmar and I were very attached to his father. For me, despite his age, he was a great support, and a pleasant word from him had made many a thing easier for me.[1]

Perhaps because he was himself an artist, Alfred was one of the few people to have little sympathy for his youngest son's Bohemian notions. Years later Hilde related to Corrodi that he had accused his son of making a fetish of his art in order to ignore his societal duties whenever he felt like it.[2] With Alfred gone, Hilde had even less reason than before to visit Brunnen.

The double bill of *Vom Fischer* and the truncated *Ranudo* was giving Schoeck the biggest operatic success of his career. Seven of the nine performances in Zurich were sold out, and Willi Schuh's review was printed on the very first page of the *Neue Zürcher Zeitung*. Schoeck himself conducted three of the performances. *Vom Fischer* would soon become his most often-performed opera, not least because it is equally suited to concert performance. Werner Reinhart admitted in private that he preferred it that way, writing to Conrad Beck on 10 February that "in the concert hall . . . the work comes across much more strongly and in a much more direct manner than on the stage."[3] The success enjoyed everywhere by *Vom Fischer* must have convinced Schoeck that his decision to embark on a neoclassical path was the right one. His growing status received further confirmation at the turn of this year with the publication of the first full-length book devoted to him: Hans Corrodi's *Othmar Schoeck: Eine Monographie,* published in Leipzig and Frauenfeld. Its author received no thanks from his subject, but the book did get good reviews, such as that of Karl Heinrich David in a special Schoeck issue of the *Schweizerische Musikzeitung* on 15 January 1931.

As usual, operatic success now led Schoeck to look around for a new topic. On 15 March 1931 after the end of the Zurich run, he went for a drink with Corrodi and Hermann Hesse in the Corso Restaurant and moaned that he wanted to write a full-length opera again but didn't have a libretto. If it was intended to prompt Hesse into making an offer, then it failed. Like a pair of ill-fated lovers, when Hesse had wanted to write an opera with him, Schoeck had not; and whenever Schoeck would later suggest it, Hesse would refuse. He was hardly an obvious choice as a librettist, given that his gifts were more lyrical than dramatic, though it would have been fascinating all the same. Schoeck was in private highly critical of Hesse's latest novels (*Narziss and Goldmund* and *Steppenwolf*)—"He's been ruined by Freud," he claimed—but never lost his love of the poetry ("As a poet, he's immortal," he declared).[4] Hesse's continuing admiration for Schoeck found expression in his *Journey to the East,* published later in the spring, in which he was one of several of Hesse's Swiss friends to receive a mention by name.

After the family turmoil and the hustle and bustle of his opera performances, Schoeck took a spring break to Bellinzona and Brissago, then set off with Hilde in mid-April for a holiday on the Mediterranean, staying at the Hotel Pardigon near St. Tropez. It was Reinhart who had recommended it, and since he was visiting Stravinsky in Nice at the time, he also took the trouble to call by. The Schoecks returned home via Marseille, Avignon, and Arles. This year was punctuated by holidays; in June, Hilde and Schoeck (together) spent two weeks at the Weidhof, where Schoeck made regular day-trips to Meersburg on the German side but also worked on a new violin sonata that was to occupy him through the summer. In August the two of them went on a car trip through the Canton of the Grisons with their friend Toni Schucany, and then Schoeck went off to spend two weeks with Rüeger in Bischofszell; his year's journeys were rounded off with a trip to see Alfred Schlenker in Constance.

One of the bêtes noires that would haunt Schoeck with increasing doggedness in his last years surfaced for the first time in the summer of 1931; it seems to have been occasioned by Hilde's buying a gramophone. For when Corrodi visited them on 9 August, he found not only the latter machine but also a Schoeck who was railing against "our [modern] times." Two weeks later Schoeck expanded on the topic on a boys' night out at the Bündnerstübli restaurant, together with Léon Oswald, Alfred Hüni, Wilfried Buchmann, and Corrodi. They discussed the current dire unemployment situation and came to the conclusion that mechanization was to blame. Schoeck declared that "the machine is evil *per se*. Machines have nowhere set man free from work but have chained him to them, enslaved them. Wherever a machine works, man is caught up in its tempo and put to the wheel."[5]

While it may be an act of overinterpretation to suggest that an innocent record player could have been the catalyst for what would become one of Schoeck's prime obsessions, its appearance in the household and his subsequent vocabulary of "machine—tempo—wheel" suggests some correlation. Perhaps Schoeck saw in the gramophone a means of "enslaving" music, of "putting it to the wheel," of "catching it up in its [own] tempo"—in other words, by capturing it, the gramophone somehow removes the music's aesthetic autonomy. There would be occasional tirades after this against the gramophone,[6] and it is noteworthy that Schoeck made almost no commercial recordings as an accompanist. He does not seem to have had any compunction in recording for radio, though this was done live; unfortunately, almost nothing of it has survived.

The fact that the gramophone had been purchased by Hilde might well have made it seem tainted from the very start, as yet another of her "modern" notions, along with equality in marriage. The sheer number of trips that Schoeck made this year, both with Hilde and without her, is striking. It was probably not because of any increased desire to see the world (for the places they visited, with the exception of the Riviera, were places that Schoeck knew like the back of his hand), but an endeavor to get away from home, away from Zurich, away from their life there together. Running away from their problems was simply followed in each case by a return home to where they'd been, and a resumption of hostilities. Corrodi had recently walked in yet again on a huge argument *chez* Schoeck. "There she goes out again, who knows where to, just because I didn't get up in time for lunch," complained Othmar. "She's not prepared to grant me the freedom that life has luckily bestowed upon me."[7] After six years of marriage, Schoeck was still unwilling to get up of a morning, and this was not the first time that Hilde had prepared lunch only to see it go cold. But it is also clear that the two of them had become adept at provoking an irate response from each other. Small wonder that they craved to get out of the house. Schoeck obviously felt that he was doing his part; he had even cast Hilde in a production of Mozart's *La finta semplice* in St. Gallen in the first half of the year. But from what we can gather, Hilde was just as unable to compromise. They were simply making each other desperately unhappy. By the last quarter of 1931 their marriage was by all accounts in a state of catastrophe, so there is a certain ironic logic in that it was now that Hilde became pregnant. Schoeck told no one until the New Year, though it seems that Hilde also kept the news from him for several weeks.

The big musical event of autumn 1931 in Zurich was the Swiss premiere of Berg's *Wozzeck* at the City Theater. Schoeck made sure to go, and he discussed it afterward in the pub. He praised its "high sense of will, the seriousness, the lack of concessions," but added that "It's really no music at all; two of the main elements are lacking: melody and rhythm. It's just harmony, and really, Schreker could do that too."[8] Corrodi remarked that *Wozzeck* reminded him a little of Schoeck's own *Penthesilea* and wondered openly if Schoeck had been at all influenced by the *Three Fragments from "Wozzeck"* that he had heard in Frankfurt in 1924. Schoeck was deeply offended and now claimed only to have heard five minutes of a rehearsal, no more—though Corrodi noted in his diary that before they had gone to the opera, Schoeck had been able to remember specific details such as the musical depiction of the lake at night in which *Wozzeck* drowns, the rising passages in the wind, and so on. It was clear to him—as it is to us, given the similarities we have already noted between the two works—that Schoeck's reaction was a white lie to cover his tracks. It is also noteworthy that Schoeck remarked of Berg's use of instrumental forms in *Wozzeck:* "It's just a sign of his own insecurity." This was probably more a comment on his own music than on Berg's, especially since he was about to embark on a work that would combine a string quartet (the ensemble and the genre) with a song cycle. Schoeck only admitted his real attitude to *Wozzeck* thirteen years later, long after Berg's death, when the passing of time had perhaps erased his need to hide any envy or influence. *Wozzeck*, he said, was "truly a masterpiece, if a very decadent one," and he confessed his regret at never having performed anything by Berg in St. Gallen.[9]

Berg came to Zurich to see the production himself, staying as a guest of Reinhart, though he attended only the final performance of 15 November 1931. We have no evidence that he and Schoeck met. But the experience of hearing *Wozzeck* complete, and of renewing his acquaintance with Berg's music, seems to have exerted some influence upon Schoeck. For he now embarked upon a work in which he came closer to the ambience of Alban Berg than he ever had before, or ever would again.

Chapter Twenty-Five

Gisela

Despite all his outward successes in 1931, a year that closed with performances of the *Elegie* in Winterthur and Romanshorn by the excellent baritone Hermann Schey, Schoeck was descending into a severe depression. He would become enraged by the slightest criticism—as when the loyal Willi Schuh dared to suggest in December that a performance he gave of Bach's *Kreuzstab Cantata* in St. Gallen had been overly "Romantic."[1] But he readily put the blame on Hilde for almost everything that he felt was out of kilter. Corrodi called by to see them just after Christmas and was told by Othmar about the pregnancy: "It's a terrible fate that this had to happen to [me]. . . . What am I supposed to do with a child? She'll only use it as a weapon against me once more, just like she uses everything as a weapon, her migraines . . . everything."[2] The fundamental reason for Hilde's dissatisfaction, he said, was her delusion ("Wahn") that he was a hindrance to her artistic career. As far as he was concerned, the main problem was his lack of sexual fulfilment. He had remained faithful to her since their marriage. But Hilde remained completely passive in bed, he told Corrodi, possessing not a whit of erotic fantasy. Even the abyss of despair into which his affair with Mary had cast him seemed now rosy in retrospect. "At least that suffering with Mary had been fruitful," he moaned, referring to the *Elegie*. He also confided to Corrodi that he was now, as then, writing some Lenau settings. But he would publish them as "songs of an unknown poet," he said, since Lenau was considered so old-fashioned the very name would make people laugh.[3] These were the beginnings of his *Notturno* for voice and string quartet.

Just a few days after this, a means of escape presented itself. Hilde left him. She packed her bags, booked a train ticket, and went to her sister's in Garmisch in southern Germany. Schoeck's friends breathed a common sigh of relief. None of them liked Hilde much, and most of them were sure she felt the same about them. The fact that she did not speak the local Swiss dialect did not help, for this linguistic adaptation was, and still is, for the Swiss a prime signifier of a foreigner's willingness to assimilate. Schoeck was now free. But to everyone's astonishment, he went after her to beg her back. To compound their astonishment yet further, she did as he asked. One might suppose that this conscious decision to remain together might have helped them in future to focus on what they had in common, not on what divided them. But nothing changed, and they continued to fight as before. As far as we know, however, this was the only time that either partner made a serious attempt to escape the other.

Perhaps in an attempt to patch things up, Schoeck and Hilde soon made a trip abroad together. Reinhart had excellent contacts in England, partly because of his behind-the-scenes work for the ISCM, and he had for some time been trying to organize a performance of the *Elegie* in London. He now succeeded, thanks to the local section of the ISCM, though it meant his giving a deficit guarantee of one hundred pounds (some two thousand francs). Schoeck gladly accepted the invitation to conduct, but since he spoke not a word of English, Reinhart—who was fluently polyglot—agreed to go along as a kind of chaperone. Schoeck was by no means unknown there. Besides Newman's favorable review of *Venus* several years before, Corrodi's biography had received a laudatory, if brief, mention in *Music and Letters* the previous October ("The book is carefully and sympathetically written, as well as being extremely well produced").[4] The Schoecks spent a week in the capital. We know nothing of what Hilde saw or did while they were there, but we know that Schoeck visited the National Gallery and the other museums and galleries on a daily basis. A trip to the London Zoo brought him face to face with a bird of paradise that so impressed him it was accorded several mentions in his correspondence. Although his postcards to Hesse and Rüeger complain of a daily greyness, Schoeck's comments to others after his return suggest that, to his surprise, he found the city congenial. He told Corrodi later that he had never felt as much at home in any other foreign city. The English character, he said, had far more in common with the Swiss than with the Germans.[5] Above all, he could barely believe how big London was.

The performance of the *Elegie* took place on 23 February 1932 in the Aeolian Hall, with Keith Falkner as baritone soloist, accompanied by members of the BBC Symphony Orchestra. The advance rehearsals had been taken by Constant Lambert, while the audience for the concert included the British composers Howard Ferguson and Gerald Finzi, both of whom were impressed by the work. A meeting between the song composers Finzi and Schoeck would have been fascinating to report on, but Howard Ferguson later recalled that none took place. Nevertheless, Schoeck made enough of an impression for him to feature, briefly, in the correspondence between Finzi and Ferguson a full twenty years later.[6] The post-concert reception was held at the home of Robert Mayer (a friend of Reinhart's). Although we know that Maurice Ravel was invited, we regrettably have no details of the event. Schoeck and Hilde apparently stayed with Keith Falkner and his wife, where communication was by necessity largely non-verbal. One morning, Schoeck appeared to express with various smiles, "mmmhs" and gestures a particularly overwhelming passion for Mrs Falkner's homemade marmalade. When he was seeing Schoeck off at the railway station, Falkner accordingly surprised him with two jars of it, handed through the window of his compartment just before departure. Falkner remembered years later the further "mmhs," gestures, and joy on Schoeck's face as he received the gift;[7] what he did not know is that the moment he was gone, the ever-polite Schoeck had turned round, his hands full of jars, and asked his neighbors' opinion in words that by all accounts ran something along the lines of "What the hell am I supposed to do with these?"[8]

Schoeck had to return to conduct a rehearsal in St. Gallen on 25 February 1932, and two days later he was in Basel to hear a concert performance of *Vom Fischer* conducted by Felix Weingartner (whose style, however, Schoeck greatly disliked). February 1932 also brought a new run of *Penthesilea* in Zurich, while the world premiere of his new violin sonata (Op. 46) took place in the Zurich Tonhalle on 3 March. Willem de Boer was accompanied by Walter Frey, but Schoeck had inadvertently also promised the premiere to Stefi Geyer, who rang him up when she learnt that she had been dropped, to give him an earful of what she thought of him. The sonata is hardly a work with immediate appeal, though it was well received by the critics. It has proved surprisingly popular in recent years, and there are currently some three CD recordings on the market. But from today's perspective its importance lies perhaps primarily as a stepping-stone in Schoeck's development toward a more contrapuntal, pared-down, neoclassical style that is neither overtly Hindemithian nor particularly indebted to Stravinsky, but with unmistakeable roots in his own late-Romantic and expressionist works of the previous decade. While writing it, Schoeck remarked to Corrodi that "all music, really, is in three parts . . . if ever a fourth voice joins them, then it's really always a harmonizing part."[9] This contrapuntal style would soon find its fullest flowering in the *Notturno,* where Schoeck's response to the poetry would transform the "cold" counterpoint of the sonata into a music of emotional impact such as he had arguably never hitherto attained.

Meanwhile, Hilde was preparing for the birth of their child. She rented another house in March 1932, this time Lettenholzstrasse 39 in Wollishofen, on the other side of town altogether. It lies not far from the city boundary, near where the Youth Hostel stands today; the tram there takes one past the former villa of the Wesendoncks, and the suburbs here are much leafier and less crowded than the area around the Nordstrasse. Thanks to its position in a triangle formed by the Lettenholzstrasse and the Marchwartstrasse, no. 39 has a bigger garden than most of the neighboring houses, and this was undoubtedly a nicer area to bring up a baby. Even today, the street is surprisingly quiet, and on Sundays one hears barely a background hum from the cars and trams that travel along the main road, just a couple of hundred meters away. Since Schoeck had already accepted living away from the center (and had gone to the lengths of begging Hilde back to him in January), he probably did not put up much of a fight this time. In any case, the last tram left for Wollishofen at 12.20 A.M., which meant he could even stay out a little later if he wished.

On 29 May Hilde gave birth to a daughter, Gisela, in the Hirslanden Clinic. Two days later, Corrodi paid a visit to Schoeck at home in Wollishofen.

I found him trembling with indignation, in an incomprehensible rage. . . . "I can't tell you what hatred I often feel toward this woman" he groaned. . . ." This

woman kills every joy in me, this woman robs me of all momentum, so that I
can't work any more . . . she kills every flower that would blossom in me. . . . you
all [his friends] are just stupid Swiss to her . . . that's these German delusions of
grandeur . . . and she told me once, "You're deceiving yourself the whole time;
only you still believe that your *Ranudo* and your *Venus* are masterpieces!"[10]

He went on to complain of Hilde's (financial) demands upon him. She was,
he claimed, in the newest clinic there was, and she had already organized for a
nanny to be at her beck and call when she came home, on top of the maid they
already had (this was at a time, *nota bene*, when the general economic malaise of
the early 1930s was bringing visible financial hardship throughout Switzerland).
He couldn't afford it, he said. And yet his tirades just as swiftly ceased: Hilde
"has magical qualities," he suddenly told Corrodi, "otherwise I'd not love her
so and I would have long separated from her. But I can't." And he was over the
moon with his child, assuring Corrodi that she looked exactly like him, with his
head, his ears, his chin, his expression (though when his friends first saw Gisela,
the only likeness anyone noticed was to Hilde). We do not know if Schoeck was
aware of the irony, but the clinic where Gisela was born lay just a hundred meters
from the Enzenbühl Cemetery, where his first daughter, Bertha, had been buried twenty-one years before.

Chapter Twenty-Six

Lost in the Stars

Early June 1932 brought the festival of the German "Allgemeiner Musikverein" back to Zurich for the first time in more than twenty years. This was still, however, an innocent gesture without the political, overtly hegemoniacal overtones that any Swiss-based German cultural happening would soon acquire under the Nazis. The festival was to have taken place in Graz in Austria, but Graz had pulled out at relatively short notice, at which Zurich had stepped into the breach. The two main events were Hindemith's oratorio *Das Unaufhörliche*, which opened the Festival, and then a performance of Schoeck's *Penthesilea* under the baton of Max Conrad in the same Zurich production that had been given four months earlier. Among those present were Paul Hindemith, Arthur Honegger, Ernst Krenek, and Ernest Bloch. Schoeck was delighted with it, though the reviews were mixed. Aloys Mooser ("snake-head" of 1923) remained unimpressed, remarking upon the work's supposed conventionality and its mish-mash of speech and song.[1] The reviewer of the *Musical Times* (one "M.U."), however, was of a different opinion. While praising the "excellent presentation" of Hindemith's oratorio and its "splendid polyphonic choruses," he felt that "the composer, though he has mastered his craft, is not yet master of himself. . . . On the other hand, the *Penthesilea* of the Swiss composer Othmar Schoeck made a big, general impression."[2]

In late June, as was his summertime wont, Schoeck went to the Weydmanns by Lake Constance for three weeks. He wrote to Reinhart, suggesting that he might want to pay him a visit, but then regretted it when he did, for Reinhart came to convey an orchestral commission from the University of Zurich for its 100th anniversary in 1933. Schoeck was still busy with the *Notturno*, but as he had an honorary doctorate from the institution, he could not say no, especially since it was Reinhart doing the asking. As it happens, Wilhelm Furtwängler had asked Schoeck to write him a small orchestral piece just a month or so before, but Schoeck had turned him down, claiming that he had neither the time nor the inclination.[3] (One wonders how many other composers have ever turned down the chance to write a work for the Berlin Philharmonic). It seems almost as if some instant karma were at work to punish him for his wilfulness, for now he had to write an orchestral piece anyway. But instead of being destined for the Berlin Philharmonic Hall, it would be doomed to performance in the University "Lichthof" in Zurich, whose booming acoustic to this day can make of flatulence a thunderclap. Schoeck accepted the commission—it was worth a thousand francs—but began making excuses for it in advance, claiming that absolute music was an anachronism, that the only really new development in it was jazz, and that he'd rather have written a cantata anyway. He hurriedly sketched the work in order not to be burdened with it for longer than necessary, and Hilde was able to notify Reinhart on 25 August that it was already finished, except for the orchestration. A few days later, emboldened by an extra twelve hundred francs that Reinhart had in the meantime slipped into their bank account,[4] Schoeck and Hilde went on an extended holiday to Salzburg, Vienna (where they saw wonderful productions of Wagner's *Meistersinger* and Weber's *Freischütz*), Trieste, and finally to Novi on the Dalmatian coast. After they arrived back home, Schoeck got the latest bad news about his university piece. Volkmar Andreae was in charge of the festive concert, but it had been agreed that Schoeck would conduct his own work (no doubt so that he could get some extra cash out of an unpleasant commitment). Now Andreae had insisted on conducting Schoeck's piece too, and so Schoeck, to his annoyance, was "asked" by the rector to step down, which he did.

Schoeck worked on the orchestration of his university commission over New Year—it was now called *Praeludium*—and continued with his *Notturno* for baritone and string quartet. On 12 January 1933 in St. Gallen, he conducted Krenek's dodecaphonic Theme and Variations for Orchestra, Op. 69, of 1931 just a few weeks before Andreae and Scherchen did the same with the Zurich Tonhalle and Winterthur Orchestras respectively. Two months later, on 25 March, Schoeck also met up with Stravinsky once more, when he came to Winterthur for a duo concert with the violinist Samuel Dushkin. Schoeck spoke of this occasion twenty years later, telling how they had spent the afternoon together, and of how he had turned the pages for Stravinsky at what was presumably the last rehearsal before the evening's concert:

> All the time that he was playing, Stravinsky pointed out the thematic working to me, which I, however, could barely recognize as such. He was dressed elegantly, spoke German and presented himself in a deft, cosmopolitan manner. Hardly surprising! After all, he has spent his whole life in the most chic places on earth! Stravinsky is interesting company, never boring, just as his music is never boring, though it's just not music to my taste![5]

There is an obvious note of envy here, and the claim that the music was not "to my taste" is somewhat disingenuous. This is the aging Schoeck speaking; the Schoeck of 1933, who had only recently written a violin sonata himself, will, no doubt, have paid particular attention to what he saw and heard in Winterthur. Stravinsky accompanied his *Duo Concertant* and his Violin Concerto (in its piano reduction). Perhaps Schoeck had the opportunity to look at the orchestral score of the latter work; what is certain is that (with the exception of his *Praeludium*), Schoeck's instrumental scoring in these years seems to betray a close acquaintance with Stravinsky's music, for there are undeniable similarities between the wide instrumental spacings employed in the scores of the latter's neoclassical works, including the violin concerto, and those of Schoeck's *Notturno* and his next opera, *Massimilla Doni*.

Schoeck was back in Winterthur in late April to accompany Helene Fahrni in his Hesse songs and Stefi Geyer in his two violin sonatas (Opp. 16 and 46—it seems that she had in the meantime forgiven him for withdrawing her from the premiere of the latter). On 29 April 1933 his *Praeludium* was given its world premiere at Zurich University by Andreae and the Tonhalle Orchestra. The program also included Wagner's *Meistersinger* Overture, and the only consolation that Schoeck had on the day was that the latter work sounded just as awful in the Lichthof acoustic as did his own. It was not really his fault but, self-critical as he was, he still reworked the score thoroughly before its next performance (in its revised form it was accepted later that year by Universal Edition, his first work to appear with them). The *Praeludium* is Schoeck's most successful work for symphony orchestra, though there is admittedly little in his oeuvre to compare it with. At times one can clearly hear how the composer has struggled to wrest it from his imagination. Toward the end, the student song "Gaudeamus igitur" makes an appearance, as in Brahms's famous *Academic Festival Overture,* and the work closes with a slightly forced pomposity reminiscent of the Respighi of the *Pines of Rome.* Schoeck later claimed to have had the motto "Geist und Arbeit" in mind while composing it ("spirit and work," or "mind and work"), and said he had wanted to portray the "pedantry" of scholarship in it.[6] While all this sounds like a poor excuse for a lack of inspiration, the work is itself really quite enjoyable.

While Schoeck was scratching his head about his scoring, Switzerland's neighbors to the north had other concerns. Adolf Hitler had been appointed chancellor of Germany on 30 January 1933, and the Nazi Party had acted swiftly to extend its control over all parameters of German life. The burning of the Reichstag on 27 February provided a useful excuse to persecute Communists and other supposed oppositional elements, and the "Ermächtigungsgesetz" of 24 March—just seven weeks after Hitler had come to power—concentrated all power in the hands of the executive, essentially turning Germany into a one-party state. Schoeck's reaction to all this was mixed. At first he had expressed criticism of the Nazis. There were then moments in the ensuing weeks when he commented that they were perhaps also clearing out much that was bad. But by May he was in no doubt that they were "barbarians": it was, he said, a "revolt of the Pharisees against freedom."[7] He would not always be quite so forthright. For a man who his apologists would later claim was wholly unpolitical, he was perhaps surprisingly perspicacious; he had in fact already realized that he could profit personally from what was happening in Germany—his own moderately modern aesthetic was after all a far cry from the dodecaphony of Schoenberg that the Nazis despised. But he insisted that this was precisely not what he wanted. Again, he would not prove quite so forthright when temptation came his way.

The world premiere of the *Notturno*, Op. 47, took place on 18 May in the small hall of the Zurich Tonhalle. Schoeck, with some trepidation, took it upon himself to offer a financial guarantee for the concert, which was devoted to his works alone. He need not have worried, for despite precious little advertising it was sold out. First he accompanied Loeffel in *Wanderung im Gebirge,* then Willem de Boer in his Second Violin Sonata. Finally, Loeffel sang the *Notturno,* accompanied by de Boer's Zurich String Quartet. According to Walter Schädelin, the impact of the last work was so great that there were ten seconds of silence before storms of applause broke out.[8] The subsequent reviews confirmed the work's immense success. The praise was certainly justified. Schoeck here combines abstract and vocal forms as he had done in many previous works, but he manages to avoid the faults of, say, *Lebendig begraben,* where he was unable to sustain the drama at its close. Furthermore, the strength of inspiration in the *Notturno* is simply far higher than in a work such as *Vom Fischer,* though in formal terms the latter is no less assured.

The *Notturno* is in five movements; it sets ten poems altogether. The inner movements set one poem each, while the first has four and the last, three. There is no "story" as in *Lebendig begraben,* but as the work's title suggests, there is an overall tenor of darkness. All the poems except the tenth are by Lenau. "I've never been able to end with Lenau," said Schoeck several years later, "I wanted to lead myself and the listener out of the depression."[9] The intensely depressing first movement, he said, "is about marriage. I left Lenau's titles out [namely "Liebe und Vermählung," "Love and Marriage"], as they are far too obvious."[10] Another time, he remarked: "I regret not having written the line 'Der immer naht, ihr immer doch zu fehlen' above [the first movement], for this line guided me during the composition."[11] This is a line from the second song of the movement, which tells of the "changeable, deceptive fate of love and marriage" by using the metaphor of a woodland rose in bloom and the brook that flows along before her, who is always drawing near to her, but always fails to reach her ("Der immer naht, ihr immer doch zu fehlen"). Derrick Puffett has pointed out that "Schoeck takes the line and applies it as a principle affecting every level of the composition." He continues:

> The notion of vain pursuit can . . . [imply] something following something else, but always lagging behind; something imitating something else, but not quite exactly; things that normally happen together being staggered or kept apart; something being deflected from its course, frustrated, or forestalled. These ideas can be conveyed in music by techniques of counterpoint, variation, and interruption, and Schoeck's first movement makes full use of such techniques.[12]

At the line in question there sounds a theme that is then used as the first subject of a subsequent sonata-form interlude for string quartet alone, marked *Andante appassionato;* even the second subject is derived from it (see ex. 26.1). But the subject itself is a near-quotation of the "Mary" theme from the piano piece "Consolation" and the final scene of *Venus,* from fifteen years before (and is almost at the same pitch as in the latter):

Example 26.1. *Notturno,* Op. 47, first movement, m. 90, Andante appassionato (first violin). Copyright 1933 by Universal Edition. See also Exx. 13.1 and 13.2.

It is no coincidence that Schoeck had told Corrodi, just at the time when he began work on the *Notturno,* that "at least that suffering with Mary had been fruitful," for the *Notturno* seems to have represented for him an attempt to rekindle the creative spark that had led to his earlier works. To judge from the remarks he made at the time, he was aware that his recent music bore little trace of the white-hot inspiration that Mary had inspired. Conjuring up her metaphorical shade to help him overcome his present shortcomings might thus have been a perfectly conscious act. It certainly worked, for it is generally accepted that the *Notturno* displays Schoeck at the very height of his powers (it would even impress Alban Berg in early 1935[13]). But it is noteworthy that the "Mary" theme is never given in its original form. The Andante appassionato alone features some forty transformations of it (they are described in detail by Puffett[14]), but none of them identical to the real source. It is a musical expression of that trick of memory we all know, whereby a familiar tune haunts one's mind but evades all attempts to notate its precise contours. This mirrors perfectly the motto of the movement. This interlude probably represented several intermingled desires on the part of Schoeck. Its mantra-like reiteration of the "Mary" theme in its multitude of transformations is on the one hand a quasi-shamanic summoning up of a former muse to aid him in the present. On the other, given that Schoeck was at the time in a deeply troubled relationship, this sudden obsession with Mary's theme—"always drawing near her, but never reaching her"—is surely also an expression of loss, of regret that things had not worked out differently a decade before, of an ideal that can never more be attained. In this sense, the avoidance of exact quotation could signify Schoeck's intention (whether subconscious or no) to "hide" these now illicit desires. Hilde, as yet, knew nothing of Mary. But for Schoeck this perhaps made the act of concealment even more necessary.

In the last song of the first movement (also the final poem that Lenau wrote before he descended into madness), the poet looks down into a river and sees his own soul flowing past, weighed down with sorrow. The second movement of the *Notturno* is an instrumental scherzo with trio, in which the narrator describes a nightmare. The recapitulation of the scherzo overlaps with the end of the trio in a superb dramatic stroke. The third movement, cast as a rondo, is highly chromatic, and perhaps the closest Schoeck ever came to the style of Alban Berg. The brief fourth movement is a desolate depiction of autumn in $\frac{5}{4}$ meter, which Schoeck later claimed to have written at the time of the *Elegie,* though in stylistic terms, with its chromaticism and the fragmentary nature of its quartet accompaniment, it firmly belongs here. The fifth and final movement opens with another version of the Mary theme, this time with its intervals expanded to span more than an octave. The first song ("Der einsame Trinker"—"The Lonely Drinker") represents a lapse in quality, noticeable only because of the compelling nature of the music before and after. The second song comprises only a two-line poem ("O solitude, how gladly I drink / From your fresh woodland well"), and there then follows an interlude in sonata form as a kind of parallel to that of the first movement (though here there is no development section). The final song is a setting of one of Gottfried Keller's last poetic sketches. When Schoeck's friend René Niederer brought it to his attention, he sketched it on the back of a visiting card, though in doing so he missed out three words by mistake (and intuitively improved it in the process, as he thereby removed a repetition of the word "Auge," "eye"). In this brief prose poem, the narrator addresses the "Heerwagen," the constellation known in English as the "Plough," and imagines his soul being carried along on it, "innocent, as a child; I shall look far into the distance to see whither we are bound." This poem might even have appealed to Schoeck on account of its superficial similarity to the final text (by Stefan George) of Schoenberg's Second String Quartet—the work that in its combining of the genres of string quartet and lied was the *Notturno*'s most significant precursor. Both texts are cast in the first person, both tell of other planets or stars, and both end with the poet soaring away in a quasi-pantheistic merging with the universe.

Schoeck sets this final poem as a chaconne. A final transformation of Mary's theme is heard at its opening, with expanded intervals, hovering above the long-held whole-note chords of the accompaniment. It soon sounds again, in augmentation, in the first violin, accompanied by fragments of itself in even greater augmentation, repeated over and over in the lower strings (see ex. 26.2). Its contours haunt the remainder of the song.

In its gradual process of transformation, the "Mary" theme has already left its original form far behind. On the final page of the score it seems to dissolve away altogether until at the end—as the narrator's soul is carried away into the stars—barely a memory of it remains. Whether or not this "casting off" of Mary's theme was for Schoeck an act of personal catharsis acted out in the very substance of his music, the overall effect of the final song is undoubtedly cathartic for the listener after all the conflict that has preceded it.

We do not know how Hilde reacted to the *Notturno,* though the manner in which it proclaimed to the world her marital strife must have caused her deep embarrassment. When Schoeck took her on a few days' holiday to Paris straight after the premiere, it was perhaps meant to divert them both from the problems he had so directly depicted in his music. The *Notturno*'s first and third movements in particular are among the darkest creations to have come from Schoeck's imagination, and their depiction of the abyss of depression surely has few parallels in their time. But the final Keller setting, with its predominantly "white-note" harmony, somehow succeeds in resolving all the torments that have gone before. Where *Lebendig begraben* had failed to carry through its dramatic trajectory to its close, the *Notturno* saves its finest moments till the very end.

Example 26.2. *Notturno,* Op. 47, fifth movement, final song; chaconne accompaniment with a transformation of "Mary's theme" in the first violin. Copyright 1933 Universal Edition. "[Plough, mighty] constellation of the Teutons, you who travel with constant, calm [motion . . .]."

Chapter Twenty-Seven

Whores and Madonnas

Schoeck's publishers were far from enamored with the *Notturno*. Breitkopf turned it down, as they had *Wanderung im Gebirge*. Hug took on the latter work, but Schoeck was reluctant to have the *Notturno* published at home, as he was sure that his compatriots would cease to take him seriously if his biggest works were not published abroad. Universal Edition had just accepted the *Praeludium*, and they now also agreed to publish the *Notturno* when the Swiss Musicians' Association donated a thousand francs for the purpose. Hug did bring out his next opus number, however: the Cantata Op. 49, written in the second half of 1933. This is an odd work for an odd ensemble—seven movements, all to texts by Eichendorff, for small men's chorus, solo baritone, three trombones, tuba, piano, and percussion. The piano had been Karl Heinrich David's idea—Schoeck had shown him the score at an early stage, only to be assured that the tuba player would have a heart attack "after ten measures" if he did not change the instrumentation to lighten his load.[1] Not only was this Schoeck's first substantial choral work since *Trommelschläge*, but it is also his only unashamedly "political" work. While its target is clearly the totalitarianism that was dominant to the north, it takes "jingoism" in general ("Vaterländerei") firmly in its sights, admonishing the listener to hold fast to moral values. Certainly, no thinking person in Zurich could at this time have had any doubts about the nature of the Nazi regime. After Hitler's assumption of power there had been an increasing number of refugees finding their way into Switzerland, many of whom were active in fields of artistic endeavor. Within a matter of weeks in early 1933, Ferdinand Rieser, the director of the Zurich Schauspielhaus, began collecting about him men and women of the theater who were now *non grata* in Germany. By the opening of the next season, his ensemble already included names such as Therese Giehse, Kurt Hirschfeld, Ernst Ginsberg, and Teo Otto.[2]

At the time that he wrote the cantata, Schoeck was presumably preparing himself for the next season's concerts in St. Gallen, which included a fascinating program on 23 November 1933 that featured Debussy's Two Nocturnes, Stravinsky's Suite from *Petrushka*, Prokofiev's Violin Concerto, Op. 19, and Ravel's Piano Concerto in G (this last work, composed just two years earlier, would not feature on the concert programs of Zurich or Winterthur until 1944 and 1948 respectively). To what extent Schoeck was influenced by the sounds he discovered in the scores of Ravel and Prokofiev we cannot know precisely, though the cantata sounds so different from his previous works that it is tempting to suppose there must be a concrete reason for it. It has never entered the repertoire, though it is one of Schoeck's most inventive scores, taking him unexpectedly into a sound-world that we associate far more with Kurt Weill, and it deserves to be heard more often.

Schoeck spent part of the summer of 1933 in the company of Toni Schucany on a driving tour through the Dolomites to Venice. Otherwise, the summer months were spent mostly in Brunnen, and partly with Hilde in nearby Rigi-Klösterli. Autumn brought the first performances in eleven years of his opera *Venus,* again at the Zurich City Theater. It was directed by Karl Schmid-Bloss, who had sung the part of Raimund at the world premiere but had now advanced to the position of overall director of the house; the conductor was Robert F. Denzler. Denzler had in the meantime made a name for himself in Berlin, but when the Nazi takeover made things difficult for non-German nationals, he had returned as music director to his old institution in Zurich.

Horace was sung by Artur Cavara, a lyric tenor from Latvia who had sung at the Kroll Opera in Berlin under Klemperer. Denzler, said Schoeck afterward, conducted the work better than he could have done himself.[3] A few changes were made to the opera, apparently at Schmid-Bloss's insistence,[4] the main one being the omission of Simone's appearance at the very end. As we have already observed, the original *pianissimo* ending of *Penthesilea* had been similar to the ending of *Venus.* Just as Schoeck had changed *Penthesilea* to end with a "bang," so he now did the same with *Venus,* writing an abrupt close after Horace's final monologue and death. But whereas the big bang of *Penthesilea* better suits the latent expressionism of the drama, the new ending to *Venus* just sounds truncated. Schoeck confessed to having written several possible endings, though we shall never know if the ones he discarded were better or weaker, as no sketches survive.

Schoeck's feelings toward Germany continued to sway between a grudging aquiescence in the status quo and something akin to germanophobia. This inability to reconcile his love and hatred for the nation, for its people, and (most of all) for "the German woman" in general (and thus Hilde in particular) would become increasingly pronounced over the coming years. The varied stance of his friends reflected the divisions within Schoeck himself. One or two were sympathetic to the Nazi cause—a son of Ernst Isler was an ardent supporter, as was René Niederer—while there were those, such as Hermann Hesse and Willi Schuh, whose opposition was quite clear. (Schuh, although still only an up-and-coming music journalist, had risked much by adding his name to the public protest against the manner in which the Nazis had harangued Thomas Mann in early 1933.) Then there were others, Corrodi first among them, who harbored grave reservations about the methods of the Nazis but who, like many in Western Europe, saw them as a useful bulwark against the supposedly far greater evils of Soviet Communism. Corrodi, however, was also an anti-Semite. He was thus upset when Schoeck gave his *Notturno* to Universal Edition, and he wrote in his diary:

Just now, when—as he himself says—he often gets anonymous letters from people who see in him the true German composer of the present day—just now he turns away from his German publishers and casts himself into the arms of the Viennese Jews![5]

Not only did Universal Edition have prominent members of staff who happened to be Jewish, but it was also the acknowledged publisher of contemporary music and thus by definition "suspect" to both anti-modernists and anti-Semites. Corrodi's diary records occasional anti-Semitic remarks that Schoeck made during their common visits to bars, and we have no reason to doubt their veracity. But we must nevertheless be cautious when investigating anti-Semitism on Schoeck's part, real or latent, for Corrodi is our only documentary source, and he was obviously keen to give particular weight to any remark that might be construed as reflecting his own prejudices. And even here the evidence remains scanty, and Corrodi devotes far more space to his distress at Schoeck's dislike of the Nazis. On 11 February 1934, for example, he wrote that Schoeck was indulging in "orgies of hatred against everything that is happening to the north of the Rhine." He went on: "His fanaticism even goes so far that he said yesterday: he himself had less fear of the Bolshevists."[6] That was something that Corrodi could not possibly comprehend. The many hundreds of Schoeck's letters that have survived contain no racist remarks of any kind.

Perhaps the most accurate barometer of Schoeck's real attitude is the list of soloists with whom he worked in St. Gallen in the 1930s. While he continued to work with his favorite German musicians, even when they had an unproblematic relationship with the Nazi regime (such as Walter Gieseking, who would be blacklisted by all four Allies after 1945,[7] or Elly Ney), he also engaged many Jewish soloists. These included Rudolf Serkin and Bronisław Huberman (in the 1934–35 season), Nathan Milstein and Emanuel Feuermann (1935–36 season; Milstein again in the 1937–38 season), and Artur Schnabel (in the 1936–37 season). Some had already taken a public stance against the Nazis, such as Huberman, a committed Zionist, who in the months before he played in St. Gallen had turned down a high-profile offer from Furtwängler to play in Nazi Germany; another was Adolf Busch, who was not Jewish but had openly opposed the Nazis' policies, and who performed with Schoeck in the 1934–35 season. Schoeck also conducted music by composers deemed unpalatable by the Nazis. In late 1936 he conducted Hindemith in the latter's viola concerto *Der Schwanendreher* (another case of Schoeck's programming tactics preempting both the Winterthur and Zurich orchestras). And a few weeks later, on 14 January 1937, he conducted Krenek's dodecaphonic "Fragments from *Karl V*," just a matter of months after their world premiere at the Barcelona ISCM, at a time when the opera was, to all intents and purposes, banned in the composer's native Austria. Admittedly, the above-mentioned Jewish soloists disappear from Schoeck's programs after the outbreak of war in 1939—but that was because they had all left continental Europe by then. He did, however, continue to conduct works that were banned in Germany until the very end of his conducting career (the 1940–41 season being something of an exception, as discussed in chapter 31 below). And when Carl Flesch managed to flee from Nazi-occupied Europe in 1943, Schoeck would be one of the first to engage him as a soloist.

While Schoeck's programming policy thus seems to belie any suggestion that he was somehow sympathetic to the policies of the Nazi regime, it would also be erroneous to regard it as intentionally demonstrative of anti-Nazi sentiments, for he did not make any attempt to distance himself from Germany when the authorities there showed an increasing interest in him and his music. But it does make evident the fact that Schoeck made no active effort to ingratiate himself to those north of the border, and this should be borne in mind as we investigate the chronology of his actions in the ensuing years. The only effort that Schoeck really seems to have made in the 1930s was to ignore politics altogether, both in his musical activities—with the early exception of his cantata—and in his personal life. He even managed to surprise Corrodi. For while the latter in his diary from the autumn of 1933 onwards recorded Schoeck's repeated harsh criticism of the Germans in general and of the Nazis in particular, he also expressed astonishment that Schoeck continued to associate happily with someone like René Niederer, who was devoted to the National Front, the Swiss Nazi Party. As odd as it may seem to us that Schoeck could ignore aspects of his friends that did not appeal to him, he was apparently able to do so.

The aspect of Schoeck's life that seems most to have surprised his friends at this time was not his politics or lack of them but his joy in fatherhood. He carried photos of Gisela with him everywhere, he loved playing with her, and even happily looked after her (albeit with a maid to help him out) whenever Hilde went off on her own to visit family in Germany. The brief film footage that we possess of the Schoecks in the 1930s, made by his friend Josi Magg, is silent. But we need no sound to be able to observe that whenever Gisela enters the picture, she is at the center of her doting father's attention, while Hilde seems to stand somehow apart even when she is in the middle of things. Gisela was also in large part responsible for Schoeck's latest operatic project. As noted before, the success of any of his operas would always prompt Schoeck into a Pavlovian grubbing around for a new topic. He had found none after the success of *Vom Fischer*, but he seems to have been more determined after the recent run of *Venus*. Twenty years later Werner Vogel interviewed Rüeger about the genesis of this next opera. Rüeger said he had suggested Balzac's "Gambara" as a possible topic—a strange tale of a penniless composer inventing new instruments and writing an operatic trilogy—but that Schoeck had decided instead to turn another story from the same volume into an opera: "Massimilla Doni." In February 1934 Corrodi wrote in his diary that René Niederer was responsible for having suggested it. Whatever the opera's precise origins, Corrodi noted in horror that it was a glorification of adultery, and that all of Schoeck's friends were advising him against it.

In the novella, the noblewoman Massimilla Doni has, for familial/political reasons, been married off to the aging rake Duke Cattaneo. He is now impotent, finds pleasure only in his protégé, the singer Clara Tinti, and expects his wife to find sexual fulfilment elsewhere. Massimilla loves the young aristocrat Emilio, but her religious scruples prevent her from committing adultery. A twist of the plot has Emilio seduced by Tinti; the story ends when Massimilla, prompted by Emilio's fatherly friend Vendramin, agrees to take the place of Tinti in Emilio's bed, thus reconciling her "ideal" love of Emilio with the physical reality of sexual love. Tinti herself is united with the tenor Genovese. At the close of the novella, the author announces that Massimilla is expecting Emilio's child. The action takes place in Venice, with the city's theatrical milieu as its backdrop.

Rüeger recalled twenty years later that Schoeck had asked him to write the libretto in the summer of 1934, but that he had

> found it wasn't a topic that could enthral today's theatergoer, couldn't agree to it, and so declined. But obviously, the novella expressed something that deeply moved Schoeck at the time. He urged me on, complained he had already noted the themes for the individual characters, the music was as good as finished, and he couldn't just let it rest now. . . . He left me no peace until I . . . wrote the libretto.[8]

The "something" was apparently two things. One of them was Gisela. "The yearning for a child should be at the center of the work," Schoeck told Corrodi. The other was the loss of virginity. In conversation with Corrodi later that year, Schoeck referred to Emilio's seduction by Tinti and confessed: "We've all been through this conflict. . . . if I hadn't been seduced by such a woman of experience, I'd still today be as chaste as Joseph."[9] Sadly for the inquisitive biographer, the identity of Schoeck's Tinti remains uncertain, though a remark of Armin Rüeger's, quoted in chapter 5 above, suggests that it could well have been Bertha Liebert. Certainly the fact that Bertha had borne him his first child would provide a link between the twin themes of *Massimilla*—acquiring sexual experience and becoming a father. Schoeck's new-found joy of parenthood had perhaps prompted him to dwell on thoughts of his first daughter, now long dead. But the contours of the "Consolation" theme (and of its chromatic, descending bass accompaniment) also seem to wind their way through much of Massimilla's music in the first act, if in a manner more elliptical than in the *Notturno. Massimilla Doni*, it seems, is full of ghosts from the past.

While Schoeck was busy constructing his rarified opera plot, he was at the same time finding that politics could impinge directly on his life and work. His cantata and "Die Drei" received their world premieres on 1 March 1934 in a concert of the chamber choir "Chambre 24" under their director Max Graf. Although Schoeck's friends saw the former work as a polemic against the Nazis, those who did not know him seem to have felt that it mocked their beloved Swiss democracy instead. Corrodi even heard the choir members cursing it openly in the Kronenhalle after the premiere. And on 17 April Schoeck at last experienced the "New Germany" palpably, if at one remove. Edwin Fischer was conducting his own chamber orchestra in a performance of the *Elegie* in the Beethovensaal in Berlin, with Loeffel as soloist, before an audience that included the Swiss ambassador. After the first two numbers, a man went up onto the podium to speak to Fischer, and at the same time, someone began whistling at the back of the hall. Another then jumped up, shouting "Jews are playing here! Out with the Jews!," then "Out with Guttmann! Out with Wolff!" They eventually found out that they had mistaken the Beethovensaal for the Bechsteinsaal, where two such named musicians were apparently due to perform on the same evening. In the interval they tried to apologize to Fischer and the ambassador, and after the interval some of them mounted the podium to explain that they had been sent to the wrong hall, though this only caused laughter in the audience. Blows were exchanged at the back of the hall before the concert was able to continue (which, astonishingly, it did).[10] It turned out that Fischer himself had provided a number of free tickets for "SA members of limited means," and that these had been given to the men in question, who along the way received instructions from higher up that they should disrupt the concert. This incident was widely reported in the press except, of course, in Hugo Rasch's review for the Nazi Party's daily paper, the *Völkischer Beobachter*, on 19 April. Although a Swiss citizen, Fischer cultivated a close relationship with the Nazi authorities (in recognition of his devotion, in spring 1938 he would receive a signed photograph of the *Führer* in a silver frame).[11]

Shortly after the events in Berlin, the first-ever festival devoted to Schoeck's music took place in Bern, from 22 to 29 April 1934. It was organized by Fritz Brun, with Max Wassmer—a local patron of the arts and friend of Hesse—as the financial guarantor. Schuh began the week with a lecture (printed soon after by Hug), and there followed performances of the *Postillon, Lebendig begraben,* the *Präludium, Notturno, Elegie, Vom Fischer un syner Fru,* and various songs and chamber works; *Venus* was also staged at the City Theater. The participants included Brun, Helene Fahrni, Durigo, Loeffel, the Bern String Quartet, and Schoeck himself. The festival was reviewed widely in the press, with even the *Völkischer Beobachter* sending its music critic, Erwin Bauer. On 27 April he published a hymn of praise to Schoeck's lieder entitled: "Othmar Schoeck—ein deutscher Musiker" ("Othmar Schoeck—a German musician"). There was also a talk on Swiss radio by a "Herr Brawand," whose idyllic depiction of Schoeck's marital joy caused guffaws of mirth among his drinking friends, with Alfons Magg performing an impromptu send-up for their benefit (all behind Schoeck's back, of course).[12]

Early June brought another performance of *Venus,* this time back in Zurich, coupled with the *Wandbild,* as part of the 100th anniversary celebrations of the Zurich City Theater. The adulation being showered upon Schoeck had no impact on his domestic circumstances, however. Hardly any of Schoeck's friends visited the Lettenholzstrasse any more—when Léon Oswald ventured there in the spring, he ran straight into a huge argument and afterward wished that he had never bothered.[13] Schoeck told Corrodi in June how he fantasized about running off with Gisela. But he knew that her mother would always get custody, and he could not bear the prospect of life without his daughter. "We men are always the weaker sex, and women use all means against us," he complained.[14]

When Schoeck went off for his annual working holiday at the Weidhof in June that year, he returned early, after just two weeks. He explained to Hilde that he wanted to make good a promise to take her on a trip to the Albis. She was astonished; he had never before been this considerate. But she also noticed that he was constantly depressed, as if "paralyzed." The truth was more complicated, though we do not know whether he came clean of his own accord or whether she wheedled it out of him: he had met Mary de Senger. How, where, and why remain a mystery, nor do we know just how intimate that meeting had been. Hilde had no idea who she was. But she now gave Schoeck a clear choice (as she recalled over two decades later): either he had to break off all contact with Mary, in which case their marriage would continue, or she would leave him for good and take Gisela with her. He chose the former. Hilde neither forgot nor forgave her rival, and her rancor would be undying.

Hilde now left for a summer holiday on Sylt, making sure to take Gisela and their maid with her—presumably to give Schoeck a taste of what life would be like if he changed his mind. He went to Brunnen, where he continued work on his opera, of which, however, he had little text as yet. But he busied himself writing motives for the different characters, sketching out the orchestral introduction to the first act, and so forth. At exactly this time in Hertenstein, some ten miles to the west of Brunnen, Sergei Rachmaninoff sat in his recently completed Villa Senar, writing his Rhapsody on a Theme of Paganini. Despite their geographical proximity—Rachmaninoff spent his summers in Hertenstein until leaving for his final American exile in 1939—we have no record of either composer taking any notice of the existence of the other.

Schoeck's nephew Georg, at the time an inquisitive boy of ten, has given us a record of Schoeck's composing habits in this summer and the next, when he was working on *Massimilla*:

> Since Schoeck regularly composed until two, sometimes three in the morning, he urgently needed his morning slumber and never appeared until toward half past one in the afternoon. The *table d'hôte* was of course finished by then, but care was taken to keep the set menu warm for him. . . . at about quarter past two, after the black coffee that he always needed, as he said, for the "ascent onto the glacier," he stood up with great self-discipline and walked off in his swaying gait. . . . We had placed his piano in a small, bare room with an irregular floorplan, the so-called No. 38. . . . All he wanted was quiet and not to be disturbed, and that was what he found there, behind closed shutters and drawn curtains. . . .

Dinner was at half past seven. At that time, I was sent up to fetch him. I always remained listening in front of the door for a moment. I heard him walk up and down in the room; after long intervals he would play a chord or a tricky harmonic progression softly on the piano, obviously only for control purposes (I hardly ever heard him play anything that hung together). Mostly I had to knock two or three times before he reacted. When I then opened the door, a cloud of smoke would hit me: the room was full of the fog of the Toscanellis that he smoked while he worked, though not as many as one might have thought, for when he composed he would forget to inhale, and so he mostly held only a cold stump between his lips. But the ashtrays were overflowing with burnt-out matchsticks.—He looked at me, without seeing me; it always lasted quite a while before he awoke from his trance and sent me off with the explanation that he'd be right there (which then usually took another half hour).

We all met in the "Stubli" [the family living-cum-dining room]. My father soon had to go to the tiresome hotel guests, but in the evening one could at least rely on the other brothers. Their discussions . . . were less about art than about the desolate situation of the world. . . .

Toward ten o'clock the meal was finally over. Ralph and Paul went down to the Rössli [a pub/restaurant in the village below] . . . and Othmar disappeared again into the upper regions, for now the most fruitful time of the day began for him. In order not to disturb the sleep of awkward hotel guests, he had brought with him a damping mechanism that could be folded down into the inside of the piano. Ghostly noises were all that remained of the piano's sound, but these obviously were perfectly sufficient for him to exercise control over what he was writing.[15]

Chastity was the order of the day until Hilde returned to Zurich at the end of the summer, which was a matter of much frustration to Schoeck. But as much as he then wished her back, her return merely set off their arguments once again. Nor was she any more popular with his friends, for in early August, two of them had begun arguing openly about which of them desired to strangle her the most.[16] When Corrodi ventured out to the Lettenholzstrasse on 25 September, he inevitably walked into another disastrous situation, for Hilde had just taken Schoeck to task for going out late the night before with Willem de Boer and Ernst Morgenthaler.

Schoeck had recently been affected by events across the border once more, though again only indirectly. One of the German critics attending the "Schoeck week" in Bern had been a certain Willi Schmid from Munich, long an admirer of Schoeck's music. But his name was identical with that of someone on the hit-list on the "Night of the Long Knives" at the beginning of July 1934, when Hitler arranged for the murder of his second-in-command Ernst Röhm and a host of other opponents real and imagined. One of the appointed murder squads in Munich had a "Willi Schmid" on their list, and in order to find him, they looked up his address in the phone book. The name is about as frequent in Germany as its English equivalent, "William Smith," but since common sense was no prerequisite for Nazi hitmen, they turned up instead at the critic's apartment and killed him (presumably taking any protestations of innocence as adequate proof of guilt). We do not know what happened to the other Willi.

At the end of 1934 two of Schoeck's friends in Germany, Paul Hindemith and Wilhelm Furtwängler, also became victims of the Nazis, though it was their careers, not their lives, that were put in jeopardy. The former was regarded as "degenerate" by leading Nazis (Hitler included), and when the latter defended him in print on 25 November, the resulting "Hindemith Case," as it became known, forced Furtwängler to resign from his post with the Berlin Philharmonic, and Hindemith to take indefinite leave from the Hochschule für Musik in Berlin. By autumn 1934 Schoeck's opinion of matters north of the border was, at least for the moment, unequivocal: "All the Germans . . . are off balance. The whole nation is sick."[17]

Chapter Twenty-Eight

"*. . . he can write music all right . . .*"

On 14 and 15 January 1935 Schoeck conducted his *Lebendig begraben* in the Zurich Tonhalle, with Loeffel as soloist; Bruckner's Fourth Symphony comprised the rest of the program. A couple of days later, a man dressed as a tramp knocked at the door of Schoeck's home on the Lettenholzstrasse. When the door opened, he asked, in German: "Does the man live here who composed *Lebendig begraben*? I'd like to meet him."[1] It was James Joyce. He was visiting Zurich to see his opthalmologist, Alfred Vogt, and—being a music lover—had ventured into the Tonhalle for the concert on the fourteenth. He wrote to his daughter-in law the next day as follows:

> Helen, please go out and buy Kassell's German-English, English-German Dictionary and sit down with Giorgio to study, first of all, the text of Gottfried Keller's poem sequence Lebendig begraben which I forward under separate cover together with piano score for bass voice by Othmar Schoeck. I heard this sung last night by the Bern bass Fritz [*sic*] Loeffel . . . bought the score just now and have rung up Prof. Fehr to ask O.S. to sign it for Giorgio. . . . If I can judge by last night he stands head and shoulders above Stravinsky and Antheil as composer for orchestra and voice anyhow. I did not know Keller wrote this kind of gruesome-satiric semi-pious verse but the effect of it on any audience is tremendous. . . . Schoeck is a type rather like Beckett who gets up at 2.30 P.M. his wife says. But I hope to catch him before he falls asleep again. But he can write music all right.[2]

Soon thereafter he invited Schoeck and his wife out to a slap-up dinner and gave Schoeck a copy of *Ulysses*, in French translation, inscribed "homage de son admirateur James Joyce / Zürich le 22 janvier 1935." While Schoeck was being thus feted by the leading literary modernist, one of the leading musical modernists was admiring his *Notturno* at a Viennese performance sung by Loeffel and organized by Krenek. It was Alban Berg, who had one of his pupils pass on his compliments to the composer—though with the remark that the singer had not pleased him as much as the work.[3] This was merely the first of several major international performances that Schoeck enjoyed in the first half of 1935. Loeffel also sang the *Notturno* in Amsterdam in March, while the same month saw Stefi Geyer and Franz-Josef Hirt perform Schoeck's recent Violin Sonata in London in a "Swiss evening" financed by Reinhart that also included some of Schoeck's songs. Mosco Carner's review in the *Schweizerische*

Musikzeitung praised Stefi's "manly, firm bowing" and the ease and precision of the soprano soloist, Sophie Wyss[4] (the same who would give the first performance of Benjamin Britten's *Our Hunting Fathers* and *Les illuminations* in 1936 and 1940 respectively). Schoeck's next Viennese concert came in early April 1935, when Loeffel sang the *Elegie* under the young Swiss conductor Max Sturzenegger. Four days later he was in Winterthur to sing *Lebendig begraben* under Scherchen at the annual Swiss *Tonkünstlerfest*.

Schoeck attended neither the Viennese concerts nor the one in London, for he was busy in Switzerland with his St. Gallen concert series (February saw him conducting Mahler's *Lied von der Erde* once again). On 2 April he made sure to attend the Swiss premiere of Hindemith's *Mathis der Maler* Symphony, though he found it "empty inside"[5] (the opera as a whole would please him more when he saw it three years later). Then one Friday evening in April 1935, just before Easter, Schoeck happened to be sitting in the Kronenhalle when Ernst Morgenthaler arrived to meet a friend by the name of Felix Speiser, with whom he was about to embark on a driving holiday to Madrid. When Morgenthaler mentioned their plans, Schoeck promptly invited himself along (he would thus seem not to have been overly superstitious, as Arthur Honegger had been involved in a serious car accident on just such a trip to Spain, one year before). Speiser just as promptly agreed, and within two days they were on their way, traveling in a freezing open car through Provence to Biarritz, where Schoeck saw the Atlantic for the first time, then to San Sebastian in the Basque country. After that came Burgos, and finally Madrid, where Speiser left Schoeck and Morgenthaler. They spent several days there, struggling to order beer and food in a language neither understood, and wandering through the Prado, where Morgenthaler was overwhelmed by Dürer and Goya, while Schoeck was attracted most by a Giorgione. They also attended a bullfight, at which six bulls were slaughtered right in front of them—"which we at first found shocking, though we soon grew used to it," recalled Morgenthaler. Schoeck's most abiding memory of the Madrid visit was of an evening at the theater where they understood not a word but marvelled all the more at the "pantomimic abilities of the actors." They returned home by train, taking a long detour via Paris.[6]

Joyce was not the only literary great who was in Zurich in early 1935. Thomas Mann had settled in Switzerland after having had to leave Nazi Germany, and his son Michael was now taking violin lessons with Willem de Boer. The latter celebrated his fiftieth birthday with a concert in the Zurich Tonhalle on 7 May, playing the concertos by Beethoven and Schoeck, plus Andreae's Rhapsody for Violin and Orchestra.[7] This concert brought Schoeck and Thomas Mann together for the first time. Although they never became close, they maintained a healthy respect for each other as artists, and they would meet on a sporadic basis over the ensuing years, both before and after Mann's exile in the United States.

Loeffel's run of Schoeck performances abroad continued on 4 June 1935, when he sang the *Notturno* in Hamburg with the Fehse Quartet at the annual

German music festival. Schoeck was invited to attend, but he was hesitant to do so—it was his first important invitation to attend a performance in Nazi Germany, and he was wary about its being used for political purposes. He claimed that he did not have the money to go, but Ernst Isler took him at his word and appealed successfully for the Swiss Musicians' Association to give him the necessary funds. Schoeck felt he could not now say no, and so he went, taking Hilde with him. He promised Elsbeth Mutzenbecher that he would call on her in Hamburg—though once he was there, he did so only after Hilde, out of a sense of duty, had dragged him to a telephone booth and made him ring her up. After the concert he, Hilde, and Elsbeth went out for a meal together. To his astonishment the two women got on famously. It was, so he said later, "a feast for gourmets to behold."[8] Many years later, after Schoeck's death, the two women even took to holidaying together.

The reviews from Hamburg were excellent, and the praise his work received seems to have smoothed over any residual worries that Schoeck had harbored about the trip. He was surprised to find little obvious trace of the new regime and its policies, though he told Corrodi that it felt as if everyone was remaining silent out of fear. There was certainly no excuse for him to be naive about what was happening in Germany. This same year had already seen the much-vaunted publication in Zurich of Wolfgang Langhoff's *Die Moorsoldaten,* an account of the thirteen months he had just spent in the concentration camp of Börgermoor. Langhoff was now a regular in the ensemble at the Zurich Schauspielhaus, and he bore the scars of his imprisonment for all to see and hear: his torturers had knocked his teeth out.

After his return to Switzerland Schoeck retired to the Weidhof with Gisela to work on *Massimilla,* then spent most of the summer alone in Brunnen before making another trip to the Weidhof. He made a concerted effort to complete the draft of his new opera before the distractions of the new concert season began in the autumn, and he was able to return to Zurich in early October with the finished sketch. Just a few days later, in mid-October 1935, he came into direct contact with Nazi functionaries for the first time. He was invited to nearby Freiburg im Breisgau for a conference of the "Alemannischer Kulturbund," or "Alemannic Cultural Union," only to find—as he really should have known— that it was an openly Nazi event. He afterward claimed that he had gone only because the program had announced a performance of his Second String Quartet by a string orchestra, an idea that he had long harbored for the work. His *Praeludium* was also being performed, about whose orchestration he had been so unsure. So while his curiosity was probably genuine, it perhaps also served to hide his embarrassment at having attended a conference where, as he related afterwards, a horde of Nazi "Gauführer" were present. Even worse, in between the movements of his quartet—played by just the usual four instruments—the writers Alfred Huggenberger and Hermann Burte recited verses. Burte was already an ardent supporter of the Nazis, while Huggenberger—a Swiss—was a known sympathizer. Another Swiss Nazi who was present was the writer Jakob Schaffner. Schoeck found these fellow Swiss participants the most distasteful of all, for he said they talked just like the Nazis and obviously couldn't wait for the Nazi "Schweinerei" to take over Switzerland too. Of Schaffner in particular, he said: "There's something untrustworthy, false about that man." He added that he had "had to keep myself hard in check in order not to blurt something out; it would have been so easy to answer him"[9]—but if it had been so easy, then he would have done. And he did not.

He did not, probably because he was getting more and more performances in Germany. He went to Nuremberg to hear Heinrich Rehkemper sing the *Notturno* in early December (and was much impressed by both the performance and its reception). But he was still happily mixing with the emigrants, too. He had conducted for the indisposed Andreae in the Tonhalle in November, with Rudolf Serkin as the soloist in Schumann's *Concert Allegro*, Op. 134. He had then socialized with Thomas Mann at the post-concert reception given by Lilly Reiff; afterward he was full of praise for Mann's intelligence and his use of language. Mann noted in his diary: "Friendship with Schoeck, who enthused about the Wagner article"—meaning his *Sufferings and Greatness of Richard Wagner*, the lecture that had so annoyed the Nazis.[10]

Schoeck's popularity in Germany continued. In January 1936 Loeffel and Sturzenegger performed the *Elegie* in Munich. Schoeck did not attend, for he spent the month in Brunnen, orchestrating *Massimilla*, and then had to go to St. Gallen to conduct a concert on the sixteenth (which comprised a project dear to his heart, namely the first Swiss performance of the complete *Má Vlast* by Smetana). He then spent a few days with Hilde in Arosa (where they bumped into Thomas and Katia Mann[11]). But he did now admit to Corrodi that things in Germany in the past couple of years had "strangely" altered in his favor. Now even the Berlin State Opera had expressed an interest in *Massimilla*—its new director being the gifted opportunist Clemens Krauss, confidant of Richard Strauss and successor to Erich Kleiber after the latter had resigned in protest at Nazi policies. Schoeck was accordingly planning a visit to Berlin to play the work to him.

Schoeck played his new opera through to his friends in late February 1936— Corrodi, Isler, and the usual suspects. But they were perplexed by it. Some were shocked at its "immorality," while others, such as Armand Bally, couldn't understand why an essentially pubertal conflict—hesitation about "going all the way"—should be made into a full-length opera. They kept their reservations from Schoeck, however. He also played it through to Krenek in March, when he visited Vienna for two concerts of his music—one in the Swiss Embassy on 4 March, in which he accompanied Wolfgang Schneiderhan and Loeffel, then another on 7 March, at which *Lebendig begraben* (with Loeffel), excerpts from *Erwin und Elmire*, the *Dithyrambe*, and the serenade from *Don Ranudo* were on the program. An unnamed journalist from the *Neues Wiener Tagblatt* published a brief interview with him on 7 March, in which he was quoted as confirming that he did not belong to any particular "movement" in composition, but "I'm certainly not reactionary!" We do not know of Krenek's opinion on *Massimilla*, but Alfred Schlee from Universal Edition was also present at the play-through and immediately announced his interest in taking on the work.

Since his own new opera featured a soprano seductress, it should perhaps not surprise us that Schoeck took the trouble to attend a performance of Berg's *Lulu Suite* under Hermann Scherchen in April (Berg had died the previous December, before completing the opera). Schoeck said afterward: "One can't deny its quality, and there is some greatness about it. Berg is in human terms more significant than Schoenberg . . . but this music is so colorful it's actually gray . . . it never really blossoms . . . it smells like hyacinths in a room where a corpse is laid out."[12] Such witticisms, however, were most typical for him when he felt unwilling or unable to praise a work that had particularly impressed him.

As for his own opera, Dresden was now expressing a more concrete interest in its premiere than had Berlin. His old supporter Fritz Busch had been hounded out of his directorship two years before, and his position taken over by Karl Böhm at the express wish of Adolf Hitler.[13] But Böhm was no stranger to Schoeck's music, for he had already conducted his orchestral *Praeludium* in a concert at the Dresden Opera House in autumn 1934. So in early May Schoeck traveled there to play *Massimilla* himself to Böhm and his colleagues. They were impressed with the music, but less happy about the "permissive" nature of the text. "That kind of thing isn't possible any more in the New Germany," Böhm and Co. told him. The matter of Massimilla's adultery was far too immoral, and certainly no bed could be allowed to be visible on stage (even though the final scene actually takes place in a bedroom). Schoeck pointed out that Strauss's *Rosenkavalier* begins with bedroom adultery. "Not even a *Rosenkavalier* would be allowed to pass today," they replied.[14]

Whatever hesitation Schoeck might have felt, he nevertheless acquiesced and went back to Rüeger; together they made the necessary alterations to the libretto. Schoeck sent their revised text to Böhm in Dresden, who in turn had to submit it to the office of Joseph Goebbels. It was passed at some point during the year, though we do not know how long the process took. Massimilla was now no longer married to the old Duke, but only his fiancée (premarital sex apparently being allowed where extramarital was not). All mention of beds was excised, as was the actual bed at the end of the opera. Instead, the final scene would take place outside the bedroom, with the lovers emerging from it in post-coital song, assuring each other that they are "eternally yours." This means that Massimilla enters the bedroom, undresses (presumably), loses her virginity to Emilio, and then puts her clothes back on again to emerge unruffled and perfectly satisfied after just a few pages of score. Given Schoeck's vast experience, he will hardly have believed that a full personal service in three minutes is likely to convince any woman to commit herself eternally. But in the theater, the strength of the music makes of it an absurdity with which one's suspension of disbelief can just about cope. By making Massimilla a fiancée instead of a wife, however, the whole plot and its conflicts become more or less irrelevant. If she is not married, then she cannot have scruples about committing adultery. But this does not seem to have bothered Schoeck, who wanted to see his work performed at an acknowledged "great" opera house.

It is unclear whether Schoeck's acquiescence in this matter was seen in Germany as proof of his general willingness to compromise, and whether or not this might have then made him an even more attractive "target" for Nazi propaganda. It would be wrong to think of Nazi music policy as some monolithic edifice, or to assume that what a composer did in one city would automatically be registered elsewhere. Nor should we underestimate, however, the importance to the Nazis of Schoeck and his fellow creative artists from German Switzerland. The Nazi regime had already lost many prominent men of science and the arts and was being subjected to much outside criticism—the latest reason being Hitler's remilitarization of the Rhineland in March 1936. But the Nazis had early on recognized the propaganda value of culture, and they were keen to lure prominent foreign artists into the Reich as a means of gaining international legitimacy. Schoeck was just one of many whose favor was curried. In his case, however, there were two added attractions. First, he was not (or no longer) a modernist but was writing music in the 1930s that bore a firm late-Romantic stamp and thus coincided more or less with the current Nazi aesthetic. Secondly, he was a German Swiss who shared his language and culture with his neighbors to the north and was himself of German descent (a fact repeated again and again in German newspapers during the Third Reich). Hitler's goal was pan-Germanism, in other words the unification of all "ethnic" Germans in one greater Germany. Bringing together the German-speaking areas of Austria, Czechoslovakia, Poland, and elsewhere was thus of prime importance to him, and the German Swiss knew well that they too were a natural target for incorporation into the Reich. Schoeck would soon be subjected to numerous attempts to make him appear supportive of Nazi policies, or at the least unlikely to express opposition to them. He would not always acquiesce. His wife in later years told the Swiss composer Rolf Urs Ringger that at some point in the mid-1930s Schoeck was offered a job in Berlin but had turned it down since neither he nor Hilde wanted it.[15] In other cases, however, he would prove far more malleable.

Schoeck completed the scoring of the first act of *Massimilla* by the beginning of July 1936, sent off the vocal score for typesetting—his proofreaders were Willi Schuh and Schoenberg's son-in-law Felix Greissle[16]—and shortly afterward signed a contract for the work with Universal. He received no fee and would get only a percentage of sales once all the publishing costs had been paid. But at least he had, for once, made his arrangements with a publisher well in advance of the premiere. He spent most of the summer in Brunnen as usual, returning to Zurich in good time for the celebrations organized around his fiftieth birthday on

1 September. The *Schweizerische Musikzeitung* published a birthday article on the day itself, while the various Swiss newspapers also brought an assortment of congratulatory articles. Hesse dedicated to him the poem "A dream of Josef Knecht," published in *Die Zeit* (Knecht being the hero of his work-in-progress *Das Glasperlenspiel*, not published until 1943), while Hermann Burte published a hexameter poem in the *Neue Zürcher Zeitung* entitled "Schoeck plays *Penthesilea*," which sadly displays none of the elegance or lyricism that characterize many of his earlier dialect poems. Nor was Schoeck impressed,[17] but he at least managed to pen a few gracious words of thanks three weeks later. (Burte had expected a more effusive response and would complain to Werner Reinhart six months later of Schoeck's "dreadful Zurich hubris," and that he had "never responded" to the poem).[18]

There were more publications to celebrate the occasion. Breitkopf & Härtel brought out a pocket score of *Vom Fischer*—the only stage work of Schoeck's to be put on sale in that format in his lifetime. Corrodi brought out a second, revised, edition of his biography, and this was reviewed once more as far away as England, where *Music and Letters* praised it as "an admirably produced volume."[19] This time, however, Corrodi had competition, for Willi Schuh published a slim volume entitled *Festgabe der Freunde* ("Festive Gift of the Friends"), which contained some musicological investigation, but mostly—as the title suggests—reminiscences of Schoeck's friends, including Corrodi himself, David, Hubacher, Fritz Brun, Andreae, and Hesse.[20] Although only 133 pages long, it sets a standard quite different from Corrodi's biography. Whereas Corrodi endeavored to appear objective but instead remained stuck fast in semi-hagiography, Schuh accepted that his friendship with the composer would limit his scope and so gave the anecdotal free reign. As a result, his little book is both honest and fascinating.

The first big event for Schoeck's birthday was a concert in the Zurich City Theater on the day itself, at which his old choirs, the Lehrergesangverein and the Men's Chorus of Aussersihl, performed various works, including the mammoth *Trommelschläge*. The program also featured the Serenade, Op. 1, and three numbers from *Erwin und Elmire;* it ended with the first act of *Venus*. There was a huge reception afterward in the "Waag" guildhouse, funded by Reinhart, which over a hundred people attended. Andreae gave a speech, as did a representative of Schoeck's native canton of Schwyz and also a relative from the Fassbind side, whose glowing portrait of Schoeck the devoted husband drew open mirth from among his friends.

The birthday celebrations continued with the first concert in the new season at the Zurich Tonhalle on 29 September, in which Andreae conducted de Boer in Schoeck's Violin Concerto and the Gemischter Chor in the *Dithyrambe*, while Schoeck conducted *Vom Fischer* in the second half. In the *Schweizerische Musikzeitung*, David noted the "hearty ovations" accorded the composer.[21] On 4 October Ernst Wolters conducted excerpts from *Don Ranudo* and *Erwin und Elmire* in Winterthur, as that town's contribution to the festivities. On 9 October Schoeck accompanied Ilona Durigo in the Zurich Tonhalle in what was her final recital before she returned to her native Hungary. The program also included her fellow Swiss-Hungarian Stefi Geyer, in a performance of Schoeck's Violin Sonata in D Major, Op. 16. Three weeks later, on 29 October, Stefi played Schoeck's Violin Concerto in St. Gallen under the composer's baton; the second half again comprised a concert performance of *Vom Fischer*, with Loeffel, Maria Bernhard-Ulbrich, and the tenor Ernest Bauer. The concert was followed by yet another reception. This was the first-ever season in which the radio began to broadcast Schoeck's orchestral concerts from St. Gallen, though no recordings of them have survived.[22] Late November took Schoeck to Thun for another mini-festival, organized by the same August Oetiker who had arranged the first-ever Schoeck concert twenty-eight years earlier.

Schoeck's correspondence with Hesse provides us with a rare insight into his feelings during the hullabaloo that surrounded him in the autumn of 1936. He wrote to Hesse on 27 September to thank him for his birthday greetings, for the poem, and for the "jewel" of a chapter he had written for Schuh's book. Hilde, he said, had gone off to Frankfurt for five weeks of singing (though whether he meant concerts or auditions, we do not know). But Gisela was with him and was "enchanting company" (see fig. 28.1) He continued that he was relieved that the "birthday fuss" was over:

In essence, I found it terrible, even though it brought so much of beauty and so much that was unforgettable. But it is embarrassing to be bombarded from all sides with "Darling of the muses" and "Master," when one in private has to survive real wrestling matches with the smallest details, be it only a matter of eighth- or sixteenth-note rests, details over which one often almost loses one's sanity.[23]

Schoeck hardly ever spoke about the process of composition to anyone, and there are very few mentions of it in Corrodi's copious diaries. This silence was almost certainly, at least in part, in order to maintain for others the mystery of inspiration that was part of his "Romantic" understanding of himself as an artist. But this was a mystery in which he too believed, as if the thing that was most precious might be lost if it were named. But his relationship with Hesse was different. Hesse was a famous creative artist—far more famous than Schoeck—and the more senior of the two by several years. They corresponded only rarely, but Schoeck seems to have felt no need to hide behind the superficial joviality that one finds in much of his other correspondence. The above passage, albeit brief, confirms what we should in any case be able to deduce from his exquisitely calligraphed scores: that they are not mere intuitive Romantic outpourings, as early commentators like Corrodi wanted the world to believe, but the product of a composer who was often engaged in an intense struggle with his material.

Figure 28.1. Schoeck and Gisela at the time of his fiftieth birthday, 1936. Courtesy of Othmar Schoeck Gesellschaft.

In the midst of all this birthday fuss, Schoeck stumbled upon a poem that attracted him, "Die Sternseherin" ("The Stargazer") by Matthias Claudius. The works of Claudius are little known today, nor were they much more popular in Schoeck's day. He is remembered best on account of his poem "Der Tod und das Mädchen" ("Death and the Maiden")—and only because it was set by Franz Schubert. Claudius came from northern Germany and achieved fame through the journal *Der Wandsbecker Bote,* which he edited from 1771 to 1775. He attracted contributions from Goethe and others and also published many of his own poems in it. The *Bote* was named after its place of publication, which was also where Claudius lived: Wandsbek (*sic*), today a suburb of greater Hamburg. Schoeck set the "Sternseherin" to music and then moved on to several other poems by Claudius that he found appealing. By January 1937 he had sixteen settings altogether (a seventeenth came a little later), and named the collection *Das Wandsbecker Liederbuch* ("Wandsbeck Songbook"). Schoeck mentioned in conversation with Loeffel that he had here created a "new form"—though he was presumably referring only to the four little piano interludes that are used to modulate from the first to the second song in each of the four groups that make up the cycle (entitled "Love," "Nature," "Man"—in the sense of "humankind"—and "Death"). The use of the word "Liederbuch" for the work's title, rather than "Zyklus," brings to mind the Goethe and Mörike "songbooks" of Hugo Wolf, which have no overall form but rather offer a representative "portrait" of the poet.

Claudius's verse is marked by a naive, pious sensibility. But it seems that it was precisely the poet's straightforward attitude to matters of good and evil, faith and belief that appealed to Schoeck. Furthermore, there is a strong pacifist element in these songs, and even, in the wonderfully dissonant "Der Krieg" ("War"), a horror at human conflict (see ex. 28.1). This poem, written in 1779 in protest at the war between Austria and Prussia, repeats over and again "It is war, and I desire to have no guilty part in it."

This is one of the few really fine songs in the cycle. Another is "Auf den Tod einer Kaiserin" ("On the Death of an Empress"—which in Claudius was "of *the* Empress," written on the death of Maria Theresa in 1780). Its text runs:

> She made peace! That is my poem.
> She was her people's happiness and blessing;
> And she encountered death as a friend,
> Full of comfort and confidence.
> A conqueror of the world cannot do that.
> She made peace! That is my poem.

The reference to a "conqueror of the world" ("Welt-Eroberer") is here an obvious reference to the dictators of Schoeck's own day, in particular to Hitler, whose expansionist ambitions were no secret. In this cycle Schoeck was making both a direct statement against war and in favor of peace and an oblique one against would-be "conquerors of the world"—all laudable sentiments. But at the same time he was doing nothing concrete to distance himself from Nazi Germany. Perhaps he even regarded this cycle as proof enough of his beliefs, and that it somehow "canceled out" in moral terms his increasingly problematical role in music life north of the border. On 18 December 1936, for example, Robert F. Denzler had conducted the Berlin Philharmonic in a performance of Schoeck's *Vom Fischer* in a Swiss/German "exchange concert" at the Singakademie in Berlin with great success. This was arguably Schoeck's most prestigious international concert to date. Ironically, the one person who saw through it all was the very person who was feeding Schoeck's domestic Germanophobia: Hilde. It was all empty success, she claimed, all just for political reasons, and Othmar, she mocked in that same December, had become "the court composer of the Nazis."[24] This did little to improve marital harmony. But while she was undoubtedly exaggerating, and while her mockery was probably intended as just another metaphorical stick with which to beat her husband, his undoubted anger at it merely confirms that he knew she was, in part, quite right.

Example 28.1. The dissonant opening of "Der Krieg" from *Das Wandsbecker Liederbuch,* Op. 52. Copyright 1937, 1965 by Universal Edition. "It is war, it is war! O angel of God, stop it, and intervene!"

Chapter Twenty-Nine

Tea with (Ms.) Hitler

Just a few weeks into 1937 Hilde received further confirmation of Schoeck's gradual appropriation by the Nazis, when the University of Freiburg im Breisgau made a discreet approach to see if he would accept the first "Erwin von Steinbach Prize." Recently founded by a German-American, its purpose was to honor artists from the Alemannic region who had made a particular contribution to German culture. "Alemannic" here refers to the old Germanic tribes from the geographical area that today covers southwest Germany, Luxembourg, eastern France, and northern Switzerland, and it is still used to denote the similar dialects spoken throughout the region. The prize itself was named after the mediaeval architect of Strasbourg's Cathedral. Strasbourg had long been a German town but had belonged to France for some two hundred years before being annexed by Germany after the Franco-Prussian War of 1870–71 and had then lapsed back to France after 1918. By naming their new prize after the architect of a then "foreign" cathedral, the Nazis were effectively declaring a proprietary right to the city itself. Their aim was thus, yet again, a pan-Germanic one: to prove that the German-speaking peoples belonged to one greater culture and should be brought into the greater Reich. The very fact that Freiburg University sounded out Schoeck in private is proof enough that the prize was political in nature and that it was feared he might refuse it. But he did not hesitate to accept. The official announcement of the award was dated 1 March, with the ceremony itself planned for late April. Schoeck saw in the prize merely an act of official recognition for his music—though it also, *nota bene,* brought him several thousand francs.

The announcement was obviously timed to gain the maximum of publicity, for the premiere of *Massimilla Doni* took place just one day later in Dresden, on 2 March 1937. Schoeck arrived in late February for the final rehearsals. The dress rehearsal proved an unnerving experience, for when it ended, only one of the hundred people present began to clap—and he stopped when no one else joined in. After this embarrassed silence in the auditorium, Schoeck grumbled: "I'll think it over carefully before I write another opera." But the premiere itself went splendidly, and Schoeck was astonished at the standard of performance that Böhm and the Dresden ensemble achieved. The cast included Felicie Hüni-Mihacsek (Massimilla), Rudolf Dittrich (Emilio), Torsten Ralph (Genovese), Erna Sack (Tinti), and Arno Schellenberg (Vendramin), while the directing team was the same as for Strauss's *Schweigsame Frau* two years before, namely Böhm in the pit, plus Max Hofmüller (director) and Adolf Mahnke (set design) (see fig. 29.1). The chorus had been rehearsed by Karl Maria Pembaur. In the *Völkischer Beobachter* of 4 March Hans Schnoor praised the "triumphant per-formance" and Schoeck's "beautiful, poetic music," stressing the highly lyrical nature of the score; Heinz Joachim wrote in the *Frankfurter Zeitung* of 5 March that the opera brought "surprising new sounds" from Schoeck—such as Tinti's coloratura and the duet of the two old aristocrats in the first act—but added that his "real strength . . . still lies in the lyrical aspect." Heinrich Strobel wrote of "one of the most notable world premieres of recent years" in the *Berliner Tagblatt* on 3 March. Others, such as Heinrich Zerkaulen in the *Schlesischer Zeitung* of 4 March, could not resist the continuing temptation to bring Schoeck into the Germanic fold and wrote: "The Swiss Othmar Schoeck belongs, in the full mean-ing of the word, 'to us.'" Perhaps the best review of the work—certainly one of the most percipient—appeared, surprisingly, in English: in the *Musical Times,* where "R.E." wrote that Tinti was, "so to speak, the Strauss-Zerbinetta raised to a high power, both in point of temperament and in the prodigality of her colora-tura." He continued:

> (Her part proves to be the most dazzling display of coloratura in modern musi-cal literature.) The Duchess Massimilla Doni, the rival of Tinti, does not seem to belong to the generation of 1830 . . . but rather to the period of Dante . . . the lyrical strains characterizing the figure of Massimilla form the fundamen-tal chord of the opera and pronounce the final word, which reconciles all opposing elements. These ethereally soaring lines represent the most lovely music for which we have to thank the Swiss composer. The effect of these lyri-cal melodies is enhanced by contrast with the rapidity and brilliance of the Tinti scenes and the realism of the street scenes, by the humorous boldness in which a canon, a fugato, and tarantella rhythms are hurled into the ensembles. Schoeck's work is full of a peculiar tension of its own.[1]

The majority of the German-language critics, however, felt that the opera was laden with rather too much aesthetics. Robert Oboussier—himself a fine composer—wrote in the *Deutsche Allgemeine Zeitung* of 4 March that Schoeck retained the "perspective" of a song composer, which resulted in an essentially undramatic, "psychological/epic aspect"; he also remarked on the importance in this opera of "Sprechgesang," accompanied in often aphoristic manner by the orchestra. It is a "music of permanent transitions," he wrote. An even more measured appraisal was given by a member of the audience of 18 March, Pro-paganda Minister Joseph Goebbels, who wrote the next day in his diary: "well-staged, glorious voices. The work quite good in part, otherwise very artificial and pale. Not a special acquisition ['Acquisition']. Certainly won't last. The orches-tra plays wonderfully under Böhm."[2] Hilde was not impressed either, claiming that Schoeck's Massimilla was just a male fantasy of a whore and a Madonna in the same person. Josef von Vintschger recalled Hilde berating her husband

Figure 29.1. Erna Sack (Tinti) and Rudolf Dittrich (Emilio) in *Massimilla Doni*, Dresden, 1937. Courtesy of Zentralbibliothek Zürich.

Figure 29.2. A henpecked Schoeck in Dresden, 1937. Courtesy of Zentralbibliothek Zürich. "I'll show you how to compose when I get you home."

about this in a Dresden restaurant. "I'll show you how to compose when I get you home," she said, and von Vintschger—an avid amateur photographer, camera ready to hand—had the quickwittedness to take a snapshot of Schoeck's furious glance at his wife (see fig. 29.2).[3]

While the general tenor of the reviews was good, and while Rüeger was praised by some, the criticisms that were made still centered on the libretto itself, on its "undramatic" qualities, and on the kind of music that it had supposedly occasioned Schoeck to write. The reactions were similar after the Swiss premiere of the work under Denzler just eleven days later, on 13 March in Zurich. There Massimilla was played by Judith Hellweg, Tinti by Julia Moor, Genovese by Max Hirzel (who had now moved from Dresden back to his native Zurich), and Vendramin by Marko Rothmüller, a Croatian baritone and sometime composition pupil of Alban Berg. Schoeck's Zurich friends found the libretto overburdened with ideas; they felt that it prevented the composer's natural lyricism from taking flight. David even allowed himself rare criticism in his review for the *Schweizerische Musikzeitung,* writing: "The text lies like a frost on the music, undermines it, and prevents its natural power from unfolding in purely musical form."[4] The one friend of Schoeck's who declared unconditional love for the work was James Joyce, who came to Zurich just to see it and went to every performance.

There is undoubtedly a lot of aesthetic discussion in the opera. But since we know that Rüeger always provided Schoeck faithfully with what he wanted, we must assume that he did not force anything upon him. He had been allowed a little more time to write his libretto for *Massimilla* than had been the case with *Don Ranudo* or *Venus,* and it is without doubt the finest of the three, with many felicitous moments. Nor was Schoeck's rapid *parlando* style (what the German critics called his "Sprechgesang") in any way forced upon him, for its development can be traced back through his songs of recent years. There are passages as far back as *Wanderung im Gebirge* that are not dissimilar to the *parlando* of *Massimilla.* And when Schoeck does decide to give full rein to his lyrical gift, the results are startling.

We can also perceive clearly in the scoring of *Massimilla* one of the most individual traits that Schoeck's music displays in these years. The different instrumental voices are often spaced so that large gaps occur between them, and it is done with such skill that the resultant sound is both lush and highly transparent. Unless the listener is particularly attentive, he does not notice just how thin the textures often look on paper. As we have already observed, such spacings can be found in the *Notturno,* and they are almost certainly inspired by Stravinsky's neoclassical works. Schoeck's harmonies in *Massimilla,* however, are neither neoclassical nor modernistic, but typically late-Romantic. This combination of Romantic harmony with quasi-Stravinskyan scoring results in a highly personal sound that arguably sets Schoeck apart from most of his contemporaries. But the strengths of *Massimilla* do not just lie in its orchestration. While there are weak patches, where the *parlando* style is too *parlando* and too little stylish, the score offers many delights. The first scene of the second act, for example, when Tinti improvises coloratura to the duke's strange musings on his solo violin while singing/speaking in *Sprechgesang* is one of Schoeck's strangest inventions and quite compelling. The intermezzo before the third scene—a beautiful waltz with filigree orchestration—is one of Schoeck's finest orchestral pieces and ought to be performed regularly on its own; and the short fourth scene combines the low woodwind and strings to create autumnal textures reminiscent of Alban Berg before climaxing with an aria for Massimilla herself that reaches an unusually sumptuous, Puccinian climax before subsiding back into the autumnal colors with which it began (see ex. 29.1). The close of the opera—where the music is virtually identical to the close of the first scene—is once again Stravinskyan in its technical means but Schoeckian in its harmony. It utilizes the same technique that Schoeck had pilfered from *Petrushka* for use in his *Penthesilea,* whereby a

motive of just a few notes is given simultaneously in its original and in diminution. Here, though, it has a specific dramatic function. The melody is a lullaby
that is hummed by Massimilla in the first scene, but in the last it is sung by an
offstage children's choir, signifying the fact that the heroine is now pregnant
(shades of the "unborn children" from Strauss's *Frau ohne Schatten,* perhaps). By
superimposing the lullaby upon itself in diminution, Schoeck creates a hypnotic
effect. The manner in which it languidly moves in and out of sync with itself is
reminiscent of the state of half-sleep in which one drifts in and out of consciousness (see ex. 29.2).

Massimilla Doni is also of historical interest beyond its own undoubted
merits, for it is oddly prescient of the final opera of Richard Strauss, *Capriccio.* The latter, subtitled "A Conversation Piece for Music," has its origins in
a libretto by Giovanni Battista de Casti (1724–1803) entitled *Prima la musica
e poi le parole* ("First the Music and Then the Words") that Stefan Zweig discovered in August 1934—not long after Schoeck had decided on *Massimilla*
as his next opera topic. Zweig was Strauss's librettist at the time but withdrew
from further collaboration because of the older man's readiness to work with
the Nazis. The final libretto of *Capriccio* was by Strauss himself, in collaboration with Clemens Krauss. Both operas make frequent use of rapid *parlando*
for aesthetic debates centring on opera, and in each case it is an aristocratic
female patron—the Duchess Massimilla on the one hand, Countess Madeleine
on the other—who is called upon to resolve them. Both operas feature two
"Italian singers"—a tenor and a soprano—though they play a major role in the
plot of *Massimilla* while remaining of little consequence in *Capriccio.* It seems
unlikely that Strauss ever saw *Massimilla,* though it would be surprising if he
had heard absolutely nothing about it, given that he and Schoeck had several
mutual friends and colleagues, including Karl Böhm and Willi Schuh. Or perhaps this is another example of a topic simply being "in the air," as we saw with
the several *Penthesilea* operas of the mid-1920s.

There was a reception at the Hotel Bellevue after *Massimilla*'s opening night
in Dresden. To Schoeck's delight, one of those present was Klara May. Her now
deceased second husband had been Karl, his favorite childhood author, whose
Schatz am Silbersee had provided him with the topic of his first-ever operatic venture more than three decades earlier. She invited him to tea at her home in
nearby Radebeul on the fifth, which he readily accepted. He took along von
Vintschger and another friend from St. Gallen who had made the journey to
the premiere, Adolf Güntensperger (nicknamed "Günti"). To their joint consternation, however, Mrs May had taken it upon herself to invite one of her best
friends too, the wife of the local architect Martin Hammitzsch, Angela, née Hitler, a half-sister of the *Führer.* Angela had long been closer to Adolf than any of
his other siblings and had at his request moved to the Berghof in the 1920s in
order to run the household there. It was her daughter from a first marriage, Geli
Raubal, who had become Hitler's favorite but had committed suicide in 1931.

Example 29.1. Massimilla's aria from the fourth scene of *Massimilla Doni,* Op. 50. Copyright 1936 by Universal Edition. "[Holy] Mother, thank you! This humility awakens a happiness in me that I have never known! Give me the strength to tell him how I love him!"

After falling out with her brother in 1936, Angela had moved to Dresden and married again.

Despite being temporarily *non grata* in the Chancellery, much of her conversation, according to von Vintschger's reminiscences, still centered on the wondrous works of brother Adolf: how he loved the books of Karl May, how he would not even allow himself to be disturbed by high matters of state if he was reading a favorite passage, and how witty he was ("What would our father say if he could have experienced this?" she reported having asked her brother after his investiture as Reichskanzler, whereupon Adolf had replied: "He'd ask: 'D'you get a good pension too?'"). When pushed for his opinion on The New Germany, Schoeck, according to von Vintschger, got away with mumbling pleasantries, embarrassed assurances that he was an artist who understood nothing of politics, and clumsy attempts to change the subject (". . . but don't the art galleries have marvellous treasures here in Dresden . . . ?").[5] Despite her age, Mrs May was far from unpolitical, and later she even arranged for the corpse of her half-Jewish first husband—along with that of his Jewish mother—to be exhumed on racial grounds from the May Mausoleum, then cremated and buried elsewhere. When she died on 31 December 1944, Klara May's obituary notice featured not a cross but the pagan "rune" preferred by the Nazis.[6]

Aside from his dealings with the Dresden opera authorities, this was Schoeck's first close personal contact with highly placed Nazi sympathizers. He would soon learn that his claim to be an uncomprehending artist would not hold water with everyone.

Example 29.2. *Massimilla Doni*, Op. 50, final scene. Copyright 1936 by Universal Edition. The passage in original and diminution is marked by brackets.

Chapter Thirty

Aryanizing Music

On Sunday 25 April 1937 Schoeck was awarded the Erwin von Steinbach Prize at a ceremony in the main hall of the University of Freiburg im Breisgau, just across the German border. The guests included representatives from the universities of Basel, Bern, and Zurich and from the Nazi Party and the Wehrmacht, plus various colleagues such as Werner Reinhart, Hermann Burte, Ernst Isler, and Hans Corrodi. The program began with a Bach Toccata for organ. Then Josef Peilscher played Schoeck's Violin Sonata Op. 16, accompanied by Hans Rosbaud (better known today for his work as a conductor). Friedrich Metz, the rector of Freiburg University, gave a *laudatio* in which he remarked that although the political borders of the region were sacrosanct, it was "a tragic, inevitable fate" that the Alemannic peoples had been split between four countries (Switzerland, Germany, France, and Luxembourg). Schoeck's German roots were yet again stressed, and his year of study with Reger in Leipzig was held up as further proof of his belonging to the German tradition. Schoeck declined to make a reply to the speech, offering instead a few carefully chosen words of thanks and expressing the wish that his music should speak for itself. He thereupon conducted a shortened version of the *Elegie* with Loeffel and members of the Freiburg opera orchestra. This was the last time that the two men would perform the work together. There was a reception afterward in the Zähringer Hof, then a trip up the Schauinsland (the local "mountain") where a folklore group sang for the party, including in their performance two songs to texts by Hermann Burte.[1]

The left-wing Swiss press did not take kindly to their leading composer's accepting a prize from a potential enemy power. Their annoyance was fueled by the version of Metz's speech that the German news agency now cleverly circulated to the media at home and abroad, and which the social-democratic Zurich paper *Das Volksrecht* quoted in gleeful horror on 27 April: "[Schoeck] is an artist who has presented Germany with innumerable works of Aryan art." They gave their article the heading "Othmar Schoeck is Aryanized" ("Othmar Schoeck wird aufgenordet") and commented: "Our people have no right to require of our artists that they turn down foreign honors.... *But Switzerland needs men who do not bend the knee*" (emphasis original). One day later the *Volksrecht* published a letter sent in by H[ans] C[orrodi], in which the writer insisted that the version of the Rector's speech that was read out in Freiburg was quite different from the one quoted in the newspaper: "Not a word was spoken of Aryan art ... it is obvious that Schoeck could not turn down the prize. His operas depend on the great stages of Germany." The editors of the *Volksrecht* then added that Schoeck should rather take his cue from Arturo Toscanini or Thomas Mann.

Schoeck was furious. He said to Corrodi: "What has Toscanini or his business got to do with me? As a Swiss, I'm neutral." When they next met, he also asked rhetorically: "Who in Germany would perform anything of mine any more if I were to turn down in such an insulting manner an honor that was accorded to me? And who in Switzerland would make good the damage done to me?"[2] To make matters worse, he now acquired vocal support from the Swiss Nazi Party. They too had their own newspaper, *Die Front,* and on 3 May it brought a front-page article supporting Schoeck's decision to accept the prize and denouncing the attacks being made upon him by the "Jewish, Masonic, and Marxist Interna-tionale" (*sic*). Nor did the matter end there: a week later, on 11 May, *Die Front* featured a front-page article by Jakob Schaffner, in which he wrote:

> The man honored here, Othmar Schoeck, is in political terms utterly spotless. He stands in no way close to National Socialism. It is impossible to judge him and treat him in this as I am judged and treated, for example. . . . Othmar Schoeck will in his whole life never have been so embarrassingly perplexed.

Schaffner—whose earlier, deservedly high reputation as a novelist never recovered from his association with Nazism—is here a far cleverer propagandist than the bullish editors of the newspaper. They were happy to rant and rave, whereas Schaffner cunningly claimed Schoeck for his cause by ostensibly distancing him from it. For what Schaffner writes here is perfectly true, and he must have been overjoyed that Schoeck's actions had given him the opportunity to take a super-ficially more "measured" stance than his socialist opponents.

The secretive manner in which the prize was first offered to Schoeck sug-gests that he was being offered an easy way out. It was the last time he would be offered one. Had he quietly turned down the prize, his subsequent life might have been so much easier. It is impossible to know whether or not his career in Germany might have suffered. But probably not, as long as he did not make his stance public. It was expedient to accept the prize; but expediency is not a category of moral justification. This decision, made so soon after his easy acqui-escence in the changes to *Massimilla* for Dresden, proved to be just one more step on a long, slippery slope that would in six years lead to personal and profes-sional catastrophe.

The next step came very soon after, and it too was taken unhesitatingly. In mid-May 1937 Schoeck traveled to Berlin to conduct a concert on the radio comprising Max Reger's *Beethoven Variations* and extracts from *Massimilla.* He took René Niederer along—presumably because he had good friends in the capital. After his return, Niederer told their friends that he had made full use while there of the opportunities for easy sex that had presented themselves, but that Schoeck had abstained, remaining instead faithful to Hilde throughout. He

claimed that Schoeck not only had an insurmountable fear of catching a sexually transmitted disease but was also terrified that Hilde would learn of his infidelity, divorce him, and take away their child.

After Berlin Schoeck traveled to Dresden to see *Massimilla* again—in particular to hear for the first time a new intermezzo that he had written to be inserted
between the fifth and sixth scenes. He was back in Zurich in good time for his
opera's performances at the June International Festival. *Massimilla* did not have
the biggest billing, as that was reserved for the world premiere of Alban Berg's
unfinished *Lulu* on 2 June. This premiere—which Berg's status as a "degenerate" composer had made impossible in Germany—marked a highpoint for the
Zurich City Theater, establishing it as a "safe haven" for art, just as the Schauspielhaus in Zurich had become for the spoken theater. The world's press flocked
there as they had never flocked before. The theater's next yearbook proudly
printed extensive excerpts from the reviews in the *New York Times,* the *Christian
Science Monitor,* the *Times* of London, *Le Figaro,* and elsewhere.[3] Schoeck attended
Lulu and reacted with the same mixture of admiration and ambivalence as when
he had heard the *Lulu* Suite just over a year before. Corrodi went too but was
shocked, and he now wrote a review with the title "Musical Bolshevism," in
which he criticized the "morals" of the Wedekind plays on which the opera was
based and went on to describe twelve-note music as "musical communism" on
the strangely logical grounds that it makes all the notes "equal," allowing none
to assume "leadership" (he here used the loaded word "Führertum")—just as
Communism, he maintained, had as its aim "to bring all men down to the same
level." He sent it off to several German newspapers and journals including the
Völkischer Beobachter, where it was readily accepted.[4] It did him no good and was
registered with much displeasure in Zurich.

Corrodi's article was also discussed openly when he, Schoeck, and their
friends met at the pub. Ernst Isler was vehemently critical, and Corrodi noted
that Schoeck too said he "had gone too far."[5] As far as we are aware, Corrodi
had never written music reviews of any kind except of works by Schoeck, nor
had he ever before indulged in such polemics. The exception that he made
here would return to haunt him at the end of World War II, and this article—
with good reason—is still quoted as a prime example of the absurd extremes
of Nazi music criticism. This misses the real point, however, for it is really all
about the one man whose name is studiously left unmentioned in it: Schoeck.
Corrodi was furious that *Massimilla* should have been given less attention than
Lulu. The world, it seemed to him, cared less for the "healthy" tonality
of Schoeck's opera than it did for the twelve-tone "immorality" that was *Lulu*.
But the only way that Corrodi could make the world take notice was to be
as polemical as possible, and to write with a vocabulary that would appeal to
Nazi newspaper editors (for no one else was likely to publish anything quite
so negative about Berg). Corrodi seems not to have noticed the plain statistic
that *Massimilla,* with eight performances in the season, was actually performed

more times than Puccini's *Tosca*, Bizet's *Carmen*, or Strauss's *Rosenkavalier; Lulu*
was given just four times.[6] Ironically, nor is the sexual roundabout of *Lulu* very
far removed from what we observe in *Massimilla*.

Seeing *Massimilla* on stage had set Schoeck on a hunt for a new libretto. In
late June he went to the Weidhof in order to start preparing for what he had
decided was to be *Das Schloss Dürande* ("Dürande Castle"), based on the novella
by Eichendorff that Hermann Hesse had recommended as an opera topic almost
thirty years earlier. Rüeger was once more asked to provide the words, but he
refused, citing lack of time and inclination. Schoeck's next choice was Hermann
Burte. He wrote an undated letter to Burte from the Weidhof, presumably in
late June or early July 1937:

> Dear Burte,
> Shall we make an opera together? I have a topic: *Das Schloss Dürande* by
> Eichendorff! It's quite a mixture of Kät[h]chen [von Heilbronn, by Kleist],
> [Michael] Kohlhaas [also by Kleist], and Romeo and Juliet, and above it all an
> Eichendorffian heaven. . . . I'd be *blissful* if you'd take the bait![7]

We do not have Burte's reply, though Schoeck's subsequent postcard to him of
31 July makes it clear that the bait was taken.

Why Burte? The answer—though we have no direct proof—lies clearly with
Werner Reinhart, who was the patron of both men. He had long wanted to find
Schoeck a "real poet" to work with, and he had known that Burte had for several
years harbored a desire to write a libretto. Burte is best remembered today for
his Nazi-inspired texts, but we can assess him fairly only if we consider his earlier achievements. Burte was born Hermann Strübe in Maulburg, near Freiburg
im Breisgau, in 1879. Like Schoeck, he had first studied painting and also
remained faithful to this art form throughout his life. He turned to literature
in the early years of the twentieth century, at which time he adopted the pseudonym "Burte." His early novel *Wiltfeber, der ewige Deutsche* ("Wiltfeber, the Eternal
German"), published in 1912, was highly successful, though it is mentioned in
the literature today mostly on account of its "blood and soil" ethos. He was also
an experienced playwright. His *Katte*, for example, was first performed at the
National Theater of Mannheim in 1914 and enjoyed many further productions
in the 1920s and 1930s, with none other than Gustaf Gründgens taking the role
of Frederick the Great in a 1922 production at the Theater in der Kommandan-
tenstrasse, Berlin.[8] Burte's dialect poetry is of a higher order than his plays, with
the collection *Madlee* of 1923 serving to establish him as the most significant Alemannic poet in southern Germany since Johann Peter Hebel. These poems have
been accorded praise even by those who did not share Burte's politics (such as
Willi Schuh). Burte was jointly awarded the first-ever Kleist Prize in 1912 (later
prizewinners included Fritz von Unruh in 1914, Bertolt Brecht in 1922, and

Carl Zuckmayer in 1925), and in 1927 he was awarded the Schiller Prize jointly with von Unruh and Franz Werfel.

Burte's politics were at least as well known as his writings: he was a committed Nazi, and he made no bones about it. On 13 August 1936, for example, he had (unsuccessfully) tried to interest the "Reichsdramaturg" Rainer Schlösser in a new text for Handel's oratorio *Judas Maccabeus,* whose hero Burte had modelled unashamedly on Hitler: "The de-Jewishing of the topic and the text has to start at the central point, at the heart of the matter: the Jewish hero has to give way to a German one! And there is only One—and no Other."[9] Nor did Burte escape the attention of the great and famous—Thomas Mann's diaries, for example, make it clear that he registered with displeasure Burte's Nazi posturings.[10] Several of Schoeck's friends even feared that Burte might write him an overtly Nazi libretto. Schoeck himself acknowledged the danger of it but insisted that he would then refuse to set the text to music. This merely seems to confirm both that Burte was not his own choice and that there was no naivety on his part in acquiescing in it. Schoeck was not to be tested directly, for the political aspect is almost absent from the surface of Burte's libretto. He was no fool and will not have wanted to provoke Schoeck—or embarrass Werner Reinhart—by writing openly Fascist *agit-prop.* Schoeck's prime concern over the next two years was in fact to be far more basic: Burte proved dreadfully slow in providing his text. In any case, Schoeck was at this time still convinced that events in Europe could only improve. He said to Corrodi in August 1937: "Reason will still be victorious at the close, and raw violence will come to an end." When Corrodi expressed his belief that matters would in fact only worsen, Schoeck countered him by saying that "without this hope he could not live."[11]

Das Schloss Dürande begins in Provence just before the Revolution of 1789. Count Armand Dürande is in love with Gabriele, the sister of his gamekeeper, Renald. The latter discovers the liaison, assumes that his master is trifling with his sister, and so sends her off to their aunt in a local convent. Armand leaves for Paris, but Gabriele follows him in secret, disguised as a gardening boy. Renald shadows them in turn, and in his anti-aristocratic fervor gets caught up in the revolutionary movement in the capital. The scene then changes back to Dürande Castle, where Armand and Gabriele find each other again and declare their love. But Renald has followed them too, storms the castle at the head of a mob, and in the ensuing chaos shoots both the lovers dead. He comes to his senses, realizes the enormity of his error, and blows up the castle with himself in it.

The plot has its problems from the start—if the count is so in love with Gabriele, why does he blithely abandon her and go off to Paris? How can one show her clandestine pursuit of him to Paris and back again without her stage persona exuding puppy-dog subservience? And how can one portray Renald's obsessive devotion to his sister without his appearing both unsympathetic and potentially incestuous? The early-Romantic, naive ambience of Eichendorff's novella allows one to suspend one's disbelief in all these matters. But the plot poses more problems in a post-Freudian age, and Burte was hardly the man to solve them. Rüeger, with his undoubted literary sensibility, might well have understood the probable pitfalls of the story. So this could be an added reason why he declined to collaborate on it.

Burte sent his first, brief, draft of the libretto to Schoeck on 18 September 1937, writing from Rilke's former home, the tower of Muzot that Reinhart owned. His letter should have been a warning sign that each man had a quite different approach to the topic. Burte suggested five acts with the following settings: the first in front of the gamekeeper's house; the second at the convent; the third at the "Red Lion," the inn of the Jacobins in Paris; the fourth at the Paris chateau of the Count; and the fifth at Dürande Castle. But Burte then added: "What is there really to prevent Victor [i.e., Armand] Dürande and Gabriele Dubois from getting each other? . . . Eichendorff ends by killing everyone in the novella. But an opera may end happily, affirmatively, like a fairy tale!"[12] Schoeck wrote back soon thereafter as follows (the letter is undated):

> The topic is *unequivocably tragic*. All possible prerequisites for a happy end are lacking. Sadly! I'm all for a good ending, but it doesn't work in this case. The greatness of all these characters lies in the fact that they are shrouded in tragedy. Without this, all their actions suddenly become small and insignificant. . . . Before my inner eye, I see the castle rising over the forests before a bright evening sky as a visionary admonition that everything has to come to an end in the course of time and generations. . . . Do you want to leave out the old [count] Dürande [Armand's father]? He would make a good figure and an even better symbol. And in Paris—don't we need a second woman there, as a counterpart to Gabriele?

Schoeck's last two suggestions were taken on board. But for over a month he heard nothing more from Burte. Corrodi took the opportunity to send Schoeck an anonymous sketch for a first act of a *Dürande* libretto. It remained unused, as had Corrodi's previous libretti, but Schoeck did decide to make use of two poems by Eichendorff (neither from the *Dürande* novella) that Corrodi had incorporated into his text: "Die Verlassene" ("The Abandoned Girl") and "Der verirrte Jäger" ("The Hunter Gone Astray"). The next letter that Schoeck sent Burte, from St. Gallen on 19 October, ran as follows:

> Dear, dear Burte!
> ?
> I'll soon explode because of Schloss Dürande!
> Always your
> Schoeck.

The two men met in November when they attended another meeting of the "Alemannic Cultural Circle" in Freiburg im Breisgau, then again at the Fluh in early December.

Burte was finally able to deliver the first act of *Dürande* before Christmas. By the end of the year Schoeck was already claiming to be both well into it and happy with Burte's verses. By the following February, when Hilde and Gisela were on holiday in the Engadine, the act was finished. It must have seemed as though progress might be even swifter than had been the case with his previous operas. This was despite Schoeck's heavy concert schedule at St. Gallen, which included performances of Beethoven's Ninth Symphony, Schumann's "Rhenish," Brahms's First, Bruckner's First, Dvořák's G-major Symphony, and the "Unfinished" and "Great" Symphonies by Schubert. Schoeck celebrated the end of this season in early April with a long trip to Italy in the company of the pianist Paul Baumgartner, who had often played under his baton in St. Gallen. They spent some ten days in Rome before Schoeck moved further south alone to Naples, where a brother of Toni Schucany showed him the sights, including Pompei and Vesuvius. Schoeck's holiday meant missing the world premiere of his *Wandsbecker Liederbuch* in Zurich on 6 April 1938, performed by Alice and Walter Frey. But his trip is perplexing for another reason, too: on 12 March 1938 Hitler had annexed Austria. Italy had for several years been the principal guarantor of Austria's independence but was now forced to stand by and watch the country be gobbled up by its northern Fascist rival. To take a holiday to Italy within three weeks of the *Anschluss* suggests either that Schoeck was utterly unconcerned at the political fragility of Central Europe, or—perhaps more likely—that he felt this might be his last chance to see the sights of Rome and Naples before the situation deteriorated further. After all, his interpretation of *Das Schloss Dürande* was based on the transience of all things.

The results of the *Anschluss* were soon to be felt in German Switzerland, for it was now (apart from a few small enclaves in the East) the only German-speaking part of Europe that was not ruled from Berlin. The Zurich Schauspielhaus and Opera were to profit from this fact as more emigrants arrived, desperate to find work at any price. Ferdinand Rieser resigned as director of the Schauspielhaus in the first half of 1938, but the tradition he had established since 1933 was maintained by his successor, Oskar Wälterlin, under whose courageous direction the house became world-renowned, especially for its premieres of works by Bertolt Brecht in the midst of World War II. But the impact of the *Anschluss* on Switzerland was in some cases far more direct: one of the violinists in Schoeck's St. Gallen orchestra, the Austrian national Willy Müller, was at this time visited by several Nazis, who insisted that his loyalties lay with the new "Greater Germany" across the border; however, he stayed in Switzerland instead and would survive the ensuing years unscathed.[13]

As it happens, Schoeck's music was now being used to help celebrate the resurgent Reich. On 13 March, one day after German troops had crossed the

Austrian border, Rudolf Schulz-Dornburg (a former fighter pilot and an acquaintance of Hermann Göring) conducted a radio concert in Cologne for "Heldengedenktag," the "Day for the Commemoration of Heroes." His program included Reger's awful *Patriotic Overture,* Siegfried Wagner's *Die heilige Linde* Overture, pieces by Beethoven and Handel, Schoeck's *Trommelschläge,* and the closing movement from Hans Heinrich Dransmann's *Einer baut ein Dom* ("A Man Builds a Cathedral"), a cantata celebrating the "German renaissance" under Hitler.[14] *Trommelschläge,* as we have seen, had been composed out of anger at World War I, and its modernist idiom was hardly what the Nazis would normally have promoted. But if its twelve drummers were loud and the horns whooped enough, then the work's ironic intent could easily be drowned out (let us not forget Aloys Mooser's barbed comment of almost two decades earlier that the work was best fit for performance on Berlin's Siegesallee).

Schoeck spent five days at the Fluh in mid-May 1938—where it seems that Burte met him and read from his latest sketches for the libretto—and then returned to Zurich for the June Festival before spending the rest of the summer at the Weidhof and in Brunnen, working on the second act of *Dürande.* The festival this year offered yet another notable world premiere, Hindemith's *Mathis der Maler* under Denzler's baton on 28 May. The production was supervised in part by the composer himself, who had at last exiled himself from Nazi Germany. The premiere took place just four days after the Nazis opened their exhibition of "degenerate music" in Düsseldorf, in which Hindemith's music featured large. As with *Lulu* a year before, the world's press was in attendance in Zurich—the yearbook of the City Theater later remarked with pride that the *Times* in London had even sent a reporter by airplane to cover *Mathis,* and the BBC, two reporters.[15] The work's reception was highly positive. Karl Heinrich David's three-page review was the first article in the *Schweizerische Musikzeitung* of 15 June; it praised the theater's "extraordinary deed" in bringing the work to life.[16] He also included a sideswipe against Corrodi's year-old criticism of *Lulu* as "musical Bolshevism." There followed an equally glowing review by Hans Ehinger of the world premiere of Honegger's *Jeanne d'Arc au bûcher* ("Joan of Arc at the Stake"), which Paul Sacher had conducted in Basel on 12 May.[17]

Schoeck attended the premiere of *Mathis,* which was obviously a must for everyone on the Zurich scene. He had been irritated by the "eternal fugati" in Hindemith's *Mathis der Maler* Symphony, and while he still found that "Hindemith has no melodic gift at all . . . he can't sing," he was nevertheless impressed: "Hindemith's best achievement is the figure of little Regina. The scene of Mathis and this little child in the wood is really touching . . . but the best scene is probably the one of the Peasants' Revolt."[18] The extensive coverage given to the world premieres of both *Mathis* and *Jeanne d'Arc,* not least in the local Swiss journal, can only have made him wish his new opera were further advanced. He was now hot on Burte's heels with the composition of it, not unlike the situation with Rüeger during their work on *Don Ranudo* and

Venus twenty years before. But Burte was not as easy to cajole, for he had a far different sense of self-worth. During the course of the summer of 1938, Burte was subjected to a series of letters and postcards in which Schoeck urged him to supply more text. Thus on 20 July, "The IInd act is as good as finished! . . . may I soon have the IIIrd?" on the thirtieth, "The IInd act is finished. . . . *Please* send me *immediately* what you have finished of the IIIrd so that I don't sit around empty"; and on 6 August from Brunnen: "If you're not quite so far with the 3rd, then *please* [underlined three times] send me immediately what you read to me at the Fluh." On 10 August Schoeck was able to confirm receipt of the next instalment of the libretto, and more on the twenty-seventh. But even basic issues of the plot had not yet been finalized between them, for Burte was now planning a love scene for Gabriele and Armand in Paris in the third act. Schoeck pointed out tactfully that if the two lovers come together here, then the last act becomes pointless. He got his way.

To Schoeck's horror, Burte was already planning to publish his as-yet-unfinished libretto as a fragment. The reason was money—Burte's correspondence with Reinhart makes it clear that he was constantly in need of cash. It is not clear what he spent his money on, for he lived alone, with no one to support except himself, and we can probably assume that Reinhart financed his writing holidays in Muzot. It seems that his plays were no longer being performed often enough to give him a proper income, though it is also obvious that he harbored grave delusions of grandeur. Two years later he would write to Reinhart: "I use every, but every opportunity to increase my meager income through writing articles, poems, giving lectures for societies—[but] this is no artistic activity: I can only with great difficulty imagine a Rilke doing this!"[19] Schoeck was able to dissuade Burte from publishing anything yet—but just days later, Burte was instead selling the manuscript of his incomplete libretto to Reinhart, in exchange for a "first, part payment" of 600 Reichsmark "by Tuesday." Reinhart confirmed the money transfer on 15 August.

The third act was finished and delivered to Schoeck only in autumn 1938, by which time the new concert season in St. Gallen had begun to eat into his time. Although the programs for his eight concerts this year were not as meaty as those of the year before, the first half of the season nevertheless included Debussy's *La mer* and Reger's *Böcklin Suite*, neither of which Schoeck had conducted before, and which will have cost much time to prepare. Nor were personal relations with Burte making things any easier. The latter wrote to Reinhart on 21 October 1938 over his differences with Schoeck:

> The building of Dürande Castle is progressing again, after the two "masters" had differing opinions over the third . . . act, and I simply didn't want to speak out, *on your account*. . . . I am trying to find my way into the passageways of Sch's thoughts, as well as one can, so that so much trouble and work isn't for nothing.

It seems as if Burte was already looking for a scapegoat to blame in case things went really wrong. On 18 November 1938 Schoeck tried a carrot: "D . .hm [*sic*; presumably Dr Böhm] from Dresden lets us know that he would like the world premiere and would like to read the text. Can I promise it to him soon?" But Böhm got nothing yet, for the text was still far from finished.

Schoeck received a new honor this same November when he, Hilde, and Gisela were given honorary citizenship of Canton Schwyz by the cantonal parliament. Schoeck rarely set much store by such things, and his reaction is not known. When a further "honor" was suggested by Corrodi and friends early in the New Year—the creation of a "Schoeck Society" to promote the man and his music—Schoeck declined, as both he and Hilde felt it would win him no more friends and would risk turning others against him.[20]

Schoeck's main concern in early 1939 was still to prise more text from his librettist. The fourth and last act arrived in March, just as the St. Gallen season ended, so Schoeck was able to immerse himself in the work straightaway. A performance of *Penthesilea* at the Zurich June Festival in 1939—at which Furtwängler was also present—served to buoy his spirits, though the latter's insistence that the opera should be performed in Berlin would in fact bring no such results. The summer of 1939 was spent at the Fluh, at the Weidhof, and in Brunnen, and on 18 August Schoeck wrote to Hesse that he had finished his opera. According to Corrodi (who was normally precise in recording facts and dates), *Dürande* was not completed until 31 August. The two dates are not incompatible, for Schoeck might have "finished," but then spent a couple of weeks going over the sketch, making final corrections and changes. However, since the opera ends with the destruction of the old order, this date was perhaps a convenient one to choose in retrospect in order to heighten the appearance of the work's topicality.

From our perspective the incessant bickering between composer and librettist from the summer of 1938 onwards seems akin to fiddling while Rome burns. While Schoeck and Burte were arguing over whether or not Gabriele and Armand should meet in Paris, Chamberlain, Hitler, Mussolini, and Daladier were meeting in Munich to guarantee "peace in our time," while sacrificing the Sudetenland and its population to the increasingly rapacious Nazis. A few weeks later, in the night of 9 November, after the assassination in Paris of a German consular official, the Nazis unleashed a supposedly "spontaneous" pogrom, now known as "Kristallnacht," in which 250 synagogues and countless Jewish schools and houses were destroyed across Germany. Some twenty thousand people were arrested and several dozen murdered. And while the life of Germany's Jewish population was becoming a living hell, the rest of the world was doing its best to prevent them leaving. It was at the express request of the Swiss authorities that a "J" stamp was put in the passports of German Jews in the last months of 1938, whereupon their border officials were ordered to deny entry into Switzerland to German citizens who were, or were suspected of being, Jews.[21] But the rest of the world was equally callous. An international conference at Evian-les-Bains in France had from 6 to 15 July 1938 debated which of the thirty-two countries in attendance might be prepared to open their borders to Jewish emigrants—and had failed to reach any decision. The total number of refugees that Switzerland would accept in the coming years from Nazi Germany and the occupied countries—almost 300,000 including interned soldiers—was proportionally far higher than the number accepted by any of the western Allies. And while any statistical discussion in the context of genocide cannot but prompt a degree of moral revulsion, it is a simple fact that, had the United States, Britain, and the latter's colonies and dominions opened their borders in time to a similar per capita number of immigrants, then the number accepted would have been far higher than the millions who would instead soon perish in the Holocaust. There is no moral excuse for the behavior of the Swiss authorities toward those refugees whom they turned away, but nor is any country of the West in a position to cast the first stone.

According to Corrodi's version of events, after Schoeck completed his draft of *Dürande* in Brunnen, he left early on 1 September to climb the nearby Niederbauen in order to clear his mind. When he returned that evening, he learnt of Germany's declaration of war on Poland. When the ultimatum issued by England and France was ignored, those two countries in turn declared war on Germany on 3 September. On postcards he sent to friends, Schoeck quoted from the poem "Der Krieg" by Matthias Claudius, which he had set in his *Wandsbecker* cycle: "And I desire no guilty part in it."[22] The otherwise laudable acknowledgement of this "desire" naturally aims to hide the awareness of any possibility of a "guilty part." To adhere to these sentiments was going to prove more difficult than Schoeck could ever have imagined.

Chapter Thirty-One

Arms and the Man

In August 1939 Schoeck assured Werner Reinhart that he would complete the orchestration of *Das Schloss Dürande* in the following winter. That would have made late 1940 a realistic date for the world premiere. But Burte was already impatient. Just over a month after delivering the fourth and final act to Schoeck, he had complained to Werner Reinhart that Schoeck was composing too slowly. This was absurd, given that Schoeck had all along been setting his text with remarkable rapidity and that the opera was his longest ever—some two and a half hours of music. His real reason was probably to impress upon Reinhart that he, Burte, had now fulfilled his part, and that the blame for any future delay lay solely with Schoeck.

Reinhart wrote to Burte on 31 August 1939 to inform him that the opera was finished, adding that Schott was interested in the opera and that Burte should provide them with his corrected version of the text. He added: "The 'Meschugge' Edition has apparently also sounded out Schoeck. But I warned him urgently against any steps in that direction and told him that you would never give your libretto to them. . . . we should win *Berlin* for [the opera], I think." (The "Meschugge" Edition is a reference to Universal Edition that was presumably meant to be humorous to the anti-Semitic Burte.) Schott did get to see the libretto of *Dürande* in the autumn of 1939 but promptly turned it down. And in any case, the orchestration was proving intractable. The outbreak of war had sent Schoeck tumbling into a prolonged deep depression that made it difficult for him to work, and served to heighten his increasingly erratic Germanophobia. The German closest to hand upon whom he could vent his anger was his wife, who complained to Corrodi that he had developed a "pathological hatred" of the Germans and was making her his personal scapegoat for the whole crisis in Europe.[1] She took Gisela off to Davos for five weeks in early 1940, but things were no better when she came back. It is easy for us to explain his behavior, for it was really he who was "collaborating" with a Nazi, and he was neither willing to alter the fact nor able even to acknowledge it. The threat of German invasion increased dramatically in the early months of 1940, and Schoeck must have felt at some level that his actions were a betrayal of all he believed in and of everyone he loved. He had family and friends doing their Swiss military service, of whom by the law of averages a good number would have been killed had the German army crossed the border. To put the blame for everything on Hilde was probably the easiest way to assuage his own complex feelings of guilt.

As Schoeck's depression worsened, so his pace of work slowed down. On 25 April 1940 Reinhart informed Burte that Böhm had turned down the premiere of the opera after having read the libretto. One wonders how many people had to reject the opera on the basis of its text before anyone would be prepared to admit that the problem was the text itself. But there is no sign that any of the participants in this strange, sad farce ever allowed themselves to utter the obvious. While a knowledge of German is necessary to grasp the true awfulness of Burte's text, those possessed of the merest smattering of the language can still recognize the banality of the rhymes and rhythms. Here, then, are just two brief samples:

Act 1:

Gabriele:
. . . Wie friedlich in die Kammer
Der Mond, der liebliche, scheint!
O Himmel! Weh und Jammer!
Das tut wie eiserne Klammer!
Mein Bruder, der stolze, weint!
. . .
Lebe wohl, du Försterlinde,
Ihr Hunde, Katze, du Fink!
Ich ziehe im Morgenwinde.
Fahre wohl, o Heimat, ich finde
Den Weg ohne Wort und Wink.

["How peacefully the dear moon shines into the room! O heaven! Woe and misery! It feels like clamps of iron! My brother, the proud one, is crying! . . . Farewell, thou linden tree of the foresters, dogs, cat, and finch! I leave with the morning breeze. Farewell my homeland, I will find the way without word or sign."]

Act 2:

Renald:
Nicht um das Geld
In aller Welt,
Sondern die Seele
Von Gabriele!
Um ihrer Jugend
Bewahrte Tugend,
Um ihre Reinheit
In der Gemeinheit
Vornehmer Mache
Geht hier die Sache!

["Not for the money in all the world, but the soul of Gabriele! It's about protecting the virtue of her youth and her purity from the vulgarity of noble sham!"]

All four acts are full of similar stuff. We can only surmise that Burte's status as a prominent Nazi was what prevented men such as Willy Strecker and Karl Böhm from saying precisely what they must have thought of the text. Not everyone was negative about the work, however, for in April 1940 Schoeck received two letters of interest. One was from the opera in Kassel, the other from Berlin, with the former apparently more concrete than the latter. Both wanted him to visit in order to play them his opera. Schoeck sent the letters to Reinhart, begging for his advice.

The enclosed letters cause me despair and embarrassment! The idea of any journey abroad is terrible at the moment. If our opera absolutely has to be performed abroad, then at an important place. To console ourselves with Kassel doesn't please me at all. Then one could do it just as well in Zurich. . . . What should I do? . . . a world premiere in Switzerland would not be out of place at the moment. But what would the publisher say? I just don't know what to do![2]

Reinhart invited him to come and discuss the matter, and in the meantime wrote to Burte to sketch out the situation. The latter wrote back on 29 April that "Schoeck should go [to Berlin], of course . . . Kassel is thoroughly provincial, nothing more." On 2 May Burte wrote again to Reinhart, stating that he would gladly go to Berlin with Schoeck, since he knew some influential people (though he does not say who they were). The rejection by Böhm in Dresden was felt keenly, since he had conducted the world premiere on 13 April 1940 of another Swiss opera, *Romeo und Julia* by Heinrich Sutermeister (1910–95), a former Orff pupil. Within months it had been performed across Germany and Switzerland and was enjoying the kind of operatic success of which Schoeck had always dreamed, but which would for ever elude him. "This success is far too big; it's suspicious," he said. "Only the Meyerbeers and the [Hermann] Sudermanns have had such a great success."[3]

It is possible that *Romeo und Julia*'s triumph was what held Schoeck back from either giving his opera to Kassel or insisting on a Swiss premiere. He had for several years been the undisputed ruler of the composing scene in German Switzerland, and after Sutermeister's *Romeo*, the older man might have seen it as ceding his primacy to have (in his words) "consoled himself" with a lesser place for *his* new opera. But whatever he and Reinhart might have decided upon, everything was for the moment put on hold when Germany began its attack on the western front on 10 May 1940. Schoeck wrote the next day to the Berlin Opera to offer them first option on *Dürande*, but he also immediately abandoned all plans to travel there. According to Reinhart, a festival of Schoeck's music had been planned in Paris of all places, but the German war machine put a stop to that, too. Germany had invaded Denmark and Norway in April and was now overrunning the Netherlands, Belgium, Luxembourg, and France just as swiftly, forcing France to sign an armistice on 22 June. This rapid conclusion of hostilities in the west and north, coupled with the entry of Italy into the war on 10 June, meant that Switzerland was now completely surrounded by the Axis powers. It was the only democracy left in western Europe, and Hitler's threatening rhetoric led many to feel that a German invasion was now inevitable.

Schoeck was panicking. Gisela had fallen ill with scarlet fever on 10 May, just as the news came through of the German invasion in the west. Since Lake Zurich was a natural defensive boundary, and since the Zurich Cantonal Hospital lies on the "wrong" bank—the one that the Germans would have occupied easily in the course of any invasion—Schoeck took his daughter instead to the hospital in Lachen in Canton Schwyz, much further down the lake but on the southern, "safe," side of it. When the immediate panic abated, Gisela was brought back home and put in quarantine on the first floor. Corrodi also noticed a sudden change in Schoeck's vocabulary when he spoke of the Nazis after France's capitulation: Hitler was now "at least a man with a great social conscience," he had muttered.[4] Schoeck was terrified—after all, it would not be wise to be seen to be a Germanophobe if Hitler was about to take over the country. It is also noteworthy that Schoeck's symphony concerts for the next St. Gallen season, due to begin on 24 October, were to feature almost solely works from the Austro-German canon. Of the seven concerts in total, there were to be three "Beethoven evenings" (denoted thus in the program) and one "Mozart-Haydn evening"; apart from Tchaikovsky's Sixth Symphony, Berlioz's *Roman Carnival Overture*, and a few songs by Schoeck himself, the other composers represented in the season were restricted to Schubert, Schumann, Brahms, Weber, Gluck, and Wagner. The military situation naturally meant that many of the younger male players would be away on military service, which would in turn make adventurous programming difficult. But if an invading German army had occupied St. Gallen in the coming months, they would have had no cause to alter the programming of its symphony orchestra.

The Swiss authorities, however, were doing all they could to prevent any further threat of invasion. On 25 June 1940, three days after the French capitulation, the Swiss president, Marcel Pilet-Golaz, gave a radio speech about the new situation in Europe, making it clear that there would have to be major concessions to the new order. Many interpreted this as a serious sign of defeatism, and it prompted the head of the Swiss Army, General Henri Guisan, to a grand gesture in order to restore morale. He gathered the whole officer corps at the Rütli Meadow opposite Brunnen—the mythical founding spot of the Swiss Confederation over 600 years earlier—and spoke for a few minutes on the readiness of the Swiss Army to defend its country against any aggressor. Guisan and his strategists made known their defensive plan in the case of invasion: the Army would immediately sacrifice the lowlands—including Zurich, Geneva, and Basel—and withdraw into a fortified enclave or "réduit" in the Alps, from where they would continue to fight and inflict the highest possible casualties on the invader.

The Army's combat readiness, or appearance thereof, succeeded in strengthening the country's resolve. In fact, it worked so well that for years afterward the legend remained in general currency that the steadfastness of Guisan and his troops had saved the day. There was some truth in it. The German Wehrmacht felt that Switzerland's difficult terrain would make it a hard nut to crack, and it is possible that they even overestimated the probable strength of Swiss resistance. Crucially, they knew that the Swiss intended to blow up the Gotthard Tunnel if defeat seemed inevitable, which would have robbed Germany of one of its most important transport routes to its ally, Italy. But as Guisan well knew, his bullish strategy was paired with massive concessions on the political and economic front that were largely hidden from the general population. The two strategies worked in tandem. Whether the one without the other would have sufficed to keep Hitler at bay is impossible to tell. For the next five years, Switzerland allowed sealed railway carriages to travel through the Gotthard from Germany to Italy and back, conveying munitions and occasionally troops; the country's financial centers served as clearing institutions, exchanging stolen gold and other treasures for valuable hard currency; the Swiss armaments industry sold its wares north of the border, essentially providing the Nazis with munitions factories safe from Allied bombs; and the Swiss electricity grid provided badly needed energy for the southern regions of Germany. When much of this information became widely known in the late 1990s, it prompted considerable shock in the world's media. But if anyone seriously believed that Switzerland could have survived World War II intact without making far-reaching concessions to the vastly more powerful countries that surrounded it, then they were being hopelessly naive.

Once Gisela's health had improved, Schoeck's immediate concern was once again his opera. In July 1940 he and Hilde went on holiday to Rigi-Klösterli, where he hoped to continue with the scoring of it. But he found it difficult to make progress and so relocated to the Weidhof, where he had always been able to work. By the end of August, he had completed roughly half of the orchestration of the opera. Burte, however, was getting increasingly impatient, so much so that he stopped using Reinhart as a go-between and instead wrote to Schoeck directly to tell him how he felt. The letter has not survived, though we do have Schoeck's reply of 7 September 1940:

Dear Mr Burte,
    You are quite right when you say that the dawdling finally has to stop. It would have been even better if had stopped about two years ago, when I waited yearningly for the text every month and every half year, for in that case, our opera would have long been performed. You know how

understanding I was about these delays back then. So the rather school-masterly tone that you now adopt, toward me of all people, is quite unde-served. . . . I am working "like an ox" [*sic*] on the score (there are about 1000 pages!). I'm now beginning the third act.

The letter reads as if Schoeck swiftly worked his anger out of his system, for it ends in far more accommodating fashion. According to Hilde, however, he was at this time suffering from terrible mood swings, in which furious rages would alternate with moments of depression when he would burst into tears. His work on *Dürande* was ruining his health, she said. He was regularly working on the score until four in the morning and was so straining his eyes that he now had to put on his glasses to be able to eat.[5]

There was also good news this month, however, for Alfred Schlee of Universal Edition came to Zurich in late September to hear Schoeck play through *Dürande*. Willi Schuh and Corrodi were also asked along. But Schlee arrived two hours late, during which time Schoeck began to rage against the Germans. When Hilde came into the room, he declared her perfume to be "digusting" and proceeded to open all the windows. Hilde somehow kept her cool, and remained for the play-through. It took three hours, which everyone found too long except Schoeck, who was determined that no cuts should be made at all. Corrodi wrote in his diary afterward that neither he, Schuh, nor Hilde liked the libretto. We do not know Schlee's reaction to it, but either it did not bother him or he found the music strong enough to overcome it, for Universal soon accepted the work. Perhaps Schlee thought that taking on an opera co-written by a known Nazi might help to mitigate Universal's reputation in Germany.

Proof enough that the current manpower situation did not prevent ambitious conductors from performing difficult contemporary repertoire is provided by the fact that Luc Balmer—formerly one of Busoni's Swiss students in Berlin, and since the mid-1930s based in Bern—conducted the Bern City Orchestra in a broadcast performance of Schoeck's *Lebendig begraben* on 21 October 1940. This performance is worthy of note for three reasons: it is the earliest surviving recording of the work; it documents the interpretation of Felix Loeffel, Schoeck's preferred soloist for the part; and among those listening in was none other than James Joyce. He had fled from Paris earlier in the year, when the Germans had invaded. He had then tried to gain entry into Switzerland from Vichy France, but it had been denied him on the grounds that he was supposedly Jewish. "I'm not a Jew from Judea, but an Aryan from Eire," had been his retort. Then it was claimed that having such an eminent writer might provide unwelcome competition for native Swiss writers. Not until two Zurich friends had put up a guarantee of Fr. 20,000, and not until he had given the names of a number of prominent citizens who could vouch for him (Schoeck included) was he allowed to enter the country. While he was waiting for an answer, he stayed in Saint-Gérard-le-Puy, just across the border, and it was there that he happened to be sitting in a café on the evening of 21 October, twiddling with the knob of a radio. To his astonishment, the strains of *Lebendig begraben* emerged from across the ether, which he took as a good omen. He was allowed into Switzerland almost two months later, and shortly before Christmas he was back in the Kronenhalle with Schoeck and his drinking companions, telling them the whole story. But less than a month afterward, on 13 January 1941, Joyce died in the Rotkreuzspital from a perforated stomach ulcer. He was buried in the Fluntern Cemetery up the hill, near the Zurich Zoo.

Late 1940 also saw Schoeck's one concrete contribution to the Swiss military machine with the world premiere of his *Military March* (woo 40) on 23 November in the Zurich Congress House, as part of an army concert attended by General Guisan himself. Schoeck had written it sometime earlier in the year, and it had been scored for military band by Hans Heusser (1892–1942), a native of St. Gallen who had belonged to the Zurich Dadaists during World War I. It was not unusual for a composer to leave the scoring of his wind band music to others, and of the three occasional marches that Schoeck composed, he in fact scored none of them himself. This march was the only new work that Schoeck composed that year.

Schoeck's St. Gallen season came to an end on 6 March 1941 with his last "Beethoven evening," comprising performances of the "Pastoral" and "Eroica" Symphonies. But he still could not concentrate wholly on *Dürande*, for in February he had begun an extended series of radio programs entitled "The Songs of Othmar Schoeck," which lasted into May. It was Corrodi who had brought it about, and it partnered Schoeck with many of the best Swiss singers in broadcasts of his songs. But instead of showing gratitude, Schoeck merely blamed Corrodi for having "burdened" him. Hilde was allocated a slot on 19 May and was judged afterward to have done an excellent job. She had suffered terribly from stagefright—after all, she had not sung in public for several years and had never before performed in public with her husband. Even worse, Schoeck had apparently refused to rehearse with her. Their program was devoted to Eichendorff songs, and Schoeck at least let his wife give one world premiere among them, of "Trost," Op. 51, no. 3.

Two weeks earlier, on 5 May 1941—a year later than originally scheduled—Schoeck had played through his new opera for Robert Heger and Erich von Prittwitz-Gaffron from the Berlin State Opera. Prittwitz-Gaffron was there as the deputy of Heinz Tietjen, the artistic director; the Strasbourg-born conductor Heger (Nazi Party member no. 5917569) was an old acquaintance of Schoeck's, for he had studied composition with Lothar Kempter in Zurich forty years before. That these Berlin theatrical representatives were in Zurich at this time was somewhat ironic, for their visit coincided almost exactly with the world premiere of a work by a man who had fled their city just a few years earlier: Brecht's *Mutter Courage*, which was first performed at the Zurich Schauspielhaus on 19 April 1941, with Therese Giehse in the title role.

Schoeck's new opera was accepted immediately for Berlin. But this was by no means the end of his problems, for the State Opera itself had suffered a direct hit from Allied bombs just a month before and now had to be rebuilt. The Kroll Opera was being considered as an alternative venue, but in any case, the premiere could not take place before early 1942, they said. Hilde wrote to Reinhart on 6 May to tell him of the work's acceptance; Schoeck wrote to Burte to tell him too, one day later, and it was announced to the public by Heger in Berlin one week after that. The scoring was still not finished, however, and Schoeck left for the Weidhof in early June in order to continue with it. As usual, he spent the summer alternately there, in Brunnen, and back home in Zurich, though he also spent the last two weeks of July as Reinhart's guest in Winterthur. Burte joined them there, and Schoeck played through the opera for him before they left.

The political situation in Switzerland eased after Hitler's invasion of the Soviet Union on 22 June 1941. If most available German divisions were being sent to the East, then it followed that the danger of Switzerland's being invaded would recede with them. The country's concert life continued as normal. On 30 August Schoeck conducted the Orchestra of La Scala Milan at the Lucerne International Festival in a concert comprising Schubert's "Unfinished" and "Great" Symphonies (see fig. 31.1). Schoeck was dazzled by the orchestra, and its members were by all accounts delighted with him, applauding him in rehearsal after the first movement of the *Unfinished*. The concert itself earned a fifteen minutes of applause.

Schoeck's program for the coming season at St. Gallen looked more "normal" than had that of the year before. Alongside the staples—Beethoven, Mozart, Haydn, Brahms, and Schubert—there were works by Berlioz, César Franck, Maurice Ravel (*Ma mère l'oye*), and Saint-Saëns, as well as by Schoeck's Swiss contemporaries Walter Lang, Fritz Brun, Paul Müller-Zürich, Karl Heinrich David, and Max Haefelin. Schoeck was able to finish the orchestration of *Dürande* on 1 October, just under a month before his season began on 30 October 1941 with a concert celebrating the twenty-fifth anniversary of his debut in St. Gallen. Stefi Geyer performed his Violin Concerto, the "Frohsinn" Chorus sang his *Dithyrambe,* and Loeffel, Maria Bernhard-Ulbrich, and Ernest Bauer sang in a concert performance of *Vom Fischer.* Schoeck was at this time considering abandoning his conducting career altogether, with only financial need keeping him on the podium. But as far as outside reports are concerned, he seems to have been at the height of his powers as a conductor. He had his technical limitations—his concertmaster in St. Gallen in the late 1930s, Karl Neracher, remembered his once getting lost in a score by Stravinsky, at which he simply held his baton vertically, drew circles in the air and watched the first violins until he found his place again.[6] But reports of his interpretation of the Romantics suggest that for that repertoire he was a conductor of the first order. The composer and Beethoven scholar Willy Hess, who for several years earned his living as an orchestral bassoonist in Winterthur under Hermann Scherchen, was a down-to-earth vegetarian teetotaller disinclined to hagiography. He nevertheless wrote as follows about the times that he traveled to St. Gallen to play as an extra there:

Figure 31.1. Schoeck conducting the Orchestra of La Scala Milan in Lucerne, 1941. Courtesy of Zentralbibliothek Zürich.

It is unforgettable to me how Schoeck swept all the musicians along in the rehears-als for his *Dithyrambe* [presumably in St. Gallen on 30 October 1941], how he sang along with unimaginable expressive power, how he jubilated with us, how his eye seemed to reflect every tiny nuance of the music, how he submerged the music in the souls of his singers until this brilliant work glowed in perfect beauty as if it were being played and sung by a single, gigantic instrument.

And what an experience was his performance of Bruckner's Eighth Sym-phony in 1941! One felt oneself no longer a member of an orchestra, but become an instrument upon which the master Schoeck himself was play-ing . . . he rehearsed and filed away until he had extracted the very last of what we were capable—not in matters of technical perfection, but in musical expression. I have played in this marvel of a symphony three times: under Schoeck, Furtwängler, and Keilberth, with the latter two in the original ver-sion that has since become available. But Schoeck's performance remains unforgettable to me.[7]

Hess's description of Schoeck's conducting, including his comparison with Furt-wängler, has been confirmed by other witnesses, including Neracher. Schoeck conducted many times on the radio, mostly in Switzerland and occasionally in Germany, but with the sole exception of the brief fragments from *Vom Fischer* in 1940, already mentioned above, all his recordings seem to have been either lost or destroyed (in the 1950s the Swiss Radio unthinkingly gave many miles of tape recordings to the local firefighters to burn as part of their training program). But if contemporary reports are accurate in suggesting that his piano playing and his conducting were similar in every way, then Schoeck's many recordings as a pianist do offer us some kind of measuring rod by which to judge him. And his playing is situated clearly in the "rubato" tradition to which Furtwängler belonged (as did Nikisch and Wagner before him), in which flexibility of tempo plays a vital role.

We must beware, however, of using the lack of extant recordings of Schoeck's conducting as an excuse to offer unthinking praise. Willi Schuh's private opin-ion of Schoeck as a conductor, for example, was not overly complimentary (and differed notably from his high opinion of him as an accompanist). He confirmed that Schoeck lacked good technique and was no "Orchestererzieher" ("orches-tra trainer"), and he remarked that Schoeck tended to over-romanticize. And for these very reasons the committee of the St. Gallen orchestra, he said, occa-sionally had heated debates about him.[8] All the same, the reports of Hess and others make the lack of recordings of Schoeck as conductor all the more regret-table. What we can state categorically is that during the 1920s and early 1930s Schoeck invested much time and energy in bringing the latest European music to the Swiss public, and for this alone he deserves a place in the annals alongside his more famous contemporaries Scherchen and Ansermet. This aspect of his career has consistently been overlooked, just as his modernist credentials as a composer were for so long ignored or hidden. His concerts regularly featured the recent music of Ravel, Honegger, Stravinsky, Krenek, Hindemith, and others at a time when such programming would have been audacious anywhere, let alone in little Catholic St. Gallen. Furthermore, this supposedly arch-exponent of Austro-German Romanticism showed a particular affinity for what was happening in Paris, not just in the case of the composers already mentioned, but also in his championing the music of his younger Swiss contemporaries, such as Conrad Beck and Paul Müller-Zürich, who had trained there and come under the influence of the Parisian neoclassical aesthetic.

Schoeck's conducting career would be cut short by ill health before the end of the war, which means that he was no longer active on the podium by the time of the rapid expansion of the postwar recording industry. Since Schoeck regarded conducting as primarily a means to earn money, and a means that he never expressed regret at putting behind him, he would perhaps be far less concerned about this loss than we are. But we do him a great disservice by ignoring his contribution as a conductor. And if we examine properly the aesthetic displayed in his concert programs, this can in turn aid us in understanding Schoeck the composer.

Chapter Thirty-Two

Castles in the Air

When Schoeck finished the scoring of *Dürande* in early October 1941, the premiere was still a long way off. One man at least, Corrodi, had summoned up the courage to tell him what he thought of Burte's text. Early in the year he had offered to write the words into the score for Schoeck, was horrified at its "cataract of trivialities," and wrote in his diary:

> I made no bones about my dislike of the libretto. Schoeck admitted that Burte loved rhymes . . . and that it was full of awful doggerel. "But you have no idea what I've had to muck out already, what junk!!" But the thing did have its good side, he said: besides many bad verses, Burte now and then wrote a good one, and the verses were fluid, not ponderous . . . anyway, most of it would not be understood and would disappear in the music. The important things were prominent enough, and the music serves to bind what often doesn't go together or jumps from one thing to another.[1]

It is difficult to reconcile this Schoeck, content with a good line "now and then," with the man so admired by Hermann Hesse and others for his literary sensibility. The only plausible explanation is that he felt bound to Burte by his quarter-century-long debt to their patron Reinhart. Nothing boded well for the future of the work. Burte, however, was already dreaming of bigger and better things, and Schoeck did not figure in them. On 20 September 1941 he wrote to Reinhart as follows:

> In Munich . . . [I] was captivated by a wonderful performance of R. Strauss's *Salome,* whose music veritably exudes the carefree freshness of youth, courage, and brilliant invention (oh! Where is Schloss D??) . . . to write a text for this musician, that would be a happy business; he's significant enough to grant the librettist his say, too, and to acknowledge it! How nice that he also belongs among your Rychenberg guests!

This presumably means that the insignificant Schoeck is to pave Burte's way to a collaboration, also implicitly to be organized by Reinhart, with his other, more significant, composing guest, Strauss. Burte's other correspondence with Reinhart leaves no doubt as to the immensity of his ambition.

The premiere of *Dürande* was now planned for the coming March (1942), shortly after Heger was to return from a tour with the State Opera to occupied Cracow, where Hans Frank, the music-loving "Butcher of Poland," resided in the opulent Wawel Royal Palace (Heger was no stranger to crossing the boundaries between the musical and the political, as he had eight years earlier conducted a festival performance of Wagner's *Meistersinger* for Hitler's birthday in Berlin).[2] But *Dürande* was soon postponed yet again, this time to autumn 1942, because the parts and vocal score were not yet ready. Willi Schuh had originally intended to prepare the vocal score, but he seems to have miscalculated seriously the time he had at his disposal (having also taken on the editorship of the *Schweizerische Musikzeitung* a few months before). So after just a few pages he abandoned what would have been a mammoth task. Since he also knew of *Dürande*'s difficult history to date, perhaps he decided it would be wise to keep his distance from it. So Universal Edition hired Anton von Webern for the job, and he began work on it in August 1941. There has been much speculation that Reinhart might have been involved in procuring the job for him, though there is no proof, and Webern was at this time making a number of vocal scores for Universal Edition in order to earn some cash. On 28 February 1942 Webern wrote to his friend Willi Reich in Zurich: "I've finished another vocal score, this time of a monster of almost 1,000 pages of score!" He was paid 1,500 marks for his trouble.

Schoeck had composed almost nothing new since finishing the sketch of *Dürande* in late summer 1939, but a few days after his jubilee concert in St. Gallen on 30 November 1941 he began work on a new song cycle to poems by Gottfried Keller. This was his first cycle to use the poet's words exclusively since *Lebendig begraben* fifteen years earlier. Its eventual title would be *Unter Sternen* ("Under [the] Stars"). Although it would take well over a year to complete, in musical terms it became Schoeck's most closely unified song cycle, thanks to his obsessive use of the same cadential formula throughout.

While Schoeck spent the first half of 1942 conducting in St. Gallen, doing the necessary corrections to the score of *Dürande* and working on his new cycle, Burte and Reinhart were getting worried about the progress of the war. Burte was still giving his laudatory Hitler speeches—"We're still useful, and that's the main thing!" he wrote to Reinhart on 2 April 1942—while Reinhart wrote back six days later to complain:

> For decades now, England has been placing itself more and more into the hands of the Jews. The [*Times*] *Literary Supplement* has long been a reliable "barometer" for me in this. . . . So we can only hope that Germany finishes off the Bolsheviks. I yearn to be able to exchange ideas with you once again.

Reinhart's political views have never been closely investigated, probably because of the immense, largely positive influence that his family has long exerted on life in Winterthur. Oddly, there are enough contrary passages in his correspondence to suggest that he had no real sympathy with anti-Semitism, just as his unstinting support for the Communist Hermann Scherchen is proof that he was no line-toeing would-be Fascist. But documents have also surfaced over the past two decades to suggest that Reinhart's real politics were far further to the right than hitherto suspected. There is a letter from Stravinsky to Reinhart of 27 March 1930—published only in expurgated form in the English-language edition of the composer's correspondence—that obviously refers to conversations held during his recent visit to Winterthur, and which runs:

> There were things that gave me real pleasure . . . [such as] your campaign against the Masons! I did not know that you were not indifferent to these antichrists, and this, together with your disgust, as conscious as it is natural (I hope), toward universal Jewry (of which the Freemasons are merely the servants). All that fills me with joy![3]

Unless the entire Reinhart archives are at some future point opened to scholars, we will not know whether Reinhart seriously shared any of Stravinsky's astonishing sentiments. But the fact that Reinhart could let down his guard when corresponding with a Nazi such as Burte—indeed, that he felt close to the ghastly man at all—suggests that Stravinsky's comments were not made in a vacuum. Nothing of this sort appears in Reinhart's correspondence with Schoeck. So perhaps the contrast between Schoeck's beliefs and those shared by his librettist and patron can also help us to understand why he must have felt increasingly trapped by *Dürande*. Whatever the reasons, the castle was now becoming a prison to him.

Schoeck at least found one refuge away from *Dürande*, Burte, and Reinhart in the first half of 1942. His last concert of the St. Gallen season was on 19 March, with Reger's *Hiller Variations*, Strauss's *Till Eulenspiegel*, and the masterly neoclassical Viola Concerto by Paul Müller-Zürich. Hilde and Gisela were away in Davos, so Schoeck took the opportunity to spend Easter at Casa Venosta, a house in Orselina in Italian Switzerland that belonged to Josef von Vintschger. Although a chemist by profession, von Vintschger was possessed of wide intellectual and cultural interests and a keen sense of humor. He was also as generous as he was wealthy, and at Casa Venosta he and his family would over the coming years provide Schoeck with a home from home in his beloved Ticino, where he could work and rest as he liked. A sure sign of the affection that Schoeck bore him is the fact that von Vintschger even received occasional composition lessons—for Schoeck had otherwise always refused steadfastly to give instruction in composition to anyone. It was at Casa Venosta that Schoeck composed his only work of 1942 besides the songs of *Unter Sternen:* a brief piece for chorus and orchestra entitled *Für ein Gesangfest im Frühling* ("For a Song Festival in Spring"), also to a text by Keller. Its subtle orchestration, sadly, cannot hide the fact that it is a pale rerun of the *Wegelied* (also to a patriotic Keller text) of 1913.

Dürande was still not ready, but three of Schoeck's earlier operas were this year taken up once more by theaters in Germany: *Vom Fischer* was performed at the Elbing City Theater, *Erwin und Elmire* in Giebichenstein Castle in an open-air production of the Halle City Theater, and on 2 May the Leipzig Opera put on a production of *Penthesilea* conducted by Paul Schmitz and directed by Wolfram Humperdinck (the son of the composer Engelbert). Schoeck attended none of these. After finishing the *Gesangfest,* he resumed work on *Unter Sternen.* He went to the Weidhof in June to continue with the cycle, and by July he had finished fifteen songs. During the summer he pondered whether or not to orchestrate them, or perhaps to alternate the accompaniment between piano and an ensemble, but in the end he kept just the piano. In October 1942 the city of Zurich offered him three thousand francs as a commission for a new work. He first turned it down, but when he mentioned that he was already busy with a large-scale cycle, he was offered the money "to complete it" and accepted gladly. Bt the end of December he had completed all twenty-five songs of the cycle as it stands today. Two of them—"Frühlingsglaube" and one unnamed other—were given their first performance by Loeffel on 29 January 1943 at the (re-)consecration of the Wasserkirche in Zurich (the "Water Church"—a church on a little island in the Limmat that had for many years served as the city library, then as a piano showroom, and was now given back its original function). Three weeks later, on 18 February, Schoeck conducted Loeffel in *Lebendig begraben* in St. Gallen in what would prove to be their last-ever joint performance of the work.

The premiere of *Dürande* was still being postponed with regularity. It had been fixed for 21 February 1943—shortly after Heger was due to return from conducting Bruckner in occupied Belgium[4]—but in early 1943 it was shifted to 25 March instead. Zurich was already planning the Swiss premiere for the following June. In mid-February Schoeck called together a number of friends and colleagues to play them the opera: Corrodi, Léon Oswald, Ernst Isler, Josi Magg, Karl Heinrich David, and others. Their congratulations sounded hollow, wrote Corrodi in his diary; David even excused himself after the first act.[5] Whatever his friends thought, Schoeck was still the most important composer in eastern Switzerland, and a full-length opera from his pen was highly newsworthy. So on 1 March the *Schweizerische Musikzeitung* brought a special "Schoeck" issue to celebrate the forthcoming premiere. Corrodi had the task of producing the article "*Das Schloss Dürande:* From Eichendorff's Novella to Hermann Burte's Libretto," in which he managed to avoid mentioning Burte's name at all until half a page from the end. He even allowed himself some mild criticism, veiled in barbed praise: "thanks to the character of the verses, which have a proverbial turn of expression and are full of folksong-like metaphors—there are in my opinion all too many!—Burte achieves a certain proximity to Eichendorff."[6] Willi Schuh's achievement was similarly virtuosic: of the thirty-two music examples in his article on the music of the opera, only one quoted from Burte's text, while the librettist's name appears twice in the first paragraph, and never after it. Hermann Spelti's general article on Schoeck's operatic oeuvre failed to mention either Rüeger or Burte.[7]

Schoeck was uncertain as to whether he should attend the Berlin premiere of *Dürande*. He wanted to, for it had an all-star cast that included Maria Cebotari, Willi Domgraf-Fassbaender, Josef Greindl, and Peter Anders. The director was Wolf Völker and the sets were by Emil Preetorius. But the Allied bombing raids were becoming more frequent and more dangerous. An indirect hit on the opera house made a further postponement necessary, this time until 1 April. The general state of things in Europe could hardly have been worse right now. In the first two months of 1943 the British and Americans had made the unconditional surrender of the Axis powers their principal war aim, Goebbels had made his infamous declaration of "total war," the Americans had begun the systematic bombardment of German cities, the doomed Warsaw Ghetto Uprising had begun, and the Battle of Stalingrad was finally lost with the surrender of the German Sixth Army. Signs of dissent in Germany, such as the anti-Nazi leaflets distributed by the White Rose group, were brutally repressed; the group's leaders, Hans and Sophie Scholl, were tried by a kangaroo court and guillotined on 22 February 1943, just four days after being arrested.

The mood in Switzerland toward their belligerent neighbors was not improved by the introduction of rationing for bread in October 1942, then for milk a month later (and this in a country for which the milk cow was and has remained an iconic symbol). The anti-Fascist stance of the theatrical community in Zurich was further underlined by the world premiere of Brecht's *Der gute Mensch von Sezuan* at the Schauspielhaus on 4 February 1943 (the premiere of his *Leben des Galilei* followed six months later, on 9 September).

Hilde's sister wrote from Germany, urging Othmar to stay at home. Schoeck's friends begged him not to go. But then Robert Heger wrote on 18 March to assure him that his accommodation had been chosen with great care. He did add, however, that the Berlin suburbs were now no longer safe. In the end, Schoeck was unable to resist the temptation. In his last concert in St. Gallen for the season, on 25 March, he conducted two works that were banned in Nazi Germany: the Violin Concerto and the "Scottish" Symphony by Felix Mendelssohn—almost as if he had planned the program in advance in order to make some gesture, however futile, against the policies of the regime that he was due to visit. He then traveled to Berlin, arriving just before the dress rehearsal. Isler and Schuh also went (separately) to review the premiere; Adolf Güntensperger was also present. Burte, however, was not. He must have seen the Schoeck issue of the *Schweizerische Musikzeitung* from which he had been more or less excluded, and wrote to Reinhart on 12 April:

> Just as I wanted to travel to Berlin to the premiere of "S.D." the news arrived that the husband of Katharina Huegin [Burte's niece], who lives here in Flax, had been killed on the eastern front. . . . I could not go, all the more since the *manner* of the publisher, the composer, his personal scribe Corrodi, and as a result of them the State Opera, quite simply, with time, became too stupid for my taste—and so I stayed at home and do not regret it.

Among Schoeck's operatic premieres, *Dürande* is the only one whose standard of performance we can judge, for some three-quarters of an hour of music have survived from a radio recording that was considered lost for half a century until it turned up in the archives of the Zurich Radio Studio and was released on CD in the mid-1990s.[8] The performance is simply superb. Heger, said Schoeck, had done everything right. The public on the night was apparently also enthusiastic—at least until the final scene, for the technical department of the opera had outdone itself in the destruction of Dürande Castle at the very end. Among those present was the Swiss Ambassador Hans Frölicher, who later recalled how Renald had disappeared into a hidden door, whereupon there was a huge explosion followed by flashing lights, dust, and then darkness. When the lights went up, one saw nothing but rubble where the castle had stood.[9] The audience screamed, thinking that Allied bombs had struck yet again, and it was a long time before everyone realized it was all just theater. The fact that the opera's premiere took place on 1 April seems macabrely appropriate.

Chapter Thirty-Three

Goering's Bullshit

The premiere was followed by a reception offered by Frölicher. Goebbels had been invited but to Schoeck's relief did not turn up. Elsbeth had come all the way from Hamburg for the event, and Hilde's sister was also there. Ernst Isler telegraphed his first, brief impressions home, which appeared in the *Neue Zürcher Zeitung* on 2 April: "In libretto and composition the work is a markedly great opera." The German reviews were hardly less enthusiastic. On 3 April Karl Holl wrote in the *Frankfurter Zeitung:*

> What the born song composer had to fear and avoid was the epic breadth of the tale . . . perhaps it was in anticipation of these dangers that Schoeck this time quite consciously ensured the collaboration of a poet of quality, who . . . could be trusted to have a strong sense of reality and a certain security in his grasp of the dramatic.

Fritz Stege in the *Hamburger Tageblatt* of 2 April praised the work's instrumentation and the orchestral use of the piano, while Walter Abendroth in the *Berliner Lokalanzeiger* of 2 April wrote of Burte's "remarkable taste" in adapting Eichendorff. In the *Dresdner Zeitung* of 2 April Karl Laux gushed: "In the land of Eichendorff and Burte, Schoeck has found a home." Only a few—such as Hermann Heger in the *Neue Leipziger Tageszeitung* of 3 April—dared to make any negative comments about Burte's incessant rhyming couplets. Otherwise, the press was unanimous: *Der Führer* in Karlsruhe, *Der Mittag* in Düsseldorf, *Der Alemanne* in Freiburg, the *Berliner Illustrierte,* the *Hamburger Fremdenblatt,* the *Königsburger Allgemeine Zeitung:* all across the Reich, the German press response was glowing.

The tenor of the reviews in Germany should not surprise us. The composer was from a country that the Nazis needed for both munitions and hard currency, and which they would have incorporated into their Reich, had they won the war. The librettist, as everyone knew, was a faithful Nazi. And it would have been unthinkable for anyone to have criticized a major premiere at the State Opera in the capital of the Reich, performed by some of the best singers in the world. All the same, it looked as though Schoeck at last had achieved the spectacular operatic success of which he had long dreamed.

The success was short-lived. Given the tragi-comic nature of the opera's genesis and first performance, there is an absurd logic in that the first man to speak the truth openly about Burte's libretto was none other than Hermann Goering. He had not attended the premiere, but he took the trouble to procure a copy of the text shortly afterward. On 14 April he sent a telegram to Heinz Tietjen, just a hundred meters or so down the road at the State Opera (we keep the punctuation here as close as possible to Goering's original):

> Have just read the libretto of the opera Schloss Dürande that's being performed at the moment it is incomprehensible to me how the State Opera could perform this utter bullshit ["Bockmist," literally "billy-goat dung"]. The librettist must be an absolute madman. Every person to whom I've read just a few lines refuses to listen to any more even for a comedy or as a complete farce it's too stupid. I'm astonished that our members took on such idiotic roles. They should have refused en masse to sing this utter bullshit. I assume that you have not yet read the text yourself. Either the dramaturge or Professor Heger is guilty of this scandal. How could Professor Heger praise it to me in Rome . . .
>
> Heil Hitler
> Goering Reichsmarschall[1]

The singers were promptly found to have "outside commitments" and the work disappeared from the program of the State Opera.

Willi Schuh's long review of the premiere in the *Schweizerische Musikzeitung* of 1 May 1943 is typical of his careful, measured style, emphasizing the positive while tactfully allowing the reader to register the negative. He was full of praise for the music, stressing how it was in many ways a "synthesis" of many of the traits of Schoeck's previous operas, from the passion of *Venus* via the mercilessness of *Penthesilea* and the formal mastery of *Vom Fischer* to the "delicacy" of *Massimilla*. While he acknowledged Burte's having provided suitably dramatic situations, he was at last more open about the libretto's weaknesses:

> The intention to achieve a "folksy" stylization, using as his means a proliferation of rhymes that play a less then happy role, has seduced [Burte] into using for long stretches an unintentionally pretentious tumult of rhymes— now carefree, now contrived or pathetic, the embarrassment of which somehow slipped imperceptibly past the otherwise ever-sensitive ear of the composer, who embraced them with the same love as he did the magical verses of Eichendorff.[2]

Schuh was still being relatively diplomatic, though we should not underestimate his courage. The April issue of the *Musikzeitung* had included an article entitled "The Military, the Radio, and Claude Debussy" by Edward Staempfli (the same whose youthful symphonic poem Schoeck had rehearsed in St. Gallen in the mid-1920s). In it he extolled the virtues of Debussy's music, which "stands fast in our culture like a dam against the waves of the Teutonic barbarism that threaten us."[3] This was strong stuff, given Switzerland's continuing precariousness in Europe, and it prompted harsh criticism of both Staempfli and Schuh in the German press.[4]

Robert Denzler was due to conduct the Swiss premiere of *Dürande* on 5 June, as part of the Zurich June Festival. Among the singing coaches involved in the production was the young Georg Solti, who had found himself stranded in Switzerland at the start of the war and had survived thanks to the generosity of a number of locals, ranging from the tenor Max Hirzel, whom he coached regularly, to Werner Reinhart. His position had become more secure upon winning the piano section of the International Competition in Geneva in autumn 1942, where his program had included Schoeck's Toccata, Op. 29, no. 2. He was at this time living in Zurich with his girlfriend, Gertrud Marchev (the daughter of Ernst Zahn, a poet and longtime chairman of the City Theater Board), though her name is omitted from his memoirs.[5] Half a century later Marchev's son still remembered how Solti would make everyone at home guffaw by singing time and again the worst lines from *Dürande,* a particular favorite being "Ah, Hölle, Tod und Fluch! Hier liegt ihr Busentuch!" ("Ah, hell, death and curses! Here lies the kerchief from her breast!").[6] Denzler became ill and pulled out of the premiere—or had he perhaps realized that it was going to be a public relations disaster? In any case, the theater decided that the best man to replace him was Solti. According to Emil Bächthold, who was chorus director at the time, Denzler made a rapid recovery when he heard the news, determined that he was not going to be replaced "by a Jew."[7] Despite his advocacy of music branded as "degenerate" by the Nazis, what hardly anyone knew at the time was that Denzler was a party member himself.

The Zurich production had a "somewhat improvisatory character" (thus Schuh in the *Schweizerische Musikzeitung*), though the singers of the three main roles—Julia Moor (Gabriele), Max Lichtegg (Armand), and especially Marko Rothmüller (Renald)—were found worthy of praise.[8] Not only did *Dürande* have to compete on the festival program with a stellar *Tristan und Isolde* featuring Max Lorenz and Kirsten Flagstad under the baton of Karl Böhm, but the timing of its premiere could hardly have been worse. In June 1943 many in Zurich were once more afraid that the Germans might invade in an attempt to deflect attention from their losses in North Africa and on the Eastern Front. It was considered tantamount to betrayal that their leading composer had written an opera to a libretto by a known Nazi and had traveled to the heart of Germany to see it performed. The ghastliness of Burte's text now provided a perfect reason to attack the opera and its composer. In the interval of the premiere, Corrodi heard the work being torn apart. Afterward, when Schoeck went off on his own to a reception with the high and mighty, Hilde complained bitterly to his friends of how he had "wasted" his music on Burte's drivel.

The *Neue Zürcher Zeitung* printed a review by Schuh on 7 June—they avoided Isler this time—in which he managed to be almost civil: "The linguistic forms appear unsatisfying: the uninhibited piling up of short, rhymed verses and the

254   GOERING'S BULLSHIT

fatal playing with 'leitmotivic' rhyme (Seele—Gabriele) overwhelm the few strophes that are worthy of the poet of *Madlee*." Other critics were not as gentle. In
the *Tat* on 8 June Robert Oboussier expressed his astonishment that Schoeck
"could put up with such an embarrassing, primitive concoction of verses as Hermann Burte offered him." He at least noted that the performance itself had
been excellent, especially the principal roles. In the *National-Zeitung Basel* on the
same day, an anonymous critic praised the music briefly but then laid into the
libretto at length:

> We had believed that the genre of the "revolution opera" . . . had had its day.
> Schoeck is of a different opinion. He has taken up the hackneyed theme again
> and let a libretto be hammered together by the Alemannic poet Hermann
> Burte, whose banal rhyming couplets leave little to be desired in the way of
> sansculottish nonchalance and vulgarity. Gone are those poetic reflections and
> allegories that Armin Rüeger had once brought to our lyricist of the stage;
> gone too those malleable, gently flowing strophes on which the music of *Don
> Ranudo, Venus,* and *Massimilla Doni* once soared . . . How was it possible that
> [Schoeck's] musical imagination could be kindled by such platitudes?

If Rüeger read this, he would have been utterly perplexed. After years of endur-
ing harsh, often unjust criticism, his work had now become a paragon of poetic
beauty. But the critic probably knew Rüeger's libretti no better than did those
who had torn them apart in the past—he had become merely a useful tool
with which to attack Burte (and, by extension, Schoeck himself). There were
also those among Schoeck's colleagues who took delight in his being toppled
from his pedestal. The composer and pianist Emil Frey even took the trouble
to compose a three-page parody entitled "Upon Hearing a Performance of
Othmar Schoeck's 'Schloss Dürande'" in which the rhyme "Gabriele—Seele" is
used even more insistently than in the opera itself, accompanied by a cabaret-
like oompah bass.[9]

It is also possible that some of the critics had been spurred on by knowledge
of Burte's latest book, a collection of speeches entitled *Sieben Reden von Burte*
and published in the first quarter of the year in occupied Strasbourg. They offer
the worst of Burte, in excess. Besides subjecting the reader to a surfeit of anti-
Semitism, the book also raises Hitler to an almost godlike level: "There came a
new man, from deep inside the people. He nailed up new theses and set up new
tablets and he has created a new people, risen up from the same depths where
great poetry originates: from the mothers, from the blood and the soil." Even
the notoriously erratic prose style of *Mein Kampf* is here praised as "poetry."[10] It
is difficult to read Burte's book today without experiencing feelings of near-phys-
ical disgust. If any of the Swiss critics in mid-1943 had come across this volume
of astonishing sophistry, it will only have emboldened them in their decision to
tear *Dürande* apart.

Example 33.1. *Das Schloss Dürande,* Op. 53, act 4, the closing love duet in Anton von Webern's vocal score. Copyright 1942, 1970 by Universal Edition. In performance, the $\frac{6}{4}$ meter is perceived as a brisk, (Richard) Straussian waltz-time. Gabriele: "My dearest, with you, with you!" Armand: "[Gabrie-]le, you here, you here!" Together: "Blessed are we! In this place, in this time, but not a dream, only blessed[ness]."

Schuh's description of the music to *Dürande* as a kind of synthesis of what had gone before it was no mere phrase of convenience. While there is nothing in it akin to the near-atonality of *Penthesilea,* the revolutionary act and the close in the doomed castle have passages of great dissonance such as one does not find in *Massimilla.* And there is much in it of the melodic strength of *Venus* or even *Erwin und Elmire.* Armand's aria with the huntsmen's chorus at the end of act 1 is one of the score's finest moments. It was no doubt inspired by the original Eichendorff poem that Schoeck sets here: the sun rises over the woodlands to the accompaniment of a male-voice choir and hunting horns in B-flat major, all redolent of the early German Romanticism of Weber's *Freischütz* or Wagner's *Tannhäuser,* but imbued with an immense, irresistible *Schwung.* At times it seems as if Schoeck had invested all the subtlety of his craft in the one area over which he had sole control, namely the orchestration, which is glorious throughout. There are heavy hints of Richard Strauss, as in the final love duet in waltz-time (see ex. 33.1), though there are also frequent Korngoldian overtones. It would be wrong, however, to assume that this accessibility was simply a concession to the German authorities, for it was a logical consequence of Schoeck's development since the late 1920s. Overall, however, the libretto is too awful to allow the music to take flight. As Robin Holloway wrote in a review of the CD release of the excerpts from the world premiere: "For every flicker of quality there is mediocrity and boredom in plenty, especially where lusty choruses and the *Marseillaise* are involved. The Act 4 love-duet comes to life a little, and the snatch of its finale, more in Schoeck's dissonant vein than before, kindles fire at last."[11]

The failure of *Dürande*—dropped from the State Opera's program in Berlin, mocked and spurned by the critics at home—was a crushing blow. Schoeck had for years been protected by a coterie of friendly critics such as Corrodi, Isler, David, and, to a lesser extent, Willi Schuh. While the author of the fierce review in the *National-Zeitung* apparently felt it too risky to put his name to his words, it was clear to all and sundry that Schoeck was untouchable no more. It was his own fault, too. German late-Romantic opera is full of mediocre libretti, ranging from Max von Schillings's *Mona Lisa* to Richard Strauss's *Liebe der Danae.* But there are few that are quite as bad as *Dürande.* And now that everything had gone as badly as it possibly could, we can only guess at the depths of depression to which Schoeck succumbed. He seems to have sought some comfort by rushing into a new operatic project, for at the time of the Zurich premiere of *Dürande* he was once more considering an opera on *Meister Pfriem* and *Bruder Lustig.* When Hilde sensibly pointed out that an opera needs a proper plot to begin with, she earned a torrent of verbal abuse.[12] In late June Schoeck came downstairs with a packed suitcase and left for the Weidhof without having said a word to her in advance about his planned absence. This was no working holiday like previous years, for he was quite incapable of composing. He was back in Zurich in July for another visit from Heger and Prittwitz, who wanted to discuss the possibility of the State Opera doing guest performances of *Dürande* in Kassel. Their condition, however, was a series of cuts and changes to the libretto. Schoeck agreed, and although the Kassel plans were finally abandoned, these alterations would be included when the Zurich City Theater took up the opera again in the following autumn.

Regardless of his depression, Schoeck's concert commitments continued. Just four days after the Zurich premiere of *Dürande* he had accompanied Helene Fahrni in a lieder recital in Winterthur that coupled his own songs with a selection by Grieg. His concert season in St. Gallen began in the autumn as usual, and there were other conducting engagements in Winterthur and Zurich in October and November, including a concert performance of the final scene of *Venus,* with Julius Patzak as soloist, in the former city. Schoeck and Loeffel gave the world premiere of his latest cycle, *Unter Sternen,* on 8 October in the smaller Tonhalle hall in Zurich. But it was half empty, and several friends whose attendance could normally be guaranteed were notable by their absence—such as Andreae, Morgenthaler, and Hermann Haller. The next day *Dürande* began its second and last run in Zurich, but the house was also half full, which was unusual for a Saturday evening. Schuh wrote in the *Neue Zürcher Zeitung* on 11 October that the suppression of the worst rhymes had been greatly to the work's benefit. But no one seemed to be listening any more. Ernst Isler was complaining of how his enthusiastic review of the previous April had done as much damage to his reputation as a critic as had the opera itself to Schoeck. After three performances *Dürande* was dropped. It would not be performed again for another fifty years.

The scorn that has been heaped upon the libretto of *Schloss Dürande* has long served to cushion it from critical attention. There is much in it, however, that warrants a closer look. It was not uncommon in the early years of the Third Reich for the Nazis to draw parallels between the French revolutionaries of 1789 and the hated Russian Bolsheviks of 1917. This is precisely what Burte does. The revolutionary scene in the opera takes place in a pub called the "Red Lion," and although the color of the lion is the same as in Eichendorff, Burte here has his revolutionary leader quote indirectly from the Communist Manifesto: "People of Paris! What have you got to lose? Only your chains and nothing else!"[13] The potential revolutionaries who have congregated in the Red Lion are, according to Burte, "deserter-soldiers, failed lawyers, runaway scribes, the unemployed, political agitators, gardeners, and servants from the palace"—in other words, a *Lumpenproletariat* of utter losers. When Gabriele takes fright at this mob in the Red Lion, she says in wonderment to the Count's faithful old servant Nicole: "so many wild fellows, with a lust for blood in their eyes." He replies "This is the first wave of the great red flood." And the Countess Morvaille—the only figure in the opera who was Burte's own creation—refers to Renald as follows: "How I hate that fellow with his impertinent threats. He already has the grimace of the red rebellion!" She longs for a leader who will "wake up" the nation. "I seek the man who will bring salvation to the land!," she cries, hoping that she has found him in Armand Dürande. All this is reminiscent of the "Deutschland erwache!" ("Germany awake!") slogans of the Nazis that echo through Burte's other writings. In a speech he gave to the German "Dichtertreffen" ("poets' conference") in the National Theater in Weimar in November 1940, Burte referred to Hitler's visit in 1922 to Wagner's son-in-law, the proto-Fascist Houston Stewart Chamberlain, and said:

> The suffering man [Chamberlain] recognizes in the man before him the German hero, the chosen one of the Norns, the savior and redeemer of the nation: blessed and comforted, he can finally find sleep once again, because he feels that *the awakener is there and Germany awakes!* [Burte's italics][14]

And in "The Essence and Importance of Grabbe the Poet," dating from the early 1940s, he wrote tautologically: "The people, reawakened ["auferweckt"] by a genius, by a leader from out of its own depths, has woken up" ["ist wach geworden"].[15] Besides his Hitler cult, there are two further, related, themes from Burte's writings of this time that are to be found encoded just below the surface of his libretto. The one is "purity of blood" and the other is anti-Semitism. Burte insists that purity of the blood is the guarantor of victory, and he maintains that whoever possesses "lower" blood is doomed to defeat. "Today we are not just busy defeating [the English] in war," he wrote, "but are overcoming them spiritually thanks to the strength of our blood, which is purer than theirs."[16] And what of those who supposedly possess the least "pure" blood? Here Burte leaves us in no doubt: they are the Jews, "the evil enemy of the human race"[17] (and thus implicitly not "human" themselves).

Burte's libretto repeatedly stresses the "purity of blood" of both Gabriele and Armand—which in his worldview can only mean their "Aryan" heritage. The prioress says of Armand that he is "Genuine and noble, of the best blood!" while the old count sings that Gabriele is "A fresh young girl, not noble, but of blood pure and good." And when Gabriele sings of herself and Armand, she insists that "even though he might be noble, I am still of good stock." Being "of good stock" was essential in Nazi Germany, where one had to prove one's lineage to be free of "Jewish blood." It is thus noteworthy that when Renald joins the revolutionaries, he sings: "Broken are all the ties of blood that I bore [in me]." This implies that he is now cut off from the (Aryan) "bloodline" of Gabriele. Following Burte's skewed logic, it means, quite simply, that he has become a Jew.

The characters in the opera who are of "purer" blood then begin to refer to Renald as a "wild animal," and in the end even as a "monster" ("Untier"). According to the Countess Morvaille, "The monster is coming nearer, we need to act, we have to defend ourselves, bring powder, guns and lead, bring all our faithful followers! For [our] salvation give us weapons, only weapons!" Renald thus undergoes a deliberate process by which he is turned first into a "red revolutionary" of "lesser" blood (thus in Burte's terms: a "Jewish Bolshevik"), and then into a non-human who must be exterminated in order to bring salvation for those of "higher" blood. The closer one looks at Burte's libretto, the more it becomes clear that it reflects with uncanny accuracy the racist, genocidal policies of the régime its author so adored.

Armand is not, however, the *Führer* that Morvaille is looking for. He is a decadent, pleasure-loving French aristocrat who would rather be relaxing at his castle by the Mediterranean: "I want to go fishing and hunting instead of bothering with ministers," he says. He claims to miss Gabriele, but he only ever really shows any interest in her when he is actually with her. So where is Morvaille's leader to be found? She gives us the answer at the end of the opera when she joins the nuns fleeing from their convent, heading "for the Tirol! This holy land." Her final words are: "A man must appear. The world is out of joint. I greet the One who will come, who will scorn the world and steer it!" In Eichendorff's novella, the nuns leave for Germany; but here, their place of refuge is to be Austria, which Morvaille implies will be the "holy land" that will provide the leader of the future. Burte's personal Hitler cult was by now, it seems, second nature to him.

Just before Renald destroys the castle at the close, the Count's faithful servant Nicole kneels beside the dead bodies of Armand and Gabriele, aware that remaining with them will mean his certain death. He sings "I will remain faithful, just as they did" before being blown up. To be "faithful" here, then, is synonymous with pointless self-sacrifice. His master dead, Nicole—who never once questions the hierarchical structures that he serves—has no further meaning in life. For us this seems strangely prescient of the suicide of Goebbels after the death of Hitler. Altogether, the cataclysm at the end of the opera is from today's perspective a strange foreboding of the end of the Third Reich. This interpretation is not completely far-fetched, though in Burte's case at least, we know that it goes wholly against what he had intended. On 18 April 1943 Corrodi wrote in his diary:

> The deep contrast between [Schoeck's] conception [of the work] and that of . . . Burte was something of which he did not become aware: [Burte] naturally sees in Renald's madness an embodiment of Jacobinism, that is, transferred to today's context, of Bolshevism, while Schoeck saw it as an embodiment of National Socialism.[18]

There is no reason to believe that Corrodi was here trying to mitigate Schoeck's involvement in *Dürande*. The Swiss ambassador in Berlin, too, had recognized in the character of Renald a typically "uncompromising, fanatical, totalitarian National Socialist."[19] And Corrodi was in any case writing while the opera still seemed to be a great success. But in his biography of 1956 he placed particular emphasis on the irony of Schoeck's portrayal of "imminent downfall" having been first performed in the capital of the Reich. The publication in 1976 of Goering's telegram seemed to confirm *Das Schloss Dürande* as a work of almost anti-Fascist intent. But Goering's criticism was directed solely against Burte's doggerel and had nothing to do with politics.

The opera seems to have developed a peculiar dynamic of its own early on. And if we hunt for the source of the problem, we find one single common denominator: money. With the example of Hofmannsthal before him, Burte dreamed of the (financial) success that was the lot of a successful librettist; Schoeck too dreamed of a great operatic success that would have freed him from all financial worries; and Werner Reinhart believed that he—that is, his money—could bring together two artists who otherwise had nothing in common. Schoeck was bound to Reinhart because he was financially dependent upon him; and it was this dependence that he will have hoped to break with the financial success of *Dürande*. But in a vicious circle that was surely one source of his depression, Schoeck could only hope to break the financial dependence on his patron by accepting artistic dependence on the librettist whom his patron had chosen for him. It might be an act of over-interpretation to suggest that Reinhart somehow needed Schoeck's dependence and so (unconsciously) provided him with the librettist most likely to ensure that he would never break free; but that is precisely what happened.

One does not have to be an apologist for Schoeck to find Burte unsympathetic. His writings and his correspondence display unequivocally a man whose opinion of himself is vastly greater than his actual gifts could merit, who is shameless in his pursuit of fame and money, and who seems to have cared not one iota about the fate of the real human beings he so blithely wrote off as being somehow less than human. The German expression "Schreibtischtäter" is the most apt for him: someone who committed no physical crime, but whose activities at his writing desk were such that he should be regarded as no less guilty for it. Burte's letters to Reinhart from the final months of the war do nothing to improve our picture of him. They ooze hypocrisy, extolling the mercy of God (implicitly for him alone) and now suddenly insisting that he had never desired to "hurt the feelings of any individual Jew" (which is specious, given that he had long regarded "the Jews" as not properly human and thus supposedly incapable of any capacity for feeling). Burte stresses that he will "do his duty [what duty? To whom?] to the bitter end"—but then proceeds to beg Reinhart to procure him asylum in Switzerland (which he did not). After the war Burte was placed under house arrest for a while but was then set free. He seems never to have pondered just how generous was the clemency shown toward him.

We come across Burte's name today almost solely in connection with his *Sieben Reden,* which are repeatedly cited as one of the most insidious instances of pseudo-literary Nazi propaganda. It is in one sense a pity that this should all overshadow Burte's earlier, fine dialect poetry, but he had only himself to blame. To castigate Burte, however, does not exonerate Schoeck. While we must in all fairness place him in perspective—it is a well-known fact that there were many composers who actively compromised themselves with the Nazis to a far greater degree—the existence of greater wrongs does not cancel out the smaller ones. Schoeck had no liking for the Nazis, and Corrodi was probably right that he saw his Renald as one of them. They were "barbarians" to him. Yet it was in full awareness of their barbarity that he agreed to do business with them. The *Dürande* affair ensured that a whiff of political unsoundness would dog Schoeck's reputation for decades to come. And the fault was his alone.

Just as Wagner's Parsifal has only to ask a single question to attain salvation for himself and those around him, so Schoeck needed only to say a single word to extricate himself: "No." He had ample opportunity for it. He could have said it when Reinhart suggested Burte as a librettist (a negative response at this stage would hardly have turned Reinhart against him); he could have said it when Burte delivered the libretto to him; and he could have said it when Burte and

Reinhart pressed him to accept a premiere in Germany. Surely few people were in those times given so many chances to say the right thing. Schoeck kept hoping that someone else—essentially Reinhart—would say "no" for him. But this was Schoeck's decision to take, no one else's, and the longer he waited, the less chance there was of anyone else taking it for him. In a moment of frustration toward the end of 1943, Hilde remarked to Corrodi that Gabriele was Schoeck's dream woman once more, keen to debase herself and ready to follow her man around like a little puppy. Renald, she said, was really Schoeck himself. While she was probably right about Gabriele, Hilde was otherwise wrong. If Schoeck is to be compared with any of the characters in his opera (always a fraught exercise with a composer), then he is not Renald but Count Armand, who knows what the right thing is that he must do but is unwilling or unable to do it. In fact, Armand is merely the last in a long line of Schoeck's male operatic "heroes"— starting with Erwin, progressing through Horace, Achilles, the Fisherman, and Emilio—who remain passive, who depend upon others to take their decisions for them, or who simply cast themselves at the mercy of a stronger woman.

Das Schloss Dürande is a wonderful score. While it is not Schoeck's finest, it is arguably the one that has the richest palette of musical invention. But its libretto is so drenched in Nazisms that it will in future at best be heard only in concert or on CD. We will never see *Dürande* in its original form on stage again, nor should we; and the world is a little the better for it.

Chapter Thirty-Four

Collapse

There now came at least one concrete sign that Schoeck had not been wholly ostracized at home. This was the "Zurich Music Prize," a newly created award of which Schoeck was made the first recipient. The presentation took place on 21 November 1943 and was accompanied by a short recital of Schoeck's songs, in which he accompanied the contralto Elisabeth Gehri, a superb singer whom he rightly regarded as a worthy successor to Durigo.[1] (The extant recording of the event shows both pianist and singer at the height of their powers). The *laudatio* was given by the eminent Goethe scholar Emil Staiger. If this occasion served to lift Schoeck's spirits, then they will have been cast down again when news came through of the Allied bombing raid that was made on Leipzig in the early hours of 4 December. Besides costing almost two thousand lives, the raid destroyed most of the city center and the whole of the publishing district. The houses of two of Schoeck's publishers, Hug and Breitkopf & Härtel, were among those destroyed, and all their stock was burned. The year's bad news was not yet over, for Ilona Durigo died in her native Budapest at Christmas, aged only 62. She had in fact visited Switzerland just a few weeks earlier (her son still lived in Zurich), and had given her final Swiss recital in Wettingen on 5 September.

The strain of this chain of catastrophes was not being borne by Schoeck alone, for as usual he was venting his anger on Hilde. In mid-December Hilde gave Gisela to friends to look after and booked herself into a clinic in Küsnacht for a few days, unable to bear her domestic situation any longer. Schoeck went off to St. Gallen, where he was once again mulling over plans for an opera on "Bruder Lustig" and "Meister Pfriem"; a St. Gallen friend by the name of Schoelly was apparently already writing a libretto. Once again it came to nothing; Schoeck was more or less incapable of composing anything at all. He managed to complete a five-measure song to honor Reinhart on his coming sixtieth birthday ("Spruch," Op. 51, no. 6), but even that took him weeks of work. In January 1944 he was in St. Gallen again, this time for a performance of *Unter Sternen* with Loeffel. Robert Müller, the critic of the local *St. Galler Tagblatt,* published a review on 17 January in which he complained in mild terms of the "declamatory" style of the vocal part. He went on to state that he knew his views "would not be appreciated everywhere . . . but the composer should not be left unclear as to the effect [of his music]. There is a superfluity of panegyrical praise at his disposal." The Swiss reviews of *Dürande* had enraged Schoeck, but now his fury at music critics in general and Müller in particular knew no bounds. Müller often wrote reports on St. Gallen concerts for the *Schweizerische Musikzeitung* (and had in the past published glowing accounts of Schoeck's performances). According to Corrodi, Schoeck now rang Willi Schuh to insist that he refrain from using Müller in future. Schuh, to his credit, said no.[2] Perhaps to make his point, Schuh included a shortened but undiluted version of Müller's review in the journal on 15 March.[3] Müller might not have dared to write such a review, had it not been for the deluge of criticism heaped upon *Dürande* the previous year. But he does have a point, for the danger of "monotony" (Müller's word) is a very real one in this cycle. It is muted in tone almost throughout, and the fact that every song cadences in the same manner—with a "false relation," the minor resolving onto the major mode—probably reinforced Müller in his opinion (one of the songs, "In der Trauer," even takes this cadential formula as its harmonic basis throughout). But in a sensitive performance, what might otherwise smack of sameness takes on an obsessive, almost hypnotic quality that is unique in Schoeck's oeuvre and can be utterly compelling. *Unter Sternen* is not as inspired as Schoeck's cycles of the 1920s and early 1930s, but it just about succeeds in turning its relative lack of inspiration into its major strength (see ex. 34.1). His later cycles would not all be so lucky. As for that cadential formula, Derrick Puffett has pointed out that it is identical to that used by William Walton at the close of his Viola Concerto—a work that Schoeck had had the opportunity to get to know when it was performed in Winterthur on 8 February 1931[4]—and which in turn had as its source Hindemith's *Kammermusik* No. 5, which Schoeck had himself conducted in January 1929, with the composer as soloist. As already mentioned in chapter 24 above, Hindemith's false relation had also left its mark on *Vom Fischer* several years before.[5]

Example 34.1. *Unter Sternen*, Op. 55, the close of "In der Trauer." Copyright 1945 by Universal Edition. Note the minor-major final cadence typical of the songs of this cycle. ". . . and must now leave without sadness and without joys!"

Schoeck's second-to-last concert program of the St. Gallen season was on 9 March 1944, and it comprised Schumann's "Spring" Symphony and Brahms's First Symphony. During the first half, the concertmaster Karl Neracher noticed how Schoeck kept clutching at his heart. He was called to the podium three times after the end of the Schumann but looked pale and exhausted. He then collapsed offstage. Hans Bärlocher was present at the concert as usual, and it was he who took control of the situation and sent for a doctor immediately. Schoeck had conducted the last movement under intense pain and now screamed constantly at Bärlocher: "Du bisch schuld, du bisch Schuld"—"You're to blame"— implicitly for overworking him and bringing about the collapse.[6] The doctor diagnosed a heart attack, administered morphine, and had him taken to Bärlocher's house to recuperate. As Schoeck knew all too well, Bärlocher was to blame for nothing at all. After the events of the previous year something had had to happen; something had had to change. But Schoeck had as ever been unable or unwilling to take any concrete steps to change anything at all, so in the end nature did it for him. He would never conduct again.

Chapter Thirty-Five

The People at Home

Some two weeks after his collapse, Schoeck was moved back home. This was just at the moment when a production of his *Venus* in Bern under Kurt Rothenbüh-ler was receiving excellent reviews, especially for its Horace, Libero de Luca.[1] While this presumably cheered Schoeck up, he was too sick to attend in person. He further missed the world premiere of his *Gesangfest im Frühling* on 12 April, also in Bern under Rothenbühler. Paul Rossier, Schoeck's doctor, ascribed his heart attack to excessive smoking and to rotting teeth roots. Schoeck had long had an inordinate fear of the dentist, and his refusal to look after his teeth had now had drastic consequences (despite his fierce opposition, the rotting teeth were pulled by the end of the year). Nor was he the only invalid at home, for Hilde too became ill in late March and was put in the bedroom next to her husband's. She was up again before him, however. Not until 1 May did his doc-tors let him get out of bed: "From today onwards I am allowed to measure out with shuffling steps my immeasurable space for the first time . . . that makes roughly two or three steps in the room, and still I prefer to sit down soon after this particular achievement," he wrote to Rüeger. He was as yet without a piano, for it was another fortnight before he could go down to his music room on the ground floor.

During his month's bedridden convalescence, Schoeck had received through the post a copy of the *Bodenseebuch, 1944* (this year's "[Year-]Book of Lake Con-stance") from Hermann Hesse. It contained an article by Hesse on the minor Zurich poet Heinrich Leuthold (1827–79) and a sample of his work: the short lyric cycle *Spielmannsweisen* ("Songs of a Minstrel"). This tale of a Zurich artist whose poems reflect the chasm that he felt between himself and his public was bound to speak to Schoeck (as was the fact that Leuthold, too, had written a *Pen-thesilea*). *Spielmannsweisen* runs: "And if my song . . . that I learnt in foreign lands is not understood by the sensible people at home, and if they do not understand my mourning tones, and if they say: ' . . . These are not the songs of the people, you have grown foreign to us,' then I will hang up my harp on the next tree." Hesse wrote of Leuthold as follows:

> The fact that these childlike emotions in the poet's soul could become music, that this poor, melancholy, helpless man could . . . give himself passionately to the magic of singing the sufferings of his heart in ever more tender, ever finer, ever more hovering tones, so that the content of the song is gradually forgot-ten through the delight and the art of the singing of it . . . that this exists, that

it is possible, herein precisely lies the secret of poetry and its power over us. Even the sick man or the weak, even he who is incapable of action or business—if he is a poet, he can do nothing other than praise life, love his sufferings, and turn his pain into song.[2]

". . . if he is a poet . . ."—or a composer, presumably. Schoeck wrote back to Hesse: "Your two pages on Leuthold . . . have moved me deeply. Your genius has once more hit the bullseye, as so often before, and I thank you with my whole heart."[3] So much of this article was bound to strike a chord with Schoeck that it is almost as if Hesse had written it with his friend in mind, in the wake of *Dürande* when Schoeck was, like Leuthold, "incapable of action."

Since his heart attack Schoeck had been haunted by a musical theme. In a further example of serendipity, the arrival of the *Bodenseebuch* had more or less coincided with a commission from Hermann Scherchen for a work for voice and harp for the next summer's Gstaad festival (the unusual combination was because Scherchen's lover was the eminent Zurich harpist Emmy Hürlimann). So the theme that haunted him now became the opening four measures of a setting of Leuthold's cycle, the accompaniment of a harp being perfect for a set of songs about a minstrel. Schoeck had been all but unable to compose for a year, yet now, *Spielmannsweisen*, Op. 53—he kept Leuthold's title for his own—was completed within just a few weeks.

A sudden awareness of the proximity of death must surely lead us to reassess our priorities, putting successes and failures into perspective and perhaps even freeing us from burdens that had hitherto seemed unbearable. And it is clear that something had changed dramatically within Schoeck's psyche since 9 March 1944, for he had, at a stroke, overcome the block to his creativity that had left him sterile for a year. He was now as fluent as ever. It is notable, too, that he wrote to Hesse: "*Your* two pages on Leuthold . . . have moved me deeply. *Your* genius has once more hit the bullseye" (my emphasis). It was thus not really Leuthold who provided Schoeck with his new *Einfall,* but Hesse, "as so often before." Leuthold was already well known to Schoeck, who had set his poem "Der Waldsee" ("The Woodland Lake") in July 1907. It is perhaps significant that this song was written just a few months after an unhappy love affair (as outlined in chapter 2 above) had prompted him to set Hesse's "Vorwurf." From the perspective of spring 1944, those few months might well have telescoped into a moment in time. Did the coupling of Hesse and Leuthold in the *Bodenseebuch* perhaps prompt memories of Schoeck's Leuthold and Hesse songs of 1907, and thus also of the post-adolescent love that had been his source of inspiration? Schoeck had let himself be inspired by memories of lost love before—the *Notturno* is a prime example, with its obsessive use of Mary's "theme" from over a decade earlier. In his later years, Schoeck remarked of Hesse: "In his poems, I find an atmosphere that speaks to me . . . but Hesse is for me simply a memory of youth ["eine Jugenderinnerung"]." Since the two men did not become properly acquainted until Schoeck had left his youth behind him, he presumably does not mean Hesse the man but his poems, and the memories of a first, lost love with which they were intertwined.

As an "answer" to the "people at home" who had not "understood" him, *Spielmannsweisen* signifies a retreat from Schoeck's former ostensible position that music and politics are independent, separate entities. On the other hand, its largely diatonic harmony also places it at a far remove from the dissonance that had characterized long passages of *Dürande*. This cycle is unashamedly tonal and "popular" in intent, far more so than either of the operas that he had written for performance in Nazi Germany. While we have already noted Schoeck's gradual post-*Penthesilea* progression away from the borders of atonality, *Spielmannsweisen* is positively demonstrative in its stylistic simplicity. This simplicity would become a hallmark of much of Schoeck's music in his final years.

By late June 1944 Schoeck was well enough to go to the Weidhof to recuperate further. From there he wrote to Hesse in July: "Despite all the forbidden things imposed upon me, [it is] as glorious [here] as ever, with the exception of the satanic tremors that for several days now have every morning echoed over the peaceful, summery Lake Constance." After the Normandy landings of 6 June, the Allies had established an unassailable presence on the Continent. And as the German airforce was gradually depleted and the strength of the Allied squadrons grew, the number and severity of bombing raids on Germany increased. Nor was Switzerland safe, for on several occasions Allied bombers hit cities in the north of the country. This was always explained away as navigational mistakes caused by "bad weather," and the raids were followed by profuse apologies, though there were long-lasting suspicions that Switzerland's continuing economic support of Nazi Germany might have prompted the Allies to allow a few "mistakes" as a means of chastisement. On 1 April 1944 the US Airforce bombed Schaffhausen, killing several dozen people and doing much material damage. Even Zurich and Basel suffered a few direct hits. One of the teenage maids employed by the Schoecks during the war could still, half a century later, recall vividly one such Allied bombing scare. Hilde and Gisela were away, and she was alone at home with Schoeck. The air sirens sounded; and in order to distract her from the possible danger, Schoeck took her to the music room, sat her down, and played the piano to her for the evening. Not long after, she was compelled to find another job, for Willi Schuh and his wife had decided that it was inappropriate for her to be left alone with Schoeck and insisted that Hilde do the "decent" thing and replace her. Not until the former maid read the German edition of my first book on Schoeck in the mid-1990s and learnt of Schoeck's youthful sexual escapades did she understand Schuh's moral puritanism. Schoeck, she assured me, had never been anything other than gentlemanly toward her.[4]

In July 1944 Schoeck moved from the Weidhof and its daily tremors to the little village of Männedorf on the eastern bank of Lake Zurich, some ten miles southeast of the city (though today, the houses stretch almost without a break from the metropolis to the other end of the lake). There he stayed with Alma Staub and her family in their big villa close to the lakeside. Alma had known Hilde for two decades, and Schoeck had also visited her on occasion since the late 1930s. Now, her house became one of his preferred refuges. Alma was rich and knew how to mother him and spoil him—just as the Weydmanns had always done—and like them, she knew when to leave him alone to get on with his work. *Spielmannsweisen* was given its first performance in Gstaad on 6 August with the tenor Willy Frei, accompanied by Emmy Hürlimann. Schoeck was not well enough to travel into the mountains to hear it, so he listened to it on the radio instead. The critical reception was muted but at least devoid of anything negative. The experience prompted him to embark on another Leuthold cycle, of much wider scope. Right from the start he chose twenty-six poems to set to music, half of which were finished by Christmas. It was to be less of a cycle than a "songbook" again, like the *Wandsbecker Liederbuch* (though without its brief piano interludes). It represents a step back from the simplicity of *Spielmannsweisen,* but not far back enough. *Der Sänger* includes some fine songs, such as "Trauer," which Puffett reckoned "can rank with Schoeck's best," though he added rightly that "there are many more . . . [that display the] poverty-stricken quality of the material."[5] There are worrying signs here of repetition, of a kind that will become frequent—even the opening of the cycle is itself a variant of the opening of *Spielmannsweisen* (see exx. 35.1 and 35.2).

Schoeck had not yet given up hope of embarking on another large-scale project. But he was to leave opera well alone. Instead, he wrote to Hesse on 24 November 1944 to sound him out about an oratorio project:

> Wouldn't it be good if, in all peace and quiet, we could together create an oratorio-like work. For the topic, I'm thinking of Flaubert's *La Légende de Saint Julien l'hospitalier* ["The Legend of St. Julien the Hospitaler"]. . . . How beautiful it is that it is precisely the animals that hate and overcome the animal in man. And the grandiose way that all is resolved at the end! It would have to be a kind of passion with a narrator and several soloists as representatives of the characteristics of Julien (Evil, Goodness) and Julien himself as the main figure. And around it all, and in between, related choruses of bigger and smaller size.

Hesse's reply has not survived, but it was obviously in the negative, for Schoeck mentions the project no more. He continued with his new Leuthold cycle, finishing it by February 1945. The impasse of the early 1940s was now firmly behind him. This month was also framed by important performances. On 5 February Stefi Geyer and friends played his Second String Quartet in the Zurich Tonhalle, while on the twenty-eighth, Loeffel and Paul Baumgartner performed *Unter Sternen* in Winterthur. April and May brought *Venus* in Zurich, under Kurt Rothenbühler, the same man who had conducted the work in Bern a year

Example 35.1. *Spielmannsweisen*, Op. 56, opening of the first song, "O Frühlings-hauch, o Liederlust." Copyright 1946 by Universal Edition. "O breath of spring, o joy of song, how you stir my emotions!"

Example 35.2. *Der Sänger*, Op. 57, opening of "Leidenschaft" ("Passion"), the first song. Copyright 1951 by Universal Edition. The first measure is harmonically almost identical to the first two bars of Ex. 35.1.

before. The world premiere of *Der Sänger* took place in St. Gallen on 17 May with the tenor Ernst Haefliger, accompanied by Schoeck in his first public performance since his heart attack. It was also the first world premiere of Schoeck's ever to take place in St. Gallen, and the press response was devoid of the criticism that had so enraged the composer in early 1944. On 19 May the critic of the *St. Galler Tagblatt* ("R.-I.") wrote effusively of the spontaneous, "grateful jubilation" that "erupted" in the audience, of the "perfection" of the performance, of the "appreciative astonishment" that the work occasioned, and much more besides.

Haefliger (1919–2007), a pupil of Karl Erb, had come to prominence when Robert Blum engaged him to sing in the world premiere of Frank Martin's *Le vin herbé* in 1941. Three years after Schoeck's death, Haefliger wrote to Werner Vogel to offer his memories of their first rehearsal together:

> Schoeck greeted me at [the door of] his house in a friendly manner, but with few words. He soon sat down at the grand piano and began to play, without any further explanations. And from that moment on it seemed as if the room, the instrument, had cast a spell on me. Barely had he touched the keys and played a few measures and there could be no more doubt or uncertainty about the rhythm or the expression of a work. It sufficed to listen to him in order to see every composition arise before you. . . . We played and sang the cycle through again and again. . . . Schoeck said now and then softly: "Let's do that once more," then at the end, "I think we've got it now." . . . Merely the aura of his playing and his personality were enough in rehearsal to mould the work as he himself experienced it in his imagination.[6]

The tone of Haefliger's reminiscences strikes one today as akin to the accounts of nineteenth-century Wagnerians who were granted the privilege of touching the hem of the Master's cloak. But Haefliger was no minor, overawed provincial singer. He was already an international star who had no need to glorify or romanticize his relationship with any composer. And his account of Schoeck's overwhelming musical presence corresponds to many other reminiscences of those who knew him. While any biographer of the early twenty-first century will tend to regard such effusions with a little cynicism, one cannot ignore what eye- and earwitnesses assure us was the objective truth.

Chapter Thirty-Six

The Reckoning

When one today reads contemporary reports of Switzerland's concert life from the first half of 1945, it seems almost as if nothing untoward was happening in the world. But the world outside was rapidly collapsing. Warsaw fell to the Red Army in mid-January, the Americans and British crossed the Rhine into Germany in March, and by mid-April the Soviets had occupied Vienna. Fearful of his future in the splintering Nazi state, Wilhelm Furtwängler sneaked across the Austrian border into Switzerland in late January and was soon conducting as a guest in Winterthur. On 11 April Robert Heger conducted a concert of the Berlin Philharmonic that Furtwängler had left behind. Appropriately enough, it included the final scene from Wagner's *Götterdämmerung*.[1] Hitler celebrated his birthday on 20 April in his bunker in Berlin, surrounded by the Red Army. He committed suicide on 30 April, and on 8 May Germany at last capitulated.

Switzerland had for some five years lived in fear of a German invasion, and the removal of that threat now sparked off reprisals, both against German nationals who were Nazi sympathizers and against Swiss nationals who were thought to have been too friendly toward the Axis powers. The Swiss authorities—cautious to the last—did not close the German Embassy in Bern until 7 May. By 9 May the newspapers were reporting that the Nazi Party was now banned in the country and that the police were raiding the houses of its members and confiscating all propaganda material. Dozens of German citizens were summarily packed off across the border. Furtwängler had problems, too, for he was regarded by many as having been a willing representative of the Nazi regime. When he planned to conduct in Zurich just a few weeks after taking refuge in Switzerland, he found himself faced with threats of street protests and had to withdraw. Paul Sacher organized a petition in protest at the Zurich City Council's treatment of him. It was signed by many of the leading Swiss musicians, including Frank Martin and Schoeck, as well as prominent anti-Fascists such as the composer and broadcaster Adolf Brunner.[2]

Furtwängler was allowed to stay in Switzerland, and he soon set up home in a villa in Morges, from where he later commuted to Berlin upon being reappointed as the conductor of the Philharmonic. Richard Strauss arrived in Switzerland in the autumn of 1945, supposedly penniless,[3] though in fact suffering merely from temporary problems of liquidity. He lived in the same grand hotels that had been his favorites in earlier times (such as the Verenahof in Baden), played his favorite card-game "skat" with visitors, and now wrote works for rich patrons such as Paul Sacher and Werner Reinhart. There was some public indignation at his presence in Switzerland, but a set of rich, powerful friends ensured that he continued to live in comfort.

Hans Corrodi was not so lucky. He had already undergone an investigation in mid-1944 after having been accused of spreading Nazi propaganda in the Küsnacht Teacher Training College, where he worked. The resultant report had left no doubt that the charges were unfounded, and it had noted that his students supported him without exception. But in May 1945 things were different. Public feeling in Switzerland demanded that an example be made of those who were deemed in some way to have crossed the boundaries of the politically permissible. So Corrodi was investigated once again, and on 18 May 1945 he was interrogated for several hours on the articles he had written on Schoeck for German newspapers in recent years. The final report confirmed once more that he could in no wise be described as a National Socialist and that he had never belonged to any political party, let alone a Fascist one. But an article from 1938, in which he had stressed the "German-ness" of Schoeck's Eichendorff songs, and also his use of the word "Führertum" in his review of *Lulu* in 1937 were now deemed "un-Swiss" ("unschweizerisch"). To his credit, Schoeck wrote a letter to the Cantonal government in September 1945 in support of Corrodi—albeit at the insistence of Hilde, who felt it her husband's duty to stand up for his friend and biographer. This was only the second time in over thirty years, Corrodi noted in his diary, that Schoeck had performed such an act of friendship (he was obviously counting them carefully).[4] But it was to no avail, as Corrodi was sacked from his teaching job on 31 October 1945. He went to court and eventually salvaged his honor—for there was hardly a case against him—but he was from now on reduced to teaching at an evening school in order to support his wife and two sons.

Corrodi was just one of many such convenient scapegoats at the time. The most famous case was that of the so-called "Two Hundred": prominent men from all walks of life who in 1940 and 1941 had petitioned the Swiss government to take conciliatory action toward Nazi Germany, most particularly in muzzling certain sections of the Swiss press, in order not to provoke retaliation from the north. Now, after the war, their names were made public, and they were subjected to a storm of protest.[5] But while the Two Hundred were being vilified, the men who had arguably profited most from business with Nazi Germany now emerged from the war untainted, untouched, and much richer. One of the richest was the banker Adolf Jöhr, who went on to help fund Richard Strauss's Swiss exile and was rewarded with the dedication of one of the *Four Last Songs*.

The Swiss music world also saw much bigger casualties than Corrodi. The director of the City Theater, Karl Schmid-Bloss, German in origin but a long-time Swiss resident, was forced to resign from his post in mid-1947 on account of (unproved) accusations of Nazi sympathies. The city's natural choice for his successor was Robert Denzler, who for years had been the musical director under Schmid-Bloss and had now been intriguing behind the scenes to get his job. But Denzler had reckoned without the intrigues of others, and one of his younger colleagues (apparently Victor Reinshagen[6]) now leaked out the fact that Denzler, unbeknownst to almost anyone, had himself been a member of the Nazi Party during his years working in Berlin. So Denzler was hounded out of his post too.

Corrodi's fate was eased in the coming years when his wife became a highly successful novelist (under the pseudonym "Marga Markwalder"). But his propaganda work for Schoeck also seems to have had repercussions in a manner that he could not have anticipated. At about the time of the *Dürande* affair in 1943, Thomas Mann—by now resident in California—began work on a new novel, *Doktor Faustus,* the tale of a modern composer who enters into a pact with the Devil and embarks upon a remarkable compositional development before collapsing into syphilitic insanity twenty-five years later. The influence on the novel of the twelve-tone system of Arnold Schoenberg is well documented, as are the parallels between Mann's composer, Adrian Leverkühn, and Friedrich Nietzsche. But Mann naturally drew on many more sources too. Shortly after the book's publication, Corrodi wrote in his diary on 18 November 1947:

> Of course I bought it just after it appeared, as the case had to interest me quite particularly: for in it, a high school teacher tells the life of his friend, the great composer Leverkühn. (Perhaps Mann happened upon this topic through my Schoeck book?)

Corrodi had sent Mann a copy of his biography of Schoeck on 4 December 1934, when Mann was still living in Switzerland, though he was realistic enough to expect his biography to slumber away unread on Mann's bookshelves. What he could not know was that Mann did indeed read the book, in the early 1940s, when he was beginning work on *Faustus*. On 27 July 1943 Mann wrote in his diary: "Read in the evening in Korrodi's [*sic*] book on Schoeck, because of the musical descriptions." One day later he wrote: "Read in the book on Schoeck"; and two days after that: "—in the book on Schoeck, to give me a little help ["aushilfsweise"]."[7] Mann had read many books for that purpose, as he confirmed six years later in his tale of the genesis of his novel *Die Entstehung des Doktor Faustus* (though he did not mention Corrodi in it).[8] Mann's copy of Corrodi's biography is held today by the Thomas Mann Archives at the Eidgenössische Technische Hochschule Zürich, and a perusal of it confirms that many places have been marked in pencil. Mostly there is just a vertical line in the margin, though a few passages—presumably those that Mann found most interesting or useful—are underlined. Here and there one also finds an exclamation mark or a question mark.

There are certain passages in *Faustus* that could well have been influenced directly by Corrodi. One of the passages underlined by Mann is Corrodi's description of a modulation from F major to A major in Schoeck's early song "Die Einsame," Op. 10, no. 2. In *Faustus,* Leverkühn's musical talent first becomes obvious toward the end of the seventh chapter, when his Uncle Niko overhears him improvise a modulation on the harmonium, from F major to A major.[9] There are also certain biographical parallels between Leverkühn and Schoeck. They both went to study in Leipzig on the recommendation of teachers there— Leverkühn in 1905 to study with Kretzschmar, Schoeck two years later to go to Reger. Both teachers insist on their writing instrumental music, while both Schoeck and Leverkühn prefer vocal music; nevertheless, each of the composers writes a single orchestral piece during his studies (the *Ratcliff Overture* and *Meeresleuchten* respectively), and both these works receive their first performance under the auspices of the Swiss Musicians' Association. Despite aesthetic differences with their pupils, Kretzschmar and Reger help their students to get their first songs published. Both teachers also leave their position in Leipzig after just a few years to become a kapellmeister elsewhere: Kretzschmar in Lübeck after five years in Leipzig, Reger in Meiningen after four years. And as it happens, both Kretzschmar and Schoeck composed an opera based on Eichendorff's *Das Marmorbild*. There is a possible similarity between Corrodi's oblique description of Schoeck's affair with Mary de Senger and that between Leverkühn and "Esmerelda," and there is also, of course, the odd fact (though one that Mann could not have deduced from Corrodi) that both composers employed a musical cipher to represent their beloved and allowed this to thread its way through their oeuvre for many years (the theme from the last act of *Venus* in the case of Schoeck, the motive "Hetera Esmerelda" in Leverkühn). One final, more peripheral point of contact (though of this Mann could hardly have been aware) is the fact that Mann consciously used Nietzsche's failed attempt to marry Mathilde Trampedach as the model for his love triangle of Leverkühn-Marie Godeau-Rudi Schwerdtfeger; for Mathilde was, of course, Mary de Senger's mother.

The really fascinating similarity between Leverkühn and Schoeck, however, lies in the person of their biographer: Zeitblom and Corrodi respectively. After raising the possibility of an influence in his diary, Corrodi dropped the matter immediately as being too absurd to contemplate. In his *Entstehung des Doktor Faustus*, Mann wrote:

> At what time I took the decision to place the medium of the "friend" between me and the object . . . is not clear from my notes of the time. . . . To convey the daemonic through a means that was undaemonic in exemplary fashion . . . was in itself an odd idea, and more or less a way out.[10]

The notion that Mann could no longer remember when he made one of the most important decisions in his novel seems improbable. But if Corrodi had indeed been the prime means of inspiration for the figure of Zeitblom, then Mann would not have admitted it just two years after publishing *Faustus*. While a novelist will hardly base any of his characters on a single person from real life, Zeitblom's descriptions of his self-sacrificing friendship with Leverkühn—in full awareness that the friendship is largely one-sided—are strikingly reminiscent of Corrodi's attitude toward Schoeck. Like Mann above, Corrodi also uses the word "dämonisch" in his diary to describe Schoeck, his personality, and his creativity. And just as Zeitblom rarely mentions his own family in his account of the life of his friend, so too are Corrodi's wife and sons almost absent from his extensive "Schoeck diary." It is as if Mann had, in some uncanny fashion, read between the lines of Corrodi's biography to discern the deepest secrets of the biographer himself, and then incorporated them into his novel. When faced with a friendship such as Corrodi's with (or "for") Schoeck, one naturally assumes that it might have some homoerotic basis. But as mentioned in the introduction above, all the other evidence points away from any such leanings on the part of either man—and as we have also already observed, when Corrodi himself heard that rumors existed about his own sexuality, his diary records brief incomprehension, then moves on. In this context, Mann's spelling mistake in his own diary entry of 27 July 1943 is revealing, for he writes "Korrodi," not "Corrodi." Both forms of the name indeed exist, and they are neither rare nor particularly common. But in Mann's day, there was one "Korrodi" who was known in all intellectual circles, namely Eduard Korrodi, chief literary critic of the *Neue Zürcher Zeitung* and a man of immense influence. That he was also gay was an open secret—Hans Corrodi even mentioned Korrodi's sexual orientation in his diary on 9 August 1931. If Corrodi had helped to inspire Mann to the figure of Zeitblom, and if Mann had indeed confused "Corrodi" with "Korrodi," albeit only subconsciously, then this could naturally have had repercussions on the depiction of the relationship between Leverkühn and his biographer.

In Zeitblom's attitude toward Leverkühn Corrodi found a personification of his own subservience toward Schoeck. Had he taken the trouble to investigate the figure of Zeitblom any more closely than he did, he would have been confronted with many questions about his own life, none of them particularly pleasant. For in his case it was not the composer but the biographer who had signed a "Faustian pact." He had sworn himself to Schoeck in the belief that he was documenting the life and work of the greatest musical genius of the age. He sacrificed almost everything to him: his time, his energy, his money, his reputation, and even his livelihood. Toward the end of his life, he seems to have half-realized that his "pact" was a chimera. He had paid a huge price but had received precious little in return. As time went on, the likelihood receded more and more that the world would ever honor Schoeck as the great man that Corrodi had so idolized, but this meant too that Schoeck's chronicler would now never receive the recognition that he obviously longed for. Without a Goethe there is no Eckermann. When Corrodi locked away his diaries in two Swiss libraries, only to be opened long after his death, he did so perhaps not just to spare his idol from being revealed as the man he was, warts and all, but also because he feared that those diaries might be acknowledged as little more than an internal monologue: a note of credit in a self-minted currency that was never going to be legal tender.

Chapter Thirty-Seven

Transfigured Summer Nights

On 12 May 1945, just a few days before the premiere of *Der Sänger*, the Bern Music Society—the organization responsible for the Bern City Orchestra—wrote to Schoeck to ask for a new orchestral work for the coming winter concert season. Schoeck replied in non-committal fashion, pointing out his precarious state of health and refusing to say either yes or no. His dislike of commissions had still not left him. He soon began sketching out an orchestral piece all the same. Then Gisela came home one day from school, full of enthusiasm for a poem they had just read there: "Sommernacht" ("A Summer's Night") by Gottfried Keller. Schoeck knew the poem already, as he had wanted to set it to music for his Keller cycle *Unter Sternen*. It had eluded him then, but now he decided to make the poem the basis for his new orchestral work. The result was a "pastoral intermezzo" for string orchestra—essentially a short tone poem—with the same title as the poem itself. He finished it in July at the Weidhof.

Schoeck's health was far from fine this summer. A loss of appetite was one of the main symptoms (a cruel blow to a man who took great pleasure in good food). Nor were matters helped by the news that the little house he had rented on the Lettenholzstrasse for the past thirteen years was about to be sold. Schoeck was offered the chance to buy it, but it was beyond his means. Then Werner Reinhart stepped in, bought the house, and gave it to the family as a gift. "How in all the world can I repay you for everything you have already done for me and my loved ones?" Schoeck wrote effusively on 17 September.[1] He accordingly dedicated his next work, the Suite in A-flat for string orchestra, Op. 59, to Reinhart. This he wrote during a prolonged stay in Brunnen in October and November 1945 (he returned in time to give the first Zurich performance of *Der Sänger* together with Haefliger on 22 November).

Sommernacht was given its first performance in Bern under Luc Balmer on 17 December 1945. It was performed in Winterthur and Zurich in the few weeks thereafter and has since become Schoeck's most often-performed instrumental work both at home and abroad. Although it is lightweight in comparison to Schoeck's large-scale works of the 1920s and 1930s, it is highly tuneful, effectively scored, and wonderfully atmospheric. The poem on which it is based tells of an old Alpine tradition—whether true or invented by the poet is unclear—whereby in the middle of the night the people of a village would harvest the crops belonging to a widow or an orphan who was unable to do the job. As a preface to the score, published by Hug in 1946, Schoeck, however, included not Keller's poem but a brief text of his own that purports to be a synopsis of it. The content remains similar, but whereas Keller's descriptions are primarily visual (he was also, after all, a gifted painter)—"summer's stars beam brightly"; "the fireflies glimmer through the bush"; "a nocturnal silver glittering of the scythes moves through the golden crops," and so on—Schoeck's are aural. His text runs:

> On a starbright summer's night, young country folk, moved by feelings of gratitude, harvest the ripened wheat in the field of an orphan or widow who has no one to help with the work. The swishing of the scythes, the cries of joy, and the sound of the accordion betray the happy hustle and bustle of this old, beautiful tradition, until the crowing of the cock in the morning, the song of the awakening birds, and the early pealing of the bells call the valiant, secret helpers to their own heavy work.[2]

The music, in fact, has more in common with Schoeck's text than with Keller's poem. This probably has several explanations. Schoeck was here confronted with the age-old problem of program music: how does one combine a literary program with the forms of instrumental music? He answered it by distilling from Keller's poem a mildly sentimental, arch-shaped narrative in which the peasants arrive, do their work, and then go home again. In musical terms this becomes the exposition, development, and recapitulation of a somewhat free sonata form. This form, however, is itself heavily subordinate to the work's ornamental, ono-matopoeic elements—almost none of them in Keller—which themselves acquire a formal function in that they are what remain most vividly in the memory of the listener: the chirping of crickets, the "happy cries" of the peasants, the strains of the accordion, and the birdsong of the early morning (in which the "Forest Murmurs" from Wagner's *Siegfried* are never far away). In fact, Schoeck's text reads as if he were trying to explain Keller's poem to a class of schoolchildren. And herein, perhaps, lies the real "inspiration" for the piece: Gisela Schoeck, for it was through her mediation that Schoeck had engaged with a text that two years before had left him wholly uninspired. On the first pencil sketch for *Sommernacht* we find numerous sketches for his introductory text, too, which suggests that this really was conceived at the beginning of the work and served as its basis throughout the process of composition. Keller, it seems, more or less disappeared from the genesis of the work at an early stage.

Sommernacht is in every sense an attempt to conjure up a pristine, untouched, ideal world. There may be orphans and widows in it, but they have happy, grateful peasant friends to stand by them. Here no one is left to suffer alone; loss finds its compensation; no money changes hands; and no one questions his place in the scheme of things. *Sommernacht* really has more in common with the dreamy, early Romantic ambience of Eichendorff's *Diary of a Good-for-Nothing* than with Gottfried Keller, and its contented widows and orphans are a far cry from the women and children that we all know from the postwar newsreels, scratching through the rubble of the ruined cities of Germany. *Sommernacht* was, of course, composed in the only part of Central Europe where an "untouched world" could be found. It is ironic that it recreates an imagined world before the loss of innocence and yet does so from a standpoint where that world in a sense still existed. In 1945 it surely could not have been composed anywhere else in Europe except in Switzerland, where questions of guilt or innocence were already being swept under the carpet.

Sommernacht's musical language seems to support such a reading. Not only is it thoroughly tonal, but it is typical of Schoeck's post-*Dürande* style in that it no longer has the feeling of tonality "after the fall" as we discussed above with regard to Schoeck's neoclassical works such as *Vom Fischer*. In those works, even where the surface is at its most "innocent," one is still aware of darker subterranean currents. Here, the "innocence" is unquestioned and unquestioning, as if Schoeck were trying to convince his listener (and himself) that the only path he had ever trodden was the present one of musical simplicity. It is noteworthy that this is also the first of Schoeck's works to include a reference to Grieg: the opening piano motive of the song "Møte" from the late song cycle *Haugtussa*, Op. 67, is quoted more or less verbatim in the first violin in the exposition of *Sommernacht*, though in D, not in the original F (see exx. 37.1 and 37.2).

Schoeck had long been fond of Grieg's music—most recently, Gieseking had played the piano concerto under him in St. Gallen in December 1939, he had conducted the *Holberg Suite* there on 5 February 1942, and as mentioned above, he had accompanied Helene Fahrni in a Grieg/Schoeck song recital on 9 June 1943 in Winterthur. The influence of Grieg's songs—in particular of *Haugtussa*—would become clearly discernable in much of Schoeck's post-*Dürande* music.

And yet, if *Sommernacht* were nothing more than a derivative conjuring-up of a romantic-utopian agrarian state peopled by unquestioningly happy peasants, it would hardly be as rich in ideas and as compelling to the listener as it is: it would sound as hollow as, say, the Suite in A-flat that Schoeck wrote just after it. The reason for the massive discrepancy in quality between the two works lies not just in the fact that the one is programmatic, the other abstract (abstractions had never been Schoeck's strongpoint), but also in the fact that *Sommernacht* is very much a personal act of remembrance of things past. This is underlined by a quotation—twice—from the opening of the penultimate song from his *Elegie*, "Dichterlos," which tells of the joyless fate of the artist ("I must suffer for all, I must blossom for all, but when the blossoms turn to fruit, they will long have buried me"). *Dürande* had failed, his publishing houses were destroyed, and the German culture that had long been his lifeblood must have seemed as destitute as the country itself. Schoeck felt more and more that the essentially Romantic aesthetic that he espoused was now of little value in the postwar world; and he began to develop an intense fear of being forgotten. Perhaps he felt that his fate was to be that of his "valiant, secret helpers" who complete their task in darkness and then by the morning light have departed, unseen by those who enjoy the fruits of their work. The final chord of *Sommernacht* seems to suggest that Schoeck did not want to know. It comprises a D-major chord held over a dominant seventh chord in F major. It is marked "NB! Very long fermata, until the sound has almost completely died away." Schoeck is so caught up in his memories that he wishes to prolong the final moment for as long as possible. In a sense, the work does not "finish" at all, for its last chord never resolves. Did Schoeck want to avoid an "ending" because he feared the reaction of a potentially hostile audience? In any case, the resolution comes not with the last chord but in the moment of silence that is, as it were, "composed" into it, between the dying away of the dissonance and the applause that the composer desired so badly.

Example 37.1. Grieg: "Møte," from the song cycle *Haugtussa;* first measure of the piano accompaniment.

Example 37.2. Schoeck: *Sommernacht,* Op. 58, first violin at figure 6. Copyright 1956 by Hug & Co.

Chapter Thirty-Eight

Silent Lights

We do not know if Schoeck attended the world premiere of Richard Strauss's *Metamorphosen* in Zurich on 25 January 1946 under Paul Sacher, though we can be sure that he attended the first performance of Strauss's new oboe concerto under Andreae in the Zurich Tonhalle a month later, on 26 February, because the program also included the Zurich premiere of *Sommernacht*. Strauss's new work naturally overshadowed everything else in the press. If Schoeck wondered why he had been so repudiated over *Dürande* while the former president of the *Reichskulturkammer* was being welcomed with open arms, one could not blame him. There is no record of Schoeck and Strauss having met during the latter's Swiss "exile," though Schoeck's friends were certainly divided in their opinion of the older man. Schuh (already the biographer-in-waiting) was doing all he could to ease Strauss's position in Zurich, while Hermann Hesse—three of whose poems Strauss would soon set to music, thanks to Schuh's mediation—was keeping his distance on account of Strauss's inability "to withstand the devil."[1]

Even if Schoeck felt in any way sidelined by the presence of Strauss in Zurich, it did not affect his composing. In early March 1946 he went to stay once more with Alma Staub and her family in Männedorf. They had planned a visit of three weeks for him, but it turned into nine. He certainly enjoyed the material comforts on offer in the Villa Staub, but nor was he idle, for in those nine weeks he composed a new songbook comprising twenty-eight songs to texts by Conrad Ferdinand Meyer. In July Schoeck retired to Italian Switzerland with the von Vintschgers, and it was there, after an evening spent with Hesse in nearby Montagnola, that he composed a piano postlude to the last song of his Meyer songbook, "Jetzt rede du!" ("You Speak Now!"). The whole set, entitled *Das stille Leuchten* ("The Silent Shining" or "The Calm Light"), was given its first performance by the contralto Elsa Cavelti, accompanied by the composer, on Schoeck's sixtieth birthday, 1 September, in the small hall of the Zurich Tonhalle. It was sold out, which must have been heartening for the composer after his half-full halls during the months of the *Dürande* affair. After the concert he had a get-together with his friends Corrodi, Brun, Andreae, Oetiker, Alma Staub, and others. Among the birthday telegrams that arrived was one from Furtwängler that read: "You are one of the very few who have continued the great line of German music-making and have held firm to it to this day."[2]

The birthday celebrations continued on 14 September in Winterthur with the world premiere of the Suite in A flat under Scherchen, and this was followed on 17 September with another Zurich performance of *Sommernacht* under Andreae, plus two arias from *Massimilla Doni*. Schoeck and Cavelti performed *Das stille Leuchten* once more on 4 October, this time in Kilchberg, where its poet had lived and died. Another birthday concert, conducted by Hans Erismann, took place in Romanshorn on the shores of Lake Constance on 10 October. Other concerts followed: Andreae conducted the Zurich premiere of the Suite on 5 November, there was a Schoeck concert in Thun on the sixteenth, and then on 20 November *Erwin und Elmire* was performed at the St. Gallen City Theater, coupled with Schoeck's Serenade, Op. 1, the latter performed as a ballet. The end of November brought a production of *Penthesilea* in Zurich, with Cavelti in the title role. Elsbeth, who had come all the way from Hamburg, was among the guests there. She had lived through the bombing raids that had laid waste to the city, and she had gone completely gray. Hilde and Gisela spent New Year at Rigi-Kaltbad, while Schoeck went to a party at Alma Staub's. He played in the New Year, appropriately enough, with his song from *Das stille Leuchten* entitled "Neujahrsglocken" ("New Year's Bells").[3]

Das stille Leuchten confirms Schoeck's recent interest in specifically Swiss writers. In fact, since 1941 he had set almost no texts to music by anyone who was not Swiss. First there was the Keller cycle *Unter Sternen*, then came the two Leuthold sets, and now the Meyer settings. The most likely reason is also the most obvious: it was a means of distancing himself from Germany. The poems that Schoeck set in *Das stille Leuchten* confirm this "patriotic" tendency, for there are several overtly nationalistic ones among them—albeit "nationalistic" in a very Swiss way, focusing on the natural beauty of the land, not on anything even vaguely militaristic. In "Firnelicht" ("Icelight"), the poet writes: "I have never boasted about my homeland, and yet I love her from my heart! In my being and in my poetry, icelight is everywhere, the great, quiet shining. What can I do for my homeland before I go to rest in my grave? What can I give that will elude death? Perhaps a word, perhaps a song, a little quiet shining!" The piano postlude that Schoeck added to the last song takes up the music from this passage. Josef von Vintschger, who was there when it was composed, later wrote: "In the pencil sketch one can read between the last, grandiose chords: *This* I can do for my homeland! It is Schoeck's personal answer to Conrad Ferdinand Meyer's question."[4]

This desire to do something "patriotic," whether to prove to the Swiss critics of *Dürande* that they were mistaken to attack him or, just as likely, as a personal act of exoneration, is perhaps also the reason for the sudden influence that we can detect of Edvard Grieg in Schoeck's post-*Dürande* music. For he offered a prime example of a composer who had established a national musical identity in a country that had previously been as dependent upon Germany as had Switzerland. Furthermore, Grieg's musical "nationalism" was one that was both stylistically accessible and unsullied by party politics. Schoeck, keen to prove his own patriotism in the wake of implicit accusations of his complicity with the Nazis, could have chosen no better composer to emulate.

Example 38.1. "Yodeling" motive from "Ich würd' es hören," in *Das stille Leuchten,*
Op. 60 (m. 6). Copyright 1949 by Universal Edition. The motive also appears in the
song with the first three notes in augmentation.

The yodelling-like motive that dominates "Ich würd' es hören" in *Das stille
Leuchten* is reminiscent of the same motive from "Møte" in Grieg's *Haugtussa*
that appears in Schoeck's *Sommernacht.* Although it is here more of a paraphrase—the notes are essentially "reordered"—it is at least pitch-specific,
though Schoeck cleverly (if subconsciously) turns a Norwegian pseudo-"yoik"
into a Swiss alphorn-yodel by adding an F sharp, thus mimicking the sharpened
subdominant characteristic of the Alpine instrument (see ex. 38.1).

Besides its stylistic proximity to Grieg, *Das stille Leuchten* also features two musical quotations of foreign material. One is a self-quotation. In "Der Reisebecher"
("The Travel Mug"), the narrator happens upon a travel mug that prompts a
flood of memories of his youth. Here Schoeck quotes from his own "Reiselied"
of almost forty years before, in slow motion and triple time, as a kind of lullaby (the effect is strangely moving). The other quotation comes at the end of
"Requiem," when the narrator hears the bell of the Kilchberg church tolling;
here, as Hans-Joachim Hinrichsen has observed, Schoeck quotes from the chorale "Wenn ich einmal soll scheiden" ("When at Last I Must Depart"), which
Bach had used in his *St. Matthew Passion.*[5]

Schoeck's recent interest in orchestral music—more specifically in the possibilities of a string ensemble—found further confirmation in early 1947. Hilde took
Gisela off to Rigi-Kaltbad, but Othmar stayed at home and began work on a concerto for cello and strings. After his birthday concert in Romanshorn the previous
October, the daughter of a wealthy doctor from the area had asked him for a cello
concerto, and this was now his catalyst. He had played chamber music with his
cellist brother Walter since they were boys, and so he knew well the instrument's
possibilities. He had even made a few brief sketches for such a concerto back in
the early 1930s, but it seems that he did not refer back to them now.

The first movement of the concerto was finished by March 1947, the second not long after, and on 29 May he gave a private premiere of these two
movements with Paul Grümmer as part of a "Schoeck evening" organized at
the home of Renée Schwarzenbach-Wille in Horgen, in belated celebration
of his sixtieth birthday. Hermann Schey sang the *Notturno* to the accompaniment of the Winterthur String Quartet, and Schoeck accompanied Hilde in a
performance of *Spielmannsweisen.* This seems to have been their first concert in
front of a live audience. By June 1947 Schoeck had finished all four movements

of the concerto and thereupon left for his customary visit to the Weidhof. When the lakeside summer heat became unbearable, he left early to join Hilde and Gisela at Rigi-Klösterli. It was at about this time, too, that he played his new work to the French cellist Pierre Fournier, who immediately asked to be assigned the world premiere.

With the exception of *Sommernacht,* Schoeck had given all of his most recent big works to Universal Edition in Vienna—*Unter Sternen, Spielmannsweisen, Der Sänger, Das stille Leuchten,* and the Suite in A flat for strings—and intended to place his new concerto with them too. But he was in a hurry, presumably because of the prospect of a premiere with Fournier, and Universal could not promise to have the score and parts ready by the end of the year. So he gave it instead to Hug, who paid him a thousand francs for it, plus a promise of 10 percent royalties. Like everyone in Austria, Universal was suffering from the general postwar paper shortage—the proofs of Schoeck's *Spielmannsweisen,* for example, arrived printed on the back of Victor Fleming's *Arabella, holde Blume der Sierra* ("Arabella, Lovely Flower of the Sierra").

September 1947 took Othmar and Hilde for a week to Alma Staub's villa, where they also performed a selection from *Das stille Leuchten* for the Zurich Lyceum Club, whom Alma had invited *en masse* to her house. To Hilde's astonishment, Schoeck was now, over twenty years into their marriage, beginning to take her seriously as a singer. More than that, she told Corrodi, her husband was starting to understand that he had treated her badly and was showing signs of remorse. "Othmar is like a changed man; you can hardly recognize him any more," she told him.[6] And in conversation with Corrodi, Schoeck was himself now singing the praises of marriage as an institution, just as he had many years before maligned it as an unnatural state of being. Schoeck's brush with death in 1944 had left him physically dependent on others—even walking upstairs alone could be difficult—and this seems to have helped change his attitude toward Hilde, and hers to him. While we would be unwise to assume that all matters of conflict between them were now conveniently forgotten, concrete proof that the two parties were definitely out of their trenches and parleying came in December 1947, when Schoeck embarked upon a new songbook. The poet this time was not Swiss; it was Eduard Mörike (1804–75), from southern Germany. The forty songs of the collection would take two years to complete, and they would be accorded a dedication unique in Schoeck's oeuvre: "To my dear wife." Mörike had long been one of Schoeck's favorite poets, though he had always hesitated to set him to music because of the example of Hugo Wolf, who had composed so many fine settings in his own Mörike songbook. Schoeck now managed to avoid those poems that Wolf had already set, with one exception: "Das holde Bescheiden," which he wished to use as the overall title of his songbook.

Volkmar Andreae conducted Fournier in the world premiere of the Cello Concerto on 10 February 1948, in Zurich, followed by a further performance in Winterthur on the eighteenth, this time under Scherchen's baton. Fournier was awarded the dedication of the work—though he promptly put it aside, leaving Schoeck wishing that he had dedicated it instead to the wealthy doctor's daughter who had asked for it in the first place.[7] He now continued work on his Mörike collection, halting briefly to set one of the poems for choir and organ instead—"Zu einer Konfirmation" ("For a Confirmation")—so that it might be sung at Gisela's own confirmation on 14 March. The local choir found it too difficult, however, and so it was sung as a solo (which version then found its way into print as part of *Das holde Bescheiden*). In April 1948 the Zurich City Theater put on a new production of *Vom Fischer,* which Schoeck himself praised as the best he had ever seen. This was the fourth of his operas that Zurich had staged in the space of less than five years. But all this interest in his music did little to alter his increasing conviction that he was out of fashion in the postwar world. He was not completely wrong, for a new generation of composers was rapidly turning its back on the late-Romantic aesthetic that had been popular under the Nazis and that was thus increasingly regarded as tarred with the brush of Fascism. The first Summer School for New Music had been held in Darmstadt in 1946; the first Twelve-Tone Congress would take place in Milan in May 1949; and when Andreae retired from the Tonhalle Orchestra in 1949, he would be replaced by the former Schoenberg pupil Erich Schmid. The modernists were by no means hostile to Schoeck (Schmid in particular would prove one of his finest interpreters), but the aesthetic winds of change were obvious to everyone. Schoeck's half-hearted jokes about it merely confirm how worried he was. He should rename Mörike "Mö-Rilke," he mocked, as that would "sound less reactionary."[8]

In June 1948 Schoeck completed the longest song of the new set, "Besuch in Urach" ("Visit to Urach"), which he placed at the very end; it is another of his expansive retrospective glances at happier days, in the manner of "Jugendgedenken" or (more recently) "Jetzt rede du!" It lasts over a quarter of an hour, and while the ritornello-like use of its opening music might risk a charge of monotony in a performance that is not carefully paced, this is still one of Schoeck's finest songs of all—Robin Holloway has remarked of it that, after the stylistic uncertainties of *Dürande,* the composer's "gift is [here] again on-course."[9] Later that month Schoeck was back at the Weidhof, where Hilde and Gisela joined him for a week soon after. They were then picked up by von Vintschger, who drove them all to his villa in Orselina, where the climate was much warmer: north of the Alps it had been an unusually cold summer. After their return to Zurich Schoeck fell into a deep depression, raging against everything and everyone—against the old criticism of *Unter Sternen* from St. Gallen in 1944, Furtwängler's "monstrous arrogance," and Hindemith's "big-mouthed pomposities." Thomas Mann was now "the comedian and entertainer of a decaying world." Corrodi noted that Schoeck refrained from uttering similar loathings about Schoenberg—otherwise one of his favored scapegoats these days—probably because Schoeck had heard through the grapevine that he had expressed praise of the *Elegie.*[10] What

Example 38.2. The climax of "Besuch in Urach," the final song of *Das holde Bescheiden*, Op. 62. Copyright 1956 by Universal Edition. "O valley, you, the other threshold of my life! You, the quiet hearth of my deepest powers! You, the marvelous home of my love! I leave you, farewell!"

Schoenberg had actually said was "O wüsst ich doch den Weg zurück"[11] ("Oh, if only I knew the way back"), a quotation from Brahms's song "Heimweh II," Op. 63, no. 8, to a poem by Karl Groth. The text of the song continues: "den lieben Weg zum Kinderland!" ("the dear way back to the land of childhood"), and it describes a yearning for a state of being in which blissful inaction is sanctioned by an all-encompassing mother-love. What Schoeck seems to have interpreted as praise we might tend to read as an ironic comment on the trajectory of the *Elegie*, with its closing depiction of the soul at evening, safe in (a very tonal) harbor. But when one considers that the 1930s and 1940s had seen repeated attempts by Schoenberg to write again in a tonal idiom, most of them unsuccessful, then perhaps his words were not quite so ironic after all.

While Schoeck's view of his contemporaries seemed to be increasingly dependent upon the constant ebb and flow of his depression, his relationship with his wife—for so many years the victim of such mood swings—seemed to be improving constantly. They were rehearsing his Mörike songs regularly, and he found her interpretation of them "uniquely beautiful." She was now his undoubted soloist of choice to give their world premiere. Schoeck and Hilde gave a dress rehearsal of the first set of the songbook at Alma Staub's villa in mid-April 1949, and it was Alma who drove them to Stuttgart for the songs' world premiere on 25 April 1949 as part of a "Swiss Cultural Week." The reaction of public and critics alike was positive, and the visit as a whole brought back a flood of memories for Schoeck. It was his first visit to Germany since his fateful attendance of the *Dürande* premiere in 1943. Stuttgart was under American control, though just a month later, on 23 May, the Allied zones would unite to form the new Federal Republic of Germany.

After the concert Schoeck wrote that same day to Hesse, himself a native of the region, that:

> The Stuttgarters enjoyed their Mörike in my apparel with understanding, enthusiasm, and gratitude. . . . Hilde sang splendidly. . . . We drove along many paths that I once wandered with Rüeger back in [19]13. . . .
>
> In the countryside you hardly see any destruction. Everything was as familiar to me as it was back then. . . . nothing has happened to this corner of god's world . . . unlike in Ulm, where really only the cathedral with its tower stands untouched and sublime, looming up into heaven above a ghastly wasteland.[12]

Hilde was less impressed with what she saw. Since it was her first visit to her homeland after the devastation of the war, her horror at the "moonscape" that was Ulm, or the "stench" in Stuttgart, is understandable. She had no rosy-spectacled memories of youthful woodland wanderings through which to observe the deprivations of the present.[13]

Schoeck spent most of July and August 1949 at Rigi-Klösterli with Hilde and Gisela, where they were joined for a week by Werner Vogel and his wife. Vogel, some thirty years younger than Schoeck, had begun to work as Hilde's occasional répétiteur in 1942. As Schoeck began to spend more and more time at home after his heart attack and concurrently began accompanying his wife himself, Vogel's visits took on a more social aspect and centered increasingly on the composer himself. They would often play piano duets together—Schubert, Mozart, or Schoeck's own works—and Schoeck allowed Vogel occasional glimpses into the creative process. Vogel's diary of their week's holiday together is fascinating, less for any musical information—of which there is relatively little—than for its insights into Schoeck's other interests. He lists the names of all the mountains and glaciers one can see from the terrace of the hotel at Rigi-Kulm, speculates cogently about the etymology of mountain names, discusses how painters from Rembrandt to Frans Hals to Corot have transposed color effects from the real world into paint on canvas, recites from memory from the dialect poems of Meinard Lienert, discusses "immediacy" in the poetry of Goethe and Uhland, and much more. While Vogel's awe of the older man is obvious on every page, he endeavors to record things as accurately as possible and thereby confirms a side of Schoeck that we also know from Corrodi's diary and other sources: he was a widely read man of broad interests, possessed of considerable wit and a love of word-play. Given to moodiness to be sure, but someone who was used to being liked by others and who naturally formed the center of attention. Vogel made regular entries in his diary until just after Schoeck's death, and although the final years are marked by the composer's increasing bitterness toward everything modern in art, the broad scope of their conversations remains to the last.

On 8 September 1949 Richard Strauss died at his home in Garmisch. He and Schoeck had never really known each other, though they had many mutual friends and colleagues and had on occasion crossed each other's paths. Strauss had once called Schoeck a "Swiss Pfitzner,"[14] and Schoeck had often referred disparagingly to the older man's music ("artificial silk" had been his latest jibe).[15] But Strauss had been the most prominent representative of the strand of late-Romanticism to which Schoeck himself belonged, and whose values he felt were now under threat. Most of the other prominent Austro-German late-Romantics of Strauss's generation were already long dead—Franz Schreker, Max von Schillings, Alexander von Zemlinsky—while Hans Pfitzner, too, had died just a few months before, on 22 May 1949. We do not know how Schoeck reacted to the news of Strauss's death, but the notion that he was becoming the "last Romantic"—an epithet applied to him with some regularity in his final years—was not one that pleased him. It merely meant that he was becoming more and more alone.

Chapter Thirty-Nine

Fair Measure

Hilde was due to give the Swiss premiere of the first group of the Mörike songs in October 1949, but this had to be postponed when she became ill with migraines and neuritis in the late summer. She entered hospital in October but was soon allowed to move to Alma Staub's villa to recuperate. Othmar was already there, preferring the comfort of the Villa Alma to coping wifeless at home. He was also composing this autumn, having accepted a commission for the centenary of the Singing Association of Canton Schwyz. He chose a short, mildly patriotic poem by Gottfried Keller, "In Duft und Reif," in which the poet imagines the figure of Liberty wandering through the night, turning an autumnal landscape into a vision of spring. Schoeck set it for male voice choir, strings, four brass, and percussion, and gave it the title *Vision*. It is one of his finer late works, with its felicitous orchestration serving to distract one from the fact that it repeats the same cadential formulae that we find time and again in his post-*Dürande* works.

The delayed Swiss premiere of a selection from *Das holde Bescheiden* took place in Zurich on 16 March 1950, with Hilde and Schoeck giving repeat performances in various places large and small over the coming months, from Winterthur in March to Meersburg (just across the border in Germany) in July. Although Schoeck frequently complained that his music was not much performed, the facts tell a different story. Wolfgang Schneiderhan and colleagues performed Schoeck's Second String Quartet in March 1950, the Zurich City Theater put on *Erwin und Elmire* and *Das Wandbild* in June, and the same month saw the world premiere of *Vision*. July 1950 brought further proof of the lasting peace between Hilde and Schoeck, when they and Gisela spent two weeks together in Brunnen. This was the first time that all three had been there together. Another trip to Rigi-Klösterli followed, after which Schoeck went to Alma Staub's for September. Throughout the summer and autumn he was working on another "official" commission, this time a work to commemorate the six-hundredth anniversary of the admission of Canton Zurich into the "Eidgenossenschaft" in 1351 (the loose federation of tiny states that many centuries later became the Swiss Confederation). He had been asked for either a cantata or an orchestral work and had decided, unusually, upon the latter. This autumn also saw Schoeck undergo a rigorous diet prescribed by his doctors. It improved his health but was then undermined by a chocolate binge at Christmastime that saw him gain several kilos again. Hilde remarked to Corrodi how Schoeck was overwhelmed by an insatiable hunger for the good things in life, which she ascribed to his conviction that his time was now limited. He felt, she said, that his life's dreams and hopes would remain unfulfilled. Memories of his youth were also haunting him. They had recently received a gift of ten thousand francs from the estate of Max Thomann in St. Gallen, and for a while they thought of building a new house on the same land where the chalet had once stood where Schoeck had been so happy forty years before.[1] In the end they decided to stay where they were. But the chalet now reappeared with regularity in Othmar's dreams.

Hilde and Schoeck continued their joint *lieder* recitals in November 1950. On the ninth they performed the first set from *Das holde Bescheiden* in Lucerne, then gave the world premiere of the second set in Zurich on 30 November—including the first performance of "Besuch in Urach." Further concerts followed in other Swiss cities—Schaffhausen in January 1951 and St. Gallen in February. Schoeck became ill during the last of these, however, and was thereafter stuck at home with a bad flu for almost a month. He was well enough after that to attend a matinée performance of his *Postillon*, the Violin Concerto, and other works in Basel, though stomach problems and arthritis soon followed. He was now working on a new concerto for horn, of which he had finished the slow middle movement by the end of January. He was also still attending concerts occasionally. Furtwängler came to the Tonhalle Orchestra as a guest conductor on 5 and 6 March 1951, and Schoeck was there. He claimed not to be impressed. Vogel quoted him as saying of the "Pastoral" Symphony that "Furtwängler makes four slow movements out of it. . . . Everything with him is 'expression.'"[2] Furtwängler made a point of visiting Schoeck every now and then; he regarded him as a kindred spirit in a world increasingly dominated by the "evils" of atonality. Schoeck, however, did not appreciate Furtwängler the composer, and after attending a performance of his Second Symphony in Winterthur in 1949 had declared him devoid of the "creative spark."[3] Josef von Vintschger later recalled having met Schoeck on the street at some point in the early 1950s, just after a visit from Furtwängler. Schoeck was visibly exhausted, and he gasped to his friend: "He played through one of his symphonies to me—it lasted *for hours*" ("es isch *stundelang gangè*"—the emphasis was von Vintschger's).[4]

It was apparently in early 1951 that Schoeck and Hilde made a private gramophone recording of four songs from *Das holde Bescheiden* (they have since been released on the Jecklin CD label), namely "Auf einen Klavierspieler," "Mein Fluss," "Restauration," and "Besuch in Urach."[5] The last of these had to be recorded on several sides, so Schoeck simply made an impromptu half-cadence at the end of each side. "Besuch in Urach" in particular is taxing for the pianist and even more so for the singer, as the vocal line lies very high. Despite the wrong notes common in Schoeck's recordings after his heart attack, this set of four songs is testament once more to his musicality and his ability to judge mood and tempo to perfection. But Hilde surprises one too. There is no denying that the song stretches her vocal abilities almost to breaking point (an element of striving is in fact inherent to the piece itself), but she carries it off well, offering proof enough that the frequent underhand criticism of her singing among Schoeck's friends was not a little unjust.

Das holde Bescheiden is the only one of Schoeck's songbooks that was not intended to be performed all at one time, though the reason is quite obvious: it is far too long. Even a complete rendering of either of the two halves of the set can prove tiring. Upon receiving the published songs for review, Colin Mason wrote in the *Musical Times:* "[They] are all dull and unoriginal."[6] If he had only allowed himself a brief perusal, then his reaction is comprehensible, for the songs are harmonically conventional. They repeat many of the formulae of *Das stille Leuchten,* in particular a harmonic sequence from "Firnelicht" that Schoeck seems to have associated with his "Swissness"—*this I can do for my homeland*—and which appears in the very first song of the new set, "Widmung," and in many thereafter. The self-quotations continue in the second song, which at the mention of "the sounds of the shepherd's flute" gives us the opening "yodel" of "Ich würd' es hören," also from *Das stille Leuchten* (the melody that seems to be a paraphrase of Grieg, as mentioned earlier). While there are a few really lovely songs here (such as "Erinna an Sappho," "Mein Fluss," and "Besuch in Urach"), the general impression is one of a dilution of stylistic possibilities. The strongest outside influence on the songbook remains Grieg, with the similarities sometimes verging on plagiarism: the piano's F-major arpeggios with an added major sixth in "Mein Fluss," for example, are obviously pilfered from "Blåbaer-Li" in *Haugtussa.* Nevertheless, "Mein Fluss" is a wonderful song possessed of an energy rare in Schoeck's late music, and it somehow manages to swallow its influences, if not wholly to digest them.

On 21 April 1951 *Don Ranudo* was performed once again at the Zurich City Theater. A semi-rehabilitated Denzler was the conductor, thirty-two years after having conducted the work's world premiere, and he earned particular praise from Schuh in the *Neue Zürcher Zeitung.*[7] The producer was Oskar Wälterlin, while the cast included Max Lichtegg as Gonzalo, Alois Pernerstorfer as Ranudo, and Edith Oravez as Leonore. The version performed was one more of the many compromises to which the work had been subjected. It was, so Schuh reported, essentially the two-act version made for Dresden in 1930, but with several scenes added to make a "quasi three-act" version. Schoeck even composed four extra pages for the finale—the last alteration that he would make to the work.[8] He almost missed the opening night, as he had suffered another semi-collapse just weeks before and was for a while so weak that when he needed to go from his bedroom to the bathroom Hilde had to half-carry him. Arthritis was now a problem too, as was his heavy wine consumption, which his two doctors, Paul Rossier and Josef Zimmermann, were powerless to curb. He was constantly endeavoring to play them off against each other, listening to whichever one gave the most lenient advice. When neither was lenient enough, he would go and badger Rüeger for a better opinion instead.[9]

On 2 June 1951, Schoeck's *Festlicher Hymnus,* the work he had written for Zurich's anniversary, was given its world premiere in the Grossmünster by the Tonhalle Orchestra under Erich Schmid. The *Hymnus* is partly programmatic, for Schoeck conceived it as the mountains of the original Swiss cantons (including his own) calling to Zurich. He accordingly began the work with the "yodel" from "Ich würd' es hören." But this vague "program" could not inspire him as had his daughter's rendition of Keller's poem in the case of *Sommernacht,* and the *Hymnus* meanders on for a total of 262 bars. One has the feeling throughout that one has heard the music somewhere before—and one usually has, for it quotes from most of the post-*Dürande* songbooks and cycles. One is never sure, however, whether the composer is aware of it, or whether by simplifying his harmonic language he has so reduced his musical possibilities that self-quotation is now the last-remaining means of generating notes when his inspiration fails him. Willi Schuh, for one, did not think that it was conscious.[10] He at least managed some kind words about the piece in his review for the *Schweizerische Musikzeitung,* as did the local papers the *Tages-Anzeiger* and *Die Tat* of 5 and 14 June repectively. But the *Hymnus* proves only that when no words were involved, there was nothing left to inspire Schoeck. It must count as one of the saddest works ever to slink from his pen.

After the premiere of the *Hymnus,* Schoeck went to the Weidhof to finish off his Horn Concerto. He and Hilde resumed their run of recitals with a concert on the Mainau peninsula in Lake Constance on 8 July. His health had improved in the climate near the lake, so while Hilde and Gisela took a holiday on the island of Sylt—the same place that Othmar had so enjoyed while working on *Vom Fischer*—he felt well enough to accept an invitation from von Vintschger to go on a car trip through Austria. They saw Innsbruck and Salzburg ('still the most beautiful city I know," said Schoeck), stopped off at St. Florian to visit Bruckner's grave, and then drove on to Vienna. Their cemetery tour continued there with visits to the graves of Beethoven, Schubert, Brahms, and Wolf, while Schoeck also insisted on descending into the catacombs of St. Stephen's Cathedral, where the bones of countless men and women lie neatly stacked. One might expect that a composer who could feel his own end drawing nigh might wish to avoid such close proximity to the dead, but it was not the case. They then swung round southwards, traveling via Bolzano along Lake Garda and the Lago Maggiore, past Schoeck's old haunt Brissago, to von Vintschger's villa in Orselina, where Schoeck now spent several weeks finishing the instrumentation of his Horn Concerto. He also completed an orchestral version of "Besuch in Urach" there—the first time that he had ever taken an existing song and orchestrated it after the fact (he also intended to orchestrate "Mein Fluss," though he never did; this is a shame, for it would surely benefit from orchestral treatment[11]). Perhaps the success of Strauss's *Four Last Songs,* which since their posthumous premiere under his friend Furtwängler in London on 22 May 1950 had already been performed all over the world, had suggested to him that there might be a market for orchestral songs in his late-Romantic idiom.

Schoeck was back in Zurich in late August, in good time for the celebrations being planned for his sixty-fifth birthday. He wrote to Reinhart of his Austrian tour: "It did me good to see something of the world once more." A few days later, on 29 August, Reinhart died, and his funeral took place on 1 September, Schoeck's birthday. If Schoeck worried about his financial future after Reinhart's death, then it would prove unnecessary, for Reinhart's heirs continued to give him his allowance just as before.

There was a plethora of concerts to celebrate Schoeck's birthday, and the usual hymns of praise in the Swiss press. While the *Dürande* affair was not wholly forgotten, it seems that most people had moved on—or rather, they had moved back to the kind of adulation common in the pre-*Dürande* era, if no longer quite as effusive. It was only with Schoeck that it did not seem to register. The main Zurich concert took place on 4 September in the Tonhalle under Erich Schmid, comprising the *Festlicher Hymnus,* a concert performance of *Vom Fischer,* and the Violin Concerto played by Stefi Geyer. Numerous concerts followed in and around Zurich, while in late September there was a Schoeck concert in Thun that climaxed in the announcement by the town president that Thun would now boast the first street in Switzerland to be named after the composer: the "Othmar Schoeck Weg." On 1 October it was Bern's turn to honor him. Loeffel sang the *Elegie* (for the forty-fifth time in his career, noted the *Schweizerische Musikzeitung*), Ernst Haefliger sang the world premiere of the orchestral version of "Besuch in Urach," and then various choral works and the *Hymnus* in its Bern premiere rounded things off. After a performance of songs from *Das holde Bescheiden* that he and Hilde gave in Basel in late November, Schoeck even received a conciliatory letter from Hermann Burte, who had been in the audience and had judged it the "most pure performance that I have heard for a long time; it gave me much joy . . . a shame that WR [Werner Reinhart] could no longer hear it; everything is such a shame!"[12]

Chapter Forty

Rather Nice Horn

The postwar surge of interest in Schoeck's operas in his native land continued in the 1951–52 season, when the Bern City Theater put four of them on its program: *Don Ranudo, Das Wandbild, Vom Fischer,* and *Erwin und Elmire.* He had never before had his operas performed with such regularity. But still he swung in and out of depression, convinced that his music was being ignored. Hindemith's triumphant return to Europe to take up the Chair of Musicology at Zurich University prompted much envy. He had been the man of the moment in Zurich when his *Mathis der Maler* was premiered in 1938, and now, returning after an absence of over a decade, he had immediately become the center of attention once again. Stravinsky was also back in Europe, conquering the stage with his *Rake's Progress.* Schoeck went to see its Zurich production in December 1951 but found it "unutterably weak . . . this is music that's as dry as a beetle's arse."[1] The voices just did not "breathe" properly, he said.[2] His biggest concern in late 1951, however, was the state of his brother Paul, whose black days were even blacker than his own. Paul had experienced a severe nervous breakdown in the previous spring and had been placed in the same sanatorium where, over two decades earlier, Corrodi's father had spent his last years in a mental haze. Schoeck's worries about Paul are a leitmotif throughout his correspondence of the following months.

In December 1951 Schoeck finished the score of his Horn Concerto. It received its premiere just over a month later, on 6 February 1952 in Winterthur, with Hans Will as soloist under the baton of Victor Desarzens. The first movement is a banal march, whose opening theme is rhythmically foursquare and of such limited melodic scope that it conveys a palpable feeling of constriction. The second movement is a charming but meandering romance, whose opening quotes the first measure of "Widmung" from *Das holde Bescheiden.* The insistent use here of plagal cadences is also a frequent feature of Schoeck's post-*Dürande* music, and at times it sounds distinctly reminiscent of those in the slow movement of Dvořák's *New World Symphony* (which Schoeck had conducted more than once in St. Gallen, the last time being in December 1939). The third movement of the concerto, a fiendishly difficult hunting-horn rondo in 6/8 time, is the best of the three. It belongs to the same type as many a final movement from horn concertos since Mozart's time, and it displays the kind of abandon that one longs for in the music of Schoeck's final years. It is also the movement with the fewest reminiscences of other works. Thanks to Willi Schuh, whose dealings with Richard Strauss had served to cement a personal friendship with Ernst Roth of Boosey and Hawkes in London, this company now accepted Schoeck's Horn Concerto for publication. It would remain his only attempt to break into the Anglo-Saxon market, though at least it would prompt some interest from an unexpected quarter. The British composers Gerald Finzi and Howard Ferguson had not forgotten the London premiere of the *Elegie* twenty years before, and Finzi now took the trouble to peruse the concerto. He subsequently wrote to Ferguson: "Have a look at the Schoeck Concerto for Horn & Strings (B&H miniature score); it's rather nice, and quite playable" (he had presumably not yet looked properly at the last movement).[3] The reviewer of the score for *Music and Letters* was also mildly complimentary, writing that it was "in a light and not too original style, but . . . pleasant and competently written. Technically, it is probably one of the more exacting and exhausting horn concertos."[4]

The concerto was received well at its premiere, though this did little to improve Schoeck's current depression. He was still worried about Paul, who seemed to improve early in the New Year, only for a relapse to claim him soon afterward. Hilde told Corrodi that Schoeck was loath to leave home for any reason and was often unable to sleep at night.[5] He was also dwelling increasingly on the past. In January 1952 he had begun to revise the violin sonata that he had written while a student at the Zurich Conservatory. Sadly, his revisions did nothing to make a weak work any stronger. Only the Dvořákian last movement has any fire to it. Prompted by Werner Vogel, Schoeck also made a piano version of his *Serenade*, Op. 1 in the first half of the year. He was still composing original works, however, and in April and May he set four sonnets by Eichendorff as a brief song cycle dedicated to the memory of Werner Reinhart. He first thought of calling it "Der heilige Quell" or "Der ewige Quell" ("The holy/eternal source"), explaining: "What Reinhart did—it all comes from the same source . . . he was able to enthuse about things, he was true and honest."[6] But he finally decided on *Befreite Sehnsucht* instead ("Liberated Longing"), taking his cue from a line in the sonnets. He first set the poems for voice and piano, but very soon he decided to orchestrate them, which he did in the course of the summer.

The piano version of the sonnets is distressingly thin. They are saved by their orchestration, which somehow transforms them utterly, making of them one of the finest works of Schoeck's last years. The cycle also profits from its relative brevity—the four songs run into each other and last in total about twelve minutes. Not even the statutory self-quotation seems out of place ("Firnelicht" once again, this time—significantly—at the mention of those whose task it is to tend the "holy flame"). The decision to orchestrate might in fact have been prompted by Furtwängler, who wrote to Schoeck on 6 May 1952: "I've been asked if I would conduct a concert in Winterthur next year (25 February). I would like to do it, and in memory of Werner Reinhart. Couldn't you—an idea I've just had—write something by then that I could premiere? (a small orchestral piece)." Perhaps Schoeck was still pondering the international success of Strauss's *Four Last Songs*. While the final flowering that Strauss there achieves is of a different order altogether from

Schoeck's four sonnets, the orchestration of both works is equally luminous, and *Befreite Sehnsucht* would not need to fear being put on the same program.

On 8 May 1952 Schoeck gave what would be his last-ever public performance in Zurich, when he accompanied the soprano Margrit Vaterlaus in a Tonhalle concert. He and Hilde were soon back across the border in Germany for a song recital in Baden-Baden as part of a week of events organized by Erich von Prittwitz-Gaffron (whom they knew from *Dürande* days). A recital was also planned in Vienna, as was an orchestral concert, both initiated by the Austrian conductor Herbert Häfner, whose acquaintance Schoeck had made through Alma Staub.[7] But it all came to nothing, for Häfner died of a heart attack while conducting a concert at that year's ISCM World Music Days in Salzburg on 28 June. Four days later Paul Schoeck committed suicide by drowning himself in the River Aare. His funeral took place in Brunnen on 4 July, though Othmar was unable to attend, as he and Hilde had to sing that same day at Hesse's seventy-fifth birthday celebrations in Lindau.[8] While there is no specific mention in the sources, Hilde's extensive comments to Corrodi on Othmar's mental state at this time, especially after Paul's death, suggest that she feared that her husband might follow his brother into some form of breakdown. She claimed that Schoeck was suffering from delusions that amounted to a persecution complex. When Erich Schmid became ill before he was due to conduct the *Festlicher Hymnus* in autumn 1952, his place was taken at short notice by Volkmar Andreae. Not surprisingly, the septuagenarian Andreae replaced the *Hymnus*, which he had never before conducted, with a Beethoven overture. But Schoeck—so Hilde said—had flown into a rage, insisting that this was all part of a conspiracy against him.[9] Corrodi's diaries also relate such emotional outbursts on the part of the composer.

It has in recent years become something of a fad to psychoanalyze creative artists posthumously. Schoeck is perhaps as good a candidate as any other, for certain well-documented aspects of his mental make-up correlate with known symptoms of bi-polar disorder: his irregular sleeping patterns, his bouts of feverish creative activity alternating with periods of inactivity and deep depression, and his heavy drinking, which was perhaps a means of stabilizing his moods in either of the two phases. The problems of his brother Paul and their mother might also suggest some genetic predisposition to mental illness. But since Hilde remains our principal witness, we must also consider that any supposed signs of instability in her husband could have served for her as convenient "proof" that she had been the innocent party throughout their years of marital strife. Nor is Corrodi a wholly reliable source. For as his diary entries imply, his approach to biography meant that any sign of "madness" in Schoeck was merely further proof of the man's place in the pantheon of troubled Romantic geniuses. Yet for all his recurrent depression, Schoeck enjoyed an active performing career for almost half a century, and there is no proof of concert cancellations due to poor mental health, nor any reports outside his immediate circle of erratic behavior onstage or off (give or take the odd rehearsal tantrum that was par for the course with many conductors of his day). There is proof enough in all the sources that as his health declined Schoeck felt increasingly depressed, lonely, and neglected. But this would in most people be a natural reaction to physical debilitation. And he remained lucid enough to the last to compose and to discuss art, music, and world events, while his ironic sense of humor—to judge from assorted accounts—never deserted him. Hilde's repeated claims to Corrodi of Schoeck's manias must be noted, though they raise more questions than they answer.[10]

Befreite Sehnsucht was given a private first performance *chez* Alma Staub on Schoeck's next birthday, 1 September 1952. He and Hilde performed the second set from *Das holde Bescheiden* in Winterthur a month later, and on 27 November they took part in a Hesse evening in Zollikon. But halfway through the evening Schoeck felt unable to continue, and so handed over the accompaniment to his daughter Gisela, who had earlier in the year completed her piano diploma (and was also proving just as gifted a singer). This was the last time that Schoeck played in public. Perhaps he himself suspected that his performing career was now over. It also, to all intents and purposes, meant the end of Hilde's career, too.

Schoeck was at this time reminiscing regularly about his childhood and youth in conversation with Vogel, and he admitted to having problems sleeping at night. His continuing depression found expression in December when he set Hesse's poem "Im Nebel" to music—a text that claims "to live is to be lonely . . . everyone is alone." Yet another pessimistic Hesse text found favor with him in January 1953, this time *Maschinenschlacht,* which he began to set for a cappella male-voice choir in fulfilment of a commission from the Harmonie Chorus— the same whose vice-director he had been over forty years before. Hesse's poem tells of the battles between man and the machines that dominate his existence. Schoeck had long been complaining of the rapidity of technical developments in the brave new world of postwar Europe (when driving past the new Zurich airport once with Alma Staub, he had non-sequitured in despair: "There's no wonder that all culture is going to the dogs when you can get in here and get out in Chicago the next morning").[11] Hesse's text and the commission now gave him the opportunity to express all these feelings in music. Schoeck was already considering a companion piece, a setting of Hesse's poem "Gestutzte Eiche" ("Pruned Oak" or "Lopped Oak"), though he did not actually compose it until the end of the year, to fulfil a commission from the Male Voice Choir of Thun.[12] Here the poet compares himself to an oak tree whose branches have been mercilessly cropped, just as the world has mocked what was "soft and tender" in him; but as the oak will each time sprout new leaves, so his soul, too, remains indestructible and at peace with the world.

On 25 February 1953 Furtwängler conducted the Reinhart memorial concert in Winterthur about which he had told Schoeck the previous spring. Schoeck had wanted Hilde to sing the world premiere of *Befreite Sehnsucht,* but Winterthur had refused, pointing out that she had already sung one recital in their present season. Schoeck had then suggested Haefliger, but had again received a negative response. As a compromise solution, *Sommernacht* was chosen, and accordingly it was performed between Franck's Symphony in D Minor and Tchaikovsky's *Pathétique*. This was the first time that Furtwängler had conducted one of Schoeck's works (he conducted it again later the same year, while on tour in Germany). Sadly, no recording of his interpretation survives. For all his occasional criticism of his colleague, Schoeck's underlying admiration for Furtwängler as a conductor is clear. He remarked to Werner Vogel:

> When Furtwängler makes crescendi and stringendi in a Brahms symphony, then it comes from a quite different source than when Stokowski does it . . . music is something magical; somehow this magic plays a role in conducting . . . incidentally, I've also heard a Haydn symphony from him that was simple, slim, and transparent in a manner that I would not have thought possible. . . . What's important, what's decisive, is the manner of the beat.[13]

In April 1953 Schoeck was once more able to see one of his operas on the Zurich stage: *Vom Fischer*, with Manfred Jungwirth as the flounder, Hedwig Müller-Bütow as the fisherwoman, and Richard Müller as the fisherman. It was sandwiched between a stage version of Sutermeister's early radio opera *Die schwarze Spinne* ("The Black Spider") and a balletic interpretation of Rolf Liebermann's orchestral piece *Furioso*. Schoeck was unhappy with the production and even unhappier with what he felt was the meager applause it reaped; he later told Vogel that he had never seen the opera performed as he would like. The audience should actually see the sea, he said, for the variations represented the increasing tempestuousness of the waters. "Movement is important in this fisher's tale, because it is precisely the act of remaining in one state that the fisherwoman doesn't want."[14]

The Zurich premiere of the Horn Concerto on the following 13 May was a success, though its coupling with Stravinsky's Symphony in C prompted Schoeck into a harangue against "the destruction of tonality" as an "act akin to those of Genghis Khan"[15]—even though Stravinsky's symphony (as the title suggests) is neoclassical and thoroughly tonal. Schoeck admitted to Vogel that he was now busy writing some "piano studies," with the implication that they would be demonstrably free from any hint of Genghis-isms. A few days later Schoeck received a written invitation to become a Corresponding Member of the Bavarian Academy of Arts. He was at first somewhat horrified and had Hilde make enquiries to ensure that an acceptance on his part would not actually compel him to "correspond" with anyone (he still did not like writing letters). It did not, of course, and so he accepted.

Schoeck was composing his new piano pieces at the instrument itself. He told Vogel at length about all the great composers of the past who had used the piano as a composing aid, thus offering an implicit justification of what was obviously his own practice. What had previously been merely a means of control while composing was now, it seems, a necessary crutch, which in turn suggests that the act of composition was an increasingly difficult one. Schoeck admitted that there were sometimes "hours when nothing goes right."[16] He was also hampered at the piano by a ligament problem that meant he could no longer stretch the little finger of his left hand. Just a fortnight later, on 4 June 1953, he accompanied the local soprano Silvia Gähwiller in a radio recording that was to be his last "public" performance of any kind. Over thirty years later Gähwiller recalled how she had told Schoeck of her inability to sing the A♭ below middle C that is required in "Frühlingsruhe" (Op. 20, no. 4) when performed in the original key. Schoeck—who could have transposed the song into any key at will—assured her that he knew her voice well enough and that she would manage it easily to his accompaniment. To judge from her manner of telling the tale, Schoeck (by now 66 years old) was flirtatiously insistent in a manner that made feminine acquiescence inevitable. They accordingly performed the song in the original key; and he was right, as we can clearly hear on the CD release of their recording, where Gähwiller descends to her lowest register with seeming ease.[17]

At some point in June 1953 Schoeck left to spend a few days with Alma Staub in Männedorf. He now had the opportunity to renew his acquaintance with Thomas Mann and family, who in their American exile had become friendly with Alma Staub's daughter and were themselves once more resident just outside Zurich. Schoeck and Hilde performed *Befreite Sehnsucht* for Alma and her guests, and Mann's positive reaction improved Schoeck's opinion of the writer considerably. The rest of the summer he spent alternately in Brunnen with his brothers and at the tower of Muzot in Canton Valais. This was Schoeck's first-ever visit to the place where Rilke had spent his final years. He had difficulty in negotiating the circular staircase to his living quarters, where to his astonishment there were no windows, only narrow slits once intended for defending archers. But his health improved in the country air, and he found the atmosphere conducive to working on his new "piano studies"—later to be entitled *Ritornelle und Fughetten* ("Ritornelli and Fughettas") and grouped in pairs, one of each. He was also bemused by the constant stream of "Rilke disciple-ettes" who would arrive and pester the housekeeper for access to the Master's last place of residence.[18]

Schoeck returned to Männedorf in late August to continue work on his new piano pieces, and it was there that he learnt of the death of his brother Walter on 8 October. He had collapsed of a heart attack while playing one of Othmar's songs on his cello, accompanied by his son Georg. The funeral took place in Brunnen. Now only Ralph was left to tend the family home, though Georg did his best to return at weekends to help keep the place in order. Schoeck had lost two brothers in the space of less than eighteen months; Ralph would survive all three of his siblings.

The world premiere of *Befreite Sehnsucht* finally took place on 9 December 1953 in Winterthur, with the German soprano Annelies Kupper singing under the baton of Victor Desarzens. Schoeck was delighted with Kupper: she had understood the work instinctively, he said, without his having to explain anything. This is hardly surprising, since she was already a world star of vast experience, who just over a year before had sung the title role in the posthumous world premiere of Strauss's *Liebe der Danae*. A live recording survives of her singing *Befreite Sehnsucht* with the Tonhalle Orchestra under Rosbaud from a couple of years afterward, and she carries the work off with marvellous *Schwung*. She told Schoeck that she regarded the work as "aktuell," namely "of contemporary relevance." This pleased him immensely, as he now seemed to need every little endorsement that he still had something pertinent to say to the world.[19]

Chapter Forty-One

Sleepless in Wollishofen

The successful premiere of *Befreite Sehnsucht* did nothing to alleviate Schoeck's general depression. He was again having difficulty falling asleep, and when he did, he was plagued by nightmares from which he would awake bathed in sweat. He would then wash in cold water and return to bed, lying awake until the cycle of sleep, nightmares, and waking would finally begin again. There was an undeniable, terrible irony in that what had for years been the bane of his wife's existence—his inability to sleep normal hours—was now his own. He tried reading at night to occupy himself, with Homer's *Odyssey* one of the works that he kept at his bedside.[1] Later he resorted to writing out from memory Bach chorales, or passages from classical masterpieces of which he was fond, such as the opening pages of the Finale to Mozart's "Jupiter" Symphony. He would then correct them the next morning (Vogel once saw a nighttime manuscript copy of Bach's "O Haupt voll Blut und Wunden," at the end of which Schoeck had later scribbled "five mistakes"[2]).

Nor was the fate of his new work for the Harmonie Chorus proving any kinder to him than had his brief, inauspicious collaboration with the choir half a century before. The Harmonie was still made up of the élite of Zurich society, and its committee members were already upset because their new conductor, Hans Erismann, had not consulted them before commissioning a work from Schoeck. Even worse, when *Maschinenschlacht* arrived, it was interpreted by several of the choir's businessmen and factory owners as a subversive attack on the technological base of the current Swiss economic upswing. Today Hesse's text seems particularly topical, as the very machines created to improve our lives are belching out the toxins that are destroying the planet. We are also, perhaps, more in awe of Nobel Prize–winning writers than was the case in the early 1950s. Awe was not on the Harmonie's agenda. They called an extraordinary general meeting and decided to replace the "offensive" references to factory owners and the like with something more innocuous. Although offended, Schoeck acquiesced in the text changes, as did Hesse (though only to please his friend, not the factory owners).

Not all was black clouds, however. On 2 February 1954 the young Dietrich Fischer-Dieskau sang *Lebendig begraben* in the Tonhalle under Erich Schmid. Schoeck had been asked to make a few alterations to the score to make its bass tessitura better suited to Fischer-Dieskau's baritone, which he did without demur. He was overwhelmed by Fischer-Dieskau's interpretation, declaring it "phenomenal," the fulfilment of his dreams for the work. His enthusiasm was shared by the critics, first among them Willi Schuh in the *Schweizerische Musikzeitung*, who praised the singer's ability both to illuminate the small-scale pictorial moments and to place everything in the context of a large-scale formal structure.[3] Fischer-Dieskau was just as taken with Schoeck's music. Although only twenty-eight years old, he was already established internationally, and 1954 was also to be the year of his debuts in Bayreuth and the United States. He never forgot Schoeck. Over the next forty years he recorded *Lebendig begraben,* the *Notturno, Unter Sternen, Das stille Leuchten,* the Hesse songs Op. 44, numerous individual songs, and finally, in collaboration with the mezzo-soprano Mitsuko Shirai, *Das holde Bescheiden.*

Just over a month later, on 6 March 1954, Schoeck's early violin sonata was given its world premiere in its recently revised version. Stefi Geyer was the soloist, accompanied by Walter Frey. Also on the program were the Bass Clarinet Sonata, *Spielmannsweisen,* and the *Wandsbecker Liederbuch,* sung by Haefliger and Silvia Gähwiller. The series of first performances of Schoeck's music continued on 29 April when Gisela Schoeck played five pairs from the *Ritornelle und Fughetten* at an evening organized by the Zurich Writers' Association, and then on 4 June when the Harmonie finally sang the neutered *Maschinenschlacht.* After the first half of the latter concert, however, Schoeck suffered a semi-collapse and had to be taken home. He was admitted into the Cantonal Hospital six days later, where he spent almost two weeks as the doctors endeavored to strengthen his heart.[4]

Maschinenschlacht enjoyed what seems to have been only a modest success at its premiere. What was probably of even greater concern to Schoeck was that getting new works performed did not necessarily guarantee them a publisher. Breitkopf and Bärenreiter had both turned down *Befreite Sehnsucht,* Hug had turned down the early violin sonata (though they would relent two years later), and Universal had recently decided to publish *Das holde Bescheiden* only because Schoeck was paying them to do so. The Swiss were not the only people to take offense at *Maschinenschlacht.* Breitkopf & Härtel had expressed a keen interest in the piece, but when they saw it they were taken aback, for—as Schoeck wrote to Hesse—they could not publish such a text "just when everything is moving forward so well; there were hardly any strikes, the helicopters had been such a help in Holland, all through the blessing brought by machines; no! impossible!" They were keen to have *Die gestutzte Eiche,* for they found it a suitable metaphor for "the young Germany rising up again."[5] This piece was assigned to Hug instead, however, as a reward for an offer to publish *Maschinenschlacht.* Hesse again acquiesced graciously in the matter of its text, requesting only that the work's title upon publication should read "after Hermann Hesse" instead of "by."[6]

The tiny company of Symphonia Verlag in Basel finally proved willing to publish *Befreite Sehnsucht* in its piano version later that year, taking the *Ritornelle und Fughetten* into its program at the same time. The latter work, at just over half an hour in length, is not only Schoeck's longest by far for his own instrument but is in total as long as any other instrumental work in his oeuvre. It is also more uneven than any of the others. Schoeck was nevertheless proud of it, telling Vogel that:

The theme for each fugue is taken from the preceding ritornello . . . You must study these fugues sometime; you'll be amazed at everything that's in them! . . . Writing fugues is fun to me; fugal writing, after all, is an ancient principle. But the most important thing is that beautiful music results from the contrapuntal work.[7]

One of Schoeck's long-time favorite sayings was "Ist die Not am grössten, ist die Fuge am nächsten" ("Where the need is greatest, a fugue is closest to hand." In other words: when a composer gets stuck, he will write a fugue to help him out).[8] Regrettably, it is all too true of his own *Ritornelle und Fughetten,* most of which are weak, dull, or both. Writing in *Notes* upon their publication, William Flanagan dismissed them as "neo-Baroque charades both scholarly and academic, idiomatic and ultra-conservative."[9]

A few of the Ritornelli are stronger than the rest. The very first, for example, with its melodic chains of fourths, is delightful. But others sound like botched reminiscences of earlier, much better works, remembered as if through a glass darkly. The fifth ritornello sounds as if Schoeck were trying desperately, but in vain, to recall his "Consolation"—as if it were one of those memory exercises with which the composer occupied himself in his waking nights. The little fugues, however, have few mitigating moments. Willi Schuh once remarked that Schoeck would fill whole manuscript books with counterpoint exercises because he regarded it as one of his weaknesses and wanted to prove that he, too, could write counterpoint.[10] The irony of this is that he had nothing to prove at all, for the counterpoint in his works of the late 1920s and 1930s is superb, far more complex than anything in his *Fughetten.* Schoeck had already included a brief fugal passage in his *Befreite Sehnsucht* and would do so in his next cycle, too. Without exception, all these late fugues and fugatos are the weakest point in their respective oeuvres. Schoeck was more desperate than ever to prove his adherence to "ancient principles." But all they prove is that his inspiration was failing fast.

Chapter Forty-Two

Echoes and Elegies

Schoeck spent most of August 1954 in Brunnen with Ralph. The summer saw Dennis Brain play the British premiere of his Horn Concerto at the Edinburgh Festival, in an all-Swiss concert given by the Collegium Musicum Zürich under Paul Sacher. W. R. Anderson wrote in the *Musical Times* that the concerto was "an easier-going, older-fashioned piece, in which Dennis Brain made the mastery of this intensely difficult instrument sound as simple as shelling peas."[1] Schoeck's health made it impossible for him to attend. But he was also busy composing. October saw him back in Brunnen, this time to work on some Lenau settings for a new orchestral cycle. He had never lost his high regard for Lenau—"the only truly musical poet," he had remarked just two years before—but had not set any of his poems since the *Notturno* in the early 1930s. In mood, this new cycle is also perhaps closest to the *Notturno,* except that it is even darker yet. There is no hint of a narrative; it is a half-hour rumination on death, depression, and despair. The first setting that Schoeck composed was of the double sonnet "Einsamkeit" ("Loneliness"), which asks rhetorically "Have you ever found yourself on a moor, utterly alone, loveless, without God? . . . The whole world is sad to the point of despair." The subsequent poems that he set were hardly any jollier. "Der Kranich" considers the crane departing for the South to avoid the winter. The similarities between Schoeck's crane and Schubert's crow in the latter's *Winterreise*—in import as in name ("Kranich" and "Krähe")—were undoubtedly intentional. The song that really upset Schoeck's friends, however, was "Der falsche Freund," about the false friends who desert one whenever problems arise. Nor was this a momentary fit of ingratitude on his part, for in his final years he repeatedly spoke of writing an opera based on Shakespeare's *Timon of Athens*. His explanation, recalled von Vintschger, was that "Timon too had given those around him much during his lifetime, but later earned only ingratitude for it. He, Schoeck, was being sidelined more and more, not just in musical terms, but in human terms too."[2] His depression was now also magnified by Gisela's absence, as she had recently gone to study singing in Munich.

Schoeck's health deteriorated as winter approached, as did his emotional state, almost as if immersing himself in Lenau's poems were making things even worse. He was physically unable to bear strong emotion. A song recital that Elsa Cavelti had given in Zurich on 1 October had left his heart racing throughout the night. In December 1954 he wrote to Hesse: "I feel really washed-out; circulation problems, congestion of the blood, etc. etc. my food doesn't taste right, nor does the wine. I had a bad summer and early winter; let's see what the doctors manage to do."[3] But he didn't like what his doctors wanted. They forbade him more than two cups of tea a day, so he drank ten. He would then pump himself full of sleeping tablets but—not surprisingly—still could not sleep. And when he heard at the turn of the year that Zurich was planning a "Schoeck week" to celebrate his seventieth birthday in 1956, he openly began to doubt whether he would live to see it.[4] But his health soon improved enough for him to continue work on his new songs, and he finished all thirteen by February 1955 (grouping the two "Einsamkeit" sonnets as one in order to avoid the unlucky number). He called his new cycle *Nachhall* ("Echo"), which had originally been intended as the title for the *Elegie* over thirty years before. And, just as he had closed both the *Elegie* and *Notturno* with a setting of another poet (Eichendorff and Keller respectively), he added a single Matthias Claudius setting to close *Nachhall*, in order not to end on a depressive note. This poem, "O du Land," was only four lines long: "O thou land of essence and of truth, for ever everlasting, I long for you and your clarity, I long for you." Schoeck was at first unsure how to set it—two different, discarded settings have also survived. He then decided to use an instrumental form (much as he had done with his chaconne at the end of the *Notturno*), and so set it as a chorale prelude. He referred to this particular song as his "requiem." The successive deaths of various old friends in these months will only have brought home the reality of his own mortality. The most recent was that of Hans Bärlocher from St. Gallen, who died in early 1955. The last movement of the *Notturno* was played at his funeral.

Schoeck had in recent months been repeatedly reminiscing to Vogel about his youth, and the New Year appropriately brought his first and last numbered works in close proximity. On 26 January 1955, Paul Baumgartner gave the first performance of Schoeck's recent piano arrangement of his Serenade Op. 1, while Gisela performed the *Ritornelle und Fughetten*, Op. 68, in their entirety on the radio on 11 March. A radio broadcast of *Penthesilea* under Denzler with Res Fischer and Heinz Rehfuss in the main roles raised Schoeck's spirits a little, and April took him to Winterthur for performances of his *Festlicher Hymnus* and *Befreite Sehnsucht* (the latter once more with Annelies Kupper). According to Corrodi's diary, Schoeck had been supposed to accompany Loeffel in *Das stille Leuchten* in Bern at this time, though there is no mention of this in the other sources, and it would have been quite impossible for him, both physically and emotionally.[5]

Corrodi now stepped in with a new form of entertainment for Schoeck. His wife's novel-writing career was going so well that they were able to buy their first-ever car. Their primary aim was not personal enjoyment but to bring a little variety into Schoeck's life by taking him on day trips into the countryside. After a ride over the Albispass to the monastery church of Muri on 30 April, Corrodi noted in his diary that Schoeck was as cheerful as he had ever seen him. But he could not help noticing how "the illness has ravaged his face."[6] And for all his cheer, they still had to listen to his misanthropic musings: Brahms and Keller had enjoyed recognition and earned money, said Schoeck. "Their final years were full of light; over mine lies impenetrable darkness."[7]

Schoeck finished orchestrating *Nachhall* in Zurich at the beginning of July 1955. As usual, part of the summer was spent at the Villa Alma in Männedorf, and when he returned he composed what was to be his last piece of vocal music: a setting for two-part children's choir and piano of Ludwig Uhland's poem "Einkehr"—a jolly little thing about an apple tree, and one of the poems that children used to learn by heart at school. It was a commission from the Pestalozzi children's village in Trogen on the occasion of its tenth anniversary (another commission for the same event was Michael Tippett's *Bonny at Morn*). Proof that Schoeck was far from forgotten then came from Vienna, when the Austrian President Julius Raab invited him to Beethoven's *Fidelio* under Böhm for the reopening of the State Opera on 5 November. But Schoeck felt that the physical strain of the journey would be too much for him. When Corrodi suggested that he could fly instead, he said "I'm not going to start that now."[8]

The world premiere of *Nachhall* took place in the Zurich Tonhalle on 6 December 1955, with Elsa Cavelti and the Tonhalle Orchestra under the baton of Erich Schmid. Although Cavelti was by now a big name on the international scene, Schoeck had really wanted Fischer-Dieskau instead. Nevertheless, the performance was a great success, and Schoeck even managed to climb unaided onto the stage in order to acknowledge the applause. The reaction of the press was reminiscent of the old days. In the *Tages-Anzeiger* on 12 December, Fritz Gysi wrote: "Who of today's [composers] would know how to orchestrate in such a tender, diaphanous, truly poetic manner? [This is a cycle] that we must count among Schoeck's most brilliant creations."

The reaction of the critics to *Nachhall* was generous at best. While it cannot be ruled out that they really believed it to be a masterpiece, it is far more likely that they wished to be kind to their foremost local composer, who was quite clearly marked by death. Indeed, Schoeck had announced his approaching end in an almost ostentatious manner through his choice of text in the cycle. If a composer with advanced heart disease writes a song cycle that deals directly and repeatedly with the topic of death, how could a reviewer possibly criticize it without appearing devoid of heart himself? Perhaps the response was also colored by a realization that with the deaths of Willy Burkhard in the previous June and of Arthur Honegger on 27 November, Schoeck was now one of the few significant composing names that Switzerland had left, and he should be treated with deference.

The music of *Nachhall* is at times weak. All the same, there is nothing here—with the exception of the amateurish fugato placed before the penultimate song—that quite plumbs the awful depths of the *Ritornelle und Fughetten*. The presence of words was still guaranteed to raise Schoeck's level of inspiration by a notch or two. But even Willi Schuh admitted in his last years that he would willingly drop some six songs from the cycle (wincing visibly when mentioning the dreadful "Der falsche Freund"). He added, in the cycle's defense, that there

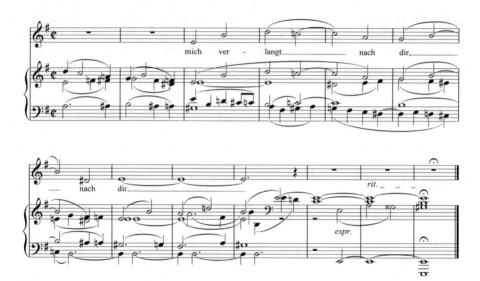

Example 42.1. *Nachhall*, Op. 70, close of the final song. Copyright 1956 by Universal Edition. Note the "pointless withholding" of the tonic in the bass until the last three measures. ". . . I long for you, for you."

were still "some fine things" in it.[9] Derrick Puffett was of a similar opinion. He found two songs impressive: the "grimly Mussorgskian" "Der Kranich," and "Niagara," but continued: "*Nachhall* represents a final deterioration of Schoeck's powers. . . . The open "horn" harmony of "Nachhall" [the opening song] simply goes on revolving for too long . . . "Der falsche Freund," after a promising beginning, proceeds to make nothing out of something."[10] Puffett saves his harshest criticism for the final song, the chorale prelude, on account of its "rhythmic lifelessness . . . [and] the many awkward anticipations and delayed resolutions caused by the aimlessness of the inner parts."[11] It is easy to concur with him. The cycle is worth an occasional airing, and a sensitive performance that respects Schoeck's insistence on avoiding slow tempi[12] can bring out the best in even the weaker songs (a radio recording made by Niklaus Tüller under Jean-Marie Auberson in Basel in 1977, regrettably never released commercially, goes a long way to smoothing over the work's inconsistencies). As was the case with *Befreite Sehnsucht*, the work's fine instrumentation (noted by Gysi) manages to make the music sound better than it really is (so to speak). That overly prolonged "horn" harmony of the opening song, for example, is more than mitigated by the instrumentation, which conjures up echo effects as one might hear from alphorns played in the mountains. But there is simply too much second-rate music in *Nachhall* for the cycle to be saved as a whole by even the finest orchestrator.

    Nachhall was on one level intended to convey a notion of loss, of transience. After all, it is quite openly about death and despair. But the palpable sense of loss one gains from it is not the one that the composer intended: it conveys a loss of inspiration, a loss of direction, a loss of the ability—as intimated in the very first chapter of this book—to express loss itself. The final song, which Schoeck himself called his "requiem," is as weak as Puffett says it is. But the distressing meandering of its instrumental parts is less a result of Schoeck's inability to provide direction than of his decision to avoid it altogether. Schoeck knew full well what his final destination was, and that it was rapidly approaching. So in his "requiem" he does everything to postpone his arrival. Puffett remarks upon the "pointless withholding of the bass E" (the tonic) in the measures before the final cadence, but in fact the withholding (admittedly "pointless" in musical terms) is in fact the point (see ex. 42.1). Like *Sommernacht,* this too is a work that does not want to end. Schoeck's very choice of the word "requiem" to describe the song is telling, for that is a ritual text to be read after death. By coupling the title of a "post-mortem" text to a piece that by its very act of composition is proof that he lives, it is as if Schoeck is trying to erase any notion of the moment that inevitably lies between them: that "point of arrival," the moment of death itself.

Chapter Forty-Three

Running on Empty

Schoeck had experienced few real setbacks in the past five years. Admittedly, it was not always easy to find a music publisher, but this was understandable in postwar Europe when publishers were flush with money only if they happened to have a blockbuster or two in their catalogue, such as Orff's *Carmina Burana* in the case of Schott. And while Schoeck was not enjoying many international performances, he was privileged in that international artists of the calibre of Fischer-Dieskau, Dennis Brain, Annelies Kupper, Ernst Haefliger, and Elsa Cavelti were singing and playing his works. 1956 was the year of his seventieth birthday, and celebratory concerts were being organized across Switzerland. Corrodi was finalizing a new edition of his biography, and Vogel was spending hours meticulously preparing a thematic catalogue of Schoeck's complete oeuvre. But none of this made any difference to Schoeck's depression. He saw only amateurs and provincial talents among his interpreters, with the obvious exception of Fischer-Dieskau, and he moaned about the money being "wasted" on the publication of Vogel's catalogue.[1] Once Schoeck was stuck in his black-dog days, nothing was going to rescue him, and every silver lining had a cloud. In early 1956, Hilde warned Corrodi not to visit before three in the afternoon, as her husband's moods before that hour were too awful to cope with. Early in the New Year Schoeck showed Vogel two new ritornelli and fugues that he had composed for piano. They were the last compositions that he would finish. For the next twelve months he would write nothing at all.

The year's first big event for Schoeck took place on 14 March 1956, when he was awarded the Hans Georg Nägeli Medal by the city of Zurich—an annual music award named after the composer and publisher who had shaped the music life of the city in the early nineteenth century. The city president, Emil Landolt, made the presentation, and the ceremony included a performance of *Der Sänger* by Haefliger, accompanied by Gisela in her most high-profile concert to date. One day later Erich Schmid conducted Heinz Rehfuss in *Gaselen* in the Tonhalle, while on 20 March Loeffel sang the *Notturno* in Bern. The Basel City Theater gave a "festive performance" of *Penthesilea* on 17 April, with Elsa Cavelti and Derrik Olsen in the main roles, and two days after that Schoeck finally signed a contract with Hug for the publication of his early violin sonata. The "preliminary" birthday celebrations of the first half of the year reached a climax in Zurich on 4 May, when Paul Sacher conducted a Schoeck concert with the Collegium Musicum Zürich. The orchestra played *Sommernacht*, Dennis Brain was once more the soloist in the Horn Concerto, and Dietrich Fischer-Dieskau sang the *Notturno* with string orchestra. Schoeck was bowled over by the musicality and technical perfection of both soloists. A radio recording of the concert survives, of which thus far only the Horn Concerto has been released on CD. Brain's performance is breathtaking. The main celebrations were naturally planned around Schoeck's actual birthday on 1 September. In anticipation of the mental and physical stress that they would bring, he withdrew to Brunnen in July for several weeks in order to rest and summon up his energies (see fig. 43.1). He returned in mid-August and soon began complaining that the "Schoeck week" planned in Zurich for early September was merely an excuse so that the powers-that-be (whoever they might be) could ignore him all the more in the years thereafter. In fact, the Zurich theater had offered to produce whichever opera he desired on his birthday. He had chosen *Venus,* and the prospect of seeing it again left him sleepless at night. *Venus* opened on his birthday itself, and he was so tense that he became drenched in sweat and had to leave his seat several times to go to the bathroom. Victor Reinshagen conducted, Marko Rothmüller played Raimond, Ingeborg Bremert was Simone, and Libero de Luca sang Horace. Since he had last sung the role, de Luca had left the Zurich ensemble to carve out an international career in Europe and the Americas. Rothmüller was now one of the stars of Covent Garden and would move to the New York Met three years later; Bremert would sing in the world premiere of Henze's *Elegy to Young Lovers* in 1961. For Zurich to go to these lengths to cast an opera that Schoeck had himself chosen as his "birthday present" naturally belies his obsession that he was being ignored by the world and that those performing his music were mere provincials.

The birthday greetings were now flooding in; Alois Hába, Otto Klemperer, Paul Hindemith, and numerous others sent their best wishes. Vogel's thematic catalogue appeared, as did the third, vastly expanded, edition of Corrodi's biography, and the *Schweizerische Musikzeitung* once more devoted an issue to him. Breitkopf & Härtel sent a silver cup that particularly pleased Schoeck because, he said, the last composer to receive one had been Jean Sibelius.[2] On 2 September Schoeck and his family were driven by Dr Zimmermann to Ottobeuren, the small town just across the border in southern Germany that is famous for its former Benedictine Abbey. There, in the "Kaisersaal" (the "Emperor's Hall"), the President of Bavaria presented him with the "Grosses Verdienstkreuz" of the German Federal Republic (roughly equivalent to the British OBE)—an honor that meant much to the composer. The musical part of the ceremony was provided by the Zurich String Quartet, who played the first movement of Schoeck's Second Quartet, and Dietrich Fischer-Dieskau, who, to the accompaniment of Margrit Weber, sang fifteen songs selected by the composer from across his oeuvre. A migraine prevented Fischer-Dieskau from attending the meal afterward. When Schoeck was told, he left the other guests and went up to his room to thank him again in person. He was delighted at the plan for the two artists to record the songs that they had performed, though he would not live to hear the results, as it was another two years before Deutsche Grammophon released them

Figure 43.1. Schoeck's last summer, Brunnen, 1956. Courtesy of Georg Schoeck.

on LP. This selection remains perhaps the finest set of any of Schoeck's songs on record—not just because it presents Fischer-Dieskau at his youthful best, but also on account of the superb accompaniment of Margrit Weber.

Zurich's "Schoeck week" was officially begun on Sunday 9 September in the Pfauen Theater, with speeches by Hans Corrodi and the federal councilor Philipp Etter, followed by performances of the Second String Quartet and the cantata *Vom Fischer*. Afterward the city of Zurich hosted a banquet at its official reception villa, the "Muraltengut" in Wollishofen, not far from where the Schoecks lived. On 11 September Erich Schmid conducted a concert performance of *Vom Fischer* in the Tonhalle with Elsa Scherz-Meister, Loeffel, and Haefliger as soloists; the program also included *Trommelschläge* and the Cello Concerto, with James Whitehead as soloist. The other concerts this month included *Wandersprüche* with Haefliger and *Das stille Leuchten* with Cavelti on 13 September, then another Tonhalle concert on the eighteenth, this time under Hans Rosbaud, with *Dithyrambe*, *Nachhall*, and the Violin Concerto (the soloists being Elsa Cavelti and Anton Fietz). The impact of the standing ovation that Schoeck received at the end of the concert was lessened by the fact that, as on 11 September, the Tonhalle was only half full.

Brunnen and Thun put on Schoeck concerts on 29 September (Schoeck attended the former), then others followed in Lucerne, St. Gallen, and Bern. At the last performance of *Venus* in Zurich, Corrodi saw how Schoeck sat huddled in a corner, utterly exhausted by the experience.[3] In late November, *Massimilla* was given in Bern, followed by a reception offered by Schoeck's old friend Max Wassmer. The half-empty house at its second night sent Schoeck into a deep depression for several weeks, and he managed to upset the cast by omitting to go backstage to thank them.[4] St. Gallen brought *Don Ranudo* toward the end of the year, while Kassel in Germany put on *Penthesilea* a few weeks later (though ill health prevented Schoeck from going to see it). And on 1 December a bust of Schoeck by Hermann Hubacher was presented to the University of Zurich (see fig. 43.2). It is far from Hubacher's best work, and it ended up spending many years behind the Music Department's photocopying machine. Schoeck was pleased, however, with a pencil portrait that Hubacher also did at this time and which appeared in the birthday number of the *Schweizerische Musikzeitung*. Schoeck was not a great fan of busts. When he heard that Brunnen was planning a "Schoeck monument" down by the lake, he was horrified at the prospect of meeting himself face to face while wandering where he had played as a child. (When Brunnen finally did create a monument, after Schoeck's death, it was to be a statue by Josef Bisa representing Schoeck's Venus.)

On 12 December 1956 Stefi Geyer died in Zurich. She had been ill for a long time, but the inevitability of the end did not soften the blow for Schoeck. "The brilliant Stefi Geyer has died." he wrote to Hesse, "That makes me very sad. Many household gods departed with her."[5] Stefi's funeral took place two days later in the Wasserkirche. Schoeck did not attend, being stuck at home—so

Figure 43.2. Schoeck and Hubacher's bust, late 1956. Courtesy of Zentralbibliothek Zürich.

Hilde explained to Corrodi—with a bad flu. That same evening, however, Vogel visited to find Schoeck in what seemed to be the best of health. But he avoided mentioning Stefi the whole evening, as did Vogel. Perhaps attending her funeral would have conjured up memories that were too overwhelming. But there was no escaping the flood of reminiscences that came upon him now. The death of the writer Robert Walser on Christmas Day 1956 prompted memories of the writer's brother Karl, the artist, long since dead, whom Schoeck had known on account of their both being fond of Rigi-Klösterli. And when Vogel visited Schoeck in early January, he found him once more brimming with anecdotes, this time of James Joyce, prompted by the recent production of *Massimilla,* the opera that Joyce had loved so much. Schoeck also admitted to Vogel that he was composing again, for the first time in a year. On 19 January 1957, he told him: "Today, I finished the first movement of a cello sonata. In the coda I've tried something a little new and united fragments of both the main themes to create a new one." He spoke warmly of Beethoven's cello sonatas and of how he had often played them with his brother Walter. It was clear to Vogel that it was familial memories above all that had prompted this renewed interest in the instrument, though he suspected that James Whitehead's admirable performance of the Cello Concerto in the previous September had been a contributing factor.[6]

On 6 February 1957 Schoeck went to Winterthur for a belated birthday concert. Victor Desarzens conducted the first movement of the Suite in A flat, then Gisela accompanied the American tenor Herbert Handt in *Spielmannsweisen,* after which Handt sang the orchestral version of "Besuch in Urach." The concert concluded with *Vom Fischer,* sung by Handt, Sylvia Gähwiller, and Fritz Mack. In the *Neue Zürcher Zeitung* of 9 February Schuh had only praise for the musicians, and he noted how Gisela's art of accompaniment reminded him in its impulsiveness and subtlety of her father. This was the last concert that Schoeck would ever attend. His health had deteriorated since the turn of the year, and on top of his heart problems he was also suffering from hemorrhoids. He worked "as if possessed" at his new cello sonata, Hilde later recalled, "using every minute that his sufferings allowed him." But just as Schoeck's body was slowly shutting down, so too was his inspiration draining away. He would often be unable to continue composing and would cry to Hilde, his hands pressed to his chest and his face distorted in pain: "It won't work any more, it just won't work any more."[7] He managed to complete three movements of the sonata, but they are depressingly thin. The "new idea" that he tried in the coda of its first movement really existed only in his mind, for the thematic and harmonic ideas of the movement—indeed, of the whole sonata—are well-nigh indistinguishable from each other. More than ever, Schoeck's compositional process here seems to comprise an extended doodling around the same few progressions that we know from *Das stille Leuchten* and the works thereafter. It is as if Schoeck were now adding more and more water to the mortar that held together the building blocks of his music.

Ever since Beethoven, there has been a discussion of "late style" in music, a discussion that has often been divorced from the actual age of the composer (Beethoven was himself only 56 at the time of his death). The two principal, and contradictory, interpretations of "lateness" are on the one hand that the "late works" of a composer represent decay, and on the other that they represent a culmination, even a summation of his work. But all musings on "lateness" postulate to some degree that death leaves its traces on a composer's music even as it stalks him unobserved. We are the ones left to discover and decode them, and to deduce from them how the composer dealt with both his mortality and the end of it: an end imminent often only to us, in retrospect. Schoeck knew all too well of its imminence. But although many of his friends tended generously to the view that his last works exuded "the light of happiness and the shadow of suffering in a manner no longer of this earth,"[8] his last works show no sign of concentrated energies, no final summoning up of his powers, no culmination, but instead a palpable letting-go. The aimlessness of his cello sonata betrays a composer who is, in creative terms, already almost dead.

Schoeck began to show symptoms of a mild influenza on Wednesday, 6 March 1957, coughing and sneezing.[9] He stayed in bed. The next day, Hilde said, he was deeply depressed. He could not sleep that night, and when Hilde went into his room at eight in the morning on the eighth, she found him groaning and gasping for air. He asked for camomile tea. She brought it, but he was unable to drink from the cup and had to be fed with a spoon. His condition worsened, but he refused everything that Hilde suggested, crying "No, no, no." He wanted to go to the bathroom but could not get up. Hilde tried to half-carry him there but was too weak, whereupon he collapsed back onto the bed. She then rang Dr Zimmermann, who arrived soon afterward, gave Schoeck some injections, and then decided that he must be taken to the hospital at once. Schoeck did not want to go, and kept asking "Must it be? Must it be?" It took an hour for the ambulance to arrive. As he was carried out on a stretcher just before ten o'clock, Schoeck stroked Zimmermann's hand and tried to say something to Gisela, but was too weak to be coherent. Hilde sat up front, while a paramedic sat next to Schoeck in the back. He heard him sigh twice as they went under the railway bridge on their way into the city. They pulled up on the Mythenquai, not far from the Tonhalle, but Schoeck's heart had already stopped. They drove back to Zimmermann's house for him to confirm the death, then returned to the Lettenholzstrasse and placed Schoeck on the chaise longue in his music room, near the piano.

Hilde rang Corrodi shortly afterward, and he notified Swiss Radio. He then rang the city president, Emil Landolt, who promised that the city would both organize the memorial service in the Fraumünster the following Tuesday and provide a permanent grave in the Manegg Cemetery, not far from Schoeck's home (graves in Zurich are not normally kept in perpetuity but are razed after twenty-five years). Margrit Corrodi then rang Philipp Etter of the Swiss Federal Council, an old acquaintance of the composer. Schoeck's body remained in his music room for the rest of the day and the evening, in order for his friends to come and pay their final respects. His nephew Georg arrived in the afternoon to help Hilde and Gisela with the necessary arrangements. Soon, as the *Neue Zürcher Zeitung* reported with a poetic touch, the music room "could barely contain the fullness of the flowers of spring."[10]

Schoeck was laid to rest in the Manegg Cemetery at two in the afternoon on Tuesday, 12 March, in a plot that was half-ringed by fir trees. The coffin was lowered, the vicar spoke a few words, and then Hilde and Gisela cast a bunch of carnations into the grave before departing for the Fraumünster to be in time for the official memorial service at three. As can be seen on the press photos, the church was overflowing with both people and flowers. The vicar, Karl Maurer, spoke a few words, then Erich Schmid conducted members of the Tonhalle Orchestra in Mozart's *Masonic Funeral Music*, K. 477. Maurer gave a sermon based on the parable of the talents from the Gospel according to St. Matthew and offered a biographical sketch of the composer. His glowing reference to Schoeck's "exemplary marriage," however, prompted a fit of coughing from one of the composer's astonished friends from St. Gallen. The Tonhalle Orchestra played the fourth movement of the Suite in A-flat, after which Maurer read a hagiographical text prepared by Corrodi entitled "At Othmar Schoeck's Bier." It was then the turn of Rudolf Wittelsbach, director of the Zurich Conservatory. He spoke officially on behalf of the various music institutions that were represented in the church, from the Tonhalle to the Swiss Musicians' Association; his "almost objective tone" was later praised by the *Neue Zürcher Zeitung*. The occasion closed with the last two songs from the *Elegie*, sung by Loeffel.

Letters and cards of condolence flooded in. Among them was one from Mary, whom Hilde had first refused to notify of Schoeck's death. Hilde had several years before compelled Schoeck to burn all his old letters from other girlfriends, but Mary was still the one woman of whom she would remain jealous to the last. Schuh, however—ever correct—had insisted that Mary be notified.

Hilde had first considered having a wooden cross erected at Schoeck's grave, but this was considered too "Catholic" by everyone else, and so she later had a simple stone pillar placed there, on which were chiselled the words of the final, four-line poem from Schoeck's *Nachhall:* "O land of essence and of clarity . . . I long for you." (At the time of writing, just over fifty years later, the pillar is covered with moss, the writing on it barely legible with the exception of Hilde's own name, which was added after she was buried there too, in 1990.)

A fortnight after the funeral, on 25 March 1957, Corrodi visited Hilde at home to see how she was coping. She wasn't. Now that everything was over, all her frustrations of the past three decades had welled up within her and could be held back no longer. "*That wretch!*" ("Schuft") she raged about her husband—and everything came tumbling out, about the horrendous reception that Schoeck's "evil" mother had given her on her first visit to Brunnen, how Schoeck had supposedly gone well-nigh insane over *Penthesilea*'s mediocre reviews, how she had hated his brother Walter and he her, and much, much more. The years since Othmar's heart attack had been far better than those before—that had not been a pretense—and he had at last begun to take her seriously as a musician. When ill health had forced him to retire from the podium, the time she had spent performing with him had become time spent tending him. But now that was all gone, too. They had argued furiously at times; but she did not even have that anymore. Now she was simply left on her own. The several hundred condolence messages that she received would only have brought home how the world saw her: the widow of a public figure, an appendage to someone else, a postscript to another, to someone more significant, someone who was still more signifi-cant than she, even when he was dead. And she surely knew that she would be forgotten once the news of his death was news no longer. She was only in her late fifties, but to all intents and purposes she had no independent existence and now never would. Her daughter was a grown woman, no longer dependent on her: but she too had at times been a pawn between them, and this also was a game that Othmar had won, for he was the one Gisela idolized. And as the years went on, the physical resemblance between Gisela and her father would become increasingly uncanny.

When Hilde's rage had abated, there was little to fill the space it had occupied. Her letters to Hesse and his wife Ninon over the next few years—two of Othmar's friends with whom she seems to have felt some empathy—circle depressingly around the absence that she feels: "I'm not quite myself at the moment; 8 March is the anniversary of Othmar's death," she wrote on 7 February 1959; and one year later, on 14 March 1960, she wrote: "On 8 March, it's now three years since Othmar is no longer here." The speeches at Schoeck's memorial service had told of the riches that he had left to the world. But the world did not concern Hilde, nor could it; and it seems that she felt he had left her only emptiness.

Epilogue

The compositional development of Othmar Schoeck mirrored that of many of his contemporaries, from Strauss to Bartók: Romantic beginnings in the wake of Wagner and Brahms led inexorably to the cusp of atonality (and occasionally beyond it), from which there was then a retreat (an admittedly loaded word) into an aesthetic variously neoclassical or neo-Romantic or both. The return to tonality of Bartók, Strauss, Stravinsky, and others has been much investigated, and in the case of those composers who emigrated to the United States in the 1930s it has often been postulated that it was the need to make a living in the New World that encouraged them to write in a more accessible idiom. But this is tantamount to asserting that American audiences are less cultivated, less intelligent than European ones. While this arrogance matches perfectly the anti-American cultural chauvinism that has long been latent in Europe, we must not forget that every composer has to earn a living, and a composer who is compelled to find his feet in a new environment—be it New York, California, or anywhere else on the globe—will probably endeavor to ingratiate himself as quickly as possible in order to meet his basic needs. For a composer to "remain true" to his art and end up starving in a Bohemian garret rather than compromise his modernity and live, is a concept far more attractive to romanticizing musicologists than it ever has been to composers themselves. Furthermore, in all the composers whose development matches the tonal-atonal-tonal trajectory, one can observe an organic development in their style, independent of place of residence, that makes their return to tonality in retrospect no surprise at all. Our long-time preoccupation with modernism can also serve to obscure the fact that the composers in question are sometimes more individual after their "return" to tonality than they were when they had abandoned it. One might even say: all modernist composers are somehow alike; but each post-modernist composer is post-modern in his own way.

As we have seen, Schoeck had already started to back away from atonality in the late 1920s, well before the Nazis in Germany declared the atonal to be "degenerate." But Schoeck's is an unusual case for two reasons: for the rapidity with which he all but abandoned tonality in the first place, and for the equal rapidity with which he regained it. For a brief period in the mid-1920s Schoeck was even close to the forefront (or "a" forefront) of musical development, when he moved from (near-)atonality into a partly jazz-inspired neoclassicism with undoubted constructivist tendencies. And as we have also noted above, Schoeck's "retreat" from modernism is significant because in one sense it did not take place. His reappropriation of tonality in a late-Romantic harmonic idiom retained important technical and formal elements from his modernist experiments. The resultant tension informs some of his most compelling music.

To claim that Schoeck's "modernistic" music of the 1920s and early 1930s might be his finest is something of a platitude, for the notion of aesthetic "progress" as a virtue that so dominated the musical and musicological discourse of the 1950s to 1970s has not yet been wholly abandoned. But even if one were to reject any notion of progress as an aesthetic category, one could still not deny that it was in his more "progressive" works that Schoeck was at the height of his powers. It was in them that he made the highest demands on his intellect, his technique, and his ear and also achieves the greatest emotional impact on the listener.

If there was a "turning point" in Schoeck's style, it was arguably not in the 1920s at the time of his foray in and out of modernism—for such shifts, however swift, can in retrospect be understood as beholden to an overarching stylistic consistency—but after the *Dürande* catastrophe. The demonstrative tonality of *Spielmannsweisen* was but a portent of things to come. There are some fine works in his later years, but the general trajectory of his stylistic development seems to involve taking away from his music the very things that had made it interesting in the first place, beginning with dissonance. This stylistic shift after the double blow of *Dürande* and his heart attack occurred when the composer had been silent for over a year—one of the longest such silences in his whole compos-ing career. Composers can fall silent for many reasons; but in Schoeck's case, it seems clear that the reasons were both psychological and political.

We cannot overestimate the dilemma with which Schoeck felt confronted after *Dürande*. Since 1937 he had invested most of his energies into a single work, a work of far greater length than anything he had hitherto conceived, and with which he had hoped, finally, at the age of nearly sixty, to conquer the operatic stage and set the scene for an old age free of financial dependence on others. He failed. Not only did he fail to win over the German operatic public with *Dürande,* but he had through the circumstances of its composition and per-formance also lost the goodwill of (to quote from *Spielmannsweisen*) "the people at home." This was compounded by the subsequent destruction of his German publishing houses and all those cities north of the border where he had enjoyed his many past successes, for it must now have seemed that his future lay in the hands of his countrymen alone—those same people at home whom he had "betrayed" in the eyes of some (and perhaps even, in the end, of himself) by his flirtation with Nazi Germany.

Between completing *Dürande* and embarking upon his Mörike songs in the late 1940s, Schoeck devoted himself solely to Swiss authors, both in his songs (Keller, Leuthold, and Meyer) and in his little tone poem *Sommernacht* (Keller). In his instrumental works he restricted himself for the next few years to forces that were likely to be available in even the most stringent of postwar circumstances. Herein lies undoubtedly the main reason why this master of instrumental color, whose infallible ear was able to combine woodwind, brass, string, and keyboard timbres in a manner arguably equal to any of his con-temporaries, now wrote a series of orchestral works for strings only (*Sommer-*

nacht, the Suite, and the Cello and Horn Concertos). But this was not enough. His models had always been German—primarily Schubert, Schumann, Wolf, and Strauss—so how was he to assuage his compatriots in a world in which the Germanic seemed unutterably tainted with Fascist militarism? From our perspective, the obvious intellectual decision would have been what the Germans call a "Flucht nach vorne," a flight into the forefront, an embracing of the very aesthetic that Fascist militarism had endeavored to obliterate, such as we observe in the work of the younger postwar generation of composers who adopted Schoenbergian (or Webernian) dodecaphony. The twelve-note route had not necessarily been an impossibility for Schoeck. He had experimented twenty years before with a quasi-serial treatment of his material, and there were passages in his *Notturno* that in their harmonic and contrapuntal complexity were close in style and spirit to Berg's *Lyric Suite.* Although the reception of Schoeck's music in the decades before and after his death repeatedly stressed his status as an "intuitive," Romantic artist, we have already seen in chapters 20 and 23 above that this "Romantic intuition" was paired with a highly developed constructivist streak. Nevertheless, those experiments lay well behind him when he reached the crossroads of 1943/44. And while he did admire Berg, he seems never really to have liked the dodecaphonic music of Schoenberg, nor even those works of Krenek that he had once ventured to conduct in St. Gallen. If he were keen to please his Swiss public, anything more modern than his most recent works would have scuppered his chances for good. Furthermore, to adopt the twelve-note method would have entailed intensive study and a huge investment of intellectual energy. At a time when Schoeck barely had the strength to walk down to his piano in the music room, such a commitment would have been both unthinkable and a physical impossibility.

There was no available role model for a Swiss composer eager to demonstrate his Swissness, for while the Swiss remain today charmingly patriotic, their music, like their literature and their cuisine, has tended to follow the trends in those countries whose languages they share: Germany, France, and (to a lesser degree) Italy. As we mentioned in our opening chapter, there has never been a Swiss national school of composition. The only models to which Schoeck could turn for examples of a national music divorced from overtly political considerations (at least in the eyes of the public in the mid-1940s) were the Czechs (Dvořák foremost among them) and the Scandinavians, primarily Grieg. It was no empty phrase when Schoeck insisted in his *Das stille Leuchten* that "*This* I can do for my homeland," for it was proof of a concrete endeavor to create a music that was both specifically Swiss, and—implicitly—as accessible to his fellow countrymen as, say, was the music of Grieg or Dvořák to theirs (it is perhaps worth remembering that he had conducted works by both composers on the same evening, shortly after the outbreak of World War II: the *New World Symphony* and Grieg's Piano Concerto, on 14 December 1939). Yet in all this, Schoeck was at least fifty years too late. The kind of folk-influenced music that Grieg had composed was hardly viable in the post-Second-World-War world, nor in the late-Romantic, harmonically complex idiom of which Schoeck was a master. This therefore offers us an added explanation for the "watering down" of his harmonic style in these years, for there simply was no example to hand of a composer writing a "national" music using the kind of dissonance that we find in Schoeck's finest works. Had he been able to become acquainted with the music of someone such as Geirr Tveitt in Norway, he would have found that there were indeed alternative ways of expressing national feeling within a more modernist aesthetic—though whether he would have found Tveitt's music at all appealing is another matter altogether.

The manner in which Schoeck returns in *Spielmannsweisen* to a straightforward, largely functional harmony is so insistent that it seems intent on trying to convince us (and perhaps the composer himself) of what it is not. As discussed in chapter 35 above, there is nothing in the notes of *Spielmannsweisen* to suggest that its composer had once ventured to the very bounds of tonality. It mimics the same happy innocence that is the lot of Schoeck's peasants in *Sommernacht* and it, too, aspires to create a (sound) world in which there is somehow no "sin." For where there is neither sin nor awareness of it, there can be no guilt. This, surely, is the crux of the matter for a composer aware of his moral failure with *Dürande*, yet unwilling to admit it. The incessant repetition of the same (tonal) melodic and harmonic formulae, referred to in chapter 39 and elsewhere above, is in this reading merely another means for the "guilty" party to cover his tracks, substituting repetition for content in his arguments.

Schoeck's efforts to become a specifically "Swiss" composer after *Dürande* found receptive ears just where he probably would not have expected it. In 1959—twenty years after the composer had scuppered the idea himself—a Schoeck Society was founded. Its first president was Philipp Etter, who moved with ease from his job as a member of the Swiss Federal Council to president of the new society. The founders were essentially those who had known the composer personally—Willi Schuh, Hans Corrodi, Adolf Güntensperger, Max Wassmer, and others—and served for some of them, at least in its early years, as a kind of "Ersatz" for him. Thus Corrodi's "Schoeck diary" undergoes a natural transition into a "diary of the Schoeck Society." What was particularly appealing—though no one would have admitted it at the time—was the convenient absence of the one man who could have got in the way of what the society wanted, for he was already dead: Schoeck himself. And the other person who could have got in the way was rapidly pushed to the sidelines: Hilde, who had never been liked, and was now accused behind her back of organizing unspecified "opposition" to the society's activities.[1] They would probably not have been happy unless she had committed *sati* back in 1957. Within a year of its founding, the society in any case became mired in crisis, with several of its leading members, Schuh and Vogel among them, resigning from the board. While it emerged from this intact, for many years thereafter the society functioned as if it were some kind of semi-secret men's club, its top members jockeying for position according to which of them had enjoyed the greatest proximity to the composer himself. Proposals to fund the publication of the composer's correspondence or his radio recordings were rejected because this would have made the public aware on the one hand of Schoeck's occasionally idiosyncratic grammar and orthography, and on the other hand of his wrong notes. Criticism of him was for years implicitly taboo, and it is a testament to Schoeck's late success in portraying himself as a quintessentially "Swiss" composer that he and his music became intimately linked to the Swiss establishment through the offices of "his" society, which in its first decades was headed by several prominent citizens, including one former head of state and two colonels from the army. His political faux-pas with *Dürande* was now left ignored and unmentioned. But given the society's close links to government, the military, and big business, this should not surprise us, for these were the areas of Swiss society that had made far bigger concessions to Nazi Germany than Schoeck had ever done (Society President Philipp Etter had in fact been Interior Minister of Switzerland throughout the war). Inasmuch as Schoeck's human peccadillos were admitted, such as his early sexual license, they were glossed over by the society's gentlemen with a locker-room grin, a nudge, and a wink and otherwise explained away as the idiosyncracies of a genius to whom normal societal rules did not apply.

Corrodi himself was to all intents and purposes rehabilitated. In its early years the society funded the publication of various of his texts in brochure form, continuing his hagiographical treatment of the composer. The publication of large extracts from Werner Vogel's diaries in 1965 did not please Corrodi, who seems to have felt himself to be the composer's only reliable mouthpiece. But as we observed in the introduction above, Vogel's portrait of the artist merely confirmed the one that Corrodi had long been propagating actively, namely that of Schoeck the intuitive Romantic anti-modernist. These were years when the musical avant-garde was flourishing in Switzerland, led from the Basel Conservatory by Klaus Huber, Pierre Boulez, Karlheinz Stockhausen, and others. The Schoeck Society's leading members were open about their vehement opposition to such trends, and they called upon Schoeck himself as their source of authority. The society's annual reports are full of anti-modern sentiments. In 1971, for example, the president, Franz Kienberger, wrote:

> There are signs that the young generation has had its fill of their protest against every kind of display of emotion . . . it might be possible for a while to have strictly structured art, preferably mechanically produced . . . but then the human nature that has been so violated will make itself known once more . . . and that would be when Othmar Schoeck's time has come.[2]

Just over a year later, as a response to the latest annual general meeting of the society, the young Hermann Danuser wrote a stinging rebuke of the society's lack of critical engagement with Schoeck's music, of its insistence on "praising 'Erg-riffen-sein' as the highest human virtue," and of its intention to "save Schoeck's work in its purity . . . for future generations.'"[3] The society's answer in its next annual report was that "what is really regrettable is the fact that many people, especially young people, use the ready-made clichés of a one-sided, superficial, sociological/societal viewpoint and thereby simply block one's access to the work of art itself." The society's vocabulary in these years verges at times peril-ously close to the anti-modern terminology of Nazi Germany. In a sense, the soci-ety was merely completing the project that Schoeck had embarked upon after *Dürande:* it was turning him into a composer of specifically local significance. To be sure, it was achieving this by linking him with a deeply conservative aesthetic-political agenda that also made him unpalatable to the younger generation and in turn restricted the reach of his music altogether. But one cannot deny that there was a certain perverse logic to it all.

Schoeck was not the only late-Romantic to suffer neglect in the 1960s and 1970s, for his fate was shared by Hans Pfitzner, Franz Schreker, and Alexan-der von Zemlinsky, among others. Schoeck even enjoyed a trump card denied to most of them, in that Dietrich Fischer-Dieskau never stopped performing and recording his music. And the society itself did help to fund several wor-thy projects, such as an LP recording of a concert performance of *Penthesilea* at the Lucerne Festival in 1973. The late 1980s and 1990s saw an opening up of the society, though its decision to plough most of its energies into a complete edition of the composer's works has remained controversial on account of the vast sums and large time-frame involved, and the fact that many of Schoeck's works (except for his full opera scores) were already available in reliable edi-tions that had been supervised (in some cases meticulously) by the composer himself. Internal wranglings even led to the establishment of more than one set of Schoeck archives. The 1990s did, however, bring several productions of *Penthesilea* in Switzerland and Germany, two of *Venus,* and a complete edition of Schoeck's songs on CD (the last of these thanks to the idealism and initiative of the Zurich CD producer Hans Jecklin). The Swiss labels Claves, MGB, Novalis, and Guild also released much of Schoeck's other music on CD. Many of these projects were supported by the Schoeck Society.

Schoeck has nevertheless failed to enjoy the same international resurgence of popularity that has been the lot of Zemlinsky, Pfitzner, and others. His posi-tion is made more difficult by the fact that his best works are vocal and thus inti-mately connected to the German language. But most of all, it seems, he has still to escape altogether a whiff of parochialism. His two great Swiss contemporaries Frank Martin and Arthur Honegger do not suffer from this—though they admit-tedly spent a large portion of their lives abroad, in Holland and France respec-tively. The fact that they both wrote significant non-vocal works and that they are seen as belonging to "international" modernist movements (Honegger as a mem-ber of *Les Six,* Martin as one of Switzerland's first twelve-note composers) makes them more palatable to an international public, even though Schoeck's works of the mid-1920s are at least as "progressive" as the music of either of them. While one cannot reduce the reasons for Schoeck's lack of fame to a single common denominator, it remains undeniable that the Schoeck who was propagated in the literature in his last years and after his death, and who became the iconic figurehead of the Schoeck Society, was not the innovative, liberal modernist of the 1920s but a tired, grumpy old representative of an outmoded, politically reactionary Romanticism. Schoeck must bear at least some responsibility for this, as he paved the way for it by his "reinvention" of himself after his heart attack as a quasi-national composer in a watered-down Romantic style derived from old-fashioned models.

This "Schoeck as quasi-national composer" is intimately bound up with the "anti-modernist Schoeck," and with the convergence of Schoeck himself and the "Schoeck" constructed largely by Hans Corrodi. The key to understanding this phenomenon lies surely in the fact that both Schoeck and Corrodi had been ostracized, albeit in different ways, for their close contact with Nazi Germany. Schoeck's reaction was a mixture of guilt and anger; the guilt, though never expressed openly, shows itself in his adherence to Swiss poets and in his insistence upon what he "can do for my homeland," while his anger had a number of possible objects. It could not be directed against the most obvious party, "the people at home" who had reviled him, as they constituted the "homeland" he now wished to serve; nor was his long-suffering wife any longer an obvious target, as he was physically dependent upon her after his heart attack—and she had in any case been critical of his exploits north of the border. Fluidity is in the nature of anger, and in his unwillingness to blame himself in the *Dürande* debacle, Schoeck seems to have been compelled to find a suitable Other on which to project his wrath. The candidate that was readiest to hand was the one that had already been constructed for him by Corrodi: the modern, and all those that promoted it. Schoeck now began to merge almost imperceptibly with Corrodi's "Schoeck," the biographer's construct—the Swiss composer faithful to traditional Romantic values, alone preserving the holy flame of art from the unjust attacks of the modernists. As we have already seen in the course of this book, a similar dichotomy had long existed within him; indeed, this modernist/conservative dualism lies at the very heart of his aesthetic. We have already investigated at length the intellectual energies and ambition that drove Schoeck into modernist exploration in the 1920s. But his earliest male artistic role model had been a well-to-do painter-father whose art was both rooted in the traditions of the nineteenth century, and utterly divorced from everyday economic reality. Furthermore, the other artists with whom the composer came into regular contact in his youth—the hotel guests—will have appeared perpetually indolent, as whenever Schoeck met them they were on holiday. The world of art and music must to a certain extent have appeared to the young, impressionable Schoeck a world of values that were as fixed, unchanging, and inactive as the stuffed vulture hanging from the ceiling of the family villa, or the preserved insects and never-to-be-hatched birds' eggs in his father's atelier. So when his aesthetic world came crumbling down after *Dürande* and his heart attack, a flight into a womb-like, received "Romantic" aesthetic must have seemed the most natural escape route.

As J. M. Coetzee has remarked, albeit in a different context: "Once paranoid discourse is entered upon and its dynamic takes over, the intentions of the other cannot but be hostile, since they are constituted by one's own projections."[4] Schoeck's "modernist" enemy was perhaps the most potent one for him, because it was within himself. Unable to face his guilt over *Dürande*, and yet somehow desperate to assuage it, he now began to fight the supposed "enemy" without by excising all modernist traces within. And since the enemy's guilt was merely a self-created projection of his own, the active excision of those traces only made him more aware of their presence, prompting in turn yet another round of excision, and another, and another. This paranoia became a self-sustaining automaton that in musical terms found its goal in the anaemic nothingness of the late Cello Sonata. And while his stage works had in fact never been performed more often than in the 1950s, nor had he ever enjoyed finer international interpreters, all he himself saw was increasing neglect. And this vicious circle did not cease to be after his death, for Corrodi continued to feed it in the years to come, when he created in his writings a Schoeck who was a mirror of his own deeply felt feelings of rejection. The third edition of his Schoeck biography, published just months before the composer's death, soon became the standard postwar work on him. It is itself little short of paranoid in its hatred of the modern world with its "idols: fashion, money, and the press,"[5] of the "degeneracy" of modern art ("entartet"—he had not yet abandoned his old Nazi phraseology[6]), of the latterday "poisoning" of the "moral foundations of life,"[7] and of "the thick covering of the rubble of civilization under which the eternal springs of true creativity lie buried."[8] And all the while, Corrodi is unable to stop complaining of how Schoeck—for him the last man to tap those "eternal springs"—has been ignored and excluded. It is by now almost impossible to untangle biography from autobiography in Corrodi's writings. This paranoia, shared by the aging composer and his would-be Eckermann, essentially became for many years the ruling ideology of the Schoeck Society that Corrodi helped to create. *Auf einsamen Wegen* ("On Lonely Paths") was the title of a brochure he penned on the fifth anniversary of Schoeck's death and which was published by the society. In it he sums up once more all his main themes: the neglect, the "dehumanization" of man and art by the avant-garde, Schoeck's music as a light in the darkness—and of course the implication, illogical but inevitable, that on his "lonely paths" Schoeck is in fact not alone but accompanied by Corrodi and his fellow society members. For how could Corrodi describe those "lonely paths" if he was not treading them himself?[9]

That "tired and grumpy," anti-modern Schoeck is, if not alive and kicking, then still twitching and far from dead. A glance at the list of concerts held in Switzerland for the fiftieth anniversary of the composer's death in 2007 makes for somewhat depressing reading. For while the superb *Notturno* does make an appearance, the works that seem most popular in the land of his birth, and which presumably still determine the commonly held conservative picture of the composer (or perhaps merely confirm it), are *Sommernacht,* the First String Quartet, and the early and late songs (that is, the most tonal ones). But the Schoeck of the interwar years, while less obviously "Swiss," is no less authentic, and far more in tune with our own times. Here was a man who scoffed at the conservative establishment; a liberal democrat whose open sympathies for the Allies in World War I had been in defiance of the opinion of most of his German Swiss countrymen; a man whose liberality in sexual matters went beyond fulfilling his own needs to encompass an easy tolerance of those whose desires were other than his own; a modernist who looked as much to Paris for aesthetic guidance as to Vienna and Berlin; a conductor whose active support of the new was in the 1920s arguably on a par with just about any of his colleagues in central Europe; and a composer possessed of an unmistakeably individual style, much of whose oeuvre deserves to be permanently in the repertoire, and of which, say, half a dozen works—foremost among them *Lebendig begraben* and *Notturno*—can bear comparison with the acknowledged masterpieces of their age. This is the Schoeck whose music was admired by Alban Berg, Fritz Busch, Arthur Honegger, Wilhelm Furtwängler, Hermann Hesse, and James Joyce; and he is a composer who is no less cosmopolitan than his compatriots Martin and Honegger. Indeed, Switzerland's position at the center of Europe has long made of Zurich, Schoeck's home, one of the most cosmopolitan, most vibrantly international cities on the continent. To deny this element in Schoeck's life and music, as was done for so long, is thus, ironically, to deny him one of the very qualities that in effect help to make him "Swiss." If his countrymen should prove willing to let this "cosmopolitan" Schoeck have the precedence that he deserves over his later, "provincial" incarnation, then perhaps we, too, might in fact find that the voice with which he speaks to us is individual in a way that also makes him specifically Swiss. The one need not obscure the other; and his "people at home," together with us, would be the richer for it.

Othmar Schoeck

Concise Work Catalogue and Discography

This catalogue is based on various sources, beginning with Werner Vogel's *Thematisches Verzeichnis* of 1956; it includes original programs, contemporary reviews, and information more recently gathered by the editors of the Schoeck Complete Edition and published there. For reasons of space, work information is in general restricted to title, text author(s), year of composition, instrumentation, current publisher, and the first performance.

Recordings of Schoeck's works are included with each work entry. Since many of Schoeck's works have appeared in compilations of various sorts, the format chosen here makes it easier for the reader to find a recording of a particular work. For reasons of space and practicality, however, we have here restricted ourselves to CD recordings.

Most of the manuscripts of Schoeck's works are held by the Zentralbibliothek Zürich, which also possesses the largest collection of sound recordings of his music (including many digital transfers of Swiss radio recordings). Its Schoeck homepage furthermore has precise information on the whereabouts of almost all known manuscripts of Schoeck. For further information, see its electronic library catalogue at http://opac.nebis.ch, its catalogue of manuscripts at http://zb-sps.uzh.ch/cgi-bin/populo/hss.pl, and its Schoeck homepage at www.zb.uzh.ch/sondersa/musik/Schoeck/Schoeck.htm (accessed June 2008).

Abbreviations

Performing forces

pic—piccolo	hn—horn
fl—flute	tpt—trumpet
afl—alto flute	trbn—trombone
ob—oboe	btrbn—bass trombone
eng hn—cor anglais	tb—tuba
cl—clarinet	

bcl—bass clarinet
bn—bassoon
cbn—contrabassoon
timp—timpani
perc—percussion
cast—castanets
cym—cymbal(s)
glock—glockenspiel
tamb—tambourine
tamt—tam-tam
trgl—triangle
xyl—xylophone
vn—violin
va—viola
vc—cello
db—double bass
str—strings

hp—harp
org—organ
pf—piano
cel—celeste

S—soprano
A—alto, contralto
T—tenor
B—bass

Other abbreviations

FP—first performance
Instr.—instrumentation
Publ.—publication
LCE—Lieder, Complete Edition (the recordings of Schoeck's songs on CD produced
    by Jecklin, Zurich, in the 1990s)

woo—without opus numbers

I. Stage Works

woo 4

Am Silbersee

Opera in three acts after Karl May's *Der Schatz im Silbersee*. Libretto by Walter
    Schoeck.

ca. 1901

Dramatis personae: Old Shatterhand—Winnetou—Bob—Jim—captain—Cornell—
    sailors—passengers—emigrants—"Men of the West"—Indians

Instr.: fl—2vn, vc—pf

Recording (performing version by Dieter Stalder): Claudia Schmidlin (soprano);
    Markus J. Frey (bass-baritone); Regula Jucker (speaker); Martin Schmidlin
    (cl); Veronika Stalder (vn); Dieter Stalder (pf). Harmonium-Museum Liestal,
    HMP 0404–2

woo 80
Der Ehri
Singspiel for voices and piano. Libretto after Karl May, presumably by one or more of
the Schoeck brothers
Fragment, 1901?
Dramatis personae: Helmsman—Capt'n—Charly—Potomba—Bob—sailors

woo 123
[*Gnom und Elfschwesterlein*]
Singspiel for voices and piano. Libretto presumably by one or more of the Schoeck
brothers
Fragment, 1903?
Dramatis personae: Elfschwesterlein (Little elf sister)—little elf—gnome (Rough-
beard)—charcoal burner boy—princess

woo 88
Die Gänsehirtin am Brunnen
Singspiel for voices and piano. Libretto after the Grimm fairy tale, presumably by
one or more of the Schoeck brothers
According to the draft score, the following accompanying ensemble was intended: fl,
cl—trbn, tb—timp—str
Fragment, 1903?
Dramatis personae: Goose-girl—witch—Lieschen—Roland

woo 93
Josephine
Singspiel for voices and piano. Libretto anonymous (by Othmar Schoeck and
friends?)
Fragment, ca. 1903?
Dramatis personae: Landlord—old woman—Josephine.
FP: ca. 1903 in the "Ochsensaal" on Kreuzplatz in Zurich (by Schoeck and his school-
friends)

woo 69
Das Glück in der Heimat
"Large popular festival play of the 'Japanesen' [i.e. Shrovetide carnival] Society in
Jeddo Schwyz," by Jakob Grüninger.
For SATB chorus and orchestra
"Chor der Priester und Priesterinnen"
"Gesang der jungen Krieger"
1906
Instr.: 2fl, 2cl—2hn, 3tpt, 2trbn, tb—timp—str
FP: 13 Jan. 1907, Schwyz

Op. 25
Erwin und Elmire
Songs for the singspiel by Goethe, with a prelude and an interlude

1911–16

Dramatis personae: Erwin—tenor; Elmire—soprano; Olympia—contralto; Bernardo—bass.

Instr.: pic, 2fl, 2ob, 2cl, 2bn—2hn, 2tpt—timp, trgl—hp, cel—str

Leipzig: Breitkopf & Härtel

FP: 11 Nov. 1916, Zurich City Theater (cond. Robert F. Denzler)

Recordings: Jeannette Fischer (Elmire); Mareike Schellenberger (Olympia); Tino Brütsch (Erwin); Hans Christoph Begemann (Bernardo); Zurich Chamber Orchestra, cond. Howard Griffiths. CPO 999 929–2

Elmire's arias "Mit vollen Atemzügen" and "Sieh mich, Heil'ger": Annette Joel-Brun; Radio Orchestra Beromünster, cond. Jean-Marie Auberson. Jecklin Edition JD 714–2

Op. 27

Don Ranudo

Comic opera in four acts after a comedy by Ludvig Holberg. Libretto by Armin Rüeger

1917–18, rev. 1920, 1930, and 1951

Dramatis personae: Don Ranudo di Colibrados, an old nobleman—bass; Dona Olympia, his wife—contralto; Maria, their daughter—soprano; Gonzalo de las Minas, a young count—tenor; Pedro, a servant of Ranudo—baritone; Leonore, Olympia's maid—soprano; Gusman, Gonzalo's servant—baritone; a Moor, vegetable seller—tenor; a bailiff—tenor; a woman—soprano; a man in the crowd—tenor; a priest—silent role; people, market women, retinue of the "Moorish Prince"—chorus (SATB); people of the court—silent

Place: A small Spanish town, ca. 1750

Instr.: 2pic, 2fl (2 also pic), 2ob (2 also eng hn), 3cl (3 only in act 3), bcl, 2bn—4hn, 3tpt, 3trbn, btrbn—timp, perc (tamb, side drum, bass drum, cym, trgl, tamt)—hp—str

Publ.: Leipzig: Breitkopf & Härtel

FP: 16 Apr. 1919, Zurich City Theater (cond. Robert F. Denzler)

FP, revised, two-act version: 3 Oct. 1930, Dresden State Opera (cond. Fritz Busch)

Op. 28

Das Wandbild

A scene and a pantomime by Ferruccio Busoni

1918

Dramatis personae of the scene: Antique dealer; Novalis, a student; Dufait, his friend

Characters in the pantomime: Priest—baritone; giant; Novalis; girl; her female companions—women's chorus (SA)

Date and place of the scene: an antique shop on the Rue St. Honoré in 1830

Date and place of the pantomime: the spirit world of the Chinese

Instr.: fl (also pic), ob, eng hn, cl, bcl, bn, cbn—hn, tpt, trbn—timp, perc (trgl, side drum, tamb, tamt, bass drum, chains, hammer, cym)—hp, cel—str

Publ.: Leipzig: Breitkopf & Härtel

FP: 2 Jan. 1921, City Theater in Halle (cond. Oskar Braun)

Recording: The opening number, "The Mechanical Clock," is on Guild GMCD 7189 (Andrew Zolinsky, pf)

Op. 32
Venus
Opera in three acts after a novella by Mérimée. Libretto by Armin Rüeger
1919–21, rev. 1933
Dramatis personae: Baron de Zarandelle—tenor; Horace, his nephew—tenor; Simone, Horace's fiancée (later wife)—soprano; Mme de Lauriens, Simone's mother—contralto; Raimond, Simone's cousin, an officer—baritone; Lucile, Simone's friend—soprano; the unknown girl (silent role); Martin, Zarandelle's gardener—baritone; a gardener—baritone; first servant—baritone; second servant—baritone; wedding guests, peasants, servants, children—chorus (SATB, children's choir)
Date and place: A country chateau in southern France, ca. 1820
Instr.: pic, 2fl, 2ob, eng hn, 2cl, bcl, 2bn, cbn—4hn, 3tpt, 3trbn, tb—timp, perc (side drum, bass drum, glock, tamb, cast, tamt, xyl)—hp, cel, pf—str
Publ.: Leipzig: Breitkopf & Härtel
FP: 10 May 1922, Zurich City Theater (cond. Othmar Schoeck)
FP, revised version: 26 Nov. 1933, Zurich City Theater (cond. Robert F. Denzler)
Recording: Frieder Lang (Baron de Zarandelle); Lucia Popp (Simone); James O'Neal (Horace); Hedwig Fassbender (Mme de Lauriens); Boje Skovhus (Raimond); Zsuzsa Alföldi (Lucile); Konstantin Beier (Martin and first servant); David Otto (gardener and second servant); Kammerchor Heidelberg; Knabenkantorei Basel; Philharmonische Werkstatt Schweiz, cond. Mario Venzago. MGB CD 6112

Op. 39
Penthesilea
After the tragedy by Heinrich von Kleist, in one act
1923–25, rev. 1927
Dramatis personae: Penthesilea, Queen of the Amazons—mezzo-soprano; Prothoe, Amazon princess—soprano; Meroe, Amazon princess—soprano; high priestess of Diana—contralto; priestess—soprano; Achilles, king amongst the Greeks—baritone; Diomedes, king amongst the Greeks—tenor; a herald—baritone; Greeks and Amazons—chorus (SATB)
Place: A battlefield near Troy
Instr.: fl (also pic), 2pic (also fl), ob (also eng hn), 6cl, 2cl in E flat, 2bcl, cbn—4hn, 4tpt, 4trbn, tb—stierhorn—timp, perc (side drum, bass drum, cym, trgl, rute, tamt)—2pf—4 solo vn, str (only va, vc, db). Offstage: 3tpt
Publ.: Kassel: Bärenreiter
FP: 8 Jan. 1927, Dresden State Opera (cond. Hermann Kutzschbach)
FP, revised version: 15 May 1928, Zurich City Theater (cond. Max Conrad)
Recordings: Helga Dernesch (Penthesilea); Jane Marsh (Prothoe); Mechthild Gessendorf (Meroe); Marjana Lipovšek (high priestess); Gabriele Sima (priestess); Theo Adam (Achilles); Horst Hiestermann (Diomedes); Peter Weber (herald); ORF Choir; ORF Symphony Orchestra, cond. Gerd Albrecht. Orfeo C 364 942 B

Yvonne Naef (Penthesilea); Renate Behle (Prothoe); Susanne Reinhard (Meroe); Ute Trekel-Burkhardt (high priestess); James Johnson (Achilles); Stuart Kale (Diomedes); Cheyne Davidson (herald/captain); Imke Büchel ("Chief of the Amazons"); Czech Philharmonic Chorus, Brno; Peter Fiala (chorus master); Basel Symphony Orchestra, cond. Mario Venzago. Pan Classics 510 118–2 (now released as MGB 6232)

A concert suite from the opera, arr. Andreas Delfs, has been recorded by the Swiss Youth Symphony Orchestra, cond. Delfs, on Claves Digital CD 50–920

Op. 43
Vom Fischer un syner Fru
Dramatic cantata for three solo voices and orchestra
Text from Philipp Otto Runge's "Platt" dialect version of the Grimm fairy tale
For stage or concert performance
1928–30
Dramatis personae: Wife—soprano; fisherman—tenor; flounder—bass (in the orchestra pit, out of sight)
Instr.: 2fl (2 also pic), 2ob (2 also eng hn), 2cl, 2bn, cbn—3hn, tpt, btrbn—timp, perc (side drum, cym, tamt, wind machine, thunder machine)—pf—str
Publ.: Leipzig: Breitkopf & Härtel
FP: 3 Oct. 1930, Dresden State Opera (cond. Fritz Busch)
First concert performance: 16 Jan. 1931, St. Gallen (St. Gallen City Orchestra, cond. Othmar Schoeck)
Recording (excerpts): Maria Bernhard-Ulbrich (wife); Ernest Bauer (fisherman); Felix Loeffel (flounder); Swiss Radio Orchestra Beromünster, cond. Othmar Schoeck. Uranus URA 601

Op. 50
Massimilla Doni
Opera in 4 acts (6 scenes)
Libretto by Armin Rüeger after the novel by Honoré de Balzac
1934–36
Dramatis personae: Duke Cattaneo, an old eccentric, patron of Tinti—tenor; Capraja, his friend, patron of Genovese—baritone; Emilio Memmi, a young nobleman—tenor; Prince Vendramin, his older friend—baritone; Genovese, a tenor—tenor; Duchess Massimilla Doni, wife (or fiancée) of the Duke—soprano; Tinti, a singer—coloratura soprano; guests, servants, stage personnel, gondoliers, street vendors, children—(SATB, children's choir)
Date and place: Venice, ca. 1830
Instr.: 2fl (2 also pic), 2ob (2 also eng hn), 2cl, bcl, 2bn, cbn—4hn, 3tpt, 3trbn, tb—timp, perc (bass drum, cym, tamt, side drum, trgl, xyl)—hp, pf (onstage)—str
Publ.: Vienna: Universal Edition
FP: 2 Mar. 1937, Dresden State Opera (cond. Karl Böhm)
Recording: Hermann Winkler (Duke Cattaneo); Harald Stamm (Capraja); Josef Protschka (Emilio Memmi); Roland Hermann (Vendramin); Edith Mathis (Massimilla Doni); Celina Lindsley (Tinti); Deon van der Walt (Genovese); Annette Küttenbaum (page/maid/shepherd/fruit-seller); Ulrich Ress (theater director/

newspaper-seller); Florian Giertzuch (gondolier); Cologne Radio Choir and the Cologne Radio Symphony Orchestra, cond. Gerd Albrecht. Koch Schwann Musica Mundi 314 025 K3

Op. 53
Das Schloss Dürande
Opera in 4 acts. Libretto by Hermann Burte, after the novella by Joseph von Eichendorff
1937–41
Dramatis personae: Armand, the young count of Dürande—tenor; the old count, his father—tenor; the prioress of Himmelpfort—contralto; Countess Morvaille—soprano; Renald Vomholz, the count's gamekeeper—baritone; Gabriele, his sister—soprano; Nicole, the count's valet—bass-baritone; a gamekeeper—baritone; a gardening boy—tenor; a helper—soprano; a popular speaker—tenor; Buffon, the landlord—baritone; a lawyer, later a commissar—tenor; a journeyman—baritone; a soldier—baritone; an other (revolutionary)—tenor; a policeman—baritone; an officer of the watch—baritone; 1st huntsman—tenor; 2nd huntsman—baritone; 3rd huntsman—tenor; 4th huntsman—baritone; 5th huntsman—baritone; a Parisian—tenor; a voice—tenor; helpers, nuns, vintners, hunters, servants, police, revolutionaries, children—chorus (SATB, children's choir)
Date and place: Provence and Paris at the time of the French Revolution of 1789
Instr.: 2fl (2 also pic), 2ob (2 also eng hn), 2cl, bcl, 2bn, cbn—4hn, 3tpt, 3trbn, tb—timp, perc (trgl, side drum, bass drum, cym, tamt, tamb, xyl, glock, bells in G, E, D)—hp, pf—str
Onstage music (behind the stage): 2fl (also pic), 4hn, 3tpt, side drum, glock, pf, cel, org
Publ.: Vienna: Universal Edition
FP: 1 Apr. 1943, Berlin State Opera (cond. Robert Heger)
Recording (excerpts from the FP on 1 Apr. 1943): Peter Anders (Armand); Maria Cebotari (Gabriele); Josef Greindl (Nicole); Marta Fuchs (Morvaille); Willi Domgraf-Fassbaender (Renald); Ret Berglund (prioress); Otto Husch (gamekeeper); Vasso Argyris (popular speaker); Benno Arnold, Leo Laschet, Fritz Marcks, Hans Wrana, Felix Schneider (hunters); Berlin State Opera, cond. Robert Heger. Jecklin JD 292–2

WoO 115
[*Bruder Lustig und Meister Pfriem*]
(opera)
Only a few brief undated sketches are extant (1943?)

II. Orchestral Works

Schoeck's orchestral works have been published in their entirety as series 3, vols. 21 and 22 of *Othmar Schoeck: Sämtliche Werke*, ed. **Victor Ravizza and Gérard Dayer** respectively (Zurich: Hug, 1995 and 1997).

WOO 25
Symphonischer Satz
1906
Instr.: pic, 2fl, 2ob, 2cl, 2bn—4hn, 2tpt, 2trbn, tb—timp—hp—str
FP: 31 Mar. 1906, Zurich (cond. Lothar Kempter Sen.)

Op. 1
Serenade
1906–7
Instr.: fl, ob, cl, bn—hn—str
FP: 23 Mar. 1907, Zurich (cond. Othmar Schoeck)
Recording: English Chamber Orchestra, cond. Howard Griffiths. Novalis 150 070–1

WOO 99
[Piece in B-flat major]
Fragment (short score), ca. 1907?

WOO 29
Ouvertüre zu William Ratcliff by Heinrich Heine (*William Ratcliff Overture*)
1907–8
Instr.: pic, 2fl, 2ob, 2cl, 2bn—4hn, 4tpt, 2trbn, btrbn, tb—timp, tamt—str
FP: 1 Jun. 1908, Baden (Zurich Tonhalle Orchestra, cond. Othmar Schoeck)

WOO 101
["Italian Sinfonietta"?]
Fragment, 1910
Instr.: 2fl, 2ob, 2cl, 2bn—2hn, 2tpt, 2trbn—str

WOO 105
Schleppend
Fragment (short score), 1916?
Note: handwritten note by Hans Corrodi on the manuscript: "für Orchester (Moiry-
    gletscher, 1916?)"

Op. 27
Serenade (intermezzo from *Don Ranudo*)
1930
Instr.: ob, eng hn—str
FP: 3 Oct. 1930, State Opera in Dresden, cond. Fritz Busch
Recording: Silvia Zabarella (ob); Martin Zürcher (eng hn); Musikkollegium Winter-
    thur, cond. Werner Andreas Albert. CPO 999 337–2

Op. 48
Präludium
For orchestra

1932–33
Instr.: 2fl (2 also pic), 2ob, 2cl, 2bn, cbn—4hn (or 6 or 8 hn *ad lib*), 3tpt, 3trbn, tb—timp, perc (cym, trgl, side drum, bass drum, tamt)—pf—str
FP: 29 Apr. 1933, Zurich (Zurich Tonhalle Orchestra, cond. Volkmar Andreae)
Recording: Musikkollegium Winterthur, cond. Werner Andreas Albert. CPO 999 337–2

Op. 58
Sommernacht
Pastoral intermezzo for string orchestra after the poem by Gottfried Keller
1945
FP: 17 Dec. 1945, Bern (Bern City Orchestra, cond. Luc Balmer)
Note: Also exists in an arrangement by the composer for pf duet
Recordings: Deutsche Kammerakademie Neuss, cond. Johannes Goritzki. Claves Digital CD 50–8502
Camerata Bern, dir. Ana Chumachenko. MGB CTS-M 69
Festival Strings Lucerne, cond. Rudolf Baumgartner. Gallo CD 799
English Chamber Orchestra, cond. Howard Griffiths. Novalis 150 106–2
Orchestre d'Auvergne, cond. Armin Jordan. Saphir LVC 1052
Swiss Chamber Orchestra, cond. Emmanuel Siffert. Gall GLL 1075

Op. 59
Suite in A-flat Major
For string orchestra
1945
FP: 14 Sept. 1946, Winterthur (Winterthur City Orchestra, cond. Hermann Scherchen)
Note: Also exists in an arrangement by the composer for pf duet
Recordings: Musikkollegium Winterthur, cond. Werner Andreas Albert. CPO 999 337–2
South West German Chamber Orchestra, Pforzheim, cond. Vladislav Czarnecki. EBS 6145
English Chamber Orchestra, cond. Howard Griffiths. Novalis 150 070–1
Adagio from the Suite: Festival Strings Lucerne, cond. Rudolf Baumgartner. Gallo CD-934

Op. 64
Festlicher Hymnus
For large orchestra
1950
Instr.: pic, 2fl, 2ob, 2cl, 2bn, cbn—4hn, 3tpt, 3trbn, tb—timp, perc (cym, trgl, bass drum)—str
FP: 2 Jun. 1951, Zurich (Zurich Tonhalle Orchestra, cond. Erich Schmid)
Note: Also exists in an arrangement by the composer for pf duet

III. Band Music

woo 28
Concert March
For the "Eidgenössisches Schützenfest" (the "Swiss National Shooting Festival") in
    Zurich in 1907
Not orchestrated. See **Piano Music (for Two and Four Hands)**

woo 36
March (in B-flat Major)
For the Brunnen "Harmoniemusik" (wind band)
Scored for wind band by Victor Burkhardt
1922?

woo 40
Military March Scored for wind band by Hans Heusser
1940
Publ.: Zurich: Hug & Co.
FP: 23 Nov. 1940, Zurich (cond. Hans Richard)

IV. Works for Solo Instrument(s) and Orchestra

Schoeck's concertante works have been published in their entirety as series 3, vol. 23
    of *Othmar Schoeck: Sämtliche Werke*, ed. **Beat A. Föllmi** (Zurich: Hug, 2001).

woo 124
Piano Concerto
Fragment, ca. 1912?

Op. 21
Concerto (*Quasi una fantasia*) in B-flat Major for Violin and Orchestra
1910–12
Instr.: 2fl, 2ob, 2cl, 2bn—2hn, 2tpt—timp—str
FP: 1st movement, 21 May 1911, Vevey
all three movements (with pf accompaniment): 28 Feb. 1912, Berlin (Willem de
    Boer, vn; Othmar Schoeck, pf);
all three movements with orchestra: 19 Mar. 1912, Bern (Willem de Boer, vn; Bern
    City Orchestra, cond. Fritz Brun)
Recordings: Ursula Bagdasarjanz (vn); Radio Orchestra Monte Ceneri, cond. Fran-
    cesco d'Avalos. BAG CD 004
Bettina Boller (vn); Swiss Youth Symphony Orchestra, cond. Andreas Delfs. Claves
    Digital CD 50–920
Stefi Geyer (vn); Zurich Tonhalle Orchester, cond. Volkmar Andreae. Jecklin Edition
    JD 715–2. Also on Dante Records LYS 398

Ulf Hoelscher (vn); English Chamber Orchestra, cond. Howard Griffiths. Novalis
150 070–1
Hansheinz Schneeberger (vn); Sinfonietta Wetzikon, cond. Christoph Müeller. Swiss
Pan SP 51.704
Emmy Verhey (vn); BBC Scottish Symphony Orchestra, cond. Jerzy Maksymiuk. MGB
CD 6117

Op. 27
Serenade (Intermezzo from *Don Ranudo*)
Instr.: ob, eng hn—strings
See **Orchestral Works**

woo 114
[Two movements of a cello concerto?]
Fragment, ca. 1931?

Op. 61
Concerto for Cello and String Orchestra
1947
FP: 1st and 2nd movements, with pf accompaniment, 29 May 1947, Horgen (Paul
Grümmer, VC; Othmar Schoeck, pf);
all four movements with orch, 10 Feb. 1948, Zurich (Pierre Fournier, vc; Zurich Ton-
halle Orchestra, cond. Volkmar Andreae)
Recordings: Julius Berger (vc); South West German Chamber Orchestra, Pforzheim,
cond. Vladislav Czarnecki. EBS 6145
Johannes Goritzki (vc and cond.); Deutsche Kammerakademie Neuss. Claves Digital
CD 50–8502
Antoine Lederlin (vc); Orchestre d'Auvergne, cond. Armin Jordan. Saphir LVC 1052
Christian Poltéra (vc); Malmö Symphony Orchestra, cond. Tuomas Ollila. BIS-CD
1597

woo 108
[Piano concerto]
Fragment, 1949/1950?

Op. 65
Concerto for Horn and String Orchestra
1950–51
FP: 6 Feb. 1952, Winterthur (Hans Will, hn; Winterthur City Orchestra, cond. Victor
Desarzens)
Recordings: Radek Baborák (hn); Prague Chamber Orchestra, cond. Jiri Belohlávek.
Supraphon SPR 3348
Dennis Brain (hn); Collegium Musicum Zürich, cond. Paul Sacher. Jecklin Edition
JD715–2
Andrew Joy (hn); Cologne Radio Symphony Orchestra, cond. Wolf-Dieter Hauschild.
Capriccio CD 10 443

Marie Luise Neunecker (hn); NDR Radio Philharmonic Orchestra, Hanover, cond. Uri Mayer. Koch Schwann 3–6412–2

Bruno Schneider (hn); Musikkollegium Winterthur, cond. Werner Andreas Albert. CPO 999 337–2

Bruno Schneider (hn); Orchestre de Chambre de Genève, cond. Thierry Fischer. MGB CD 6117

Zbigniew Zuk (hn); Leopoldinum Chamber Orchestra, Wrocław, cond. Jan Stanienda. Zuk Records ZKRR 71088

V. Chamber Music

WOO 55
Suite (one movement)
Instr.: vc, pf?
ca. 1902?

WOO 84
Allegro
Instr.: vc, pf
Fragment, ca. 1902?

WOO 86
Allegro
Instr.: vn, pf?
Fragment, ca. 1902?

WOO 89
[Piece in G major]
Instr.: melody instrument, pf?
Fragment, ca. 1903?

WOO 61
Sommer
Instr.: vn, vc, pf
Fragment, 1903?

WOO 63
Abend-Gebet
Instr.: vc, pf
1903

WOO 22
Sonata in D Major
Instr.: vn, pf
1905, rev. 1952

Publ.: Zurich: Hug & Co.
FP 1st version: 28 Oct. 1908, Thun (Hans Kötscher, vn; Othmar Schoeck, pf)
FP 2nd version: 6 Mar. 1954, Zurich (Stefi Geyer, vn; Walter Frey, pf)
Recordings: (1st version): Paul Barritt (vn); Catherine Edwards (pf). Guild GMCD
    7142
(2nd version): Simone Zgraggen (vn); Ulrich Koella (pf). Claves CD 50 2503
Martin Gelland (vn); Lennart Wallin (pf). VMM 2017
Matthias Wollong (vn); Patricia Pagny (pf). MGB CD 6163.

woo 26
Minuet and Trio
Instr.: str quartet
1906 or 1907
FP: 20 Nov. 1996, Zurich (Julia Schröder, Kevin Griffiths, vn; David Friedeberg, viola;
    Martina Brotbeck, cello)

woo 70
Albumblatt
Instr.: vn, pf
1908
FP: August? 1908 (Stefi Geyer, vn; Othmar Schoeck, pf)
Recordings: Ursula Bagdasarjanz (vn); Gisela Schoeck (pf). BAG CD 002
Paul Barritt (vn); Catherine Edwards (pf). Guild GMCD 7142
Matthias Wollong (vn); Patricia Pagny (pf). MGB CD 6163
Simone Zgraggen (vn); Ulrich Koella (pf). Claves CD 50 2503

woo 71
Waltz
Instr.: str quartet
ca. 1908?

woo 72
Fuga a 4 voci, 2 soggetti (Bach)
Instr.: str quartet
ca. 1908?
FP: 16 Nov. 1997, Zurich-Witikon (Kammerorchester der Kirchgemeinde Witikon,
    cond. Chris Walton)
Note: an arrangement of Fugue No. 23 (BWV 892) from J. S. Bach's *Well-Tempered
    Clavier*, book 2

woo 73
[Movement in C]
Instr.: str quartet
ca. 1908?

woo 100
[Trio in D major]

Inst.: vn, va, vc?
Fragment, ca. 1907?

Op. 16
Sonata in D Major
Instr.: vn, pf
1908–9
Publ.: Zurich: Hug & Co.
FP: 29 Apr. 1909, Zurich (Willem de Boer, vn; Othmar Schoeck, pf)
Recordings: Ursula Bagdasarjanz (vn); Gisela Schoeck (pf). BAG CD 002
Paul Barritt (vn); Catherine Edwards (pf). Guild GMCD 7142
Ulrich Lehmann (vn); Charles Dobler (pf). Ex Libris CD 6043
Gerhard Taschner (vn); Edith Farnadi (pf). MDG 6420985
Matthias Wollong (vn); Patricia Pagny (pf). MGB CD 6163
Simone Zgraggen (vn); Ulrich Koella (pf). Claves CD 50 2503

WoO 75
String Quartet Movement in B-flat Major
ca. 1908/1909?
Publ.: Winterthur: Amadeus
FP: 2 Jan. 1986, Zurich (Ustemer Quartet)
Note: completed by Werner Vogel
Recording: Minguet Quartet. MDG Scene MDG 603 0665–2

WoO 125
[String quartet movement in A-flat minor]
Fragment, ca. 1910?

WoO 126
[String quartet movement in D minor]
Fragment, ca. 1910?

Op. 23
String Quartet in D Major
1911–13
Publ.: Leipzig and Zurich: Hug & Co.
FP: 14 Jun. 1913, St. Gallen (Zurich String Quartet)
Recording: Minguet Quartet. MDG Scene MDG 603 0665–2

WoO 133
"Fliessend"
Instr.: melody instrument, pf
Fragment

WoO 102
[Sonata movement in E]
Instr.: vn, pf

Fragment, 1914
Recording: Matthias Wollong (vn); Patricia Pagny (pf). MGB CD 6163

WOO 103
[Fugue]
Instr.: 3vn, vc?
Fragment, 1915

WOO 104
[Fugue]
Instr.: str quartet?
Fragment, 1915

WOO 76
Fugue for 3 Voices
Instr.: 2vn, vc?
1915

WOO 35
Andante
Instr.: cl, pf
1916
Publ.: Zurich: Hug & Co.
FP: 8 Jun. 1949, Geneva (Pierre de Bavier, cl; Luise von Walther, pf)
Note: from an unfinished clarinet sonata in G

WOO 77
Scherzo
Instr.: vn, va, vc
1917?
Publ.: in *Dissonanz* 34, 1992, reconstructed by Chris Walton
FP: 20 Nov. 1996, Zurich (Julia Schröder, vn; David Friedeberg, va; Martina Brotbeck, vc)
Recording: Oliver Lewis (vn); Tim Grant (va); Justin Pearson (vc). Guild GMCD 7189

WOO 135
[Fragment for string quartet]
early 1920s?

Op. 37
String Quartet in C Major
1923
Publ.: Leipzig: Breitkopf & Härtel
FP: 29 Nov. 1923, Zurich (Zurich String Quartet)
Recordings: Minguet Quartet. MDG Scene 603 0665–2
Amar Quartet. MGB CD 6238

Op. 41
Sonata for Bass Clarinet and Piano
1927–28
Publ.: Leipzig: Breitkopf & Härtel
FP: 22 Apr. 1928, Lucerne (Wilhelm Arnold, bcl; Fritz Müller, pf)
Recordings: Henri Bok (bcl); Rainer Klaas (pf). Clarinet Classics CNS 0026
Renate Rusche (bcl); Werner Hagen (pf). MDG Scene 1 Sc63072
Version for bn, pf: Dag Jensen (bn); Midori Kitagawa (pf). MDG 603 0831–2

Op. 46
Sonata in E
Instr.: vn, pf
1931
Publ.: Leipzig and Zurich: Hug & Co.
FP: 3 Mar. 1932, Zurich (Willem de Boer, vn; Walter Frey, pf)
Recordings: Ursula Bagdasarjanz (vn); Gisela Schoeck (pf). BAG 002
Paul Barritt (vn); Catherine Edwards (pf). Guild GMCD 7142
Abraham Comfort (vn); Hadassa Schwimmer (pf). Comiotto Collection CO 1
Ulrich Lehmann (vn); Charles Dobler (pf). Ex Libris CD 6043
Matthias Wollong (vn); Patricia Pagny (pf). MGB CD 6163
Simone Zgraggen (vn); Ulrich Koella (pf). Claves CD 50 2503

woo 113
[Fragment for string quartet in A-flat major]
late 1940s?

woo 107
[Fragment for string quartet in C minor]
late 1940s?

woo 116
Drängend bewegt
Instr.: vn, vc, pf
Fragment, late 1940s?

woo 47
Sonata
Instr.: vc, pf
1957
Publ.: Kassel: Bärenreiter
FP: 1 May 1958, Zurich (James Whitehead, vc; Gisela Schoeck, pf)
Note: Schoeck only completed the first three movements.
Recordings: Johannes Goritzki (vc); David Levine (pf). Claves CD 50–8908
Christian Poltéra (vc); Julius Drake (pf). BIS-CD 1597

VI. Piano Music (for Two and Four Hands)

Unless otherwise stated, all works below are for piano solo.

Schoeck's piano music has been published in its entirety as series 4, vol. 18 of *Othmar Schoeck: Sämtliche Werke*, ed. Erik Levi (Zurich: Hug, 2005).

woo 48
Adagio
ca. 1898?

woo 49
Sonatina
ca. 1901?
Note: one movement only

woo 50
Theme for a Scherzo
ca. 1901?

woo 81
Nocturne
pf?
Fragment, ca. 1901?

woo 58
Fröhlich
1902?

woo 97
[Piece in A major]
pf?
Fragment, ca. 1905?

woo 28
Concert March
pf duet
1907
FP: 10 Nov. 1998, Zurich (students of the Lucerne Conservatory)
Note: composed as a piano duet for the "Eidgenössisches Schützenfest" (the "Swiss National Shooting Festival") in Zurich in 1907. It was to have been scored for band but was deemed too difficult.

woo 127
[Fugue in C minor]

Fragment, ca. 1907–8?
Note: a counterpoint exercise

woo 128
[Two-part Invention in C major]
Fragment, ca. 1907–8?
Note: a counterpoint exercise

woo 32
Waltz
1910?
Recording: Jean Louis Steuerman. MGB CD 6146

woo 134
[Fugato]
pf?
Fragment, ca. 1915?

woo 79
Souvenires [sic] de Brissago (O mia sole!). Walzer
pf?
1915?
Recording: Jean Louis Steuerman. MGB CD 6146

woo 121
Sorrento!
pf?
1917?
Note: The melody is similar to that of "Torna a surriento," by Ernesto de Curtis
Recording: Jean Louis Steuerman. MGB CD 6146

Op. 29
Two Piano Pieces
1919
Consolation
Toccata
Recordings: Werner Bärtschi. Jecklin Edition JS 306–2
Charles Dobler. Ex Libris CD 6043
Lorris Sevhonkian. Ambitus amb 97906
Jean Louis Steuerman. MGB CD 6146

woo 106
Rondo
Fragment, 1919
Note: intended as the third of the piano pieces Op. 29 but used instead in the ball
    music of the second act of the opera *Venus*

woo 36
March
pf duet (i.e., a short score)
For the Brunnen "Harmoniemusik" (wind band)
1922?
See also **Band Music**

woo 38
[Piece in A major]
ca. 1928
Recordings: Jean Louis Steuerman. MGB CD 6146
Charles Dobler. Ex Libris CD 6043

Op. 58
Sommernacht
pf duet
Arrangement by the composer of his Pastoral Intermezzo for string orchestra, made
    in August 1945

Op. 59
Suite in A-flat Major
pf duet
Schoeck's arrangement, made in 1945, of his original version for strings

Op. 64
Festlicher Hymnus
for pf and for pf duet
Arrangements by the composer of his orchestral work, both made in 1950

Op. 1
Serenade
arr. of this orchestral work by the composer, 1952
FP of this arrangement: 26 Jan. 1955, Zurich (Paul Baumgartner)
Recordings: Charles Dobler. Ex Libris CD 6043
Jean Louis Steuerman. MGB CD 6146

Op. 27
Serenade (Intermezzo from *Don Ranudo*)
arr. by the composer, 1952
Recording: Jean Louis Steuerman. MGB CD 6146

Op. 68
Ritornelle und Fughetten (*Ritornelli and Fughettas*)
1953
FP: 11 Mar. 1955, Zurich (Gisela Schoeck)
Note: there are eight each of the ritornelli and fughettas.
Recording: Jean Louis Steuerman. MGB CD 6146

woo 46
Two Ritornelli and Fughettas
in G Minor
in E Minor
1955?
Recording: Jean Louis Steuerman. MGB CD 6146

VII. Voice and Piano

Unless otherwise stated, the works below are for one solo voice with piano accompaniment.

The songs up to and including Opus 17, as well as those early songs without opus number, have been published in series 1, vol. 1 of *Othmar Schoeck: Sämtliche Werke,* ed. Lukas Meister (Zurich: Hug, 2004).

woo 51
"Es liegen Veilchen dunkelblau" (Hermann von Gilm)
1900
FP: 28 Jun. 1996, Brunnen (Otto Georg Linsi, tenor; Thomas Grabowski, pf)

woo 2
"Nachtgesang" (Johann Wolfgang von Goethe)
1900

woo 1
"Das Grab" (Johann Gaudenz von Salis-Seewis)
1901?
FP: 28 Jun. 1996, Brunnen (Otto Georg Linsi, tenor; Thomas Grabowski, pf)

woo 52
"Ständchen von Busch" (Wilhelm Busch)
1901?

woo 6
"Kinderliedchen (Ach, wer doch das könnte!)" (Victor Blüthgen)
1902
FP: 22 Oct. 1994, Lugano (Otto Georg Linsi, tenor; Chris Walton, pf)
Recording: Peter van Hulle (tenor); Edward Rushton (pf). Guild GMCD 7237

woo 59
"Johanniswürmchen" (anon.)
1902

woo 60
"Der öde Garten" (Karl von Gerok)
1902

WoO 5
"Geistesgruss" (J. W. von Goethe)
1902?

WoO 53
"Melodie zur Comment-Buch-Weihe" (Othmar Schoeck?)
See **Choral Works with Accompaniment**

WoO 56
"Volkslied" (anon.)
1902?
FP: 28 Jun. 1996, Brunnen (Otto Georg Linsi, tenor; Thomas Grabowski, pf)
Recording: Peter van Hulle (tenor); Edward Rushton (pf). Guild GMCD 7237

WoO 57
"Kinder[lied ohne Worte]" [*sic*] (without text)
1902?

WoO 82
"Die Wasserlilie" (Heine)
Fragment, 1902?

WoO 83
"Gesang der Mädchen aus *Johannes*" (Hermann Sudermann)
2 voices, pf
Fragment, 1902?

WoO 85
"O Springquell munterer Schwätzer" (Paul Schoeck)
Fragment, ca. 1902?

WoO 87
["Harfenspieler"] (J. W. von Goethe)
Fragment, ca. 1902?

WoO 112
"Ernte" (anon.)
1902?

WoO 136
"Nur wer's glaubt, der hält's für wahr" (anon.)
1902?

WoO 137
"Es hieng [*sic*] an einer Blume" (anon.)
Fragment, ca. 1902?

woo 3
"KTV-Kantus" (M. Lutz)
See **Choral Works with Accompaniment**

woo 7
"Lieb Seelchen, lass das Fragen sein" (Hans von Hopfen)
1903

woo 8
"Selbstbetrug" (J. W. von Goethe)
1903

woo 9
"Der Gast" (Theodor Fontane)
1903

woo 10
"Gleich und gleich" (J. W. von Goethe)
1903

woo 11
"Über den Bergen" (Carl Busse)
1903
FP: 18 May 1996, Venice (Erika Bill, soprano; Giorgio Agazzi, pf)

woo 65
"Schweizerlied" (anon.)
1903
FP: 28 Jun. 1996, Brunnen (Otto Georg Linsi, tenor; Thomas Grabowski, pf)

woo 12
"Mai" (Paul Barsch)
1903

woo 67
"Perlen" (anon.)
1903
FP: 22 Oct. 1994, Lugano (Otto Georg Linsi, tenor; Chris Walton, pf)
Recording: Peter van Hulle (tenor); Edward Rushton (pf). Guild GMCD 7237

woo 13
"Kindergottesdienst" (Karl von Gerok)
1903?

woo 64
"Thatsache" (Richard Dehmel)
1903?

FP: 28 Jun. 1996, Brunnen (Otto Georg Linsi, tenor; Thomas Grabowski, pf)

woo 66
"Schlaf ein, lieb Kind" (Hermann Sudermann)
1903?
FP: 7 Jul. 1982, Brunnen (Frieder Lang, tenor; Margrit Speiser, pf)
Recording: Louise Innes (mezzo-soprano); Edward Rushton (pf). Guild GMCD
    7237

woo 90
[Song? in E-flat major, 3/4 time] (without text)
Fragment, ca. 1903?

woo 91
[Song? in E-flat major, *alla breve*] (without text)
Fragment, ca. 1903?

woo 92
"Kennst du das Land" (J. W. von Goethe)
Fragment, ca. 1903?

woo 94
["Primula veris"] (Nikolaus Lenau)
Fragment, ca. 1903?

woo 111
"Spätherbst" (Paul Schoeck)
ca. 1903?

woo 95
"Stille Sicherheit" (Lenau)
Fragment, 1904

woo 14
"Vergangenheit" (Lenau)
1904
Recording: William Coleman (baritone); Edward Rushton (pf). Guild GMCD 7237

woo 68
"Gefunden" (J. W. von Goethe)
1904
FP: 22 Oct. 1994, Lugano (Otto Georg Linsi, tenor; Chris Walton, pf)
Recording: Peter van Hulle (tenor); Edward Rushton (pf). Guild GMCD 7237

woo 96
"Am einsamen Strande plätschert die Flut" (Heinrich Heine)
Fragment, ca. 1904?

WOO 15
"Wiegenlied" (August Heinrich Hoffmann von Fallersleben)
1904/5?
Publ.: Zurich: Hug, 1959

WOO 16
"Das Fräulein am Meere" (Heinrich Heine)
1905
FP: 22 Oct. 1994, Lugano (Otto Georg Linsi, tenor; Chris Walton, pf)
Recording: Peter van Hulle (tenor); Edward Rushton (pf). Guild **GMCD** 7237

WOO 17
"Scheideblick" (Nikolaus Lenau)
1905
FP: 28 Jun. 1996, Brunnen (Otto Georg Linsi, tenor; Thomas Grabowski, pf)

WOO 18
"Stummer Abschied" (anon.)
1905
Recording: William Coleman (baritone); Edward Rushton (pf). Guild **GMCD** 7237

WOO 19
"Lebewohl!" (Nikolaus Lenau)
1905
Recording: William Coleman (baritone); Edward Rushton (pf). Guild **GMCD** 7237

Op. 2
Drei Schilflieder von Lenau
1905
    1. "Drüben geht die Sonne scheiden"
       FP: 23 Jan. 1910, Zurich (Anna Schabbel-Zoder; Othmar Schoeck, pf)
    2. "Trübe wird's, die Wolken jagen"
       FP: 25 Nov. 1917, St. Gallen (Ilona Durigo, contralto; Othmar Schoeck, pf)
    3. "Auf geheimem Waldespfade"
Recording: Cornelia Kallisch (mezzo-soprano); Till Körber (pf), on *LCE* vol. 4. Jecklin Edition JD 674–2

WOO 129
["Am Grabe Höltys"] (Nikolaus Lenau)
Fragment, 1905?

WOO 138
"Leis rauscht der See" (anon.)
Fragment, 1905?

WOO 131
[Song in D-flat major, without text]

Fragment, ca. 1907?

woo 98
"Einkehr" (Emanuel Geibel)
Fragment, ca. 1907?

Op. 3
Sechs Gedichte von Uhland
1. "Ruhetal." 1903
   FP: 22 Mar. 1908 in Greiz (Frieda Hollstein, soprano; Othmar Schoeck, pf)
2. "Die Kapelle." 1905
   FP: 29 Apr. 1909, Zurich (Rudolf Jung, baritone; Othmar Schoeck, pf)
3. "Abschied." 1905?
   FP: 7 Dec. 1905, Zurich (Emmi Gysler, soprano; Othmar Schoeck?, pf)
4. "Lebewohl." 1905
   FP: 2 Feb. 1906, Zurich (Emmi Gysler, soprano; Othmar Schoeck, pf)
5. "Scheiden und Meiden." 1907
   FP: 24 Jan. 1923, Zurich (Alfred Flury, tenor; Othmar Schoeck, pf)
6. "Auf den Tod eines Kindes." 1907.
   FP: 5 Mar. 1916, Zurich (Max Krauss, baritone; Othmar Schoeck, pf)
Recordings (nos. 1–4): Cornelia Kallisch (mezzo-soprano); Till Körber (pf), on *LCE* vol. 4. JD 674–2
(Nos. 5, 6): Christine Schäfer (soprano); Wolfram Rieger (pf), on *LCE* vol. 1. JD 671–2
(No. 3): Hanna Matti (mezzo-soprano); Christoph Demarmels (pf). MGB CD 6118

Op. 4
Drei Lieder von Heine
1. "Sommerabend." 1904
   FP: 2 Feb. 1906, Zurich (Emmi Gysler, soprano; Othmar Schoeck, pf)
2. "Warum sind denn die Rosen so blass?" 1906
   FP: 13 Dec. 1906, Zurich (Adele Bloch, soprano; Othmar Schoeck, pf)
3. "Wo?" 1906. For voice, vn, pf
   FP: 7 Jan. 1907, Zurich (Thekla Rosenstiel, soprano; William Ackroyd, vn; Friedrich Niggli, pf)
Recordings: Juliane Banse (soprano); Dietrich Henschel (baritone); Christine Ragaz (vn); Wolfram Rieger (pf), on *LCE* vol. 5. Jecklin Edition JD 675–2
(No. 2): Hanna Matti (mezzo-soprano); Christoph Demarmels (pf). MGB CD 6118

Op. 5
Drei Gedichte von Lenau
1. "Himmelstrauer." 1905
   FP: 12 Oct. 1941, Zurich (Felix Loeffel, bass; Othmar Schoeck, pf)
2. "An die Entfernte." 1907
   FP: 29 Apr. 1909, Zurich (Alfred Flury, tenor; Othmar Schoeck, pf)
3. "Frühlingsblick." 1907
   FP: 20 Oct. 1907, Zurich (Adele Bloch, soprano; Ernst Isler, pf)

Recordings (No. 1): Cornelia Kallisch (mezzo-soprano); Till Körber (pf), on *LCE* vol. 4. Jecklin Edition JD 674–2

(Nos. 2, 3): Christine Schäfer (soprano); Wolfram Rieger (pf), on *LCE* vol. 1. JD 671–2

(No. 3): Silvia Gähwiller (soprano); Othmar Schoeck (pf). Jecklin Edition JD 714–2

Op. 6
Sechs Lieder
For high voice
1. "Die Verlassene" (Schwabian folk song). 1905
   FP: 3 Jun. 1909, Stuttgart (Hedwig Schmitz-Schweiker; Othmar Schoeck, pf)
2. "Schifferliedchen" (Gottfried Keller). 1906
   FP: 2 Feb. 1906, Zurich (Emmi Gysler, soprano; Othmar Schoeck, pf)
3. "Vor der Ernte" (Conrad Ferdinand Meyer). 1905
   FP: as no. 2
4. "Alle meine Wünsche schweigen" (Paul Schoeck). 1906
   FP: 18 Sept. 1975, Solothurn (Christa Tschumi; Magdalena Vonlanthen, pf)
5. "Marienlied" (Novalis). 1907
   FP: 20 Oct. 1907, Zurich (Adele Bloch, soprano; Ernst Isler, pf)
6. "Mandolinen" (Paul Verlaine). 1907
   FP: 4 Nov. 1936, Zurich (Ria Ginster, soprano; Othmar Schoeck, pf)

Recordings: Christine Schäfer (soprano); Wolfram Rieger (pf), on *LCE* vol. 1. JD 671–2

(No. 5): Ernst Haefliger (tenor); Karl Grenacher (pf). Jecklin-Disco JD 504–2

(Nos. 3, 4): Austin Miskell (tenor); John Taylor (pf). Cambria CBA 1038

Op. 7
Drei Lieder
For low voice
1. "Bei der Kirche" (Armin Rüeger). 1905
2. "Septembermorgen" (Eduard Mörike). 1905
3. "In der Herberge" (from the "Schi-King": Li-Tai-Pe). 1907
   FP: 20 Oct. 1907, Zurich (Adele Bloch, soprano; Ernst Isler, pf)

Recordings: Nathan Berg (baritone); Julius Drake (pf), on *LCE* vol. 2. JD 672–2

(No. 3, arr. vc, pf): Christian Poltéra (vc); Julius Drake (pf). BIS-CD 1597

Op. 8
Vier Gedichte von Hermann Hesse
1906
1. "Elisabeth"
   FP: 13 Dec. 1906, Zurich (Adele Bloch, soprano; Othmar Schoeck, pf)
2. "Aus zwei Tälern"
   FP: 12 Nov. 1919, Winterthur (Alfred Flury, tenor; Ernst Radecke, pf)
3. "Auskunft"
   FP: as no. 1
4. "Jahrestag"
   FP: as no. 1

Recordings: Juliane Banse (soprano); Dietrich Henschel (baritone); Wolfram Rieger (pf), on *LCE* vol. 5. JD 675–2
(Nos. 2,3): Dietrich Fischer-Dieskau (baritone); Margrit Weber (pf). DG 463 513–2
(No. 3): Christine Walser (mezzo-soprano); Wendy Waterman (pf). MDS Records MDS 3017

WoO 27
"Vorwurf" (Hermann Hesse)
1907
Recording: Dietrich Henschel (baritone); Wolfram Rieger (pf), on *LCE* vol. 5. JD 675–2

Op. 9
Zwei Gesänge
For baritone
　　1. "Die Verklärende" (Michelangelo). 1907
　　　　FP: 28 Oct. 1908, Thun (Rudolf Jung, baritone; Othmar Schoeck, pf)
　　2. "Du, des Erbarmens Feind" (Dante, trans. Richard Zoozmann). 1906
　　　　FP: 25 Mar. 1942, Zurich (Felix Loeffel, bass; Othmar Schoeck, pf)
Recording: Nathan Berg (baritone); Julius Drake (pf), on *LCE* vol. 2. JD 672–2

Op. 10
Drei Gedichte von Eichendorff
　　1. "Erinnerung." 1907
　　　　FP: 30 May 1908 in Baden (Rudolf Jung, baritone; Othmar Schoeck, pf)
　　2. "Die Einsame." 1907
　　　　FP: 20 Oct. 1907, Zurich (Adele Bloch, soprano; Ernst Isler, pf)
　　3. "Guter Rat." 1907
　　　　FP: 29 Apr. 1909, Zurich (Adele Bloch, soprano; Othmar Schoeck, pf)
Recordings: Juliane Banse (soprano); Wolfram Rieger (pf), on *LCE* vol. 5. JD 675–2
(Nos. 1, 2): Elisabeth Grümmer (soprano); Aribert Reimann (pf). Orfeo d'Or, C 506 001
(No. 1): Austin Miskell (tenor); John Taylor (pf). Cambria CBA 1038

Op. 12
Zwei Wanderlieder von Eichendorff
　　1. "Reiselied." 1908
　　　　FP: 22 Mar. 1908, Greiz (Frieda Hollstein, soprano; Othmar Schoeck, pf)
　　2. "Wanderlied der Prager Studenten." 1907
　　　　FP: 17 Mar. 1908, Leipzig (Max Kühne; Othmar Schoeck, pf)
Note: Schoeck's archives contain a fragmentary arrangement of no. 2 for voice and orchestra
Recordings: Christine Schäfer (soprano); Wolfram Rieger (pf), on *LCE* vol. 1. JD 671–2
(No. 1): Samuel Zünd (baritone), Jeroen Sarphati (pf). Deluc Productions

Op. 13
Drei Lieder von Heine und Wilhelm Busch

1. "Vergiftet sind meine Lieder" (Heinrich Heine). 1907
   FP: 19 Mar. 1983 in Wald (Paul Späni, tenor; Hansheinrich Hotz, pf)
2. "Ja, du bist elend" (Heine). 1907
   FP: 3 Jun. 1909 in Stuttgart (Hedwig Schmitz-Schweiker; Othmar Schoeck, pf)
3. "Dilemma" (Busch). 1907
   FP: 28 Oct. 1908 in Thun (Rudolf Jung, baritone; Othmar Schoeck, pf).
Recordings: Dietrich Henschel (baritone); Wolfram Rieger (pf), on *LCE* vol. 5. JD
   675–2
(No. 3): Hanna Matti (mezzo-soprano); Christoph Demarmels (pf). MGB CD 6118

Op. 14
Vier Lieder
For lower voice
1. "An meine Mutter" (Eduard Mörike). 1907
   FP: 17 Mar. 1908, Leipzig (Max Kühne; Othmar Schoeck, pf)
2. "Das Schlummerlied" (Adolf Frey). 1907
3. "Schöner Ort" (Adolf Frey). 1907
   FP: 19 Mar. 1915, Zurich (Adele Bloch, soprano; Reinhold Laquai, pf)
4. "Schlafen, nichts als schlafen" (Friedrich Hebbel). 1907
   FP: 23 Jan. 1910, Zurich (Anna Schabbel-Zoder, soprano; Othmar Schoeck, pf)
Recordings: Cornelia Kallisch (mezzo-soprano); Till Körber (pf), on *LCE* vol. 4. JD
   674–2
(No. 1): Elisabeth Gehri (contralto): Othmar Schoeck (pf). Jecklin Edition JD 714–2

Op. 15
Sechs Lieder
For medium and high voice
1. "Der Waldsee" (Heinrich Leuthold). 1907
2. "Nun quill aus meiner Seele" (Paul Schoeck). 1907
   FP: 21 Feb. 1909, Zurich (Rudolf Jung, baritone; Othmar Schoeck, pf)
3. "Frühlingsfeier" (Uhland). 1907/8
   FP: 14 Nov. 1909, Zurich (Rudolf Jung, baritone; Othmar Schoeck, pf)
4. "In der Fremde" (Eichendorff). 1908
   FP: 29 Apr. 1909, Zurich (Alfred Flury, tenor; Othmar Schoeck, pf)
5. "Erster Verlust" (Goethe). 1908
   FP: 28 Oct. 1908, Thun (Rudolf Jung, baritone; Othmar Schoeck, pf)
6. "Peregrina" (Mörike). 1908
   FP: 16 Mar. 1937, Burghalde (Dora Wyss, soprano; Max Rüegg, pf)
Recordings: (Nos. 1, 2, 3, 5, 6): Cornelia Kallisch (mezzo-soprano); Till Körber (pf),
   on *LCE* vol. 4. JD 674–2
(Nos. 4, 5): Christine Schäfer (soprano); Wolfram Rieger (pf), on *LCE* vol. 1. JD
   671–2
(No. 3): Silvia Gähwiller (soprano); Othmar Schoeck (pf). Jecklin Edition JD 714–2
(No. 6): Dagmar Pecková (mezzo-soprano); Irwin Gage (pf). Supraphon, SU 3434–2

Op. 17
Acht Lieder

1. "Im Sommer" (Georg Jacobi). 1907
  FP: 29 Nov. 1936, Thun (Helene Fahrni, soprano; Othmar Schoeck, pf)
2. "Im Herbste" (Uhland). 1908
  FP: 29 Apr. 1909, Zurich (Adele Bloch, soprano; Othmar Schoeck, pf)
3. "Der Kirchhof im Frühling" (Uhland). 1908
  FP: 21 Feb. 1909, Zurich (Rudolf Jung, baritone; Othmar Schoeck, pf)
4. "Peregrina II" (Eduard Mörike). 1909
  FP: 29 Apr. 1909, Zurich (Rudolf Jung, baritone; Othmar Schoeck, pf)
5. "Gekommen ist der Maie" (Heine). 1904
  FP: as no. 4
6. "Auf einer Burg" (Eichendorff). 1909
  FP: 10 Jan. 1924, Kreuzlingen (Felix Loeffel, bass; Othmar Schoeck, pf)
7. "Erinnerung" (Eichendorff). 1909
  FP: as no. 2
8. "Der frohe Wandersmann" (Eichendorff). 1909
  FP: 14 Nov. 1909, Zurich (Rudolf Jung, baritone; Othmar Schoeck, pf)

Recordings: (Nos. 2, 3, 4, 6): Cornelia Kallisch (mezzo-soprano); Till Körber (pf), on *LCE* vol. 4. JD 674–2

(Nos. 1, 5, 7, 8): Christine Schäfer (soprano); Wolfram Rieger (pf), on *LCE* vol. 1. JD 671–2

(No. 4): Dietrich Fischer-Dieskau (baritone); Margrit Weber (pf). Deutsche Grammophon 463 513–2

(No. 3): Silvia Gähwiller (soprano); Othmar Schoeck (pf). Jecklin Edition JD 714–2

(No. 4): Elisabeth Gehri (contralto); Othmar Schoeck (pf). Jecklin Edition JD 714–2

(No. 4): Ernst Haefliger (tenor); Karl Grenacher (pf). Jecklin-Disco JD 504–2

(Nos. 2, 3, 5): Hanna Matti (mezzo-soprano); Christoph Demarmels (pf). MGB CD 6118

(No. 4): Austin Miskell (tenor); John Taylor (pf). Cambria CBA 1038

(No. 4): Dagmar Pecková (mezzo-soprano); Irwin Gage (pf). Supraphon, SU 3434–2

woo 31
Mir glänzen die Augen (Gottfried Keller)
1910?

woo 132
Präömion
Fragment, 1912?

Op. 19a
Lieder nach Gedichten von Goethe
1. "Herbstgefühl." 1909
  FP: 12 Dec. 1909, Zurich (Rudolf Jung, baritone; Othmar Schoeck, pf)
2. "Dämmrung senkte sich von oben." 1911
  FP: 18 Nov. 1911, Zurich (Ilona Durigo, contralto; Othmar Schoeck, pf)
3. "Mailied." 1910
  FP: 2 Apr. 1911, Zurich (Rudolf Jung, baritone; Othmar Schoeck, pf)
4. "Mit einem gemalten Band." 1912

FP: 30 Jan. 1914, Zurich (Ilona Durigo, contralto; Othmar Schoeck, pf)
5. "Rastlose Liebe." 1912
   FP: 23 Mar. 1915, Bern (Ilona Durigo, contralto; Othmar Schoeck, pf)
6. "Sorge." 1910
   FP: 21 Feb. 1941, Zurich (Ria Ginster, soprano; Othmar Schoeck, pf)
7. "Ungeduld." 1914
   FP: 21 Nov. 1924, Zurich (Emmy Krüger, soprano; Othmar Schoeck, pf)
8. "Parabase." 1914
   FP: 5 Mar. 1916, Zurich (Max Krauss, baritone; Othmar Schoeck, pf)
Publ.: Leipzig: Breitkopf & Härtel
Recordings: Juliane Banse (soprano); Dietrich Henschel (baritone); Wolfram Rieger
   (pf), on *LCE* vol. 5. JD 675–2
(No. 2): Dietrich Fischer-Dieskau (baritone); Margrit Weber (pf). Deutsche Gram-
   mophon 463 513–2
(No. 4): Ria Ginster (soprano); Paul Baumgartner (pf). Testament TES 0132
(Nos. 1, 4): Ria Ginster (soprano); Gerald Moore (pf). Preiser Records, PSR 89227
(No. 4): Ernst Haefliger (tenor); Karl Grenacher (pf). Jecklin-Disco JD 504–2
(No. 2): Dagmar Pecková (mezzo-soprano); Irwin Gage (pf). Supraphon, SU 3434–2
(Nos. 1, 2): Christoph Prégardien (tenor); Michael Gees (pf). CPO 999685
(Nos. 2, 4): Gunnel Sköld (contralto); Jan Bülow (pf). Gallo CD 1035

Op. 19b
Lieder aus dem west-östlichen Divan von Goethe
1. "Nachklang." 1915
   FP: 5 Mar. 1916, Zurich (Max Krauss, baritone; Othmar Schoeck, pf)
2. "Suleika und Hatem." 1915
   FP: 21 Feb. 1941, Zurich (Ria Ginster, soprano; Othmar Schoeck, pf)
3. "Suleika." 1915
   FP: 18 Jan. 1928 (Clara Wirz-Wyss, soprano; Othmar Schoeck, pf)
4. "Drei Lieder aus dem *Buch der Betrachtungen*":
   1 "Haben sie von deinen Fehlen." 1915
      FP: as no. 1
   2 "Höre den Rat, den die Leier tönt." 1915
      FP: Oct. 1917, Vienna (Hans Duhan, baritone; Othmar Schoeck, pf)
   3 "Wie ich so ehrlich war." 1915
      FP(?): 31 Oct. 1943, Männedorf (Hilde Schoeck, soprano; Othmar Schoeck, pf)
5. "Unmut." 1915
   FP: 19 Jan. 1929, Zurich (Heinrich Rehkemper, baritone; Othmar Schoeck,
   pf)
6. "Selige Sehnsucht." 1911
   FP: as no. 1
7. "Fünf venezianische Epigramme":
   1 "Warum leckst du dein Mäulchen." 1906
   2 "Eine einzige Nacht an deinem Herzen." 1907
   3 "Wie sie klingeln, die Pfaffen!" 1906
   4 "Seh' ich den Pilgrim." 1906
   5 "Diese Gondel vergleich ich." 1906

FP (all five): Oct. 1917, Vienna (Hans Duhan, baritone; Othmar Schoeck, pf)
Publ.: Leipzig: Breitkopf & Härtel
Recordings: Juliane Banse (soprano); Dietrich Henschel (baritone); Wolfram Rieger (pf), on *LCE* vol. 5. JD 675–2
(Nos. 1, 4/3, 7/5): Dietrich Fischer-Dieskau (baritone); Margrit Weber (pf). Deutsche Grammophon 463 513–2
(No. 1): Christoph Prégardien (tenor); Michael Gees (pf). CPO 999685
(No. 1): Gunnel Sköld (contralto); Jan Bülow (pf). Gallo CD 1035

Op. 20
Lieder nach Gedichten von Uhland und Eichendorff
1. "Auf ein Kind" (Uhland). 1908
   FP: 12 Dec. 1909, Zurich (Rudolf Jung, baritone; Othmar Schoeck, pf)
2. "An einem heitern Morgen" (Uhland). 1910
   FP: 2 Apr. 1911, Zurich (Rudolf Jung, baritone; Othmar Schoeck, pf)
3. "Dichtersegen" (Uhland). 1910
   FP: as no. 2
4. "Frühlingsruhe" (Uhland). 1905
   FP: 22 Apr. 1920, Lucerne (Ilona Durigo, contralto; Othmar Schoeck, pf)
5. "Wein und Brot" (Uhland). 1910
   FP(?): 22 Mar. 1918, Zurich (Heinrich Pestalozzi; Othmar Schoeck, pf)
6. "Abendwolken" (Uhland). 1910
   FP: 5 Mar. 1916, Zurich (Max Krauss, baritone; Othmar Schoeck, pf)
7. "Abschied" (Eichendorff). 1909
   FP: 18 Nov. 1911, Zurich (Ilona Durigo, contralto; Othmar Schoeck, pf)
8. "Auf meines Kindes Tod" (Eichendorff). 1914
   FP: as no. 6
9. "Der Kranke" (Eichendorff). 1913
   FP: 30 Jan. 1914, Zurich (Ilona Durigo, contralto; Othmar Schoeck, pf)
10. "Abendlandschaft" (Eichendorff). 1914
    FP: 23 Mar. 1915, Bern (Ilona Durigo, contralto; Othmar Schoeck, pf)
11. "Der Gärtner" (Eichendorff). 1914
    FP: 19 May 1941, Zurich (Hilde Schoeck, soprano; Othmar Schoeck, pf)
12. "Umkehr" (Eichendorff). 1914
    FP: 11 Feb. 1924, Bern (Felix Loeffel, bass; Fritz Brun, pf)
13. "Nachtlied" (Eichendorff). 1914
    FP: 30 Apr. 1916, Thun (Maria Philippi, contralto; Othmar Schoeck, pf)
14. "Nachruf" (Eichendorff). 1910
    FP: as no. 9
Publ.: Leipzig: Breitkopf & Härtel
Recordings: (Nos. 1, 4, 6, 7, 8, 9, 10, 12, 14): Cornelia Kallisch (mezzo-soprano); Till Körber (pf), on *LCE* vol. 4. JD 674–2
(Nos. 2, 3, 5, 11, 13): Christine Schäfer (soprano); Wolfram Rieger (pf), on *LCE* vol. 1. JD 671–2
(No. 5): Ulf Bästlein (baritone); Stefan Laux (pf). Ars Musici ARM 1237
(Nos. 1, 14): Dietrich Fischer-Dieskau (baritone); Margrit Weber (pf). Deutsche Grammophon 463 513–2

(No. 14): Karl Erb (tenor); Bruno Seidler-Winkler (pf). Preiser Records PSR 89208

(No. 4): Silvia Gähwiller (soprano); Othmar Schoeck (pf). Jecklin Edition JD 714–2

(Nos. 8, 14): Elisabeth Grümmer (soprano); Aribert Reimann (pf). Orfeo d'Or, C 506 001

(No. 2): Ernst Haefliger (tenor); Karl Grenacher (pf). Jecklin-Disco JD 504–2

(No. 14): Wolfgang Holzmair (baritone); Imogen Cooper (pf). Philips 464 991

(Nos. 8, 10): Arthur Loosli (bass-baritone); Karl Grenacher (pf). Jecklin-Disco JD 535–2

(Nos. 8, 14): Dagmar Pecková (mezzo-soprano); Irwin Gage (pf). Supraphon, SU 3434–2

(No. 13): Margherita Perras (soprano); Othmar Schoeck (pf). Testament TES 0132

(No. 14): Heinrich Schlusnus (baritone); Sebastian Peschko (pf). Preiser Records PSR 89216

(Nos. 1, 4, 7, 8, 9, 13, 14): Gunnel Sköld (contralto); Jan Bülow (pf). Gallo CD 1035

(Nos. 13, 14): Oliver Widmer (baritone); Till Alexander Körber (pf). Atlantis ATL 96 206

(No. 7): Samuel Zünd (baritone); Jeroen Sarphati (pf). Deluc Productions

Op. 24a
Lieder nach Gedichten von Lenau, Hebbel, Dehmel und Spitteler

1. "Lenz" (Nikolaus Lenau). 1910
   FP: 30 Jan. 1914, Zurich (Ilona Durigo, contralto; Othmar Schoeck, pf)
2. "Stumme Liebe" (Lenau). 1913
   FP: 19 Jan. 1929, Zurich (Heinrich Rehkemper, baritone; Othmar Schoeck, pf)
3. "An die Entfernte" (Lenau). 1914
   FP: 9 Jan. 1924, Zurich (Ilona Durigo, contralto; Othmar Schoeck, pf)
4. "Die drei Zigeuner" (Lenau). 1914
   FP: 23 Mar. 1915, Bern (Ilona Durigo, contralto; Othmar Schoeck, pf)
5. "Das Heiligste" (Friedrich Hebbel). 1914
   FP: 25 Mar. 1942, Zurich (Felix Loeffel, bass; Othmar Schoeck, pf)
6. "Manche Nacht" (Richard Dehmel). 1911
   FP: as no. 1
7. "Das bescheidene Wünschlein" (Carl Spitteler). 1910
   FP: 29 Jan. 1910, Frankfurt (Rudolf Jung, baritone; Othmar Schoeck, pf)
8. "Glöckleins Klage" (Spitteler). 1910
   FP: 28 Feb. 1910, Zurich (Emmi Gysler, soprano; Othmar Schoeck, pf)
9. "Der Hufschmied" (Spitteler). 1909
   FP: as no. 7
10. "Eine Unbekanntschaft" (Spitteler). 1910
    FP: as no. 8

Publ.: Leipzig: Breitkopf & Härtel

Recordings: Lynne Dawson (soprano); Cornelia Kallisch (mezzo-soprano); Jürg Dürmüller (tenor); Nathan Berg (baritone); Julius Drake (pf), on *LCE* vol. 6. Jecklin Edition JD 676–2

(Nos. 4, 9): Gunnel Sköld (contralto); Jan Bülow (pf). Gallo CD 1035

Op. 24b
Lieder nach Gedichten von Spitteler, Gamper, Hesse und Keller
1. "Ein Jauchzer" (Carl Spitteler). 1910
   FP: 28 Feb. 1910, Zurich (Emmi Gysler, soprano; Othmar Schoeck, pf)
2. "Jünger des Weins (I)" (Gustav Gamper). 1915
   FP: 5 Mar. 1916, Zurich (Max Krauss, baritone; Othmar Schoeck, pf)
3. "Jünger des Weins (II)" (Gamper). 1915
   FP: Oct. 1917, Vienna (Hans Duhan, baritone; Fritz Brun, pf)
4. "Kennst du das auch?" (Hermann Hesse). 1906
5. "Was lachst du so?" (Hesse). 1906
   FP: 2 Dec. 1925, Zurich (Emmy Krüger, soprano; Othmar Schoeck, pf)
6. "Frühling" (Hesse). 1911
   FP: 30 Jan. 1914, Zurich (Ilona Durigo, contralto; Othmar Schoeck, pf)
7. "Keine Rast" (Hesse). 1914/15
   FP: 23 Mar. 1915, Bern (Ilona Durigo, contralto; Othmar Schoeck, pf)
8. "Das Ziel" (Hesse). 1914
   FP: as no. 7
9. "Ravenna" (Hesse). 1913
   FP: as no. 6
10. "Jugendgedenken" (Gottfried Keller). 1914
    FP: 30 Apr. 1916, Thun (Maria Philippi, contralto; Othmar Schoeck, pf)
Publ.: Leipzig: Breitkopf & Härtel
Recordings: Lynne Dawson (soprano); Cornelia Kallisch (mezzo-soprano); Jürg Dürmüller (tenor); Nathan Berg (baritone); Julius Drake (pf), on *LCE* vol. 6. Jecklin Edition JD 676–2
(No. 3): Ulf Bästlein (baritone); Stefan Laux (pf). Ars Musici ARM 1237
(Nos. 4, 7, 8, 9, 10): Dietrich Fischer-Dieskau (baritone); Margrit Weber (pf). Deutsche Grammophon 463 513–2
(No. 8): Kathrin Graf (soprano); Rainer Boesch (pf). Jecklin Szene Schweiz JS 270/1–2
(Nos. 7, 9): Arthur Loosli (bass-baritone); Karl Grenacher (pf). Jecklin-Disco JD 535–2
(No. 7): Gunnel Sköld (contralto); Jan Bülow (pf). Gallo CD 1035
(No. 7): Christine Walser (mezzo-soprano); Wendy Waterman (pf). MDS Records MDS 3017
(No. 7): Oliver Widmer (baritone); Till Alexander Körber (pf). Atlantis ATL 96 206

Op. 30
Zwölf Eichendorff-Lieder
1. "Waldeinsamkeit!" 1918
   FP: 8 Apr. 1920, Zurich (Ilona Durigo, contralto; Othmar Schoeck, pf)
2. "Kurze Fahrt." 1918
   FP: 1 Jun. 1919, Burgdorf (Hanna Brenner, contralto; Othmar Schoeck, pf)
3. "Winternacht." 1918
   FP: as no. 1
4. "Im Wandern." 1918
   FP: as no. 2

5. "Sterbeglocken." 1918
6. "Ergebung." 1918
   FP: as no. 2
7. "Nachklang." 1917
   FP: 6 Jan. 1918, Cologne (Ilona Durigo, contralto; Otto Neitzel, pf)
8. "Der verspätete Wanderer." 1917
   FP: 11 Feb. 1924, Bern (Felix Loeffel, bass; Fritz Brun, pf)
9. "Nacht." 1917
   FP: 22 Mar. 1918, Zurich (Heinrich Pestalozzi, baritone; Othmar Schoeck, pf)
10. "Lockung." 1917
    FP: as no. 1
11. "An die Lützowschen Jäger." 1917
    FP: as no. 8
12. "Auf dem Rhein." 1917
    FP: as no. 7

Publ.: Leipzig: Breitkopf & Härtel
Note: Schoeck arranged no. 12 for male chorus, pf; see **Choral Works with Accompaniment**
Recordings: Nathan Berg (baritone); Julius Drake (pf), on *LCE* vol. 2. Jecklin Edition JD 672–2
Jean-Pierre Gerber (bass); Ursula Weingart (pf). Swiss Broadcasting Corporation CD110297
Michael Leibundgut (bass); Ute Stoecklin (pf). Guild GMCD 7254
(No. 6): Elisabeth Grümmer (soprano); Aribert Reimann (pf). Orfeo d'Or, C 506 001
(Nos. 1, 7, 12, 4): Arthur Loosli (bass-baritone); Karl Grenacher (pf). Jecklin-Disco JD 535–2
(No. 7): Dagmar Pecková (mezzo-soprano); Irwin Gage (pf). Supraphon, SU 3434–2
(Nos. 4, 6, 12): Gunnel Sköld (contralto); Jan Bülow (pf). Gallo CD 1035
(Nos. 6, 7, 12): Samuel Zünd (baritone); Jeroen Sarphati (pf). Deluc Productions
(Nos. 3, 7, 9 arr. vc, pf): Christian Poltéra (vc); Julius Drake (pf). BIS-CD 1597 ·

Op. 31
Fünf Lieder
1. "Madrigal" (Michelangelo). 1917
   FP: Jan. 1922, Bern (Felix Loeffel, bass; Othmar Schoeck, pf)
2. "Die Kindheit" (Hesse). 1914
   FP: 9 Jan. 1924, Zurich (Ilona Durigo, contralto; Othmar Schoeck, pf)
3. "Im Kreuzgang von St. Stefano" (Hesse). 1917
   FP: 1 Jun. 1919, Burgdorf (Hanna Brenner, contralto; Othmar Schoeck, pf)
4. "Ruheplatz" (Anacreon-Mörike). 1915
   FP: 30 Jan. 1942, Zurich (Elisabeth Gehri, contralto; Othmar Schoeck, pf)
5. "Epigramm" (Goethe). 1906
   FP: 21 Feb. 1941, Zurich (Ria Ginster, soprano; Othmar Schoeck, pf)

Publ.: Leipzig: Breitkopf & Härtel

Recordings: Nathan Berg (baritone); Julius Drake (pf), on *LCE* vol. 2. Jecklin Edition
  JD 672–2
(Nos. 2, 3): Dietrich Fischer-Dieskau (baritone); Margrit Weber (pf). Deutsche
  Grammophon 463 513–2
(No. 3): Ernst Haefliger (tenor); Karl Grenacher (pf). Jecklin-Disco JD 504–2
(No. 3): Gunnel Sköld (contralto); Jan Bülow (pf). Gallo CD 1035
(No. 5, arr. vc, pf): Christian Poltéra (vc); Julius Drake (pf). BIS-CD 1597

Op. 33
Zwölf Hafis-Lieder (Hafez reworked by Georg Friedrich Daumer) 1919/20
  1. "Ach, wie schön ist Nacht und Dämmerschein"
     FP: 7 Oct. 1921, Zurich (Ilona Durigo, contralto; Othmar Schoeck, pf)
  2. "Höre mir den Prediger"
     FP(?): 3 Aug. 1923, Vienna (Heinrich Rehkemper, baritone; Othmar Schoeck,
     pf)
  3. "Das Geschehne, nicht bereut's Hafis"
  4. "Ach, wie richtete, so klagt' ich"
     FP: 13 May 1922, Zug (Felix Loeffel, bass; Othmar Schoeck, pf)
  5. "Wie stimmst du mich zur Andacht"
  6. "Meine Lebenszeit verstreicht"
  7. "Ich roch der Liebe himmlisches Arom"
  8. "Ich habe mich dem Heil entschworen"
     FP: as no. 1
  9. "Lieblich in der Rosenzeit"
     FP(?): as no. 2
  10. "Horch, hörst du nicht vom Himmel her"
     FP: as no. 1
  11. "Nicht düstre, Theosoph, so tief!"
     FP: as no. 4
  12. "Sing, o lieblicher Sängermund"
     FP: as no. 1
Publ.: Leipzig: Breitkopf & Härtel
Recordings: Niklaus Tüller (baritone); Christoph Keller (pf), on *LCE* vol. 3. Jecklin
  Edition JD 673–2
(No. 1): Dietrich Fischer-Dieskau (baritone); Margrit Weber (pf). Deutsche Gram-
  mophon 463 513–2
(Nos. 1, 10): Gunnel Sköld (contralto); Jan Bülow (pf). Gallo CD 1035
(No. 1): Oliver Widmer (baritone); Till Alexander Körber (pf). Atlantis ATL 96 206

Op. 34
Der Gott und die Bajadere (Goethe)
1921
Publ.: Leipzig: Breitkopf & Härtel
FP: 7 Oct. 1921, Zurich (Ilona Durigo, contralto; Othmar Schoeck, pf)
Recording: Niklaus Tüller (baritone); Christoph Keller (pf), on *LCE* vol. 3. Jecklin
  Edition JD 673–2

woo 78
Sommerabend (Müllenhof [first name unknown])
1921
FP: 8 Nov. 1991, Zurich (Niklaus Tüller, baritone; Christoph Keller, pf)
Note: *nach & für René* [*sic*] *bearbeitet* ("arranged after and for René," i.e., an arrange-
    ment by Schoeck of a song by Renée Zürcher, later the wife of Paul Schoeck)
Recording: Niklaus Tüller (baritone); Christoph Keller (pf), on *LCE* vol. 3. Jecklin
    Edition JD 673–2

woo 37
"Die Entschwundene" (Gottfried Keller)
1923
FP: 9 Jan. 1924, Zurich (Ilona Durigo, contralto; Othmar Schoeck, pf).
Recording: Niklaus Tüller (baritone); Christoph Keller (pf), on *LCE* vol. 3. Jecklin
    Edition JD 673–2

Op. 35
Drei Lieder nach Gedichten von Keller, Storm und Eichendorff
    1. "Fahrewohl" (Gottfried Keller). 1928
    2. "April" (Theodor Storm). 1928
    3. "Gottes Segen" (Eichendorff). 1928
Publ.: Leipzig: Breitkopf & Härtel
FP (all three): 4 Oct. 1929, Zurich (Ilona Durigo, contralto; Othmar Schoeck, pf)
Recordings: Juliane Banse (soprano, no. 3); Dietrich Henschel (baritone, nos. 1, 2);
    Wolfram Rieger (pf), on *LCE* vol. 7. Jecklin Edition JD 677–2
(No. 2): Ulf Bästlein (baritone); Charles Spencer (pf). Dabringhaus und Grimm,
    MDG 603 1234–2

Op. 44
Zehn Lieder nach Gedichten von Hermann Hesse
1929
    1. "Nachtgefühl"
    2. "Magie der Farben"
    3. "Verwelkende Rosen"
    4. "Abends"
    5. "Mittag im September"
    6. "Blauer Schmetterling"
    7. "Pfeifen"
    8. "Sommernacht"
    9. "Für Ninon"
    10. "Vergänglichkeit"
Publ.: Leipzig: Breitkopf & Härtel
FP: 25 Mar. 1930, St. Gallen (Felicie Hüni-Mihacsek, soprano; Othmar Schoeck, pf)
Recordings: Dietrich Fischer-Dieskau (baritone); Karl Engel (pf). Deutsche Gram-
    mophon 463 513–2

Lynne Dawson (soprano); Cornelia Kallisch (mezzo-soprano); Jürg Dürmüller (tenor); Nathan Berg (baritone); Julius Drake (pf), on *LCE* vol. 6. Jecklin Edition JD 676–2
(No. 9): Arthur Loosli (bass-baritone); Karl Grenacher (pf). Jecklin-Disco JD 535–2
(Nos. 5, 9): Gunnel Sköld (contralto); Jan Bülow (pf). Gallo CD 1035
(Nos. 6, 7, 9): Christine Walser (mezzo-soprano); Wendy Waterman (pf). MDS Records MDS 3017

woo 118
"Eine Kompanie Soldaten" (Alfred Hein)
1920s or 1930s?
FP: 2 Dec. 1997, Baden (Switzerland) (Otto Georg Linsi, tenor; Madeleine Nussbaumer, pf)
Note: An arrangement of the song of the same name by Willy Kaufmann, a friend of the composer

Op. 45
Wanderung im Gebirge
A cycle of poems ("Gedichtfolge") by Nikolaus Lenau
1930
  1. "Erinnerung"
  2. "Aufbruch"
  3. "Die Lerche"
  4. "Der Eichwald"
  5. "Der Hirte"
  6. "Einsamkeit"
  7. "Die Ferne"
  8. "Das Gewitter"
  9. "Der Schlaf"
  10. "Der Abend"
Publ.: Leipzig and Zurich: Hug & Co.
FP: 7 Feb. 1931 in Winterthur (Willy Rössel, baritone; Othmar Schoeck, pf)
Recordings: Niklaus Tüller (baritone); Christoph Keller (pf), on *LCE* vol. 3. Jecklin Edition JD 673–2
Olaf Bär (baritone); Helmut Deutsch (pf). Denon Records

Op. 51
Sechs Lieder nach Gedichten von Eichendorff und Mörike
  1. "Nachtgruss" (Joseph von Eichendorff). 1931
    FP: 25 Oct. 1931, Bern (Felix Loeffel, bass; Othmar Schoeck, pf)
  2. "Motto" (Eichendorff). 1934
    FP: 27 Apr. 1934, Bern (Ilona Durigo, contralto; Othmar Schoeck, pf)
  3. "Trost" (Eichendorff). 1934
    FP: 19 May 1941, Zurich (Hilde Schoeck, soprano; Othmar Schoeck, pf)
  4. "Er ist's" (Eduard Mörike). 1937

    FP: 30 Jan. 1942, Zurich (Elisabeth Gehri, contralto; Othmar Schoeck, pf)
5. "Septembermorgen" (Mörike). 1937
    FP: as no. 4
6. "Spruch" (Mörike). 1943
    FP: 5 Feb. 1947, Winterthur (Fritz Mack, bass; Othmar Schoeck, pf)
Publ.: Zurich: Hug & Co.
Recordings: Juliane Banse (soprano, nos. 1, 4, 5); Dietrich Henschel (baritone, nos. 2, 3, 6); Wolfram Rieger (pf), on *LCE* vol. 7. Jecklin Edition JD 677–2
(No. 5): Ernst Haefliger (tenor); Karl Grenacher (pf). Jecklin-Disco JD 504–2
(No. 2): Elisabeth Grümmer (soprano); Aribert Reimann (pf). Orfeo d'Or, C 506 001

Op. 52
Wandsbecker Liederbuch
Song cycle ("Liederfolge") after poems by Matthias Claudius
1936–37; a sketch for no. 10 exists on a page of manuscript paper from the years 1922–23
1. "Die Liebe"
2. "Phidile"
3. "Ein Wiegenlied, bei Mondschein zu singen"
4. "Als er sein Weib und's Kind schlafend fand"
5. "Die Natur"
6. "Der Frühling"
7. "Die Sternseherin"
8. "Kuckuck"
9. "Ein Lied, hinterm Ofen zu singen"
10. "Abendlied"
11. "Der Mensch"
12. "Die Römer"
13. "Der Schwarze in der Zuckerplantage"
14. "Der Krieg"
15. "Auf den Tod einer Kaiserin"
16. "Der Tod"
17. "Spruch"
Publ.: Vienna: Universal Edition
FP: 6 Apr. 1938, Zurich (Alice Frey, soprano; Walter Frey, pf)
Recordings: Juliane Banse (soprano, nos. 2, 3, 5, 6, 7, 10, 15); Dietrich Henschel (baritone, nos. 1, 4, 8, 9, 11, 12, 13, 14, 16, 17); Wolfram Rieger (pf), on *LCE* vol. 7. Jecklin Edition JD 677–2
(Nos. 5, 6): Silvia Gähwiller (soprano); Othmar Schoeck (pf). Jecklin Edition JD 714–2

WoO 130
Nachhall (Gottfried Keller)
1940

Op. 55

Unter Sternen

Songs ("Lieder und Gesänge") for medium voice after poems by Gottfried Keller

1941–43

1. "Trost der Kreatur"
2. "Sonnenuntergang"
3. "Siehst du den Stern"
4. "Stille der Nacht"
5. "Unter Sternen"
6. "Abendlied an die Natur"
7. "Unruhe der Nacht"
8. "Aus den Waldliedern I"
9. "Aus den Waldliedern II"
10. "Stilleben (aus den Rheinbildern)"
11. "Das Tal (aus den Rheinbildern)"
12. "Abendlied"
13. "Wir wähnten lange recht zu leben"
14. "Flack're, ew'ges Licht im Tal"
15. "Die Zeit geht nicht"
16. "Trübes Wetter"
17. "Frühgesicht (aus den Rheinbildern)"
18. "Frühlingsglaube"
19. "In der Trauer"
20. "Den Zweifellosen I"
21. "Den Zweifellosen II"
22. "Tod und Dichter"
23. "An das Herz"
24. "Aus: Ein Tagewerk I"
25. "Aus: Ein Tagewerk II"

Publ.: Vienna: Universal Edition

FP: 8 Oct. 1943, Zurich (Felix Loeffel, bass; Othmar Schoeck, pf)

Recordings: Dietrich Fischer-Dieskau (baritone); Hartmut Höll (pf). Claves CD 50–8606

Roman Trekel (baritone); Christoph Keller (pf), on *LCE* vol. 8. Jecklin Edition JD 678–2

(Nos. 17, 24, 25): Dietrich Fischer-Dieskau (baritone); Margrit Weber (pf). Deutsche Grammophon 463 513–2

(No. 18): Silvia Gähwiller (soprano); Othmar Schoeck (pf). Jecklin Edition JD 714–2

(Nos. 11, 12): Oliver Widmer (baritone); Till Alexander Körber (pf). Atlantis ATL 96 206

(Nos. 1, 3, 10, 12, 15, 16, arr. Rolf Urs Ringger for voice and orchestra): Nathan Berg (baritone); English Chamber Orchestra, cond. Howard Griffiths. Novalis 150 106–2

Op. 56
Spielmannsweisen
Song cycle ("Liederfolge") for high voice and harp or piano after poems by Heinrich
    Leuthold
1944
1. "O Frühlingshauch, o Liederlust"
2. "Die Ströme ziehn zum fernen Meer"
3. "Ich bin ein Spielmann von Beruf"
4. "Und wieder nehm' ich die Harfe zur Hand"
5. "Mein Herz ist wie ein Saitenspiel"
6. "O Lebensfrühling, Blütendrang"

Publ.: Vienna: Universal Edition
FP: 6 Aug. 1944, Gstaad (Willi Frey, tenor; Emmy Hürlimann, hp)
Recordings: Ernst Haefliger (tenor); Catherine Eisenhoffer (hp). Gallo CD 622
Bernhard Hunziker (tenor); Jean-Jacques Dünki (pf). MGB CD 6179
Kurt Streit (tenor); Gudrun Haag (hp), on *LCE* vol. 9. Jecklin Edition, JD 679–2

Op. 57
Der Sänger
Song cycle ("Liederfolge") for high voice after poems and strophes by Heinrich Leuthold
1944–45
1. "Leidenschaft"
2. "Muttersprache"
3. "Liederfrühling"
4. "Waldeinsamkeit"
5. "Vorwurf"
6. "Rechtfertigung"
7. "Abkehr"
8. "Waldvögelein"
9. "Aus dem Süden"
10. "Riviera"
11. "Nacht, Muse und Tod"
12. "Sapphische Strophe"
13. "Sonnenuntergang"
14. "Warnung"
15. "Heimweh"
16. "Rückkehr"
17. "Einst"
18. "An meine Grossmutter"
19. "Trauer"
20. "Der Waldsee"
21. "Im Klosterkeller"
22. "Trinklied"
23. "Distichen, Strophenlied im Tone einer Schnitzelbank"
24. "Spruch"
25. "Unmut"
26. "Trost"

Publ.: Vienna: Universal Edition
FP: 17 May 1945, St. Gallen (Ernst Haefliger, tenor; Othmar Schoeck, pf)
Recordings: Frieder Lang (tenor); Ruth Lang-Oester (pf). Koch Schwann 3–1091–2
Kurt Streit (tenor); Wolfram Rieger (pf), on *LCE* vol. 9. Jecklin Edition, JD 679–2
(Nos. 20, 22, 24): Ernst Haefliger (tenor); Othmar Schoeck (pf). Jecklin Edition JD
    714–2
(Nos. 8, 12): Ernst Haefliger (tenor); Karl Grenacher (pf). Jecklin-Disco JD 504–2

Op. 60
Das stille Leuchten
Song cycle ("Liederfolge") for medium voice after poems by Conrad Ferdinand
    Meyer.
1946
Geheimnis und Gleichnis
  1. "Das heilige Feuer"
  2. "Liederseelen"
  3. "Reisephantasie"
  4. "Mit einem Jugendbildnis"
  5. "Am Himmelstor"
  6. "In einer Sturmnacht"
  7. "In Harmesnächten"
  8. "Lenzfahrt"
  9. "Frühling Triumphator"
  10. "Unruhige Nacht"
  11. "Was treibst du, Wind?"
  12. "Hochzeitslied"
  13. "Der Gesang des Meeres"
  14. "Der römische Brunnen"
  15. "Das Ende des Festes"
  16. "Die Jungfrau"
  17. "Neujahrsglocken"
  18. "Alle"
Berg und See
  19. "Der Reisebecher"
  20. "Das weisse Spitzchen"
  21. "Göttermahl"
  22. "Ich würd' es hören"
  23. "Firnelicht"
  24. "Schwarzschattende Kastanie"
  25. "Requiem"
  26. "Abendwolke"
  27. "Nachtgeräusche"
  28. "Jetzt rede du!"
Publ.: Vienna: Universal Edition
FP: 1 Sept. 1946, Zurich (Elsa Cavelti, contralto; Othmar Schoeck, pf)
Recordings: Hedwig Fassbender (mezzo-soprano); Aziz Kortel (pf), on *LCE* vol. 10.
    Jecklin Edition JD 680–2

Dietrich Fischer-Dieskau (baritone); Hartmut Höll (pf). Claves CD 50–8910

(Nos. 3, 15, 28): Dietrich Fischer-Dieskau (baritone); Margrit Weber (pf). Deutsche Grammophon 463 513–2

(Nos. 3, 15, 26): Oliver Widmer (baritone); Till Alexander Körber (pf). Atlantis ATL 96 206

(Nos. 8, 19, 22, 25, 26, arr. Rolf Urs Ringger for voice and orchestra): Nathan Berg (baritone); English Chamber Orchestra, cond. Howard Griffiths. Novalis 150 106–2

(No. 19, arr. vc and pf): Christian Poltéra (vc); Julius Drake (pf). BIS-CD 1597

woo 44
Wiegenlied
Text and melody by Johannes Jaeger, arr. for voice and piano by Othmar Schoeck
1947
In Johannes Jaeger, *Du Kindlein in der Wiege* (Basel: Heinrich Maier, 1952), 32–35
Recording: Juliane Banse (soprano); Wolfram Rieger (pf), on *LCE* vol. 7. Jecklin Edition JD 677–2

Op. 62
Das holde Bescheiden
Songs ("Lieder und Gesänge") after poems by Eduard Mörike
1947–49
  1. "Widmung"
Natur
  2. "An einem Wintermorgen, vor Sonnenaufgang"
  3. "Gesang zu zweien in der Nacht"
  4. "Am Walde"
  5. "An Philomele"
  6. "Auf der Teck (Rauhe Alb)"
  7. "Das Mädchen an den Mai"
  8. "Im Park"
  9. "Mein Fluss"
Liebe
  10. "Lose Ware"
  11. "Ritterliche Werbung (Englisch)"
  12. "Die Schwestern"
  13. "Schön-Rotraut"
  14. "Peregrina"
  15. "Zu viel"
  16. "Nachts am Schreibepult"
  17. "Aus der Ferne"
  18. "Nur zu!"
Betrachtung
  19. "Auf eine Lampe"
  20. "Nachts"
  21. "Antike Poesie (An Goethe)"
  22. "Erinna an Sappho"
  23. "Johann Kepler"

"Fünf Sprüche"
24. "Keine Rettung"
25. "Nach dem Kriege"
26. "In ein Autographen-Album"
27. "Impromptu (An Mörikes Hündchen Joli)"
28. "Die Enthusiasten"
29. "Trost"
30. "Auf ein Ei geschrieben"
31. "Auf einen Klavierspieler"
32. "Restauration (Nach Durchlesung eines Manuskriptes mit Gedichten)"
Glaube
33. "Gebet"
34. "Der Hirtenknabe (Zu einer Zeichnung L. Richters)"
35. "Auf ein Kind (das mir eine ausgerissene Haarlocke vorwies)"
36. "Zu einer Konfirmation"
In der Krankheit
37. "Muse und Dichter"
38. "Auf dem Krankenbette"
39. "Der Geprüfte"
Rückblick
40. "Besuch in Urach"

Publ.: Vienna: Universal Edition

FP: 1st series (1–18) 25 Apr. 1949, Stuttgart (Hilde Schoeck, soprano; Othmar Schoeck, pf); 2nd series (19–40) 30 Nov. 1950, Zurich (ditto)

Note: Schoeck wrote a version of no. 40 for high voice and orchestra. See **Voice and Orchestra**

Recordings: Dietrich Fischer-Dieskau (baritone, nos. 3, 4, 5, 6, 8, 10, 11, 12, 13, 14, 16, 19, 20, 21, 23, 26, 27, 29, 30, 32, 33, 34, 35, 36, 37, 38); Mitsuko Shirai (mezzo-soprano, nos. 1, 2, 7, 9, 15, 17, 18, 22, 24, 25, 28, 31, 39, 40); Hartmut Höll (pf). Claves CD 50–9308/9

Ian Bostridge (tenor, nos. 3, 4, 5, 9, 10, 11, 13, 14, 16, 17, 19, 20, 21, 23, 26, 27, 29, 32, 33, 37, 38); Lynne Dawson (soprano, nos. 1, 2, 3, 6, 7, 8, 12, 15, 17, 18, 22, 24, 25, 28, 30, 31, 34, 35, 36, 39, 40); Julius Drake (pf), on *LCE* vol. 11. Jecklin Edition JD 681/2–2

(No. 18): Ernst Haefliger (tenor); Karl Grenacher (pf). Jecklin-Disco JD 504–2

(Nos. 6, 8, 20) Elisabeth Grümmer (soprano); Aribert Reimann (pf). Orfeo d'Or, C 506 001

(Nos. 9, 31, 32, 40): Hilde Schoeck (soprano); Othmar Schoeck (pf). Jecklin Edition JD 714–2

woo 45
"Im Nebel" (Hermann Hesse)
1952
Publ.: Wiesbaden: Breitkopf & Härtel
Recording: Dietrich Henschel (baritone); Wolfram Rieger (pf), on *LCE* vol. 7. Jecklin Edition JD 677–2

woo 109
"O du Land" (Matthias Claudius).
1954/55?
FP: 2 Dec. 1997, Baden (Switzerland) (Otto Georg Linsi, tenor; Madeleine Nussbaumer, pf)
Note: Presumably conceived as the final song of the cycle *Nachhall,* Op. 70, for voice
and orchestra, but never orchestrated. Not identical with either Op. 70, no. 12
or woo 110

woo 110
["O du Land"] (Matthias Claudius)
1954/55?
FP: 2 Dec. 1997, Baden (Switzerland) (Otto Georg Linsi, tenor; Madeleine Nussbaumer, pf)
Note: Presumably conceived as the final song of the cycle *Nachhall,* Op. 70, for voice
and orchestra (as woo 109 above). Not identical with either Op. 70, no. 12 or
woo 109

VIII. Voice and Organ

Op. 11
Drei geistliche Lieder
For baritone and organ.
   1. "Psalm" (Paul Schoeck). 1906
      FP: 21 Mar. 1906, Zurich (Othmar Schoeck, baritone; Johannes Luz, organ)
   2. Psalm 23. 1907
      FP: 20 Mar. 1907, Zurich (Othmar Schoeck, baritone; Johannes Luz, organ)
   3. Psalm 100. 1907
      FP: as no. 2
Publ.: Leipzig: Hug & Co.
Recordings: Nathan Berg (baritone); Oskar Birchmeier (organ), on *LCE* vol. 2. Jeck-
lin Edition JD 672–2
Gotthold Schwarz (baritone); Rolf Schönstedt (organ). Thorofon, Tho CTH 2336

Op. 62, no. 36
"Zu einer Konfirmation" (Eduard Mörike)
For voice and organ or harmonium or piano, published as part of the cycle *Das holde
Bescheiden* for voice and piano

IX. Voice and Orchestra

Op. 12, no. 2
"Wanderlied der Prager Studenten" (Joseph von Eichendorff)
For voice and orchestra

Fragment, undated
Instr.: 2fl, 2ob, 2cl, 2bn, cbn—3hn, 2tpt—timp—str
Note: an unfinished arrangement by the composer of the second of his *Zwei Wander-lieder von Eichendorff* for voice and piano

Op. 36
Elegie
Song cycle ("Liederfolge") after poems by Nikolaus Lenau and Joseph von Eichendorff
1915 (no. 21), 1921–22 (the rest)
 1. "Wehmut" (Eichendorff)
 2. "Liebesfrühling" (Lenau)
 3. "Stille Sicherheit" (Lenau)
 4. "Frage nicht" (Lenau)
 5. "Warnung und Wunsch" (Lenau)
 6. "Zweifelnder Wunsch" (Lenau)
 7. "Waldlied" (Lenau)
 8. "Waldgang" (Lenau)
 9. "An den Wind" (Lenau)
 10. "Kommen und Scheiden" (Lenau)
 11. "Vesper" (Eichendorff)
 12. "Herbstklage" (Lenau)
 13. "Herbstgefühl" (Lenau)
 14. "Nachklang" (Eichendorff)
 15. "Herbstgefühl" (Lenau)
 16. "Das Mondlicht" (Lenau)
 17. "Vergangenheit" (Lenau)
 18. "Waldlied" (Lenau)
 19. "Herbstentschluss" (Lenau)
 20. "Verlorenes Glück" (Lenau)
 21. "Angedenken" (Eichendorff)
 22. "Welke Rose" (Lenau)
 23. "Dichterlos" (Eichendorff)
 24. "Der Einsame" (Eichendorff)
Instr.: fl, ob (also eng hn), 2cl (2 also bcl)—hn—timp, tamt—pf—str
Publ.: Leipzig: Breitkopf & Härtel
FP: 19 Mar. 1923, Zurich (Felix Loeffel, bass; members of the Zurich Tonhalle Orchestra, cond. Othmar Schoeck)
Recordings: Peter Lagger (bass); Camerata Zürich, cond. Räto Tschupp. Classic Pick 470–115
Arthur Loosli (bass-baritone); Berner Kammerensemble, cond. Theo Hug. Jecklin Disco JD 510–2
Klaus Mertens (bass-baritone); Mutare Ensemble, cond. Gerhard Müller-Hornbach. NCA, MA 95 04 808
Andreas Schmidt (baritone); Musikkollegium Winterthur, cond. Werner Andreas Albert. CPO 999 472–2

Op. 40

Lebendig begraben

Fourteen songs ("Gesänge") for voice (bass) and orchestra, after the cycle of poems
of the same name by Gottfried Keller

1926

1. "Wie poltert es!"
2. "Da lieg' ich denn"
3. "Ha! was ist das?"
4. "Läg' ich, wo es Hyänen gibt"
5. "Horch! Stimmen und Geschrei"
6. "Als endlich sie den Sarg hier abgesetzt"
7. "Horch—endlich zittert es durch meine Bretter!"
8. "Da hab' ich gar die Rose aufgegessen"
9. "Zwölf hat's geschlagen"
10. "Ja, hätt' ich ein verlassnes Liebchen nun"
11. "Wie herrlich wär's"
12. "Der erste Tannenbaum, den ich gesehn"
13. "Der schönste Tannenbaum, den ich gesehn"
14. "Und wieder schlägt's—ein Viertel erst"

Instr.: 2fl (both also pic), 2ob (2 also eng hn), 2cl, bcl, 2bn, cbn—4hn, 2tpt, 3trbn,
tb—timp, perc (bass drum, cym, rute, side drum, tamt, trgl, xyl)—cel, hp, org,
pf—str—chorus (AB).

Publ.: Leipzig: Breitkopf & Härtel

FP: 2 Mar. 1927, Winterthur (Thomas Denijs, bass; Winterthur City Orchestra, cond.
Othmar Schoeck)

Recordings: Dietrich Fischer-Dieskau (baritone); Radio Symphony Orchestra Berlin,
cond. Fritz Rieger. Claves CD 50–8610

Günter von Kannen (bass); Orchestra of the Zurich Opera, cond. Ralf Weikert.
Atlantis Digital ATL 96 205

Felix Loeffel (bass); Swiss Radio Orchestra Beromünster, cond. Luc Balmer. Uranus
URA 601

Op. 62, no. 40

Besuch in Urach (Eduard Mörike)

For high voice and orchestra

1948; orchestral version: July 1951 in Orselina

Instr.: 2fl, 2ob, 2cl, 2bn—4hn, 3tpt, 3trbn—timp, perc (bass drum, cym, trgl, tamt)—
pf—str

FP: 1 Oct. 1951, Bern (Ernst Haefliger, tenor; Bern City Orchestra)

Note: An orchestral version by the composer of his song of the same title for voice
and piano

Op. 66

Befreite Sehnsucht

Song cycle ("Liederfolge") for high voice and orchestra after four sonnets by Joseph
von Eichendorff

1952

Sonnet 1: "So viele Quellen von den Bergen rauschen"
Sonnet 2: "So eitel künstlich haben sie verwoben"
Sonnet 3: "Ein Wunderland ist oben aufgeschlagen"
Sonnet 4: "Wer einmal tief und durstig hat getrunken"
Instr.: fl, 2ob, 2cl, 2bn—2hn—timp—hp—str
Publ.: Zurich: Hug & Co.
FP: 9 Dec. 1953, Winterthur (Annelies Kupper, soprano; Winterthur City Orchestra, cond. Victor Desarzens)
Recording: Annelies Kupper (soprano); Zurich Tonhalle Orchestra, cond. Hans Rosbaud. BMG 74321306202

Op. 70
Nachhall
Song cycle ("Liederfolge") for medium voice and orchestra after poems by Nikolaus Lenau and Matthias Claudius
1954–55
  1. "Nachhall" (Lenau)
  2. "Einsamkeit" (two sonnets) (Lenau)
  3. "Mein Herz" (Lenau)
  4. "Veränderte Welt" (Lenau)
  5. "Abendheimkehr" (Lenau)
  6. "Auf eine holländische Landschaft" (Lenau)
  7. "Stimme des Windes" (Lenau)
  8. "Der falsche Freund" (Lenau)
  9. "Niagara" (Lenau)
  10. "Heimatklang" (Lenau)
Zwischenspiel
  11. "Der Kranich" (Lenau)
  12. "O du Land" (Claudius)
Instr.: fl, 2 ob (also eng hn), 2 cl, 2 bn—2 hn, tpt—timp, perc (tamt, cym, xyl)—pf—str
Publ.: Vienna: Universal Edition
FP: 6 Dec. 1955, Zurich (Elsa Cavelti, contralto; Zurich Tonhalle Orchestra, cond. Erich Schmid)
Recording: Arthur Loosli (bass-baritone); Chamber Ensemble of Radio Bern, cond. Theo Loosli. Jecklin-Disco JD 535–2

X. Voice with Obbligato Accompaniment

woo 62
In der Dorfschenke (Margarete Bentler)
For voice, fl(?), vn, vc, pf
1903

Op. 4, no. 3
"Wo?" (Heinrich Heine)
For voice, vn, pf

See **Voice and Piano**
Op. 38
Gaselen
Song cycle ("Liederfolge") after poems by Gottfried Keller
For baritone, fl, ob, bcl, tpt, perc (one player: cym, side drum, tamt, trgl), pf
1923
1. "Unser ist das Los der Epigonen"
2. "O heiliger Augustin im Himmelssaal"
3. "Der Herr gab dir ein gutes Augenpaar"
4. "Wenn schlanke Lilien wandelten"
5. "Nun schmücke mir dein dunkles Haar"
6. "Perlen der Weisheit sind mir deine Zähne"
7. "Ich halte dich in meinem Arm"
8. "Berge dein Haupt, wenn ein König vorbeigeht"
9. "Mich tadelt der Fanatiker"
10. "Verbogen und zerkniffen war der vordre Rand an meinem Hut"
Publ.: Leipzig: Breitkopf & Härtel
FP: 23 Feb. 1924, Winterthur (Felix Loeffel, bass; cond. Othmar Schoeck)
Recording: Nathan Berg (baritone); William Bennett (fl); Neil Black (ob); Andrew
    Crowley (tpt); Julian Poole (perc); Ian Watson (pf), cond. Howard Griffiths.
    Novalis 150 106–2

Op. 42
Wandersprüche
Song cycle ("Liederfolge") after poems by Joseph von Eichendorff
For tenor or soprano, cl, hn, perc (one player: cym [hanging], glock, side drum,
    sleigh bells, tamt, timp, trgl), pf
1928
1. "Es geht wohl anders, als du meinst"
2. "Herz, in deinen sonnenhellen Tagen"
3. "Was willst auf dieser Station?"
4. "Die Lerche grüsst den ersten Strahl"
5. "Wenn der Hahn kräht auf dem Dache"
6. "Der Sturm geht lärmend um das Haus"
7. "Ewig muntres Spiel der Wogen"
8. "Der Wand'rer von der Heimat weit"
Publ.: Leipzig: Breitkopf & Härtel
FP: 16 Mar. 1929, Zurich (Felicie Hüni-Mihacsek, soprano; cond. Othmar Schoeck)
Recording: Jörg Hering (tenor); Thea King (cl), Frank Lloyd (hn); James Holland
    (perc); Ian Watson (pf), cond. Howard Griffiths. Novalis 150 106–2

Op. 47
Notturno
Five Movements for String Quartet and Voice (Baritone)
1931–33
1a. "Liebe und Vermählung, erste Stimme" (Nikolaus Lenau)
1b. "Liebe und Vermählung, zweite Stimme" (Lenau)

1c. *Andante appassionato*
1d. "Der schwere Abend" (Lenau)
1e. "Blick in den Strom" (Lenau)
2a. *Presto*
2b. "Traumgewalten" (Lenau)
3. "Ein Herbstabend" (Lenau)
4. "Waldlieder" No. 9 (Lenau)
5a. "Der einsame Trinker" No. 1 (Lenau)
5b. *Allegretto*
5c. "Impromptu" (Lenau)
5d. *Allegretto tranquillo*
5e. "Heerwagen, mächtig Sternbild der Germanen" (Gottfried Keller)
Publ.: Vienna: Universal Edition
FP: 18 May 1933, Zurich (Felix Loeffel, bass; Zurich Tonhalle Quartet)
Recordings: Olaf Bär (baritone); Carmina Quartet. Denon Records CO 18085
Christian Gerhaher (baritone); Rosamunde Quartet UPC/EAN 0289 476 6995 (1)/
    ECM 2061
Klaus Mertens (bass-baritone); Minguet Quartet. NCA 60133–215
François le Roux (baritone); Stanislas Quartet. Gallo CD-842
Kurt Widmer (baritone); Amati Quartet. Atlantis ATL 96 206

Op. 56
Spielmannsweisen
Song cycle ("Liederfolge") for a high voice and harp or piano
See **Voice and Piano**

XI. Choral Works with Accompaniment

All the choral works have been published in series 2, vol. 8 of *Othmar Schoeck: Sämtliche Werke*, ed. Bernhard Billeter (Zurich: Hug, 2002).

woo 53
Melodie zur Comment-Buch-Weihe (Othmar Schoeck?)
For unison chorus, pf
ca. 1902?

woo 3
KTV ["Kantonsschul-Turnverein"]-*Kantus* (M. Lutz)
For unison chorus, pf
1903?
For the arrangement for male chorus, see **A Cappella Choral Works**, "Studenten-
lied," woo 117

woo 69
Das Glück in der Heimat
see **Stage Works**

Op. 18

Der Postillon (Nikolaus Lenau)

For tenor solo, small male chorus [TTBB], orch (or pf).

1909

Instr.: 2fl, 2ob, 2cl, 2bn—4hn—timp—str

FP: 19 Mar. 1911, Bern (Liedertafel Bern; Bern City Orchestra, cond. Fritz Brun) and (simultaneously) in Zurich (Alfred Flury, tenor; Männerchor Zürich; Zurich Tonhalle Orchestra, cond. Volkmar Andreae)

Recordings: Martin Homrich (tenor); MDR Radio Choir; MDR Symphony Orchestra, cond. Mario Venzago. Claves Records CD 50–2701

Ernst Haefliger (tenor); Wettinger Kammerchor and Seminarchor Wettingen; Wettinger Chamber Orchestra, cond. Karl Grenacher. Jecklin-Disco JD 504–2

Op. 22

Dithyrambe (Goethe)

For double chorus [SATB, SATB], large orchestra, and organ

1911

Instr.: 3fl, 3ob, 3cl, 3bn, cbn—6hn, 3tpt, 3trbn, tb—timp, cym—org—str

FP: 19 Mar. 1912, Bern (Cäcilienverein Bern; Bern City Orchestra, cond. Fritz Brun)

Recording: MDR Radio Choir; MDR Symphony Orchestra, cond. Mario Venzago. Claves Records CD 50–2701

Op. 24

Wegelied (Gottfried Keller)

For male chorus [TTBB] and orchestra

1913

Instr.: pic, 2fl, 2ob, 2cl, 2bn—4hn, 2tpt, 3trbn, tb—timp, perc (side drum, bass drum, cym)—str

FP: 23 May 1914, Bern (the Liedertafel of Bern and Basel plus the Männerchor Zürich; Bern City Orchestra, cond. Fritz Brun)

Recording: MDR Radio Choir; MDR Symphony Orchestra, cond. Mario Venzago. Claves Records CD 50–2701

Op. 26

Trommelschläge (Walt Whitman, trans. Johannes Schlaf)

For mixed chorus [SATB] and large orchestra

1915

Instr.: pic, 2fl, 3ob, 3cl, 3bn, cbn—8hn, 4tpt, 3trbn, tb—2 timp, perc (cym, bass drum, side drum, tamt, 6 further side drums)—org—str

FP: 5 Mar. 1916, Zurich (Lehrergesangverein Zürich; Zurich Tonhalle Orchestra, cond. Othmar Schoeck)

Recording: MDR Radio Choir; MDR Symphony Orchestra, cond. Mario Venzago. Claves Records CD 50–2701

Op. 30, no. 12

Auf dem Rhein (Eichendorff)

For male chorus [TTB], pf
1943
FP: 5 Nov. 1943, Zurich (Männerchor Chambre XXIV, cond. Max Graf; Othmar
Schoeck, pf)
Note: An arrangement of the solo song Op. 30, no. 12

Op. 49
Kantate nach Gedichten von Eichendorff
For baritone solo, small male chorus [TTB], 3trbn, tb, pf, perc (side drum, bass
drum, tamt, cym); or with perc, pf alone
1933
1. "Motto"
2. "Geistesgruss"
3. "Der neue Rattenfänger"
4. "Ratskollegium"
5. "Vision"
6. "Mahnung"
7. "Spruch"
FP: 1 Mar. 1934, Zurich (Männerchor Chambre 24, cond. Othmar Schoeck)
Recording: Ralf Lukas (bass-baritone); MDR Radio Choir; Steffen Schleiermacher
(pf); Eckart Wiegräbe, Lutz Grützmann, Fernando Günther (trbn); Bernd
Angerhöfer (tb); Gerd Schenker, Sven Pauli (perc), cond. Mario Venzago.
Claves Records CD 50–2701

woo 41
Kanon (Othmar Schoeck)
For mixed voices [SATB], pf
1941
FP: 25 Jan. 1942, Bern (Lehrergesangverein Bern)

Op. 54
Für ein Gesangfest im Frühling (Gottfried Keller)
For male chorus [TTBB] and orchestra
1942
Instr.: 2fl, 2ob, 2cl, 2bn—4hn, 3tpt, 3trbn, tb—timp, perc (trgl, cym, bass drum)—str
FP: 12 Apr. 1944, Bern (Berner Liedertafel; Bern City Orchestra, cond. Kurt Rothen-
bühler)
Recording: MDR Radio Choir; MDR Symphony Orchestra, cond. Mario Venzago.
Claves Records CD 50–2701

Op. 62, no. 36
Zu einer Konfirmation (Eduard Mörike)
For mixed chorus [SATB] with organ or harmonium (or pf), or a cappella ad lib.
1948
Note: composed before the solo version of Op. 62, no. 36
Recordings: The Choir of Gonville and Caius College; Jeremy Bines (organ), cond.
Geoffrey Webber. Guild GMCD 7177

MDR Radio Choir; Franz Zimpel (organ), cond. Howard Arman. Claves Records CD 50–2701

Op. 63
Vision (after the poem "In Duft und Reif" by Gottfried Keller)
For male chorus [TTB], tpt, 3trbn—perc (timp, trgl, cym)—str
1949
FP: 25 Jun. 1950, Lachen (Männerchor Lachen, cond. Rudolf Sidler)
Recording: MDR Radio Choir; MDR Symphony Orchestra, cond. Mario Venzago. Claves Records CD 50–2701

Op. 69
Zwei zweistimmige Lieder for children's or women's chorus with piano accompaniment
1. "Spruch" (Christian Morgenstern). 1941
2. "Einkehr" (Ludwig Uhland). 1955
    FP: 23 Sept.1956, Trogen (children of the Pestalozzi Village, cond. Ernst Klug)
Recording: MDR Radio Choir; Justus Zeyen (pf), cond. Howard Arman. Claves Records CD 50–2701

XII. A Cappella Choral Works

All the choral works have been published in series 2, vol. 8 of *Othmar Schoeck: Sämtliche Werke,* ed. Bernhard Billeter (Zurich: Hug, 2002).

WOO 139
Was ist des Schweizers Vaterland? (anon.)
TTBB?
Fragment, ca. 1900?

WOO 54
Nun ist der selt'ne Tag erschienen (anon.)
For mixed chorus [SATB]
1902?
Note: in the above volume of the *Sämtliche Werke* (p. 16), Bernhard Billeter suggests convincingly that the text might have been written by either Schoeck or one of his brothers on the occasion of a family birthday or wedding, and that Emanuel Geibel's poem "Nun ist der letzte Tag erschienen" served as a model.

WOO 20
Agnes (Eduard Mörike)
For mixed chorus [SATB]
1905
FP: 28 Oct. 1908, Thun (Cäcilienverein, cond. August Oetiker).
Recording: Wettinger Kammerchor and Seminarchor Wettingen, cond. Karl Grenacher. Jecklin-Disco JD 504–2

WOO 21
's Seeli (Meinrad Lienert)
For male chorus [TTBB]
1905
FP: 1905 (?), Zurich (cond. Carl Attenhofer)
Recording: Wettinger Kammerchor and Seminarchor Wettingen, cond. Karl Grenacher. Jecklin-Disco JD 504–2

WOO 119
[Psalm 150: "Alles was Odem hat, lobe den Herrn"; in D-flat major]
For mixed chorus [SATB]
Fragment, ca. 1905?
Note: Presumably a counterpoint exercise from Schoeck's years at the Zurich Con-
servatory

WOO 120
[Psalm 150: "Alles was Odem hat, lobe den Herrn"; in C major]
For mixed chorus [SATB]
Fragment, ca. 1905?
Note: Presumably a counterpoint exercise from Schoeck's years at the Zurich Con-
servatory

WOO 23
Ein Vöglein singt im Wald (Anna Ritter)
For mixed chorus [SATB]
1906/7
FP: 28 Oct. 1908, Thun (Cäcilienverein, cond. August Oetiker)
Recordings: Wettinger Kammerchor and Seminarchor Wettingen, cond. Karl Gre-
nacher. Jecklin-Disco JD 504–2
Vokalensemble Cantuccelli, cond. Elisabeth Fischer. CANTU 1999 IFPI LA41

WOO 24
Es ist bestimmt in Gottes Rat (Ernst von Feuchtersleben)
For mixed chorus [SATB]
1906/7
FP(?): Apr. 1911, Thun (by a solo SATB quartet: Clara Wirz-Wyss, A. Günther, Franz
Müller, Fritz Haas; it is unclear if this work was sung with conductor)
Recordings: Wettinger Kammerchor and Seminarchor Wettingen, cond. Karl Gre-
nacher. Jecklin-Disco JD 504–2
Vokalensemble Cantuccelli, cond. Elisabeth Fischer. CANTU 1999 IFPI LA41

WOO 74
[*Firnelicht* (Conrad F. Meyer)]
For male chorus [TTBB]
ca. 1908?

Note: The music is without text; the title was added to the manuscript at a later date by Werner Vogel, presumably acting on information from the composer. Meyer's poem fits the music, but only if portions of the text are repeated.

woo 30
Sehnsucht (Joseph von Eichendorff)
For male chorus [TTBB]
1909
FP: 14 Nov. 1909, Zurich (Männerchor Aussersihl, cond. Othmar Schoeck)
Recordings: Wettinger Kammerchor and Seminarchor Wettingen, cond. Karl Grenacher. Jecklin-Disco JD 504–2
Vokalensemble Cantuccelli, cond. Elisabeth Fischer. CANTU 1999 IFPI LA41

woo 33
Frühling und Herbst (free translation by Gian Bundi from the Romansh of Gian Singer)
For mixed chorus [SATB]
1912
FP: Jun. 1912, Bern (Cäcilienverein, cond. Fritz Brun)

woo 34
's Liedli (Meinrad Lienert)
For mixed chorus [SATB]
1915
FP: 30 Apr. 1916, Thun (Cäcilienverein, cond. August Oetiker)

woo 34 (revised)
's Liedli (Meinrad Lienert)
For SATB chorus
before 1931
Note: only the opening is identical with the first "version" of this setting; the two should rather be considered as different works.

woo 39
Die Drei (Lenau)
For male chorus [TBB]
1930
FP: 1 Mar. 1934, Zurich (Männerchor Chambre 24, cond. Max Graf)
Recordings: MDR Radio Choir, cond. Howard Arman. Claves Records CD 50–2701
Schmaz (Schwuler Männerchor Zürich), cond. Karl Scheuber. PolyGram 523 992–2

woo 122
[*Spottkanon*] (Othmar Schoeck)
For 3 voices
1940
Note: This rudimentary canon, the object of which was supposedly Adolf Hitler, was sketched on the back of an envelope. Whether intentionally or not, it is similar

to the Witch's motive from Engelbert Humperdinck's *Hänsel und Gretel* (and is here in the same key as it first appears in that opera).

WOO 42
Nachruf (Uhland)
For three-part choir [SAB]
1943

WOO 43
Zimmerspruch (Uhland)
For male chorus [TTBB]
1947
FP: 26 Jun. 1948, Bern (Männerchor "Frohsinn" of Brunnen)
Recordings: MDR Radio Choir, cond. Howard Arman. Claves Records CD 50–2701
Wettinger Kammerchor and Seminarchor Wettingen, cond. Karl Grenacher. Jecklin-
    Disco JD 504–2

Op. 62, no. 36
Zu einer Konfirmation (SATB)
For the original choral version, see **Choral Works with Accompaniment**

Op. 67a
Maschinenschlacht (Hermann Hesse)
For male chorus [TTBB]
1953
FP: 4 Jun. 1954, Zurich (Sängerverein Harmonie, cond. Hans Erismann)
Recording: MDR Radio Choir, cond. Howard Arman. Claves Records CD 50–2701

Op. 67b
Gestutzte Eiche (Hesse)
For male chorus [TTBB]
1953
FP: 30 Oct. 1954, Thun (Männerchor Thun, cond. Heiner Vollenwyder)
Recording: MDR Radio Choir, cond. Howard Arman. Claves Records CD 50–2701

WOO 117
Studentenlied (Rosemarie Dunkel)
For male chorus [TTBB]
ca. 1955?
FP: 15 Dec. 1956, Bern (Berner Singstudenten, cond. Heiner Vollenwyder)
Note: this is an arrangement for four voices of the *KTV-Kantus*, WOO 3, with a new
    text. The arrangement was presumably made by the composer himself.

Notes

Introduction

1.   See, for example, Adrian Wolfgang Martin, *Othmar Schoeck und der schweizerische Geist* (St. Gallen: Tschudy, 1957).

2.   The term is common in discussions of Swiss art, but was, to my knowledge, first used in the context of Schoeck's music by Jürg Stenzl. It was a major feature in the discussions during the first Othmar Schoeck Congress, in Bern in 1986.

3.   I am grateful to Beat Föllmi of the Schoeck Complete Edition for permission to peruse the shorter version of Corrodi's unpublished biography, "Das Leben Othmar Schoecks (gekürzte Fassung)." The longer version was for a while available for consultation to editors of the Complete Edition (see, e.g., Michael Baumgartner's introduction to Schoeck's *Massimilla Doni*, in *Sämtliche Werke* series 3, vol. 16 [vocal score], ed. Baumgartner, 9–14, here 9, n. 1), but its whereabouts are now unknown (communication from the editors, 4 July 2008). Margrit Corrodi told me about her husband's biography during our conversations in 1988.

4.   See Chris Walton, "Der Zeitblom von Erlenbach: Thomas Mann, *Doktor Faustus* und Hans Corrodi," in CWZ, 92–103, here 101.

5.   HCD, 15 Feb. 1916.

6.   Ludwig Wittgenstein, *Lectures and Conversations on Aesthetics, Psychology and Religious Belief,* ed. Cyril Barrett (Oxford: Blackwell, 1978), 44.

7.   WVG.

8.   WVG, 175.

9.   DPS.

10.   Charles Cattin, "Textwahl und -zusammenstellung der Lenau-Gedichte in den Liederzyklen *Elegie—Notturno—Nachhall* als Othmar Schoecks künstlerische Tat" (undergraduate diss., University of Neuchâtel, 1973).

11.   Stefanie Tiltmann-Fuchs, "Studien zu Othmar Schoecks Liederfolgen für Singstimme und Orchester" (PhD diss., University of Cologne, 1975).

12.   Canisius Braun, "Othmar Schoeck in St. Gallen: Zur Rezeption der Schoeckschen Programmgestaltung" (undergraduate diss., University of Zurich, 1989).

13.   Michael Baumgartner, "Studien zu Othmar Schoecks Oper *Massimilla Doni*" (undergraduate diss., University of Zurich, 1999).

14.   Beat A. Föllmi, "Einleitung," in Föllmi, ed., *Die Worte vergrössern—Schoecks Opern im Spiegel der Kulturwissenschaften: Bericht über das zweite Internationale Symposium Othmar Schoeck in Luzern, 13. und 14. August 1999* (Zürich: Othmar-Schoeck-Gesellschaft, 2000), 7–11, here 7.

15.   "Honegger" offers 13 hits, but two are theses by Marc Honegger with no connection to the composer Arthur.

Chapter One

1. Theophil F. Wiget, "Othmar Schoeck und Brunnen," *Mitteilungen des Historischen Vereins des Kantons Schwyz* 74 (1982): 87–94, here 87.
2. WVG, 93.
3. WVG, 94.
4. WVG, 122.
5. See Georg Vohmann-Falk, *Brunnen-Ingenbohl: Üses Dorf, üsi Gmeind, üsi Lüüt* (Brunnen: Hohener-Vohmann, 1991), 181–82.
6. See, for example, Karl Baedeker, *Die Schweiz nebst den angrenzenden Teilen von Oberitalien, Savoyen und Tirol: Handbuch für Reisende*, 34th ed. (Leipzig: Baedeker, 1911), 120.
7. Rigbie Turner, "Richard Strauss to Cäcilie Wenzel: Twelve Unpublished Letters," *19th-Century Music* 9, no. 3 (Spring 1986): 163–75, here 171.
8. See Michael Meyer, *Strindberg: A Biography* (Oxford & New York: Oxford University Press, 1987), 159.
9. See WVG, 93.
10. WVG, 56.
11. HCD, 11 Oct. 1921.
12. Ann Bridge (pseudonym of Mary Dolling Sanders O'Malley), *Portrait of My Mother* (London: Chatto & Windus, 1955), 175–76.
13. HCD, 5 Jan. 1935.

Chapter Two

1. Related to me by Grosser's daughter in April 2007.
2. HCD, 31 Dec. 1923.
3. See Ingeborg Schreiber, *Max Reger in seinen Konzerten* (Bonn: Dümmlers Verlag, 1981), 2:308–9.
4. Quoted in WVZ, 44.

Chapter Three

1. Unpublished letters from Schoeck to Rüeger of 20 and 9 May 1907 respectively.
2. WVG, 128.
3. Werner Vogel, ed., *Euer dankbarer Sohn: Schoecks Leipziger Briefe* (Winterthur: Amadeus, 1985), 65.
4. Friedrich Huch, Diary in the Braunschweig Stadtarchiv, shelf mark G IX 24:42, quoted in full—as are the letters from Huch to Schoeck—in CWZ, 30–35.
5. Letter of late Nov./early Dec. 1907 from Schoeck to his parents, in Vogel, *Euer dankbarer Sohn*, 64.
6. See Rudolf Zipkes, *Leben und Wirken der Sängerin Adele Zipkes-Bloch* (Zurich: n.p., 1996), 29.
7. WVG, 130.
8. Zipkes, *Leben und Wirken der Sängerin Adele Zipkes-Bloch*, 19.
9. Joseph Haas, "Max Reger als Lehrer," in *Reden und Aufsätze* (Mainz: Schott, 1964), 83.

10.   Vogel, *Euer dankbarer Sohn*, 74.

11.   Georg Schoeck, "Schoeck und Reger," in *Varius Idem: Festlieder und Gelegentliches*, by Georg Schoeck, ed. Elisabeth Schoeck-Grüebler (Brunnen: Soli invicto, 1994), 158.

12.   HCD, Jan. 1919.

13.   Letter of Busoni to Volkmar Andreae, 6 Oct. 1919, in Joseph Willimann, ed., *Der Briefwechsel zwischen Ferruccio Busoni und Volkmar Andreae, 1907–1923* (Zurich: Hug, 1994), 98–99, here 99.

Chapter Four

1.   Werner Vogel, *Euer dankbarer Sohn: Schoecks Leipziger Briefe* (Winterthur: Amadeus, 1985), 80.

2.   Elisabeth Schoeck-Grüebler, "Kunst und Brot: Othmar Schoeck und sein erster Verleger," *Neue Zürcher Zeitung*, 14/15 Feb. 1987.

3.   HCD, 10 May 1912.

4.   Elisabeth Schoeck-Grüebler, ed., *Post nach Brunnen: Briefe an die Familie, 1908–1922* (Zurich: Atlantis Musikbuch-Verlag, 1991), 23–24.

5.   See Inge van Rij, *Brahms's Song Collections* (Cambridge: Cambridge University Press, 2006), 184–86.

6.   HCD, 18 Mar. 1922.

7.   Anon., "Othmar Schoeck," *Vereinsorgan des Männerchor Aussersihl Zürich* 5, no. 7 (August 1916): 120–22, here 120.

8.   Schoeck-Grüebler, *Post nach Brunnen*, 40.

9.   Schoeck to Rüeger, 18 Aug. 1909.

10.   WVG, 130.

11.   See the photographs in Georg Vohmann-Falk, *Brunnen-Ingenbohl: Üses Dorf, üsi Gmeind, üsi Lüüt* (Brunnen: Hohener-Vohmann, 1991), 34–40.

12.   WVZ, 74.

13.   HCD, 13 Jul. 1930.

14.   Malcolm Gillies, ed., *The Bartók Companion* (Portland: Amadeus, 1994), 469.

15.   HCD, 13 Jul. 1930 and 22 Sept. 1921; Corrodi here records Schoeck's reminiscences of much earlier conversations with Furtwängler.

Chapter Five

1.   See Margrit Joelson-Strohbach, ed., *Briefe an Hans Reinhart* (Winterthur: W. Vogel, 1985), 28.

2.   WVG, 108–9.

3.   The tempi on the CD recording by the MDR Choir and Symphony Orchestra under Mario Venzago (on Claves 50–2701) are as close to perfect as one could wish for.

4.   HCD, 23 Aug. 1931.

5.   Hermann Hesse, ed., *Eichendorffs Gedichte und Novellen* (Berlin: Deutsche Bibliothek, 1913), vii.

6.   Hermann Hesse, *Gesammelte Briefe*, ed. Ursula and Volker Michels, vol. 1 (Frankfurt am Main: Suhrkamp, 1973), 226.

7.   Männerchor Aussersihl Zürich, *Vereinsorgan und Reiseblatt* 1, no. 5 (28 Feb. 1911): 84.

8. HCD, 15 Aug. 1928.
9. Quoted in WVZ, 78.
10. HCD, 10 Jul. 1912.
11. See Anon., "Othmar Schoeck," in *Vereinsorgan des Männerchor Aussersihl Zürich* 5, no. 7 (Aug. 1916): 120–22, here 121.
12. WVZ, 87.
13. HCD, 16 Feb. 1936.
14. Corrodi, "Richard Wagner" (unpublished article).
15. Corrodi, "Der Gott und die Bajadere" (unpublished article).

Chapter Six

1. Hans Corrodi, *Othmar Schoeck: Bild eines Schaffens* (Frauenfeld: Huber, 1956), 64.
2. HCD, 13 Jul. 1930.
3. Hans Corrodi, "Das Leben Othmar Schoecks (gekürzte Fassung)," 42.
4. HCD, 2 Mar. 1914.
5. This correspondence, recently acquired by the Zentralbibliothek Zurich, is subject to copyright restrictions, so may not be quoted directly here.
6. Quoted in Georg Schoeck, *Varius Idem: Festlieder und Gelegentliches* (Brunnen: Soli invicto, 1994), 150.
7. HCD, 18 May 1950.

Chapter Seven

1. "Aus dem Tagebuch unseres im Kriege gefallenen Mitgliedes Hermann Kaltenbach," *Vereinsorgan des Männerchor Aussersihl Zürich* 4, no. 10 (15 Jun. 1915): 206–14; no. 11 (1 Sept. 1915): 228–36; and no. 12 (22 Oct. 1915): 248–51.
2. Hans Corrodi, "Das Leben Othmar Schoecks (gekürzte Fassung)," 48.
3. PSR 2:206.
4. *Vereinsorgan des Männerchor Aussersihl Zürich* 4, no. 9 (3 Feb. 1915): 167.

Chapter Eight

1. See, e.g., HCD, 11 Oct. 1935.
2. Georg Herbst's concert review in the *Tages-Anzeiger*, 11 Mar. 1916.
3. On *Othmar Schoeck: Chorwerke*, Claves Records, CD 50–2701.
4. WVG, 129.
5. Elisabeth Schoeck-Grüebler, *Post nach Brunnen: Briefe an die Familie* (Zurich: Atlantis Musikbuch-Verlag, 1991), 121.
6. See PSR 3:334.
7. See Hansjörg Pauli, *Hermann Scherchen, 1891–1966* (Zurich: Hug, 1993), esp. 16–18.
8. Conversation with Karin Schoeller-Gottlieb, Rheinfelden, 30 Sept. 1987.
9. See Hans Bärlocher, *Othmar Schoeck und St. Gallen: Erinnerungen.* (Zurich: [Hug], 1945), especially 1, 2, and 4, and Canisius Braun, "Othmar Schoeck in St. Gallen: Zur

Rezeption der Schoeckschen Programmgestaltung" (undergrad. diss., University of Zurich, 1989), 16–17.

10.   HCD, 12 Nov. 1916.

11.   Georg Schoeck, *Varius Idem: Festlieder und Gelegentliches*, ed. Elisabeth Schoeck-Grüebler (Brunnen: Soli invicto, 1994), 151.

Chapter Nine

1.   WVG, 71.

2.   HCD, 2 Mar. 1934.

3.   Related by Daniell Revenaugh on 17 Mar. 1998.

4.   Letter from Elsbeth Mutzenbecher, 5 Aug. 1985. See also WVG, 141.

5.   HCD, 19 May 1921.

6.   See Ferruccio Busoni's "Die Einheit der Musik und die Möglichkeiten der Oper," in *Wesen und Einheit der Musik* (Berlin: Max Hesses Verlag, 1956), 10–30, here 21–22.

7.   See the letter from Ernst Georg Wolff to Werner Reinhart of 16 May 1917 in PSR, 3: 336.

8.   I am grateful to Antony Beaumont for information on the dating of the libretto. E-mail of 31 Jan. 2006.

9.   Corrodi: "Im Kampf der Waffen und Gesänge" (unpublished article), 6.

10.   Communication from Ray Holden on 22 May 2006.

11.   Quoted in Erich H. Mueller von Asow, *Richard Strauss: Thematisches Verzeichnis* (Vienna: Doblinger, 1962), 2:661.

12.   Elisabeth Schoeck-Grüebler, *Post nach Brunnen: Briefe an die Familie* (Zurich: Atlantis Musikbuch-Verlag, 1991), 130–31.

Chapter Ten

1.   See Fritz Müller, *Friedrich Hegar: Sein Leben und Wirken in Briefen; Ein halbes Jahrhundert Zürcher Musikleben, 1865–1926* (Zurich: Atlantis Musikbuch-Verlag, 1987), 214.

2.   "A Singer" from the Aussersihl Chorus, reminiscing in WVZ, 62.

3.   One Carl Kleiner from the LGV, reminiscing in Werner Vogel, *Euer dankbarer Sohn: Schoecks Leipziger Briefe* (Winterthur: Amadeus, 1985), 116.

4.   Corrodi reminiscing about his days in the LGV, quoted in Vogel, *Euer dankbarer Sohn*, 118.

5.   WVZ, 119–20.

6.   Letter to the present writer, 5 Aug. 1985.

7.   Told to me by one of Rüeger's daughters in 1987.

8.   HCD, 26 Mar. 1957.

9.   Bruno Fritzsche and Max Lemmenmeier, "Auf dem Weg zu einer städtischen Industriegesellschaft," in *Geschichte des Kantons Zürich*, vol. 3: *19. und 20. Jahrhundert*, ed. Fritzsche, Lemmenmeier, Mario König, Daniel Kurz, and Eva Sutter (Zurich: Werd Verlag, 1994), 158–249, here 245–46. For prices of basic foodstuffs in Switzerland from 1914 to 1920, see Eidgenössisches statistisches Bureau, *Statistisches Jahrbuch der Schweiz, 1920* (Bern: A. Francke, 1921), 277.

10.   WVG, 141.

11. Ferruccio Busoni, "Von der Zukunft der Oper," in *Wesen und Einheit der Musik* (Berlin: Max Hesses Verlag, 1956), 61–64, here 63.
12. HCD, 18 Mar. 1922.
13. HCD, 11 Aug. 1922.

Chapter Eleven

1. HCD, 12 Sept. 1918, and Walter Schädelin's diary, 30 Sept. 1918. In her reminiscences in WVZ, Mary gives 12 August as the date she met Schoeck. Corrodi wrote that their first meeting was in early September and assumed that the three days in Lausanne were spent immediately afterwards. We cannot know who was right, though it seems unlikely that Mary would have got the date wrong.
2. Schädelin, Diary, 30 Sept. 1918.
3. Letter from Schoeck to Rüeger, undated, but from Oct. 1918.
4. See also DPS, 36.
5. HCD, Jan. 1919. I am indebted to Harry Joelson for identifying Lise Stiefel (later Rioult-Stiefel, after her marriage to a French naval officer). She lived until 1996. See also "100jährige Winterthurerin" by "ldb," *Die Landbote*, 24 Dec. 1994.
6. Willimann, ed., *Der Briefwechsel zwischen Ferruccio Busoni und Volkmar Andreae, 1907–1923* (Zurich: Hug, 1994), 73.
7. Ferruccio Busoni, *Briefe an seine Frau*, ed. Friedrich Schnapp (Erlenbach & Leipzig: Rotapfel, 1935), 330.

Chapter Twelve

Epigraph. Schoeck to Rüeger from Brissago on 12 May 1919.
1. Elisabeth Schoeck-Grüebler, *Post nach Brunnen: Briefe an die Familie, 1908–1922* (Zurich: Atlantis Musikbuch-Verlag, 1991), 138.
2. Ferruccio Busoni, "Von der Zukunft der Oper," in *Wesen und Einheit der Musik* (Berlin: Max Hesses Verlag, 1956), 61–64, here 63.
3. WVG, 94.
4. Rainer Maria Rilke, *Die Briefe an Frau Goldi Nölke aus Rilkes Schweizer Jahren* (Wiesbaden: Insel-Verlag, 1953), 16.
5. Rilke, *Die Briefe an Frau Goldi Nölke*, 19.
6. Harry Graf Kessler, *Tagebücher, 1918–1937*, ed. Wolfgang Pfeiffer-Belli (Frankfurt am Main: Insel-Verlag, 1961), 218–20.
7. I am grateful to Charles Beer, a descendant of Antonietta, for information on his family history. E-mails of 6 Aug. 2007.
8. "The Vegetation of the Island of St. Léger in Lago Maggiore," *Journal of the Royal Horticultural Society* 38 (1913): 503–14.

Chapter Thirteen

1. A death-bed confession from the lover to her daughter, who in turn told the present writer. The source must here remain anonymous.

2.   HCD, 3 Jul. 1919.

3.   HCD, 10 Oct. 1919.

4.   Schoeck-Grüebler, *Post nach Brunnen*, 147

5.   John Barbirolli, "Speech to the New York Philharmonic-Symphony League on 1 November 1938," in *Glorious John: A Collection of Sir John Barbirolli's Lectures, Articles, Speeches and Interviews*, ed. Raymond Holden (Uttoxeter, UK: The Barbirolli Society, 2007), 133–42, here 141.

6.   Georg Solti, "with assistance from Harvey Sachs," *Solti on Solti: A Memoir* (London: Chatto & Windus, 1997), 57.

7.   Diary of Walter Schädelin, 4 Jan. 1920, manuscript.

8.   Mooser published his comments in *La Suisse* in June 1920, and they were translated by Hans Trog and published in the *Neue Zürcher Zeitung* on 15 June.

9.   Walter Schädelin, Diary, 14 Jun. 1920.

10. Walter Schädelin, Diary, 15 Jun. 1920.

Chapter Fourteen

1.   Rüeger's reminiscences as retold by Georg Schoeck to the author, 15 Aug. 1985.

2.   See Dieter Borchmeyer, *Drama and the World of Richard Wagner* (Princeton: Princeton University Press, 2003), 111 and 117–18.

3.   Review by Fritz Kreis in *St. Galler Tagblatt*, evening edition, 14 Oct. 1920, quoted in Canisius Braun, "Othmar Schoeck in St. Gallen: Zur Rezeption der Schoeckschen Programmgestaltung," (undergrad. thesis, University of Zurich, 1989), 76–77.

4.   Comments by Kreis in *St. Galler Tagblatt*, evening edition, 25 Oct. 1920, quoted in Braun, "Othmar Schoeck in St. Gallen," 77–78.

5.   Braun, "Othmar Schoeck in St. Gallen," 78–79, here 78.

6.   *St. Galler Tagblatt*, evening edition, 2 Nov. 1920, quoted in Braun, "Othmar Schoeck in St. Gallen," 80–82.

7.   WVG, 114.

8.   WVG, 163.

9.   HCD, 19. May 1921.

10. Hans Corrodi, "Im Ansturm auf das Theater" (unpublished article), 6.

11. HCD, 3 Jun. 1921.

12. For statistics on wages in Switzerland ca. 1920, see Eidgenössisches statistisches Bureau, *Statistisches Jahrbuch der Schweiz, 1920*, 281–83.

13. Conversation with Karl Neracher, St. Gallen, 5 Jun. 1987.

14. Hermann von Glenck, Diary, 7 Oct. 1921. Von Glenck had to leave Zurich just before the concert, so sadly his diary records nothing of the performances.

15. HCD, 26 Mar. 1957.

16. HCD, 4 Nov. 1921.

17. Another possibility would be Emma's sister, Gertrud Maria; Emma was a piano teacher, Gertrud a singing teacher. Letter from the St. Gallen City Archives to the present writer.

18. HCD, 4 Nov. 1921.

19. I am grateful to Verena Naegele for bringing Cavelti's attendance to my attention. Although many reference works give Cavelti's year of birth as 1914, it was in fact 1907.

20. HCD, 18 Mar. 1922.

21. HCD, 16 Apr. 1922

22. HCD, 11 Apr. 1922.

23. Ernest Newman in the *Sunday Times*, 21 May 1922.
24. HCD, 30 May 1928 and 2 Jun. 1933.
25. Robin Holloway, "Smiling Through," *The Musical Times* 137, no. 1846 (Dec. 1996): 22–26, here 25.
26. HCD, 14 Feb. 1926.
27. HCD, Apr. 1923.
28. HCD, 17 Jun. 1922 and 6 Jul. 1922.

Chapter Fifteen

1. HCD, 6 Jul. 1922.
2. HCD, 30 Aug. 1922.
3. Schädelin, Diary, 23 Sept. 1922.
4. Conversation with Sibyll Güntensperger, Lala's daughter, 1986.
5. WVZ, 172.
6. HCD, 12 Aug. 1922.
7. HCD, 26 Jan. 1924.

Chapter Sixteen

1. See Willi Schuh, "Eine Art Zauberflötestoff, zwei Grimm-Märchen," in *Neue Zürcher Zeitung*, 30/31 Aug.1986.
2. HCD, 18 Jul. 1923.
3. PSR, 2:208.
4. Honegger, quoted in WVZ, 154.
5. Related to me by Georg Schoeck in April 2007.
6. PSR, 3:340.
7. HCD, 18 Jul. 1923.
8. HCD, 28 Jul. 1923.
9. PSR, 2:14–18.
10. Arthur Honegger, "Souvenirs sur Othmar Schoeck," *SMZ* 86, nos. 8/9 (1 Sept. 1946): 324.
11. *SMZ* 63, no. 19 (1 Sept. 1923): 256–57.
12. Edwin Evans, "Donaueschingen and Salzburg Festivals," *The Musical Times* 64, no. 967 (1 Sept. 1923): 631–35, here 633.
13. Alban Berg, *Briefe an seine Frau*, ed. Helene Berg (Munich, Vienna: Langen, Müller, 1965), 524.
14. Hans Corrodi, "Von neuer Musik" (unpublished article), 5.
15. Conversation with Lala's daughter, Sibyll Güntensperger, in 1986.
16. HCD, 19 and 27 Aug. 1923.

Chapter Seventeen

1. Conversation with Angelie's daughter in Rheinfelden, 30 Sept. 1987.
2. HCD, 10 Sept. 1923.

3. PSR, 2:211.
4. DPS, 179.
5. DPS, 188.
6. DPS, 182.
7. Conversation with Georg Schoeck, Mar. 1986.
8. DPS, 197–99.
9. Max Deutsch, quoted in Walter Szmolyan, "Die Geburtstätte der Zwölftontechnik," *Österreichische Musikzeitschrift* 26, no. 3 (Mar. 1971): 113–126, here 118.
10. WVG, 129.
11. Erwin Stein, "Neue Formprinzipien," *Musikblätter des Anbruch* 6 (1924): 286–303.
12. DPS, 199.
13. DPS, 200.

Chapter Eighteen

1. HCD, 2 Nov. 1923, 10 Nov. 1923 and 25 Nov. 1923.
2. Canisius Braun, "Othmar Schoeck in St. Gallen: Zur Rezeption der Schoeckschen Programmgestaltung" (undergraduate thesis, University of Zurich, 1999), xxxi.
3. HCD, 26 Jan. 1924.
4. HCD, 24 Feb. 1924, and Corrodi, "Die *Gaselen*" (unpublished article).
5. David to Hermann von Glenck, quoted in Walton, "'... er möchte eben überall in vorderster Linie stehen ...': Schoecks *Penthesilea* im Urteil seiner Zeitgenossen," *Dissonanz* 61 (Aug. 1999): 14–16, here 15.
6. HCD, 23 Mar. 1924 and 25 Apr. 1924.
7. WVZ, 164.
8. Walter Schenk, "Das Tonkünstlerfest in Frankfurt am Main," *Die Musik* 16, no. 2 (Aug. 1924): 812.
9. HCD, 17 Jun. 1924.
10. Hilde's reminiscences were written for (and perhaps with?) Vogel and are given here as in WVZ, 169–72.
11. HCD, 18 Jun. 1924, and Hans Corrodi, "Hilde Bartscher" (unpublished article).
12. Corrodi, "Hilde Bartscher."
13. HCD, 6 Jul. 1924.
14. HCD, 6 Jul. 1924, 30 Oct. 1924, and Corrodi, "Hilde Bartscher."
15. Anton Haefeli, *IGNM: Die Internationale Gesellschaft für Neue Musik: Ihre Geschichte von 1922 bis zur Gegenwart* (Zurich: Atlantis Musikbuch-Verlag, 1982), 105.
16. All information on the 1924 program is taken from Haefeli, *IGNM*, 482
17. Anon., "Music in the Provinces," *The Musical Times* 65, no. 979 (1 Sept. 1924): 843–47, here 846.

Chapter Nineteen

1. HCD, 30 Oct. 1924.
2. WVZ, 310.

3. I am grateful to Harry Joelson-Strohbach of the Winterthur Stadtbibliothek and Jörg Obrecht of the Zurich Tonhalle for information on the programs of the Winterthur City Orchestra and the Zurich Tonhalle Orchestra respectively.

4. PSR, 2:207.

5. HCD, 7 Feb. 1925.

6. David to Hermann von Glenck, quoted in Walton, "'. . . er möchte eben überall in vorderster Linie stehen . . .': Schoecks *Penthesilea* im Urteil seiner Zeitgenossen," *Dissonanz* 61 (Aug. 1999): 14–16, here 15.

7. Anton Haefeli, *IGNM: Die Internationale Gesellschaft für Neue Musik; Ihre Geschichte von 1922 bis zur Gegenwart* (Zurich: Atlantis Musikbuch-Verlag, 1982), 483.

8. PSR, 3:345.

9. Quoted in WVZ, 167–68.

10. See CWZ, 109.

11. Corrodi only discovered this twenty years later, recording it in his diary on 13 Jun. 1946.

12. Karl Heinrich David, "Geheilte Liebesnot," in *Othmar Schoeck: Festgabe der Freunde zum 50. Geburtstag,* ed. Willi Schuh (Erlenbach: Eugen Rentsch, 1936), 68.

13. HCD, 16 Oct. 1925.

14. Elisabeth Schoeck-Grüebler, *Post nach Brunnen: Briefe an die Familie, 1908–1922* (Zurich: Atlantis Musikbuch-Verlag, 1991), 165–66.

15. Conversation with Angelie's daughter in Rheinfelden, 30 Sept. 1987.

16. The "blood-red windows" were still there when my wife and I were married in Zurich in 1994. Our witness, Elisabeth Schoeck-Grüebler, sitting on my left, remarked as the mid-morning sun flooded the room: "Gäll, dr bluetrosige Schimmer vom Giacometti!" The windows are extraordinarily beautiful.

17. Related to the present writer by more than one friend of the composer.

18. HCD, 27 Mar. 1957.

19. HCD, 26 Mar. 1957.

20. HCD, 31 Jan. 1926.

21. HCD, "end of April" 1923.

22. David, "Geheilte Liebesnot," 69.

23. HCD, 4 Jun. 1927.

24. Haefeli, *IGNM,* 148.

25. HCD, 11 Jul. 1926.

26. HCD, 1 Nov. 1926.

27. HCD, 7 Nov. 1926.

28. HCD, 4 Jun. 1927, and conversation with Willi Schuh in 1985.

29. HCD, 7 Nov. 1926.

Chapter Twenty

1. Rüeger's diary of 10 Jan. 1927, quoted in Hans and Sylvia van der Waerden, "Nachklang: Die Freundschaft zwischen Othmar Schoeck und Armin Rüeger" (talk given to the Literaria Bischofszell on 12 Nov. 1986, unpublished), 18.

2. PSR, 2:214.

3. HCD, 26 Mar. 1957.

4. See CWZ, 108–11.

5. See CWZ, 123–25.

6. Hans-Joachim Hinrichsen, "Das 'Wesentliche des Kleist'schen Dramas'? Zur musikdramatischen Konzeption von Othmar Schoecks Operneinakter 'Penthesilea,'" *Archiv für Musikwissenschaft* 59, no. 4 (2002): 267–97, here 288.

7. Quoted in WVZ, 176.

Chapter Twenty-One

1. Conversation with Edward Staempfli in Berlin, 1992.

2. See Theodor W. Adorno, "Walter Herbert," *Der Rabe—Magazin für jede Art von Literatur* 61 (2002): 179.

3. HCD, 14 Feb. 1926.

4. DPS, 235.

5. WVG, 116.

6. Conversation with Franz Ludwig von Senger, 28 Nov. 1986.

7. HCD, 9 Jul. 1927.

8. Letter from Hüni to Krebs of 16 Aug. 1927, and from Hüni to Schoeck of 22 Aug.

9. PSR, 3:347–48.

10. PSR, 2:213.

11. PSR, 1:140–42.

12. HCD, 22 Jun. 1927.

13. HCD, 19 Jul. 1927.

14. HCD, 20 Apr. 1928.

15. PSR, 3:348.

16. Hermann von Glenck to Karl Heinrich David, quoted in Walton, "'. . . er möchte eben überall in vorderster Linie stehen . . . ,'" 14–16, here 15–16.

17. Quoted in Walton, "'. . . er möchte eben überall in vorderster Linie stehen . . . ,'" 16.

18. Anton Haefeli, *IGNM: Die Internationale Gesellschaft für Neue Musik; Ihre Geschichte von 1922 bis zur Gegenwart* (Zurich: Atlantis Musikbuch-Verlag, 1982), 156.

19. As I can confirm from having chaired several local ISCM juries.

20. As told by von Vintschger during our several meetings in St. Gallen in the mid-1980s.

Chapter Twenty-Two

1. HCD, 26 May 1930.

2. WVG, 153.

3. Cosima Wagner, *Die Tagebücher*, vol. 1 (Munich and Zurich: Piper, 1976), 498.

4. Georg Schoeck, "Einige Aussprüche von Othmar Schoeck," in *Varius idem: Festlieder und Gelegentliches* (Brunnen: Soli invicto, 1994), 150–54, here 151.

5. WVG, 35 and 50.

6. Schoeck to Hesse from Zurich, 6 Jun. 1929, quoted in WVZ, 195.

7. Schoeck to Hesse from Lübeck, 18 Aug. 1929, quoted in WVZ, 198.

8. Schoeck to Hesse from Lübeck, 18 Aug. 1929, quoted in WVZ, 198.

9. PSR, 3:353.

10. See Hans Corrodi, *Othmar Schoeck: Bild eines Schaffens* (Frauenfeld: Huber, 1956), 178.

Chapter Twenty-Three

1.   HCD, 27 Oct. 1929, and letter from Breitkopf to Schoeck of 16 Sept. 1929.
2.   Hindemith to David, 29 Oct. 1929.
3.   HCD, 27 Oct. 1929.
4.   PSR, 3:354.
5.   Related in a personal conversation by Josef von Vintschger in 1988.
6.   Conversation with Willi Schuh in 1985.
7.   Letter from Breitkopf to Schoeck of 6 Sept. 1930.
8.   WVZ, 310.
9.   The beginning and the end of the work were preserved in the archives of the Zurich Radio Studio and have been published on Uranus URA 601.
10.   Derrick Puffett, "Walton, Hindemith, Schoeck"; letter to the editor, *The Musical Times* 123, no. 1672 (Jun. 1982), 392.
11.   HCD, 21 Oct. 1930 and 4 Jan. 1931.

Chapter Twenty-Four

1.   PSR, 3:354.
2.   HCD, 27 Mar. 1957.
3.   PSR, 3:356.
4.   HCD, 7 Jun. 1931.
5.   HCD, 23 Aug. 1931.
6.   WVZ, 33.
7.   HCD, 23 Aug. 1931.
8.   HCD, 28 Oct. 1931.
9.   HCD, 23 Jan. 1944.

Chapter Twenty-Five

1.   HCD, 3 Jan. 1932.
2.   HCD, 3 Jan. 1932.
3.   HCD, 3. Jan. 1932.
4.   Review by Sc. G, *Music and Letters* 12, no. 4 (Oct. 1931): 420.
5.   HCD, 2 Mar. 1932. Also postcards from Schoeck to Hesse and Rüeger of 20 and 22 Feb. respectively.
6.   See Howard Ferguson and Michael Hurd, eds., *Letters of Gerald Finzi and Howard Ferguson* (Woodbridge, UK: Boydell Press, 2001), 280. Howard Ferguson could still recall the performance of the *Elegie* in conversation with the present writer in 1992.
7.   This anecdote is based on reports from Keith Falkner to Peter Palmer.
8.   Reminiscences of Ursula Schädelin.
9.   HCD, 23 Aug. 1931.
10.   HCD, 1 Jun. 1932.

Chapter Twenty-Six

1.   Robert Aloys Mooser, *Regards sur la musique contemporaine, 1921–1946* (Lausanne: Rouge, 1946), 162–63.

2.   M.U., "The Tonkünstlerfest at Zürich" *The Musical Times* 73, no. 1076 (1 Oct. 1932): 940.

3.   HCD, 1 Jun. 1932. Furtwängler's letter to Schoeck of 26 May 1932 is published in Othmar-Schoeck-Gesellschaft, *Jahresbericht über das neunzehnte Vereinsjahr, 1977/78*. ([Zurich]: Othmar-Schoeck-Gesellschaft, 1978), 6.

4.   See PSR, 3:362.

5.   WVG, 103.

6.   HCD, 4 Oct. 1933.

7.   HCD, 8 May 1933.

8.   See WVZ, 209.

9.   WVG, 165.

10.   WVG, 72.

11.   WVG, 43.

12.   DPS, 304–5.

13.   Alban Berg passed on his praise via friends of Schoeck. Communication from Niklaus Tüller in 1988.

14.   DPS, 331–32.

Chapter Twenty-Seven

1.   HCD, 2 Mar. 1934.

2.   See Curt Riess, *Zürcher Schauspielhaus: Sein oder Nichtsein; Der Roman eines Theaters* (Zürich: Buchklub Ex Libris, 1963), 83–135.

3.   HCD, 26 Nov. 1933.

4.   HCD, 29 Nov. 1943.

5.   HCD, 8 Jul. 1933.

6.   HCD, 11 Feb. 1934.

7.   Toby Thacker, *Music after Hitler, 1945–1955* (Aldershot, UK: Ashgate, 2007), 119.

8.   WVZ, 222.

9.   HCD, 29 Jul. 1934.

10.   *Neue Zürcher Zeitung*, 18 Apr. 1934.

11.   See Fred K. Prieberg, *Handbuch deutscher Musiker, 1933–1945* (n.p.: Prieberg, 2004), 1573–75.

12.   HCD, 29 Apr. 1934.

13.   HCD, 22 Apr. 1934.

14.   HCD, 2 Jun. 1934.

15.   Georg Schoeck, "Schoeck zur Zeit der Massimilla in Brunnen," in *Varius Idem: Festlieder und Gelegentliches* (Brunnen: Soli invicto, 1994), 154–58, here 155–57.

16.   HCD, 11 Aug. 1934.

17.   HCD, 25 Sept. 1934.

Chapter Twenty-Eight

1. Related to the present writer by Hans Vogt in April 1986; he had heard the tale from Hilde Schoeck.
2. See Stuart Gilbert, ed., *Letters of James Joyce* (London: Faber & Faber, 1957), 356.
3. Communication from Niklaus Tüller.
4. *SMZ* 75, no. 8 (15 Apr. 1935): 315.
5. HCD, 3 Apr. 1935.
6. Morgenthaler's reminiscences are given in WVZ, 216–19, though the year given there for the trip is 1936. Other, contemporary sources, such as Corrodi's diary, confirm that the year was in fact 1935.
7. See Thomas Mann, *Tagebücher, 1935–1936*, ed. Peter de Mendelssohn (Frankfurt am Main: Suhrkamp, 1978), 96.
8. HCD, 11 Jun. 1935.
9. HCD, 27 Oct. 1935.
10. Mann, *Tagebücher*, 201.
11. Mann, *Tagebücher*, 243.
12. HCD, 8 Apr. 1936.
13. See the entry "Karl Böhm" in Prieberg, *Handbuch deutscher Musiker, 1933–1945* (n.p.: Prieberg, 2004), 604.
14. HCD, 22 May 1936.
15. Rolf Urs Ringger, "Othmar Schoeck—oder: Die Zukunft eines Musikers," in *Von Debussy bis Henze: Zur Musik unseres Jahrhunderts* (Munich & Zurich: Piper, 1986), 165–75, here 170.
16. See Michael Baumgartner, "Einleitung," in *Massimilla Doni*, series 3, vol. 16 of Schoeck, *Sämtliche Werke*, ed. Baumgartner (vocal score) (Zurich: Hug & Co. Musikverlage, 2000), 9–14, here 12.
17. Georg Schoeck later recalled his uncle's comments upon opening the newspaper that morning.
18. Letter of 21 Apr. 1937.
19. Review of the revised version of Corrodi's biography of Schoeck by "S. G.," *Music & Letters* 18, no. 2 (Apr. 1937): 212–13.
20. Schuh, ed., *Othmar Schoeck: Festgabe der Freunde zum 50. Geburtstag* (Erlenbach: Eugen Rentsch, 1936).
21. Review by Karl Heinrich David, *SMZ* 76, no. 20 (15 Oct. 1936): 556.
22. Canisius Braun, "Othmar Schoeck in St. Gallen: Zur Rezeption der Schoeckschen Programmgestaltung" (undergrad. diss., University of Zurich, 1989), 18.
23. Schoeck to Hesse, 27 Sept. 1936, quoted in part in WVZ, 221.
24. HCD, 28 Dec. 1936.

Chapter Twenty-Nine

1. R. E., "Othmar Schoeck's 'Massimilla Doni,'" *Musical Times* 78, no. 1130 (Apr. 1937): 367.
2. Joseph Goebbels, *Die Tagebücher*, ed. Elke Fröhlich, part 1, vol. 3 (Munich: Institut für Zeitgeschichte, 1987), 84.
3. Reminiscences of Josef von Vintschger, 1988.

4. David's review in *SMZ* 77, no. 7 (1 Apr. 1937): 178–79, here 178.

5. Typescript reminiscences of Josef von Vintschger (Mar. 1937).

6. See Hans-Dieter Steinmetz, "Karl Mays Grabmal in Radebeul," at http://karl-may.leo.org/kmg/seklit/JbKMG/1995/12.htm, accessed Mar. 2007. The site features a facsimile of Klara May's obituary notice.

Chapter Thirty

1. See the various reports of the occasion, e.g., Anon., "Verleihung des Erwin von Steinbach-Preises" in *Der Führer*, 26 Apr. 1937; "Verleihung des Erwin-von-Steinbach-Preises an Dr. h.c. Othmar Schoeck (Zürich)," *Freiburger Zeitung*, Apr. 26, 1937.

2. HCD, 4 May 1937.

3. Karl Schmid-Bloss, "Drei Stunden im Weltinteresse," in *Zürcher Stadttheater: Jahrbuch 1937/38*, 16: 8–15.

4. Corrodi, "Musikalischer Bolschewismus in der Oper: Zur Uraufführung der Oper 'Lulu' von Alban Berg in Zürich," *Die Musik* 29, no. 10 (Jul. 1937): 46. It also appeared in the *Völkischer Beobachter* on June 6.

5. HCD, 17 Oct. 1937.

6. Anon. (presumably Karl Schmid-Bloss), "Im Stadttheater fanden in der Spielzeit 1936/37 356 Veranstaltungen statt." in *Zürcher Stadttheater: Jahrbuch 1937/38*, 16:34–37, here 34.

7. Schoeck's letters to Burte are in the Burte Archives in Maulburg.

8. See Wolf Borchers, "Männliche Homosexualität in der Dramatik der Weimarer Republik," (PhD diss., University of Cologne, 2001), 583.

9. Prieberg, *Handbuch deutscher Musiker, 1933–1945* (n.p.: Prieberg, 2004), 2631.

10. Thomas Mann, *Tagebücher, 1935–1936*, ed. de Mendelssohn (Frankfurt am Main: Suhrkamp, 1978), entry of 10 Nov. 1935, 204.

11. HCD, 12 Aug. 1937.

12. Burte to Schoeck from Muzot, 18 Sept. 1937.

13. Braun, "Othmar Schoeck in St. Gallen: Zur Rezeption der Schoeckschen Programmgestaltung" (undergrad. diss., University of Zurich, 1989), 18.

14. Prieberg, *Handbuch deutscher Musiker*, 1445–46.

15. Karl Schmid-Bloss, "Rückschau auf die Spielzeit 1937/38 des Zürcher Stadttheaters," in *Zürcher Stadttheater: Jahrbuch 1938/39*, 17:6–13, here 10.

16. Karl Heinrich David, "Paul Hindemith: *Mathis der Maler*," *SMZ* 78, no. 12 (15 Jun. 1938): 313–16.

17. Hans Ehinger, "Arthur Honegger: *Jeanne d'Arc au bûcher*," *SMZ* 78, no. 12: 316–19.

18. HCD, 30 May 1938.

19. Letter from Burte to Reinhart from Lörrach, 18 Mar. 1940.

20. PSR, 3:368–72.

21. See Alfred Häsler, *Das Boot ist voll . . . Die Schweiz und die Flüchtlinge, 1933–1945* (Zurich and Stuttgart: Fretz & Wasmuth, 1967), 328–29.

22. HCD, later addition to the entry of 20 Nov. 1939.

Chapter Thirty-One

1. HCD, 18 Mar. 1940.

2. Undated letter of Apr. 1940 from Schoeck to Reinhart, quoted in PSR, 2:232–33.

3. HCD, 27 Apr. 1940.
4. HCD, 3 Jul. 1940.
5. HCD, 12 Sept. 1940.
6. Conversation with Karl Neracher, St. Gallen, 5 Jun. 1987.
7. Willy Hess, "Hinter den Kulissen: Momentbilder und Anekdoten eines Orchestermusikers," in *Der Landbote*, 1 Nov. 1991.
8. Conversations with Willi Schuh, 1984 and 1985.

Chapter Thirty-Two

1. HCD, 26 Apr. 1941.
2. See Prieberg, *Handbuch deutscher Musiker. 1933–1945* (n.p.: Prieberg, 2004), 2764.
3. See PSR, 3:75–76. See also Richard Taruskin, *Defining Russia Musically: Historical and Hermeneutical Essays* (Princeton & Oxford: Princeton University Press, 2000), 455.
4. See Prieberg, *Handbuch deutscher Musiker*, 2764.
5. HCD, 21 Feb. 1943. In WVZ, 255, Josi Magg is quoted as giving 25 Feb. as the day of the play-through.
6. Hans Corrodi, "'Das Schloss Dürande': Von Eichendorffs Novelle zu Hermann Burtes Textbuch," *SMZ* 83, no. 3 (Mar. 1943): 72–74, here 74.
7. Willi Schuh, "Idée und Tongestalt in Schoecks 'Schloss Dürande,'" and Hermann Spelti, "Betrachtungen zu Othmar Schoecks Opernschaffen," both in *SMZ* 83, no. 3 (Mar. 1943): 74–83 and 83–85 respectively.
8. On Jecklin JD 292–2.
9. See Hans Frölicher, *Meine Aufgabe in Berlin* (Bern: Büchler, 1962), 104.

Chapter Thirty-Three

1. This telegram is given as a facsimile in Heinz Stuckenschmidt, *Zum Hören geboren: Ein Leben mit Musik meiner Zeit* (Munich: Piper, 1979), 149. In the original everything is capitalized throughout.
2. Willi Schuh, "Betrachtungen zu Othmar Schoecks *Schloss Dürande*: Uraufführung an der Berliner Staatsoper (1. April)," *SMZ* 83, no. 5 (May 1943): 156–59, here 156.
3. Edward Staempfli, "Militär, Radio und Claude Debussy," *SMZ* 83, no. 4 (Apr. 1943): 125–26, here 126.
4. Editorial in *Musik im Kriege* 1 (1943): 35.
5. See Georg Solti, *Solti on Solti: A Memoir* (London: Chatto & Windus, 1997), especially 45–63.
6. Conversation with Robin Marchev in 1995.
7. Conversation with Bächthold in 1997.
8. See Willi Schuh, "Zürcher Opernwochen," *SMZ* 83, no. 7 (1 Jul. 1943): 236–37, here 236.
9. This parody is to be found in Frey's archives in the Zentralbibliothek Zürich.
10. Burte, *Sieben Reden von Burte* (Strasbourg: Hünenburg, 1943), 27–29.
11. Holloway, "Smiling Through," *The Musical Times* 137, no 1846 (Dec. 1996): 22–26, here 24.

12. HCD, 6 Jun. 1943.

13. See Karl Marx & Friedrich Engels, *Manifest der Kommunistischen Partei* (Moscow: Verlagsgenossenschaft Ausländischer Arbeiter in der UdSSR, 1935), 48.

14. Burte, *Sieben Reden*, 27.

15. Burte, *Sieben Reden*, 78.

16. Burte, *Sieben Reden*, 78.

17. Burte, *Sieben Reden*, 182.

18. HCD, 18 Apr. 1943.

19. Hans Frölicher, *Meine Aufgabe in Berlin* (Bern: Büchler, 1962), 104.

Chapter Thirty-Four

1. Corrodi, "Das Leben Othmar Schoecks (gekürzte Fassung)," chapter "Unter Sternen," 47.

2. HCD, 23 Jan. 1944.

3. *SMZ* 84, no. 3 (15 Mar. 1944): 100.

4. See PSR, 2:225.

5. See Puffett, "Walton, Hindemith, Schoeck," *The Musical Times* 123, no. 1672 (Jun. 1982): 392.

6. Conversation with Karl Neracher, St. Gallen, 5 Jun. 1987.

Chapter Thirty-Five

1. See, e.g., the reviews by "Gr.," *Berner Tagblatt*, Mar. 28, 1944, and by Schuh, *SMZ* 84, no. 5 (1 May 1944): 202–3.

2. Hesse, "Über einen vergessenen Dichter," in *Das Bodenseebuch, 1944* (Ulm: Karl Höhn, 1944), 92–93.

3. Letter from Schoeck to Hesse of Apr. 1944.

4. Private correspondence with the lady in question in 1995.

5. DPS, 394.

6. Quoted in WVZ, 274.

Chapter Thirty-Six

1. Prieberg, *Handbuch deutscher Musiker 1933–1945* (n.p.: Prieberg, 2004), 2764.

2. Prieberg, *Handbuch deutscher Musiker*, 1868–72.

3. See Ernst Roth's strange reminiscences of a penniless Strauss devoid of business sense in *The Business of Music: Reflections of a Music Publisher* (London: Cassell, 1969), 181.

4. HCD, 14 Sept. 1945.

5. See Gerhart Waeger, *Die Sündenböcke der Schweiz: Die Zweihundert im Urteil der geschichtlichen Dokumente, 1940–1946* (Olten & Freiburg im Breisgau: Walter-Verlag, 1971), esp. 254–62.

6. Conversation with Emil Bächthold in 1997.

7. Thomas Mann, *Tagebücher, 1940–1943*, ed. Peter de Mendelssohn (Frankfurt am Main: Fischer, 1982), 606–7.

8.   Thomas Mann, *Die Entstehung des Doktor Faustus* (Frankfurt am Main: Fischer Taschenbuch Verlag, 1984), 31.

9.   See Hans Corrodi, *Othmar Schoeck: Eine Monographie* (Frauenfeld & Leipzig: Huber, 1931), 31, and chapter 7 of Thomas Mann, *Doktor Faustus* (Frankfurt am Main: Fischer Taschenbuch Verlag, 1990).

10.   Mann, *Die Entstehung des Doktor Faustus*, 24.

Chapter Thirty-Seven

1.   PSR, 3:385.

2.   Schoeck, foreword to *Sommernacht* (Zurich: Hug, 1946).

Chapter Thirty-Eight

1.   PSR, 2:191.

2.   See Furtwängler, *Briefe*, ed. Frank Thiess (Wiesbaden: Brockhaus, 1964), 149.

3.   See WVZ, 283.

4.   WVZ, 280.

5.   Hans-Joachim Hinrichsen, "Linerarität: Bach, Ernst Kurth und Othmar Schoeck," in *Nähe aus Distanz: Bach-Rezeption in der Schweiz*, ed. Urs Fischer, Hinrichsen, and Laurenz Lütteken (Winterthur: Amadeus, 2005), 219–47, here 242–45.

6.   HCD, 18 Nov. 1947.

7.   HCD, 14 Jun. 1949.

8.   WVG, 27.

9.   Holloway, "Smiling Through," *The Musical Times* 137, no 1846 (Dec. 1996): 22–26, here 24.

10.   HCD, 1 Sept. 1948 and 20 Oct. 1948, 1 Jan. 1949.

11.   Verbal communication to the author from Josef von Vintschger, 1987.

12.   Schoeck to Hesse, 25 Apr. 1949. Quoted in WVZ, 288–89.

13.   HCD, 30 Apr. 1949.

14.   Conversation with Willi Schuh in Aug. 1984.

15.   HCD, 14 Jun. 1949.

Chapter Thirty-Nine

1.   See the letter from Hilde to Werner Reinhart of 3 Dec. 1950, in PSR, 3:397.

2.   WVG, 48.

3.   Corrodi, "Das Leben Othmar Schoecks (gekürzte Fassung)," chapter "1949," 37.

4.   Conversation with Josef von Vintschger, 1987.

5.   Jecklin Edition JD 714–2

6.   Colin Mason, "New Music," *The Musical Times* 97, no. 1366 (Dec. 1956): 647–49, here 648.

7.   Willi Schuh, Review of *Don Ranudo*, in the *Neue Zürcher Zeitung*, 24 April 1951.

8.   See PSR, 3:393–96.

9.   HCD, 27 Feb. 1951, 20 Mar. 1951, 22 Mar. 1951, and 17 Apr. 1951.

10. Conversation with Schuh in 1985.
11. See WVG, 164.
12. Letter of 28 Nov. 1951.

Chapter Forty

1. HCD, 11 Dec. 1951.
2. WVG, 103.
3. In Ferguson and Hurd, eds., *Letters of Gerald Finzi and Howard Ferguson* (Woodbridge, UK: Boydell Press, 2001), 280.
4. Anon., Review of Schoeck's Concerto for Horn & Strings, *Music & Letters* 34, no. 2 (Apr. 1953): 176.
5. HCD, 27 Mar. 1952.
6. WVG, 80.
7. See Alma Staub's reminiscences in WVZ, 295–96.
8. Hans Corrodi, "Das Leben Othmar Schoecks (gekürzte Fassung)," chapter "1952," 28.
9. HCD, 14 Oct. 1952.
10. I am grateful to Mercedes Pavlicevic for advice here.
11. HCD, 9 Oct. 1949.
12. WVG, 118.
13. WVG, 81.
14. WVG, 111.
15. WVG, 113.
16. WVG, 113.
17. Conversation with Silvia Gähwiller in Zurich, 1987. The songs can be heard on Jecklin Edition JD 714-2.
18. WVG, 114.
19. WVG, 115.

Chapter Forty-One

1. WVG, 95.
2. WVG, 154.
3. Willi Schuh, Review of *Lebendig begraben*, SMZ 94, no. 3 (1 Mar. 1954): 103–4, here 104.
4. WVG, 122.
5. Schoeck to Hesse, Jul. 1954, also quoted in WVZ, 311–12.
6. Hesse to Schoeck in Jul. 1954, also quoted in WVZ, 312.
7. WVG, 114–15.
8. See, for example, Georg Schoeck, "Einige Aussprüche von Othmar Schoeck," in *Varius Idem: Festlieder und Gelegentliches*, ed. Elisabeth Schoeck-Grüebler (Brunnen: Soli invicto, 1994), 150–54, here 154.
9. William Flanagan, Review of *Ritornelle und Fughetten*, Notes 2nd series 13, no. 4 (Sept. 1956): 706.
10. Conversation with Willi Schuh, 1985.

Chapter Forty-Two

1. W. R. Anderson, "The Edinburgh Festival," *The Musical Times* 95, no. 1340 (Oct. 1954): 555–56, here 556.
2. WVZ, 312–13.
3. Quoted in part in WVZ, 312.
4. HCD, 1 Jan. 1955.
5. HCD, 25 Apr. 1955.
6. HCD, 2 May 1955.
7. HCD, 25 May 1955.
8. HCD, 10 Nov. 1955.
9. Conversation in 1985.
10. DPS, 424–25.
11. DPS, 426.
12. WVG, 165.

Chapter Forty-Three

1. HCD, 5 Feb. 1956.
2. WVG, 171.
3. HCD, 19 Oct. 1956.
4. HCD, 8 Dec.1956.
5. WVZ, 323.
6. WVG, 182.
7. HCD, 11 Mar. 1957.
8. Thus Vogel on the Cello Sonata, in WVZ, 332.
9. The description of Schoeck's final hours is based heavily on the two sources closest to the family, namely WVG, 183–84 and HCD, 8 Mar. 1957.
10. "At," *Neue Zürcher Zeitung*, Mar. 13, 1957.

Epilogue

1. This is disussed in greater detail in CWZ, 164–66.
2. Franz Kienberger, "Geleitwort," in Othmar-Schoeck-Gesellschaft, *Jahresbericht über das zwölfte Vereinsjahr 1970/71*: 1.
3. Hermann Danuser, "Reaktionäre Meisterverehrung," *National-Zeitung Basel*, 9 Dec. 1972.
4. J. M. Coetzee, "The Work of the Censor: Censorship in South Africa," in *Giving Offense: Essays on Censorship* (Chicago & London: University of Chicago Press, 1996), 185–203, here 200.
5. Corrodi, *Othmar Schoeck: Bild eines Schaffens* (Frauenfeld: Huber, 1956), 267.
6. Corrodi, *Othmar Schoeck: Bild eines Schaffens*, 408.
7. Corrodi, *Othmar Schoeck: Bild eines Schaffens*, 414.
8. Corrodi, *Othmar Schoeck: Bild eines Schaffens*, 6.
9. Corrodi, *Auf einsamen Wegen: Zu Othmar Schoecks fünftem Todestag* (Zurich: Othmar-Schoeck-Gesellschaft, 1962).

Bibliography

Schoeck's Complete Works

Othmar Schoeck: Sämtliche Werke
This is an ongoing project. The following volumes have appeared so far:
Series 1: Lieder. Vol. 1: Lieder aus der frühen Schaffenszeit 1 (bis 1910). Edited by
Lukas Meister. Zürich: Hug & Co. Musikverlage, 2004.
Series 2: Chorwerke. Vol. 8: Werke für gemischten Chor, Männerchor, Frauen- oder
Kinderchor, a cappella oder mit Begleitung. Edited by Bernhard Billeter. Zur-
ich: Hug & Co. Musikverlage, 2002.
Series 3: Bühnenwerke: Vol. 10: Erwin und Elmire. Edited by Patrick Müller and
Beat A. Föllmi. Zurich: Hug & Co. Musikverlage, 2008.
Vol. 11: Don Ranudo. Edited by Thomas Seedorf. Zurich: Hug & Co. Musikverlage,
1999.
Vol. 15: Vom Fischer un syner Fru. Edited by Hans Oesch. Zurich: Hug & Co.
Musikverlage, 2003.
Vol. 16c: Massimilla Doni. Edited by Michael Baumgartner. Zurich: Hug & Co.
Musikverlage, 2000.
Series 4: Instrumentalmusik. Vol. 18: Werke für Klavier. Edited by Erik Levi. Zurich:
Hug & Co. Musikverlage, 2005.
Vol. 21: Werke für kleines Orchester und für Streichorchester. Edited by Victor
Ravizza. Zurich: Hug & Co. Musikverlage, 1995.
Vol. 22: Werke für grosses Orchester. Edited by Gérard Dayer. Zurich: Hug & Co.
Musikverlage, 1997.
Vol. 23: Werke für ein Soloinstrument und Orchester. Edited by Beat A. Föllmi. Zur-
ich: Hug & Co. Musikverlage, 2001.

Unpublished Material

Baumgartner, Michael. "Studien zu Othmar Schoecks Oper *Massimilla Doni*." Under-
graduate diss., University of Zurich, 1999.
Borchers, Wolf. "Männliche Homosexualität in der Dramatik der Weimarer Repub-
lik." PhD diss., University of Cologne, 2001.
Braun, Canisius. "Othmar Schoeck in St. Gallen: Zur Rezeption der Schoeckschen
Programmgestaltung." Undergraduate diss., University of Zurich, 1989.
Cattin, Charles. "Textwahl und -zusammenstellung der Lenau-Gedichte in den Lie-
derzyklen *Elegie—Notturno—Nachhall* als Othmar Schoecks künstlerische Tat."
Undergraduate diss., University of Neuchâtel, 1973.

Corrodi, Hans. Diaries, 1912–57.
———. "1914."
———. "1918."
———. "Als die 'Elegie' entstand."
———. "Als 'Don Ranudo' entstand."
———. "Auf Franz Schuberts Spuren."
———. "Dada, Soso und Dadacacapopo."
———. "Don Ranudo tritt ins Rampenlicht."
———. "Elsbeth."
———. "'Erwin und Elmire.'"
———. "Ferien im Walliser Hochgebirge."
———. "Feruccio [*sic*] Busoni."
———. "Die 'Gaselen.'"
———. "'Der Gott und die Bajadere.'"
———. "Hilde Bartscher."
———. "Himmlische und irdische Liebe."
———. "Hugo Wolf."
———. "Ilona Durigo."
———. "Im Ansturm auf das Theater."
———. "Im Kampf der Waffen und Gesänge."
———. "In Leipzig als Schüler Max Regers."
———. "'Jugendgedenken.'"
———. "Das Leben Othmar Schoecks (gekürzte Fassung)."
———. "Neue Gesichter in Schoecks Freundeskreis."
———. "Othmar Schoecks Freundeskreis (um 1922)."
———. "Paris und Salzburg: Von neuer Musik."
———. "Richard Wagner."
———. "Schoeck dirigiert Mozart—und verzichtet auf weitere Schwerarbeit."
———. "Schoeck führt Hugo Wolfs 'Corregidor' auf."
———. "Schoeck macht Karriere . . . [*sic*]: I: Dirigent der St. Galler Sinfoniekonzerte."
———. "Schoecks Vaterhaus."
———. "Schoecks zweites Liederbündel."
———. "'Seele, banger Vogel du . . .' [*sic*]."
———. "Die Uraufführung der 'Venus.'"
———. "Die Venus beherrscht die Stunde: Sommer 1920."
———. "Von neuer Musik."
———. "Was Othmar Schoeck (und andere) von Kindheit und Jugendjahren erzählte."
———. "Weg von der Schulbank und hinein ins tätige Leben."
———. "Winterliches Intermezzo."
———. "Der 'Zirkus Haller' im Café Schneebeli."
———. "Zürich horcht auf, Thun schwärmt."
Glenck, Hermann von. Diary, 1921, held by the Zentralbibliothek Zürich.
Huch, Friedrich. Diary, January 1908, held by the Braunschweig Stadtarchiv.
Neracher, Karl. "Erlebtes bei Schoeckproben."
Schädelin, Walter. Diaries, 1918–22. Held by Schädelin's heirs.

Van der Waerden, Hans, and Silvia van der Waerden. "Nachklang: Die Freundschaft zwischen Othmar Schoeck und Armin Rüeger" [talk given on 12 Nov. 1986 to the Literaria Bischofszell].

Vintschger, Josef von. "Reise-Episoden." Printed in part in Werner Vogel, *Othmar Schoeck: Leben und Schaffen.*

Published Material

Abendroth, Walter. Review of *Schloss Dürande. Berliner Lokalanzeiger,* 2 Apr. 1943.

Aber, Adolph. Review of *Penthesilea. Leipziger Neueste Nachrichten,* 10 Jan. 1927.

Adorno, Theodor W. "Walter Herbert." *Der Rabe—Magazin für jede Art von Literatur* 61 (2002): 179.

Anderson, W. R. "The Edinburgh Festival." *The Musical Times* 95, no. 1340 (Oct. 1954): 555–56.

Anon. "Aus dem Tagebuch unseres im Kriege gefallenen Mitgliedes Hermann Kaltenbach." *Vereinsorgan des Männerchor Aussersihl Zürich* 4, no. 10 (15 Jun. 1915): 206–14; no. 11 (1 Sept. 1915): 228–36; and no. 12 (22 Oct. 1915): 248–51.

———(presumably Karl Schmid-Bloss). "Im Stadttheater fanden in der Spielzeit 1936/37 356 Veranstaltungen statt." *Zürcher Stadttheater: Jahrbuch,* 16 (1937/38): 34–37.

———. "Music in the Provinces." *The Musical Times* 65, no. 979 (1 Sept. 1924): 843–47.

———. "Othmar Schoeck." *Vereinsorgan des Männerchor Aussersihl Zürich* 5, no. 7 (Aug. 1916): 120–22.

———. Review of Schoeck's Concerto for Horn & Strings. *Music & Letters* 34, no. 2 (Apr. 1953): 176.

Asow, Erich H. Mueller von. *Richard Strauss: Thematisches Verzeichnis* 2. Vienna: Doblinger, 1962.

Ball, Hugo, and Emmy Hennings. *Damals in Zürich.* Zurich: Verlag der Arche, 1978.

Barbirolli, John. "Speech to the New York Philharmonic-Symphony League on 1 November 1938." In *Glorious John: A Collection of Sir John Barbirolli's Lectures, Articles, Speeches and Interviews,* ed. Raymond Holden, 133–42. Uttoxeter, UK: The Barbirolli Society, 2007.

Bärlocher, Hans. *Othmar Schoeck und St. Gallen: Erinnerungen.* Zurich: [Hug], 1945.

Baumgartner, Michael. "'Verfluchte Sirene' und 'hohe Frau'—Die Darstellung der bipolaren Weiblichkeit in Massimilla Doni." In Föllmi, *Die Worte vergrössern. Schoecks Opern im Spiegel der Kulturwissenschaften: Bericht über das zweite Internationale Symposium Othmar Schoeck in Luzern, 13. und 14. August 1999,* 31–50.

Berg, Alban. *Briefe an seine Frau,* ed. Helene Berg. Munich, Vienna: Langen, 1965.

Bonjour, Edgar. *Geschichte der schweizerischen Neutralität.* Vol. 5: 1939–45. Basel and Stuttgart: Schwabe, 1970.

Borchmeyer, Dieter. *Drama and the World of Richard Wagner.* Princeton, NJ: Princeton UP, 2003.

Bridge, Ann. *Portrait of My Mother.* London: Chatto & Windus, 1955.

Brosche, Günter, ed. *Richard Strauss—Clemens Krauss: Briefwechsel; Gesamtausgabe.* Tutzing, Germany: Schneider, 1997.

Burte, Hermann. *Sieben Reden von Burte.* Strasbourg: Hünenburg, 1943.

Busoni, Ferruccio. *Briefe an seine Frau.* Edited by Friedrich Schnapp. Erlenbach, Switzerland, & Leipzig: Rotapfel, 1935.

———. *Selected Letters.* Edited and translated by Anthony Beaumont. London: Faber & Faber, 1987.

———. *Wesen und Einheit der Musik.* Berlin: Max Hesses Verlag, 1956.

Coetzee, J. M. "The work of the Censor: Censorship in South Africa." In *Giving Offense: Essays on Censorship,* 185–203. Chicago & London: University of Chicago Press, 1996.

Corrodi, Hans. *Auf einsamen Wegen: Zu Othmar Schoecks fünftem Todestag.* Zurich: Othmar-Schoeck-Gesellschaft, 1962.

———. "Musikalischer Bolschewismus in der Oper: Zur Uraufführung der Oper 'Lulu' von Alban Berg in Zürich." *Die Musik* 29, no. 10 (Jul. 1937): 46.

———. *Othmar Schoeck: Bild eines Schaffens.* Frauenfeld: Huber, 1956.

———. *Othmar Schoeck: Eine Monographie.* Frauenfeld & Leipzig: Huber, 1931; 2nd revised edition, 1936.

Danuser, Hermann. "Reaktionäre Meisterverehrung." *National-Zeitung Basel,* 9 Dec. 1972.

David, Karl Heinrich. "Paul Hindemith: *Mathis der Maler.*" *SMZ* 78, no. 12 (15 Jun. 1938): 313–16.

———. Review of the Zurich premiere of *Massimilla Doni. SMZ* 77, no. 7 (1 Apr. 1937): 178–79.

Dreyfus, Kay. *The Farthest North of Humanness: Letters of Percy Grainger, 1901–1914.* Basingstoke, UK: Macmillan, 1985.

E., R. [*sic*]. "Othmar Schoeck's 'Massimilla Doni.' *Musical Times* 78, no. 1130 (Apr: 1937): 367.

Ehinger, Hans. "Arthur Honegger: *Jeanne d'Arc au bûcher.*" *SMZ* 78, no. 12:316–19.

Eidgenössisches statistisches Bureau. *Statistisches Jahrbuch der Schweiz 1920,* Bern: A. Francke, 1921.

Engeler, Margaret. *Briefe an Volkmar Andreae: Ein halbes Jahrhundert Zürcher Musikleben, 1902–1959.* Zurich: Atlantis Musikbuch-Verlag, 1986.

Evans, Edwin. "Donaueschingen and Salzburg Festivals." *The Musical Times* 64, no. 967 (1 Sept. 1923): 631–35.

Fauser, Annegret. "'... den muss aus Liebe Schönheit töten': Klang—Körper—Frau." In Föllmi, *Die Worte vergrössern,* 51–73.

Ferguson, Howard, and Michael Hurd. *Letters of Gerald Finzi and Howard Ferguson.* Woodbridge, UK: Boydell Press, 2001.

Fischer, Kurt von. *Arthur Honegger.* Zurich: Hug, 1978.

Flanagan, William. Review of *Ritornelle und Fughetten. Notes,* 2nd series 13, no. 4 (Sept. 1956): 706.

Föllmi, Beat A. "Nach Süden nun sich lenken: Die Krise der Gattung Oper als metadiegetischer Kommentar." In Föllmi, *Die Worte vergrössern,* 83–104.

———. *Praktisches Verzeichnis der Werke Othmar Schoecks.* Zurich: Othmar Schoeck-Gesellschaft, 1997.

———, ed. *Die Worte vergrössern. Schoecks Opern im Spiegel der Kulturwissenschaften: Bericht über das zweite Internationale Symposium Othmar Schoeck in Luzern, 13. und 14. August 1999.* Zurich: Othmar Schoeck-Gesellschaft, 2000.

Föllmi, Beat A., and Michael Baumgartner. *Das Streichquartett in der zweiten Hälfte des 20. Jahrhunderts: Bericht über das dritte Internationale Symposium Othmar Schoeck in Zürich, 19. und 20. Oktober 2001.* Tutzing, Germany: Hans Schneider, 2004.

Fritzsche, Bruno, Max Lemmenmeier, Mario König, Daniel Kurz, and Eva Sutter, eds. *Geschichte des Kantons Zürich.* Vol. 3: *19. und 20. Jahrhundert.* Zurich: Werd Verlag, 1994.

Frölicher, Hans. *Meine Aufgabe in Berlin.* Bern: Büchler, 1962.

Furtwängler, Wilhelm. *Briefe.* Edited by Frank Thiess. Wiesbaden: Brockhaus, 1964.

G., S. Review of Corrodi's revised biography of Schoeck. *Music & Letters* 18, no. 2 (Apr. 1937): 212–13.

G., Sc. Review of Corrodi's biography of Schoeck. *Music and Letters* 12, no. 4 (Oct. 1931): 420.

Gilbert, Stuart, ed. *Letters of James Joyce.* London: Faber & Faber, 1957.

Gillies, Malcolm. *The Bartók Companion.* Portland: Amadeus, 1994.

Glaus, Beat. *Die Nationale Front: Eine Schweizer faschistische Bewegung, 1930–1940.* Zurich, Einsiedeln & Cologne: Benziger, 1969.

Goebbels, Joseph. *Die Tagebücher.* Edited by Elke Fröhlich. Part 1, vol. 3. Munich: Institut für Zeitgeschichte, 1987.

Gysi, Fritz. Review of *Nachhall. Tages-Anzeiger,* 12 Dec. 1955.

Haas, Joseph. *Reden und Aufsätze.* Mainz: Schott, 1964.

Haefeli, Anton. *IGNM: Die Internationale Gesellschaft für Neue Musik: Ihre Geschichte von 1922 bis zur Gegenwart.* Zurich: Atlantis Musikbuch-Verlag, 1982.

Häsler, Alfred. *Das Boot ist voll . . . Die Schweiz und die Flüchtlinge, 1933–1945.* Zurich & Stuttgart: Fretz & Wasmuth, 1967.

Heger, Hermann. Review of *Schloss Dürande. Neue Leipziger Tageszeitung,* 3 Apr. 1943.

Hess, Willy. "Hinter den Kulissen: Momentbilder und Anekdoten eines Orchestermusikers." *Der Landbote,* 1 Nov. 1991.

Hesse, Hermann, ed. *Eichendorffs Gedichte und Novellen.* Berlin: Deutsche Bibliothek, 1913.

———. *Gesammelte Briefe.* Edited by Ursula Michels and Volker Michels. Vol. 1. Frankfurt am Main: Suhrkamp, 1973.

———. "Über einen vergessenen Dichter." In *Das Bodenseebuch, 1944.* Ulm: Karl Höhn, 1944, 92–93.

Hinrichsen, Hans-Joachim. "Linerarität: Bach, Ernst Kurth und Othmar Schoeck." In *Nähe aus Distanz: Bach-Rezeption in der Schweiz,* ed. Urs Fischer, Hinrichsen, and Laurenz Lütteken, 219–47. Winterthur: Amadeus, 2005.

———. "Das 'Wesentliche des Kleist'schen Dramas'? Zur musikdramatischen Konzeption von Othmar Schoecks Operneinakter 'Penthesilea.'" *Archiv für Musikwissenschaft* 59, no. 4 (2002): 267–97.

Holl, Karl. Review of *Schloss Dürande. Frankfurter Zeitung,* 3 Apr. 1943.

Holloway, Robin. "Safe Haven for Genius." In Georg Schoeck, *Varius Idem: Festlieder und Gelegentliches,* edited by Elisabeth Schoeck-Grüebler, 322–23. Brunnen: Soli invicto, 1994.

———. "Schoeck the Evolutionary." In *On Music: Essays and Diversions, 1963–2003,* 173–79. Brinkworth, UK: Claridge Press, 2003.

———. "Smiling Through." *The Musical Times* 137, no. 1846 (Dec. 1996), 22–26.

Isler, Ernst. *Othmar Schoeck, "Penthesilea": Führer durch die Musik des Werkes.* Zurich: Hüni, 1928.

———. Review of *Schloss Dürande. Neue Zürcher Zeitung,* 2 Apr. 1943.

———. Reviews of *Penthesilea. Neue Zürcher Zeitung,* 10 Jan. 1927 and 11 Jan. 1927.

Joelson-Strohbach, Margrit. *Briefe an Hans Reinhart.* Winterthur: W. Vogel, 1985.

Kälin, Wernerkarl. *Paul Schoeck, 1882–1952: Eine Dokumentation.* Schwyz: Kulturkommission des Kantons Schwyz, 1982.

Kessler, Harry Graf. *Tagebücher, 1918–1937.* Edited by Wolfgang Pfeiffer-Belli. Frankfurt am Main: Insel-Verlag, 1961.

Kienberger, Franz. *Othmar Schoeck.* Zurich: Hug, 1975.

Krenek, Ernst. *Selbstdarstellung.* Zurich: Atlantis-Verlag, 1948.

Kunze, Stefan, and Hans Jürg Lüthi, eds. *Auseinandersetzung mit Othmar Schoeck: Internationales Othmar-Schoeck-Symposion Bern, 22.-24. Oktober 1986.* Zurich: Atlantis Musikbuch-Verlag, 1987.

Laux, Karl. Review of *Schloss Dürande. Dresdner Zeitung,* 2 Apr. 1943.

ldb. "100jährige Winterthurerin." *Die Landbote,* 24 Dec.1994.

Loeffel, Felix. "Erinnerung an Othmar Schoeck." Bern: Othmar-Schoeck-Gesellschaft, 1963.

Loertscher, Alfred. *François de Senger: Editeur malgré lui.* Lausanne: 30 jours, 1985.

[Lütolf, Max, ed.] *Zur Gesamtausgabe der Werke Othmar Schoecks.* Zurich: Othmar Schoeck-Gesellschaft, 1996.

Mann, Thomas. *Doktor Faustus.* Frankfurt am Main: Fischer Taschenbuch Verlag, 1990.

———. *Die Entstehung des Doktor Faustus.* Frankfurt am Main: Fischer Taschenbuch Verlag, 1984.

———. *Tagebücher, 1935–1936.* Edited by Peter de Mendelssohn. Frankfurt am Main: Suhrkamp, 1978.

———. *Tagebücher, 1940–1943.* Edited by Peter de Mendelssohn. Frankfurt am Main: Fischer, 1982.

Männerchor Aussersihl Zürich, *Vereinsorgan und Reiseblatt* 1, no. 5 (28 Feb. 1911): 84.

Martin, Adrian Wolfgang. *Othmar Schoeck und der schweizerische Geist.* St. Gallen, Switzerland: Tschudy, 1957.

Marx, Karl, and Friedrich Engels. *Manifest der Kommunistischen Partei.* Moscow: Verlagsgenossenschaft Ausländischer Arbeiter in der UdSSR, 1935.

Mason, Colin. "New Music." *The Musical Times* 97, no. 1366 (Dec. 1956): 647–49.

Meyer, Michael. *Strindberg: A Biography.* Oxford & New York: Oxford University Press, 1987.

Misch, Ludwig. Review of *Penthesilea. Berliner Lokalanzeiger,* 10 Jan. 1927.

Mooser, Robert Aloys. *Regards sur la musique contemporaine, 1921–1946.* Lausanne: rouge, 1946.

Müller, Fritz. *Friedrich Hegar: Sein Leben und Wirken in Briefen; Ein halbes Jahrhundert Zürcher Musikleben, 1865–1926.* Zurich: Atlantis Musikbuch-Verlag, 1987.

Müller, Robert. Review of *Unter Sternen. St. Galler Tagblatt,* 17 Jan. 1944.

Oboussier, Robert. Review of *Massimilla Doni. Deutsche Allgemeine Zeitung,* 4 Mar. 1937.

———. Review of *Schloss Dürande. Die Tat,* 8 Jun. 1943.

Othmar Schoeck-Gesellschaft. *Jahresbericht.* Zurich: Schoeck-Gesellschaft, 1959.

Palmer, Peter. "Othmar Schoecks Opern: Eine Kritik der reinen Unvernunft?" In Föllmi, *Die Worte vergrössern,* 75–82.

Pauli, Hansjörg. *Hermann Scherchen, 1891–1966.* Zurich: Hug, 1993.

Prieberg, Fred K. *Handbuch deutscher Musiker, 1933–1945.* N.p.: Prieberg, 2004.

Puffett, Derrick. "Schoecks Opern: Ein Beitrag zur Frage der Gattung am Beispiel der Opern *Venus, Penthesilea* und *Vom Fischer un syner Fru.*" In *Schweizer Theaterjahrbuch* no. 45, ed. Dorothea Baumann, 45–63. Bonstetten, Switzerland: Theaterkultur-Verlag, 1984.

———. *The Song Cycles of Othmar Schoeck.* Bern: Peter Lang, 1982.

———. "Walton, Hindemith, Schoeck"; Letter to the Editor. *The Musical Times* 123, no. 1672 (Jun. 1982): 392.

R.-I. Review of *Der Sänger. St. Galler Tagblatt,* 19 May 1945.

Riess, Curt. *Zürcher Schauspielhaus: Sein oder Nichtsein; Der Roman eines Theaters.* Zurich: Buchklub Ex Libris, 1963.

Rij, Inge van. *Brahms's Song Collections.* Cambridge: Cambridge University Press, 2006.

Rilke, Rainer Maria. *Die Briefe an Frau Goldi Nölke aus Rilkes Schweizer Jahren.* Wiesbaden: Insel-Verlag, 1953.

Ringger, Rolf Urs. "Othmar Schoeck—oder: Die Zukunft eines Musikers." In *Von Debussy bis Henze: Zur Musik unseres Jahrhunderts,* 165–75. Munich & Zurich: Piper, 1986.

Roth, Ernst. *The Business of Music: Reflections of a Music Publisher.* London: Cassell, 1969.

Schenk, Dietmar. *Die Hochschule für Musik zu Berlin: Preussens Konservatorium zwischen romantischem Klassizismus und Neuer Musik, 1869–1932/33.* Stuttgart: Franz Steiner, 2004.

Schenk, Walter. "Das Tonkünstlerfest in Frankfurt am Main." *Die Musik* 16, no. 2 (Aug. 1924): 812.

Schmid-Bloss, Karl. "Drei Stunden im Weltinteresse." *Zürcher Stadttheater: Jahrbuch* 16 (1937/38): 8–15.

———. "Rückschau auf die Spielzeit 1937/38 des Zürcher Stadttheaters." *Zürcher Stadttheater: Jahrbuch* 17 (1938/39): 6–13.

Schnoor, Hans. Review of *Penthesilea. Dresdner Anzeiger,* 18 January 1927.

Schoeck, Georg. *Die Welt des jungen Othmar Schoeck.* Einsiedeln, Switzerland: Kulturkommission des Kantons Schwyz, 1986.

———. *Varius Idem: Festlieder und Gelegentliches.* Edited by Elisabeth Schoeck-Grüebler. Brunnen: Soli invicto, 1994.

Schoeck, Othmar. Foreword to *Sommernacht.* Zurich: Hug, 1946.

Schoeck-Grüebler, Elisabeth. "'Ein junger Komponist aus der Nachbarschaft.': Ein gestrichener Nebensatz in Inglins *Werner Amberg.*" *Neue Zürcher Zeitung,* 24/25 Jul. 1993.

———. "Kunst und Brot: Othmar Schoeck und sein erster Verleger." *Neue Zürcher Zeitung,* 14/15 Feb. 1987.

———, ed. *Post nach Brunnen: Briefe an die Familie, 1908–1922.* Zurich: Atlantis Musikbuch-Verlag, 1991.

Schoenberg, Arnold. *Harmonielehre.* 3rd edition. Vienna: Universal Edition, 1923.

Schreiber, Ingeborg. *Max Reger in seinen Konzerten.* Vol. 2. Bonn: Dümmlers Verlag, 1981.

Schuh, Willi. "Eine Art Zauberflötestoff, zwei Grimm-Märchen." *Neue Zürcher Zeitung,* 30/31 Aug. 1986.

———. "Betrachtungen zu Othmar Schoecks *Schloss Dürande:* Uraufführung an der Berliner Staatsoper (1. April)." *Schweizerische Musikzeitung* 83, no. 5 (1 May 1943): 156–59.

———. "Idée und Tongestalt in Schoecks 'Schloss Dürande.'" *Schweizerische Musikzeitung* 83, no. 3 (Mar. 1943): 74–83.

———, ed. *Othmar Schoeck: Festgabe der Freunde zum 50. Geburtstag.* Erlenbach, Switzerland: Eugen Rentsch, 1936.

———. Review of *Lebendig begraben. SMZ* 94, no. 3 (1 Mar. 1954): 103–4.

———. Review of *Schloss Dürande. Neue Zürcher Zeitung,* 7 Jun. 1943.

———. Review of Schoeck's seventieth-birthday concert in Winterthur. *Neue Zürcher Zeitung,* 9 Feb. 1957.

———. "Zürcher Opernwochen." *Schweizerische Musikzeitung* 83, no. 7 (Jul. 1943): 236–37.

Solti, Georg, "with assistance from Harvey Sachs." *Solti on Solti: A Memoir.* London: Chatto & Windus, 1997.

Spelti, Hermann. "Betrachtungen zu Othmar Schoecks Opernschaffen." *Schweizerische Musikzeitung* 83, no. 3 (Mar. 1943): 83–85.

Staempfli, Edward. "Militär, Radio und Claude Debussy." *Schweizerische Musikzeitung* 83, no. 4 (Apr. 1943): 125–26.

Starobinski, Georges. "*Le Notturno op. 47 d'Othmar Schoeck: Le quatuor à cordes confronté aux exigences du lied.*" In Föllmi and Baumgartner, *Das Streichquartett in der zweiten Hälfte des 20. Jahrhunderts: Bericht über das dritte Internationale Symposium Othmar Schoeck in Zürich, 19. und 20. Oktober 2001,* 111–30.

Stege, Fritz. Review of *Schloss Dürande. Hamburger Tageblatt,* 2 Apr. 1943.

Stein, Erwin. "Neue Formprinzipien." *Musikblätter des Anbruch* 6 (1924): 286–303.

Steinberg, Jonathan. *Why Switzerland?* Cambridge: Cambridge University Press, 1976.

Steinmetz, Hans-Dieter. "Karl Mays Grabmal in Radebeul." http://karlmay.leo.org/kmg/seklit/JpKMG/1995/12/htm, accessed Mar. 2007.

Stuckenschmidt, Heinz. *Zum Hören geboren: Ein Leben mit Musik meiner Zeit.* Munich: Piper, 1979.

Sulzer, Peter. *Zehn Komponisten um Werner Reinhart.* Vols. 1–3. Winterthur: Stadtbibliothek Winterthur, 1979, 1980, 1983.

Szmolyan, Walter. "Die Geburtstätte der Zwölftontechnik." *Österreichische Musikzeitschrift* 26, no. 3 (Mar. 1971): 113–26.

Tappolet, Claude. *Hugo de Senger, 1835–1892: Un grand animateur de la vie musicale à Genève au XIXe siècle.* Geneva: Tribune, 1985.

Taruskin, Richard. *Defining Russia Musically: Historical and Hermeneutical Essays.* Princeton & Oxford: Princeton University Press, 2000.

Thacker, Toby. *Music after Hitler, 1945–1955.* Aldershot, UK: Ashgate, 2007.

Tiltmann-Fuchs, Stefanie. *Othmar Schoecks Liederzyklen für Singstimme und Orchester. Studien zum Wort-Ton-Verhältnis.* Regensburg: Gustav Bosse, 1976.

Turner, Rigbie. "Richard Strauss to Cäcilie Wenzel: Twelve Unpublished Letters." *19th-Century Music* 9, no. 3 (Spring 1986): 163–75.

U. M. "The Tonkünstlerfest at Zürich." *The Musical Times* 73, no. 1076 (1 Oct. 1932): 940.

Unabhängige Expertenkommission Schweiz—Zweiter Weltkrieg. *Die Schweiz und die Goldtransaktionen im Zweiten Weltkrieg: Veröffentlichungen der Unabhängigen Expertenkommission Schweiz—Zweiter Weltkrieg.* Vol. 16. Zurich: Chronos, 2002.

Vogel, Werner. *Euer dankbarer Sohn: Schoecks Leipziger Briefe.* Winterthur: Amadeus, 1985.

———. *Othmar Schoeck im Gespräch.* Zurich: Atlantis, 1965.

———. *Othmar Schoeck: Leben und Schaffen im Spiegel von Selbstzeugnissen und Zeitgenossenberichten.* Zurich: Atlantis Musikbuch-Verlag, 1976.

———. *Thematisches Verzeichnis der Werke von Othmar Schoeck.* Zurich: Atlantis, 1956.

———. *Wesenszüge von Othmar Schoecks Liedkunst.* Zurich: Juris-Verlag, 1950.

Vogler, Carl. *Der Schweizerische Tonkünstlerverein im ersten Vierteljahrhundert seines Bestehens: Festschrift zur Feier des 25-jährigen Jubiläums.* Zurich: Tonkünstlerverein, 1925.

Vohmann-Falk, Georg. *Brunnen-Ingenbohl: Üses Dorf, üsi Gmeind, üsi Lüüt.* Brunnen, Switzerland: Hohener-Vohmann, 1991.

W, J. F. Review of *Penthesilea.* *Dresdner Neueste Nachrichten,* 11 Jan. 1927.

Waeger, Gerhart. *Die Sündenböcke der Schweiz: Die Zweihundert im Urteil der geschichtlichen Dokumente, 1940–1946.* Olten & Freiburg im Breisgau: Walter-Verlag, 1971.

Wagner, Cosima. *Die Tagebücher.* Vol. 1. Munich & Zurich: Piper, 1976.

Walton, Chris. "'. . . er möchte eben überall in vorderster Linie stehen . . .': Schoecks *Penthesilea* im Urteil seiner Zeitgenossen." *Dissonanz* 61 (Aug. 1999): 14–16.

———. *Othmar Schoeck: Eine Biographie.* Mainz & Zurich: Atlantis Musikbuch-Verlag, 1994.

———. "Othmar Schoeck und die Japanesen." *Neue Zürcher Zeitung,* 24/25 Jul. 1993.

———. *Othmar Schoeck und seine Zeitgenossen.* Winterthur: Amadeus, 2002.

———. "Schoenberg's Alpine Wanderer: Erich Schmid at 100." *The Musical Times* 1896 (Winter 2006): 7–24.

———. "Storks and Ostriches: An Early Parody of Strauss's *Ariadne auf Naxos.*" *Tempo* 59, no. 232 (Apr. 2005): 40–47.

Walton, Chris, and Antonio Baldassarre, eds. *Musik im Exil: Die Schweiz und das Ausland, 1918–1945.* Bern: Peter Lang, 2005.

Wiget, Theophil F. "Othmar Schoeck und Brunnen." *Mitteilungen des Historischen Vereins des Kantons Schwyz* 74 (1982): 87–94.

Willimann, Joseph, ed. *Der Briefwechsel zwischen Ferruccio Busoni und Volkmar Andreae, 1907–1923.* Zurich: Hug, 1994.

Wittgenstein, Ludwig. *Lectures and Conversations on Aesthetics, Psychology and Religious Belief.* Edited by Cyril Barrett. Oxford: Blackwell, 1978.

Zipkes, Rudolf. *Leben und Wirken der Sängerin Adele Zipkes-Bloch.* Zürich: n.p., 1996.

Index

woo 35, 62, 341; Bass Clarinet Sonata Op. 41, 161–62, 164–65, 173, 176, 301, 342; Cello Sonata woo 47, 313–14, 324, 342; *Drängend bewegt* for piano trio woo 116, 342; *Fliessend* woo 133, 340; Fragment for string quartet in A-flat major woo 113, 342; Fragment for string quartet in C minor woo 113, 342; Fragment for string quartet woo 135, 341; *Fuga a 4 voci, 2 soggetti (Bach)* woo 72, 339; Fugue for string quartet woo 104, 341; Fugue for three violins and cello woo 103, 341; Fugue for two violins and cello woo 76, 341; Minuet and Trio for string quartet woo 26, 23, 339; Movement in C for string quartet woo 73, 339; Piece in G major woo 89, 338; *Sommer* for piano trio woo 61, 20, 338; Sonata for bass clarinet Op. 41, 5; Sonata movement for violin in E woo 102, 340; String quartet movement in A-flat minor woo 125, 340; String quartet movement in B-flat Major woo 75, 340; String quartet movement in D minor woo 126, 340; String Quartet Op. 23, 44, 46–47, 49, 129, 325, 340; String Quartet Op. 37, 117, 123, 129, 206, 268, 288, 309, 311, 341; Suite for cello and piano woo 55, 338; Trio in D major for string trio woo 100, 339; Violin Sonata in D major woo 22, 21, 23, 33, 294, 301, 308, 338; Violin Sonata Op. 16, 33–34, 36, 45, 190, 211, 223, 340; Violin Sonata Op. 46, 181, 186, 189–91, 204, 342; *Waltz* for string quartet woo 71, 339

Schoeck, Othmar, works of (choral works with accompaniment): *Auf dem Rhein* Op. 30, no. 12, 376; *Dithyrambe* Op. 22, 44–45, 51, 58, 155, 207, 210, 241, 243, 311, 376; *Für ein Gesangfest im Frühling* Op. 54, 247–48, 265, 377; *Kanon* woo 41, 377; *Kantate nach Gedichten von Eichendorff* Op. 49, 195, 198–99, 377; *Der Postillon* Op. 18, 36, 41–42, 58, 71, 155, 200, 289, 376;

Trommelschläge Op. 26, 57–60, 93, 195, 210, 230, 311, 376; *Vision* Op. 63, 288, 378; *Wegelied* Op. 24, 49, 51, 58, 155, 247, 376; *Zu einer Konfirmation* Op. 62, no. 36, 284, 377; *Zwei zweistimmige Lieder* Op. 69, 378

Schoeck, Othmar, works of (individual vocal titles): "Der Abend" Op. 45, no. 10, 363; "Abendheimkehr" Op. 70, no. 5, 373; "Abendlandschaft" Op. 20, no. 10, 357; "Abendlied" Op. 52, no. 10, 364; "Abendlied" Op. 55, no. 12, 365; "Abendlied an die Natur" Op. 55, no. 6, 365; "Abendwolke" Op. 60, no. 26, 367; "Abendwolken" Op. 20, no. 6, 357; "Abkehr" Op. 57, no. 7, 366; "Abschied" Op. 3, no. 3, 351; "Abschied" Op. 20, no. 7, 357; "Ach, wie richtete, so klagt' ich" Op. 33, no. 4, 361; "Ach, wie schön ist Nacht und Dämmerschein" Op. 33, no. 1, 361; "Alle meine Wünsche schweigen" Op. 6, no. 4, 352; "Alle" Op. 60, no. 18, 367; "Alles was Odem hat, lobe den Herrn" woo 119, 379; "Alles was Odem hat, lobe den Herrn" woo 120, 379; "Als endlich sie den Sarg hier abgesetzt" Op. 40, no. 6, 372; "Als er sein Weib und's Kind schlafend fand" Op. 52, no. 4, 364; "Am einsamen Strande plätschert die Flut" woo 96, 349; "Am Grabe Höltys" woo 129, 350; "Am Himmelstor" Op. 60, no. 5, 367; "Am Walde" Op. 62, no. 4, 368; "An das Herz" Op. 55, no. 23, 365; "An den Wind" Op. 36, no. 9, 371; "An die Entfernte" Op. 5, no. 2, 351; "An die Entfernte" Op. 24a, no. 3, 358; "An die Lützowschen Jäger" Op. 30, no. 11, 360; "An einem heitern Morgen" Op. 20, no. 2, 357; "An einem Wintermorgen, vor Sonnenaufgang" Op. 62, no. 2, 368; "An meine Grossmutter" Op. 57, no. 18, 366; "An meine Mutter" Op. 14, no. 1, 354; "An Philomele" Op. 62, no. 5, 368; "Angedenken" Op. 36, no. 21,

Eastman Studies in Music